"Composed in the style of the great medieval *catenae*, this new anthology of patristic commentary on Holy Scripture, conveniently arranged by chapter and verse, will be a valuable resource for prayer, study and proclamation. By calling attention to the rich Christian heritage preceding the separations between East and West and between Protestant and Catholic, this series will perform a major service to the cause of ecumenism."

AVERY CARDINAL DULLES, S.J.
Laurence J. McGinley Professor of Religion and Society
Fordham University

"The initial cry of the Reformation was *ad fontes*—back to the sources! The Ancient Christian Commentary on Scripture is a marvelous tool for the recovery of biblical wisdom in today's church. Not just another scholarly project, the ACCS is a major resource for the renewal of preaching, theology and Christian devotion."

TIMOTHY GEORGE
Dean, Beeson Divinity School, Samford University

"Modern church members often do not realize that they are participants in the vast company of the communion of saints that reaches far back into the past and that will continue into the future, until the kingdom comes. This Commentary should help them begin to see themselves as participants in that redeemed community."

ELIZABETH ACHTEMEIER
Union Professor Emerita of Bible and Homiletics
Union Theological Seminary in Virginia

"Contemporary pastors do not stand alone. We are not the first generation of preachers to wrestle with the challenges of communicating the gospel. The Ancient Christian Commentary on Scripture puts us in conversation with our colleagues from the past, that great cloud of witnesses who preceded us in this vocation. This Commentary enables us to receive their deep spiritual insights, their encouragement and guidance for present-day interpretation and preaching of the Word. What a wonderful addition to any pastor's library!"

WILLIAM H. WILLIMON
Dean of the Chapel and Professor of Christian Ministry
Duke University

"Here is a nonpareil series which reclaims the Bible as the book of the church by making accessible to earnest readers of the twenty-first century the classrooms of Clement of Alexandria and Didymus the Blind, the study and lecture hall of Origen, the cathedrae of Chrysostom and Augustine, the scriptorium of Jerome in his Bethlehem monastery."

GEORGE LAWLESS
Augustinian Patristic Institute and Gregorian University, Rome

"We are pleased to witness publication of the
Ancient Christian Commentary on Scripture. It is most beneficial for us to learn
how the ancient Christians, especially the saints of the church
who proved through their lives their devotion to God and his Word, interpreted
Scripture. Let us heed the witness of those who have gone before us in the faith."

METROPOLITAN THEODOSIUS
Primate, Orthodox Church in America

"Across Christendom there has emerged a widespread interest
in early Christianity, both at the popular and scholarly level. . . .
Christians of all traditions stand to benefit from this project, especially clergy
and those who study the Bible. Moreover, it will allow us to see how our traditions are
both rooted in the scriptural interpretations of the church fathers while at
the same time seeing how we have developed new perspectives."

ALBERTO FERREIRO
Professor of History, Seattle Pacific University

"The Ancient Christian Commentary on Scripture fills a long overdue need for scholars and
students of the church fathers. . . . Such information will be of immeasurable
worth to those of us who have felt inundated by contemporary interpreters and novel theories
of the biblical text. We welcome some 'new' insight from the
ancient authors in the early centuries of the church."

H. WAYNE HOUSE
Professor of Theology and Law
Trinity University School of Law

Chronological snobbery—the assumption that our ancestors working without benefit of
computers have nothing to teach us—is exposed as nonsense by this magnificent
new series. Surfeited with knowledge but starved of wisdom, many of us are
more than ready to sit at table with our ancestors and listen to their holy
conversations on Scripture. I know I am.

EUGENE H. PETERSON
Professor Emeritus of Spiritual Theology
Regent College

"Few publishing projects have encouraged me as much as the recently announced Ancient Christian Commentary on Scripture with Dr. Thomas Oden serving as general editor. . . . How is it that so many of us who are dedicated to serve the Lord received seminary educations which omitted familiarity with such incredible students of the Scriptures as St. John Chrysostom, St. Athanasius the Great and St. John of Damascus? I am greatly anticipating the publication of this Commentary."

FR. PETER E. GILLQUIST
Director, Department of Missions and Evangelism
Antiochian Orthodox Christian Archdiocese of North America

"The Scriptures have been read with love and attention for nearly two thousand years, and listening to the voice of believers from previous centuries opens us to unexpected insight and deepened faith. Those who studied Scripture in the centuries closest to its writing, the centuries during and following persecution and martyrdom, speak with particular authority. The Ancient Christian Commentary on Scripture will bring to life the truth that we are invisibly surrounded by a 'great cloud of witnesses.'"

FREDERICA MATHEWES-GREEN
Commentator, National Public Radio

"For those who think that church history began around 1941 when their pastor was born, this Commentary will be a great surprise. Christians throughout the centuries have read the biblical text, nursed their spirits with it and then applied it to their lives. These commentaries reflect that the witness of the Holy Spirit was present in his church throughout the centuries. As a result, we can profit by allowing the ancient Christians to speak to us today."

HADDON ROBINSON
Harold John Ockenga Distinguished Professor of Preaching
Gordon-Conwell Theological Seminary

"All who are interested in the interpretation of the Bible will welcome the forthcoming multivolume series Ancient Christian Commentary on Scripture. Here the insights of scores of early church fathers will be assembled and made readily available for significant passages throughout the Bible and the Apocrypha. It is hard to think of a more worthy ecumenical project to be undertaken by the publisher."

BRUCE M. METZGER
Professor of New Testament, Emeritus
Princeton Theological Seminary

ANCIENT CHRISTIAN COMMENTARY ON SCRIPTURE

NEW TESTAMENT
I*a*

MATTHEW 1-13

EDITED BY
MANLIO SIMONETTI

GENERAL EDITOR
THOMAS C. ODEN

InterVarsity Press
Downers Grove, Illinois

InterVarsity Press
P.O. Box 1400, Downers Grove, IL 60515-1426
World Wide Web: www.ivpress.com
E-mail: email@ivpress.com

InterVarsity Press® is the book-publishing division of InterVarsity Christian Fellowship/USA®, a student movement active on campus at hundreds of universities, colleges and schools of nursing in the United States of America, and a member movement of the International Fellowship of Evangelical Students. For information about local and regional activities, write Public Relations Dept., InterVarsity Christian Fellowship/USA, 6400 Schroeder Rd., P.O. Box 7895, Madison, WI 53707-7895, or visit the IVCF website at <www.intervarsity.org>.

Spine photograph: Byzantine Collection, Dumbarton Oaks, Washington, D.C. Pendant cross (gold and enamel). Constantinople, late sixth century.

Cover photograph: Scala/Art Resource, New York. View of the apse. S. Vitale, Ravenna, Italy.

ISBN-10: 0-8308-1486-8
ISBN-13: 978-0-8308-1486-2

Printed in the United States of America ∞

Library of Congress Cataloging-in-Publication Data

Matthew 1-13/edited by Manlio Simonetti.
        p. cm.—(Ancient Christian commentary on Scripture. New Testament; 1a)
    Includes bibliographical references (p.) and indexes.
    ISBN 0-8308-1486-8 (cloth: alk. paper)
    1. Bible. N. T. Matthew I-XIII—Commentaries. I. Simonetti, Manlio. II. Series.
    BS2575.3 .M29 2001
    226.2'077'09—dc21   2001026465

P	28	27	26	25	24	23	22	21	20	19	18	17	16	15	14	13	12	11	10
Y	28	27	26	25	24	23	22	21	20	19	18	17	16	15	14	13				

CONTENTS

GENERAL INTRODUCTION

The Ancient Christian Commentary on Scripture (hereafter ACCS) is a twenty-eight volume patristic commentary on Scripture. The patristic period, the time of the fathers of the church, spans the era from Clement of Rome (fl. c. 95) to John of Damascus (c. 645-c. 749). The commentary thus covers seven centuries of biblical interpretation, from the end of the New Testament to the mid-eighth century, including the Venerable Bede.

Since the method of inquiry for the ACCS has been developed in close coordination with computer technology, it serves as a potential model of an evolving, promising, technologically pragmatic, theologically integrated method for doing research in the history of exegesis. The purpose of this general introduction to the series is to present this approach and account for its methodological premises.

This is a long-delayed assignment in biblical and historical scholarship: reintroducing in a convenient form key texts of early Christian commentary on the whole of Scripture. To that end, historians, translators, digital technicians, and biblical and patristic scholars have collaborated in the task of presenting for the first time in many centuries these texts from the early history of Christian exegesis. Here the interpretive glosses, penetrating reflections, debates, contemplations and deliberations of early Christians are ordered verse by verse from Genesis to Revelation. Also included are patristic comments on the deuterocanonical writings (sometimes called the Apocrypha) that were considered Scripture by the Fathers. This is a full-scale classic commentary on Scripture consisting of selections in modern translation from the ancient Christian writers.

The Ancient Christian Commentary on Scripture has three goals: the renewal of Christian *preaching* based on classical Christian exegesis, the intensified study of Scripture by *lay* persons who wish to think with the early church about the canonical text, and the stimulation of Christian historical, biblical, theological and pastoral *scholarship* toward further inquiry into the scriptural interpretations of the ancient Christian writers.

On each page the Scripture text is accompanied by the most noteworthy remarks of key consensual exegetes of the early Christian centuries. This formal arrangement follows approximately the traditional pattern of the published texts of the Talmud after the invention of printing and of the *glossa ordinaria* that preceded printing.[1]

---

[1]Students of the Talmud will easily recognize this pattern of organization. The Talmud is a collection of rabbinic arguments, discussions and comments on the Mishnah, the first Jewish code of laws after the Bible, and the Gemara, an elaboration of the Mishnah. The study of Talmud is its own end and reward. In the Talmud every subject pertaining to Torah is worthy of consideration and analysis. As the Talmud is a vast repository of Jewish wisdom emerging out of revealed Scripture, so are the Fathers the repository of Christian wisdom emerging out of

Retrieval of Neglected Christian Texts

There is an emerging felt need among diverse Christian communities that these texts be accurately recovered and studied. Recent biblical scholarship has so focused attention on post-Enlightenment historical and literary methods that it has left this longing largely unattended and unserviced.

After years of quiet gestation and reflection on the bare idea of a patristic commentary, a feasibility consultation was drawn together at the invitation of Drew University in November 1993 in Washington, D.C. This series emerged from that consultation and its ensuing discussions. Extensive further consultations were undertaken during 1994 and thereafter in Rome, Tübingen, Oxford, Cambridge, Athens, Alexandria and Istanbul, seeking the advice of the most competent international scholars in the history of exegesis. Among distinguished scholars who contributed to the early layers of the consultative process were leading writers on early church history, hermeneutics, homiletics, history of exegesis, systematic theology and pastoral theology. Among leading international authorities consulted early on in the project design were Sir Henry Chadwick of Oxford; Bishops Kallistos Ware of Oxford, Rowan Williams of Monmouth and Stephen Sykes of Ely (all former patristics professors at Oxford or Cambridge); Professors Angelo Di Berardino and Basil Studer of the Patristic Institute of Rome; and Professors Karlfried Froehlich and Bruce M. Metzger of Princeton. They were exceptionally helpful in shaping our list of volume editors. We are especially indebted to the Ecumenical Patriarch of Constantinople Bartholomew and Edward Idris Cardinal Cassidy of the Pontifical Council for Promoting Christian Unity, the Vatican, for their blessing, steady support and wise counsel in developing and advancing the Drew University Patristic Commentary Project.

The outcome of these feasibility consultations was general agreement that the project was profoundly needed, accompanied by an unusual eagerness to set out upon the project, validated by a willingness on the part of many to commit valuable time to accomplish it. At the pace of three or four volumes per year, the commentary is targeted for completion within the first decade of the millennium.

This series stands unapologetically as a practical homiletic and devotional guide to the earliest layers of classic Christian readings of biblical texts. It intends to be a brief compendium of reflections on particular Septuagint, Old Latin and New Testament texts by their earliest Christian interpreters. Hence it is not a commentary by modern standards, but it is a commentary by the standards of those who anteceded and formed the basis of the modern commentary.

Many useful contemporary scholarly efforts are underway and are contributing significantly to the recovery of classic Christian texts. Notable in English among these are the Fathers of the Church series (Catholic University of America Press), Ancient Christian Writers (Paulist), Cistercian Studies (Cistercian Publications), The Church's Bible (Eerdmans), Message of the Fathers of the Church (Michael Glazier, Liturgical Press) and Texts and Studies (Cambridge). In other languages similar efforts are conspicuously found in Sources Chrétiennes, Corpus Christianorum (Series Graeca and Latina),

---

revealed Scripture. The Talmud originated largely from the same period as the patristic writers, often using analogous methods of interpretation. In the Talmud the texts of the Mishnah are accompanied by direct quotations from key consensual commentators of the late Judaic tradition. The format of the earliest published versions of the Talmud itself followed the early manuscript model of the medieval *glossa ordinaria* in which patristic comments were organized around Scripture texts. Hence the ACCS gratefully acknowledges its affinity and indebtedness to the early traditions of the catena and *glossa ordinaria* and of the tradition of rabbinic exegesis that accompanied early Christian Scripture studies.

Corpus Scriptorum Christianorum Orientalium, Corpus Scriptorum Ecclesiasticorum Latinorum, Texte und Untersuchungen zur Geschichte der altchristlichen Literatur, Die griechischen christlichen Schriftsteller, Patrologia Orientalis, Patrologia Syriaca, Biblioteca patristica, Les Pères dans la foi, Collana di Testi Patristici, Letture cristiane delle origini, Letture cristiane del primo millennio, Cultura cristiana antica, Thesaurus Linguae Latinae, Thesaurus Linguae Graecae and the Cetedoc series, which offers in digital form the volumes of Corpus Christianorum. The Ancient Christian Commentary on Scripture builds on the splendid work of all these studies, but focuses primarily and modestly on the recovery of patristic biblical wisdom for contemporary preaching and lay spiritual formation.

Digital Research Tools and Results

The volume editors have been supported by a digital research team at Drew University which has identified these classic comments by performing global searches of the Greek and Latin patristic corpus. They have searched for these texts in the Thesaurus Linguae Graecae (TLG) digitalized Greek database, the Cetedoc edition of the Latin texts of Corpus Christianorum from the Centre de traitement électronique des documents (Université catholique de Louvain), the Chadwyck-Healey Patrologia Latina Database (Migne) and the Packard Humanities Institute Latin databases. We have also utilized the CD-ROM searchable version of the Early Church Fathers, of which the Drew University project was an early cosponsor along with the Electronic Bible Society.

This has resulted in a plethora of raw Greek and Latin textual materials from which the volume editors have made discriminating choices.[2] In this way the project office has already supplied to each volume editor[3] a substantial read-out of Greek and Latin glosses, explanations, observations and comments on each verse or pericope of Scripture text.[4] Only a small percentage of this raw material has in fact made the grade of our selection criteria. But such is the poignant work of the catenist, or of any compiler of a compendium for general use. The intent of the exercise is to achieve brevity and economy of expression by exclusion of extraneous material, not to go into critical explanatory detail.

Through the use of Boolean key word and phrase searches in these databases, the research team identified the Greek and Latin texts from early Christian writers that refer to specific biblical passages. Where textual variants occur among the Old Latin texts or disputed Greek texts, they executed key word searches with appropriate or expected variables, including allusions and analogies. At this time of writing, the Drew University ACCS research staff has already completed most of these intricate and prodigious computer searches, which would have been unthinkable before computer technology.

The employment of these digital resources has yielded unexpected advantages: a huge residual database, a means of identifying comments on texts not previously considered for catena usage, an efficient and cost-

---

[2]Having searched Latin and Greek databases, we then solicited from our Coptic, Syriac and Armenian editorial experts selections from these bodies of literature, seeking a fitting balance from all available exegetical traditions of ancient Christianity within our time frame. To all these we added the material we could find already in English translation.

[3]Excepting those editors who preferred to do their own searching.

[4]TLG and Cetedoc are referenced more often than Migne or other printed Greek or Latin sources for these reasons: (1) the texts are more quickly and easily accessed digitally in a single location; (2) the texts are more reliable and in a better critical edition; (3) we believe that in the future these digital texts will be far more widely accessed both by novices and specialists; (4) short selections can be easily downloaded; and (5) the context of each text can be investigated by the interested reader.

effective deployment of human resources, and an abundance of potential material for future studies in the history of exegesis. Most of this was accomplished by a highly talented group of graduate students under the direction of Joel Scandrett, Michael Glerup and Joel Elowsky. Prior to the technology of digital search and storage techniques, this series could hardly have been produced, short of a vast army of researchers working by laborious hand and paper searches in scattered libraries around the world.

Future readers of Scripture will increasingly be working with emerging forms of computer technology and interactive hypertext formats that will enable readers to search out quickly in more detail ideas, texts, themes and terms found in the ancient Christian writers. The ACCS provides an embryonic paradigm for how that can be done. Drew University offers the ACCS to serve both as a potential research model and as an outcome of research. We hope that this printed series in traditional book form will in time be supplemented with a larger searchable, digitized version in some stored-memory hypertext format. We continue to work with an astute consortium of computer and research organizations to serve the future needs of both historical scholarship and theological study.

The Surfeit of Materials Brought to Light

We now know that there is virtually no portion of Scripture about which the ancient Christian writers had little or nothing useful or meaningful to say. Many of them studied the Bible thoroughly with deep contemplative discernment, comparing text with text, often memorizing large portions of it. All chapters of all sixty-six books of the traditional Protestant canonical corpus have received deliberate or occasional patristic exegetical or homiletic treatment. This series also includes patristic commentary on texts not found in the Jewish canon (often designated the Apocrypha or deuterocanonical writings) but that were included in ancient Greek Bibles (the Septuagint). These texts, although not precisely the same texts in each tradition, remain part of the recognized canons of the Roman Catholic and Orthodox traditions.

While some books of the Bible are rich in verse-by-verse patristic commentaries (notably Genesis, Psalms, Song of Solomon, Isaiah, Matthew, John and Romans), there are many others that are lacking in intensive commentaries from this early period. Hence we have not limited our searches to these formal commentaries but sought allusions, analogies, cross-connections and references to biblical texts in all sorts of patristic literary sources. There are many perceptive insights that have come to us from homilies, letters, poetry, hymns, essays and treatises, that need not be arbitrarily excluded from a catena. We have searched for succinct, discerning and moving passages both from line-by-line commentaries (from authors such as Origen, Cyril of Alexandria, Theodoret of Cyr, John Chrysostom, Jerome, Augustine and Bede) and from other literary genres. Out of a surfeit of resulting raw materials, the volume editors have been invited to select the best, wisest and most representative reflections of ancient Christian writers on a given biblical passage.

For Whom Is This Compendium Designed?

We have chosen and ordered these selections primarily for a general lay reading audience of nonprofessionals who study the Bible regularly and who earnestly wish to have classic Christian observations on the text readily available to them. In vastly differing cultural settings, contemporary lay readers are asking how they might grasp the meaning of sacred texts under the instruction of the great minds of the ancient church.

Yet in so focusing our attention, we are determined not to neglect the rigorous requirements and needs of academic readers who up to now have had starkly limited resources and compendia in the history of exegesis. The series, which is being translated into the languages of half the world's population, is designed to serve public libraries, universities, crosscultural studies and historical interests worldwide. It unapologetically claims and asserts its due and rightful place as a staple source book for the history of Western literature.

Our varied audiences (lay, pastoral and academic) are much broader than the highly technical and specialized scholarly field of patristic studies. They are not limited to university scholars concentrating on the study of the history of the transmission of the text or to those with highly focused interests in textual morphology or historical-critical issues and speculations. Though these remain crucial concerns for specialists, they are not the paramount interest of the editors of the Ancient Christian Commentary on Scripture. Our work is largely targeted straightaway for a pastoral audience and more generally to a larger audience of laity who want to reflect and meditate with the early church about the plain sense, theological wisdom, and moral and spiritual meaning of particular Scripture texts.

There are various legitimate competing visions of how such a patristic commentary should be developed, each of which were carefully pondered in our feasibility study and its follow-up. With high respect to alternative conceptions, there are compelling reasons why the Drew University project has been conceived as a practically usable commentary addressed first of all to informed lay readers and more broadly to pastors of Protestant, Catholic and Orthodox traditions. Only in an ancillary way do we have in mind as our particular audience the guild of patristic academics, although we welcome their critical assessment of our methods. If we succeed in serving lay and pastoral readers practically and well, we expect these texts will also be advantageously used by college and seminary courses in Bible, hermeneutics, church history, historical theology and homiletics, since they are not easily accessible otherwise.

The series seeks to offer to Christian laity what the Talmud and Midrashim have long offered to Jewish readers. These foundational sources are finding their way into many public school libraries and into the obligatory book collections of many churches, pastors, teachers and lay persons. It is our intent and the publishers' commitment to keep the whole series in print for many years to come and to make it available on an economically viable subscription basis.

There is an emerging awareness among Catholic, Protestant and Orthodox laity that vital biblical preaching and teaching stand in urgent need of some deeper grounding beyond the scope of the historical-critical orientations that have dominated and at times eclipsed biblical studies in our time.

Renewing religious communities of prayer and service (crisis ministries, urban and campus ministries, counseling ministries, retreat ministries, monasteries, grief ministries, ministries of compassion, etc.) are being drawn steadily and emphatically toward these biblical and patristic sources for meditation and spiritual formation. These communities are asking for primary source texts of spiritual formation presented in accessible form, well-grounded in reliable scholarship and dedicated to practical use.

The Premature Discrediting of the Catena Tradition

We gratefully acknowledge our affinity and indebtedness to the spirit and literary form of the early traditions of the catena and *glossa ordinaria* that sought authoritatively to collect salient classic interpretations of ancient exegetes on each biblical text. Our editorial work has benefited by utilizing and adapting those traditions for today's readers.

It is regrettable that this distinctive classic approach has been not only shelved but peculiarly misplaced for several centuries. It has been a long time since any attempt has been made to produce this sort of commentary. Under fire from modern critics, the catena approach dwindled to almost nothing by the nineteenth century and has not until now been revitalized in this postcritical situation. Ironically, it is within our own so-called progressive and broad-minded century that these texts have been more systematically hidden away and ignored than in any previous century of Christian scholarship. With all our historical and publishing competencies, these texts have been regrettably denied to hearers of Christian preaching in our time, thus revealing the dogmatic biases of modernity (modern chauvinism, naturalism and autonomous individualism).

Nineteenth- and twentieth-century exegesis has frequently displayed a philosophical bias toward naturalistic reductionism. Most of the participants in the ACCS project have lived through dozens of iterations of these cycles of literary and historical criticism, seeking earnestly to expound and interpret the text out of ever-narrowing empiricist premises. For decades Scripture teachers and pastors have sailed the troubled waters of assorted layers and trends within academic criticism. Preachers have attempted to digest and utilize these approaches, yet have often found the outcomes disappointing. There is an increasing awareness of the speculative excesses and the spiritual and homiletic limitations of much post-Enlightenment criticism.

Meanwhile the motifs, methods and approaches of ancient exegetes have remained shockingly unfamiliar not only to ordained clergy but to otherwise highly literate biblical scholars, trained exhaustively in the methods of scientific criticism. Amid the vast exegetical labors of the last two centuries, the ancient Christian exegetes have seldom been revisited, and then only marginally and often tendentiously. We have clear and indisputable evidence of the prevailing modern contempt for classic exegesis, namely, that the extensive and once authoritative classic commentaries on Scripture still remain untranslated into modern languages. Even in China this has not happened to classic Buddhist and Confucian commentaries.

This systematic modern scholarly neglect not only is seen among Protestants but is widespread among Catholics and even Orthodox, where ironically the Fathers are sometimes piously venerated while not being energetically read.

So two powerful complementary contemporary forces are at work to draw our lay audience once again toward these texts and to free them from previous limited premises: First, this series is a response to the deep hunger for classical Christian exegesis and for the history of exegesis, partly because it has been so long neglected. Second, there is a growing demoralization in relation to actual useful exegetical outcomes of post-Enlightenment historicist and naturalistic-reductionist criticism. Both of these animating energies are found among lay readers of Roman, Eastern and Protestant traditions.

Through the use of the chronological lists and biographical sketches at the back of each volume, readers can locate in time and place the voices displayed in the exegesis of a particular pericope. The chains (catenae) of interpretation of a particular biblical passage thus provide glimpses into the history of the interpretation of a given text. This pattern has venerable antecedents in patristic and medieval exegesis of both Eastern and Western traditions, as well as important expressions in the Reformation tradition.

The Ecumenical Range and Intent

Recognition of need for the Fathers' wisdom ranges over many diverse forms of Christianity. This has necessitated the cooperation of scholars of widely diverse Christian communities to accomplish the task fairly and in a balanced way. It has been a major ecumenical undertaking.

Under this classic textual umbrella, this series brings together in common spirit Christians who have long distanced themselves from each other through separate and often competing church memories. Under this welcoming umbrella are gathering conservative Protestants with Eastern Orthodox, Baptists with Roman Catholics, Reformed with Arminians and charismatics, Anglicans with Pentecostals, high with low church adherents, and premodern traditionalists with postmodern classicists.

How is it that such varied Christians are able to find inspiration and common faith in these texts? Why are these texts and studies so intrinsically ecumenical, so catholic in their cultural range? Because all of these traditions have an equal right to appeal to the early history of Christian exegesis. All of these traditions can, without a sacrifice of intellect, come together to study texts common to them all. These classic texts have decisively shaped the entire subsequent history of exegesis. Protestants have a right to the Fathers. Athanasius is not owned by Copts, nor is Augustine owned by North Africans. These minds are the common possession of the whole church. The Orthodox do not have exclusive rights over Basil, nor do the Romans over Gregory the Great. Christians everywhere have equal claim to these riches and are discovering them and glimpsing their unity in the body of Christ.

From many varied Christian traditions this project has enlisted as volume editors a team of leading international scholars in ancient Christian writings and the history of exegesis. Among Eastern Orthodox contributors are Professors Andrew Louth of Durham University in England and George Dragas of Holy Cross (Greek Orthodox) School of Theology in Brookline, Massachusetts. Among Roman Catholic scholars are Benedictine scholar Mark Sheridan of the San Anselmo University of Rome, Jesuit Joseph Lienhard of Fordham University in New York, Cistercian Father Francis Martin of the Catholic University of America, Alberto Ferreiro of Seattle Pacific University, and Sever Voicu of the Eastern European (Romanian) Uniate Catholic tradition, who teaches at the Augustinian Patristic Institute of Rome. The New Testament series is inaugurated with the volume on Matthew offered by the renowned Catholic authority in the history of exegesis, Manlio Simonetti of the University of Rome. Among Anglican communion contributors are Mark Edwards (Oxford), Bishop Kenneth Stevenson (Fareham, Hampshire, in England), J. Robert Wright (New York), Anders Bergquist (St. Albans), Peter Gorday (Atlanta) and Gerald Bray (Cambridge, England, and Birmingham, Alabama). Among Lutheran contributors are Quentin Wesselschmidt (St. Louis), Philip Krey and Eric Heen (Philadelphia), and Arthur Just, William Weinrich and Dean O. Wenthe (all of Ft. Wayne, Indiana). Among distinguished Protestant Reformed, Baptist and other evangelical scholars are John Sailhamer and Steven McKinion (Wake Forest, North Carolina), Craig Blaising and Carmen Hardin (Louisville, Kentucky), Christopher Hall (St. Davids, Pennsylvania), J. Ligon Duncan III (Jackson, Mississippi), Thomas McCullough (Danville, Kentucky), John R. Franke (Hatfield, Pennsylvania) and Mark Elliott (Hope University Liverpool).

The international team of editors was selected in part to reflect this ecumenical range. They were chosen on the premise not only that they were competent to select fairly those passages that best convey the consensual tradition of early Christian exegesis, but also that they would not omit significant voices within it. They have searched insofar as possible for those comments that self-evidently would be most widely received generally by the whole church of all generations, East and West.

This is not to suggest or imply that all patristic writers agree. One will immediately see upon reading these selections that within the boundaries of orthodoxy, that is, excluding outright denials of ecumenically received teaching, there are many views possible about a given text or idea and that these different views may be strongly affected by wide varieties of social environments and contexts.

The Drew University project has been meticulous about commissioning volume editors. We have sought out world-class scholars, preeminent in international biblical and patristic scholarship, and wise in the history of exegesis. We have not been disappointed. We have enlisted a diverse team of editors, fitting for a global audience that bridges the major communions of Christianity.

The project editors have striven for a high level of consistency and literary quality over the course of this series. As with most projects of this sort, the editorial vision and procedures are progressively being refined and sharpened and fed back into the editorial process.

Honoring Theological Reasoning

Since it stands in the service of the worshiping community, the ACCS unabashedly embraces crucial ecumenical premises as the foundation for its method of editorial selections: revelation in history, trinitarian coherence, divine providence in history, the Christian *kerygma, regula fidei et caritatis* ("the rule of faith and love"), the converting work of the Holy Spirit. These are common assumptions of the living communities of worship that are served by the commentary.

It is common in this transgenerational community of faith to assume that the early consensual ecumenical teachers were led by the Spirit in their interpretive efforts and in their transmitting of Christian truth amid the hazards of history. These texts assume some level of unity and continuity of ecumenical consensus in the mind of the believing church, a consensus more clearly grasped in the patristic period than later. We would be less than true to the sacred text if we allowed modern assumptions to overrun these premises.

An extended project such as this requires a well-defined objective that serves constantly as the organizing principle and determines which approaches take priority in what sort of balance. This objective informs the way in which tensions inherent in its complexity are managed. This objective has already been summarized in the three goals mentioned at the beginning of this introduction. To alter any one of these goals would significantly alter the character of the whole task. We view our work not only as an academic exercise with legitimate peer review in the academic community, but also as a vocation, a task primarily undertaken *coram Deo* ("before God") and not only *coram hominibus* ("before humanity"). We have been astonished that we have been led far beyond our original intention into a Chinese translation and other translations into major world languages.

This effort is grounded in a deep respect for a distinctively theological reading of Scripture that cannot be reduced to historical, philosophical, scientific or sociological insights or methods. It takes seriously the venerable tradition of ecumenical reflection concerning the premises of revelation, apostolicity, canon and consensuality. A high priority is granted here, contrary to modern assumptions, to theological, christological and triune reasoning as the distinguishing premises of classic Christian thought. This approach does not pit theology against critical theory; instead, it incorporates critical methods and brings them into coordinate accountability within its overarching homiletic-theological-pastoral purposes. Such an endeavor does not cater to any cadre of modern ideological advocacy.

Why Evangelicals Are Increasingly Drawn Toward Patristic Exegesis

Surprising to some, the most extensive new emergent audience for patristic exegesis is found among the expanding worldwide audience of evangelical readers who are now burgeoning from a history of revivalism that has often been thought to be historically unaware. This is a tradition that has often been caricatured as critically backward and hermeneutically challenged. Now Baptist and Pentecostal laity are rediscovering the history of the Holy Spirit. This itself is arguably a work of the Holy Spirit. As those in these traditions continue to mature, they recognize their need for biblical resources that go far beyond those that have been made available to them in both the pietistic and historical-critical traditions.

Both pietism and the Enlightenment were largely agreed in expressing disdain for patristic and classic forms of exegesis. Vital preaching and exegesis must now venture beyond the constrictions of historical-critical work of the century following Schweitzer and beyond the personal existential story-telling of pietism.

During the time I have served as senior editor and executive editor of *Christianity Today*, I have been privileged to surf in these volatile and exciting waves. It has been for me (as a theologian of a liberal mainline communion) like an ongoing seminar in learning to empathize with the tensions, necessities and hungers of the vast heterogeneous evangelical audience.

But why just now is this need for patristic wisdom felt particularly by evangelical leaders and laity? Why are worldwide evangelicals increasingly drawn toward ancient exegesis? What accounts for this rapid and basic reversal of mood among the inheritors of the traditions of Protestant revivalism? It is partly because the evangelical tradition has been long deprived of any vital contact with these patristic sources since the days of Luther, Calvin and Wesley, who knew them well.

This commentary is dedicated to allowing ancient Christian exegetes to speak for themselves. It will not become fixated unilaterally on contemporary criticism. It will provide new textual resources for the lay reader, teacher and pastor that have lain inaccessible during the last two centuries. Without avoiding historical-critical issues that have already received extensive exploration in our time, it will seek to make available to our present-day audience the multicultural, transgenerational, multilingual resources of the ancient ecumenical Christian tradition. It is an awakening, growing, hungry and robust audience.

Such an endeavor is especially poignant and timely now because increasing numbers of evangelical Protestants are newly discovering rich dimensions of dialogue and widening areas of consensus with Orthodox and Catholics on divisive issues long thought irreparable. The study of the Fathers on Scripture promises to further significant interactions between Protestants and Catholics on issues that have plagued them for centuries: justification, authority, Christology, sanctification and eschatology. Why? Because they can find in pre-Reformation texts a common faith to which Christians can appeal. And this is an arena in which Protestants distinctively feel at home: biblical authority and interpretation. A profound yearning broods within the heart of evangelicals for the recovery of the history of exegesis as a basis for the renewal of preaching. This series offers resources for that renewal.

Steps Toward Selections

In moving from raw data to making selections, the volume editors have been encouraged to move judiciously through three steps:

Step 1: *Reviewing extant Greek and Latin commentaries.* The volume editors have been responsible for examining the line-by-line commentaries and homilies on the texts their volume covers. Much of this material remains untranslated into English and some of it into any modern language.

Step 2: *Reviewing digital searches.* The volume editors have been responsible for examining the results of digital searches into the Greek and Latin databases. To get the gist of the context of the passage, ordinarily about ten lines above the raw digital reference and ten lines after the reference have been downloaded for printed output. *Biblia Patristica* has been consulted as needed, especially in cases where the results of the digital searches have been thin. Then the volume editors have determined from these potential digital hits and from published texts those that should be regarded as more serious possibilities for inclusion.

Step 3. *Making selections.* Having assembled verse-by-verse comments from the Greek and Latin digital databases, from extant commentaries, and from already translated English sources, either on disk or in paper printouts, the volume editors have then selected the best comments and reflections of ancient Christian writers on a given biblical text, following agreed-upon criteria. The intent is to set apart those few sentences or paragraphs of patristic comment that best reflect the mind of the believing church on that pericope.

The Method of Making Selections

It is useful to provide an explicit account of precisely how we made these selections. We invite others to attempt similar procedures and compare outcomes on particular passages.[5] We welcome the counsel of others who might review our choices and suggest how they might have been better made. We have sought to avoid unconsciously biasing our selections, and we have solicited counsel to help us achieve this end.

---

[5]A number of Ph.D. dissertations are currently being written on the history of exegesis of a particular passage of Scripture. This may develop into an emerging academic methodology that promises to change both biblical and patristic studies in favor of careful textual and intertextual analysis, consensuality assessment and history of interpretation, rather than historicist and naturalistic reductionism.

In order that the whole project might remain cohesive, the protocols for making commentary selections have been jointly agreed upon and stated clearly in advance by the editors, publishers, translators and research teams of the ACCS. What follows is our checklist in assembling these extracts.

The following principles of selection have been mutually agreed upon to guide the editors in making spare, wise, meaningful catena selections from the vast patristic corpus:

1. From our huge database with its profuse array of possible comments, we have preferred those passages that have enduring relevance, penetrating significance, crosscultural applicability and practical applicability.

2. The volume editors have sought to identify patristic selections that display trenchant rhetorical strength and self-evident persuasive power, so as not to require extensive secondary explanation. The editorial challenge has been to identify the most vivid comments and bring them to accurate translation.

We hope that in most cases selections will be pungent, memorable, quotable, aphoristic and short (often a few sentences or a single paragraph) rather than extensive technical homilies or detailed expositions, and that many will have some narrative interest and illuminative power. This criterion follows in the train of much Talmudic, Midrashic and rabbinic exegesis. In some cases, however, detailed comments and longer sections of homilies have been considered worthy of inclusion.

3. We seek the most representative comments that best reflect the mind of the believing church (of all times and cultures). Selections focus more on the attempt to identify consensual strains of exegesis than sheer speculative brilliance or erratic innovation. The thought or interpretation can emerge out of individual creativity, but it must not be inconsistent with what the apostolic tradition teaches and what the church believes. What the consensual tradition trusts least is individualistic innovation that has not yet subtly learned what the worshiping community already knows.

Hence we are less interested in idiosyncratic interpretations of a given text than we are in those texts that fairly represent the central flow of ecumenical consensual exegesis. Just what is central is left for the fair professional judgment of our ecumenically distinguished Orthodox, Protestant and Catholic volume editors to discern. We have included, for example, many selections from among the best comments of Origen and Tertullian, but not those authors' peculiar eccentricities that have been widely distrusted by the ancient ecumenical tradition.

4. We have especially sought out for inclusion those consensus-bearing authors who have been relatively disregarded, often due to their social location or language or nationality, insofar as their work is resonant with the mainstream of ancient consensual exegesis. This is why we have sought out special consultants in Syriac, Coptic and Armenian.

5. We have sought to cull out annoying, coarse, graceless, absurdly allegorical[6] or racially offensive interpretations. But where our selections may have some of those edges, we have supplied footnotes to

---

[6]Allegorical treatments of texts are not to be ruled out but fairly and judiciously assessed as to their explanatory value and typicality. There is a prevailing stereotype that ancient Christian exegesis is so saturated with allegory as to make it almost useless. After making our selections on a merit basis according to our criteria, we were surprised at the limited extent of protracted allegorical passages selected. After making a count of allegorical passages, we discovered that less than one twentieth of these selections have a decisive allegorical concentration. So while allegory is admittedly an acceptable model of exegesis for the ancient Christian writers, especially those of the Alexandrian school and especially with regard to Old Testament texts, it has not turned out to be as dominant a model as we had thought it might be.

assist readers better to understand the context and intent of the text.

6. We have constantly sought an appropriate balance of Eastern, Western and African traditions. We have intentionally attempted to include Alexandrian, Antiochene, Roman, Syriac, Coptic and Armenian traditions of interpretation. Above all, we want to provide sound, stimulating, reliable exegesis and illuminating exposition of the text by the whole spectrum of classic Christian writers.

7. We have made a special effort where possible to include the voices of women[7] such as Macrina,[8] Eudoxia, Egeria, Faltonia Betitia Proba, the Sayings of the Desert Mothers and others who report the biblical interpretations of women of the ancient Christian tradition.

8. In order to anchor the commentary solidly in primary sources so as to allow the ancient Christian writers to address us on their own terms, the focus is on the texts of the ancient Christian writers themselves, not on modern commentators' views or opinions of the ancient writers. We have looked for those comments on Scripture that will assist the contemporary reader to encounter the deepest level of penetration of the text that has been reached by its best interpreters living amid highly divergent early Christian social settings.

Our purpose is not to engage in critical speculations on textual variants or stemma of the text, or extensive deliberations on its cultural context or social location, however useful those exercises may be, but to present the most discerning comments of the ancient Christian writers with a minimum of distraction. This project would be entirely misconceived if thought of as a modern commentary on patristic commentaries.

9. We have intentionally sought out and gathered comments that will aid effective preaching, comments that give us a firmer grasp of the plain sense of the text, its authorial intent, and its spiritual meaning for the worshiping community. We want to help Bible readers and teachers gain ready access to the deepest reflection of the ancient Christian community of faith on any particular text of Scripture.

It would have inordinately increased the word count and cost if our intention had been to amass exhaustively all that had ever been said about a Scripture text by every ancient Christian writer. Rather, we have deliberately selected out of this immense data stream the strongest patristic interpretive reflections on the text and sought to deliver them in accurate English translation.

To refine and develop these guidelines, we have sought to select as volume editors either patristics scholars who understand the nature of preaching and the history of exegesis, or biblical scholars who are at ease working with classical Greek and Latin sources. We have preferred editors who are sympathetic to the needs of lay persons and pastors alike, who are generally familiar with the patristic corpus in its full range, and who intuitively understand the dilemma of preaching today. The international and ecclesiastically diverse character of this team of editors corresponds with the global range of our task and audience, which bridge all major communions of Christianity.

---

[7]Through the letters, histories, theological and biographical writings of Tertullian, Gregory of Nyssa, Gregory of Nazianzus, Jerome, John Chrysostom, Palladius, Augustine, Ephrem, Gerontius, Paulinus of Nola and many anonymous writers (of the Lives of Mary of Egypt, Thais, Pelagia).

[8]Whose voice is heard through her younger brother, Gregory of Nyssa.

Is the ACCS a Commentary?

We have chosen to call our work a commentary, and with good reason. A commentary, in its plain sense definition, is "a series of illustrative or explanatory notes on any important work, as on the Scriptures."[9] *Commentary* is an Anglicized form of the Latin *commentarius* (an "annotation" or "memoranda" on a subject or text or series of events). In its theological meaning it is a work that explains, analyzes or expounds a portion of Scripture. In antiquity it was a book of notes explaining some earlier work such as Julius Hyginus's commentaries on Virgil in the first century. Jerome mentions many commentators on secular texts before his time.

The commentary is typically preceded by a proem in which questions are asked: who wrote it? why? when? to whom? Comments may deal with grammatical or lexical problems in the text. An attempt is made to provide the gist of the author's thought or motivation, and perhaps to deal with sociocultural influences at work in the text or philological nuances. A commentary usually takes a section of a classical text and seeks to make its meaning clear to readers today, or proximately clearer, in line with the intent of the author.

The Western literary genre of commentary is definitively shaped by the history of early Christian commentaries on Scripture, from Origen and Hilary through John Chrysostom and Cyril of Alexandria to Thomas Aquinas and Nicolas of Lyra. It leaves too much unsaid simply to assume that the Christian biblical commentary took a previously extant literary genre and reshaped it for Christian texts. Rather, it is more accurate to say that the Western literary genre of the commentary (and especially the biblical commentary) has patristic commentaries as its decisive pattern and prototype, and those commentaries have strongly influenced the whole Western conception of the genre of commentary. Only in the last two centuries, since the development of modern historicist methods of criticism, have some scholars sought to delimit the definition of a commentary more strictly so as to include only historicist interests—philological and grammatical insights; inquiries into author, date and setting, or into sociopolitical or economic circumstances; literary analyses of genre, structure and function of the text; or questions of textual criticism and reliability. The ACCS editors do not feel apologetic about calling this work a commentary in its classic sense.

Many astute readers of modern commentaries are acutely aware of one of their most persistent habits of mind: control of the text by the interpreter, whereby the ancient text comes under the power (values, assumptions, predispositions, ideological biases) of the modern interpreter. This habit is based upon a larger pattern of modern chauvinism that views later critical sources as more worthy than earlier. This prejudice tends to view the biblical text primarily or sometimes exclusively through historical-critical lenses accommodative to modernity.

Although we respect these views and our volume editors are thoroughly familiar with contemporary biblical criticism, the ACCS editors freely take the assumption that the Christian canon is to be respected as the church's sacred text. The text's assumptions about itself cannot be made less important than modern assumptions about it. The reading and preaching of Scripture are vital to the church's life.

---

[9]*Funk & Wagnalls New "Standard" Dictionary of the English Language* (New York: Funk & Wagnalls, 1947).

The central hope of the ACCS endeavor is that it might contribute in some small way to the revitalization of that life through a renewed discovery of the earliest readings of the church's Scriptures.

A Gentle Caveat for Those Who Expect Ancient Writers to Conform to Modern Assumptions

If one begins by assuming as normative for a commentary the typical modern expression of what a commentary is and the preemptive truthfulness of modern critical methods, the classic Christian exegetes are by definition always going to appear as dated, quaint, premodern, hence inadequate, and in some instances comic or even mean-spirited, prejudiced, unjust and oppressive. So in the interest of hermeneutic fairness, it is recommended that the modern reader not impose on ancient Christian exegetes lately achieved modern assumptions about the valid reading of Scripture. The ancient Christian writers constantly challenge what were later to become these unspoken, hidden and often indeed camouflaged modern assumptions.

This series does not seek to resolve the debate between the merits of ancient and modern exegesis in each text examined. Rather it seeks merely to present the excerpted comments of the ancient interpreters with as few distractions as possible. We will leave it to others to discuss the merits of ancient versus modern methods of exegesis. But even this cannot be done adequately without extensively examining the texts of ancient exegesis. And until now biblical scholars have not had easy access to many of these texts. This is what this series is for.

The purpose of exegesis in the patristic period was humbly to seek the revealed truth the Scriptures convey. Often it was not even offered to those who were as yet unready to put it into practice. In these respects much modern exegesis is entirely different: It does not assume the truth of Scripture as revelation, nor does it submit personally to the categorical moral requirement of the revealed text: that it be taken seriously as divine address. Yet we are here dealing with patristic writers who assumed that readers would not even approach an elementary discernment of the meaning of the text if they were not ready to live in terms of its revelation, that is, to practice it in order to hear it, as was recommended so often in the classic tradition.

The patristic models of exegesis often do not conform to modern commentary assumptions that tend to resist or rule out chains of scriptural reference. These are often demeaned as deplorable proof-texting. But among the ancient Christian writers such chains of biblical reference were very important in thinking about the text in relation to the whole testimony of sacred Scripture by the analogy of faith, comparing text with text, on the premise that *scripturam ex scriptura explicandam esse* ("Scripture is best explained from Scripture").

We beg readers not to force the assumptions of twentieth-century fundamentalism on the ancient Christian writers, who themselves knew nothing of what we now call fundamentalism. It is uncritical to conclude that they were simple fundamentalists in the modern sense. Patristic exegesis was not fundamentalist, because the Fathers were not reacting against modern naturalistic reductionism. They were constantly protesting a merely literal or plain-sense view of the text, always looking for its spiritual and moral and typological nuances. Modern fundamentalism oppositely is a defensive response branching out and away from modern historicism, which looks far more like modern historicism than ancient typological reasoning. Ironically, this makes both liberal and fundamentalist exegesis much more like each other than either are like the ancient Christian exegesis, because they both tend to appeal to rationalistic and historicist assumptions raised to the forefront by the Enlightenment.

Since the principle prevails in ancient Christian exegesis that each text is illumined by other texts and by the whole of the history of revelation, we find in patristic comments on a given text many other subtexts interwoven in order to illumine that text. When ancient exegesis weaves many Scriptures together, it does not limit its focus to a single text, as much modern exegesis prefers, but constantly relates it to other texts by analogy, intensively using typological reasoning, as did the rabbinic tradition.

The attempt to read the New Testament while ruling out all theological and moral, to say nothing of ecclesiastical, sacramental and dogmatic assumptions that have prevailed generally in the community of faith that wrote it, seems to many who participate in that community today a very thin enterprise indeed. When we try to make sense of the New Testament while ruling out the plausibility of the incarnation and resurrection, the effort appears arrogant and distorted. One who tendentiously reads one page of patristic exegesis, gasps and tosses it away because it does not conform adequately to the canons of modern exegesis and historicist commentary is surely no model of critical effort.

On Misogyny and Anti-Semitism

The questions of anti-Semitism and misogyny require circumspect comment. The patristic writers are perceived by some to be incurably anti-Semitic or misogynous or both. I would like to briefly attempt a cautious apologia for the ancient Christian writers, leaving details to others' more deliberate efforts. I know how hazardous this is, especially when done briefly. But it has become such a stumbling block to some of our readers that it prevents them even from listening to the ancient ecumenical teachers. The issue deserves some reframing and careful argumentation.

Although these are challengeable assumptions and highly controverted, it is my view that modern racial anti-Semitism was not in the minds of the ancient Christian writers. Their arguments were not framed in regard to the hatred of a race, but rather the place of the elect people of God, the Jews, in the history of the divine-human covenant that is fulfilled in Jesus Christ. Patristic arguments may have had the unintended effect of being unfair to women according to modern standards, but their intention was to understand the role of women according to apostolic teaching.

This does not solve all of the tangled moral questions regarding the roles of Christians in the histories of anti-Semitism and misogyny, which require continuing fair-minded study and clarification. Whether John Chrysostom or Justin Martyr were anti-Semitic depends on whether the term *anti-Semitic* has a racial or religious-typological definition. In my view, the patristic texts that appear to modern readers to be anti-Semitic in most cases have a typological reference and are based on a specific approach to the interpretation of Scripture—the analogy of faith—which assesses each particular text in relation to the whole trend of the history of revelation and which views the difference between Jew and Gentile under christological assumptions and not merely as a matter of genetics or race.

Even in their harshest strictures against Judaizing threats to the gospel, they did not consider Jews as racially or genetically inferior people, as modern anti-Semites are prone to do. Even in their comments on Paul's strictures against women teaching, they showed little or no animus against the female gender as such, but rather exalted women as "the glory of man."

Compare the writings of Rosemary Radford Ruether and David C. Ford[10] on these perplexing issues. Ruether steadily applies modern criteria of justice to judge the inadequacies of the ancient Christian writers. Ford seeks to understand the ancient Christian writers empathically from within their own historical assumptions, limitations, scriptural interpretations and deeper intentions. While both treatments are illuminating, Ford's treatment comes closer to a fair-minded assessment of patristic intent.

A Note on Pelagius

The selection criteria do not rule out passages from Pelagius's commentaries at those points at which they provide good exegesis. This requires special explanation, if we are to hold fast to our criterion of consensuality.

The literary corpus of Pelagius remains highly controverted. Though Pelagius was by general consent the arch-heretic of the early fifth century, Pelagius's edited commentaries, as we now have them highly worked over by later orthodox writers, were widely read and preserved for future generations under other names. So Pelagius presents us with a textual dilemma.

Until 1934 all we had was a corrupted text of his Pauline commentary and fragments quoted by Augustine. Since then his works have been much studied and debated, and we now know that the Pelagian corpus has been so warped by a history of later redactors that we might be tempted not to quote it at all. But it does remain a significant source of fifth-century comment on Paul. So we cannot simply ignore it. My suggestion is that the reader is well advised not to equate the fifth-century Pelagius too easily with later standard stereotypes of the arch-heresy of Pelagianism.[11]

It has to be remembered that the text of Pelagius on Paul as we now have it was preserved in the corpus of Jerome and probably reworked in the sixth century by either Primasius or Cassiodorus or both. These commentaries were repeatedly recycled and redacted, so what we have today may be regarded as consonant with much standard later patristic thought and exegesis, excluding, of course, that which is ecumenically censured as "Pelagianism."

Pelagius's original text was in specific ways presumably explicitly heretical, but what we have now is largely unexceptional, even if it is still possible to detect points of disagreement with Augustine. We may have been ill-advised to quote this material as "Pelagius" and perhaps might have quoted it as "Pseudo-Pelagius" or "Anonymous," but here we follow contemporary reference practice.

---

[10]Rosemary Radford Ruether, *Gregory of Nazianzus: Rhetor and Philosopher* (Oxford: Clarendon Press, 1969); Rosemary Radford Ruether, ed., *Religion and Sexism: Images of Woman in the Jewish and Christian Traditions* (New York: Simon & Schuster, 1974); David C. Ford, "Men and Women in the Early Church: The Full Views of St. John Chrysostom" (So. Canaan, Penn.: St. Tikhon's Orthodox Theological Seminary, 1995). Cf. related works by John Meyendorff, Stephen B. Clark and Paul K. Jewett.
[11]Cf. Adalbert Hamman, Supplementum to PL 1:1959, cols. 1101-1570.

What to Expect from the Introductions, Overviews and the Design of the Commentary

In writing the introduction for a particular volume, the volume editor typically discusses the opinion of the Fathers regarding authorship of the text, the importance of the biblical book for patristic interpreters, the availability or paucity of patristic comment, any salient points of debate between the Fathers, and any particular challenges involved in editing that particular volume. The introduction affords the opportunity to frame the entire commentary in a manner that will help the general reader understand the nature and significance of patristic comment on the biblical texts under consideration, and to help readers find their bearings and use the commentary in an informed way.

The purpose of the *overview* is to give readers a brief glimpse into the cumulative argument of the pericope, identifying its major patristic contributors. This is a task of summarizing. We here seek to render a service to readers by stating the gist of patristic argument on a series of verses. Ideally the overview should track a reasonably cohesive thread of argument among patristic comments on the pericope, even though they are derived from diverse sources and times. The design of the overview may vary somewhat from volume to volume of this series, depending on the requirements of the specific book of Scripture.

The purpose of the selection *heading* is to introduce readers quickly into the subject matter of that selection. In this way readers can quickly grasp what is coming by glancing over the headings and overview. Usually it is evident upon examination that some phrase in the selection naturally defines the subject of the heading. Several verses may be linked together for comment.

Since biographical information on each ancient Christian writer is in abundant supply in various general reference works, dictionaries and encyclopedias, the ACCS has no reason to duplicate these efforts. But we have provided in each volume a simple chronological list of those quoted in that volume and an alphabetical set of biographical sketches with minimal ecclesiastical, jurisdictional and place identifications.

Each passage of Scripture presents its own distinct set of problems concerning both selection and translation. The sheer quantity of textual materials that has been searched out, assessed and reviewed varies widely from book to book. There are also wide variations in the depth of patristic insight into texts, the complexity of culturally shaped allusions and the modern relevance of the materials examined. It has been a challenge to each volume editor to draw together and develop a reasonably cohesive sequence of textual interpretations from all of this diversity.

The footnotes intend to assist readers with obscurities and potential confusions. In the annotations we have identified many of the Scripture allusions and historical references embedded within the texts.

The aim of our editing is to help readers move easily from text to text through a deliberate editorial linking process that is seen in the overviews, headings and annotations. We have limited the footnotes to roughly less than a one in ten ratio to the patristic texts themselves. Abbreviations are used in the footnotes, and a list of abbreviations is included in each volume. We found that the task of editorial linkage need not be forced into a single pattern for all biblical books but must be molded by that particular book.

The Complementarity of Interdisciplinary Research Methods in This Investigation

The ACCS is intrinsically an interdisciplinary research endeavor. It conjointly employs several diverse but interrelated methods of research, each of which is a distinct field of inquiry in its own right. Principal among these methods are the following:

Textual criticism. No literature is ever transmitted by handwritten manuscripts without the risk of some variations in the text creeping in. Because we are working with ancient texts, frequently recopied, we are obliged to employ all methods of inquiry appropriate to the study of ancient texts. To that end, we have depended heavily on the most reliable text-critical scholarship employed in both biblical and patristic studies. The work of textual critics in these fields has been invaluable in providing us with the most authoritative and reliable versions of ancient texts currently available. We have gratefully employed the extensive critical analyses used in creating the Thesaurus Linguae Graecae and Cetedoc databases.

In respect to the biblical texts, our database researchers and volume editors have often been faced with the challenge of considering which variants within the biblical text itself are assumed in a particular selection. It is not always self-evident which translation or stemma of the biblical text is being employed by the ancient commentator. We have supplied explanatory footnotes in some cases where these various textual challenges may raise potential concerns for readers.

Social-historical contextualization. Our volume editors have sought to understand the historical, social, economic and political contexts of the selections taken from these ancient texts. This understanding is often vital to the process of discerning what a given comment means or intends and which comments are most appropriate to the biblical passage at hand. However, our mission is not primarily to discuss these contexts extensively or to display them in the references. We are not primarily interested in the social location of the text or the philological history of particular words or in the societal consequences of the text, however interesting or evocative these may be. Some of these questions, however, can be treated briefly in the footnotes wherever the volume editors deem necessary.

Though some modest contextualization of patristic texts is at times useful and required, our purpose is not to provide a detailed social-historical placement of each patristic text. That would require volumes ten times this size. We know there are certain texts that need only slight contextualization, others that require a great deal more. Meanwhile, other texts stand on their own easily and brilliantly, in some cases aphoristically, without the need of extensive contextualization. These are the texts we have most sought to identify and include. We are least interested in those texts that obviously require a lot of convoluted explanation for a modern audience. We are particularly inclined to rule out those blatantly offensive texts (apparently anti-Semitic, morally repugnant, glaringly chauvinistic) and those that are intrinsically ambiguous or those that would simply be self-evidently alienating to the modern audience.

Exegesis. If the practice of social-historical contextualization is secondary to the purpose of the ACCS, the emphasis on thoughtful patristic exegesis of the biblical text is primary. The intention of our volume editors is to search for selections that define, discuss and explain the meanings that patristic commentators have discovered in the biblical text. Our purpose is not to provide an inoffensive or extensively demythologized, aseptic modern interpretation of the ancient commentators on each Scripture text but to allow their comments to speak for themselves from within their own worldview.

In this series the term *exegesis* is used more often in its classic than in its modern sense. In its classic sense, exegesis includes efforts to explain, interpret and comment on a text, its meaning, its sources, its connections with other texts. It implies a close reading of the text, using whatever linguistic, historical, literary or theological resources are available to explain the text. It is contrasted with *eisegesis*, which implies that the interpreter has imposed his or her own personal opinions or assumptions on the text.

The patristic writers actively practiced *intra*textual exegesis, which seeks to define and identify the exact wording of the text, its grammatical structure and the interconnectedness of its parts. They also practiced *extra*textual exegesis, seeking to discern the geographical, historical or cultural context in which the text was written. Most important, they were also very well practiced in *inter*textual exegesis, seeking to discern the meaning of a text by comparing it with other texts.

Hermeneutics. We are especially attentive to the ways in which the ancient Christian writers described their own interpreting processes. This hermeneutic self-analysis is especially rich in the reflections of Origen, Tertullian, Jerome, Augustine and Vincent of Lérins.[12] Although most of our volume editors are thoroughly familiar with contemporary critical discussions of hermeneutical and literary methods, it is not the purpose of ACCS to engage these issues directly. Instead, we are concerned to display and reveal the various hermeneutic assumptions that inform the patristic reading of Scripture, chiefly by letting the writers speak in their own terms.

Homiletics. One of the practical goals of the ACCS is the renewal of contemporary preaching in the light of the wisdom of ancient Christian preaching. With this goal in mind, many of the most trenchant and illuminating comments included are selected not from formal commentaries but from the homilies of the ancient Christian writers. It comes as no surprise that the most renowned among these early preachers were also those most actively engaged in the task of preaching. The prototypical Fathers who are most astute at describing their own homiletic assumptions and methods are Gregory the Great, Leo the Great, Augustine, Cyril of Jerusalem, John Chrysostom, Peter Chrysologus and Caesarius of Arles.

Pastoral care. Another intensely practical goal of the ACCS is to renew our readers' awareness of the ancient tradition of pastoral care and ministry to persons. Among the leading Fathers who excel in pastoral wisdom and in application of the Bible to the work of ministry are Gregory of Nazianzus, John Chrysostom, Augustine and Gregory the Great. Our editors have presented this monumental pastoral wisdom in a guileless way that is not inundated by the premises of contemporary psychotherapy, sociology and naturalistic reductionism.

Translation theory. Each volume is composed of direct quotations in dynamic equivalent English translation of ancient Christian writers, translated from the original language in its best received text. The adequacy of a given attempt at translation is always challengeable. The task of translation is intrinsically debatable. We have sought dynamic equivalency[13] without lapsing into paraphrase, and a literary trans-

---

[12]Our concern for this aspect of the project has resulted in the production of a companion volume to the ACCS written by the ACCS Associate Editor, Prof. Christopher Hall of Eastern College, *Reading Scripture with the Church Fathers* (Downers Grove, Ill.: InterVarsity Press, 1998).

[13]The theory of dynamic equivalency has been most thoroughly worked out by Eugene A. Nida, *Toward a Science of Translating* (Leiden: Brill, 1964), and Eugene A. Nida and Jan de Waard, *From One Language to Another: Functional Equivalence in Bible Translating* (Nashville, Tenn.: Nelson, 1986). Its purpose is "to state clearly and accurately the meaning of the original texts in words and forms that are widely accepted by people who use English as a means of communication." It attempts to set forth the writer's "content and message in a standard, everyday, natural form of English." Its aim is "to give today's readers maximum understanding of the content of the original texts." "Every effort has been made to use language that is natural, clear, simple, and unambiguous. Consequently there has been no attempt to reproduce in English the parts of speech, sentence structure, word order and grammatical devices of the original languages. Faithfulness in translation also includes a faithful repre-

lation without lapsing into wooden literalism. We have tried consistently to make accessible to contemporary readers the vital nuances and energies of the languages of antiquity. Whenever possible we have opted for metaphors and terms that are normally used by communicators today.

What Have We Achieved?
We have designed the first full-scale early Christian commentary on Scripture in the last five hundred years. Any future attempts at a Christian Talmud or patristic commentary on Scripture will either follow much of our design or stand in some significant response to it.

We have successfully brought together a distinguished international network of Protestant, Catholic and Orthodox scholars, editors and translators of the highest quality and reputation to accomplish this design.

This brilliant network of scholars, editors, publishers, technicians and translators, which constitutes an amazing *novum* and a distinct new ecumenical reality in itself, has jointly brought into formulation the basic pattern and direction of the project, gradually amending and correcting it as needed. We have provided an interdisciplinary experimental research model for the integration of digital search techniques with the study of the history of exegesis.

At this time of writing, we are approximately halfway through the actual production of the series and about halfway through the time frame of the project, having developed the design to a point where it is not likely to change significantly. We have made time-dated contracts with all volume editors for the remainder of the volumes. We are thus well on our way toward bringing the English ACCS to completion. We have extended and enhanced our international network to a point where we are now poised to proceed into modern non-English language versions of ACCS. We already have inaugurated editions in Spanish, Chinese, Arabic, Russian and Italian, and are preparing for editions in Arabic and German, with several more languages under consideration.

We have received the full cooperation and support of Drew University as academic sponsor of the project—a distinguished university that has a remarkable record of supporting major international publication projects that have remained in print for long periods of time, in many cases over one-hundred years. The most widely used Bible concordance and biblical word-reference system in the world today was composed by Drew professor James Strong. It was the very room once occupied by Professor Strong, where the concordance research was done in the 1880s, that for many years was my office at Drew and coincidentally the place where this series was conceived. Today *Strong's Exhaustive Concordance of the Bible* rests on the shelves of most pastoral libraries in the English-speaking world over a hundred years after its first publication. Similarly the *New York Times's* Arno Press has kept in print the major multivolume Drew University work of John M'Clintock and James Strong, *Theological and Exegetical Encyclopedia*. The major edition of Christian classics in Chinese was done at Drew University fifty years

---

sentation of the cultural and historical features of the original, without any attempt to modernize the text" (preface, *Good News Bible: The Bible in Today's English Version* [New York: American Bible Society, 1976)]). This does not imply a preference for paraphrase, but a middle ground between literary and literal theories of translation. Not all of our volume editors have viewed the translation task precisely in the same way, but the hope of the series has been generally guided by the theory of dynamic equivalency.

ago and is still in print. Drew University has supplied much of the leadership, space, library, work-study assistance and services that have enabled these durable international scholarly projects to be undertaken.

Our selfless benefactors have preferred to remain anonymous. They have been well-informed, active partners in its conceptualization and development, and unflagging advocates and counselors in the support of this lengthy and costly effort. The series has been blessed by steady and generous support, and accompanied by innumerable gifts of providence.

Thomas C. Oden
Henry Anson Buttz Professor of Theology, Drew University
General Editor, ACCS

A Guide to Using This Commentary

Several features have been incorporated into the design of this commentary. The following comments are intended to assist readers in making full use of this volume.

Pericopes of Scripture
The scriptural text has been divided into pericopes, or passages, usually several verses in length. Each of these pericopes is given a heading, which appears at the beginning of the pericope. For example, the first pericope in the commentary on Matthew 1—13 is "1:1-17 The Genealogy of Jesus Christ." This heading is followed by the Scripture passage quoted in the Revised Standard Version (RSV) across the full width of the page. The Scripture passage is provided for the convenience of readers, but it is also in keeping with medieval patristic commentaries, in which the citations of the Fathers were arranged around the text of Scripture.

Overviews
Following each pericope of text is an overview of the patristic comments on that pericope. The format of this overview varies within the volumes of this series, depending on the requirements of the specific book of Scripture. The function of the overview is to provide a brief summary of all the comments to follow. It tracks a reasonably cohesive thread of argument among patristic comments, even though they are derived from diverse sources and generations. Thus the summaries do not proceed chronologically or by verse sequence. Rather they seek to rehearse the overall course of the patristic comment on that pericope.

We do not assume that the commentators themselves anticipated or expressed a formally received cohesive argument but rather that the various arguments tend to flow in a plausible, recognizable pattern. Modern readers can thus glimpse aspects of continuity in the flow of diverse exegetical traditions representing various generations and geographical locations.

Topical Headings
An abundance of varied patristic comment is available for each pericope of these letters. For this reason we have broken the pericopes into two levels. First is the verse with its topical heading. The patristic comments are then focused on aspects of each verse, with topical headings summarizing the essence of the patristic comment by evoking a key phrase, metaphor or idea. This feature provides a bridge by

which modern readers can enter into the heart of the patristic comment.

Identifying the Patristic Texts

Following the topical heading of each section of comment, the name of the patristic commentator is given. An English translation of the patristic comment is then provided. This is immediately followed by the title of the patristic work and the textual reference—either by book, section and subsection or by book-and-verse references.

The Footnotes

Readers who wish to pursue a deeper investigation of the patristic works cited in this commentary will find the footnotes especially valuable. A footnote number directs the reader to the notes at the bottom of the right-hand column, where in addition to other notations (clarifications or biblical cross references) one will find information on English translations (where available) and standard original-language editions of the work cited. An abbreviated citation (normally citing the book, volume and page number) of the work is provided except in cases where a line-by-line commentary is being quoted, in which case the biblical references will lead directly to the selection. A key to the abbreviations is provided on page xxxv. Where there is any serious ambiguity or textual problem in the selection, we have tried to reflect the best available textual tradition.

For the convenience of computer database users the digital database references are provided to either the Thesaurus Linguae Graecae (Greek texts) or to the Cetedoc (Latin texts) in both the appendix found on pages 297-98 and the bibliography found on pages 313-14.

Abbreviations

ACW	Ancient Christian Writers: The Works of the Fathers in Translation. Mahwah, N.J.: Paulist, 1946-.
ANF	A. Roberts and J. Donaldson, eds. Ante-Nicene Fathers. 10 vols. Buffalo, N.Y.: Christian Literature, 1885-1896. Reprint, Grand Rapids, Mich.: Eerdmans, 1951-1956; Reprint, Peabody, Mass.: Hendrickson, 1994.
CCL	Corpus Christianorum. Series Latina. Turnhout, Belgium: Brepols, 1953-.
CS	Cistercian Studies. Kalamazoo, Mich.: Cistercian Publications, 1973-.
FC	Fathers of the Church: A New Translation. Washington, D.C.: Catholic University of America Press, 1947-.
GCS	Die griechischen christlichen Schriftsteller. Berlin: Akademie-Verlag, 1897-.
MA	*Miscellanea Agostiniana*. 2 vols. Edited by Antonio Casamassa. Rome: Tipografia Poliglotta Vaticana, 1930-1931.
MKGK	*Matthäus-Kommentare aus der griechischen Kirche*. Edited by Joseph Reuss. Berlin: Akademie-Verlag, 1957.
NPNF	P. Schaff et al., eds. A Select Library of the Nicene and Post-Nicene Fathers of the Christian Church. 2nd series (14 vols. each). Buffalo, N.Y.: Christian Literature, 1887-1894; Reprint, Grand Rapids, Mich.: Eerdmans, 1952-1956; Reprint, Peabody, Mass.: Hendrickson, 1994.
PG	J.-P. Migne, ed. Patrologiae cursus completus. Series Graeca. 166 vols. Paris: Migne, 1857-1886.
PL	J.-P. Migne, ed. Patrologiae cursus completus. Series Latina. 221 vols. Paris: Migne, 1844-1864.
PL Supp	A. Hamman, ed. Patrologia Latinae Supplementum. Paris: Garnier Frères, 1958-.
PO	Patrologia Orientalis. Paris, 1903-.
RB	*Revue bénédictine*. Belgium: Abbaye de Maredsous. 1884-.
SC	H. de Lubac, J. Daniélou et al., eds. Sources Chrétiennes. Paris: Editions du Cerf, 1941-.
SSL	Spicilegium Sacrum Lovaniense: Études et Documents. Université Catholique. Louvain, 1922-.
WSA	J. E. Rotelle, ed. *Works of St. Augustine: A Translation for the Twenty-First Century*. Hyde Park, N.Y.: New City Press, 1995.

INTRODUCTION TO MATTHEW

Of the four Gospels contained in the canon of the New Testament, those of Matthew and John were the most widely read and therefore the most commented upon during the patristic age; also, the use of Matthew began far earlier than that of John. Consequently, it is no exaggeration to state that the faithful who lived between the end of the first and the end of the second centuries came to know the words and deeds of Christ on the basis of this text.

Toward the end of the first century, the *Didache* demonstrates a direct knowledge of this Gospel, and only a few years later the letter of Pseudo-Barnabas cites it as a divinely inspired Scripture: "because it should not happen, as it has been written, that many of us were called but few were chosen" (*Barnabas* 4.14 [Mt 22:14]). The first explicit mention of this Gospel dates to the third decade of the second century and is made by Papias, bishop of Hierapolis (Phrygia): "Matthew gathered the sayings [of Jesus] in the Hebrew tongue, and each person translated them as he was able" (in Eusebius *Ecclesiastical History* 3.39.16). Its use becomes more frequent with the passage of time, demonstrating the increased interest in the words and the deeds of Jesus, especially for the Sermon on the Mount. And alongside simple echoes of the text, explicit citations appear, particularly in Justin, toward the middle of the second century. To Justin we are indebted for the earliest description of the Eucharistic celebration, composed during his sojourn in Rome (*First Apology* 67), and we can be certain that among the remembrances of the apostles he mentions having read during the celebration, the Gospel of Matthew was to be found. Some decades later, about 190, the Catholic canon of the New Testament was constituted, and the Gospel of Matthew, by now in general use not only among Catholics but also among heretics (Gnostics), is given the first rank, followed by the other three Gospels.

Irenaeus is the first Catholic author to attest to the constitution of the New Testament canon, and consequently he cites the Gospel of Matthew regularly, together with the other books, as inspired Scripture on the same level as the Old Testament. Subsequent authors (Hippolytus, Tertullian, Cyprian, Novatian and others) do likewise. In fact, these writers make regular use of both the Old Testament and the New Testament, both in polemics with heretics and in teachings and admonitions of an ascetic, ethical and disciplinary nature for the community of faith. Such use also clearly implies an interpretation of the scriptural passages to fit the author's reasoning. However, for the majority of the authors mentioned, it is an implicit interpretation, not offered as an end in itself or inspired by aims that were exclusively and independently exegetical, but rather produced in connection with the subject then under consideration, such that one cannot yet consider this type of work to be explicitly exegetical literature. However, by the 160s the Valentinian Gnostic Heracleon had already composed a systematic commentary on the Gospel of John, and toward the end of the century Hippolytus introduced this innovation to the Catholic sphere, citing certain texts that serve in the interpretation of the scriptural text being commented upon, though with a preference for Old Testament texts.

For the first systematic commentary on Matthew we must wait for the mature Origen of the 240s. Given that exegetical literature developed in the West considerably later than in the East, we must wait more than a century for the first commentary on Matthew in Latin, by Hilary of Poitiers. After the appearance of these pioneering works, the Gospel of Matthew was among the most frequently commented on texts, even though much of this production, especially in Greek, has survived only in fragmentary form. A specific look at the texts used in this collection will be provided in the second part of this introduction. At present we will survey the distinctive characteristics of this exegetical literature on Matthew, considering both the external form of the various writings and the methods of interpretation adopted by the various authors.

The texts that interpret and comment on the Gospel of Matthew have come down to us in the form of commentaries and homilies. By "exegetical commentary" is meant a systematic and continuous interpretation of all or part of a book of the sacred Scriptures. Within this common term, commentaries could have had different origins. Some were conceived with the sole purpose of being written and published for reading. Others represented a homogeneous series of reworked homilies, designed for publication in a continuous exposition so as to bridge the disruptions in the passage from one homily to another. Still others derived from explanations taught in the schools, reworked more or less summarily for the purposes of publication. In the specific case of the commentaries on Matthew, Origen's commentary belongs to the last category and those of Hilary and Jerome to the first, while examples of the second type—the exegetical form favored by Ambrose—are absent. The literary form of the Christian biblical commentary was patterned after the pagan scholastic commentary, which was either grammatical or philosophical, depending on whether the texts interpreted were literary or philosophical. Among those using the grammatical pattern, rhetorical and antiquarian illustrations were fairly concise, while there was greater breadth and liberty of development in those following the philosophical pattern.

The structure of these exegetical commentaries was simple. The text that was the subject of the commentary was divided into passages that ranged in length from extremely brief to several lines long. Each passage was followed by its explanation, which aimed to illustrate the general sense of the passage and all or most of its principal details. This structural simplicity allowed the maximum freedom of scope, ranging from the twenty-five-book commentary of Origen to the commentary of Hilary in a single book. A different genre of commentary was the so-called catenae, widespread in the Greek-language area from the sixth century. These commentaries on the Scripture were put together from passages of previous exegetical works and arranged so as to furnish several interpretations for every passage of the text under consideration, each with its author. Since the bulk of Greek exegetical literature has been lost, we know of many commentaries, even those of exegetes of the first rank, only through the catena collections. For the Gospel of Matthew, this is true of Apollinaris of Laodicea, Theodore of Heraclea, Theodore of Mopsuestia and Cyril of Alexandria.

Turning to the homilies, we must first distinguish between serial and discrete homilies. The former represent an organic series of homilies preached within a short time and conceived in such a way as to interpret in a systematic fashion an entire book of Scripture or a large part of it. Collections of this sort do not differ in content from commentaries derived from organic series of homilies. The difference consists in a less extensive reelaboration of materials in the serial homily collection as compared with this type of commentary, through which the homilies preserve their character as distinct discourses, separated one from the other—even if in their sequence closely connected—by the continuity of the interpreted text. For Matthew, the most characteristic example of serial homily is John Chrysostom's ninety homilies, which cover the entire body of the Gospel. In the Latin world, we should remember the collection of homilies (*tractatus*) by Chromatius of Aquileia. Alongside these exhaustive serial collections we find numerous isolated homilies, primarily deriving from Sunday preaching, by a wide range of authors, from Augustine to Severus of Antioch, Eusebius of Emesa to Gregory the Great. While the commentary normally has a primarily didactic purpose, the homily adds a paraenetic or morally instructive aim, which can even become predominant (as often occurs in Chrysostom). Despite this more composite character, however, the patristic homily on a scriptural theme does not normally lose its specifically exegetical dimension, aimed, that is, at the interpretation of the text.

In this sense Origen was an innovator. Having begun to preach at a rather advanced age, he brought into the homily the specifically exegetical aim of the commentary, above all by dividing into passages even the biblical texts to be explained to the audience, so that the resulting explanation was continuous and complete. His method of elucidating the biblical text in public became widespread. Even when, in a later phase, the paraenetic aim joined the didactic one predominant in Origen, the habit then prevailing of breaking the read biblical text into passages and adding relevant explanation afterwards preserved the exegetical density of the homily. This prevented readings during liturgical meetings from becoming a pretext for merely generic explanations aimed only at the emotions.

The passage-by-passage explanation of the biblical text was designed to disclose the text's meaning to readers and listeners. These explanations varied widely, depending on the ability of the interpreter and on the intellectual environment by which he was influenced. While recognizing the complexity of the history of biblical exegesis in the patristic age, we may in general terms distinguish between literal and allegorical interpretation. Literal interpretation aimed at the direct explanation of the text, in order to bring out the meaning that we today call "historical." However, this type of interpretation, apart from indispensable clarifications of a geohistorical and a general antiquarian nature that it provided, could be executed at different levels of refinement and therefore in different ways and with differing results (the interested reader can take stock of this only through consultation of the texts). I will here limit myself to a brief look at certain general difficulties and interpretive tendencies regarding the interpretation of the Gospel of Matthew.

The traditional method of interpreting Scripture with Scripture, a transposition of the grammatical technique that interpreted Homer with Homer, in Gospel exegesis consisted above all in linking a given passage of the Gospels directly interpreted with the parallel passages of the other Gospels. This was done for two purposes. First, the author sought to explain the divergences among the Gospels in the recounting of the same episodes, when read in the most literal sense (e.g., the post-Easter stories). Second, a detail present in one Gospel was used to better clarify the meaning of another, in which that detail did not appear. For example, Cyril (fragment 290) observes that Jesus, during the Last Supper, conse-crated the bread and the wine after Judas departed. This detail does not appear in Matthew, but Cyril found it in John and transferred it in order to illustrate the text of Matthew. Matthew's Gospel takes pains to note in a systematic fashion how the prophecies of the Old Testament were realized in the acts of Jesus. This tendency was emphasized by the exegetes by extending the references to other texts of the Old Testament in order to accentuate the completion, through Christ, of the divine economy already in operation in the Old Testament age and aimed at the redemption of all humanity. The objective of every exegete is to demonstrate that all of Christ's deeds and words fit into a divine plan that excludes unfore-seen events and improvisations, both in the relation between Jesus and the people and in his conflict with the Jewish authorities, in a succession that develops gradually toward the conclusion that had been his aim from the beginning of his public activities. It should again be stressed that, from the fourth cen-tury on, the continuation of the trinitarian and christological polemics brought to the attention of all exegetes the advisability of stressing, in the interpretation of the Gospel text, the specific terms of their profession of faith regarding the issues of God, Christ and the Trinity. In this sense Chrysostom, but also Hilary, Jerome and Chromatius, are careful to maintain the perfect divinity of Christ and his equality with the Father, while one notices Cyril's care to affirm the copresence of the divine and human natures in Christ incarnate.

We notice immediately the frequent use of allegorical interpretation among our exegetes on Matthew. Because of the overriding historicism of this age, the modern reader is no longer familiar with this method of exegesis and may be perplexed by the frequency with which it is employed. It is therefore use-ful to preface the discussion of this subject with several general observations. In the first place I would point out the necessity, already felt by the first generation of Christians, to demonstrate over against the Jews the messianic nature of Christ on the basis of the guarantee of the Old Testament prophecies. In this climate of controversy Paul formulates the idea that Christ represents the key that allows the spiri-tual interpretation of the Old Testament, which the Jews have understood only literally. An explanation of this sort already implies the use of the allegorical interpretation, of which Galatians 4:24 is an exam-ple. Christ is sought in the Old Testament, and where the literal interpretation is insufficient, allegory is employed. In this way a historical event, while maintaining its validity at the literal level, at the higher (i.e., spiritual) level signifies Christ and the church both symbolically and prophetically: Ishmael and Isaac, in addition to their historical reality, prefigure symbolically the Jews and the Christians. This is the interpretation that modern scholars call typological (from *typos*, 1 Cor 10:6), by which events and figures of the Old Testament are assumed to prefigure persons and events in the New Testament.

This type of Christian interpretation of the Old Testament spread progressively and reached its peak in the polemic against the Gnostics and Marcionites (second century). The radical dualism of these groups led them to distinguish the supreme God revealed by Jesus from the lesser god, creator of a world considered inferior, and hence to deny the genuine and reliable revelation contained in the Old Testa-ment. This approach was fed by a widespread sentiment of disinterest in or even aversion to Old Testa-ment books, whose Hebrew origin rendered them foreign to Christians coming in ever-increasing numbers from the ranks of paganism. The most effective means of neutralizing this unfavorable view of

Old Testament revelation consisted in affirming and demonstrating that the primary aim of this revelation had been to foreshadow, through symbols and prophecies, the coming of Christ to the earth. This necessity caused the ever-increasing exploitation of the allegorical interpretation of the ancient writings (Irenaeus, Hippolytus, Tertullian).

This hermeneutical way of reasoning (*ratio*) was most fully exploited and exhaustively codified in the Alexandrian environment, where the culture of Judeo-Hellenistic origin had already sought to render Greek philosophy and the Old Testament mutually compatible, through the massive allegorical interpretation of the latter Philo. Between the end of the second century and the mid-third century, Clement first transferred Philo's tradition of exegesis to the Christian sphere, setting it alongside the traditional typology. Then Origen unified and gave coherent organization to these various methods of interpreting the Old Testament, on the basis of a philosophical plan of Platonic origin. According to this plan, the distinction of two levels of reality, sensible and intelligible, implied in the exegetical sphere the distinction between a lower level of interpretation of the sacred text, which merely illustrated its concrete (i.e., literal) meaning, for the benefit of more simple believers. A higher level was intended to illuminate—generally using the allegorical technique—the spiritual (i.e., Christian) meaning hidden beneath the veil of the words for the benefit of the more gifted and motivated faithful. The belief, inherited from Philo, that the sacred text turns away the reader who is merely curious or even malevolent, rendering its deeper meaning difficult to access through the use of symbols and hidden modes of expression, soon led to the application of the allegorical technique to the interpretation of the New Testament as well. This method of interpretation spread with great success throughout the East and later in the West. It is true that from the middle of the fourth century this method was opposed in the Antiochene environment by a reaction (Diodore of Tarsus, Theodore of Mopsuestia) that preferred the literal reading of the sacred texts over the evident excesses of certain allegorical interpretations. The general preference, however, was for the application of the allegorical method, especially for preaching and pastoral duties. Augustine also noted that readers and listeners would be more inclined to appreciate a concept if it was expressed in a veiled fashion through the use of allegory rather than through a direct, nonallegorical manner.

After this historical background, we turn to the allegorical interpretation of the Gospel of Matthew. We have already observed the great freedom of the interpreter vis-à-vis the text he is explaining. This is even more true for interpretation of an allegorical nature, especially in light of the generalized conviction of the inexhaustible richness of the divine word, *sensus spiritalis multiplex est.* That is, multiple spiritual meanings can be ascribed to the same individual passage that do not exclude but build on one another. In view of this liberty and variety, I will limit my comments to the most general tendencies.

The search for a meaning hidden beneath the words of the Gospel text could be aimed in several directions. In the vertical direction, the actions of Jesus, beyond their material reality, take on a spiritual significance: the healings performed signify above all the liberation from sin. In the horizontal direction, the backwards connection to texts of the Old Testament allowed authors to accentuate the newness of the Christian message as compared with the Hebrew tradition, while the application of Jesus' words to modern times transferred their teachings to the daily life of the church. In the great variety of technical procedures used by the exegetes, I will limit my discussion to four that were of widespread use and consequently are frequently found in the texts of our collection.

First, there is *etymological symbolism*, based on the conviction that in some manner the name expressed the nature of the designated object and consisting in the extraction of an allegorical meaning from the etymology of a Hebrew name, whether of a person or a locality. Second is *arithmetical symbolism*, based on the belief universally recognized throughout the ancient world in the mysterious meanings of numbers, above all of certain special numbers (five, seven, ten, forty, etc.) with symbolic meanings. Third is the defect in the literal sense, *defectus litterae*, which consisted in observing in the text any sort of incongruity or improbability, then passing directly to the research, via allegorization, of the true meaning of the passage in question. Fourth is *the interpretation of Scripture with Scripture*. It is important to note that this procedure, already mentioned in connection with literal interpretation, was used most frequently to produce an allegorical meaning through the juxtaposition to the passage under examination with one or more other passages related to it verbally or conceptually.

The Principal Interpretive Writings and Commentaries on Matthew

After having outlined in a general manner the characteristics of the interpretation of the Gospel of Matthew in the patristic age, we shall now examine, in equally general terms and remaining within the tripartite scheme laid out, the principal works from which this collection has been assembled.

Commentaries. I have already alluded to the importance of Origen's *Commentary on Matthew* in the exegetical history of this Gospel. One of Origen's latest works (c. 245), it was in fact not only (to our knowledge) the first such systematic commentary ever composed but also the longest by a considerable margin, consisting of no fewer than twenty-five volumes. Of the original text only volumes 10 through 17 have survived, which contain the interpretation and commentary relating to Matthew 13:36 through Matthew 22:33. Beginning with book 12, chapter 9, the Greek original is accompanied by an ancient Latin version, which is believed to date from the beginning of the fifth century and is on the whole fairly literal, though with various omissions and occasional additions with respect to the Greek text. For the part of the Gospel from 22:34 through the end of 27 a summary exposition in Latin has survived, normally called the Commentariorum Series, which is also very ancient and which provides a concise knowledge of the content of the lost books, from 18 onward. Origen's *Commentary on Matthew* was widely used by compilers of the catenae: the edition of E. Klostermann contains no fewer than 571 fragments of various length that, though of little or no use where we possess the original text and the Latin abbreviation, do provide some knowledge of Origen's interpretation of Matthew 1:1—13:35 and of Matthew 28.

As in all other commentaries by Origen, the *Commentary on Matthew* also derived from scholastic teachings and therefore contains significant traces of the manner in which this teaching was carried out. In the first place there is the ampleness—not to say the prolixity—of the explanation, which derives not only from the care with which every detail of the Gospel was illustrated for the students but still more from the characteristic manner in which the explanation was developed. Origen modeled his explanation on the style normally used in pagan schools of philosophy, based substantially on the method of *quaestiones* and *responsiones*. In this approach the text is first interpreted literally according to its obvious and clear meaning. Then Origen poses the question, which at times is drawn from a detail of the text under examination but more often springs from the juxtaposition of this text with another of the same Gospel or of a different scriptural book that in some way suggests it. This juxtaposition, which may gradually be extended to other related passages, allows the in-depth exploration of the text using a series of proposed interpretations, added one to another, with motives that are above all else heuristic: Origen is far more interested in discussing and proposing than in defining axiomatically. Frequently this exploration of the interpreted text is achieved via the technique of allegory. This is not always true, however. Even when the first explanation is allegorical (e.g., in the interpretation of the parables), one or more others are added that are also allegorical but of a more exacting nature. The key element of Origen's exegesis of the sacred text is the distinction of two levels of interpretation, one more superficial and the other deeper, which can be expressed in more than one proposed interpretation.

Given this *ratio interpretandi*, the topics considered in the interpretation of the Gospel of Matthew are extremely varied. It is sufficient to observe the tendency to spiritualize the interpretation, that is, to attribute to the actions of Jesus a meaning that transcends their naked materiality and to transfer the historical meaning of his words into the specific context of the interpretation of the Scriptures (the Pharisees do not understand the teachings of Jesus and of the Scriptures as a whole, because they are unable to go beyond their literal meaning). One should also note the interpreter's interest in the conditions of the contemporary ecclesiastical community. Employing the words of Jesus in a new context, Origen condemns the shortcomings and the deviations from the spirit of the Gospel, above all on the part of the church hierarchy.

The *Commentary on Matthew* of Hilary of Poitiers was composed approximately between the years 350 and 355, before the author was exiled in 356 to Phrygia for several years due to his opposition of the pro-Arian policies of the emperor Constans. This therefore represents one of the first works of a specifically exegetical nature to be composed in a Latin environment. There is no sign in the text as it has come down to us of the characteristics that indicate it was derived from oral preaching, still less of those typical of a scholastic exposition. Although one cannot rule out a radical reworking of a previous oral expression with a view to publication, it is more probable that the work was conceived in its earliest form exclusively to be read.

The pioneering character of the *Commentary on Matthew* in the Latin world is evident with the first reading. The structure of the commentary is, in a still simpler form, the same that we encounter in similar Greek works: the evangelical text has been divided into passages, which from time to time are followed by an explanation. But the dimensions of these explanations vary greatly: Hilary provides a lengthy and detailed explanation for certain passages, while for others he merely hints at an explanation, at times omitting it. For example, when he reaches the precepts concerning prayer (Mt 6:5-15), he refers the reader to the writings of Cyprian and Tertullian on this subject; explanations of the parable of the sower and the tares (Mt 13:1-8, 24-30) are omitted, given that—as Hilary observes—Jesus himself explained them to the disciples.

Hilary's interpretation of Matthew never suggests the use of the commentary of Origen, but he demonstrates a thorough knowledge of the hermeneutic *ratio* of the Alexandrian tradition. He adheres wholeheartedly to it: alongside the simple, literal meaning of the text he discovers a more profound and important meaning that can be revealed only through more thoughtful examination and which he reveals with extensive allegorization. In applying this interpretive principle, Hilary is confident that he is not forcing the original meaning of the scriptural story in the slightest, since this story itself is the vehicle that guides us and compels us to go beyond the merely literal meaning. Precisely this confidence leads Hilary to apply massive doses of the procedure that we have termed *defectus litterae*. Not that he doubts the truth of the events in the story, but they frequently have occurred in a manner that is at odds with what seems to him the story's logical and natural sequence, since their material occurrence was intended to foreshadow a symbolic meaning destined to come to pass in the future. For example, the behavior of Jesus in Matthew 8:18 (when Jesus flees from the mob and gives the order to depart to the other side of the Sea of Galilee) does not seem to him in harmony with Jesus' goodness. But by understanding the boat allegorically as a symbol of the church and aligning the other details of the story with it, Jesus' conduct becomes perfectly comprehensible (Mt 8:7-10). Another of Hilary's favorite hermeneutical methods is to derive an allegorical meaning from a given passage by connecting it to the preceding passage, even in cases where two episodes of the biblical story are connected merely by chronological adjacency. For example, the healing of the two blind men in Matthew 9:27 and following is interpreted in harmony with the preceding episode of the healing of the ruler's daughter. The latter symbolizes the few Jews who were to believe in Christ, and this same interpretation is extended in a more specific way to the story of the two blind men (Mt 9:9). On the strength of these hermeneutical instruments, Hilary performs an allegorical interpretation, on the whole rather unified and organic, which expands on a central theme of the Gospels: the hostility of the Jews toward Jesus and their disapproval by God. Hilary transfers this theme from Christ to the nascent church and therefore sees foreshadowed in Christ's earthly affairs the hostility of the Jews to the first Christian community, their inability to accept the new reality springing from the death and resurrection of Christ, the abolition of the old dispensation of the law and the installation of the new dispensation of grace.

Jerome composed his four-volume *Commentary on Matthew* in 398, at the request of his friend and disciple Eusebius of Cremona, as he states in the preface of the work. Here he also explains that, pressed by the departure of his friend, he had had to complete the work in the two weeks before Easter. He further states that he has been concise in his exposition and that he has used a number of sources: Origen, Hippolytus, Theophilus of Antioch, Theodore of Heraclea, Apollinaris of Laodicea and Didymus the Blind among the Greeks; Victorinus of Petovium, Fortunatian of Aquileia and Hilary among the Latins. On the basis of our existing knowledge, the debt to Origen is well documented, while Hilary seems to have been little used. Certain surviving fragments of Theodore and Apollinaris also indicate points of contact with Jerome's commentary.

The most obvious characteristics of this commentary are its brevity and, within the overall limits of this framework, its great variety. At times the explication of passages of Matthew is so brief as to be no longer than the interpreted text, while elsewhere it is considerably longer. Jerome was clearly writing in a hurried fashion and not systematically, so that he examined certain details that seemed to him interesting in themselves or for what he read about them in his sources, while he passed rapidly over many others. At times we even have the impression that we are reading a collection of explanatory glosses rather than a systematic commentary. And even when the explanation is lengthier and Jerome brings in multiple interpretations for a single biblical passage, the discourse is always streamlined and concise; one can in general conclude that he succeeded in the task set for him by Eusebius: *ut Matheum breviter exponens verbis stringerem sensibus dilatarem* (When explaining Matthew, do so briefly, with concise words where there are extended meanings). In fact, his commentary encapsulates in a relatively limited space a large quantity of material of the most varied provenance.

In the preface Jerome also claims to have carried out, at the request of Eusebius, the historical (i.e., literal) interpretation but also now and then to have inserted *intellegentiae spiritalis flores*, that is, allegorical interpretations. Indeed this type of interpretation is amply represented. In the context of this sort of composite exposition, it is possible to recognize the more personal characteristics of Jerome's exegesis in the frequent historical, antiquarian, philological and critical annotations that appear. It is clear that for the allegorical interpretation, which applies the sayings and deeds of Jesus to the events both of the future church and to each soul considered individually, he relies on his sources, Origen above all but others as well. Precisely because the perspective of the interpretation is so varied, it is impossible to identify a central interest, as in the case of Hilary. The distinguishing feature of Jerome's overall exegesis is the ability to balance the requirements of both literal and spiritual interpretation. Despite the speed of composition and the resulting disconnected and rhapsodic nature of many interpretations, he has on the whole succeeded in expressing his exegetical message, although perhaps not at its best.

Opus imperfectum in Matthaeum (OIM) was identified in the Middle Ages as a commentary on the Gospel of Matthew already passed down in incomplete form under the name of John Chrysostom. The work, which enjoyed great popularity as attested by the nearly two hundred surviving manuscripts, is divided in fifty-four homilies of varying length. This division is not original, however, since the work is not homiletic in nature but rather a commentary arranged and composed to be read. The interpretation ends with Matthew 25:46 and contains two enormous lacunae, one between homilies 22 and 23 with the omission of the interpretation of Matthew 8:11—10:15; the other, still larger, between homilies 31 and 32, with the omission of the interpretation of Matthew 13:14—18:35. The attribution of *OIM* to Chrysostom, very old but nonetheless devoid of any basis in fact (as Erasmus recognized), played an important role in the survival of the work. In all probability it would not have come down to us if it had not been shrewdly placed under the protection of that great name. In fact, the author of *OIM* was an Arian, a bishop or presbyter active in the first decades of the fifth century, in all likelihood in one of the Danube provinces, where the presence of these heretics was fairly substantial. Critics disagree whether the work was originally composed in Greek or in Latin. J. van Banning, who is preparing the critical edition of the work, hypothesizes that the original was in Latin, written in a border region where the influence of the Greek was noticeable (CCL 87b:iii). The survival of the work was also furthered by the fact that the unknown author, while carrying on a polemic with those he calls "heretics" (who are none other than the Catholics, then dominant thanks to the support of the emperor Theodosius) reveals himself an Arian in a few doctrinally complex passages. Elsewhere his arguments are predominantly moral in nature and thus largely orthodox and generic. It is from these that selections have largely been taken. Already in the late Middle Ages the doctrinally compromising passages that smacked of Arianism were modified, and this trend was continued by the first editors. Hence the edition currently available in PG 56, by B. de Montfaucon, is unsatisfactory from this point of view. These are minor imperfections, however, that do not compromise the use of a text that represents the most important commentary on Matthew written in Latin.

The author of *OIM*, who several times used Origen's commentary and perhaps that of Jerome as well, demonstrates his complete familiarity with the theory and all of the most common techniques of allegorizing exegesis in the Alexandrian tradition. He does not overlook the literal interpretation, exploited above all for moral guidance. However, he accepts wholeheartedly the conviction of Philo and Origen that the Scriptures hide beneath the veil of the words a deeper and truer meaning, on which he attempts to shed light through all of the resources that the allegorizing tradition provided him, with evident preference for etymological symbolism. His aim is to illustrate the meaning of the Gospel of Matthew in its deepest recesses, in order to bring out what he considers to be the logic, the rationality of Jesus in acting exclusively for the spiritual well-being of humanity. He does this in a dialectical manner, enumerating and illustrating in precise terms the explanation of the text both literally and spiritually. An exegesis carried out with such clarity and argumentational rigor was certain to please the Scholastics, and it is no surprise to read that St. Thomas Aquinas would have preferred to have the complete *OIM* than to be lord of Paris.

We have already seen the interest of the author in subjects of moral import: in this area his attention is directed primarily at the condition of the church, and in particular its hierarchy, whose abuses he criticizes no less than Origen had done. Moral commitment means responsibility, and our author strikes this note repeatedly, with evident awareness of the polemic between Augustine and the Pelagians, sharing the positions of the former but always intent on safeguarding the rights of free will. As a member of a fringe minority destined to diminish with every passing day, he senses acutely the precariousness of his position and that of his community. Consequently he systematically extends the traditional theme of the repudiation of the Jews for the benefit of the church of the Gentiles, to the point of including in the condemnation those people whom he considers heretics, the current heirs of the Jews due to the position of power that they hold. In order to strengthen the resolve of the remaining faithful, he invokes and emphasizes the theme of persecution, the supreme test intended to determine the perseverance and capacity for sacrifice of the few elect.

We have noted the importance of the catenae for our fragmentary knowledge of Greek exegetical texts that have not survived in their original form. The edition of J. Reuss has placed at our disposal four series of fragments, of varying length and clarity, derived from commentaries on the Gospel of Matthew by authors whose importance and chronology have direct bearing on this collection: Theodore of Heraclea (Thrace), Apollinaris of Laodicea, Theodore of Mopsuestia and Cyril of Alexandria. The last two, representatives of the rival exegetical schools of Antioch (Theodore) and Alexandria (Cyril) between the end of the fourth and the beginning of the fifth centuries, are well-known for other exegetical works that have survived in their entirety. Hence these fragments on Matthew also fit comfortably into the context of Theodore's literalist exegesis and Cyril's tendency to allegorize. It is less easy to place Apollinaris and Theodore of Heraclea—the former active in the second half of the fourth century, the latter in the first half—in their proper context. Despite their fame as exegetes, none of their works has come down to us in its entirety. The little that we know of their exegesis suggests that they had a tendency to historical, and hence literal, interpretation, but our fragments not infrequently show signs of allegorizing tendencies. It would be unwise to make a general observation of this, because experience shows that the knowledge of an exegete only through fragments, while extremely useful in coming to know certain of his specific interpretations, is insufficient to lay bare the fundamental aspects of his *ratio interpretandi*.

The characteristics shown in these fragments are the ability to exploit even faint subtleties of the biblical text in order to illustrate the reasons underlying Jesus' actions and the tendency to connect the text with passages from the other Gospels in order to broaden the meaning of these actions within the fabric of the economy of redemption. With particular reference to Theodore of Mopsuestia, even the fragments make clear his technique of explicative paraphrase, which blends the biblical story and its explanation together and is characteristic of his exegetical style. As for Cyril, even though his adoption of hermeneutical positions of the Alexandrian tradition is generally more moderate than in Origen and Didymus, the Alexandrian tradition is on the whole evident even in the fragments, which are considerably more numerous than those of the other three exegetes. I refer not only to the greater space devoted to the allegorization of the biblical text as compared with the other authors but also to the emphasis on the theme of the history of salvation to underscore the hostility of the Jews and of the pedagogical role played by Christ incarnate, in harmony with the role he had already played in the context of the Old Testament dispensation.

Serial homilies. The ninety homilies of John Chrysostom on the Gospel of Matthew were preached at Antioch while the orator was still a presbyter, probably in 390. They are on average rather lengthy and cover in a continuous and systematic fashion the entire Gospel of Matthew. While each discourse remains autonomous and complete with respect to the others, they are all tightly interconnected, proof that this exceptional oratorical tour de force was completed in a brief space of time. Chrysostom was an orator famous above all for his ability to sway the emotions, and the homilies on Matthew also demonstrate this gift in their generous employment of paraenesis and their tendency to moral interpretation, over against the explicitly exegetical nature of the text. This purpose is never sacrificed, however, since not only is adequate space devoted to exegesis, but also Chrysostom is careful to proceed in his explanation of the biblical text by systematically breaking the text into passages. Even if moral lessons are inserted throughout and the tone is always expressive, the space devoted to exegesis and paraenesis respectively are generally fairly distinct.

Although Chrysostom avoided the polemical tone dear to his master Diodore and his friend Theodore, and wisely chose to avoid taking positions that were too unilateral and therefore dangerous, he belonged to the Antiochene environment from both the doctrinal and the exegetical perspective. It is therefore no surprise that in his homilies on Matthew the explanation of the biblical text is systematically literal. The presence of any allegorical interpretation is highly unusual, but also the author takes very little care to link the words and deeds of Jesus with the great drama of the history of salvation via the connection with Old Testament texts, as is the custom in Alexandrian exegesis, which became deeply rooted in the West as well. Even the interpretation of the parables, a natural invitation to allegorical emphasis, is handled with the greatest simplicity. Chrysostom is interested first and foremost in turning the explanation of the parables into an opportunity for moral instruction. Therefore the acts of Christ interest him in their specific details. The hostility of the priests and Pharisees is for him interesting not so much as a culminating moment in the relationship between God and his people but as a sign of the ingratitude and evil that, then as now, prevents us from taking possession of our own salvation by following Christ in the faith.

Guided by this prevailing interest, the explanation follows a precise schema. Chrysostom likes to begin his interpretation of the scriptural pericope by recalling the *tote* ("Then, at that time") that so frequently opens the scriptural pericope, asking himself *pote* ("When?"). The response allows him to situate his interpretation within the plot of the scriptural account. Chrysostom explains the text vividly, in almost a visual manner, intending to make as clear as possible, in a systematic manner, the philanthropy and instruction of Jesus' actions. Even when these acts appear contradictory (at times Jesus produces the sign for which he is asked, other times he refuses), nonetheless they are always intended to achieve that which is most pedagogically useful to the onlookers at that moment. In comparison with this unlimited goodness, the wickedness of his enemies stands out with the maximum clarity. It is obvious that an exegesis that follows these principles and derives moral lessons from them has in the literal interpretation of the scriptural text its most suitable mode of expression.

Today we are thoroughly familiar with the exegesis of Chromatius, bishop of Aquileia between the end of the fourth and the first years of the fifth century, thanks to the work of several scholars, above all R. Étaix and J. Lemarié. They have identified, collected and edited his homilies, which were scattered among various collections of sermons and passed on anonymously or attributed to Jerome or Augustine. In addition to numerous separate sermons, a corpus of writings has once again been attributed to Chromatius: fifty-nine *tractati* (i.e., homilies) on the Gospel of Matthew, which are to be dated toward the end of his episcopate (after the year 400). The corpus is preceded by a homily that acts as a prologue, from which we learn the intention of the orator to interpret, with a continuous series of homilies, the whole of the Gospels. In fact the *tractati* from 1 to 48 appear as a continuous work that interprets in a systematic fashion, with very few lacunae, the Gospel of Matthew from its beginning up to 9:31. The successive *tractati* instead illustrate selected passages of the Gospel: the last concerns Matthew 18:19-35. It is clear that many homilies have been lost. On the whole the homilies of Chromatius, when compared with those of Chrysostom, are rather brief, as was common in the West, and although paraenesis always enters into the exposition, the didactic element clearly prevails. The primary aim of the exposition is to explain to the listeners the meaning of a scriptural passage that had previously been read.

Chromatius, like Hilary on whom he relies, also adheres to the guiding principles and the norms of Alexandrian exegesis. These he learned directly from Jerome's translations of the homilies of Origen, also assimilating the underlying belief that it is possible to ascribe more than one spiritual interpretation to a single biblical passage. The maxim *sensus spiritalis multiplex est* is his and appears more than once. Thus his exegesis gives the broadest scope to allegorical interpretation, in order to apply the text of the Gospel to the current condition of the church. Given his historical milieu, Chromatius has particular interest in revealing the danger posed by the many heretics active at the time, and he often takes care to recall the responsibilities, as well as the honors, incumbent on the members of the church hierarchy. But the most obvious characteristic of Chromatius's exegesis is the continuous tendency to connect the scriptural text under interpretation with Old Testament passages. He does this not so much to derive an allegorical interpretation from this juxtaposition as to underscore the unity of revelation, demonstrating how much of the Gospel message had been presaged and anticipated by the prophets and other figures of the Old Testament. Obviously Chromatius's primary interest is to familiarize his listeners with the text of the Old Testament, which, as we learn from various sources, seems at that time to have been little known in the West among the majority of the faithful. Knowledge of Chromatius's homiletic production is of unique interest, because it puts us into contact with a preaching method that, while of good quality, does not reach the heights of the great exegetes whom we have previously discussed. Instead it finds parallels in other contemporary preachers who are of a middle rank (Gaudentius of Brescia, Zeno of Verona, Gregory of Elvira) and consequently reveals what must have been the average level of the bulk of homiletic activity practiced in the Western church at that time.

Homilies and other aids. Sunday and feast-day homilies regularly rehearsed passages taken from the Gospel of Matthew for Christian audiences, and consequently it is possible through this genre to deepen our understanding of patristic exegesis of this Gospel. In order to produce a collection as varied and representative as possible, I have drawn on exegetes of all levels, from the most celebrated—like Augustine and Gregory the Great—to others of lesser fame, such as the so-called Epiphanius the Latin, a bishop of uncertain date (fifth to sixth centuries) who is meaningful for our purposes in the same way that Chromatius is. We should once again recall in the West the trio of great Italian preachers of the first half of the fifth century: Leo the Great, Maximus of Turin and Peter Chrysologus, bishop of Ravenna. In the East are Eusebius, bishop of Emesa in the first half of the fourth century, and Severus, bishop of Antioch in the first half of the sixth century, both known exclusively in translation: in Latin for the former, Syriac for the latter. The Sunday homily was by its very nature less suited than the serial homily to the development of a systematic exegesis of a previously read Gospel text. In fact, I have had to omit many homilies, in particular by Eastern authors, because their specific exegetical character appears too heavily influenced by paraenetic or general liturgical aims to be useful for the purposes of this collection. Instead, in the case of the above-mentioned orators (excepting only Eusebius and Leo), the systematic practice of dividing the interpreted text into passages has allowed emphasis to be placed—while not always in the most effective possible manner—on the specifically exegetical aim of the homily.

Within this common denominator, the texts here present the widest variety of expressive forms and explicitly exegetical content. They range from the extremely marked rhetorical tone of Peter Chrysologus, which also appears in Eusebius of Emesa even through the Latin translation, to the humble prose of Epiphanius, which nonetheless is of high quality overall. Gregory the Great also expresses himself at times in a less elementary form than he would have the reader believe. As regards the hermeneutic *ratio*, if one excepts Eusebius of Emesa, forerunner of the antiallegorical reaction in Syria and Palestine in the middle of the fourth century, the general tendency is toward an exegesis of a spiritual nature. Spiritual exegesis employed an extensive use of allegorization, given that the figurative mode of speech was expected to produce a stronger reaction in its audience and therefore to yield better effects in the pastoral context. Although Severus had preached in Antioch, a century before the stronghold of literal exegetes, he himself is very open to allegorizing. This links him to Chrysostom, his great predecessor, despite the divergence in their manner of interpretation and the tendency to limit the interpretation within the scope of Jesus' activities. Augustine and Gregory meanwhile prefer to update and generalize the spiritual sense of these activities in order to adapt them to the contemporary needs of the church and the faithful. On the whole we find exegesis of good quality being produced, with certain high points such as Augustine and Severus. This demonstrates that this centuries-old practice, enriched by theoretical reflections on biblical interpretation, had diffused, even in culturally modest circles, the principles that were to guide the interpretation of the sacred text, so as to furnish Greek and Latin exegetes with an adequate foundation.

In conclusion we will briefly examine several texts which I have used that either are not of a specifically exegetical nature or, although exegesis, do not fit into the three textual categories into which we have divided our exegetical material. I refer to the three tractates on prayer by Tertullian *(De oratione)*, Cyprian *(De dominica oratione)* and Origen *(Peri euchēs)*. Each explains the Lord's Prayer word by word, because it is the only prayer taught directly by Jesus and, as such, a compendium of all his teachings. Compared with the explanation of Tertullian, the oldest on this prayer that we know which addresses the individual believer outside of the liturgical context, Cyprian's gloss is clearly more concerned with the community. With respect to these two explanations, the interpretation of Origen follows his usual approach of a predominantly spiritual understanding of Jesus' words. In the two books of *De sermone Domini in monte* (Sermon on the Mount) by Augustine, composed in about the year 395, the explanation of the Lord's Prayer is inserted into the wider context of the interpretation of the entire Sermon on the Mount. Even in this work, the dominant theme is Augustine's concern to explain the sacred text with reference to the current condition of the church and its individual members. The resulting exegesis is predominantly moral, though with frequent doctrinal observations. The four books of *De consensu evangelistarum* (Harmony of the Gospels), which Augustine composed about the year 400, concern the contradictions that emerged from a comparison of the narratives of identical episodes in the four Gospels. Pagans in particular used these supposed contradictions to disprove the credibility of those texts. This subject had already occupied exegetes and polemicists for two centuries. Consequently, Augustine enters a well-established tradition with the freedom and originality that always characterize his scriptural approach. For the purposes of this collection, the passages of interest consider the beginning and the ending of the Gospel of Matthew.

Criteria for the Selection and Ordering of the Texts

From the foregoing exposition it is clear that the surviving patristic writings that concern the interpretation of the Gospel of Matthew are on the whole abundant, especially if compared with the quantity of material regarding the New Testament—and especially the Old Testament—that have come down to us. Obviously these writings are not equally distributed: certain essential works are incomplete (Origen, Chromatius, *OIM*) or contain explanations that are in places so abbreviated as to make them useless for our work (Hilary, Jerome). A limited number of Gospel passages have only two useful interpretations, while for others we have at our disposal ten or more, so that in such cases we are forced to select, even when this selection requires painful omissions. In the latter case the selection has been made in order to offer the widest possible range of interpretations and hermeneutical approaches. As a general principle, when the material at my disposal permits it, I have attempted to provide at least four interpretations for each passage of the Gospel, at times extending this to six or seven when the importance of the interpreted text, or of the proposed interpretations and their variety, required a certain latitude of selection.

In subdividing the material I have followed more or less the method of the ancient catenae writers, splitting Matthew into passages and presenting a series of interpretations for each passage. To divide the text I have sought to isolate units that are in some sense complete, in order to avoid the excessive fragmentation of the Gospel text. The passages are consequently of varying lengths, each containing a minimum of one verse and a maximum of eight, with the goal being from two to four. An exception is made for the parables, which at times are longer than eight verses and which I have attempted to present more cohesively. This is also the case in the genealogy of Jesus in Matthew 1:2-16. With regard to the series of interpretations that accompany and elucidate each passage, these have been arranged in the most logical way possible, without any attempt to follow the chronology of the various exegetes. Since within each passage the interpretations do not always concern the entire length of the passage, they have been arranged in order to follow the development of the passage from beginning to end. In the frequent cases in which different interpretations are given for the same Gospel text, these are set out in increasing order of complexity, beginning with the more simple interpretations of predominantly literal character and moving to the more complicated, usually allegorizing, interpretations.

The great share of the selected texts are from the commentaries and serial homilies, since only these texts allow the presentation of homogeneous interpretations of even lengthy Gospel passages. These represent the structural framework of this collection, and among them the selection was made so that every Gospel pericope is normally followed by several complete interpretations, obviously in general terms. The use of isolated homilies has allowed enriching and varying this homogeneous scheme with the addition of certain interpretations that seemed of particular significance. The exegetical texts selected and presented differ from one another not only in the manner and quantity of their interpretation but also in length, ranging from passages of a few lines to texts that fill an entire page. The only criterion governing the dimension of individual passages is that, whatever their length, they should present a discourse that is coherent and self-contained. The very nature of the collection has made it necessary to divide lengthy exegetical texts into several passages and frequently to isolate an important passage by excerpting it from its larger context. While the texts of certain exegetes are particularly suited to this type of selection (e.g., those of Jerome and Chrysostom), others have suffered from it, in particular those of Origen, given the discursive and problematic nature of his exegesis, and those of Augustine and Hilary as well. In the case of Origen the selections have been limited almost exclusively to his allegorizing interpretations. However, in order that readers of the selected passages not derive a distorted impression of this great exegete, they should keep in mind that Origen normally presupposes a literal interpretation as well. This is true not only for Origen but for other authors too. In order not to exclude interpretations of great importance, I have on several occasions had to include texts of considerable length.

Having thus explained in detail the criteria that have guided the selection and arrangement of the excerpts, I may add that these are only general indications. All are subordinate to the fundamental criterion to present a selection that, within the limits of the available space, is as rich and varied as possible. It has been the decision of the publisher, because of the abundance of excerpts, to divide the material on Matthew into two volumes, this first covering Matthew 1-13 and the second covering Matthew 14-28. This is surely in keeping with the importance the early church attributed to this Gospel. This introduction serves to orient the reader to both volumes.

THE GOSPEL ACCORDING TO MATTHEW

1:1-17 THE GENEALOGY OF JESUS CHRIST

¹The book of the genealogy of Jesus Christ, the son of David, the son of Abraham.

²Abraham was the father of Isaac, and Isaac the father of Jacob, and Jacob the father of Judah and his brothers, ³and Judah the father of Perez and Zerah by Tamar, and Perez the father of Hezron, and Hezron the father of Ram,ᵃ ⁴and Ramᵃ the father of Amminadab, and Amminadab the father of Nahshon, and Nahshon the father of Salmon, ⁵and Salmon the father of Boaz by Rahab, and Boaz the father of Obed by Ruth, and Obed the father of Jesse, ⁶and Jesse the father of David the king.

And David was the father of Solomon by the wife of Uriah, ⁷and Solomon the father of Rehoboam, and Rehoboam the father of Abijah, and Abijah the father of Asa,ᵇ ⁸and Asaᵇ the father of Jehoshaphat, and Jehoshaphat the father of Joram, and Joram the father of Uzziah, ⁹and Uzziah the father of Jotham, and Jotham the father of Ahaz, and Ahaz the father of Hezekiah, ¹⁰and Hezekiah the father of Manasseh, and Manasseh the father of Amos,ᶜ and Amosᶜ the father of Josiah, ¹¹and Josiah the father of Jechoniah and his brothers, at the time of the deportation to Babylon.

¹²And after the deportation to Babylon: Jechoniah was the father of She-alti-el,ᵈ and She-alti-elᵈ the father of Zerubbabel, ¹³and Zerubbabel the father of Abiud, and Abiud the father of Eliakim, and Eliakim the father of Azor, ¹⁴and Azor the father of Zadok, and Zadok the father of Achim, and Achim the father of Eliud, ¹⁵and Eliud the father of Eleazar, and Eleazar the father of Matthan, and Matthan the father of Jacob, ¹⁶and Jacob the father of Joseph the husband of Mary, of whom Jesus was born, who is called Christ.

¹⁷So all the generations from Abraham to David were fourteen generations, and from David to the deportation to Babylon fourteen generations, and from the deportation to Babylon to the Christ fourteen generations.

a Greek *Aram*   b Greek *Asaph*   c Other authorities read *Amon*   d Greek *Salathiel*

OVERVIEW: The divine lineage is an unfathomable mystery (ORIGEN). Christ's true humanity is revealed in Matthew's genealogy (SEVERUS). Matthew's Gospel, written first in Hebrew, prominently displays Jesus' kingly succession from David and blood lineage with Abraham (CHROMATIUS, HILARY, ANONYMOUS). The varied reports of Christ's lineage are not inconsistent due to the distinction between blood father and adoptive father (AUGUSTINE). Isaac's birth is prefigurative of the birth of Jesus, and Jacob's twelve sons prefigure the twelve apostles of the age to come (ANONYMOUS). Christ took upon himself a blood relationship to the nature that fornicated, in order to purify it (SEVERUS). Thus Rahab the harlot is unapologetically in the lineage of the Lord, as well as Zerah, who prefigures the Jews under the law; Perez, who prefigures the Gentiles and the gospel; and notably David and Bathsheba (ANONYMOUS). The relation of Joseph and Mary stands as an enduring commendation to faithful married persons of the principle that even when by common consent they maintain their continence, the marital relation can still remain and can still be called one of wedlock. Joseph was truly the husband of Mary yet without the intercourse of the flesh (AUGUSTINE).

1:1 The Genealogy of Jesus Christ

WHO WILL TELL OF JESUS' LINEAGE? ANONYMOUS: The Bible is like a storehouse of grace. For just as everyone finds whatever he desires in the storehouse of a rich man, so also does every soul find whatever is considered important in this book.

Why is it that Matthew says, "The book of the genealogy of Jesus Christ, descendant of David, descendant of Abraham," while the prophet Isaiah exclaims, "And who will tell of his lineage?"[1] Matthew is setting forth his fleshly line, while Isaiah proclaims that his divine lineage is an unfathomable mystery. INCOMPLETE WORK ON MATTHEW.[2]

JESUS' HUMANITY REVEALED IN THE GENEALOGY. SEVERUS: One must bear in mind therefore that the Evangelists, or rather the Spirit speak-

ing through them, took pains to ensure that their readers believed that Christ was truly God and truly human. Because of what they wrote, no one could possibly doubt that he is God by nature, beyond all variation, mutation or illusion, and that according to the ordered plan of God he was truly human. This is why John could say, on the one hand, "In the beginning was the Word, and the Word was with God, and the Word was God." John immediately adds, "The Word was made flesh and dwelt among us."[3] Hence Matthew wrote appropriately, "The book of the generation of Jesus Christ, the son of David, the son of Abraham." On the one hand he is not able to be counted simply from natural generation among families, since it is written, "Who shall declare his generation?"[4] He is before the centuries and of one substance with the Father himself, from the standpoint of eternity. But by this genealogy he is also numbered among the families of humanity according to the flesh. For in truth, while remaining God, Christ became man without ceasing to be God, unaltered till the end of time.

This is why there is also mention of the ancient patriarchs in the lineage, the narrative and observation of the times and vicissitudes that are indeed proper to human history. Through all this Matthew made it clear that Christ participates in our human generation and in our nature. Otherwise some might claim that he appeared in illusion and in imagination only, rather than by becoming genuinely human. Think of what might have been said if none of this had been written? CATHEDRAL SERMONS, HOMILY 94.[5]

---

[1]Is 53:8. [2]PG 56:612. The fifth-century anonymous commentary on Matthew's Gospel, *Incomplete Work on Matthew*, is a Latin catena that contains passages from Jerome, Chromatius of Aquileia and Leo the Great. It ends at Matthew 25. See *Clavis Patrum Latinorum* 707; J. Banning, "The Critical Edition of the Incomplete Work on Matthew: An Arian Source," in *Studia Patristica* 17 (Oxford: Oxford University Press, 1982), pp. 382-87; R. Étaix, "Fragments Indits de l'Opus Imperfectum in Matthaei," *Revue bénédictine* 84 (1974): 271-300. [3]Jn 1:1-2, 14. [4]Is 53:8. [5]PO 25:52-53.

WHY DAVID IS NAMED BEFORE ABRAHAM.
ANONYMOUS: Furthermore, he did not say "of Jesus Christ, Son of God" but instead "Son of David, Son of Abraham." But why then did John immediately point out the nature of his divinity by saying in the beginning of his Gospel, "In the beginning was the Word, and the Word was with God"?[6] Because John's Gospel was set in exile among the Gentiles. He wrote in the Greek language for the benefit of the Gentiles, who knew little of such matters as whether God had a Son or in what sense God had offspring. Therefore it was important to first show to the Gentiles the mystery of his incarnation, since they did not know who he was at that time. For that reason it was first necessary for them to realize that the Son of God is God. Then, because God took on flesh, John said in the next phrase that "the Word was made flesh and lived among us."[7]

Matthew instead wrote his Gospel to the Jews in the Hebrew language, just as I have already said, so that the Jews might be edified in faith. Indeed, the Jews always knew that he is the Son of God and how he is the Son of God.[8] Therefore it was unnecessary to explain to them the nature of his divinity, which they themselves knew quite well.

But why did he name David first when Abraham came before him in time? The first and straightforward reason is this: When the Evangelist proposed to recount the lineage of the Lord from Abraham, if he had first listed him as the descendant of Abraham, David would have come afterward. He realized it was necessary to return to Abraham again and to count him twice in this very place.[9] Moreover, there is the other reason that rank of kingdom is greater than rank of birth. For even if Abraham came first in time, David nevertheless came first in rank. INCOMPLETE WORK ON MATTHEW, HOMILY 1.[10]

THE LINE OF DESCENT. CHROMATIUS: Therefore St. Matthew began writing his Gospel with an introduction of this sort, saying, "This is the book of Jesus Christ, descendant of David, descendant of Abraham. Abraham begot Isaac, Isaac begot Jacob," and the rest that follows. Matthew, as I have said, tells of the second birth[11] of the Lord into flesh and for this reason traces his family line from Abraham, treating separately the tribe of Judah, until he comes down to Joseph and Mary. Since the Evangelist begins from Abraham by succession of birth and recounts in order the names of all, one may wonder why he calls Christ our Lord only the descendant of David and the descendant of Abraham in saying, "This is the book of the lineage of Jesus Christ, Son of David, Son of Abraham." At any rate, we know that the Evangelist did not say this without reason and in this order. Each of them, both Abraham and David, whether by the promise of the Lord or rank of birth, lived as a worthy predecessor in the line of Jesus Christ as to his existence in flesh. For the Lord had promised to Abraham, who by right of circumcision was the founding patriarch of the Jewish people, that from his seed all nations would be blessed. This was realized in Christ, who received his body from the line of Abraham. The apostle made an interpretation for the Galatians about this, saying, "Now the promises were made to Abraham and to his offspring. It does not say, 'And to offsprings,' referring to many; but, referring to one, 'And to your offspring,' which is Christ."[12] So also is David first among the tribe of Judah in the rank of king. And likewise God promised to this very tribe that the eternal king, Christ the Lord, would be born from the fruit of its womb. For David was the first king from the tribe of Judah, from which the Son of God received his flesh. Thus

---

[6]Jn 1:1. [7]Jn 1:14. [8]The author claims that the Jews knew of the existence of the Son of God insofar as this existence, according to the Christian interpretation of the Old Testament, is announced and therefore made known by the prophecies. [9]That is, Abraham is mentioned after David even though he preceded him in time, since with his name the Evangelist began the list of the generations. [10]PG 56:612-13. [11]The Son is eternally generated from the Father and born into flesh in the incarnation; hence it is said that his incarnate birth is second to his eternal generation. [12]Gal 3:16.

Matthew rightly counted Christ our Lord as the descendant of David and Abraham, because both Joseph and Mary are descended from these regal origins, the line of David, who himself descended from Abraham, who in faith lived as the father of nations and in flesh was the first of the Jewish people. TRACTATE ON MATTHEW 1.1.[13]

THE KINGLY SUCCESSION PRESENTED BY MATTHEW. HILARY: What Matthew publishes in order of kingly succession, Luke has set forth in order of priestly origin.[14] While accounting for each order, both indicate the relationship of the Lord to each ancestral lineage. The order of his lineage is thus duly presented, because the association of the priestly and royal tribes that was begun through David from marriage is now confirmed out of the descent from Shealtiel to Zerubbabel. And so, while Matthew recounts his paternal origin that began in Judah, Luke teaches that his ancestry was taken from the tribe of Levi. Each in his own way demonstrates the glory of our Lord Jesus Christ, who is both the eternal king and priest, as seen even in the fleshly origin of both of his ancestries. It does not matter that the origin of Joseph instead of Mary is recounted, for indeed there is one and the same blood relationship for the whole tribe. Moreover, both Matthew and Luke provide precedents. They name fathers in order not so much by their lineage as by their clan, since the tribe began from one individual and continues under a family of one succession and origin. Indeed, Christ has to be shown as the son of David and Abraham, so Matthew began in this way: "The book of the genealogy of Jesus Christ, the son of David, the son of Abraham." It does not matter who is placed in a given order as long as the whole family is understood to derive from a single source. Joseph and Mary belonged to the same kinship line. Joseph is shown to have sprung from the line of Abraham. It is revealed that Mary came from this line, too. This system is codified in law so that, if the oldest of a family

should die without sons, the next oldest brother of the same family would take the dead man's wife in marriage. He would consider his sons as received into the family of the one who had died, and thus the order of succession remains with the firstborn, since they are considered to be the fathers of those born after them in either name or birth. ON MATTHEW 1.1.[15]

EXPLAINING VARIED REPORTS OF THE LINEAGE: AUGUSTINE: Some might be perplexed by the fact that Matthew enumerates one series of ancestors, descending through David to Joseph,[16] while Luke specifies a different succession, tracing the ancestry from Joseph backwards through David.[17] It was easy for them to perceive that Joseph was able to have two fathers, one blood father by whom he was born and another adoptive father by whom he was adopted.[18] Indeed, this was the custom of adoption even among that people of God. In this way they could endow sonship upon those whom they had not given birth. Recall how Pharaoh's daughter adopted Moses[19] (and she was a foreigner). And Jacob himself adopted his own grandsons, the sons of Joseph: "And now your two sons, who were born to you in the land of Egypt, before I came to you in Egypt, are mine; Ephraim and Manasseh shall be mine, as Reuben and Simeon are. And the offspring born to you after them shall be yours."[20] In this way, too, it came about that there were twelve tribes

---

[13]CCL 9a:193-94. [14]The discrepancy between Matthew and Luke in the genealogy of Jesus was troublesome for the ancient exegetes. Hilary here explains it by deriving, from Luke, Jesus' descent from the tribe of Levi, which had no territory of its own and thus was intermingled with the other tribes. In this way the Messiah's royal (from Judah) as well as sacerdotal (from Levi) origin is revealed. [15]SC 254:90-92. Hilary provides an explanation of why Matthew's account of the ancestors of the Lord differs from Luke's. Considered together they show in a complementary way that the Lord has both priestly and kingly ancestry. Both Mary and Joseph derive from Abraham and David. [16]Mt 1:1-16. [17]Lk 3:23-38. [18]According to Matthew 1:16, Joseph was the son of Jacob; according to Luke 3:23, on the other hand, Joseph was the son of Eli. The difficulty is resolved by hypothesizing a biological and an adoptive father. [19]Ex 2:10. [20]Gen 48:5-6.

of Israel, with the tribe of Levi being given the special task of tending the temple. Along with this one there were thirteen tribes, although there had been twelve sons of Jacob. In this way it is understood that Luke included Joseph's father in his Gospel, not by whom he was begotten but by whom he was adopted. He recounted his ancestors upwards until he came to David. HARMONY OF THE GOSPELS 2.3.5.[21]

1:2 Abraham, Isaac and Jacob

HOW ISAAC'S BIRTH PREFIGURES THE BIRTH OF JESUS. ANONYMOUS: Abraham was the father of the faithful,[22] and when God wished him to be an example for the virtuous, he said to him, "Go from your country and your kindred and your father's house to the land that I will show you."[23] So that all who should wish to be the sons of Abraham might know how to receive that living land of promise, it was written, "I believe that I will see the goodness of the Lord in the land of the living."[24] . . . Those who do not wish to imitate Abraham in faith cannot be the descendants of Abraham. Then "Abraham was the father of Isaac,"[25] which itself was first interpreted as a jest. However, it is the laughter of the holy. It is not the idiotic cackling of lips but a rational joy of the heart, which was the mystery of Christ penetrating all things. For in this way Isaac was bestowed to parents who had long given up hope as a joy in their extreme old age. Isaac was not understood as a son of nature but as a son of grace. In this way Isaac was born by a Judean mother at the very end of her life as a joy for all to behold. In this same way the angel spoke to the shepherds: "Lo, I announce to you a great joy which will be for all people."[26] And in this same way the apostle said, "When the time came, God sent his Son born of a woman, born under law."[27] Although God's son was born from a virgin and Isaac from an old woman, both were born wholly beyond the expectations of nature. The former [Isaac] had delayed until after his mother was able to give birth; the latter would arrive before his mother was able to give birth.[28] The former was born from an old woman who was already failing to some extent; the latter was born from a chaste virgin. The former was born under a law that was to end; the latter under grace that would remain. INCOMPLETE WORK ON MATTHEW, HOMILY 1.[29]

HOW JACOB'S TWELVE SONS PREFIGURE THE TWELVE OF THE AGE TO COME. ANONYMOUS: Isaac then begot Esau and Jacob. This signifies two ages. Esau, who was covered with hair from head to toe, signifies the first age, which was filled completely from beginning to end with sin like the coarsest of hair. Yet Jacob, who was entirely handsome and refined, signifies the age to come. This age[30] will shine with the splendor of piety, and no harshness or stain of sin will be found in it. As Jacob held fast to Esau's heel when he left his mother's womb, he was thus named Jacob, which in Hebrew means "one who follows upon another's heels."[31] For just as the head of Jacob appeared as soon as the feet of his brother had come out, so also the beginning of the next age will appear immediately after the end of that first age. Just as Esau persecuted Jacob, the sons of that age persecute the sons of this age. And just as Jacob overcomes evil men by fleeing and not resisting, so also do his children. For just as Jacob's mother then approached him and said, "Son, listen to me and

---

[21]PL 34:1072-73; NPNF 1 6:103-4. [22]Alone among the texts quoted, this text explains each figure named in the genealogy. The interpretation is allegorical, and the allegory—derived mainly from the etymology of the names of the characters—is based on considering the Old Testament a symbolic and prophetic preparation for the New Testament, in such a way that the continuity between the Testaments—and therefore the Christian meaning of the Old Testament—is revealed. The explanation is too long to be reproduced in full and has been digested to treat only the interpretation of persons of particular historical or symbolic importance. [23]Gen 12:1. [24]Ps 27:13 (26:13 LXX). [25]Gen 25:19. [26]Lk 2:10. [27]Gal 4:4. [28]Note the ironic reversal in types: Isaac was delayed in coming until a time when his mother was beyond the natural capacity of giving birth, whereas Jesus was preexistent as divine Word even before his mother was called to give birth. [29]PG 56:613. [30]Following the advent of Christ. [31]*Supplantator*.

flee to Mesopotamia until the anger of your brother subsides,"[32] so also does the church teach its children daily. Whenever they suffer persecution, it advises, "If you have been persecuted in one city, flee to another"[33] and never avenge yourselves.[34] "Then Jacob begot Judah and his brothers."[35] Our Jacob[36] also begot the twelve apostles in spirit, not in flesh and in word, not in blood. For just as Jacob went down into Egypt with his twelve sons in order to multiply, so also did Christ descend into the world with his twelve apostles. He multiplied throughout the whole world, as the deed itself bears witness. INCOMPLETE WORK ON MATTHEW, HOMILY 1.[37]

1:3 Judah and His Descendants

HOW COULD FORNICATORS BE IN JESUS' LINEAGE? SEVERUS: It is for this reason [to show Christ's true humanity] that in this genealogy the Evangelist mentioned in his list even those who had shocking carnal relations that were inappropriate and outside the law. For Matthew wrote with due deliberation, "And Judah became the father of Perez and Zerah by Tamar" and even more plainly "And David became the father of Solomon by Uriah's wife." These were women with whom they became united by fornication and adultery. By this means the genealogy revealed that it is our very sinful nature that Christ himself came to heal. It is that very nature which had fallen, revolted and plunged into inordinate desires. When our nature fled [from God], he took hold of it. When it dashed out and ran away in revolt, he stopped it, held onto it, enabled it to return and blocked its downward spiral. This is what the words of the apostle say in this regard: "For surely it is not with angels that he is concerned but with the descendants of Abraham. Therefore he had to be made like his brothers in every respect."[38]

Christ therefore took upon himself a blood relationship to that nature which fornicated, in order to purify it. He took on that very nature

that was sick, in order to heal it. He took on that nature which fell, in order to lift it up. All this occurred in a charitable, beneficial manner wholly appropriate to God.

Although sinless, he became united to the flesh that is of the same essence as ours, which possesses an intelligent soul. It is with this premise that the gestation and conception from the Holy Spirit was spoken and the virgin birth occurred, the birth that knew not marriage or carnal union and that respected in an unspeakable manner the seal of virginal purity. CATHEDRAL SERMONS, HOMILY 94.[39]

PEREZ AND ZERAH AS TYPES. ANONYMOUS: We note how Judah became "the father of Perez and Zerah by Tamar."[40] But note how the mysteries of the Jewish and Gentile people were being anticipated: Zerah [symbolic of Israel] was the first to come forth from the womb. The midwife "took and bound on his hand a scarlet thread," signifying the Jewish people marked with the blood of circumcision. Zerah withdrew, and Perez [symbolic of the Gentiles] came out. The flesh in which Zerah had been enclosed was blocked. But the flesh in which Perez had been enclosed opened up. Therefore Perez came out first.[41] Thus the Jewish people appeared first in the light of faith, as though proceeding from the dark womb of the world. They were therefore marked with the scarlet thread of circumcision, everyone believing that this people of God would be first. But what then happened?

The law was placed before them as a hedge to stand in the way of God's judgment. Yet the law, as we learn, may impede faith and not help; as it is written: "without the law sin was dead. Once upon a time I was living without law, but when the commandment came, sin revived, and I died."[42] Thus, due to sin, the law impeded the way of the Jewish people, so they did not bring in the

---

[32]Gen 27:43-44. [33]Mt 10:23. [34]Rom 12:19. [35]Mt 1:2. [36]Christ. [37]PG 56:614. [38]Heb 2:16-17. [39]PO 25:53-54. [40]Mt 1:3. [41]Gen 38:27-30. [42]Rom 7:8-10.

light of justice. But when Christ came in due time, the hedge of the law that was between the Jews and the Gentiles was broken, as the apostle says: "[He] has broken down the dividing wall of hostility."[43] So it happened that the Jewish people, who were first to come, were held captive, while the Gentiles remained as though in the womb of the dark world. After the law was broken at Christ's bidding, with the Jewish people being excluded, the Gentiles were first to come to faith [in the gospel]. Later the Jewish people will follow, as the apostle says: "Behold, I tell you a mystery [. . .] a partial blindness only has befallen Israel, until the full number of the Gentiles should enter, and thus all Israel will be saved."[44] INCOMPLETE WORK ON MATTHEW, HOMILY 1.[45]

1:4 Salmon Fathered Boaz

RAHAB WHO LOVED ISRAEL A FIGURE OF THE CHURCH. ANONYMOUS: "Nahshon brought forth Salmon." The name Salmon is interpreted "take the vessel." Salmon married Rahab. This Rahab is said to have been a harlot from Jericho, who took in spies and envoys from the children of Israel. And when the king of Jericho sought the spies so that he might put them to death, Rahab hid them on the roof of her house and kept them safe from harm. Hearing of the deeds of the children of Israel, she loved Israel more than her own people. And this fact seems to be doubly credible to me. Since Salmon was considered noble among the children of Israel and was of the tribe of Judah and the son of the prince, he saw the faithful Rahab thus converted to goodness and beloved by God and led from Jericho at God's command and counted among the daughters of Israel. Such a wonderful woman surely deserved to become Salmon's wife.

I therefore believe, in terms of a spiritual mystery, that Rahab the harlot was a figure of the church. Though a harlot among the people and defiled by the worship of idols, she received the messengers (i.e., the apostles) of Jesus Christ into the home of her heart because of

their words. She hid them on top of the storehouse of her mind, so that the prince of the world, the devil, might not find them nor put to death those who with the sign of the scarlet cord had also been lowered down through the window. It was as though saved by the mark of the Lord's passion, led out of the world and made chaste, that she became the bride of Christ.

This Rahab, after she married Salmon, was named Rachab,[46] which is interpreted "ascent." Indeed, just as Rahab ascended bodily, having been made one of the daughters of Israel and dignified by marriage to that man, she also ascended spiritually. For although the church was once a worshiper of idols, she became the companion of angels, the bride of Christ and the daughter of God. INCOMPLETE WORK ON MATTHEW, HOMILY 1.[47]

1:5 Boaz Fathered Obed

THE UNION OF RUTH AND BOAZ BROUGHT FORTH A ROYAL NATION. ANONYMOUS: As for Salmon, which is interpreted "take the vessel," what son did he beget from Rahab? Boaz is interpreted as "in strength" or "strength in him" or "showing strength." At God's command Boaz took as his wife Ruth, who had been provided by God. In strength he brings forth children who are strong in themselves and distinguished. But those who take wives provided by the devil (i.e., with no awareness of religion) and who are not faithful bring forth children in feebleness. They are neither prominent nor strong except in doing evil. As punishment for their impious ways, they seem to have brought forth children neither in joy nor in consolation.

And so, Boaz took as his wife a Moabite woman named Ruth. I believe it is superfluous to tell how he took her, since on this subject Scripture is clear to all. We, however, will say only one thing. It was by the merit of her faith

---

[43]Eph 2:14. [44]1 Cor 15:51; Rom 11:25-26. [45]PG 56:614-15. [46]Latin *Raab* to *Rachab*. [47]PG 56:618.

that Ruth married Boaz. She viewed with indifference her own people, land and race and chose Israel. She did not shun her bereaved and foreign mother-in-law, being led by the desire of this race rather than her own. She renounced the gods of her ancestors and chose the living God, saying these words to her mother-in-law: "Do not ask me to leave you or to turn back from following you; for where you go I will go, and where you lodge I will lodge; your people shall be my people, and your God my God; where you die I will die, and there I will be buried. May the Lord do so to me and more also if even death parts me from you."[48] Therefore Boaz by the merit of Ruth's faith took her as his wife, so that through this sanctified union a royal nation might be born. INCOMPLETE WORK ON MATTHEW, HOMILY 1.[49]

1:6 Jesse Fathered David and His Dynasty

HOW DAVID PREFIGURED CHRIST AND THE CHURCH. ANONYMOUS: "Jesse brought forth David the king," for God is in the generation of the just, and the generation of the righteous shall be blessed. What can we say concerning David, whose role in Scripture is that of king? Passing over all else, we can at least say this: David prefigured Christ. David is interpreted as "able of hand" or "beloved," just as Christ was. He was strong in battle and powerful and beloved by his country. In his acts, in mercy and in his gentleness, he was prophetically anticipating Christ. But how does this apply to his unjust abuses, as distinguished from his just actions? Even in his worst sin lay the mystery of Christ and the church. David, taking delight on his high roof, saw the very beautiful Bathsheba bathing, desired her and beckoned her, though she was married to a Hittite man. There is a prefiguring even here, though it may seem unlikely. Christ, while in his high heaven and still joyful in his divinity, saw in advance the very attractive church of his people displeasing him with sordid behavior and weakening in good works, when it

was still the devil's bride. He laid eyes on her, loved her and drew her to himself.[50] INCOMPLETE WORK ON MATTHEW, HOMILY 1.[51]

SOLOMON'S BUILDING OF THE TEMPLE PREFIGURES CHRIST. ANONYMOUS: "David brought forth Solomon." Solomon is interpreted as "peaceful." He is called "peaceful" because he provided a peaceful kingdom for all the people in the territory who were peace-loving and taxpaying so he might build a temple to God, using also the ministry of the people. In this way Solomon was a figure of our peace-loving Christ, who, for all people fleeing to him in faith and paying the spiritual taxes of good works, provided a peaceful kingdom, built with living stones—not only Jews but also Gentiles—so that he might build a living temple to the living God. INCOMPLETE WORK ON MATTHEW, HOMILY 1.[52]

GOD UNASHAMED OF STOOPING TO SAVE SINNERS. SEVERUS: The Evangelist exposes and derides the passions of our race, its dishonors and ailments, to which the Word of God descended in his mercy. He descended to glorify them and raise them up by his charity. It in no way reflects badly upon the physician that he stoops to the level of those who are sick. Matthew could have written, "David became the father of Solomon by Bathsheba" (the name of the woman involved). In deriding, so to speak, adultery itself, he rather stated clearly, "And David was the father of Solomon by the wife of Uriah." He thus showed that Christ, who descended from such a degenerate race by generation, "took up our infirmities and bore the burden of our ills,"[53] as one of the prophets said. CATHEDRAL SERMONS, HOMILY 94.[54]

1:7-15 Solomon and His Descendants

---

[48]Ruth 1:16-17. [49]PG 56:618-19. [50]Here the author of the *Opus imperfectum* stretches credibility in pressing to find analogies between David and Christ, as well as Bathsheba and the church. [51]PG 56:620. [52]PG 56:621. [53]Is 53:4; Mt 8:17. [54]PO 25:55.

THE REBELLIOUS MULTITUDE ANTICIPATED.
ANONYMOUS: Solomon symbolizes the Christian people who were just beginning to flourish. Rehoboam, however, symbolizes a people in decline. When Solomon sinned in old age, the Lord let loose Satan upon him, and a crucial part of his kingdom was cut away. However, Rehoboam rejected the advice of the elders at a critical time and followed that of his young courtiers. He lost nearly his entire kingdom when ten tribes split away and appointed their own kings. Only two tribes remained under Rehoboam's rule.[55] INCOMPLETE WORK ON MATTHEW, HOMILY 1.[56]

1:16 Joseph and Mary

THE MARITAL RELATION BETWEEN JOSEPH AND MARY. AUGUSTINE: Matthew relates the human lineage of Christ in this way: After recounting the fathers from Abraham, he continues to Joseph, the husband of Mary, from whom Jesus was born. It is not fitting to think of Joseph apart from his marriage to Mary, who bore Christ as a virgin and not from intercourse with him.[57] For by his example an incomparable commendation is made to faithful married persons of the principle that even when by common consent they maintain their continence, the marital relation can still remain steadfast and still be rightly called one of wedlock, not by virtue of physical intercourse but by the heart's affection. This is especially so because it was possible for a son to be born to them without bodily embrace, which is intended within the purpose of procreation. Furthermore, Joseph should not have been denied being called Christ's father on the basis that he did not beget him through intercourse. For if he had adopted a child from another, he would have rightly been the father of one who was not even born from his own wife.

Indeed, Christ was even considered by some to be the son of Joseph, just as if he had been simply born of his flesh. But this was believed by those who did not know of Mary's virginity.

Luke says, "Jesus, when he began his ministry, was about thirty years of age, being the son (as was supposed) of Joseph."[58] Instead of naming Mary his only parent, he had not the slightest hesitation in also speaking of both parties as his parents when he says, "And the child grew and became strong, filled with wisdom; and the favor of God was upon him. Now his parents went to Jerusalem every year at the feast of the Passover."[59] Lest any imagine that by the "parents" here was meant only Mary and her blood relations, we do well to recall that preceding word of Luke: "And his father and mother marveled at what was said about him."[60] HARMONY OF THE GOSPELS 2.1.2-3.[61]

WITHOUT INTERCOURSE OF THE FLESH. AUGUSTINE: Since he thus related that Christ was born from Mary as a virgin and not as a result of intercourse with Joseph, for what reason does Matthew call him his father, if not because we understand Joseph to be truly the husband of Mary, not through intercourse of the flesh but in virtue of the genuine spiritual union of marriage? . . . All this suggests that Luke's phrase, "as was supposed," was inserted with a view of correcting those of the opinion that he was born from Joseph in the same way that others are born. HARMONY OF THE GOSPELS 2.1.3.[62]

1:17 Three Groups of Fourteen Generations

FORTY GENERATIONS IN THREE CYCLES. AUGUSTINE: This particular number of generations, totaling forty, is a sign of that laborious period in which, under the discipline of Christ

---

[55]1 Kings 11—12; cf. 2 Chron 10. [56]PG 56:621. [57]Joseph did not disengage himself from the married estate into which he entered with Mary on the ground that she gave birth not as the wedded wife of Joseph but as a virgin. [58]Lk 3:23. [59]Lk 2:40-41. [60]Lk 2:33. [61]PL 34:1071-72; NPNF 1 6:102-3*. In what way, Augustine asks, did Joseph remain the husband of Mary the virgin? Though Joseph was not the physical father, nonetheless he was a real and significant father to Jesus and continued in an enduring relation with Mary. In what follows, a single asterisk (*) indicates that the previous English translation has been dearchaized. [62]PL 34:1072.

the King, we will continue to fight against the devil. The same number was foreshadowed in both the law and the prophets, who had already solemnized a fast of forty days for the humbling of the soul (this pattern was firmly set in the narratives of Moses and Elijah, each of whom fasted for forty days).[63] The Gospel narrative itself then again foreshadowed this same number in the fast of the Lord himself, during his forty days of temptation by the devil.[64] What else does this narrative show than that condition of temptation which pertains to us through all the space of this age?[65] Christ bore this temptation in the flesh when he condescended to take upon himself our own mortality.

Add to this also that after his resurrection, it was his will to remain with his disciples on the earth not longer than forty days.[66] During this time he continued to mingle his resurrected life with theirs in the form of human intercourse. He shared with them food, which mortals need for life, even though he himself would never die. All this was done with the view of signifying to them through these forty days that although his presence would be later hidden from their eyes, he would yet fulfill what he promised when he said, "I am with you, even to the end of the world."[67]

There may be other and subtler methods of accounting for the length of this age, but the most apparent anticipations within the natural order of this number are the seasons of the years, which revolve in four successive alternations. Note also the fact that the world itself has its bounds determined by four divisions (which Scripture sometimes designates by the names of the winds, east and west, north and south).[68] The number forty then is four times the cycle-completing number ten. The number ten, of course, is itself made up by adding one, two, three and four together. HARMONY OF THE GOSPELS 2.4.9.[69]

PRIOR SALVATION HISTORY. ANONYMOUS: "So

all the generations from Abraham to David were fourteen generations." When the Evangelist could have briefly explained the number of generations by saying, "From Abraham to Christ there are forty-two generations," for what reason did he three times omit generations and divide them into three parts of fourteen generations each? Because the human situation among the Jews was changed three times, with fourteen generations cycling three times. First, from Abraham to David, they were under the judges. Second, from David to the exile, they were under the kings. Third, from the exile to Christ, they were under the high priests.

So this demonstrates that just as fourteen generations were completed three times, the state of humanity was altered. So with fourteen generations completed from the exile to Christ, the state of humanity from Christ on must be once again changed. This indeed happened. After Christ, the generations were no longer under so many judges, or so many kings or so many high priests. Rather all generations came forth under one Christ who was Judge and King and High Priest. For in those three states, only he finally had dignity.

Therefore, since the judges and kings and high priests prefigured the three offices of Christ, their beginnings were always to be understood as anticipatory figures of Christ. Joshua was the first judge; David, the first king; and Jeshua, the son of Josedech, the first high priest. No one doubts that these men were prefiguring Christ. . . . The reason why forty-two generations are given according to the flesh of Christ being born into the world is this: forty-

---

[63]Ex 34:28; 1 Kings 19:8. [64]Mt 4:1-2. [65]Between Christ's coming and his coming again. [66]Acts 1:3. [67]Mt 28:20. [68]Zech 14:4. [69]PL 34:1075; NPNF 1 6:105**. Why were there three cycles of fourteen generations, or forty generations from Abraham to David to Christ? This was to point back to the typological significance of the number forty as repeatedly foreshadowed in the law and prophets and then reappearing in the narrative of Jesus' life. In what follows, a double asterisk (**) indicates that an earlier English translation has been used with significant modifications.

two is the product of six times seven. Six, however, is the number that signifies work and toil, for the world was made in six days—it is a world made in work and toil and pain. So, appropriately, there are forty-two generations before Christ being born into the world in toil and pain, and these generations contain the mystery of work and toil. INCOMPLETE WORK ON MATTHEW, HOMILY 1.[70]

[70]PG 56:629-30.

1:18 25 THE BIRTH OF JESUS CHRIST

[18]*Now the birth of Jesus Christ[f] took place in this way. When his mother Mary had been betrothed to Joseph, before they came together she was found to be with child of the Holy Spirit;* [19]*and her husband Joseph, being a just man and unwilling to put her to shame, resolved to divorce her quietly.* [20]*But as he considered this, behold, an angel of the Lord appeared to him in a dream, saying, "Joseph, son of David, do not fear to take Mary your wife, for that which is conceived in her is of the Holy Spirit;* [21]*she will bear a son, and you shall call his name Jesus, for he will save his people from their sins."* [22]*All this took place to fulfil what the Lord had spoken by the prophet:*

[23]*"Behold, a virgin shall conceive and bear a son,*
   and his name shall be called Emmanu-el"
(which means, God with us). [24]*When Joseph woke from sleep, he did as the angel of the Lord commanded him; he took his wife,* [25]*but knew her not until she had borne a son; and he called his name Jesus.*

f Other ancient authorities read *of the Christ*

OVERVIEW: No one can explain the mystery of his birth, nor is it possible to explain (CHRYSOSTOM). His corporeal birth was in time, but his divine Sonship was before time. The one was from a virgin mother, the other from God the Father. He assumed visible flesh to demonstrate his invisible divinity (CHROMATIUS). The angel laid open to Joseph all things that were in his mind, what he felt, what he feared, and what he was resolved to do, that he might be instructed in self-restraint and consoled (CHROMATIUS, CHRYSOSTOM, ANONYMOUS). He gave to Joseph the honor of giving a name to the Savior and called him to exhibit a father's care toward the child (CHRYSOSTOM). The typological analogies between Adam's rib and Joseph's dread and between the conceptions of Elizabeth and Mary are explored (ANONYMOUS). The nativity is best understood in relation to the coming salvation and its prophetic expectation, which had been already promised by the Lord speaking through Isaiah (CHRYSOSTOM). The virgin held in her womb what the whole world could not contain (ANONYMOUS). Jesus' birth does not diminish his incorruptibility (ORIGEN). The miracle of the genealogy is that he who adopted and begot fathers was born from their sons! They were made his fathers whose son he was not; in turn he treated them with a favor by being their son (ANONYMOUS). The Virgin did not later enter into physical relations (CHRYSOSTOM), for it is not plausible that the one who bore God, who was worthy of carrying God in her womb, would subsequently have carnal relations with a man (CHROMATIUS). As Christ would later commit Mary to his disciple, so now he commits her to Joseph (CHRYSOSTOM). The angel gave to Joseph the honor that belongs to a father, that of naming the child (CHRYSOSTOM).

1:18 *How the Birth of Jesus Christ Came About*

HIS BIRTH DOES NOT DIMINISH HIS INCOR-RUPTIBILITY. ORIGEN: Why does the Evangelist make mention here of "birth," whereas at the start of the Gospel he had said "generation"? For in this place he says, "Now the birth of Jesus Christ[1] took place in this way,"[2] but there "The book of the generation."[3] . . . What then is the difference between "birth" and "generation"? How are either of them to be understood as applied to Christ?

Note that this, my spoken word, in its own proper nature, is intangible and invisible. But when it is written down in a book, in a manner of speaking, it takes on a body. It is then both seen and touched. So it is with the fleshless, bodiless Word of God. The Word is neither seen nor described according to his Godhood but becomes, through his incarnation, subject to both sight and description. For this reason there is the "book" of his "generation" as of one who is made flesh. But here the point under investigation is not why he says "book" instead of "vision" or "account" (for this has been discussed already). Rather, it is why, when Matthew had previously mentioned "generation," he here speaks of "birth." What is "birth" as distinguished from "generation"?

There is a difference between generation and

birth. For "generation," or "coming into being," is the original formation of things by God, while "birth" is the succession from others caused by the verdict of death that came on account of the transgression. And even now, "generation" has something incorruptible and sinless about it, whereas "birth" implies that which is subject to passion and sin. The Lord in his eternal generation is incapable of sin. His being born did not undermine his eternal generation, which is incorruptible. But upon being born he assumed what is passible. That does not imply that he assumed what is subject to sin. He continued to bear the original Adam incapable of being lessened, either in respect of corruptibility or as regards the possibility of sin. Hence the "generation" in the case of Christ is not according to some procession from nonbeing into being. It is rather a transition [a path, a way] from existing "in the form of God" to the taking on of "the form of a servant."[4] Hence his "birth" was both like ours and above ours. For to be born "of woman"[5] is like our birth, but to be born "not of the will of the flesh" or "of man"[6] but of the Holy Spirit is above ours. There is here an intimation, a prior announcement of a future birth to be bestowed on us by the Spirit. FRAGMENT 11.[7]

THE SIMPLE MYSTERY OF THE CONCEPTION. CHRYSOSTOM: Do not speculate beyond the text. Do not require of it something more than what it simply says. Do not ask, "But precisely how was it that the Spirit accomplished this in a virgin?" For even when nature is at work, it is impossible fully to explain the manner of the formation of the person. How then, when the

---

[1]At Mt 1:18 certain manuscripts have *genesis*, which is preferred by modern editors. Others have *gennēsis*. Origen read it thus, pointing out the difference between *genesis* in 1:1 and *gennēsis* in 1:18, indicating the birth of Jesus. His explanation takes into account the more generic meaning of *genesis*, signifying "to become, to be born, to be," as compared to the more specific *gennēsis*, meaning "to beget." [2]Mt 1:18. [3]Mt 1:1. [4]Phil 2:6-7. [5]Gal 4:4. [6]Jn 1:13. [7]GCS 41.1:19-20. Generation is the incorruptible original formation of things by God, while birth emerges from the corruptible succession out of secondary causes.

Spirit is accomplishing miracles, shall we be able to express their precise causes? Lest you should weary the writer or disturb him by continually probing beyond what he says, he has indicated who it was that produced the miracle. He then withdraws from further comment. "I know nothing more," he in effect says, "but that what was done was the work of the Holy Spirit."

Shame on those who attempt to pry into the miracle of generation from on high! For this birth can by no means be explained, yet it has witnesses beyond number and has been proclaimed from ancient times as a real birth handled with human hands. What kind of extreme madness afflicts those who busy themselves by curiously prying into the unutterable generation? For neither Gabriel nor Matthew was able to say anything more, but only that the generation was from the Spirit. But how from the Spirit? In what manner? Neither Gabriel nor Matthew has explained, nor is it possible.

Do not imagine that you have untangled the mystery merely by hearing that this is the work of the Spirit. For we remain ignorant of many things, even while learning of them. So how could the infinite One reside in a womb? How could he that contains all be carried as yet unborn by a woman? How could the Virgin bear and continue to be a virgin? Explain to me how the Spirit designed the temple of his body. THE GOSPEL OF MATTHEW, HOMILY 4.3.[8]

THE MYSTERY OF HIS DIVINITY. ANONYMOUS: Such, according to Matthew, was the exceptional genealogy of Christ. He has made it clear that Jacob begot Joseph, to whom Mary was betrothed when she bore Jesus. Yet no one hearing this should suppose that the birth of Christ came about in the same usual manner as that of his forefathers. So Matthew continues to present the special lineage of Christ, which was not like the lineage of these fathers in every respect, as we will see. How can this be so, that he stands in this lineage but stands in it differently? "After Mary had been betrothed to Joseph, she

was found to be with child before they had married." That is, the child was from a virgin but had [an adoptive, legal] human father. While enumerating his line, Matthew shows him to have descended from the seed of David according to the promises of God. But in explaining that his birth happened in a way quite beyond human nature, he reveals the mystery of his divinity. It was not fitting that the only Son of God should be born in the human way. For he was born not for himself but for humanity. He was indeed born into flesh that would undergo corruption. But Christ was born in order to heal corruption itself. Human corruption is not derived from the uncorrupted state of a virgin. It does not make sense that the only Son of God, who was born to heal corruption, might be born of a corrupt union. Humanity is born out of the necessity to exist. Christ, however, was not born out of the necessity of nature to exist but by his merciful will to save. He was appropriately born contrary to the law of human nature because he was beyond nature. Behold the strange and wonderful birth of Christ. It came through a line that included sinners, adulterers and Gentiles. But such a birth does not soil the honor of Christ. Rather, it commends his mercy.

This is the miracle: He who adopted and begot fathers was born from their sons! They were made his fathers whose son he was not. He did them a favor by being their son. They, however, offered him nothing by being his forefathers. Among men, fathers adopt whomever they wish to be their sons. This son, however, adopted fathers whom he chose for himself. Among men, sons receive the honor of birth from their fathers. But in Christ's case, the fathers received honor from the son.

The text reads, "Although his mother Mary had been betrothed to Joseph, before they married, she was found to be with child by the Holy

---

[8]PG 57:42-43; NPNF 1 10:22**. We know *that* the Lord's conception was of the Spirit, not *how*. There is no need to speculate beyond the text or require of it more than what it simply says.

Spirit." Subsequently all saints would be born from the virgin church which is betrothed to Christ. . . . Sons often imitate the example of their father. Note that Mary was betrothed to a carpenter. Christ, betrothed to the church, was about to fashion for humanity salvation in its entirety and his entire work from the wood of the cross. INCOMPLETE WORK ON MATTHEW, HOMILY 1.[9]

HIS CORPOREAL BIRTH AND HIS DIVINITY.

CHROMATIUS: For blessed Matthew, after enumerating the genealogy of Christ, added the following regarding hope for our salvation: "After Mary, mother of Jesus, had been betrothed to Joseph, she was found to be pregnant by the Holy Spirit before they were married." This is the heavenly mystery, this sacrament obscured and hidden by the Holy Spirit. Luke describes in greater detail the manner of the Lord's incarnation, for he recounts how an angel came to Mary and greeted her saying, "Hail woman full of grace,"[10] and the rest that follows. And when Mary asked him how what he had been proclaiming to her could take place—because she had never had relations with a man—he said to her, "The Holy Spirit will come upon you and the power of the Most High will overshadow you. And thus what is born from you will be called the Son of God."[11] It was right that holy Mary, who was about to conceive the Lord of glory in her womb, be informed about the Holy Spirit and the excellence of the Most High when she received into her blessed womb the Creator of the world. Indeed, both Matthew and Luke began their narratives with the corporeal birth of the Lord. John, however, addresses the issue of Jesus' divine birth in the preface to his Gospel: "In the beginning was the Word, and the Word was with God, and God was the Word. This was with God in the beginning. All things were made through him and without him nothing was made."[12] The Evangelists help us to recognize both the divine and corporeal birth of the Lord, which they describe as a twofold mystery

and a kind of double path. Indeed, both the divine and the bodily birth of the Lord are indescribable, but that from the Father vastly exceeds every means of description and wonder. The bodily birth of Christ was in time; his divine birth was before time. The one in this age, the other before the ages. The one from a virgin mother, the other from God the Father. Angels and men stood as witnesses at the corporeal birth of the Lord, yet at his divine birth there was no witness except the Father and the Son, because nothing existed before the Father and the Son. But because the Word could not be seen as God in the glory of his own divinity, he assumed visible flesh to demonstrate his invisible divinity. He took from us what is ours in order to give generously what is his. TRACTATE ON MATTHEW 2.1.[13]

1:19 Joseph's Dilemma

THE SELF-RESTRAINT OF JOSEPH. CHRYSOSTOM:

Do you not see here a man of exceptional self-restraint, freed from that most tyrannical passion, jealousy? What an explosive thing jealousy is, of which it was rightly spoken: "For the soul of her husband is full of jealousy. He will not spare in the day of vengeance."[14] And "jealousy is cruel as the grave."[15] And we too know of many that have chosen to give up their lives rather than fall under the suspicion of jealousy. But in this case it was not a matter of simple suspicion, as the burden of Mary's own womb entirely convicted her. Nevertheless Joseph was so free from the passion of jealousy as to be unwilling to cause distress to the Virgin, even in the slightest way. To keep Mary in his house appeared to be a transgression of the law, but to expose and bring her to trial would cause him to deliver her to die. He would do nothing of the sort. So Joseph determined to conduct himself now by a higher rule than the law. For now that

[9]PG 56:630. [10]Lk 1:28. [11]Lk 1:35. [12]Jn 1:1-3. [13]CCL 9a:201-2. [14]Prov 6:34 LXX. [15]Song 8:6 LXX.

grace was appearing, it would be fitting that many tokens of that exalted citizenship be expressed. It is like the sun not yet arisen, but from afar more than half the world is already illumined by its light. So did Christ, when about to rise from that womb—even before his birth—cast light upon all the world. In this way, even before her birth pains, prophets danced for joy and women foretold what was to come. And John, even before his birth, leaped in the womb. THE GOSPEL OF MATTHEW, HOMILY 4.4.[16]

JOSEPH'S INWARD MUSING. ANONYMOUS: Perhaps Joseph thought within himself: If I should conceal her sin, I would be acting against God's law, and if I should publicize it to the sons of Israel, they would stone her. I fear that what is in her womb is of divine intervention. Didn't Sarah conceive when she was ninety years of age and bring forth a child? If God caused that woman who was like dry wood to flower, what if the Godhead wanted to cause Mary to bear a child without the aid of a man?

Does the conception of a woman depend on a man? If the conception of a woman depends always on a man, doubtless when a man so desires, the woman will conceive. But in this case it is not when the man so desires that the woman conceives but when God so desires. Therefore, if a woman's conception does not depend on a man but on God, what is so incredible if God should wish to give her offspring without a man?

What shall I do then? I will put her away secretly, because it is better in an uncertain matter that a known prostitue should get off free than that an innocent person should die. It is indeed more just that an unjust person should escape justly than that a just person should die unjustly. If a guilty person should escape once, he can die another time. But if an innocent person should die once, he cannot be brought back. INCOMPLETE WORK ON MATTHEW, HOMILY I.[17]

1:20 The Angel's Reassurance

EVE AND MARY—THE WORD OF DEATH AND LIFE. CHROMATIUS: While St. Joseph, yet uninformed of so great a mystery, wanted to put away Mary quietly, he was advised in a dream by an angel who said to him, "Do not be afraid, Joseph, son of David, to take to you Mary your wife, for that which is begotten in her is of the Holy Spirit." St. Joseph is made aware of the heavenly mystery, lest he think otherwise about Mary's virginity. He is also made aware of this that he might exclude the evil of suspicion and receive the good of the mystery. The following words were said to him: "Do not be afraid, Joseph, son of David, to take to you Mary your wife, for that which is begotten in her is of the Holy Spirit," so he might acknowledge the integrity of his fiancée and the virgin birth. It was not appropriate for so great a mystery to be revealed to anyone other than Joseph, who was known to be Mary's fiancé, and no reproach of sin was attached to his name. In fact, *Joseph* translated from Hebrew into Latin means "beyond reproach." Notice here too the order of a mystery: The devil first spoke to Eve the virgin long ago, and then to a man, that he might administer to them the word of death. In the latter case, a holy angel first spoke to Mary and then to Joseph, that he might reveal to them the word of life. In the former case, a woman was chosen unto sin; in the latter case, she was chosen unto salvation. In the former case, the man fell through the woman; in the latter case, he rose through the virgin. The angel therefore said to Joseph, "Do not be afraid, Joseph, son of David, to take to you Mary your wife, for that which is begotten in her is of the Holy Spirit."

And he added, "She shall bring forth a son, and you shall call his name Jesus, for he shall save his people from their sins."[18] But this name of Lord which was given to Jesus from the virgin's womb is not new to him but old. For *Jesus*

---

[16]PG 57:44; NPNF 1 10:23**. As the sun illumines the earth before rising, so grace was illuminating the conduct of those upon whom it was soon to shine. The self-restraint of Joseph, facing a situation that might have elicited the outrage of jealousy, anticipated the forbearing grace that was coming into the world. [17]PG 56:633. [18]Mt 1:21.

translated from Hebrew into Latin means "Savior." This name is agreeable to God because he says through the prophet: "Just God and a Savior; there is none beside me."[19] Lastly, when the Lord himself would speak through Isaiah about the bodily origin of his nativity, he says, "The Lord called me from the womb, from the body of my mother he named my name." His name is certainly not strange, for Jesus was called according to the flesh (i.e., Savior, who was a Savior according to divinity). For Jesus, as we said, is rendered as "Savior." This is what he said through the prophet: "From the body of my mother he named my name."[20] And that he might more fully show us the sacrament of his incarnation, he went on to say, "He made my mouth like a sharp sword . . . he made me a polished arrow, in his quiver he hid me away."[21] By the arrow he signified his divinity; by the quiver he assumed a body from the Virgin in which his divinity was covered with a garment of flesh. TRACTATE ON MATTHEW 2.3-4.[22]

THE CONSOLATION OF JOSEPH. CHRYSOSTOM: How then did the angel assure Joseph? Hear and marvel at the wisdom of these words: "Joseph, son of David, do not fear to take Mary your wife." The angel instantly puts him in mind of David, from whose seed the Anointed One would spring. He did not allow him to be confused by the exalted title of his forefather or remind him that the promise was made to the whole race. Rather, he addresses him personally as "Joseph, Son of David." . . . By saying "fear not," he indicates that Joseph had been afraid, lest he might give offense to God by retaining an adulteress under the law. If it had not been for this, he would not have even thought of casting her out. The angel came from God to bring forward and set before him clearly what he thought to do and what he felt in his mind.

The angel did not only mention her by name but also simply called her "your wife." He would not have called her so if she had been unfaithful. Even as espoused, he speaks of her as "your wife," just as Scripture commonly calls betrothed husbands sons-in-law even before marriage.

But what is meant by "[Do not fear] to take Mary your wife"? It means to retain her in his house. For he was intending to put her away. It is as if the angelic voice prompted: "Retain her just as if she has been committed to you by God, not by her parents alone. God is committing her not for marriage but to dwell with you. By my voice he is committing her to you." Just as Christ would later commit Mary to his disciple, so now he commits her to Joseph. THE GOSPEL OF MATTHEW, HOMILY 4.6.[23]

WHY JOSEPH ALSO NEEDED A REVELATION. ANONYMOUS: Hearing Mary's words and reflecting on her life did not allow Joseph to think badly of her. But as he reflected on her conception he still was not able to think well of her completely. Joseph's mind fluctuated between two alternatives. He was fearful of keeping her, while he did not dare to betray her. It was thus necessary that Joseph also have a revelation. Mary herself had seen the angel and heard him speaking to her about her conception and that of Elizabeth. She had gone into the hill country to see Elizabeth and was reassured at the sight of her. If Mary needed this revelation, how much more did Joseph upon hearing the words of Mary's conception. . . .

Therefore the angel appeared to him for three reasons. First, lest an ignorant but just man should do an unjust thing for a just cause. Next, for the sake of her mother's honor, for if Mary had been put away—not among believers but among unbelievers—the woman could not be above foul suspicion. Third, realizing it was a holy conception, Joseph would in the future keep himself more diligently under control in her regard. . . .

---

[19]Is 43:1; Hos 13:4. [20]Is 49:1. [21]Is 49:2. [22]CCL 9a:202-4. [23]PG 57:47-48; NPNF 1 10:25-26**. The angel led Joseph through this crisis, vindicating and committing Mary to Joseph's care.

He protected himself first according to the system of justice, then out of fear of this type of birth. But why didn't the angel come to Joseph before the virgin's conception in order that he might not think what he was thinking? That he might not suffer the fate of Zacharias, who incurred the blame of unfaithfulness on the conception of his wife who was already an old woman.[24] For it was even more incredible that a virgin rather than an old woman could conceive. If this established high priest did not believe it would be feasible, how much more would his fellow countryman not believe it would be so? Incomplete Work on Matthew, Homily 1.[25]

The Exoneration of Mary. Chrysostom: The very thing which had made him afraid and for which he would have cast her out—this very thing, I say, was a just cause why he should take her and retain her in his house. This more than entirely did away with his distress. It is as if the angel were saying, "For she is not only free from unlawful sexual relations but her very conception is above all natural causes. So not only put away your fear but rejoice even more greatly, 'for that which is conceived in her is of the Holy Spirit.'"

What a strange thing he spoke of, surpassing human reasoning and all the laws of nature. How then might one be made able to believe such an announcement that would be so wholly unexpected? Only by viewing this event in relation to past disclosures in Scripture. For with this intent the angel laid open to Joseph all things that were in his mind, what he felt, what he feared, what he was resolved to do, so that he would be wholly reassured. And not only by past revelations in Scripture but also by the promise of what is yet to come does the angel win him over: "She will bear a son, and you shall call his name Jesus." The Gospel of Matthew, Homily 4.6.[26]

1:21 Joseph to Function as a Father

Joseph to Name Jesus. Chrysostom: It was as if the angel were saying to Joseph, "Do not imagine that, because he is conceived of the Holy Spirit, that you have no part in the ministry of this new dispensation. In the conception you had no part. You never touched the virgin. Nevertheless I am giving you what pertains to a father. I give you the honor of giving a name to the One who is to be born. For you, Joseph, shall name him. For though the offspring is not your own, yet you are called to exhibit a father's care toward him. So on this occasion, at this moment of giving him a name, you stand in significant relation with the one who is born." Then lest on the other hand anyone should, out of all this, suspect him to be the father, hear what follows and with what exact care the angel states it: "She shall bring forth a Son." He does not say "bring forth to you" but merely "she shall bring forth," putting it indefinitely, since it was not merely to him that she brought forth, but to the whole world. The Gospel of Matthew, Homily 4.6.[27]

Mary's Conception Compared with Elizabeth's. Anonymous: "She will bring forth a son, and you shall call his name Jesus." He did not say, "She will bear you a son," as he said to Zacharias: "Behold, your wife Elizabeth will bear you a son."[28] The woman who conceived from a man bore her husband a son. Mary's case is greater than Elizabeth's. The woman who had not conceived from a man did not bear him a son but bore only herself a son.

See in what way the similarity here follows in everything that happened with Adam. At that

---

[24]Lk 1. [25]PG 56:633-34. [26]PG 57:46; NPNF 1 10:25-26**. How did the angel vindicate Mary? Joseph's distress ended when he could grasp, under angelic instruction, that this conception is viewed not as an isolated natural occasion but in relation to the work of God the Spirit and salvation history as revealed in Scripture, and that the angelic visitor fully understood his feelings. [27] PG 57:47-48; NPNF 1 10:25-26**. The conception is wholly of the Holy Spirit, yet in being given the honor of naming the child, Joseph took on a fatherly role in relation to him. [28]Lk 1:13.

time the woman alone, tasting of the fruit of the tree, was seduced and brought forth death, but Adam did not share in her seduction. He did not sin through being seduced by the devil but because he consented to the woman's act. Likewise, submitting to the Holy Spirit, Mary alone believed, saying, "Behold, henceforth all generations shall call me blessed."[29] Joseph then actually had nothing in common with her conception, but later he was saved only by being silent and consenting. Joseph was assisted in a dream —not openly—so that even as when Adam was asleep God created the woman, so when Joseph was asleep he was given a wife by divine influence. INCOMPLETE WORK ON MATTHEW, HOMILY 1.[30]

THE SAVIOR FROM SIN. ANONYMOUS: The Evangelist here interprets the meaning of Jesus in the Hebrew language, saying, "He shall save his people from their sins." Therefore, while a doctor, who has no real power over human health, is unashamed to call himself a doctor simply because of his ability to prepare herbs, how much more worthy is the one who is called Savior, through whom the whole world is saved? INCOMPLETE WORK ON MATTHEW, HOMILY 1.[31]

1:22 Fulfilling What the Lord Had Spoken

THE COMING SALVATION. CHRYSOSTOM: Having established Joseph's faith by all means—by past expectations, by future hopes, by present grace and by the honor given to himself—the angel then rings in the prophet also to give expression in support of all these, proclaiming beforehand the good things that are to occur to the world through the Son: Sins are removed and done away. "For he will save his people from their sins."[32] Here again the coming event exceeds all human expectation. From what are the people being saved? Not from visible warfare or barbarians but something far greater: from their own sins, a work that had never been possible to anyone before. THE GOSPEL OF MAT-

THEW, HOMILY 4.7.[33]

THE PROMISE IS FROM GOD. CHRYSOSTOM: To make what he said easier to understand, the angel makes reference to Isaiah, and not to Isaiah only but to God who speaks through Isaiah. For he does not refer this saying to Isaiah as such but to the God of all. Hence he did not say simply that "All this took place to fulfill what was spoken by Isaiah" but "All this took place to fulfill what the Lord had spoken by the prophet." The mouth indeed was Isaiah's, but the oracle was wafted from above. THE GOSPEL OF MATTHEW, HOMILY 5.2.[34]

NOT BY CHANCE. ANONYMOUS: "Now all this came to pass." What is meant by "all"? That the Virgin would marry her kinsman, that she would be preserved chaste, that the angel would speak to Joseph in a dream, that he would be instructed to accept her as his wife, that the boy would be called Jesus and that the Virgin would bring forth the Savior of the world. "All this took place to fulfill what the Lord had spoken by the prophet,"[35] saying, "Behold, the virgin shall be with child and shall bring forth a son."[36] Grace is witnessed through the prophets so that the Old and New Testaments may harmonize, grace may compensate for the weakness of the learned and what was predicted long ago might not seem to happen solely by chance. INCOMPLETE WORK ON MATTHEW, HOMILY 1.[37]

1:23 Emmanuel, God with Us

GOD AMONG US. CHRYSOSTOM: Why then do they not call him Emmanuel instead of Jesus Christ? Because the text says not "you shall call" but "his name shall be called." This means that

---

[29]Lk 1:48. [30]PG 56:634. [31]Ibid. [32]Mt 1:21. [33]PG 57:47; NPNF 1 10:25-26**. An unprecedented good, salvation from sin in a form previously unimaginable, would come from this conception that Joseph was being called to confirm and this person he was called to name. [34]PG 57:56; NPNF 1 10:32. [35]Mt 1:22. [36]Is 7:14. [37]PG 56:634.

the multitude and the outcome of the events themselves will cause him to be called Emmanuel. For here he puts the event as a name. This is customary in Scripture, to substitute names for the actual events. Therefore to say "they shall call him 'Emmanuel' " means nothing else than that they shall see God among us. Admittedly God has always been among us, but never before so openly. THE GOSPEL OF MATTHEW, HOMILY 5.2-3.[38]

1:24 Joseph Did as the Angel Commanded

JOSEPH'S RESPONSE. CHROMATIUS: Joseph therefore learns from the angel about the sacrament of the heavenly mystery and happily complies with the angel's word. Rejoicing, he abides by the divine plan. He accepts holy Mary and glories in exultant praise because he was deemed worthy to hear that the virgin mother of such great majesty was called by the angel to be his wife. TRACTATE ON MATTHEW 3.1.[39]

1:25 Until Mary Bore a Son

MARY'S CONTINUING VIRGINITY. CHROMATIUS: But concerning what the Evangelist said, "And he did not know her till she had borne her firstborn son," not a few careless people insist on asking whether after the Lord's birth the holy mother Mary had relations with Joseph. But this is not admissible on the grounds of either faith or truth. Far be it indeed that after the sacrament of so great a mystery and after the birth of the sublime Lord, one should believe that the Virgin Mary was intimate with a man. Remember that Miriam the prophetess of the Old Testament (the sister of Moses and Aaron) remained a virgin unsullied by man, having beheld the light of heavenly signs after the plagues of Egypt and the parting of the Red Sea and the Lord's glory going in advance and seen in a pillar of fire and clouds. It is not plausible therefore that the Mary of the Gospel, a virgin bearing God, who beheld God's glory not in a

cloud but was worthy of carrying him in her virginal womb, had relations with a man. Noah, who was made worthy to converse with God, declared that he would abstain from the conjugal need. Moses, after hearing God calling him from the bush, abstained from conjugal relations. Now are we to believe that Joseph, the man who always did what was right, had relations with holy Mary after the birth of the Lord? TRACTATE ON MATTHEW 3.1.[40]

WHETHER "UNTIL" IMPLIES A LIMITED TIME. CHRYSOSTOM: And when Joseph had taken her, "he had no relations with her until she had borne a son." Matthew has here used the word *until* not that you should suspect that afterward Joseph did know her but to inform you that before the birth the Virgin was wholly untouched by man. But why then, it may be said, has he used the word *until*? Because it is common in Scripture that this expression is used without reference to specific, limited times. Here are three examples. First, in the narrative of the ark it was said that "the raven did not return *until* the earth was dried up,"[41] yet the raven did not return even after that limited time. Second, when discussing God the Scripture says, "You are from everlasting to everlasting,"[42] but there is no implication here that some limit is being fixed—rather the opposite. Third, when preaching the gospel beforehand and saying, "In his days may righteousness flourish, and peace abound, until the moon be no more!"[43] it is not thereby setting a temporal limit to this beautiful part of creation. So then here likewise, it uses the word *until* to make certain what was before the birth, but as to what follows, it leaves some further inference to be made. So it is necessary to learn what Matthew teaches: that the Virgin was untouched by man until the birth. But the rest is left for you to perceive, both as a

---

[38]PG 57:56-57; NPNF 1 10:32. [39]CCL 9a:208. [40]CCL 9a:208. [41]Gen 8:7 LXX, italics added. [42]Ps 90:2 (89:2 LXX). [43]Ps 72:7 (71:7 LXX).

consequence of the previous narrative and what was later acknowledged: that not even after having become a mother and having been counted worthy of a new sort of travail and a childbearing so strange, could that righteous man ever have permitted himself to have sexual relations with her. THE GOSPEL OF MATTHEW, HOMILY 5.3.[44]

SHE HELD WHAT THE WORLD COULD NOT CONTAIN. ANONYMOUS: The One whom the world was neither able to contain or worthy to receive, Mary alone was able to hold as it were in the little chamber of her womb. Joseph saw that she would remain a virgin after childbirth. He saw the mystery of the star as it shone above the child's head, and it pointed out the child to the magi who had arrived. Standing aside, he gave

testimony, for he was speechless. Further, he saw the magi in adoration, presenting their hallowed gifts. He heard them speaking about how they had come from the east to Jerusalem, following the star, which did not disdain to pay tribute to men that it might reveal God's glory. Therefore, the incomparable nativity, beyond the measure of all human nativities, manifested the divinity of the newborn child and demonstrated to Joseph the dignity of Mary who had given birth. The Evangelist thus said, "And he did not know her till she had brought forth her firstborn child." That is, he knew who she was after she had given birth. INCOMPLETE WORK ON MATTHEW, HOMILY 1.[45]

---

[44]PG 57:58; NPNF 1 10:33**. [45]PG 56:635.

2:1-8 THE VISIT OF THE MAGI

[1]Now when Jesus was born in Bethlehem of Judea in the days of Herod the king, behold, wise men from the East came to Jerusalem, saying, [2]"Where is he who has been born king of the Jews? For we have seen his star in the East, and have come to worship him." [3]When Herod the king heard this, he was troubled, and all Jerusalem with him; [4]and assembling all the chief priests and scribes of the people, he inquired of them where the Christ was to be born. [5]They told him, "In Bethlehem of Judea; for so it is written by the prophet:
[6]"And you, O Bethlehem, in the land of Judah,
are by no means least among the rulers of Judah;
for from you shall come a ruler
who will govern my people Israel.'"
[7]Then Herod summoned the wise men secretly and ascertained from them what time the star appeared; [8]and he sent them to Bethlehem, saying, "Go and search diligently for the child, and when you have found him bring me word, that I too may come and worship him."

OVERVIEW: Christ came during the reign of Herod, who was not a Jew by race but whose reign was prophesied (THEODORE OF MOPSUESTIA). Herod continutes to serve as a symbol of false devotion (GREGORY THE GREAT). Feigning adoration of the Christ child (PETER CHRYSOLOGUS), Herod would have destroyed him if only he could find him (GREGORY THE GREAT). Silent elements (a star) preached of the Christ child before he ever spoke. Later the apostles would make the Lord known to us by speaking when he was no longer present in earthly body to speak (GREGORY THE GREAT). If Herod had believed the prophecy was true, he would not have attempted to frustrate what was divinely mandated (CHRYSOSTOM). When the wicked want to do serious harm, they paint treachery in the color of humility (ANONYMOUS). Nothing restrained Herod. This is how wickedness works, stumbling over its own greed (CHRYSOSTOM). Jerusalem remained troubled by the same idolatrous affections that had previously caused them to turn from God precisely when God was pouring out his greatest benefits upon them (CHRYSOSTOM). The whole people of God was called by the name of Israel, as if by a name divinely chosen, setting them apart from other nations, as was true of the church (CYRIL OF ALEXANDRIA). God came to help the human race in the form of the Christ child, who needed help from no one else (PETER CHRYSOLOGUS).

2:1a When Jesus Was Born

HOW HEROD'S RULE WAS ANTICIPATED.
THEODORE OF MOPSUESTIA: The patriarch Jacob had already anticipated this very time precisely when he said, "The scepter shall not depart from Judah, nor the ruler's staff from between his feet, until he comes to whom it belongs."[1] Matthew brought these same prophetic testimonies forward in order to show from them that everything came about according to the words of the prophets. On the one hand, he showed that Christ would come from Bethlehem, as had been said by the prophet.[2] On the other hand, he demonstrated that this saying of Jacob prefigured that this was to occur "in the days of Herod." First then those who

ruled over Israel were from David, from the tribe of Judah (Levi's brother), until the captivity in Babylon. After these things the high priests themselves who held the leadership of the people were of the tribe of Levi, but their lineage was also traced from Judah. An intermixture had occurred between the levitical tribe—especially the high priests—and the royal tribe of Judah. Afterward, when the brothers Aristobulus and Hyrcanus came into conflict with each other and warred over the monarchy, the kingdom finally settled upon Herod, who was not a Jew by race, for he was the son of Antipater, an Idumean. And it was, in fact, during the time of his kingdom that Christ the Master appeared, when the kings and rulers from among the Jews had ceased. FRAGMENT 6.[3]

HEROD AND CHRIST. PETER CHRYSOLOGUS:
What does this mean, that it was in the time of a very malevolent king that God descended to earth, divinity entered into flesh, a heavenly union occurred with an earthly body? What does this mean? How could it happen that a tyrant could then be driven out by one who was not a king, who would free his people, renew the face of the earth and restore freedom? Herod, an apostate, had wrongly invaded the kingdom of the Jews, taken away their liberty, profaned their holy places, disrupted the established order, abolished whatever there was of discipline and religious worship. It was fitting therefore that God's own aid would come to succor that holy race without any human help. Rightly did God emancipate the race that no human hand could free. In just this way will Christ come again, to undo the antichrist, free the world, restore the original land of paradise,

---

[1]Gen 49:10. From the beginning of the second century, Genesis 49:10-11 had been interpreted (by Justin, Hippolytus, Origen, Eusebius and others) as a christological prophecy. Thus the claim that until the arrival of the Messiah there would always be a prince of the house of Judah was referred to Christ by pointing out that at the time of Jesus' birth, Herod—who was not of the Hebrew race—was the king of the Jews. [2]Mic 5:2. [3]MKGK 98.

uphold the liberty of the world and take away all its slavery. SERMONS 156.5.[4]

2:1b The Wise Men Seek Jesus

MORE THAN HUMAN LEADING. CHRYSOSTOM: A star appeared in the heavens, calling the wise men from on high. They made a long pilgrimage to worship the One who lay in swaddling clothes in a manger. The prophets of old had proclaimed his coming. These and all the other events were more than human. THE GOSPEL OF MATTHEW, HOMILY 7.3.[5]

2:2 Coming to Worship the King

DISTINGUISHING A SILENT SIGN FROM A SPOKEN PROPHECY. GREGORY THE GREAT: We must ask what it means that when our Redeemer was born, an angel appeared to the shepherds in Judea, but a star and not an angel guided the magi from the east to worship him. This was the reason: It was a reasoning being,[6] an angel, who preached to the Jews as persons capable of using their reason. But a sign and not a voice guided the Gentiles, who were not prepared to make full use of reason to know the Lord. Hence Paul says that "prophecy has been given for believers not for unbelievers, but signs have been given for unbelievers and not for believers."[7] And so prophecy has been given to the Jews as believers and not unbelievers, and signs have been given to the Gentiles as unbelievers and not believers. Note that the apostle preached our Redeemer to these same Gentiles when Jesus was already a grown man, but a star declared him to the Gentiles even when he was a small child, not yet able to perform the normal human function of speaking. It was surely reasonable both that silent elements should preach him when he was not yet speaking and that preachers should make the Lord known to us by speaking when he was already speaking. FORTY GOSPEL HOMILIES 10.1.[8]

2:3 Herod Troubled

TROUBLE IN THE HOLY CITY. CHRYSOSTOM: Since Herod was king, he was naturally afraid both for himself and for his children. But why was Jerusalem troubled? Surely the prophets had foretold him as the Savior, Benefactor and Deliverer who would come from above. But Jerusalem remained troubled by the same idolatrous affections that had previously caused them to turn from God precisely when God was pouring out his greatest benefits on them. While God was offering them new freedom, they were once again mindful only of the fleshpots of bondage in Egypt.

Note the accuracy of the prophets, who had foretold this judgment earlier: "They shall compensate for every garment that has been acquired by deceit and all clothing with restitution; and they shall be willing, even if they had been burnt with fire. For unto us a child is born, unto us a son is given."[9]

Although troubled, they nevertheless did not try to understand what was happening. They did not follow the wise men or even take any particular notice. To this extent were they both contentious and careless. This happened just when those in Jerusalem under Herod had reason to pride themselves that a king was being born among them. This had even attracted the attention of the wise from Persia. They were on the point of having everything going their way, as though their affairs were advancing toward

---

[4]CCL 24b:971-72; FC 17:267**. It is amazing that in such an evil time God chose to do such a great thing. As God sustained the Jews even during the Herodian tyranny, so will he continue to care for the new people of God. [5]PG 57:75-76; NPNF 1 10:45-46**. [6]With this juxtaposition of rational and irrational Gregory seeks to reveal the superiority of the Jews over the pagans insofar as they knew the truth revealed to them through sacred Scripture. [7]1 Cor 14:22. [8]PL 76:1110-11; CS 123:55* (Homily 8). Why was the star the guiding sign of the wise men, while the voice of an angel addressed the shepherds? Both silence and speech were employed to proclaim Jesus' coming. The Jews, as seen in the shepherds, were the recipients of prophetic voices; the Gentiles, as seen in the magi, were recipients of silent signs. [9]Is 9:5-6 LXX.

improvement. But most did not even take notice. Amid an empire that had become so magnificent, they showed little improvement.

Jerusalem had only recently been delivered from subjugation. It might have been more reasonable for them to think, *If the Persians tremble before this king now merely at his birth, wouldn't they tremble much more when he grows up? They would fear and obey him, and our situation might then be more glorious than that of the barbarians.* Even if they knew nothing of mysteries or revelations but formed their judgments only on the basis of present self-interest, they surely might have thought along these lines. But nothing like this really occurred to them, so great was their dullness in prophecy and envy in human affairs.

Such dullness and envy must be rooted out of our minds. One must be more impassioned than fire to stand up against such an array. This is why Christ said, "I am come to send fire on earth, and how I wish it were already kindled."[10] And the Spirit on this account appeared in fire. THE GOSPEL OF MATTHEW, HOMILY 6.4.[11]

2:6 A Ruler from Bethlehem

HOW THE CHURCH BECAME ISRAEL. CYRIL OF ALEXANDRIA: Jacob was called the first Israel when he beheld the ladder and, on it, the "angels ascending and descending."[12] He wrestled with the one who appeared to him. He heard him say, "Your name shall no more be called Jacob, but Israel."[13] By this name the entire people of Israel was called, as if by a name divinely chosen, setting them apart from other nations. Now, Israel means "a mind that sees God."[14] Thus the church from among the Gentiles is also called Israel, not according to the flesh but according to divine grace. FRAGMENT 11.[15]

2:7 Herod's Evil Intent

THE INTENT TO DESTROY. GREGORY THE GREAT: When Herod learned of the birth of our King, he resorted to crafty means to prevent his earthly kingdom from being endangered. He demanded that it be reported to him where the child was to be found. Pretending that he wished to worship him, he would have destroyed him if only he could find him. But of what avail is human malice against the divine plan? "There is no wisdom, no prudence, no plan against the Lord."[16] The star appeared to guide the magi. They found the newborn king and offered him their gifts. They were warned in a dream not to return to Herod. And so Herod was unable to find Jesus, whom he was seeking. Herod symbolizes all those today who, falsely seeking after the Lord, never manage to find him. FORTY GOSPEL HOMILIES 10.2.[17]

WHAT TROUBLED HEROD. CYRIL OF ALEXANDRIA: It wasn't the words of the magi that troubled Herod. It was the speculations of the legal experts about the words of the believing prophets. For the magi were seeking a king, but the Jews were declaring that Christ had been born. For this reason, turning aside the magi, Herod calls the Jews and asks them where the Christ should be born, he "whom you, having heard the magi, are now announcing." This is how the enemies of the truth may sometimes unwillingly speak the truth. They interpret the whole prophecy uselessly, failing to grasp what is necessary. FRAGMENT 10.3.[18]

2:8 Herod's Feigned Response

HEROD SENT THE MAGI. CYRIL OF ALEXANDRIA: Herod treats the magi as ambassadors.

---

[10]Lk 12:49. [11]PG 57:67-68; NPNF 1 10:40**. Due to their dullness in prophecy and envy in human affairs, the Jerusalem of Herod lost sight of its historic calling and unparalleled opportunity as they clung to bondage and idolatry. Hence they were troubled by the portent of change. [12]Gen 28:12. [13]Gen 32:28. Cyril is not quoting the Septuagint precisely. [14]Or "God rules." [15]MKGK 156-57. [16]Prov 21:30. [17]PL 76:1111; CS 123:56* (Homily 8). How was the infant protected against invasive tyrannical power? The divine economy provided for the protection of the child. [18]MKGK 156.

For after a certain manner, they had come to the King of Israel in order to intercede that there might be peace between them and the Israelites. They hoped that, for Gentiles and Jews alike, there might be "one fold, one shepherd."[19] FRAGMENT 10.[20]

NOTHING RESTRAINED HEROD. CHRYSOSTOM: The attempt to murder the child just born was not only an act of madness but also of extreme folly, since what had been said and done was enough to hold him back from any such attempt. For these were not merely natural or human occurrences. . . . Nevertheless nothing restrained Herod. This is how wickedness works—it stumbles over its own greed, always attempting vain objectives. What utter folly. So on either premise his craftiness was bizarre. It was also folly for him to think that the wise men would take him more seriously than the child whom they had come so far to see, whose identity had been confirmed by prophecy. How could Herod hope to persuade the wise men to betray this child to him, even before they had seen the One for whom they had so long hoped? Nevertheless, as many as were the good reasons to hold him back, Herod persisted with his evil attempt. . . . He must have imagined that the Jews would be so anxious to protect the child that they would never be willing to give up their national Deliverer and Savior. With all these miscalculations, he called in the wise men privately and sought to discern the timing of the star. The object of his pursuit was far more than a star. For the star, I think, must have appeared and been visible a long time before, because it took a long time for the wise men to come on their journey to find him in swaddling clothes. If the star appeared at the moment of Jesus' birth in Palestine, it would have already been seen by many in the distant east. The trip to Jerusalem would have taken quite some time.

As to Herod's murder of the children "who were two years old and under," this shows the extent of his irrational wrath and dread in trying to prevent even one from escaping. . . .

But the wise men perceive nothing of this, by reason of their exceeding awe. They would never have expected that Herod could have persisted toward such great wickedness as to attempt to form plots against a dispensation so marvelous. THE GOSPEL OF MATTHEW, HOMILY 7.2-3.[21]

PAINTING MALICE IN THE COLOR OF HUMILITY. ANONYMOUS: After Herod heard the response, he found it believable on two counts: first, it had been spoken by the priests, and second, it had been substantiated by the prophets. He did not bow in devotion to the King about to be born. Rather he harbored malice, seeking Jesus' death through deceit. The wicked may be able to understand what pertains to God when they cannot do what pertains to God. Human intellect was created by God, while human actions spring from free will. Herod saw the great devotion of the magi to Christ. He could not manipulate them with blandishments or frighten them with threats or corrupt them with gold to make them acquiesce with him in the murder of the future King. So he sought to deceive them. But it could not be that, having been lured by blandishments, they would betray the One on account of whom they had undertaken so arduous a journey. Neither could these men announce another king. They belonged to another kingdom and had no high regard for either Herod or Caesar. They could not be intimidated by anyone into betraying him, nor could they desire anything more than Christ, to whom they were bringing precious gifts from so distant a province.

Herod saw there was nothing else he could do. While sharpening his sword, he promised his devotion and painted the malice of his heart in the color of humility. Such is the habit of all wicked people when they want to do serious

---

[19]Jn 10:16. [20]*MKGK* 156. [21]PG 57:75-76; NPNF 1 10:45-46**. Was Herod merely cruel or also witless? Herod shows us how stupid wickedness can become even when it is executing its own deceptions. He was constantly stumbling over his own greed and pride, so as to become not only wicked but also foolish in every respect.

harm to someone: they feign humility and friendship. INCOMPLETE WORK ON MATTHEW, HOMILY 2.[22]

FEIGNED ADORATION. PETER CHRYSOLOGUS: "Go and search diligently for the child, and when you have found him bring me word." Appropriately did Herod say, "Bring me word," for the one who hastens to come to Christ always brings a word of renunciation[23] to the devil. When the priest says to the future Christian, "Do you renounce the devil?" the latter will answer, "I do renounce him." Properly therefore are the magi instructed to bring word to Herod, who realized he was taking the place of the devil. Satan knew how to corrupt a person.

"That I may come and worship him." He wants to lie but he cannot. He who feigned adoration will come that he might bow to abuse, kneel to inflict punishment, recline to do harm. . . . But when the clouds of treachery have passed, in the fair weather of emerging Christian faith, the magi behold again the star they had seen, preceding and leading them on. Finally they arrive at the most holy place of the Lord's birth. SERMONS 158.8-9.[24]

[22]PG 56:640. [23]It is clear that here *renuntiare* means "to announce, to make known." But Chrysologus prefers to interpret it in its more specific meaning of "to renounce." From this he deduces that every Christian must renounce Satan, symbolized by Herod. [24]CCL 24b:983.

2:9-12 THE STAR OF BETHLEHEM

[9]*When they had heard the king they went their way; and lo, the star which they had seen in the East went before them, till it came to rest over the place where the child was.* [10]*When they saw the star, they rejoiced exceedingly with great joy;* [11]*and going into the house they saw the child with Mary his mother, and they fell down and worshiped him. Then, opening their treasures, they offered him gifts, gold and frankincense and myrrh.* [12]*And being warned in a dream not to return to Herod, they departed to their own country by another way.*

OVERVIEW: The star of Bethlehem was not an ordinary star, for no other star has this capacity to guide, not merely to move but to beckon (CHRYSOSTOM). The star went ahead of the magi, showing how all the cosmic elements pay tribute to Christ (ANONYMOUS). The Son of God, who is God of the universe, was born a human being in the flesh. He permitted himself to be placed in a manger while the heavens were being upheld by the same One who was within the manger (CHROMATIUS). The wise men saw a dark and lowly stable, more fit for animals than people, in which no human would be content to retreat unless compelled by the necessity of the journey (ANONYMOUS). Realizing that the baby was a king, they offered him costly gold, the fragrance of frankincense and myrrh (ANONYMOUS). Gold symbolizes wisdom, frankincense the fragrant pursuit of holy speech, and myrrh the mortification of the flesh. We too offer myrrh to God when we employ the spice of self-restraint to keep this earthly body of ours from decomposing through decadence (GREGORY THE GREAT). It was foretold that our Lord and infant

Savior would be triumphant even at the beginning of his life in the flesh (CHROMATIUS). It was not possible for those who had come from Herod to Christ to return to Herod, so they came back by another route (ANONYMOUS). God thereby signified that he intended to heal both Babylon and Egypt (CHRYSOSTOM). So let us, like the magi, return to our home country (paradise) by another way than the way we left it (GREGORY THE GREAT).

2:9 The Star Guides the Wise Men to Jesus

AN ORDINARY HOUSE, NOT AN ORDINARY STAR. CHRYSOSTOM: "And lo, the star which they had seen in the East went before them, till it came to rest over the place where the child was." The star brought them to inquire of the Jews, that their discovery might be made evident to all, and then appeared to them again. Note how fitting was the order of events: the wise men saw the star, were received by the Jews and their king; they heard prophecy to explain what had appeared; the angel instructed them; and then they journeyed from Jerusalem to Bethlehem by the guidance of the star. From all this we learn that this was not an ordinary star, for no other star has this capacity to guide, not merely to move but to beckon, to "go before them," drawing and guiding them along their way.

The star remained after bringing them to the place, in order that the child might also be seen. For there is nothing conspicuous about the place. The inn was ordinary. The mother was not celebrated or notable. The star was needed to manifest and illumine the lowly place, until they had reached their destination at the manger. THE GOSPEL OF MATTHEW, HOMILY 7.3.[1]

THE ELEMENTS PAY TRIBUTE. ANONYMOUS: Considering the homage paid by the star, they became aware of the dignity of the king and said among themselves, "How can this be—an earthly king to whom a star pays tribute?" What

wonder, then, that with the sun of justice about to arise, the heavenly star paid tribute to him! It went before them, that it might show how all the elements pay tribute to those who seek God. Therefore, if you think it a great thing that the star paid homage to Christ, see how much greater are those things which pay tribute to you who have been made human. Look at the sun that hastens to rise for you and the moon that does not cease to shine. If the elements pay tribute to you who have been made, what wonder if the star paid tribute to Christ? If the elements pay tribute to you who are a sinner, what wonder if the star hastened before those who were seeking Christ? And if angels pay tribute to people, whom God created not out of respect for humans but for himself, what great thing is it if the elements that were created for humans should pay tribute to humans? Hearing this, it behooves us both to rejoice and to be fearful, for the greater the benefits given to humanity, all the greater will be the judgments prepared for sinners. And the star stood above the child's head, saying simply: Here he is. Though unable to point him out by speaking, it pointed him out by remaining in one place. INCOMPLETE WORK ON MATTHEW, HOMILY 2.[2]

2:10 Rejoicing Greatly

THEY FOUND WHAT THEY SOUGHT. CHRYSOSTOM: In this way marvel was linked to marvel: the magi were worshiping, the star was going before them. All this is enough to captivate a heart made of stone. If it had been only the wise men or only the prophets or only the angels who had said these things, they might have been disbelieved. But now with all this confluence of varied evidence, even the most skeptical mouths are stopped.

---

[1] PG 57:76; NPNF 1 10:46**. Did a single evidence enable their recognition? The divine economy worked in nature and through prophecy and angelic visitation to gradually bring this incomparable nativity to recognition. [2] PG 56:641.

Moreover, the star, when it stood over the child, held still. This itself demonstrates a power greater than any star: first to hide itself, then to appear, then to stand still. From this all who beheld were encouraged to believe. This is why the magi rejoiced. They found what they were seeking. They had proved to be messengers of truth. Their long journey was not without fruit. Their longing for the Anointed One was fulfilled. He who was born was divine. They recognized this in their worship. THE GOSPEL OF MATTHEW, HOMILY 7.4.[3]

WITH GREAT JOY. ANONYMOUS: "And when they saw the star they rejoiced exceedingly," because they had not been deceived in their hope but rather confirmed even more that they had not undertaken the burden of so great a journey without reason. By the sign of the star appearing to them at the time, they understood that the birth of the King was revealed to them by divine authority. Through the mystery of the star they understood that the dignity of the King who was born exceeded the measure of all earthly kings. For it was inevitable that they considered this King more glorious than the star, which devotedly paid homage to him. What else could these men do but submit to him when even the stars in the sky saw they were subject to him? How could the earth be rebellious against him upon whom the heavens waited? INCOMPLETE WORK ON MATTHEW, HOMILY 2.[4]

2:11 The Wise Men Worship and Bring Gifts

A CRADLE THE WORLD CANNOT HOLD. CHROMATIUS: Let us now observe how glorious was the dignity that attended the King after his birth, after the magi in their journey remained obedient to the star. For immediately the magi fell to their knees and adored the one born as Lord. There in his very cradle they venerated him with offerings of gifts, though Jesus was merely a whimpering infant. They perceived one thing with the eyes of their bodies but another with the eyes of the mind. The lowliness of the body he assumed was discerned, but the glory of his divinity is now made manifest. A boy he is, but it is God who is adored. How inexpressible is the mystery of his divine honor! The invisible and eternal nature did not hesitate to take on the weaknesses of the flesh on our behalf. The Son of God, who is God of the universe, is born a human being in the flesh. He permits himself to be placed in a manger, and the heavens are within the manger. He is kept in a cradle, a cradle that the world cannot hold. He is heard in the voice of a crying infant. This is the same one for whose voice the whole world would tremble in the hour of his passion. Thus he is the One, the God of glory and the Lord of majesty, whom as a tiny infant the magi recognize. It is he who while a child was truly God and King eternal. To him Isaiah pointed, saying, "For a boy has been born to you; a son has been given to you, a son whose empire has been forged on his shoulders."[5] TRACTATE ON MATTHEW 5.1.[6]

WHAT THEY SAW. ANONYMOUS: "And upon entering the house they saw the boy and his mother." Do we understand why, on seeing such a glorious sight, they delighted in the boy, the boy whom they sought as King and for whom they undertook the labor of so great a journey? Did they see a palace splendid in its marble? Did they see his mother crowned with a diadem or reclining on a gilded couch? Did they see a boy swaddled in purple and gold, a royal hallway thronged with various peoples? What did they see? A dark and lowly stable, more fit for animals than people, in which no one would be content to hide unless compelled by the necessity of the journey. They saw his mother with scarcely one tunic to her name, and that tunic was not dressy clothing for her body but a covering for her nakedness, such as a carpenter's wife might

---

[3]PG 57:77; NPNF 1 10:46-47**. [4]PG 56:641. [5]Is 9:6. [6]CCL 9a:216.

have—the garb of an immigrant. The child was covered in the most lowly swaddling clothes and placed in an even lowlier manger. The place was so confining that they could find no room to set him down.

If then they had been seeking a king of this world and thus had found him, they would have been more perplexed than delighted, because they would have undertaken the effort of so great a journey for nothing. Yet because they were seeking the heavenly king, even if they saw nothing regal in him, they were nevertheless delighted, content in the testimony of the star. Their eyes could not see an unworthy boy, because the spirit in their hearts was revealing him to them as an awesome thing. If, moreover, they had sought him as a king of this world, they would have stayed with him, as is often the case when people abandon one king and transfer their allegiance to another. Instead they adored him and returned home that they might have Jesus as the just, heavenly king over their souls and the king of their home country as ruler over their bodies. INCOMPLETE WORK ON MATTHEW, HOMILY 2.[7]

INTIMATIONS OF DIVINITY. ANONYMOUS: "And they adored him." Do you think they would have adored a boy who did not understand the honor of their adoration unless they had believed that God was in him? Therefore they did not postpone their honoring of him, as to one childishly lacking understanding. They treated him as one whose divinity is aware of everything. Even the very nature of the gifts they offered gave witness that they had a certain intimation of the infant divinity. INCOMPLETE WORK ON MATTHEW, HOMILY 2.[8]

GIFTS FIT FOR NATIONS. ANONYMOUS: "For they opened their treasure chests, and gave him gifts of gold, frankincense and myrrh." Thus they were fulfilling the acknowledgment of Christ on behalf of all nations. They were signifying the fulfillment of Isaiah's prophecy: "All

those who are in Sheba shall come, offering gold and precious stones and spreading the good news of the Lord; all the sheep of Kedar shall be gathered together, and the rams of Nebaioth shall come, and they will offer pleasing incense on your altar."[9] They recognized him at once. They opened their treasure chests. They displayed their offerings, gifts in themselves fit for nations to give. For, realizing that he was king, they offered him their elegant and costly first fruits, fit for the Holy One. They offered him gold they had stored up for themselves. Moreover, recognizing his divine and heavenly coming to them, they made an offering of frankincense, a beautiful gift like the soothing speech of the Holy Spirit. Moreover, understanding as they did that human life is but a sepulcher, they offered myrrh. INCOMPLETE WORK ON MATTHEW, HOMILY 2.[10]

OFFERING OF THE HALLOWED MIND, SPEECH AND WILL. GREGORY THE GREAT: There is something more that must be understood about the gold, incense and myrrh. Solomon testifies that gold symbolizes wisdom when he says, "A pleasing treasure lies in the mouth of the wise."[11] The psalmist bears witness to that incense which prayer offers to God when he says, "Let my prayer ascend as incense in your sight."[12] The myrrh indicates the mortification of our bodies, of which the holy church speaks of its workmen who strive even unto death on behalf of God, "My hands dripped with myrrh."[13] And so do we too offer gold to the newborn king if we shine in his sight with the brightness of the wisdom from on high. We too offer him incense if we enkindle on the altar of our hearts the thoughts of our human minds by our holy pursuit of prayer, so as to give forth a sweet smell to God by our heavenly desire. And we offer him myrrh if we mortify the vices of our bodies by our self-denial. Myrrh brings it about, as I have said,

---

[7]PG 56:641-42. [8]PG 56:642. [9]Is 60:6-7. [10]PG 56:642. [11]Prov 21:20 LXX. [12]Ps 141:2 (140:2 LXX). [13]Song 5:5.

that dead bodies do not decompose. For a dead body to decompose is the same as for the human body of ours to become a slave to the decay of dissoluteness, as is said by the prophet: "The pack animals have decomposed in their own dung."[14] This indicates fleshly minded persons who end their lives in the stench of dissoluteness. Therefore we are offering myrrh to God when we employ the spice of self-restraint to keep this earthly body of ours from decomposing through decadence. FORTY GOSPEL HOMILIES 10.6.[15]

2:12 The Wise Men Warned to Avoid Herod

THEY DEPARTED ANOTHER WAY. ANONYMOUS: Oh, the faith of the magi! They did not speak disparagingly of the warning, saying, "We have come a long way, passing through a multitude of nations, feeling no fear. We did not tremble at all before the dread kings when we were there, but we stood our ground and faithfully foretold the king who had been born and, as if to a god, we brought him worthy gifts. And now like slaves you bid us flee further and return by a different route from that we would normally travel?"

No, having already faithfully stood their ground, they did not fear to become known, nor were they ashamed to withdraw in secret. It was not possible that those who had come from Herod to Christ would return to Herod. For those who, abandoning Christ, make their way to Herod still can readily return to Christ. But those who abandon Herod and come to Christ with all their heart do not wish to return to Herod. This is to say: the one who by sinning crosses over from Christ to the devil may readily return through repentance to Christ. But those who abandon the devil for Christ do not easily return to the devil. This is because the one who has never been involved in evil but has known only innocence, so long as evil has not been experienced, is easily deceived and crosses over to the devil. But when he has had experience of

evil and has recalled the good that he has squandered, he quickly returns to God, from whom he strayed. The man who has been involved in evil, moreover, and has converted to good, so long as he rejoices in the goodness he has found and recalls the evil he has escaped, with difficulty is called back to evil. INCOMPLETE WORK ON MATTHEW, HOMILY 2.[16]

THE WILES OF THE TYRANT OVERCOME. CHROMATIUS: This is an example to us of modesty and faith, that once we have come to know and adore Christ as King, we may abandon the path we were traveling before, which was the path of error. We may now proceed by the other path, on which Christ is our guide. We may return to our place, paradise, from which Adam was driven out. This place is mentioned in the psalm as one where we will please the Lord in the land of the living.[17] Thus it was that the magi, having been advised to follow another road, frustrated the tyrant's cruel designs in their return. It was in this manner, through the magi, that the boy who was born a king became known, while at the same time the wiles of the tyrant Herod were overcome. It was predicted that our infant Lord and Savior would be triumphant even at the very beginning of his life in the flesh. This was foretold in advance by Isaiah when he said, "For before the child shall have knowledge to cry 'father' and 'mother,' the riches of Damascus and the spoil of Samaria shall be taken away before the king of Assyria."[18] By "riches of Damascus" is meant the gold that the boy, born the Son of God, received as offered to him by the magi. The "spoils of Samaria" represent the worship of idols, the superstitious error of Samaria from which he diverted those same magi. Those who previously were the prey of the devil because of their false religion became the

---

[14]Joel 1:17. [15]PL 76:1113; CS 123:58-59** (Homily 8). The gold of wisdom, the incense of prayer and the myrrh of self-denial are the gifts offered to the Christ child. [16]PG 56:643. [17]Ps 116:9 (114:9 LXX). [18]Is 8:4.

plunder of God through their knowledge of Christ. The "king of the Assyrians" refers to Herod, or in fact to the devil, to whom the magi themselves became enemies, reverencing as they did the Son of God, our Lord and Savior. TRAC-TATE ON MATTHEW 5.2.[19]

THE OTHER WAY HOME. GREGORY THE GREAT: The return of the magi "by another way" home suggests a spiritual interpretation: As they were advised to take another way, so are we. Our home country is the paradise from which we have fallen. We are forbidden to return to it. When we come to know Jesus, we can return along the way by which he returned. We left our paradise by our pride and disobedi-ence, by overvaluing visible things, by succumb-ing to the tasting of forbidden fruit. We now can return only by weeping and obedience, rejecting visible things, and by curbing our bodily appe-tites. So let us, like the magi, return to our home country by another way than the way we left it. Our evil inclination led us away from the joys of paradise. Our turning around in repentance summons us to return by another way. In this way, dearly beloved, we are being awakened to the fear of God. Be vigilant. Set before the eyes of your heart the deceitfulness of your works. Take seriously the severity of the final judg-ment. Consider how strict a judge is coming. He threatens the impenitent with terror. Yet he still gives them time for repentance. He bears with us. He puts off coming for this reason, that he may find fewer to condemn. FORTY GOSPEL HOMILIES 10.7.[20]

---

[19]CCL 9a:217-18. [20]PL 76:1113-14; CS 123:59-60** (Homily 8). By returning home by another way, the magi suggested to Gregory a broader analogy: our return home to our original relation with God by means of repentance and faith.

2:13-18 THE ESCAPE TO EGYPT

[13]*Now when they had departed, behold, an angel of the Lord appeared to Joseph in a dream and said, "Rise, take the child and his mother, and flee to Egypt, and remain there till I tell you; for Herod is about to search for the child, to destroy him."* [14]*And he rose and took the child and his mother by night, and departed to Egypt,* [15]*and remained there until the death of Herod. This was to fulfil what the Lord had spoken by the prophet, "Out of Egypt have I called my son."*

[16]*Then Herod, when he saw that he had been tricked by the wise men, was in a furious rage, and he sent and killed all the male children in Bethlehem and in all that region who were two years old or under, according to the time which he had ascertained from the wise men.* [17]*Then was fulfilled what was spoken by the prophet Jeremiah:*

[18]*"A voice was heard in Ramah,*
wailing and loud lamentation,
Rachel weeping for her children;
she refused to be consoled,
because they were no more."

OVERVIEW: Egypt, which under Pharaoh stood stubbornly against Yahweh, now became a witness to and abode of Christ (CHROMATIUS). It was not to escape death that he went down into Egypt but that he might put demons to flight and demolish death-dealing idols (ANONYMOUS). The devil, who foresaw the future of Christ, tried desperately to stop him even in his infancy. Christ fled that, in time, he might bestow on us the eternal hope of escape from oppression. In the face of persecution, it is better to flee than to recant. Yet as a grown man he would not flee the death he escaped as an infant (PETER CHRYSOLOGUS). The babies slain by Herod did not fail to attain glory immediately because of their martyrdom (HILARY). They were the first martyrs of Christ's coming (CHROMATIUS). It was Herod, not Christ, who killed the children (THEODORE OF MOPSUESTIA). Whatever the source of unjust suffering, as exemplified by the slain children, the ultimate cause is either God devising a release for us from our sins or it is God offering an exchange of sin (CHRYSOSTOM). For the babes, death brought a blessed end to their grief. For the mothers, however, the memory of their babes ever renewed their grief (ANONYMOUS). Thus it was prophetically foretold that Herod would have no power over the Lord (CHROMATIUS).

2:13 The Holy Family Flees to Egypt

BABYLON AND EGYPT. CHRYSOSTOM: But why was the Christ child sent into Egypt? The text makes this clear: he was to fulfill what the Lord had spoken by the prophet, "Out of Egypt have I called my son."[1] From that point onward we see that the hope of salvation would be proclaimed to the whole world. Babylon and Egypt represent the whole world. Even when they were engulfed in ungodliness, God signified that he intended to correct and amend both Babylon and Egypt. God wanted humanity to expect his bounteous gifts the world over. So he called from Babylon the wise men and sent to Egypt the holy family.

Besides what I have said, there is another lesson also to be learned, which tends powerfully toward true self-constraint in us. We are warned from the beginning to look out for temptations and plots. And we see this even when he came in swaddling clothes. Thus you see even at his birth a tyrant raging, a flight ensuing and a departure beyond the border. For it was because of no crime that his family was exiled into the land of Egypt.

Similarly, you yourself need not be troubled if you are suffering countless dangers. Do not expect to be celebrated or crowned promptly for your troubles. Instead you may keep in mind the long-suffering example of the mother of the Child, bearing all things nobly, knowing that such a fugitive life is consistent with the ordering of spiritual things. You are sharing the kind of labor Mary herself shared. So did the magi. They both were willing to retire secretly in the humiliating role of fugitive. THE GOSPEL OF MATTHEW, HOMILY 8.2.[2]

WHY CHRIST FLED. PETER CHRYSOLOGUS: His flight then was not occasioned by fear but by what had come through the mystery of prophecy. The Evangelist planted the seed when he thus spoke: "Take the boy and his mother and flee into Egypt." And later, "that what was written might be fulfilled: 'From Egypt have I summoned my son.'"[3] Christ fled so that he might establish the truth of the law, faith in prophecy and the testimony of the psalter. The Lord himself says, "It was needful that what was written in the law and the prophets and the psalms be fulfilled by me."[4] Christ fled for us, not for himself. Christ fled so that at the right time he might serve as a steward of the sacraments [the divine mysteries]. Christ fled so that by granting absolution he might take away

---

[1]Hos 11:1. [2]PG 57:83-84; NPNF 1 10:51-52**. The faithful are instructed to hold in memory, amid their own afflictions and hindrances, the flight of the holy family to Egypt and the return of the magi by another route. [3]Hos 11:1. [4]Lk 24:44.

the source of abuses to come and that he might give proof of faith to those who would believe. And finally, Christ fled so that he might bestow on us faith even when we have to flee, because in the face of persecution it is better to flee than to deny the faith. For Peter, because he was unwilling to flee, denied the Lord. John, lest he deny the Lord, fled. SERMONS 150.11.[5]

THE DEVIL FORESAW THE FUTURE OF CHRIST. PETER CHRYSOLOGUS: Was it Herod seeking the child, or the devil working through Herod? When Herod saw the magi for himself, he imagined in his fantasy that they had fled their governors. For Christ, though bound in swaddling clothes, though busy at his mother's breast, though keeping quiet, concealing his words, unable to walk, nevertheless transformed the magi (who had been standard-bearers of the devil) into his most faithful servants. The devil instantly realized what Christ could do when he came of age. So he spurred the Jews against him and, clever contriver that he was, impelled Herod that he might get the jump on Christ in his infancy. He hoped to deprive him of the coming emblem of his virtue, the cross, the banner of the greatest victory for us. The devil perceived that Christ would soon be restoring life to all the world with his teaching and his virtue. Even while still whimpering as a baby, Jesus was taking possession of this world from top to bottom. It was as the prophet said: "Before the child knows to cry to his father and mother he shall take the pride of Damascus and the spoils of Samaria."[6] The Jews themselves attest to this when they say, "You see how the whole world hastens after him."[7] SERMONS 150.9.[8]

PUTTING TO FLIGHT THE DEMONS OF EGYPT. ANONYMOUS: "Go into the land of Egypt." For, just like a doctor, the Lord went down into Egypt that he might visit it as it languished in error, not that he might stay there. For at first blush it seems as if he went down into Egypt in flight from Herod. The fact is that he went in

order to put to flight the demons of Egypt's error, just as Isaiah gives witness when he says, "Behold, the Lord goes down into Egypt, seated atop a swift cloud, and the idols of Egypt shall fall."[9] Do you see then that it was not to escape death that he went down into Egypt but that he might eradicate their deadly idols? For this is the only time that the Lord traveled to Egypt.

It must be noted, moreover, why he fled into Egypt by night but returned during the day. This is because, when he fled, he was fleeing the persecution of Herod. He began his return, however, after the persecutor had died. For night symbolizes the tightening of the heat of persecution, while the day represents a cooling off. INCOMPLETE WORK ON MATTHEW, HOMILY 2.[10]

2:14 Egypt Receives the Christ Child

WHILE PALESTINE PLOTS, EGYPT RECEIVES. CHRYSOSTOM: Mary, who had never even passed beyond the threshold of her own house, was commanded to undergo this long ordeal of adversity for the sake of this wonderful birth and for her own spiritual labor and development. Isn't this remarkable: While Palestine plots, it is Egypt that receives and preserves the One for whom the plots are designed! This is reminiscent of the patriarch Jacob, who also sought succor in Egypt,[11] anticipating the coming of our Lord. THE GOSPEL OF MATTHEW, HOMILY 8.2.[12]

AS A MAN CHRIST WOULD NOT FLEE DEATH. PETER CHRYSOLOGUS: Christ promised that he would come incarnate, that he would go through the phases of life, that he would announce the glory of the kingdom of heaven, that he would proclaim the way of faith and that by the power of his word alone he would put demons to flight.

---

[5]CCL 24b:938-39. [6]Is 8:4. [7]Jn 12:19. [8]CCL 24b:936-37. [9]Is 19:1. [10]PG 56:646. [11]Gen 45:25—46:7. [12]PG 57:85; NPNF 1 10:52**.

He promised that he would give sight to the blind, gait to the lame, speech to the mute, hearing to the deaf, remission for sinners and life to the dead. All these things he promised through the law and the prophets. Thus it was that Christ, when he was to become a man, was not to flee the death he escaped as an infant. SERMONS 150.10.[13]

2:15 A Son Out of Egypt

FUGITIVES EAST AND WEST. CHRYSOSTOM: There is something else here worth noticing, one touching the magi and the other touching the Child. The issue is why didn't the magi remain with the Child? And why didn't the Child remain in Bethlehem? Both had to escape as fugitives shortly after they were received with joy: the magi to Persia and the holy family to Egypt. Why? This is worthy of close examination. The magnificence of God's plan of salvation would not have been believed if he had not come in the flesh. If Jesus had fallen into the hands of Herod, his life in the flesh might have been cut off. Many circumstances were quietly ordered providentially within human history. Even while the flesh of the Christ child was in danger, some dared to imagine that he never assumed our common human flesh, that his coming was like that of a ghost. These impious ideas will ultimately destroy those who do not confess that God has come to us in the flesh in a way becoming to his deity.

As to the wise men, they were sent off quickly, commissioned to teach in the land of the Persians, having thwarted the madness of the king. Herod was allowed the opportunity to learn that he was attempting things impossible, against prophecy, and that there was still time to quench his wrath and desist from his demented plot. It is fitting to God's power not only to subdue his enemies but to do so with ease, deceiving the deceivers in a way fitting to God's almighty power. In the same way the Egyptians had earlier been deceived,[14] their wealth transferred secretly and with craft and God's power made awesome to them. THE GOSPEL OF MATTHEW, HOMILY 8.1.[15]

EGYPT THE ABODE OF CHRIST. CHROMATIUS: Joseph therefore was commanded to accept this boy about whom Isaiah had said, "For a boy has been born to you; a son has been given to you, whose rule has extended over his shoulders."[16] Now he said "a son has been given to you" because Christ the Lord was born as a boy and was counted a son of Joseph and Mary. As to his going down into Egypt, Isaiah predicted this long before the fact when he said, "Behold, the Lord sits atop a swift cloud and will come into Egypt."[17] By this statement the promise of the Lord's incarnation was clearly revealed. Since the Lord himself is invoked as "arising from on high, the sunlight of justice,"[18] it is right that he would come on a swift cloud. By this Isaiah means he would come in a hallowed body, a body weighed down by no sin and through which he covered the light of his own majesty with the envelope of the cloud of his body. Hosea as well points to this very fact when he says, "The king of Israel has been thrown down. Because Israel was small, I took delight in him. And I called my son from Egypt."[19]

After Egypt's ancient, grave sin, after many blows had been divinely inflicted upon it, God the omnipotent Father, moved by devotion, sent his Son into Egypt. He did so that Egypt, which had long ago paid back the penalty of wickedness owed under Moses, might now receive Christ, the hope for salvation. How great was God's compassion as shown in the advent of his

---

[13]CCL 24b:938. [14]In the time of Moses; cf. 1 Sam 6:6 LXX. [15]PG 57:83-84; NPNF 1 10:51**. What messianic-prophetic significance did the secretive flight of both the magi and the holy family convey? Both the magi and the holy family became fugitives, east to Persia and west to Egypt, to attest God's own humble coming in the flesh for all humanity, deceiving the deceivers in a way fitting to God's almighty power. [16]Is 9:6. [17]Is 19:1. [18]Mal 4:2; Lk 1:78. [19]Hos 10:15—11:1.

Son! Egypt, which of old under Pharaoh stood stubborn against God, now became a witness to and home for Christ. God's compassion toward Egypt was like that shown toward the magi, who deserved to know Christ the Lord. For, although the magi had for a long time dared resist the divine goodness under Moses, they now, having seen but a single star in heaven, believed in the Son of God. The cavalier magicians were handed over to punishment for their lack of faith. Others were brought to glory through faith, since they believed that God had been born in the flesh—God whom the Egyptian magicians were unwilling to recognize in all his divine excellence. TRACTATE ON MATTHEW 6.1.[20]

2:16 Herod Slaughters the Infants in Bethlehem

THE LORD'S SAFEKEEPING PROPHETICALLY FORETOLD. CHROMATIUS: For Herod, as we have said, in his desire to destroy the Savior of the world, sent word to Bethlehem and commanded that all children two years of age and under be killed, figuring the age according to the time that he had learned from the magi. He thought that his edict would reach even to the Lord himself, the source of life. The Holy Spirit had already foreseen his wickedness beforehand. Solomon, speaking for the church, had said, "Who will give to you my brother, the one who nurses at the breast of his mother?"[21] Moreover, by saying, "Who will give to you?" he was demonstrating that Herod would have no power over him who is the Lord and Prince of all powers. Thus the Lord spoke rightly when he bore witness about himself through the same Solomon: "Evil men will seek and not find me. For they hate wisdom and moreover have not partaken of the Word of God and have had no desire for it."[22] The Spirit also said through David: "Since you are the one who gave birth to me, you are my hope, my mother, from the time I nursed at your breast . . . you are my protec-

tor."[23] The blessed Moses also relates that Christ the Lord, an infant, could not have been killed while still nursing. He gave witness to this with his words, "You will not cook a lamb in the milk of its own mother."[24] In this exact statement Moses revealed the expectation that Christ our Lord would be the true Lamb of God who was to suffer at the appointed time.[25] TRACTATE ON MATTHEW 6.2.[26]

WHETHER CHRIST ABANDONED THE LITTLE SOLDIERS. PETER CHRYSOLOGUS: Why did Christ do this? Christ is the judge of thoughts and the examiner of minds. Why did he desert those whom he knew were being sought because of himself and whom he knew would be killed for his sake? He was born a king, the king of heaven—why did he neglect the standard-bearers of his own innocence? Why did he disdain an army of the same age as himself? Why did he thus abandon those who were cut down as plunder from the same cradle as himself? Was it so that he, who would become the one king, might proceed against the forces of all his enemies? Brothers, Christ did not despise his own soldiers but promoted them and granted that they might walk in victory before they lived. He enabled them to participate in a victory without struggle. He gave to them the gift of the crown even before their bodies had grown. It was Christ's will that they pass over vice for virtue, attain heaven before earth and share in the divine life immediately. Thus it was that Christ sent his soldiers ahead. He did not abandon them. He gathered up his ranks. He did not leave them behind. SERMONS 152.7.[27]

THE FIRST MARTYRS OF CHRIST. CHROMATIUS: In Bethlehem therefore all the babies were

---

[20]CCL 9a:220-21. [21]Song 8:1. [22]Prov 1:28-30. [23]Ps 71:5-6 (70:6 LXX). [24]Ex 23:19; Deut 14:21. [25]Accordingly, the law and prophets were anticipating the coming of Christ by identifying him in advance as the Lamb of God and by showing that he would not be harmed in his infancy, before his divine vocation was complete. [26]CCL 9a:221-22. [27]CCL 24b:953-54; FC 17:257-58.

slain. These innocents who died then on Christ's behalf became the first martyrs of Christ. David refers to them when he says, "From the mouths of nursing babies you have perfected praise because of your enemies, that you might bring ruin to the enemy."[28] . . . For in this persecution even tiny infants and nursing babies were killed on Christ's behalf and attained to the consummate praise of martyrs. Meanwhile the wicked king Herod was destroyed, he who had usurped the realm to defend himself against the king of the heavens. Thus it is that those blessed babes have deservedly lasted beyond others. They were the first who were worthy to die on Christ's behalf. TRACTATE ON MATTHEW 6.2.[29]

TWO YEARS OLD OR UNDER. THEODORE OF MOPSUESTIA: He gave orders that not only the children in Bethlehem but even those in the outlying districts of the town be killed, thinking that amid the multitude of those killed would be the one he was seeking. Herod ordered those who were two years old and under to be slaughtered. He had calculated such was the time that had passed from the incarnation of Christ, taking into account the time the magi had spent on their journey and that which he had spent on the throne. But Christ was taken out of Bethlehem once night had arrived. It is not possible that the birth of Christ be the cause of the killing of the children. But the disclosure of Herod's child-killing marked the beginning of a long string of wickedness. Even those who crucified Christ were not wicked at the time when they arrested Christ. Rather, they became wicked at the time when they undertook his murder. Yet for Christ's sake the children will receive a good reward, fitting to their martyrdom. FRAGMENT 9.[30]

2:17-18 *Wailing in Ramah*

THE GRIEF OF MOTHERS AND CHILDREN. ANONYMOUS: "A voice was heard in Ramah."[31] Ramah was Saul's city. Saul was of the tribe of Benjamin. Benjamin was the son of Rachel, whose memorial was near Bethlehem, where these wicked deeds were done. Therefore, since the babies were killed in Bethlehem, where there is a monument to Rachel, this is why Rachel is described as weeping.[32] . . . What he meant by "weeping" is revealed as the tears of the infants; what he meant by "wailing" is shown to be the lamenting of the mothers. For the babies wept because they were separated from their mothers. The mothers wept because they were bereft of their children, as if their insides were being torn from them. And it is possible to see greater grief in the mothers who remained behind than in the dying babies. For the children suffered a single moment of grief, because they had been separated from their mothers, not because they were being led out to death. For they did not yet possess a fear of death. The mothers, however, experienced twofold suffering: in the first place, they saw their own babies being killed; in the second place, they were themselves bereft of their children. For the children, death brought a blessed end to their grief. For the mothers, however, the memory of their babies continually renewed their grief. INCOMPLETE WORK ON MATTHEW, HOMILY 2.[33]

---

[28]Ps 8:2. [29]CCL 9a:222. [30]MKGK 99. [31]Jer 31:15; 40:1. [32]Gen 35:16-20. [33]PG 56:644-45.

2:19-23 THE RETURN TO NAZARETH

[19]*But when Herod died, behold, an angel of the Lord appeared in a dream to Joseph in Egypt, saying,* [20]*"Rise, take the child and his mother, and go to the land of Israel, for those who sought the child's life are dead."* [21]*And he rose and took the child and his mother, and went to the land of Israel.* [22]*But when he heard that Archelaus reigned over Judea in place of his father Herod, he was afraid to go there, and being warned in a dream he withdrew to the district of Galilee.* [23]*And he went and dwelt in a city called Nazareth, that what was spoken by the prophets might be fulfilled, "He shall be called a Nazarene."*

OVERVIEW: While Joseph fled into Egypt in the night of persecution, he returned from Egypt during the day of safety (ANONYMOUS). Joseph prefigured the ministry of the apostles (HILARY). Every impulse led Joseph away from Bethlehem toward Galilee (CHRYSOSTOM). Ironically it was the child who was nourishing his mother and watching over his father (ANONYMOUS). The child had priority over the parents (ANONYMOUS). The whole sense of the Scriptures attests that the expected Messiah was to be holy and hence the prototype of the Nazarene (JEROME, ANONYMOUS), a term that suggests the dual meanings of holiness and blooming (CYRIL OF ALEXANDRIA). Those are called Nazarenes who make an extraordinary vow of chastity to God, affirming that vow with the hair of their heads, which the law had commanded them to offer as a sacrifice (CHROMATIUS).

2:19 After Herod Died

HOW JOSEPH PREFIGURED THE APOSTOLATE. HILARY: After the death of Herod, Joseph was advised by the angel to return to Judea with the boy and his mother. When he returned he heard that Archelaeus, son of Herod, was king. So he was afraid to go, but the angel admonished him to cross over into the region of Galilee, and they lived in the city of Nazareth. . . . Joseph resembles the apostles to whom Christ entrusted the

spreading of the news about him. Similar to what happened with Joseph after the death of Herod, they must deal with the same people who caused the Lord to suffer. The apostles are commanded to preach to the Jews, for they were sent to the lost sheep of the house of Israel. But when they saw that the power remained in the hands of inherited faithlessness,[1] they became afraid and retreated. ON MATTHEW 2.1.[2]

2:20-21 Returning to Israel

THE PRIORITY OF THE CHILD TO THE MOTHER. ANONYMOUS: Do you see why Joseph was not chosen to be the husband of Mary, but her attendant? When she was going to and returning from Egypt, had she not been married, who would have attended her in such great need? For indeed, at first glance, Mary was nourishing a child, and Joseph was looking after her. In point of fact, however, the boy was nourishing his mother, and Joseph was being watched over. . . . Nor was it the son's glory to have that mother, but rather it was her blessing to have that son. She herself used to say as much: "Behold, now every generation will call me blessed."[3] INCOMPLETE WORK ON MATTHEW, HOMILY 2.[4]

---

[1]*Hereditariae infidelitatis.* [2]SC 254:100-102. [3]Lk 1:48. [4]PG 56:645.

2:22 Withdrawing to Galilee

IN PLACE OF HIS FATHER HEROD. CHRYSOS-
TOM: Do you perceive the alternation between
relief and danger? Joseph left foreign territory
and returned to his ancestral land, discovering
the slaughter of the children in the process.
Having left his household in Bethlehem, he
again discovers remnants of his first dangers. He
finds that the son of the tyrant is alive and ruling as king. And how was it possible that Archelaus should be king of Judea, when Pontius
Pilate was in charge? Herod's death had recently
occurred, and the kingdom had not yet been
divided. But no sooner had Herod died than his
son took power in his father's place. . . . But if
Joseph had feared to make his way to Judea, they
say, on account of Archelaus, he ought to have
been equally wary of Galilee on account of
Herod Antipas. But let us leave unexamined for
now the rest of the question as to whether he
changed his place of residence, for his every
impulse led away from Bethlehem and its confines. THE GOSPEL OF MATTHEW, HOMILY 9.4.[5]

JOSEPH WITHDREW TO GALILEE. CHRYSOS-
TOM: After the slaughter of the children
occurred, the young Archelaus was under the
impression that everything else had been taken
care of. Both the children in Bethlehem had
been eliminated and the one they were seeking
to kill. But once he saw how his father had lost
his life, Archelaus became most conscious of the
precedent and much more diligent in contending
with lawlessness. Therefore Joseph left Judea for
Nazareth, both in flight from the danger and at
the same time out of love for his home country.
And that he might be more confident, he
received a divine pronouncement from the messenger about it. THE GOSPEL OF MATTHEW,
HOMILY 9.4.[6]

2:23 Living in Nazareth

THE SENSE OF PROPHETIC SCRIPTURES SUM-
MARIZED. JEROME: If this could have been
found in the Scriptures, he never would have
said, "Because it has been spoken by the prophets," but he would rather have spoken more
plainly: "Because it has been spoken by *a*
prophet." As it is now, in speaking of prophets in
general he has shown that he has not taken the
specific words but rather the sense from the
Scriptures. "Nazarene" is understood as "holy."
Every Scripture attests that the Lord was to be
holy. We can also speak in another way of what
was written . . . in Hebrew in Isaiah: "A branch
will blossom from the root of Jesse, a Nazarene
from his root."[7] COMMENTARY ON MATTHEW
1.2.23.[8]

WHY A NAZARENE? CHROMATIUS: Our Lord
and Savior is called "the Nazarene" as much
after the name of the place, the city of Nazareth,
as from the mystery of the law. For, according to
the law, those are called Nazarenes who make an
extraordinary vow of chastity to God, maintaining that vow with the hair of their heads, which
the ordained law had commanded them to offer
as a sacrifice.[9] Therefore, because the author and
ruler of every act of sanctity and piety is Christ
the Lord, who said through the prophet, "Let
them be holy, since I am holy, says the Lord,"[10] it
was not undeservedly that he was called "the
Nazarene." It was he who, following truly what
was preordained in the law, offered as a pledge
to God the Father the sacrifice of his own body.
David spoke about this pledge when he said of
the Lord, "Just as Jacob swore an oath to the
Lord, he was offered a pledge to God."[11] The
Lord would show himself as the Nazarene at the
time when he became a creature of flesh. TRAC-
TATE ON MATTHEW 7.2.[12]

BLOOMING IN HOLINESS. CYRIL OF ALEXAN-

---

[5]PG 57:180; NPNF 1 10:58**. After Herod's death, Joseph was led
safely back to Nazareth. [6]PG 57:180; NPNF 1 10:58**. [7]Is 11:1.
[8]CCL 77:16. [9]Num 6. [10]Lev 11:44; 19:2; 20:7. [11]Ps 132:2 (131:2
LXX). [12]CCL 9a:224-25.

DRIA: But if "the Nazarene" is interpreted to mean "holy" or, according to some, as "flower," this is the designation found in many instances. For Daniel calls him "holy" or "of the holy ones." Likewise we find in Isaiah: "A branch from the stock of Jesse and its flower."[13] Even the Lord says of himself in the Song of Songs, "I am the bloom of the plain, the lily of the valleys."[14] FRAGMENT 16.[15]

NAZARENE UNDERSTOOD THROUGH ALL THE PROPHETS. ANONYMOUS: When he says "through the prophets," not "through *a* prophet," he clarifies a term derived from no specific prophetic authority. He speaks instead of the implied meaning he has gathered from all the prophets. For Jesus was called "the Nazarene" by all the prophets because he was holy. Or, per-

haps, they read other prophets, whom we do not recognize as canonical, making this assertion. For thus some have prophesied and have written, such as Nathan and Esdras. And inasmuch as it had been prophesied, this very thing Philip makes clear when he says to Nathanael, "We have found the one of whom Moses wrote in his law, as well as the prophets, and he is Jesus, the son of Joseph of Nazareth."[16] Thus did Nathanael, knowing that it had been prophesied, respond in confirmation of this very thing: "Can anything good come from Nazareth?"[17] INCOMPLETE WORK ON MATTHEW, HOMILY 2.[18]

---

[13]Is 11:1. [14]Song 2:1. [15]MKGK 158. [16]Jn 1:45. [17]Jn 1:46. [18]PG 56:646.

3:1-6 JOHN THE BAPTIST PREPARES THE WAY

[1]In those days came John the Baptist, preaching in the wilderness of Judea, [2]"Repent, for the kingdom of heaven is at hand." [3]For this is he who was spoken of by the prophet Isaiah when he said,

"The voice of one crying in the wilderness:
Prepare the way of the Lord,
make his paths straight."

[4]Now John wore a garment of camel's hair, and a leather girdle around his waist; and his food was locusts and wild honey. [5]Then went out to him Jerusalem and all Judea and all the region about the Jordan, [6]and they were baptized by him in the river Jordan, confessing their sins.

OVERVIEW: Both the prophets and John made a way and prepared it beforehand. John did not bestow the gift that was yet to come—the remission of sins—but in a timely way he readied the souls of those who would receive the God of all (CHRYSOSTOM). So within each of us the way of chastity, faith and holiness must be paved by repentance (CHROMATIUS).

John was a voice from the wilderness as distinguished from the Word promised to come (ANONYMOUS). He preached that sins against God's law could be purged by repentance (CHROMATIUS). John's garment of camel hair was chosen as a symbol of the rigorous work of evangelical repentance among not only Jews but Gentiles (PETER CHRYSOLOGUS, THEODORE of Mopsuestia), for whom he wore the skin of an unclean animal (MAXIMUS OF TURIN). He who had no use for worldly delights did not seek costly attire or succulent foods (CHROMATIUS). His food was locust—food for penance—mixed with tender mercy, honey (PETER CHRYSOLOGUS). Note that wild honey is not obtained by effort but as an undeserved, merciful gift (ORIGEN). A secure belt for the waist in every good work prepares one to be girded with the will of God for every service (HILARY). By his leather girdle John symbolically brought to repentance his generative organs (ORIGEN), so as to prepare the soul to walk in purity (JEROME). The appearance of a prophet after such a great interval of time increased Israel's amazement (CHRYSOSTOM). Confession is morally deficient when one does not believe in future judgment (ANONYMOUS). The crowds ran to John as to a man sent from God (THEODORE OF HERACLEA).

3:1 John the Baptist

IN THOSE DAYS. CHRYSOSTOM: How "in those days"? What days? He does not mean the days when Jesus was a child at Nazareth but thirty years later, when John came, as Luke also testifies.[1] Why then is it said "in those days"? It is common in Scripture to use this rhetorical device: In speaking of something that seems to come immediately after, it also refers to something that comes to pass many years later. THE GOSPEL OF MATTHEW, HOMILY 10.1.[2]

3:2 John Preaches Repentance

THE KINGDOM IS WITHIN TO JUSTIFY AND SANCTIFY. CYRIL OF ALEXANDRIA: The kingdom of heaven? This refers to justification by faith and sanctification by the Spirit. This is why it says elsewhere, "the kingdom [of heaven] is within you."[3] FRAGMENT 17.[4]

3:3 A Voice Crying in the Wilderness

THE VOICE OF ONE CRYING. ANONYMOUS: A voice or sound is an obscure utterance, manifesting no secret of the heart but signifying this only: that the one who calls out wants to say something. A word, however, is rational speech, opening the heart's mystery. While a voice as such is common to both animals and men, a word is fitting only to humans. Thus John was called a voice and not a word, because, through John, God demonstrated neither his mercies nor his justice nor his counsels prepared before the foundation of the world but only this: that God was planning to do something great in human history. Later through his Son he revealed the full mystery of his will. The Son was therefore called the Word. To "make ready the way of the Lord" meant: Repent of your sins and produce fruit worthy of repentance. INCOMPLETE WORK ON MATTHEW, HOMILY 3.[5]

PREPARING SOULS FOR PURITY. JEROME: He prepared the souls of believers in whom the Lord would walk, so he might walk in purity along the purest of paths, saying, "I will live in them and move among them, and I will be their God, and they shall be my people."[6] COMMENTARY ON MATTHEW 1.3.3.[7]

MAKING A PATH FOR THE COMING MESSIAH. CHRYSOSTOM: Both the prophet and the Baptist state the same idea even though with different words. The prophet said that one would come: "prepare the way of the Lord, make his paths straight."[8] And when John came he himself said, "Bear fruit worthy of repentance,"[9] a statement that corresponds to "prepare the way of the Lord." Both by the words of the prophets and by John's own preaching, this one thing is clear: he had arrived, making a way and preparing it beforehand. John was not bestowing the gift, which was the remission of sins, but preparing

---

[1]Lk 3:1-2. [2]PG 57:183; NPNF 1 10:61*. [3]Lk 17:21. [4]MKGK 159. [5]PG 56:647. [6]Lev 26:12; 2 Cor 6:16. [7]CCL 77:16. [8]Is 40:3. [9]Mt 3:8.

beforehand the souls of those who would receive the God of all. THE GOSPEL OF MATTHEW, HOMILY 10.3.[10]

REMOVE THE STONES FROM THE ROAD. CHROMATIUS: Hence John prepared these ways of mercy and truth, faith and justice. Concerning them, Jeremiah also declared, "Stand by the roads, and look, and ask for the ancient paths, where the good way is, and walk in it."[11] Because the heavenly kingdom is found along these ways, not without good reason John adds, "The kingdom of heaven is near."[12] So do you want the kingdom of heaven to also be near for you? Prepare these ways in your heart, in your senses and in your soul. Pave within you the way of chastity, the way of faith and the way of holiness. Build roads of justice. Remove every scandal of offense from your heart. For it is written: "Remove the stones from the road."[13] And then, indeed, through the thoughts of your heart and the very movements of your soul, Christ the King will enter along certain paths. TRACTATE ON MATTHEW 8.1.[14]

3:4 The Symbolism of John's Food and Clothing

THE GARB OF REPENTANCE. CHRYSOSTOM: It was fitting that the forerunner of the One who was to put away all the ancient ills, the labor, the curse, the sorrow and the sweat display symbols of the situation prior to the fall of Adam. This is why he neither tilled the land nor ploughed furrows nor ate bread by the sweat of his brow. Rather, his table was hastily supplied, and his clothing more easily furnished than his table, and his lodging even less troublesome than his clothing. For he needed neither roof, nor bed, nor table nor any other earthly comfort. He lived a kind of angel's life in this our flesh. For this reason John's clothing was of hair, that by his very dress he might instruct persons to separate themselves from all things human, to have nothing in common with the earth but to hasten

back to their undefiled nobility, the condition in which Adam lived before he required garments or robe. Thus John's clothing itself was symbolic of nothing less than the coming kingdom and of repentance. THE GOSPEL OF MATTHEW, HOMILY 10.4.[15]

NO COSTLY ATTIRE. CHROMATIUS: First, the heavenly life and glorious humility of John are demonstrated in his way of living. He who held the world in low regard did not seek costly attire. He who had no use for worldly delights did not have any desire for succulent foods. What need was there of fancy worldly clothing for one who was dressed with the cloak of justice? What dainty food of the earth could he desire who fed on divine discourses and whose true food was the law of Christ? Such a precursor ought to be the prophet of the Lord and the apostle of Christ who gave himself completely to his heavenly God and had contempt for the things of the world. TRACTATE ON MATTHEW 9.1.[16]

SHABBINESS SANCTIFIED. HILARY: A garment woven with camel's hair designates the peculiar clothing of this prophetic preacher. He is covered with the skins of an unclean animal. Whatever had been useless or shabby in us becomes sanctified by the prophet's clothes. ON MATTHEW 2.2.[17]

GIRDED WITH SKINS OF AN UNCLEAN ANIMAL. MAXIMUS OF TURIN: Indeed, when Christ's forerunner wore a coarse camel-hair garment, what else does it signify but that the coming Christ would be vested in the garb of a human body, thick with the coarseness of sinners, and that, girded with the skins of a most unclean animal, the Gentile people, he bore

---

[10]PG 57:187; NPNF 1 10:63*. John did not bestow the gift of forgiveness but prepared the way for its bestowal. [11]Jer 6:16. [12]Mt 3:2. [13]Is 40:4. [14]CCL 9a:228-29. [15]PG 57:188; NPNF 1 10:64**. John's way of life itself foreshadowed humanity's recovery of the human condition before its fall. [16]CCL 9a:231. [17]SC 254:104.

their very own deformity? SERMONS 88.3.[18]

A GARMENT INTENDED FOR THE HARD WORK OF REPENTANCE. PETER CHRYSOLOGUS: He could have made use of goat's hair, but there was no need for it. Rather, he wore a garment of camel's hair with nothing refined about it, nothing graceful, nothing comely. By nature it was intended for hard work and heavy burdens and consigned to utter subjection. The teacher of repentance ought to be vested with such a garment, so that those who had turned away from virtue in their education and given themselves shamelessly over to sin might be subdued by the great burden of penance, might be consigned to the rigors of reparation and experience the heavy sighs of contrition. Thus refashioned and reshaped into the form of a needle, they might obtain ample remission through the narrow opening of penance. And the Lord's words would then be fulfilled concerning a camel passing through the eye of a needle. SERMONS 167.8.[19]

WHY CAMEL'S HAIR? THEODORE OF MOPSUESTIA: Camel's hair is mentioned not merely circumstantially but in a mystery and as a type. The camel is counted neither as strictly one of the unclean beasts nor as strictly one of the clean, but it occupies a middle position and partakes of the characteristics of both. For to chew the cud, that is, to bring up again the food after it has been swallowed and direct it forward to be ground by the teeth, is proper to the clean animals.[20] This pertains to the camel. But not to part the hoof is a feature of the unclean beasts. The camel's foot is not divided, given that its nails meet together. Therefore, on this account, John was clothed with the hairs of this animal, demonstrating the call of the gospel. He showed that the kingdom of God, which John declared was at hand, was going to accept both those who were from Israel, the clean people, and those from the unclean Gentiles. To both of these he preached repentance without any distinction. FRAGMENT 12.[21]

RESTRAINED BY VIRTUE. MAXIMUS OF TURIN: As for the leather belt, what else does it demonstrate but this fragile flesh of ours, trapped in the grip of vice before the coming of Christ and which, after his coming, was restrained by virtue? Before his coming this flesh was fat through dissipation. Now by abstention it is firmly held in place. SERMONS 88.3.[22]

LOCUSTS AND WILD HONEY. ORIGEN: John ate locusts, suggesting that the people of God were being nourished by a word that traveled high aloft in the air and had not yet passed over the earth. In the second place John ate honey, which is not obtained by people through their own efforts. The honey produced under the law and the prophets was not accessible to those who were inquiring only superficially about the meaning of the Scriptures and not searching their deeper intention. FRAGMENT 41.[23]

FOOD FOR PENANCE. PETER CHRYSOLOGUS: Locusts intended for sinners worthy of chastisement are rightly considered to be food for repentance, so that bounding from the place of sin to the place of repentance the sinner may fly to heaven on the wings of forgiveness. The prophet was aware of this when he said, "I am gone, like a shadow at evening. I am shaken off like a locust. My knees are weak through fasting; my body has become gaunt . . . Save me according to your steadfast law."[24] You have heard how John was shaken off like a locust from sin to repentance. He bent his knees that he might bear the burden of repentance. His food was mixed with honey, so that tender mercy might temper the bitterness of repentance. SERMONS 167.9.[25]

3:5 People from the Area Go to Hear John's Preaching

---

[18]CCL 23:360. [19]CCL 24b:1028-29. [20]Lev 11:1-4. [21]*MKGK* 100. [22]CCL 23:360. [23]GCS 41.1:32. [24]Ps 109:23-26 (108:23-26 LXX). [25]CCL 24b:1029.

THE TONE OF JOHN'S PROPHETIC SPEECH. CHRYSOSTOM: See how great was the power of the coming of the prophet! He stirred up the people. He called them to consider the meaning of their own sins. It was indeed worthy of wonder to behold his remarkable human form, his great freedom of speech, the strength of his reproof of all as if they were children and the abundant grace beaming out from his countenance. The appearance of a prophet after such a great interval of time increased their amazement. The prophetic gift that had been absent for a long time was now returning. The very tone of his prophetic speech was strange and unusual. For they had heard none of those things of which the prophets were accustomed to speak: of wars and battles and victories below, of famine and pestilence, of the Babylonians and Persians, and the taking of the city, and the other things with which they were familiar; of heaven and its kingdom, of punishment in hell. THE GOSPEL OF MATTHEW, HOMILY 10.5.[26]

A MAN SENT FROM GOD. THEODORE OF HERACLEA: When the crowds heard of his manner of life, far surpassing normal human life, they longed to see him. For this reason, when they heard that John was nearby, they all simultaneously ran to him, as to "a man sent from God."[27] They confessed their sins in his presence so that, like a priest, he might offer up sacrifices on their behalf. FRAGMENT 13.[28]

3:6 Confessing and Being Baptized

CLEANSING BY REPENTANCE. CHROMATIUS: Therefore John exhorted those coming to him. He preached that the sins they had committed by transgressing the precepts of divine law could be cleansed by repentance. Thus by satisfying God with worthy repentance they might receive forgiveness from him who said through the prophet: "I have no pleasure in the death of anyone . . . so turn and live."[29] And again: "Turn to me, says the Lord of Hosts, and I will turn to you."[30] And again: "I am the Lord who does not remember wickedness, provided one turn from his evil ways and all his iniquities so that he may live."[31] TRACTATE ON MATTHEW 10.1.[32]

CONFESSING THEIR SINS. CYRIL OF ALEXANDRIA: The baptism of John did not provide forgiveness of sins, but it taught people to run to the baptism[33] that is for the sake of sins. FRAGMENT 18.[34]

CONFESSION AND SHAME. ANONYMOUS: Confession of sins is the testimony of a conscience that fears God. Whoever fears God's judgment will not be ashamed to confess his sins, for he who is ashamed has no fear. Indeed, perfect fear of God releases one from all feeling of shame. One's confession is morally valueless when one does not believe in the punishment of future judgment. For do we not know that the confession of sins involves shame and that this very shamefulness is itself a severe punishment? But all the more does God order us to confess our sins so we may experience shame by way of punishment. For this very thing is a part of judgment. O mercy of God, which we have so often incited to wrath! Sufficient for it is the punishment that accompanies our shame. INCOMPLETE WORK ON MATTHEW, HOMILY 3.[35]

---

[26]PG 57:189; NPNF 1 10:65**. John renewed the tone and voice of prophetic preaching. [27]Jn 1:6. [28]MKGK 60. [29]Ezek 18:32. [30]Cf. Is 45:22; Jer 15:19. [31]Ez 18:21-22 [32]CCL 9a:235. [33]This second baptism is the Christian baptism, of which John's baptism was merely a symbolic prefigurement. [34]MKGK 159. [35]PG 56:650.

3:7-12 THE BAPTISM OF REPENTANCE

[7]*But when he saw many of the Pharisees and Sadducees coming for baptism, he said to them, "You brood of vipers! Who warned you to flee from the wrath to come?* [8]*Bear fruit that befits repentance,* [9]*and do not presume to say to yourselves, 'We have Abraham as our father'; for I tell you, God is able from these stones to raise up children to Abraham.* [10]*Even now the axe is laid to the root of the trees; every tree therefore that does not bear good fruit is cut down and thrown into the fire.*

[11]*"I baptize you with water for repentance, but he who is coming after me is mightier than I, whose sandals I am not worthy to carry; he will baptize you with the Holy Spirit and with fire.* [12]*His winnowing fork is in his hand, and he will clear his threshing floor and gather his wheat into the granary, but the chaff he will burn with unquenchable fire."*

OVERVIEW: Even the Pharisees came to be baptized by John, but they did not continue faithfully in the preaching of John (CHRYSOSTOM). By reason of their deceptions they were called a brood of vipers, because by doing the will of the devil, who from the beginning was called a snake, they made themselves the devil's children (CHROMATIUS). Vipers are beautiful on the outside but on the inside full of poison (ANONYMOUS). Those who remain faithful to Abraham are his posterity in faith, but those who are unfaithful are changed into the devil's offspring (HILARY). So do not take pride in saying that we have Abraham for our father; rather, be ashamed if you are his children yet not heirs of his holiness (ANONYMOUS). God, who made everything out of nothing, can produce the softness of a tender people out of the hardest stones (JEROME). Insofar as children are given to Abraham, this is not by their possessing his flesh and spirit but by their sharing his virtue (THEODORE OF HERACLEA).

Even while bringing the axe so near to the root, John makes its cutting depend upon you. For if you repent, this axe will be laid aside without doing any harm (CHRYSOSTOM). The former world is ending, and the future world is now approaching (ANONYMOUS). The cutting and burning of the trees signifies the destruction of barren faithlessness that is being prepared for the fire of final judgment (HILARY, CHROMATIUS, CYRIL OF ALEXANDRIA). John left to the apostles the glory of spreading God's word (HILARY). Sandals here prefigure the footsteps of gospel preaching (CHROMATIUS). John states his case without compromise, yet he does not dwell on the axe alone or on the tree that is thrown into the fire but on the remission of sins (CHRYSOSTOM). The ripened fruit of believers will be stored in barns, but the chaff of unfruitful human futility is fit for the fire of judgment (HILARY). The fire is the life-giving energy of the Spirit (CYRIL OF ALEXANDRIA). Fire on the one hand is suitable for the formation and ripening of fruits. On the other hand, it is useful for destroying and consuming. As fire outperforms all the elements, so too the Almighty overpowers all gods, rulers and powers (THEODORE OF HERACLEA). The threshing floor is the church, the barn is the heavenly kingdom, and the field is this world. Therefore, like the head of the household who sends out reapers to mow down the stalks in the field and bring them to the threshing floor that he may winnow them and separate the wheat from the chaff, the Lord sends out his apostles and teachers as reapers (ANONYMOUS).

3:7 Pharisees and Sadducees Came to John

The Clash with Religious Leaders. Chrysostom: They did not continue to follow John.[1] This is what Christ meant when he later refused to disclose his own authority to the Pharisees.[2] When they refused to receive the very One of whom John was preaching, this was hardly a convincing expression of their faith. The Pharisees imagined that they had the highest regard for the prophets and Moses. But Jesus said they had disregarded Moses because they had not received the one foretold by him: "If you believed Moses, you would believe me."[3] Then he confronted them: "I also will ask you a question: now tell me, Was the baptism of John from heaven or from men?" They debated: "If we say, from heaven, he will say, why did you not believe him?"[4] From all this it was clear that they came indeed and were baptized by John, but they did not continue faithfully in the preaching of John. John's Gospel also points out their corruptness, reporting how they sent representatives to the Baptist asking, "Are you Elijah? Are you Christ?" This is why it was added: "Now they had been sent from the Pharisees."[5] The Gospel of Matthew, Homily 11.1.[6]

Brood of the Devil. Chromatius: John put it clearly to the Pharisees and Sadducees who had come to him for baptism when he said, "Brood of vipers! Who has shown you how to flee from the wrath to come? Therefore, produce fruit that matches genuine repentance."[7] Those who for a long time were called God's children are now by reason of their faults called a brood of vipers, because by doing the will of the devil, who from the beginning was called a snake, they made themselves the devil's children. "The devil is your father, and it is your will to fulfill your father's desires."[8] Tractate on Matthew 10.2.[9]

The Poison of Malice. Anonymous: "Offspring of vipers." The nature of vipers is such that when a viper bites a person, it immediately heads for water. If it does not find water, it dies.[10] So too John called those persons the offspring of vipers who, committing grave sins, hastened to baptism so that, like vipers, through water they might avoid the danger of death. Also, the nature of a viper is that it ruptures its mother's entrails in order to be born. Therefore, because the Jews who were doggedly persecuting the prophets ruptured their mother the synagogue, as the lamenting woman says in Canticles, "My mother's children were angry at me,"[11] they are called the offspring of vipers. Further, vipers are beautiful on the outside and adorned as it were, but on the inside they are full of poison. Thus John calls both hypocrites and Pharisees the offspring of vipers, because the hypocrites showed the beauty of holiness on their face while they bore the poison of malice in their hearts. Incomplete Work on Matthew, Homily 3.[12]

3:8 Fruit That Befits Repentance

Succession of Faith, Not Flesh. Hilary: He advises them to "bring forth fruit that matches repentance" and not to boast that they have Abraham as their father, for God is able to raise up children to Abraham out of stones. Indeed, succession to Abraham in the flesh is not required, but the inheritance of Abraham's faith. In this context, dignity of origin consists in examples of works. The glory of one's race lies in the imitation of faith. The devil was faithless, but Abraham was faithful. The devil was treacherous in his treatment of humanity, whereas Abraham was justified by faith. Therefore the very life and character of each person is acquired by a close relationship, so that those who are

---

[1]Mt 21:32. [2]Lk 20:1-8. [3]Jn 5:46. [4]Lk 20:5; cf. Mt 21:25-26. [5]Jn 1:24. [6]PG 57:191-92; NPNF 1 10:67-68**. [7]Mt 3:7-8. [8]Jn 8:44. [9]CCL 9a:235-36. [10]Misconceptions of the strangest sort regarding animals abounded in the ancient world and were often included in literary works (Aelian, Pliny the Elder). Such misconceptions served as starting points for the allegorical interpretation of animals named in the Scriptures, as is evidenced here. [11]Song 1:6. [12]PG 56:651.

faithful to Abraham are his posterity in faith. But those who are unfaithful are changed into the devil's offspring by their unfaithfulness. ON MATTHEW 2.3.[13]

FRUITS OF REPENTANCE. CYRIL OF ALEXANDRIA: One might say that the fruits of repentance are, by way of anticipation, faith in Christ. They are also the evangelical society that exists "in newness of life,"[14] changed from the present dullness of the letter. FRAGMENT 20.[15]

3:9 Claiming Descent from Abraham

A NOBLE FAMILY WITH CONTEMPTIBLE CHILDREN. ANONYMOUS: It is better to be born noble from a contemptible family than to be born contemptible from a noble family. As for the one who is born noble from a noble family, the glory of his nobility is not his alone, but he has it in common with his family. As for the one who is born contemptible from a contemptible family, the baseness of his contemptibility is not his alone.... Therefore do not take pride in saying that "we have Abraham for a father." Rather, be ashamed that you are his children and are not heirs of his holiness. INCOMPLETE WORK ON MATTHEW, HOMILY 3.[16]

THE POWER OF GOD TO REMAKE A PEOPLE. JEROME: "God is able from these stones to raise up children to Abraham." He calls the Gentiles stones because of their hard heart. We read in Ezekiel: "I will revive their stony heart and give them a heart of flesh."[17] He shows the hardness in a stone and the softness of flesh. In other words, this passage indicates the power of God, who made everything out of nothing and can produce a people out of the hardest stones. COMMENTARY ON MATTHEW 1.3.9.[18]

SHARING ABRAHAM'S FAITH. THEODORE OF HERACLEA: If from "stones children are given to Abraham," this is not by their possessing his flesh and spirit but by their sharing his virtue.[19]

Therefore the people of God are able to call Abraham "father." How so? Consider the following: Stones are employed by the Gentiles not only for building but also for idolatry. Besides this, remember this: the heart of the dragon is said to be as hard as a stone.[20] FRAGMENTS 15-16.[21]

CHILDREN FROM STONES. CHRYSOSTOM: Although John terrified them with his preaching, he did not permit them to fall into despair. He did not say "God has raised up" but "God is able from these stones to raise up children to Abraham." In this way he simultaneously alarmed and comforted them. THE GOSPEL OF MATTHEW, HOMILY 11.3.[22]

3:10 The Axe Laid to the Tree's Root

THE AXE LAID TO THE ROOT. CHRYSOSTOM: He did not merely say that the axe was barely "touching the root" but "laid to the root"—it is poised right next to it and shows no sign of delay. Yet even while bringing the axe so near, he makes its cutting depend upon you. For if you turn around and become better persons, this axe will be laid aside without doing any harm. But if you continue in the same ways, it will tear up the tree by the roots. So note well that the axe is neither removed from the root nor too quickly applied to cut the root. He did not want you to become passive, yet he wanted to let you know that it is possible even in a short time to be changed and saved. He first heightened their fear in order to fully awaken them and press them on to repentance. THE GOSPEL OF MATTHEW, HOMILY 11.3.[23]

THE ROOT. CYRIL OF ALEXANDRIA: He calls Christ an axe "sharper than a two-edged

[13]SC 254:104-6. [14]Rom 6:4. [15]MKGK 159. [16]PG 56:651. [17]Ezek 36:26. [18]CCL 77:17-18. [19]Abraham's virtue is faith. [20]Cf. Job 41:24 (LXX 41:15). [21]MKGK 61. [22]PG 57:195; NPNF 1 10:70**. John's preaching of repentance both terrified and offered hope, combining threat and promise. [23]PG 57:195; NPNF 1 10:70**.

sword,"[24] which was to cut off the unbelieving Jews and dissociate them from the honor and communion of the patriarchs. Those spoken of as "the root" are the fathers of old who remained well pleasing to God, those who with Abraham and as with many people in former times were holy. The unbelievers who sprang from them were cut off as fruitless branches. But the root remained, onto which those of the believing Gentiles were engrafted. And as Irenaeus reminds us, God's Word is like an axe in accordance with Jeremiah's saying: the word of the Lord is "like a pickaxe chopping stone."[25] Why am I saying that you are going to fall away? God did not spare the root. FRAGMENT 24.[26]

THE AXE. ANONYMOUS: The axe is the utter wrath of the destruction about to strike down the whole world. If that axe was prepared, why did it not strike down? And if it was not about to strike down, why was it made ready? The trees[27] of which we speak have a rational quality and have the power either to do or not to do good. Since an axe has been laid at their roots they fear being cut down, as they were called to bear fruit. An evildoer is not corrected by fear. But a good person will perish unless he has appropriate fear. Therefore, even if angry denunciation does nothing to change evildoers, it serves to distinguish the bad from the good. Note, however, that the axe is not said to be laid at the branches that they may be cut down and then restored. It is laid at the roots that they may be irretrievably eradicated. Why? Because as long as this world steeped in evil has not come to final judgment,[28] sinners are chastised but not cut away altogether. This is for two reasons. First, it was necessary for people responding to God to have a locus of action in the world, even if the world is full of iniquity. Second, with the world continuing on, there was hope that some just people might be born from the generations of the unjust. But now with the former world ending and the holy world fast approaching, sinners are not being chastised but turned out.

There is room for hope that from the generations of the unjust, some just people may possibly be born. But it would be inappropriate in this coming holy world to have people who are not holy, as it is written: The upright of heart shall inhabit the earth, but "the evildoers lie prostrate, they are thrust down, unable to rise."[29] INCOMPLETE WORK ON MATTHEW, HOMILY 3.[30]

THREAT OF DIVINE JUDGMENT. CHROMATIUS: There is no doubt this axe signifies the power of the divine word, for God says through Jeremiah the prophet: "Is not my word like fire, says the Lord, and like a hammer which breaks the rock in pieces?"[31] Therefore this axe which is laid at the very roots of interior faith in this forest of humanity always implies the severe threat of divine judgment. Unfruitful trees or barren people, bearing no fruit of faith, will be cut down and consigned to perpetual fire. TRACTATE ON MATTHEW 11.1.[32]

FAITHLESSNESS DESTROYED. HILARY: The axe laid at the roots of the trees witnesses to the power present in Christ. The cutting down and burning of the trees signifies the destruction of barren faithlessness that is being prepared for the fire of judgment. ON MATTHEW 2.4.[33]

3:11a Baptism with Water

HE WHO COMES AFTER ME. HILARY: The work of the law is now ineffectual for salvation. John appeared as a messenger of repentance to those about to be baptized. It was the task of the prophets to call people away from their sins, but it was proper to Christ to save those who believe. Thus John said that he was baptizing them for repentance. He also said that a mightier one would come whose sandals he was not

---

[24]Heb 4:12. [25]Jer 23:29 LXX (RSV: "like a hammer which breaks the rock in pieces"). [26]MKGK 160. [27]Symbolizing human beings. [28]1 Jn 5:19. [29]Ps 36:12 (35:12 LXX). [30]PG 56:652. [31]Jer 23:29. [32]CCL 9a:239. [33]SC 254:106.

worthy to untie. And he left to the apostles the glory of spreading God's word. It would be their duty to go about with their trusty feet and proclaim God's peace.[34] He therefore points ahead to the time of our salvation and judgment in the Lord, saying, "He will baptize you with the Holy Spirit and with fire."[35] On Matthew 2.4.[36]

Grace and Judgment Blended. Chrysostom: See how great is the wisdom of the Baptist in his preaching? Note how he states his case without compromise, unafraid of alarming his hearers and filling them with anxiety. Yet his very next words are mild, speaking of that which is apt to make them recover. He does not dwell on the axe alone or the tree that is cut down, burned and thrown into the fire, or the wrath to come, but also speaks of the remission of sins, the removal of punishment, righteousness, sanctification, redemption, adoption and community, a partaking of the inheritance and an abundant supply of the Holy Spirit. For to all these remedies John implicitly pointed when he said, "He shall baptize you with the Holy Spirit."[37] At once, by this very figure of speech, John witnessed to the abundance of grace. He did not say "He will give you the Holy Spirit" but "He will baptize you with the Holy Spirit." Then to specify the volatile and uncontrollable quality of divine grace he adds, "and with fire." The Gospel of Matthew, Homily 11.4.[38]

3:11b Baptism with Fire and with the Spirit

Sandals as a Biblical Type. Chromatius: Now we must focus on what is meant by these sandals from the spiritual standpoint. We know that Moses said long ago: "Put off your sandals from your feet, for the place on which you are standing is holy ground."[39] We read that Joshua the son of Nun likewise said, "Remove the latchet from your sandal."[40] But as to why they are ordered by the Lord to remove their sandals, we must understand this to be the type of a future truth. According to the law, if a man is

unwilling to accept the wife of his brother after his brother's death, he should take off his shoes, so that another may marry her and succeed by right of law.[41] As to the commandment prefigured in law, we find it fulfilled in Christ, who is the true bridegroom of the church. Therefore, because neither Moses the lawgiver nor Joshua the leader of the people could be the bridegroom of the church, not without good reason was it said to them that they should remove the sandals from their feet, because the true future bridegroom of the church, Christ, was to be expected. John says concerning him: "He who has the bride is the bridegroom."[42] To bear or loosen his sandals, John professed himself to be unworthy. The Lord himself through David revealed that these sandals signify the footsteps of gospel preaching when he says, "Upon Edom I cast my shoe";[43] through his apostles he will take the steps of gospel teaching everywhere. Tractate on Matthew 11.4.[44]

Fire of the Spirit. Cyril of Alexandria: The blessed Baptist added to the word *spirit* the active and meaningful phrase "and with fire." This was not to imply that through Christ we shall all be baptized with fire but to indicate through the designation *fire* that the life-giving energy of the Spirit is given. Fragment 27.[45]

The Fire Is to Purify. Theodore of Heraclea: The words "behind me" are used in the sense of "after me." "He who is coming" is said rather than "he who shall be revealed." The souls of the saints, in order to receive the mystery of revelation, are said to be baptized purely "in fire." This is because the Spirit first came down upon the disciples in tongues of fire, by which they were baptized and their souls made per-

---

[34]Cf. Rom 10:15. [35]Mt 3:11. [36]SC 254:106-8. [37]Mt 3:11. [38]PG 57:197; NPNF 1 10:71**. To ask whether judgment or grace was the heart of John's preaching is to miss the point: he preached both entwined. [39]Ex 3:5. [40]Josh 5:15. [41]The law of levirate marriage; Deut 25:7-9. [42]Jn 3:29. [43]Ps 60:8 (59:8 LXX); 108:9 (107:9 LXX). [44]CCL 9a:240-41. [45]MKGK 161.

fect.[46] Or because, in the age to come, all will be baptized with fire, for "everyone will be salted with fire,"[47] so that "the fire may test everyone's work, of what sort it is."[48] Fire is appointed for the material element, which in itself is neither wicked nor evil but powerful and able to purify from evil. For the power of fire is deemed to be beneficial and strong, destructive of evil things and preservative of what is better. This is why fire is associated with wisdom by the prophets. For this reason also, when God is called "a consuming fire,"[49] this is to be understood as a term and symbol not for evil but for power. As fire is the strongest of the elements and conquers everything else, in the same way God is all-powerful and almighty, able to conquer, to create, to make, to nourish, to multiply, to save, possessing authority over both body and soul. Just as fire outperforms all the elements, so too all gods, powers and rulers are no match for the Almighty.

Fire has a twofold potency. On the one hand, it is suitable for the formation and ripening of fruits and for the birth and sustenance of animals. The sun is the primary image of this power. On the other hand, fire is fit for destroying and consuming, as is the case with earthly fire. When God therefore is called a "consuming fire," able to destroy, he is being called a mighty and irresistible power. To God nothing is impossible. Concerning such a power the Savior also says, "I came to cast fire upon the earth."[50] This is a power that purifies the saints, causes material things to disappear and, we might say, educates. Fire induces fear. Its light spreads outward. FRAGMENT 18.[51]

3:12 The Wheat and the Chaff

THE THRESHING FLOOR. ANONYMOUS: The threshing floor is the church, the barn is the kingdom of heaven, and the field is the world. Therefore, like the head of the household who sends out reapers to mow down the stalks in the field and bring them to the threshing floor

that he may thresh and winnow them there and separate the wheat from the chaff, the Lord sends out his apostles and other teachers as reapers. He will cut down all the people in the world and gather them onto the threshing floor of the church, where we are to be threshed at one point and then winnowed. As the grain of wheat enclosed in the chaff cannot escape unless it has been threshed, so too it is hard for one to escape worldly encumbrances and carnal affairs while one is enclosed in the chaff, unless one has been shaken by some hardship. Note that once the full grain has been slightly shaken it sheds its chaff. If it is flimsy, it takes longer to escape. If it is empty, it never emerges but is ground in its chaff and then thrown out with the chaff. In this way, all who take delight in carnal things will be like the grain and the chaff. But one who is faithful and has a good heart, once he experiences adversity, disregards those things that are carnal and hastens to God. If he has been somewhat unfaithful, however, only with great difficulty will he go back to God. As for him who is unfaithful and empty, though he may be sorry over his circumstances, like empty grain he will emerge from the chaff—he will never leave carnal things or worldly encumbrances behind, nor will he go over to God. Rather, he will be ground up with the things that are evil and thus be cast out with the unfaithful like the chaff. INCOMPLETE WORK ON MATTHEW, HOMILY 3.[52]

THE WHEAT AND THE CHAFF. HILARY: It remains for those who have been baptized in the Holy Spirit to be consumed with the fire of judgment, for "his winnowing fan is in his hand, and he will thoroughly clean out his threshing floor and will gather his wheat into the barn; but the chaff he will burn up with unquenchable fire." The function of the fan is to separate the

---

[46]Acts 2:3. [47]Mk 9:49. [48]1 Cor 3:13. [49]Deut 4:24; Heb 12:29. [50]Lk 12:49. [51]MKGK 61-62. [52]PG 56:655.

fruitful from the unfruitful. That the decision lies in God's hands is indicated by his splendid wheat, the ripened fruit of believers, to be stored in barns. But the chaff indicates the futility of the unprofitable and unfruitful who are fit for the fire of burning judgment. ON MATTHEW 2.4.[53]

[53]SC 254:108.

3:13-17 THE BAPTISM OF JESUS

[13]*Then Jesus came from Galilee to the Jordan to John, to be baptized by him.* [14]*John would have prevented him, saying, "I need to be baptized by you, and do you come to me?"* [15]*But Jesus answered him, "Let it be so now; for thus it is fitting for us to fulfil all righteousness." Then he consented.* [16]*And when Jesus was baptized, he went up immediately from the water, and behold, the heavens were opened[g] and he saw the Spirit of God descending like a dove, and alighting on him;* [17]*and lo, a voice from heaven, saying, "This is my beloved Son,[h] with whom I am well pleased."*

g Other ancient authorities add *to him*   h Or *my Son, my (or the) Beloved*

OVERVIEW: Jesus freely accepted John's baptism in order that he might fulfill in all humility the justice of the law, that by his baptism he might validate John's ministry of baptism and that by sanctifying the waters he might show the Holy Spirit's advent in the baptism of believers (JEROME). Hence by being baptized himself, Jesus set apart for sacramental use the waters of our baptism. Yet since he committed no sin, there was no personal need for him to be baptized (HILARY, THEODORE OF MOPSUESTIA). The faithful are symbolically transferred from this present life by baptism and given that life which is to come. Jesus saw to it that this observance should be fulfilled first of all in himself (THEODORE OF MOPSUESTIA). When people saw the Son being baptized as if he might be a sinner, the question arose as to the innocence to which the Baptist gave witness (ANONYMOUS). John did not want anyone to draw the conclusion that Jesus also came to the Jordan to repent of his sins, so he immediately set this point straight by calling him both Lamb and Redeemer of all the sin that is in the world (CHRYSOSTOM). John tried to excuse himself from doing what Jesus directed him to do, because he could not conceive that baptism was necessary for the One whom he knew had come to blot out the sins of the world (CHROMATIUS).

Jesus came to do away with the curse that is appointed for the transgression of the law. So he first of all had to fulfill all the law, to bring its curse to an end (CHRYSOSTOM). He who was perfect according to the law (THEODORE OF HERACLEA) in baptism identified himself with all that belongs to human nature (ANONYMOUS). Jesus freely identified himself with the people; otherwise he would not have come with the people for John's baptism. Hence, when Jesus was baptized, a voice with the Spirit clearly proclaimed his identity as the only begotten Son (CHRYSOSTOM). The Lord was not baptized for his own sake but for ours, in order to fulfill all righteousness (CHROMATIUS). John's baptism was perfect according to the precept of the law but imperfect in that it did not supply remission of sins yet to come. It merely made people fit for receiving the perfect one (THEODORE OF MOPSUESTIA). The dove signifies meekness and reconciliation (ORIGEN), affection and steady allegiance (THEODORE OF MOPSUESTIA). The dove and the voice manifested the Son's identity both by eye and ear (HILARY). The triune teaching is concisely embedded in the voice of the Father concerning the Son through the descent of the Holy Spirit (AUGUSTINE).

3:13 Jesus Came to Be Baptized by John

WHILE JOHN WAS STILL TEACHING. ANONYMOUS: And then Christ came, so that also this witness revealed his truth. In his baptism the heavens opened and the Holy Spirit descended, the Father spoke from heaven, and through this it was made manifest that he who was baptized by John was truly more worthy than John. In the same way Lucifer came forth, but the light did not wait for the fall of Lucifer before it emerged. Even as he came forth it emerged and with its light obscured his brightness. So too in this way John's preaching came before Christ. Christ did not wait for John to complete his career before he arrived on the scene, but, while John was still teaching, he appeared. Thus in comparing the teaching and work of Jesus and John, John's work and role is constantly diminishing. Hence, after Jesus began preaching to all those who were flocking to him, John's teaching was overshadowed. INCOMPLETE WORK ON MATTHEW, HOMILY 4.[1]

WHY THE SINLESS CHRIST WAS BAPTIZED. ANONYMOUS: John went about preaching, "Repent, for the kingdom of heaven is at hand."[2] Jesus came that he might receive John's witness and confirm his preaching: "Behold the Lamb of God, who takes away the sins of the world."[3]

Thus, when some saw the sinless Christ baptized as if he were a sinner, they said to one another: "If he whose innocence the Baptist gave witness thought it necessary to have himself baptized, how can we who are covered with sins scorn repentance?" Here we must recall that John himself testified that "I baptize you with water for repentance, but he who is coming after me is mightier than I, whose sandals I am not worthy to carry; he will baptize you with the Holy Spirit and with fire." INCOMPLETE WORK ON MATTHEW, HOMILY 4.[4]

THE WATERS OF BAPTISM SANCTIFIED. HILARY: In Jesus Christ we behold a complete man. Thus in obedience to the Holy Spirit the body he assumed fulfilled in him every sacrament of our salvation. He came therefore to John,[5] born of a woman,[6] bound to the law and made flesh through the Word.[7] Therefore there was no need for him to be baptized, because it was said of him: "He committed no sin."[8] And where there is no sin, the remission of it is superfluous. It was not because Christ had a need that he took a body and a name from our creation. He had no need for baptism. Rather, through him the cleansing act was sanctified to become the waters of our immersion. ON MATTHEW 2.5.[9]

WHETHER THE BAPTIZER IS GREATER THAN THE BAPTIZED. ORIGEN: By this act Jesus showed himself to be "meek and lowly in heart,"[10] coming to those inferior to him, doing all that followed in order to humble himself and become obedient "unto death."[11] It is not always the case that the one who baptizes is greater than the one who is baptized. Ananias was not

---

[1]PG 56:657. [2]Mt 3:2. [3]Jn 1:29. [4]PG 56:657. [5]The baptism of Jesus by John provided difficulties for ancient exegetes: why would Jesus, immune from sin and far superior to John, subject himself to this penitential practice? In this passage from Hilary and in those that follow lies a series of interpretations that variously attempt to resolve this difficulty. [6]Cf. Gal 4:4. [7]Cf. Jn 1:14. [8]1 Pet 2:22. [9]SC 254:108. [10]Mt 11:29. [11]Phil 2:8.

greater than Paul.[12] And while Philip baptized,[13] Peter gave the Spirit through the laying on of hands.[14] FRAGMENT 52.[15]

WHY JESUS ACCEPTED JOHN'S BAPTISM. JEROME: For three reasons the Savior accepted baptism from John. First, because he was born a man, that he might fulfill all justice and humility of the law. Second, that by his baptism he might confirm John's baptism. And third, that by sanctifying the waters of the Jordan through the descent of the dove, he might show the Holy Spirit's advent in the baptism of believers. COMMENTARY ON MATTHEW 1.3.13.[16]

WHY HE WAS BAPTIZED. THEODORE OF MOPSUESTIA: Many raise the question, What in fact was the nature of this baptism with which the Lord was baptized? What did it amount to, the baptism of our Lord and Savior Jesus Christ, who, for the sake of the salvation of all, became human? As such he was to show himself to be the beginning of a certain paradoxical life on account of which he is called Adam, since for Adam's sake and for the rest of those who have arisen from Adam he becomes the beginning of everlasting life, in the same way that Adam was the original of this temporary and mortal life. This Jesus, I say, recapitulated in himself everything that pertains to our salvation. For just as he both died and rose again, we also shall do so, in the same way. Since necessarily we were to be symbolically transferred from this present life by baptism and settled in that life which is to come, he saw to it that this baptism should be fulfilled first of all in himself. In his providential dispensation of things, he had received, before all others, this baptism of adoption which is by water and the Spirit. He thereby showed this baptism to be great and honorable, in that he himself, first of all, truly accepted it. Moreover, he himself identified himself with that part of society outside the law of grace, in which we also take part. For it was fitting that the Lord, in humility of spirit, should become subject both to the prophet and Baptist,

like a common person from among the people. He was baptized that he might hallow the waters and bestow upon us, through the basin, regeneration and adoption and remission of sins and all the other blessings that came to us through baptism, prefiguring them in himself. As God, however, he is the One "who takes away the sin of the world,"[17] and as such he has no need of baptism. FRAGMENT 14.[18]

3:14 John Questions Jesus' Request

JESUS NOT THERE FOR REPENTANCE. CHRYSOSTOM: John's baptism was looking toward repentance. Its purpose was to bring hearers to the point of experiencing conviction for their offenses. John, however, did not want anyone to draw the conclusion that Jesus himself also came to the Jordan to repent of his sins. So he sets this point straight from the outset by calling him both Lamb and Redeemer of all the sin that is in the world. He who is able to take away the sins of the whole world was himself without sin. THE GOSPEL OF MATTHEW, HOMILY 12.1.[19]

WHY JOHN TRIED TO PREVENT HIM. CHROMATIUS: Jesus therefore descended to fulfill all the observances of the law, and in this context he was baptized by John in Galilee at the Jordan. But John, recognizing the Lord as his God through the Holy Spirit, declared that he was unworthy to bear his sandals. He excused himself from doing what he was directed to do, because he could not conceive that baptism was necessary for the One whom he knew had come to blot out the sins of the world. He rather pled that he himself ought to be baptized by Christ, saying, "It is I who should be baptized by you, and do you come to me?" It is as if he were saying, "I am a man. You are God. I am a sinner because I am a man. You are sinless because you

---

[12]Acts 9:10-18. [13]Acts 8:13, 38. [14]Acts 8:17. [15]GCS 41.1:36. [16]CCL 77:18-19. [17]Jn 1:29. [18]MKGK 101. [19]PG 57:203; NPNF 1 10:75**.

are God. Why do you want to be baptized by me? I do not refuse the respect you pay me, but I am ignorant of the mystery. I baptize sinners in repentance. But you have no taint of sin. So why do you want to be baptized? Why do you want to be baptized as a sinner, who came to forgive sins?" This is what John in effect was saying to the Lord. TRACTATE ON MATTHEW 12.1.[20]

3:15 Fulfilling All Righteousness

JESUS WAS BAPTIZED FOR US. CHROMATIUS: The Lord here is testing the faithful deference of service on the part of his servant, but he reveals the mystery of his dispensation by saying, "Let it be so now; for thus it is fitting for us to fulfill all righteousness," showing this to be true righteousness, that he the Lord and Master should fulfill in himself every sacrament of our salvation. Therefore the Lord did not want to be baptized for his own sake but for ours, in order to fulfill all righteousness. Indeed, it is only right that whatever someone instructs another to do, he should first do himself. Since the Lord and Master of the human race had come, he wanted to teach by his example what must be done for disciples to follow their Master and for servants their Lord. TRACTATE ON MATTHEW 13.2-3.[21]

THE LAW'S CURSE MADE VOID. CHRYSOSTOM: To this Jesus did not merely reply "Let it be so," but he added pointedly, "now." The implication: It will not be so forever. You will not always see the One for whom the prophets have longed. But for the present, permit this. And then he shows how this baptism is fitting. Why? "For thus it is fitting for us to fulfill all righteousness." The whole law is fulfilled by "all righteousness," by which all the commandments are performed. He is in effect saying, "Since then we have performed all the rest of the commandments, this baptism alone remains. I have come to do away with the curse that is appointed for the transgression of the law. So I must therefore first fulfill it all and, having delivered you from

its condemnation, bring it to an end. It is fitting for me therefore to fulfill the whole law by the same rule by which it is fitting for me to do away with the curse that is written against you in the law. This is the very purpose of my assuming flesh and coming to you." THE GOSPEL OF MATTHEW, HOMILY 12.1.[22]

ALL THAT BELONGS TO HUMAN NATURE. ANONYMOUS: How did Christ fulfill the righteousness of baptism? Without doubt according to the demands of human nature: people need to be baptized, for according to carnal nature they are all sinners. Even as he fulfilled the righteousness of baptism, he fulfilled also the righteousness of being born and of growing, of eating and drinking, of sleeping and relaxing. He also fulfilled the righteousness of experiencing temptation, fear, flight and sadness, as well as suffering, death and resurrection: that is, according to the requirement of the human nature he took upon himself, he fulfilled all these acts of righteousness. INCOMPLETE WORK ON MATTHEW, HOMILY 4.[23]

PERFECT IN THE LAW. THEODORE OF HERACLEA: When he who is perfect according to the law was baptized with the baptism of John, he became the first to achieve the perfection of the law. For this reason even Christ, who was perfect in the law, was baptized with the baptism of John. For this reason he says, "For thus it is fitting for us to fulfill all righteousness." FRAGMENT 21.[24]

MAKING US FIT TO RECEIVE THE PERFECT ONE. THEODORE OF MOPSUESTIA: The baptism of John was at one and the same time perfect and imperfect. It was perfect according to the precept of the law, but it was imperfect in that it did not supply remission of sins but merely made people fit for receiving the perfect

---

[20]CCL 9a:244. [21]CCL 9a:244-45. [22]PG 57:203; NPNF 1 10:76**.
[23]PG 56:658. [24]MKGK 63.

one. For this reason, even Christ, since he was perfect with regard to the law, was baptized with this baptism, that is, the baptism of John. And he makes this clear, saying, "For thus it is fitting for us to fulfill all righteousness." FRAGMENT 13.[25]

3:16 The Spirit Descends When Jesus Is Baptized

NOT BAPTIZED AS ONE REPENTING. CYRIL OF ALEXANDRIA: In the times before Christ's coming, those being baptized were held down in the water a longer time for the confession of sin. But Christ, being sinless, "came up immediately." For Christ was not baptized as one repenting but as one cleansing sins and sanctifying the waters. FRAGMENT 29.[26]

IN BAPTISM WE ARE IMMEDIATELY MADE CHILDREN OF GOD. ANONYMOUS: I do not understand why it states "He immediately came up from the water." What difference does it make if he came out later?[27] The Evangelist therefore could have said, "After being baptized, Jesus came out of the water." I believe that Christ's action belongs to the mystery of all those who were subsequently to be truly baptized. Thus he said "immediately." And note that he did not say "he went out" but "he came up." All those who, as members formed and established in righteousness, are worthily baptized in Christ immediately come up from the water in the sense that they advance in virtue and are raised up to heavenly dignity. Those who enter the water as carnal children of Adam the sinner immediately come up from the water as persons who have been made spiritual children of God. INCOMPLETE WORK ON MATTHEW, HOMILY 4.[28]

THE MEEKNESS OF THE DOVE. ORIGEN: Christ was baptized for our sake, in order to sanctify the waters. The Spirit descended in the form of a dove, since wherever there is reconciliation with God there is a dove, as in the case of

Noah's ark . . . announcing God's mercy to the world and at the same time making clear that what is spiritual should be meek and without wickedness, simple and without guile.[29] FRAGMENT 56.[30]

THE STEADY ALLEGIANCE OF THE DOVE. THEODORE OF MOPSUESTIA: The Holy Spirit appeared in the form of a dove, being kindly, affectionate and a lover of humanity. Although frequently pushed aside,[31] the dove nevertheless comes again to be possessed by us and does us good according to its own goodness. For the dove is an affectionate creature, a friend of humanity, who, even though mistreated by people who snatch away and eat its nestlings, does not depart from those it is accustomed to live with but remains no matter what. FRAGMENT 15.[32]

3:17 A Voice from Heaven

AN ANGELIC VOICE? APOLLINARIS: Some say that the "voice saying, 'This is my beloved Son'" was either an angelic voice serving to represent the person of the Father or else some other voice fashioned on the spot. FRAGMENT 9.[33]

BY HEARING AND BY SIGHT. HILARY: A voice from heaven thus spoke: "This is my beloved Son, in whom I am well pleased."[34] God's Son is manifested both by hearing and by sight. Both the witnesses of contemplation and the spoken word are sent from the Lord to an unfaithful people who disregard the prophets. At the same time, we knew from those who were immersed in Christ that after baptism with water the Holy Spirit would descend to us from the heavenly gates. Then we would be filled with the anointing of heavenly glory and become God's children through the adoption the Father's voice an-

[25]MKGK 100. [26]MKGK 162. [27]Here we have a typical *defectus litterae* (see pp. xlii, xliv). [28]PG 56:658. [29]Cf. Mt 10:16. [30]GCS 41.1:37. [31]Cf. 1 Thess 4:8; Heb 10:29. [32]MKGK 102. [33]MKGK 3. [34]Mt 3:17; Mk 1:11; Lk 3:22.

nounced. Truth prefigured the image of the sacrament through these very happenings. On Matthew 2.6.[35]

My Beloved Son. Chrysostom: Jesus freely identified himself with the people. For if he were not one of the people, he would not have come with the people for John's baptism. Yet this caused some to imagine that John was greater than Jesus. In order that this opinion not be entertained, when Jesus was baptized the Spirit came down, and a voice with the Spirit proclaimed the identity of the Only Begotten. The voice said, "This is my beloved Son." The voice was not identifying John but Jesus. The voice did not say this one who is baptized, but simply "this." The Spirit came in the form of a dove, drawing the voice toward Jesus and making it evident to all that "this" was not spoken of John who baptized, but of Jesus who was baptized. The Gospel of Matthew, Homily 12.2.[36]

The Father's Voice, the Son's Humanity, the Spirit's Descent. Augustine: Here then we have the Trinity presented in a clear way: the Father in the voice, the Son in the man, the Holy Spirit in the dove. This only needs to be barely mentioned, for it is so obvious for anyone to see. Here the recognition of the Trinity is conveyed to us so plainly that it hardly leaves any room for doubt or hesitation. The Lord Christ himself, who comes in the form of a servant to John, is undoubtedly the Son, for here no one can mistake him for either the Father or the Holy Spirit. It is the Son who comes. And who could have any doubt about the identity of the dove? The Gospel itself most plainly testifies: "The Holy Spirit descended upon him in the form of a dove." So also there can be no doubt whose voice it is who speaks so person-

ally: "You are my beloved Son." So we have the Trinity distinguished.... Here are the three persons of the Trinity distinguished: When Jesus came to the river, he came from one place to another. The dove descended from heaven to earth, from one place to another. The very voice of the Father sounded neither from the earth nor from the water but from heaven. These three are as it were distinguished in places, in offices and in works. But one may say to me, "Show me instead the inseparability of the triune God. Remember you who are speaking are a Catholic, and to Catholics are you speaking." For thus does our faith teach, that is, the true, the right Catholic faith, gathered not by the opinion of private judgment but by the witness of the Scriptures, not subject to the fluctuations of heretical rashness but grounded in apostolic truth. This we know, this we believe. This, though we do not see it with our eyes nor as yet with the heart, so long as we are being purified by faith, yet by this faith we most firmly and rightly maintain the Father, Son and Holy Spirit are a Trinity—inseparably one God, not three gods. But yet one God in such a way that the Son is not the Father, and the Father is not the Son, and the Holy Spirit is neither the Father nor the Son but the Spirit of the Father and of the Son. This ineffable Divinity, abiding ever in itself, making all things new, creating, creating anew, sending, recalling, judging, delivering, this Trinity, I say, we know to be at once indescribable and inseparable. Sermon 2.1-2.[37]

---

[35]SC 254:110. [36]PG 57:204; NPNF 1 10:76**. The Spirit revealed Jesus' identity directly, making clear the relation of John and Jesus. [37]PL 38:355; NPNF 1 6:259**. The Trinity is plainly revealed in the baptismal narrative. The one God, God the Father, God the Son and God the Holy Spirit, all appear explicitly in this narrative, distinguishable, yet one God.

4:1-11 THE TEMPTATION OF JESUS

[1]*Then Jesus was led up by the Spirit into the wilderness to be tempted by the devil.* [2]*And he fasted forty days and forty nights, and afterward he was hungry.* [3]*And the tempter came and said to him, "If you are the Son of God, command these stones to become loaves of bread."* [4]*But he answered, "It is written,*

"Man shall not live by bread alone,

but by every word that proceeds from the mouth of God.' "

[5]*Then the devil took him to the holy city, and set him on the pinnacle of the temple,* [6]*and said to him, "If you are the Son of God, throw yourself down; for it is written,*

'He will give his angels charge of you,'

and

'On their hands they will bear you up,

lest you strike your foot against a stone.' "

[7]*Jesus said to him, "Again it is written, 'You shall not tempt the Lord your God.' "* [8]*Again, the devil took him to a very high mountain, and showed him all the kingdoms of the world and the glory of them;* [9]*and he said to him, "All these I will give you, if you will fall down and worship me."* [10]*Then Jesus said to him, "Begone, Satan! for it is written,*

'You shall worship the Lord your God

and him only shall you serve.' "

[11]*Then the devil left him, and behold, angels came and ministered to him.*

OVERVIEW: Adam's temptation was reversed in Jesus' temptation (THEODORE OF MOPSUESTIA). The devil goes out to tempt people, but in this case it was Christ who went to confront the devil (ANONYMOUS). It was fitting that the devil be defeated in that same human flesh in whose death he had gloried (HILARY). In the forty days he provided a pattern for our fasting (ANONYMOUS). Jesus' temptation was for our instruction. Jesus did whatever was necessary for our salvation by both acting and being acted upon (CHRYSOSTOM). The forty days may have symbolic resonance with the mystical meaning of four tens (CHRYSOLOGUS), with the basic units of physical measurement, with embryonic formation (ORIGEN) or with the fact that Elijah fasted forty days. The devil was disturbed and feared

most that after he had filled the world with sins, there would now come someone to take away the sins of the world (CHROMATIUS).

It was precisely when Christ hungered that the devil made his move to tempt him (THEODORE OF MOPSUESTIA). By hunger he participates fully in our human condition except for sin (ORIGEN). The devil begins with the temptation to indulge the belly. By this same means he cast out the first man, and by this means many are still cast down (CHRYSOSTOM). In following, the Lord did not show weakness but patience; in leading, the devil did not show strength but pride (ANONYMOUS). In the wilderness the Lord had humbled the Hebrews through hunger and fed them with manna that they might know that one does not live by bread alone (ORIGEN). By the Word, not bread alone, we are fed for life with God (JEROME). That by which Adam was tempted, food, did not succeed in tempting Christ (MAXIMUS OF TURIN). It is not through miracles but by patient, long-suffering endurance that we must prevail over the devil. We should do nothing merely for show (THEODORE OF MOPSUESTIA). The devil sought to lead the Lord from the highest to the lowest things by setting him on the pinnacle of the temple (HILARY). The false arrows from the devil's own skewed view of Scripture are broken by the true shield of Scripture (JEROME).

Responding to the devil with Scripture, Jesus shows that demonic temptation must be overcome by forbearance (CHRYSOSTOM). Jesus dealt with three temptations—to gluttony, vainglory and avarice. All three recapitulated the one temptation of Adam. By this we are taught to answer all temptation with Scripture (GREGORY THE GREAT). The devil is subservient to whatever purpose God wished to happen in his providential arranging of all things (THEODORE OF MOPSUESTIA).

Every promise of the devil is intrinsically irrational, for he could not give everything to one person unless he took everything away from everybody, and if he took everything away, he would be adored by no one. The devil does not have the power to tempt God's people as long as he wishes but only as long as God permits (ANONYMOUS). When the devil was commanded to worship the Lord and him only, this was the opposite of the devil's earlier words to the Savior: "If you will fall down and worship me" (JEROME). In this way the Lord made sport of the devil, the Leviathan, as with a fishhook (CHROMATIUS). According to God's dispensation, our good angels may make themselves invisible to the devil, that they might give the devil an open space in which to tempt in order to provide moral exercise toward deeper virtue (ANONYMOUS).

4:1 Jesus Led into the Wilderness

READINESS TO FACE TEMPTATIONS. CHRYSOSTOM: The text says "then." Then when? This was after the descent of the Spirit, after the voice that was borne from above had said, "This is my beloved Son, in whom I am well pleased." Led by whom? This is marvelous. All of this was led by the Holy Spirit. For it says Jesus was "led up by the Spirit." All this was for our instruction. The Lord does whatever is necessary for our salvation by both acting and being acted upon. He submitted himself to being led up there to wrestle against the devil. Now we should not be troubled if, after our baptism, we too have to endure great temptations. We should not treat this as if unexpected but continue to endure all things nobly, as though it were happening in the natural course of things. THE GOSPEL OF MATTHEW, HOMILY 13.1.[1]

ADAM'S TEMPTATION REVERSED. THEODORE OF MOPSUESTIA: For since Adam met with luxury in paradise and, through deception, deteriorated to what is worse, it was necessary that [the Spirit] lead Christ into the wilderness in order to enfeeble the devil's force by someone greater in strength. So he fasted for forty nights and days. FRAGMENT 17.[2]

LED BY THE SPIRIT. ANONYMOUS: With the words the Evangelist added, "to be tempted by the devil," he shows that Jesus was led by the Spirit, but not as a subordinate on the command of a superior and not as a superior on the encouragement of a subordinate. He is referring not only to one who is led or drawn under another's power but also to one who acquiesces in someone's reasonable insistence.

Jesus was led to the devil to be tempted. Note that the devil goes out to people to tempt them,

---

[1]PG 57:207-8; NPNF 1 10:80**. By submitting himself to being led up by the Spirit to the wilderness to struggle against temptation, he teaches us to face our temptations.   [2]MKGK 102. Adam through deception fell from the luxury of paradise into temptation and the Fall. Hence the Spirit necessarily led Jesus into the wilderness to enfeeble the devil's force by someone greater in strength.

and it is not people who go to the devil in order to be tempted by him. And since the devil could not go against Christ, it was Christ who went against the devil. INCOMPLETE WORK ON MATTHEW, HOMILY 5.[3]

THE DEVIL DEFEATED BY THE SAME FLESH HE HAD MADE MISERABLE. HILARY: The journey into the desert, the forty-day fast, the hunger after the fast, the temptation by Satan and the Lord's response—all these are full of the effects of the great heavenly counsel. The fact he was led into the desert signifies the freedom of the Holy Spirit to offer his man to the devil and to permit the occasion of temptation and conquest, which the tempter would not have had unless he had been given it. There was in the devil therefore suspicious fear but no knowledge of the true identity of the One suspected. The devil was moved by the forty-day fast. He had knowledge of the poured-out waters of the abyss in just as many days and of the exploration of the promised land,[4] in the Mosaic law written by God.[5] He also knew that this number of years was fulfilled when the people remained in the desert with the life and condition as it were of angels.[6] Apprehensive of that time therefore in tempting him whom he considered to be a man, he acted rashly. He had enticed Adam and by deceiving him led him to death. But it was fitting, because of his wickedness and evil deed, that he be defeated by that same humanity in whose death and misfortunes he gloried. It was the devil who envied God's gifts to humanity before the temptation of Adam, who was now unable to understand God's being present in a human being. The Lord was therefore tempted immediately after being baptized. His temptation indicates how sinister are the devil's attempts especially against those who have been sanctified, for he eagerly desires victory over the saints.

Jesus did not hunger for human food but for human salvation. It was after forty days and not during forty days that he hungered. Moses and Elijah were not hungry during the same period of fasting.[7] Therefore, when the Lord hungered, the work of abstinence did not creep up on him. His strength was not depleted by his forty days of fasting. He did not abandon his nature as a man. The devil was not to be defeated by God but by the flesh, which he surely would not have dared to tempt, except in those things which he recognized were proper human needs because of the pangs of hunger. ON MATTHEW 3.1 2.[8]

4:2 Jesus Fasts for Forty Days and Nights

FORTY DAYS, THEN HUNGER. ORIGEN: For the number "forty days" is composed of four groups of ten.[9] This may be akin to the four aspects of physical reality, because the sensible world is formed out of four elements. Or it may be because a human being is formed in forty days in the womb.[10] And so that he might not, by fasting any longer than this, give anyone the notion that he had not taken on flesh in truth, he afterward was hungry, sharing all that we have "except for sin"[11] and participating in our condition through his own suffering. FRAGMENT 61.[12]

ELIJAH FASTED FORTY DAYS. THEODORE OF MOPSUESTIA: When Christ "hungered," as it is written, then the devil made his move to tempt him; for he was not wholly amazed at the fact of his fasting for forty days, since he knew that Elijah had fasted for the same length of time.[13] For this reason he took courage to attack him, think-

---

[3]PG 56:661. [4]See Num 13:25. [5]Ex 24:18. [6]Ex 16:35. [7]Cf. Ex 34:28. [8]SC 254:110-14. [9]In this passage is an example of numerical exegesis, which constructs an allegorical interpretation on the symbolical meaning attributed to numbers. The belief that numerical combinations contained hidden inner meanings was widespread in the ancient world. [10]This does not imply that before these forty days there is nothing human about the developing baby but only that its formation is clearly evident by the fortieth day. In any event, Origen grasped the analogy between the forty days of temptation in forming the new creation and the forty days of embryonic development to form the original creation of the person in the womb. [11]Heb 4:15. [12]GCS 41.1:39. [13]Cf. 1 Kings 19:8.

ing him to be a person of this kind, and not God. FRAGMENT 18.[14]

JESUS' HUNGER WAS VOLUNTARY. ANONYMOUS: He therefore fasted for forty days, and he did this for two reasons. First, that he might give us an example of fasting to ward off temptations. Second, that he might set the measure of forty days for our fasting. He hungered, furthermore, so that by not overdoing his fasting God might be manifestly understood and he might dash the devil's hope in temptation and thwart his victory. After the devil beheld him fasting for forty days, he gave up hope. It was when he realized that Christ was hungry that hope was restored. He approached him as he hungered outwardly but found that inwardly he was never hungry. And while he tempted the hungry Christ, he was conquered by the Christ who was not hungry.

To be hungry and not to eat is proper of human patience, but not to be hungry is proper of a divine nature. Therefore he who was not hungry for forty days and then became hungry demonstrates that his hunger was voluntary and not necessary. INCOMPLETE WORK ON MATTHEW, HOMILY 5.[15]

LENTEN FASTING ANTICIPATED. PETER CHRYSOLOGUS: So you see, my friends, the fact that we fast during Lent is not of human invention. The authority is divine and mystical and not taken for granted. Nor is it based on an earthly custom but on heavenly secrets. Lent [*Quadragesima*] contains the four-sided teaching of four decades of faith, because perfection is always four-sided. The number forty [*quadragesimus*] and the number ten [*denarius*], which hold sacraments both in heaven and on earth because a square is not free to open, are used to explain the undertaking of the Lord's fast. SERMONS 11.4.[16]

4:3 The First Temptation

THE DEVIL'S INTERROGATION. CHROMATIUS: The devil provokes that he might tempt him,

and the Lord follows up that he might win. The battle over this temptation is thus engaged, as the devil says to the Lord, "If you are the Son of God, command these stones to become loaves of bread." Unaware of the mystery of the divine dispensation, he frames as a question what he does not know.[17] With the voice of a doubter, he interrogates Christ and says, "If you are the Son of God . . ." Now let us see why he inquires when he doubts and why he questions when he does not know. He heard that it had been announced by the angel to the Virgin that she would give birth to the Son of God. He saw the magi, who had left behind the error of their limited knowledge, in humble adoration of the Child that was born. He saw, after the baptism, the Holy Spirit descending like a dove. He also heard the Father's voice from heaven saying, "This is my Son."[18] He heard John with a loud voice proclaiming, "This is he who takes away the sin of the world."[19] Disturbed by so much testimony therefore and now troubled by this voice, this is what he feared most of all: that after he had filled the world with sins, he heard there would now come someone to take away the sins of the world. He was frightened indeed by all these utterances, but he did not yet fully believe that the Son of God whom he had heard, whom he now beheld as a man in the flesh, would take away the sins of the world. In a terrible state of fear he seeks to find out whether these things he had heard were true. He sees the Lord fasting "forty days and nights," but he was loath to believe that this was the Son of God. He recalled that both Moses and Elijah also

---

[14]MKGK 203. [15]PG 56:664-65. [16]CCL 24:74; FC 17:58*. Christ permitted the devil to tempt him for forty days, that the devil might become entangled by the means by which he thought he might make a catch and thereby to establish for the liturgical year the pattern of forty days of penitence. [17]On the level and importance of the knowledge possessed by the devil, the ancient exegetes were highly uncertain. In interpreting the temptation of Christ they usually maintained that the devil could have an inkling of Jesus' actual identity but could not be certain. This assumption directed their interpretation of the account in Scripture. [18]Mt 3:16-17; cf. Mk 1:10-11. [19]Jn 1:29.

fasted for forty days. And so he asked to be given some sign that this was truly the Son of God. He therefore said, "If you are the Son of God, command these stones to become loaves of bread." TRACTATE ON MATTHEW 14.2.[20]

THE FIRST POINT OF ATTACK. CHRYSOSTOM: What does the devil first say? "If you are Son of God, command these stones to become loaves of bread." The focus is not upon hunger but divine Sonship. Thinking to cheat him with supposed compliments, the devil suggested, "If you are Son of God," remaining silent about his hunger in order that he not seem to allege that he indeed was hungry and not upbraiding him for it. For unaware of the greatness of the economy which was unfolding, he supposed hunger to be a reproach to him. So flattering him smoothly, he makes mention of his dignity only.

How then did Christ respond to this? In order to put down the devil's pride and signify that there was nothing shameful in Jesus' hunger nor unbecoming to his wisdom, he brings forward precisely the point that the devil had passed over in silence to flatter him. Jesus said, "Man shall not live by bread alone."

In this way the devil begins his temptation with the necessity of the belly. Mark well the craft of that wicked demon. Note at what precise point he begins his struggling and how well he remembers what he does best. For it was by this same means that he cast out the first man and then encompassed him with thousands of other evils. Now by the same means here he again weaves his deceit: the temptation to indulge the belly. So too even now one may hear many foolish people say their bad words by thousands because of the belly. THE GOSPEL OF MATTHEW, HOMILY 13.3.[21]

COMMAND THESE STONES TO BECOME LOAVES. CYRIL OF ALEXANDRIA: Wanting to draw Christ into the passion of vainglory,[22] Satan did not say to him "eat" but "work a miracle." This he did, not so that Christ would be helped, but,

as I said, in order to draw him to a pretentious act. But Christ, knowing this, did not obey him. Later he would not comply with the Pharisees when they wanted to see a sign from him. For they did not approach him with an undoubting heart, as to God, but were tempting him as a man. Let this therefore be an unfailing rule for the saints, not to show off before unbelievers upon any pretext of utility.[23] FRAGMENT 32.[24]

4:4 Living by the Word, Not by Bread Alone

THE LESSON OF THE MANNA. ORIGEN: This saying is quoted by our Savior, and it makes clear to a person with understanding that before the manna came, which was our heavenly food, we must have been in a bad way and close to starving, having spent up all our fat for food. For thus it is written: "And you shall remember all the way which the Lord your God has led you in the wilderness, that he might humble you, testing you to know what was in your heart, whether you would keep his commandments or not. And he humbled you and let you hunger and then fed you with manna, which you had not known, nor had your fathers known, in order that he might make you know that man does not live by bread alone."[25] The manna itself is a word. This is made clear from the reply Moses made to the question of the children of Israel, when they said to one another, "What is that?"[26] What then did Moses say? "This is the bread which the Lord has given you to eat. This is the word which the Lord has commanded."[27] After this the devil goes on to another defeat. FRAGMENT 63.[28]

FEEDING ON THE WORD. MAXIMUS OF TURIN: The Savior put down the devil's stratagem with

---

[20]CCL 9a:251-52. [21]PG 57:210; NPNF 1 10:81*. The first point of attack in demonic temptation is, as usual, the temptation to satisfy the belly, in response to which Jesus quotes Scripture in defense. [22]Ambition, the lust for glory, showing off. [23]However useful it may seem. [24]MKGK 162. [25]Deut 8:2-3. [26]Ex 16:15. [27]Ex 16:15-16. [28]GCS 41.1:41.

a clever response. He does not do what the devil says, lest he seem to declare the glory of his power at his adversary's will, nor does he answer that it cannot be done, since he could not deny what he had often already done. Therefore he neither gives in to the devil's petition nor rejects his inquiry. He reserves for himself the manifestation of his power and counters his adversary's stratagem with eloquence. He therefore says to him, "Not by bread alone shall man live, but by every word that proceeds from the mouth of God"—that is, not by earthly bread or by material food, whereby you deceived Adam the first man, but by the word of God, which contains the food of heavenly life. The Word of God is Christ the Lord, as the Evangelist says: "In the beginning was the Word, and the Word was with God."[29] So, whoever feeds on the word of Christ does not require earthly food, nor can one who feeds on the bread of the Savior desire the food of the world. The Lord has his own bread; indeed, the bread is the Savior himself, as he taught when he said, "I am the bread who came down from heaven."[30] About this bread the prophet says, "And bread strengthens the human heart."[31] SERMONS 51.2.[32]

NOT BY BREAD ALONE. THEODORE OF HERACLEA: The first Adam sinned by eating. Christ prevailed by self-control. He thus teaches that there is no need for us to stay far away from God, even if we are famishing. This is also a pledge of our future state, which Christ in fact inaugurated, that in the future human beings will live even without food. FRAGMENT 22.[33]

FEEDING ON GOD'S WORD. JEROME: The testimony was taken from Deuteronomy. The Lord responded in this way, for it was his purpose to overcome the devil with humility and not with power. At the same time, it should be noted that unless the Lord had begun to fast, the devil would not have had an occasion, in accordance with the passage: "My son, as you embark upon the service of God, prepare your soul for temp-

tation."[34] But the Savior's very response indicates that it was as man that he was tempted: "Not by bread alone shall man live, but by every word that comes forth from the mouth of God." So if anyone does not feed upon God's Word, that one will not live. COMMENTARY ON MATTHEW 1.4.4.[35]

DO NOTHING FOR SHOW. THEODORE OF MOPSUESTIA: If as God Jesus overcame the devil, it was no great accomplishment for him to defeat the apostate angel whom he himself had made. Nor is this victory to be ascribed to his humanity alone. But by long-suffering, he prevailed over him as man, teaching us that it is not through miracles but by long-suffering and patient endurance that we must prevail over the devil and that we should do nothing merely for show or for notoriety's sake. FRAGMENT 20.[36]

4:5-6 The Second Temptation

THE PINNACLE OF THE TEMPLE. HILARY: The devil works at temptation by leading the Lord from the highest to the lowest things to reduce him to humiliation. He set him on the pinnacle of the temple, as if towering over the laws and the prophets. He knew indeed that the angels would be prompt to minister to the Son of God, lest he dash his foot against a stone. He could trample underfoot the serpent and the adder and tread on the lion and the dragon.[37] Concerning those lower things which were taken for granted, the devil kept silent, but by mentioning the higher things, he wanted in some way to elicit obedience from the tempted One, hoping to hear an echo of his own glory in a vote of confidence from the Lord of majesty. ON MATTHEW 3.4.[38]

---

[29]Jn 1:1. [30]Jn 6:41. [31]Ps 104:15 (103:15 LXX). [32]CCL 23:51; ACW 50:125*. By the Word, not bread alone, we are fed for life with God. That by which Adam was tempted, food, did not succeed in tempting Christ. [33]MKGK 63. [34]Sir 2:1. [35]CCL 77:20. [36]MKGK 103. [37]Ps 91:13 (90:13 LXX). [38]SC 254:116.

If You Are the Son of God. Chrysostom: What can the reason be that with each temptation the devil adds, "If you are the Son of God"? He is acting just like he did in the case of Adam, when he disparaged God by saying, "In the day you eat, your eyes will be opened."[39] So he does in this case, intending thereby to signify that our first parents had been beguiled and outsmarted and had received no benefit. So even in the temptation of Jesus he insinuates the same thing, saying, "In vain God has called you Son and has beguiled you by his gift. For, if this is not so, give us some clear proof that you are from that power." And, because Christ had reasoned with him from Scripture, he does the same, bringing in the testimony of the prophet. The Gospel of Matthew, Homily 13.4.[40]

How the Devil Misinterpreted Scripture. Jerome: "Throw yourself down." It is the devil's voice by which he desires that everyone should fall down. "Throw yourself," he says. He is able to persuade, but he cannot cast down. "He will give his angels charge concerning you; and upon their hands they shall bear you up, lest you dash your foot against a stone." This we read in the ninetieth psalm.[41] Clearly the prophecy here is not about Christ but about a holy man. The devil therefore is a poor interpreter of the Scriptures. Certainly, if he really knew what was written about the Savior, he should have also said what follows in the same psalm against him: "You will tread on the lion and the adder, the young lion and the serpent you will trample underfoot."[42] Concerning the help of the angels, he speaks as though to a feeble man. Concerning his being trampled underfoot, he is silent like an artful dodger.

Jesus said to him, "It is written further, 'You shall not tempt the Lord your God.'" The false arrows from the devil's own scriptures he breaks with the true shield of the Scripture. And it should be noted that he cited the necessary testimony from Deuteronomy that he might show the sacraments of the second law. Commentary on Matthew 1.4.5-7.[43]

4:7 Not Tempting the Lord

Temptation Overcome by Forbearance. Chrysostom: What does Christ then do? He is neither indignant nor provoked but with extreme gentleness reasons with him again from the Scriptures, saying, "You shall not tempt the Lord your God,"[44] teaching us that we must overcome the devil not by miracles but by forbearance and long-suffering and that we should do nothing at all for display and vainglory. The Gospel of Matthew, Homily 13.4.[45]

Led That We Might Not Follow. Anonymous: "Then the devil took him into the holy city." When you hear the words "led by the devil," do not think of the devil's power, that he was able to lead Christ. Rather, wonder at the patience of Christ when he allowed himself to be led by the devil. Therefore, in following, the Lord did not show weakness but patience; in leading, the devil did not show strength but pride, because not understanding the willingness of Christ, it was as though he were leading an unwilling person. He was led that we might not follow the devil's will. Incomplete Work on Matthew, Homily 5.[46]

4:8 The Third Temptation

The Economy of God Expressed Even in Temptation. Theodore of Mopsuestia: The statement that the devil "led him away" has to be understood with reference to God's plan,[47] since Christ, who had foretold and sought that he should do this, had prearranged for the clear defeat of the one who should try in vain to tempt

[39]Gen 3:5. [40]PG 57:211; NPNF 1 10:82*. [41]Ps 91:11-12 (90:11-12 LXX). [42]Ps 91:13 (90:13 LXX). [43]CCL 77:21-22. [44]Mt 4:7. [45]PG 57:211; NPNF 1 10:82*. Theodore of Mopsuestia uses the same words in his Fragment 20; MKGK 102. [46]PG 56:665. [47]Economy, oikonomia.

him. For in the case of Job too it says that "the devil said to the Lord."[48] But who is so simple-minded as to suppose that the devil discusses things with God? But what he had intended, God allowed him to do, in order to demonstrate Job's indomitability. So too in the present instance, to the devil is applied whatever purpose God had wished to happen in providentially arranging all things. But as to the phrase "he showed him," it is clear that he did not show him this in substance and reality, since it is impossible to find a mountain so high that from it someone who wishes can see the whole world. Rather it was through an imaginary image, in keeping with the demon's usual custom, the clear identifying mark of which is the attempt to delude people of sound understanding by representing to them things that are not there as though they were there and things that have not happened as though they had happened. FRAGMENT 22.[49]

4:9 *Fall Down and Worship Me*

THE INCONSISTENCY IN THE DEMONIC PROMISE. ANONYMOUS: Consider how every promise of the devil is intrinsically irrational and untrue. Certainly he could not give everything to one person unless he took everything away from everybody. If he took everything away from everybody, he would be adored by no one. Remember that the devil is not adored either out of love or out of fear but because he promises and makes deals for riches. So how could the devil take everything away from everyone and give it to one person, in order to be despised by all and worshiped by one? Nor can we say that anyone could keep his own when the devil has charge of everything. There is no case in which one person is in a situation where he is subject to no one else. This has not happened, nor can it happen. Why? First, because God will not grant the devil such absolute power. Second, because of the devil himself, for in what do his joy and glory and power consist except in pride, envy, wrath, vain ambition and the like? When

these things come into play, a kingdom cannot stand in unity. It would be necessary to divide up such a kingdom into many kingdoms. But when these things do not come into play, the devil is not reverenced, nor does he reign. INCOMPLETE WORK ON MATTHEW, HOMILY 5.[50]

THE THREE TEMPTATIONS. GREGORY THE GREAT: If we look at the progression of his temptation, we see how great the struggle was that set us free from temptation. Our ancient enemy rose up against the first human being, our ancestor, in three temptations. He tempted him by gluttony, by vain ambition and by avarice. And he overcame [Adam] when tempted, because he subjugated him through consent. He tempted him by gluttony when he showed him the forbidden food of the tree and told him, "Taste it." He tempted him by vain ambition when he said, "You will be like gods." He tempted him by adding avarice when he said, "knowing good and evil." Avarice is concerned not only with money but also with high position. We rightly call it avarice when we seek high position beyond measure. If grasping at honor was not related to avarice, Paul would not have said of God's only begotten Son, "He did not think that being equal to God was something to be grasped."[51] The devil drew our ancestor to pride by stirring him up to an avaricious desire for high position.

But the means by which he overcame the first man were the same ones that caused him to yield when he tempted the second Adam. The devil tempted him by gluttony when he said, "Tell these stones to become bread." He tempted him by vain ambition when he said, "If you are the Son of God, cast yourself down." He tempted him by an avaricious desire for high position when "he showed him all the kingdoms of the world, saying, 'I will give you all these if you will fall down and worship me.'" But the devil is overcome by the second man in the same way as

---

[48]Job 1:7; 2:2. [49]*MKGK* 104. [50]PG 56:667. [51]Phil 2:6.

he boasted of overcoming the first man. He exits our heart at the same juncture where he first made his earliest inroads.

But there is something else we have to consider in this temptation of the Lord, dearly beloved. When the Lord was tempted by the devil, he answered him with the commands of sacred Scripture. By the Word that he was, he could have easily plunged his tempter into the abyss. But he did not reveal the power of his might, but he only brought forth the precepts of Scripture. This was to give us an example of his patience, so that as often as we suffer something from vicious persons we should be aroused to teach rather than to exact revenge. Consider how great God's patience is, how great our impatience. When we are provoked by some injury or threatened harm, or moved to rage, we seek revenge as far as possible. When we are unable to obtain it, we make our threats. But the Lord endured the devil's opposition, and he answered him with nothing except words of meekness. He put up with one he could have punished, so that this might all the more redound to his praise. He overcame his enemy not by destroying him but by suffering him for a while. FORTY GOSPEL HOMILIES 16.2-3.[52]

4:10 Serving Only God

THE ATTEMPT TO CORRUPT BY AMBITION. HILARY: But now for the third time, the full ambition of diabolical power is at work. The Lord was taken to a very high mountain. All the kingdoms of the world and the glory of them would be his, he was promised, if only he would fall down and worship. His answer broke through all the devil's suspicions. The devil had enticed Adam with food and led him from the glory of paradise to the place of sin—to the region of the forbidden tree. And he had corrupted him with ambition for a divine name by promising a future similar to that of the gods. In this same way all the power of the world is arrayed against the Lord. The possession of all this is offered to the devil's very Creator, so that in line with the order of the ancient deceit, he whom the devil did not entice with food nor move from place, he would now corrupt by ambition.

But the Lord's response put the matter on a higher plane. He said, "Begone, Satan! For it is written, 'The Lord your God shall you worship, and him only shall you serve.'" The devil had to live with the outcome of such great recklessness. His crimes were being discovered. He realized that the Lord his God must be adored in the man. By this effective response, the Lord gave us a decisive example. With human power having been disdained and with worldly ambition being held of little account, we also should remember that our Lord and God alone must be adored, especially when the devil's honor has become the common business of every age. After this flight of the devil, therefore, the angels ministered to Christ. With the devil overcome by the man, his head now being crushed, we now can see better the ministering service of the angels and the unfailing courtesies of the heavenly powers toward us. ON MATTHEW 3.5.[53]

THE LIMITS OF THE DEVIL'S POWER TO TEMPT. ANONYMOUS: He put an end to the devil's tempting when he said, "Get behind me, Satan!" The devil could progress no further with his temptation. But we can rightly understand and reasonably ascertain that he withdrew not as though in obedience to the command. Rather it was the divinity of Christ or the Holy Spirit in Christ who drove away the devil. This gives us great consolation, for the devil cannot tempt God's people as long as he wishes. He can tempt them only so long as Christ or the Holy Spirit who is in them allows him to. INCOMPLETE WORK ON MATTHEW, HOMILY 5.[54]

THE DEVIL'S OFFER REVERSED. JEROME: "Then Jesus said to him, 'Begone, Satan! For it is

---

[52]PL 76:1135-36; CS 123:102-4* (Homily 14).　[53]SC 254:116-18.　[54]PG 56:668.

written: the Lord your God shall you worship, and him only shall you serve.' " Satan and the apostle Peter are not condemned by the same judgment, as many may think. For to Peter it was said, "Get behind me, Satan," that is, follow me, you who are contrary to my will. But the devil heard the words "Begone, Satan"; And it was not said to him "Get behind me," as if it were a matter of simple subjection. Rather it is an instruction: "You shall worship the Lord your God and him only shall you serve." This is the opposite of the devil's earlier words to the Savior: "If you will fall down and worship me." Now he hears that it is he who should worship his Lord and God. Otherwise, "Go into the everlasting fire that has been prepared for you and your angels."[55] Commentary on Matthew 1.4.10-11.[56]

The Lord Made Sport of the Devil. Chromatius: David also prefigures this rejection of temptation when he speaks of the Lord, saying, "And the scourge did not approach his tabernacle."[57] No sin of diabolical scourge could come close to the body of the Lord. Therefore the Lord withstood temptations from the enemy that he might restore victory to humankind. He thereby made sport of the devil, according to what David also proclaimed: "That Leviathan, whom you made to sport in it."[58] And again: "He will bring low the false accuser."[59] And also: "You broke the heads of Leviathan in pieces on the water."[60] In the book of Job the Lord declared that this Leviathan would be made sport of and caught in this temptation, saying, "You will draw out Leviathan with a fishhook."[61] Tractate on Matthew 14.5.[62]

4:11 The Angels Minister to Jesus

The Permission to Tempt. Anonymous: He did not say, "The angels descended and ministered to him," so he might show that the angels were always on earth to minister to him. Rather at the Lord's behest they withdrew from him so that the devil might have room to work against Christ. If the devil were to see angels around him, he might not approach him. In this same way the devil comes invisibly to tempt the faithful. There are two permanent angels with each one of us—a good angel and a bad one. As long as the good angel is with us, the bad angel can never lead us into temptation. According to God's dispensation, however, the good angel may draw back somewhat. Well, he does not exactly draw back but hides himself, making himself invisible to the devil. For unless the good angel wishes to be recognized, he is not seen by the devil. He therefore withdraws, that he might give the devil an open space in which to tempt, and then he waits for the temptation to transpire. Incomplete Work on Matthew, Homily 5.[63]

---

[55]Cf. Mt 25:41. [56]CCL 77:22-23. [57]Ps 91:10 (90:10 LXX). [58]Ps 104:26 (103:26 LXX). [59]Ps 72:4 (71:4 LXX). [60]Ps 74:13-14 (73:13-14 LXX). [61]Job 40:24. [62]CCL 9a:255. [63]PG 56:671.

4:12-22 THE CALL OF THE FIRST FOUR DISCIPLES

[12]*Now when he heard that John had been arrested, he withdrew into Galilee;* [13]*and leaving Nazareth he went and dwelt in Caperna-um by the sea, in the territory of Zebulun and Naph-*

tali, [14]*that what was spoken by the prophet Isaiah might be fulfilled:*

[15]*"The land of Zebulun and the land of Naphtali,*

toward the sea, across the Jordan,

Galilee of the Gentiles—

[16]*the people who sat in darkness*

have seen a great light,

and for those who sat in the region and shadow of death

light has dawned."

[17]*From that time Jesus began to preach, saying, "Repent, for the kingdom of heaven is at hand."*

[18]*As he walked by the Sea of Galilee, he saw two brothers, Simon who is called Peter and Andrew his brother, casting a net into the sea; for they were fishermen.* [19]*And he said to them, "Follow me, and I will make you fishers of men."* [20]*Immediately they left their nets and followed him.* [21]*And going on from there he saw two other brothers, James the son of Zebedee and John his brother, in the boat with Zebedee their father, mending their nets, and he called them.* [22]*Immediately they left the boat and their father, and followed him.*

OVERVIEW: Jesus waited until John's imprisonment to begin the preaching of repentance (CHRYSOSTOM). When John had brought the old covenant to conclusion, Jesus "began to preach" the new, being himself the beginning of it (ORIGEN). Jesus' intention was not to trample on John's teaching but to confirm it (ANONYMOUS). No one can receive the grace of God unless he or she has been cleansed of every stain of sin by the confession of repentance (CHROMATIUS). Let the just rejoice, for their troubles are now ending. Let sinners lament, for their troubles are beginning (ANONYMOUS).

In his withdrawal to Galilee, Jesus provided a pattern for us by which we are instructed not to look for temptations or persecutions (CYRIL OF ALEXANDRIA) but to withdraw ourselves from their sphere of influence (CHRYSOSTOM). The Lord withdrew to Galilee, not because he feared death but in order that he might reserve his passion for an appropriate time and that he might set an example for us about fleeing from the danger of temptation (ANONYMOUS).

The great light is the gospel (CYRIL OF ALEXANDRIA). The light shines upon those sitting in the shadow of death, even when they were not looking for it (ORIGEN). It is appropriate that those tribes of Galilee of the Gentiles who had been first led into bodily captivity should first be brought back from spiritual captivity (ANONYMOUS). Even as the Father is light, so too is the Son light. The region and shadow of death is the region of the infernal abode into which the Savior introduced the light of his majesty upon those who were shrouded in death (CHROMATIUS).

Upon being called by Jesus, the disciples left their nets immediately. Christ seeks this kind of immediate obedience from us (CHRYSOSTOM). Those who hold onto spiritual things will be uplifted by them. Those who hold onto earthly things will be brought down by them (ANONYMOUS). You will leave behind much if you renounce earthly desires. The Lord looks to the heart and not at our material goods (GREGORY THE GREAT). Every disciple who comes to Christ must leave behind these three inordinate attachments: acts of the flesh, material goods, parents in the flesh (ANONYMOUS). The kingdom of God is worth sacrificing not only everything you have but all that you desire (GREGORY THE GREAT). Jesus neither resisted the disciples when they desired to withdraw from him, nor having withdrawn themselves, did he let them go altogether (CHRYSOSTOM). Jesus sees them not bodily but spiritually and chooses them not as apostles but because they could become apostles (ANONYMOUS). He chose illiterate, unskilled and untutored fishermen, that God's grace might be all the more apparent (CHROMATIUS). He made them fishers of men, teachers, so that with the net of God's word they might fetch people out of this delusive world, a world fluctuating and frenetic, unstable and treacherous (ANONYMOUS).

4:12 *Jesus Withdraws to Galilee*

AVOIDING PERSECUTION. CYRIL OF ALEXANDRIA: It was not out of fear that he withdrew. By doing the things he did, he taught us to escape from persecutors. He "withdrew" from Judea to the Gentiles. This showed that God removes himself to a remote part of the land of the Jews when they sin against the holy prophets and insult his deity. FRAGMENT 34.[1]

UNDER GOD'S CARE. ANONYMOUS: Undoubtedly [John's arrest][2] was permitted by God, because no one can do anything against a holy man unless God permits him to. A sinner may perhaps do something against another sinner, for the sinner is not completely under God's care. Against a man of God, however, he can undoubtedly do nothing, for "God is a shield for all those who take refuge in him."[3] And thus he says in another place: "Are not two sparrows sold for a penny? And not one of them will fall to the ground without your Father's will. But even the hairs of your head are all numbered. Fear not, therefore; you are of more value than many sparrows."[4] . . .

The Lord knew this, and he withdrew, not because he feared death but for two other reasons. First, that he might reserve his passion for an appropriate time, and second, that he might set an example for us about fleeing from the danger of temptation. It was not because he feared the danger of temptation, but because otherwise we would be unable to withstand all temptation. If he preceded us along every path of justice as our master that we might follow him as his disciples, it is clear that he did not consider what he could do but what *we* were capable of doing. Moreover, if Christ did those things which he could do and we could not do, we could not be his disciples, for we would lack the strength to follow him. INCOMPLETE WORK ON MATTHEW, HOMILY 6.[5]

4:13 *Living in Capernaum*

DO NOT LOOK FOR TEMPTATIONS. CHRYSOSTOM: Why did he withdraw? He was serving as a pattern for us in instructing us not to seek out temptation but to withdraw ourselves from its sphere of influence. It is not a matter of reproach that one does not intentionally put oneself in danger. Yet one must stand nobly when one inadvertently falls into danger. So, to teach us this and to soothe the ire of the Jewish leaders,[6] he withdrew to Capernaum, and in doing so he fulfilled the prophey of Isaiah.[7] THE GOSPEL OF MATTHEW, HOMILY 14.1.[8]

4:14-15 *The Land of Zebulun and Naphtali*

GALILEE OF THE GENTILES. ANONYMOUS: As history teaches us, these tribes were the first to cross over into Babylonia.[9] It is appropriate

---

[1]MKGK 163. [2]The author asks himself by whom John might have been given over *(traditus esset)* to Herod. [3]Ps 18:30 (17:31 LXX). [4]Mt 10:29-30. [5]PG 56:671-72. [6]For John had been arrested (Mt 4:12). [7]Is 9:1-2. "So that what had been spoken through the prophet Isaiah might be fulfilled: 'Land of Zebulum, land of Naphtali, on the road by the sea, across the Jordan, Galilee of the Gentiles—the people who sat in darkness have seen a great light'" (Mt 4:14-16). [8]PG 57:217; NPNF 1 10:86*. Why did Jesus withdraw from Galilee when he hears that John has been arrested? Temptation and danger are not to be sought but courageously withstood when they appear. They are neither to be recklessly embraced nor cravenly avoided. [9]Zebulun and Naphtali had been part of Israel and were thus sent by the Assyrians to Babylon (cf. 2 Kings 17) before the same fate befell the inhabitants of Judah.

therefore that all those whom the wrath of God has struck should first be visited by God's mercy and those who have been led into bodily captivity should first be brought back from spiritual captivity. "The people who sat in darkness have seen a great light, and for those who sat in the region and shadow of death light has dawned."[10] Jews also were sitting in darkness. Even though they were under the law, God's justice was not being manifested. Although justice was there, it had been covered over with certain figures and mysteries of carnal things. What light of justice is there in circumcision? Indeed the darkness was especially poignant under the law, which was given more to punish the hardness of our hearts than to actually bring about righteousness. As the Lord said, "For your hardness of heart he wrote you this commandment."[11] The law was not given to save but to chastise them. The law blinded them, so that, inebriated with the law, they were unable to see the great light, Christ, when he came.

There indeed were many lights among the Jews: Moses and Aaron and Joshua and the judges and prophets were all lights. Every teacher is a light to them, whom he enlightens by teaching, as is written: "You are the light of the world."[12] But Christ is the great light. In the region and shadow of death were seated the Gentiles, either because they were committing iniquities or because they were worshiping idols and demons, the worship of which was leading them to everlasting death. INCOMPLETE WORK ON MATTHEW, HOMILY 6.[13]

4:16 Light on the People Who Sat in Darkness

THE GOSPEL A GREAT LIGHT. CYRIL OF ALEXANDRIA: And the "great light" is Christ our Lord and the brightness of the gospel preaching. It is not, in fact, the law, which was likened to a lamp.[14] For this reason a lamp always burned in the tabernacle, on account of the shortness of the law's rays, which had strength to extend

their light only within the confines of the Jewish territories. Therefore the Gentiles were "in darkness," not having this lamplight. FRAGMENT 34.[15]

THE TRUE LIGHT OF REVELATION TO THE GENTILES. CHROMATIUS: The Evangelist commemorated in this passage the prophet's words: "Beyond the Jordan, Galilee of the Gentiles: the people who sat in darkness have seen a great light."[16] In what darkness? Certainly in the profound error of ignorance. What great light did they see? The light concerning which it is written: "He was the true light that illumines everyone who comes into this world."[17] This was the light about which the just man Simeon in the Gospel declared, "A light of revelation to the Gentiles and a glory for your people Israel."[18] That light had arisen according to what David had announced, saying, "A light has arisen in the darkness to the upright of heart."[19] Also, Isaiah demonstrated that light about to come for the enlightenment of the church when he said, "Arise, shine; for your light has come, and the glory of the Lord has risen upon you."[20] Concerning that light also Daniel noted, "It reveals the profound and hidden things, knowing those things which are in darkness and the light is with it,"[21] that is, the Son with the Father, for even as the Father is light, so too is the Son light. And David also speaks in the psalm: "In your light shall we see light,"[22] for the Father is seen in the Son, as the Lord tells us in the Gospel: "Who sees me, sees the Father."[23] From the true light, indeed, the true light proceeded, and from the invisible the visible. "He is the image of the invisible God," as the apostle notes.[24] TRACTATE ON MATTHEW 15.1.[25]

THE SHADOW OF DEATH. ORIGEN: He spoke of

---

[10]Is 9:2. [11]Mk 10:5. [12]Mt 5:14. [13]PG 56:672. [14]Prov 6:23; Ps 119:105 (118:105 LXX). [15]MKGK 163. [16]Mt 4:15-16. [17]Jn 1:9. [18]Lk 2:32. [19]Ps 112:4 (111:4 LXX). [20]Is 60:1. [21]Dan 2:22. [22]Ps 36:9 (35:9 LXX). [23]Jn 14:9. [24]Col 1:15. [25]CCL 9a:259.

"the shadow of death" and not simply "death." This is because of the inability of sin utterly to corrupt the soul. Such complete corruption happens to bodies in death. But sin brings forth the *shadow* of death. And the words "light is sprung up" signify that it did not spring up upon us who were looking for it, but it shone upon those who were unprepared for it. FRAGMENT 73.[26]

THE DESCENT OF THE LIGHT INTO THE DARKNESS. CHROMATIUS: Concerning this light, the Evangelist points out in the present passage: "The people who sat in darkness have seen a great light." They see not with bodily contemplation—for the light is invisible—but with the eyes of faith and in the mind's eye. Therefore he says, "The people who sat in darkness have seen a great light, and for those who sat in the region and shadow of death light has dawned."[27] Therefore not only to those who were in darkness did this light appear, but he says that a light has arisen for those sitting in the region and shadow of death. This shows that there were others who were sitting in darkness—established in the region and shadow of death. And what is this region and shadow of death if not the region of the infernal abode, about which David speaks: "Even though I walk in the valley of the shadow of death, I shall fear no evil, for you are with me"?[28] He shall not fear any evil, that is, the punishments of hell. Therefore a saving light has arisen for those who are seated in the region and shadow of death, that is, Christ the Son of God who says in the Gospel: "I am the true light. He who follows me shall not walk in darkness."[29]

He who after his venerable and life-giving passion and death went down into the region of the infernal abode suddenly introduced the light of his majesty upon those who were shrouded in death, so that he might free those who were being held among the dead in expectation of his arrival, as the Lord himself in the person of Wisdom says through Solomon: "I will go down into the depths of the earth and gaze upon all those who are asleep, and I shall enlighten those who hope in God."[30] TRACTATE ON MATTHEW 15.2.[31]

4:17 Jesus Preaches Repentance

JOHN'S PREACHING COMPARED WITH JESUS' PREACHING. ORIGEN: John's preaching of repentance[32] was not precisely the same as the preaching of Jesus, yet the Savior preaches in ways commensurable with John, for there is one God who sent them both. John first says "repent" in order to make ready a "people prepared" for God.[33] Jesus, when he has received a people who have been made ready and who have already repented, does not merely say to them, "Repent." For he does not preach in competition with the law and the prophets. When John had fulfilled the old covenant, Jesus "began to preach" the new, being himself the beginning of it. For this reason the words "he began" are not written of John, for he was an end. Moreover, the one preaches in the wilderness, the other in the midst of the people. FRAGMENT 74.[34]

THE PREACHING MINISTRY BEGINS. CHRYSOSTOM: "From that time." What time? After John was cast into prison. But why didn't he start preaching this from the beginning? What occasion did John provide? Didn't the witness of his works already make this proclamation? He began only at this time to preach in a public way, so that his unique divine identity might become recognized, of which the patriarchs and prophets had already spoken by way of anticipation, as in the voice of Zechariah: "And you, my child, will be called a prophet of the Most High."[35] And that he might leave no occasion for impetu-

---

[26]GCS 41.1:45. [27]Is 9:2. [28]Ps 23:4 (22:4 LXX). [29]Jn 8:12. [30]Cf. Sir 24:5. [31]CCL 9a:259-60. [32]Origen notes that in certain manuscripts "repent" (*metanoiete*) had been omitted. Also attested to by Justin in the second century and consequently quite ancient, this reading is considered secondary by modern editors, who prefer the more complete text. Origen's interpretation takes both readings into account. [33]Lk 1:17. [34]GCS 41.1:45. [35]Lk 1:76.

ous Pharisaic interpretations, he remarked, "For John came neither eating nor drinking, and they say, 'He has a demon.' The Son of Man came eating and drinking, and they say, 'Here is a glutton and a drunkard, a friend of tax collectors and sinners.' But wisdom is proved right by her actions."[36] It was necessary, furthermore, that he be correctly identified not by his own words alone but by another. Otherwise, even after so many and such powerful testimonies and demonstrations, they would merely dismiss him by saying "You are testifying on your own behalf; your testimony is not valid."[37] If John had said nothing, and if Jesus had first come into their midst and testified only of himself, you can imagine what they would have said. So he did not preach publically before John's coming, nor did he work miracles until John was cast into prison, lest the people be confused. THE GOSPEL OF MATTHEW, HOMILY 14.1.[38]

CONFIRMING JOHN'S TEACHING. ANONYMOUS: From the time when John was delivered, Jesus began to preach. For if he had begun to preach while John was alive, doubtless he would have belittled John, and John's preaching would have been considered superfluous compared with that of Jesus—as the light that rises at the same time with the lamplighter overshadows the lamplighter's grace. How wisely then did he begin preaching as John, was accustomed to preach: "Repent, for the kingdom of heaven is at hand."[39] His intention was not to trample on John's teaching but to confirm it all the more. For if he were to preach while John was still teaching, he might seem to be intruding on John's mission. But now, with John confined, he takes up John's teaching. There is no trampling, but confirmation. He confirmed John's teaching, that he might point him out as a true witness. INCOMPLETE WORK ON MATTHEW, HOMILY 6.[40]

NOT A PLACE. ORIGEN: "The kingdom of heaven" is not in a place but in disposition. For it is "within" us.[41] John preaches the coming of

that kingdom of heaven, which Christ the King will deliver up "to God, even the Father."[42] FRAGMENT 74.[43]

THE CALL TO REPENTANCE. CHROMATIUS: The voice of the Lord urging the people to repentance—the Holy Spirit made it known to the people that they might take heed, saying, "Today, when you hear his voice, do not harden your hearts as in the rebellion, as in the day of testing in the wilderness."[44] In the same psalm above, he made clear that he was urging the sinful people to repentance and showed the state of a repentant soul, saying, "Come, let us fall down before him and lament before the Lord who made us, for he is our God."[45] The Lord urges the people to repentance, and he promises to pardon their sins, according to Isaiah's words: "I, even I, am the one who wipes out your iniquities, and I will not be mindful of your sins. But you be mindful, declare first your iniquities that you may be justified."[46] Rightly then does the Lord urge the people to repentance when he says, "Repent, for the kingdom of heaven is at hand," so that through this confession of sins they may be made worthy to approach the kingdom of heaven. For no one can receive the grace of the heavenly God unless one has been cleansed of every stain of sin by the confession of repentance, through the gift of the saving baptism of our Lord and Savior. TRACTATE ON MATTHEW 15.3.[47]

AT HAND. ANONYMOUS: "The kingdom of heaven is at hand." This refers to the blessedness of the heavenly kingdom, which God has prepared for the faithful. The message is to prepare yourselves by penance and by patience to receive

---

[36]Mt 11:18-19. [37]Jn 8:13 NRSV. [38]PG 57:217-18; NPNF 1 10:87*. Why did he wait until John's imprisonment to begin the preaching of repentance? His unique messianic identity is best grasped in the light of John's ministry. After John's imprisonment, the time had come for his preaching to begin. [39]Mt 3:2. [40]PG 56:673. [41]Lk 17:21. [42]1 Cor 15:24. [43]GCS 41.1:45. [44]Ps 95:8 (94:8 LXX). [45]Ps 95:6-7 (94:6-7 LXX). [46]Is 43:25-26. [47]CCL 9a:260-61.

the blessedness of the heavenly kingdom. The time for receiving a reward is at hand. You who fear to do evil and desire to do good, pay heed, for the kingdom of heaven is at hand. If you are repelled by what is evil or attracted by what is good, or if you do not desire kingdoms or if you fear torments, pay heed. Let the just rejoice, for their troubles are now ending and their good fortune is beginning. Let sinners lament, for their good fortune is now passing and their troubles are beginning. No harm is being done to just people. Their troubles are over, and their good fortune beginning. The recollection of past troubles not only does not harm them but gives even greater delight. Indeed, as long as troubles are present, they seem to be oppressive. When they are a thing of the past, the memory of them is a cause for delight. But what good is it when sinners have obtained fortune and are beginning to experience trouble? For the recollection of past fortune not only does no good but becomes even disagreeable. For as long as that fortune is present, it is a source of enjoyment; when it is a thing of the past, however, the recollection of it becomes a source of annoyance. Did this preaching yield the fruit of bringing people to Christ? It sowed the word of repentance and produced virtuous preachers of justice. INCOMPLETE WORK ON MATTHEW, HOMILY 6.[48]

4:18 Simon Peter and Andrew Casting Nets

HOW MUCH DID THE POOR FISHERMEN LEAVE BEHIND? GREGORY THE GREAT: Someone may wonder: At the Lord's beckoning, what or how much did these two fishermen, who scarcely had anything, leave behind? On this, my beloved, we should attend to one's intention rather than one's wealth. That person has left behind a lot who keeps nothing for himself, who, though he has little, gives up everything. We tend to be attached to those things we own, and those things we scarcely own, we carefully hold on to. Therefore Peter and Andrew left much behind when they left behind covetousness and

the very desire to own. That person has left much behind who renounces with the thing owned the very coveting of that thing. Therefore those poor who followed Jesus left behind just as much as those less poor who did not follow him but were able to covet. So when you notice that some have left a great deal behind, you need not say to yourself, *I want to imitate those who disdain this world, but sorry, I have nothing to leave behind.* You will leave much behind, my brothers, if you renounce earthly desires. External things, however small they may be, are sufficient for the Lord, since he looks at the heart and not at our material goods. Nor does he judge by how much is involved in our sacrifice but *from* how much it is made. For if we judge by external goods, our holy merchants traded in their nets and vessels for the perpetual life of the angels. FORTY GOSPEL HOMILIES 5.2.[49]

4:19 Follow Me

HOW JESUS CALLED HIS FIRST DISCIPLES. CHRYSOSTOM: "And they left their nets, and followed him."[50] And yet John (the Evangelist) says that they were called in a different way.[51] From this it is evident that this was a second call. One may conclude this from several evidences. For there it is said that they came to him when "John had not yet been thrown into prison";[52] but here it says after he was in confinement. And there Andrew calls Peter, but here Jesus calls both. On the one hand, John says, "Jesus saw Simon coming and said, 'You are Simon, the Son of Jonah. You shall be called Cephas, which is translated Peter.'"[53] On the other hand, Matthew says that he was already called by that name, for he says,

---

[48]PG 56:674. [49]PL 76:1093; CS 123:10-11* (Homily 2). As much is given up by those following the kingdom, then, as those not following them can crave. The kingdom of God is worth everything you have and all that you desire. [50]Mt 4:20. [51]The Gospel of John recounts the call of the first apostle in a different manner (Jn 1:35-40). Chrysostom harmonizes the two accounts, admitting of two distinct calls, the first of which is described in John. [52]Jn 3:24. [53]Jn 1:42.

"Seeing Simon who was called Peter." . . . In the other instance, Andrew is seen coming into his house and hearing many things. But here, having heard one brief call, they both followed immediately. When they earlier had seen that John was in prison and that Jesus was withdrawing, it would not have been unnatural for them to return again to their own craft, fishing, having followed him at the beginning and then later having left him to fish. Accordingly, you now see that Jesus finds them actively fishing. But he neither resisted them at first when they desired to withdraw from him, nor having withdrawn themselves, did he let them go altogether. He gave way when they moved aside from him and came again to win them back. This, after all, is exactly what fishing is all about. THE GOSPEL OF MATTHEW, HOMILY 14.[51]

WHY THE LORD CHOSE FISHERMEN. CHROMATIUS: Here they proved that they were true sons of Abraham, because by a similar pattern they followed the Savior on hearing God's voice. For they immediately gave up hope of material advantage that they might seek eternal rewards. They left behind their earthly father that they might have a heavenly Father, and hence not undeservedly were they chosen. So the Lord chose fishermen who in a better way of plying their fishing trade were converted from earthly to heavenly fishing, that they might catch the human race for salvation like fish from the deep waters of error, according to what the Lord himself said to them: "Come after me, and I will make you fishers of men." It was the very same thing he had promised through Jeremiah the prophet: "Behold, I am sending for many fishers, says the Lord, and they shall catch them; and afterward I will send for many hunters and they shall hunt them."[55] So we see that the apostles are called not only fishermen but also hunters: fishermen, for in the nets of gospel preaching they catch all believers like fish in the world; hunters, for they catch for salvation by heavenly hunting those people who are roving in this world as though in the woods of error and who are living like wild animals. TRACTATE ON MATTHEW 16.2.[56]

FISHERS OF MEN. ANONYMOUS: "And he said to them, 'Come, follow me, and I will make you fishers of men.'" That is, I will make you teachers, so that with the net of God's Word you may catch people in this delusive world,[57] a world fluctuating and frenetic, unstable, treacherous and always dangerous, and never safe for anyone, where people do not walk but are borne along as though against their will.

The devil's wrath made clever use of the instability of strong desire. He lied to them that their will would be accomplished. He took delight in impelling them to evil deeds, so they may feed upon each other like big fish eating the weaker fish, lest having been removed from the water they live on the fruitful land of the body of Christ. Otherwise, having been made limbs of Christ's body, they could have lived on the fruitful earth, on the sweet and ever tranquil earth, where there is no storm that brews destruction, except perhaps for the testing of their faith and the flowering of their patience. In that body people walk safely, not being coerced. They do not devour each other but support each other.

Behold, I am not handing over to you a new gospel. It is not like another net woven with numerous narrations billowing here and there like waves of various opinions and indispensable parables, admirable virtues and manifold teachings, and bound by threats of judgments and promises of happiness. It is not made of rigid ties, or highlighted by predictions or the knowledge of occult thinking, or confessions of devils and resurrections of the dead, in order for its secure texture to diligently hold rational people captive and prevent them from exiting by any

---

[54]PG 57:218-19; NPNF 1 10:87-88**. The variant Gospel accounts should be understood as reflecting the nature of fishing itself. If the fish escape, one doesn't stop fishing. They are apt to be caught again. [55]Jer 16:16. [56]CCL 9a:264. [57]The symbolism sea=earth is of general and frequent use in ancient scriptural exegesis.

means as through some fissure overlooked by the Holy Spirit who wove that net. INCOMPLETE WORK ON MATTHEW, HOMILY 7.[58]

4:20 They Leave Their Nets to Follow Jesus

NO MIDDLE WAY. ANONYMOUS: Someone may ask, "So I cannot love riches and please Christ?" The apostles gave us a lesson in leaving behind their nets immediately, for no one can own earthly things and completely attain to heavenly things. Notice how, between the earth and the sky, there is an intermediate layer that separates both creations. This shows that between the heavenly and earthly bodies there can be no commingling. The heavenly bodies are spiritual and light, and naturally they always tend upward. The earthly bodies are heavy, and they always hang downward. So, if you hold onto spiritual things, they will bring you up; if you hold onto earthly things, they will bring you down. Therefore they left behind their nets, lest these things become more of an impediment to them than an added benefit. INCOMPLETE WORK ON MATTHEW, HOMILY 7.[59]

JESUS CHOOSES THEM FOR WHAT THEY CAN BECOME. ANONYMOUS: Before he says or does anything, he calls the apostles so nothing may be concealed from them as to Christ's words or works and they may later say in confidence: "For we cannot but speak of what we have seen and heard."[60] He sees them not bodily but spiritually, regarding not their appearance but their hearts. And he chooses them not as apostles but because they could become apostles. Just as an artist who sees precious, and not rough-hewn, stones chooses them—not because of what they are but because of what they can become. Like the sensitive artist who does not spurn the unshaped good—so too the Lord, upon seeing them, does not choose their works but their hearts. INCOMPLETE WORK ON MATTHEW, HOMILY 7.[61]

4:21 James and John Called

JESUS CHOSE THE LOWLY TO DEMONSTRATE DIVINE GRACE. CHROMATIUS: Oh, blessed are those fishermen whom the Lord chose from among so many doctors of the law and scribes, from among so many sages of the world, for the task of divine preaching and the grace of the apostolate! Worthy of our Lord, indeed, and appropriate for his preaching was that choice, so that in the preaching of his name all the greater might be the wonder of praise as the humble and lowly of the age preached his word—not that they might capture the world through the wisdom of the word but that they might liberate the human race from the error of death through the simple preaching of the faith, as the apostle says: "That your faith may not be in human wisdom but in the power of God."[62] And in another place: "But the foolish things of the world has God chosen to put to shame the wise, and the weak things of the world has God chosen to put to shame the strong, and the base things of the world and the despised has God chosen, and the things that are not, to bring to nothing the things that are."[63] Therefore he has not chosen the noble of the world or the rich, lest their preaching be suspect; not the wise of the world, lest people believe that they persuaded the human race with their wisdom; but he chose illiterate, unskilled and untutored fishermen, so that the Savior's grace might be open. TRACTATE ON MATTHEW 16.1.[64]

4:22 They Follow Immediately

IMMEDIATELY THEY LEFT THE BOAT. CHRYSOSTOM: But note both their faith and their obedience. For though they were in the midst of their work (and you know how time-consuming a chore fishing is), when they heard his command they did not delay or procrastinate. They

---

[58]PG 56:674-75. [59]PG 56:675. [60]Acts 4:20. [61]PG 56:674. [62]1 Cor 2:5. [63]1 Cor 1:27-28. [64]CCL 9a:263.

did not say, "Let us return home, and talk things over with our family." Instead, "they left everything behind and followed," even as Elisha did when he followed Elijah.[65] For Christ seeks this kind of obedience from us, such that we delay not even for a moment, though something absolutely most necessary should vehemently press in on us. THE GOSPEL OF MATTHEW, HOMILY 14.2.[66]

THE KINGDOM WORTH EVERYTHING. GREGORY THE GREAT: The kingdom of heaven has no price tag on it: It is worth as much as you have. For Zacchaeus it was worth half of what he owned, because the other half that he had unjustly pocketed he promised to restore fourfold.[67] For Peter and Andrew it was worth the nets and vessel they had left behind; for the widow it was worth two copper coins;[68] for another it was worth a cup of cold water.[69] So, as we said, the kingdom of heaven is worth as much as you have. FORTY GOSPEL HOMILIES 5.2.[70]

WHAT IS LEFT BEHIND IN DISCIPLESHIP. ANONYMOUS: Notice that Peter and Andrew are said to have left behind their nets, whereas James and John their father and a vessel. There are generally three things that each person who comes to Christ should leave behind: acts of the flesh, material goods, parents in the flesh. By leaving behind the fishing nets means leaving behind acts of the flesh; by leaving behind the vessel means material goods; by leaving behind their father, all parents. And notice that first they leave behind their nets, then their vessel and, third, their father. It is appropriate to leave behind worldly acts first, for they are particularly harmful to spiritual things. Second, worldly goods, for it is not as harmful to have something in the world as to do some act, though also to have is harmful. Last, one's parents, for they too can be harmful, though less harmful than the riches and actions of this world. So they left behind their vessel, that they might become helmsmen of the church's vessel; they left behind their nets, that they might no longer bring fish to the earthly city but people to the heavenly city; and they left behind a father, that they might become the parents of all spiritual beings. INCOMPLETE WORK ON MATTHEW, HOMILY 7.[71]

---

[65]1 Kings 19:20-21. [66]PG 57:219; NPNF 1 10:88**. Obedience requires immediate response. [67]Lk 19:8. [68]Mk 12:42. [69]Mt 10:42. [70]PL 76:1093-94; CS 123:11* (Homily 2). [71]PG 56:676.

4:23-25 JESUS MINISTERS TO THE CROWDS

[23]*And he went about all Galilee, teaching in their synagogues and preaching the gospel of the kingdom and healing every disease and every infirmity among the people.* [24]*So his fame spread throughout all Syria, and they brought him all the sick, those afflicted with various diseases and pains, demoniacs, epileptics, and paralytics, and he healed them.* [25]*And great crowds followed him from Galilee and the Decapolis and Jerusalem and Judea and from beyond the Jordan.*

OVERVIEW: Like gathering an army, the Lord gathered together his apostles, not that by their efforts he might attain glory but that he might win victory for them (ANONYMOUS). Let us also come to him, we who have many diseases of our soul that he would gladly heal. Let us ask nothing pertaining to this life but rather remission of sins for eternity. The disciples' very act of bringing others to him exhibits some preliminary faith (CHRYSOSTOM). With heavenly medicine he cures the sickness of body and soul that he might free bodies beset by the devil and restore those persons afflicted by infirmities to true and complete health (CHROMATIUS). The demons dishonor bodies, causing souls to become active in sinning and madness (ORIGEN). If we leave unattended the fountain of our ills, we should not expect that the streams that follow will be unpolluted (CHRYSOSTOM).

4:23 Jesus Teaches, Preaches and Heals

JESUS' HEALINGS PROPHESIED. CHROMATIUS: Isaiah predicted this would happen when he said, "He himself took our infirmities and bore our sickness." To this end the teacher of life and heavenly physician Christ the Lord had come that by his direction he might educate people to life and with his heavenly medicine cure the sickness of body and soul, that he might free bodies beset by the devil and restore those persons afflicted by various infirmities to true and complete health. By the word of divine power he cured the weaknesses of the body, but by the medicine of heavenly teaching he healed the wounds of the soul. David clearly noted that the wounds of the soul are healed by God alone when he said, "Bless the Lord, O my soul, and forget not all his benefits," to which he added, "who forgives all your iniquity, who heals all your diseases."[1] He is the true and perfect physician therefore who gives healing to the body and restores the soul to health: our Lord and Savior. TRACTATE ON MATTHEW 16.4.[2]

LIKE A DEVOTED DOCTOR. ANONYMOUS: He traveled throughout Galilee; like a devoted doctor he attended the seriously ill, dispensing suitable medicines for each and every ailment, because all those weak and suffering people could not come to the doctor. INCOMPLETE WORK ON MATTHEW, HOMILY 8.[3]

4:24 Bringing People to Be Healed

THROUGHOUT ALL SYRIA. CYRIL OF ALEXANDRIA: And this too needs to be added by way of explanation, that the allotment of the tribes of Zebulun and Naphtali extended to the Gentile city of Sidon. The Jews dwell there interspersed among the Gentiles to this day. Now "Zebulun" may be interpreted as a sweet smell and blessing, while "Naphtali" is a sprouted stump, that is to say, a spreading plant. And such things have believers in Christ become. Those who formerly were in Galilee, when they went forth like fragrance,[4] became worthy of divine blessing and were extended into every good thing. Now "Galilee" is interpreted under the metaphor of "circular," so those believers from Galilee are like wheels rolling against the pits of destruction. FRAGMENT 37.[5]

WHETHER FAITH WAS DEMANDED. CHRYSOSTOM: But we must ask how it could be that he demanded faith of none of those he healed. For he did not here say what we later find him saying, "Do you believe that I am able to do this?"[6] He had not yet given proof of his power. The very act of approaching him and of bringing others to him exhibited no small faith. For they brought them even long distances. They would never have brought them unless they had persuaded themselves of great things concerning him. THE GOSPEL OF MATTHEW, HOMILY 14.3.[7]

THE FOUNTAIN UNATTENDED. CHRYSOSTOM: If we have any bodily ailment, we contrive everything possible to be rid of what pains us. Yet when our soul is ailing, we delay and draw back. For this reason we are not delivered from

---

[1]Ps 103:2-3 (102:2-3 LXX). [2]CCL 9a:266. [3]PG 56:677. [4]Cf. 2 Cor 2:15-16. [5]MKGK 164. [6]Mt 9:28. [7]PG 57:220; NPNF 1 10:89**.

bodily ailments. The indispensible corrective has become for us secondary, while the dispensible secondary matters seem indispensable. While we leave unattended the fountain of our ills, we still hope to have the streams unpolluted. THE GOSPEL OF MATTHEW, HOMILY 14.3.[8]

DISTINGUISHING DISEASE AND INFIRMITY.
CYRIL OF ALEXANDRIA: If anyone asks what is the difference between "disease" and "infirmity," our answer is that an infirmity is a temporary indisposition of the body, whereas disease denotes an abiding disequilibrium of the body's elements. FRAGMENT 37.[9]

How DEMONIC TEMPTATIONS AFFECT BODILY HEALTH. ORIGEN: You will see the variety of evils in prodigality or avarice, boorishness or licentiousness, in silliness, knavery, insolence, cowardice and every opposing vice; and the soul's trials are money, fame, poverty, obscurity. And while the demons dishonor bodies, they cause souls to become active in sinning and madness. But the epileptic has a "dumb and deaf" demon.[10] Such passions trouble the soul at intervals, rendering it deaf to the saving word; as, for example, anger is a paralysis of souls, such that, when they succumb to it, their vigor is slackened both for action and for living. And "weakness" of the soul is a term used by Greeks, in a general sense, for any sickness arising from vice; more specifically, for that which is opposed to endurance, a sort of giving up in the face of patience and sufferings and anguish. FRAGMENT 77.[11]

AILMENTS OF SOUL AND BODY. ANONYMOUS: When he said "disease," this pertains to bodily ailments; when he said "every sickness," this pertains to the spiritual ailments of the soul. The ailments of the soul are not fewer than those of the body. And though he said "healing every disease and every sickness among the people," we could understand both as pertaining to bodily

ailments, so that we understand diseases as being more serious ailments, whereas sicknesses are lesser disorders. Now when he says "every disease," he includes every kind of either serious or minor ailment; but the addition of the other clause seems to be superfluous unless we understand one clause as pertaining to bodily ailments and the other to spiritual ailments. However, we could understand both clauses as pertaining to both ailments: that is, "every disease" whether bodily or spiritual, and "every sickness" whether bodily or spiritual, so that we understand disease of the soul as being some disorder, infirmity or infidelity, since a person who is subject to the disorder of avarice or lust or empty ambition suffers a disease of the soul. However, the person who ignores the mystery of God's calling is sick in faith. For many are those who are able to do good works and please God but who do not do them, for they ignore the mystery of God's calling. These persons are sick. Some people are given up to carnal ailments, so that even though they know the mystery of God's calling, they are not permitted to do good. These are the ones who have a disease. But he cured bodily ailments by the power of divinity and spiritual ailments by the word of compassion. Even as medicine benefits an ailing body, a word benefits an ailing soul. Notice, also, that he did not say first "healing every disease and every sickness" but rather "teaching and preaching the gospel of the kingdom" and then "healing." He did this for two reasons. First, because miracles of virtue build souls according to words of compassion. Therefore he says first what he judges to be more necessary. And then, because words of compassion do not set off miraculous powers, but words of truth set off miraculous powers. Therefore it was not believed that Christ was able to do mighty works because he preached

---

[8]PG 57:221; NPNF 1 10:89**. Physical sickness is a sign of the need for a much greater healing, that of the diseases of the soul. We are quick to ask for the healing of the body, while we overlook the more virulent virus. [9]*MKGK* 164. [10]Mk 9:25. [11]GCS 41.1:46.

the truth, but it was believed that he preached the truth because he was able to do mighty works. "They brought to him all who were ill and who were possessed . . . and he cured them."[12] In certain places it says, "And he cured many,"[13] as also "And all who touched him were saved."[14] But here it simply says, "And he cured them," meaning that he cured all. A new doctor going to a city and wishing to spread word of his practice treats all who come to him and does not think so much of receiving a fee as of building a reputation, but when his reputation becomes established he begins to demand a fee depending on his work. So too the Lord at the start of his preaching healed not just certain people depending on his judgment, but everyone indiscriminately. Once the entire region of Judea knew him, he sold the benefits of health at a price keyed to one's faith, saying to each person, "Be it done unto you according to your faith."[15] But not everyone, only those whom he had prepared according to his foreknowledge before they came to him. INCOMPLETE WORK ON MAT-THEW, HOMILY 8.[16]

4:25 Great Crowds Follow Jesus

WE TOO ARE CALLED TO FOLLOW HIM. CHRY-SOSTOM: Now then, let us too follow him. For we also have many diseases of our soul, and these especially he would gladly heal. With this intent he corrects that other sort, that he may banish these out of our soul.

Let us therefore come to him, and let us ask nothing pertaining to this life but rather remission of sins. For indeed he gives it even now, if we come in earnest. Since as then "his fame went out into Syria,"[17] so now into the whole world. And they indeed ran together when they heard that he healed demon-possessed people. And you, after having much more and greater experience of his power, do you not rouse yourself and run?

But whereas they left both country and friends and family, do you not endure so much as to leave your house for the sake of drawing near and obtaining far greater things? Or rather we do not require of you so much as this, but only leave your evil habits, and you can easily be made whole, even while remaining at home with your friends. THE GOSPEL OF MATTHEW, HOM-ILY 14.3.[18]

THE LORD GATHERS HIS ARMY. ANONYMOUS: Every king about to do battle against an enemy king first gathers together an army, then goes off to war. So too the Lord about to do battle with the devil first gathers together his apostles and thus begins to preach the gospel of the kingdom throughout Galilee. The taking of the devil by storm is the preaching of truth; the deadly arrow in his heart is the speaking of righteousness. Overturning him is the work of signs. The stripping of his powers is the conversion of believers. An earthly king gathers together an army that by its efforts he may attain glory. The Lord gathered together his apostles not that by their efforts he might attain glory but that by his own effort he might win victory for them. INCOM-PLETE WORK ON MATTHEW, HOMILY 8.[19]

---

[12]Mk 1:34. [13]Lk 7:21. [14]Mt 14:36. [15]Mt 9:29. [16]PG 56:678-79. [17]Mt 4:24. [18]PG 57:220; NPNF 1 10:89**. [19]PG 56:676-77.

5:1-2 PREFACE TO THE SERMON ON THE MOUNT

[1]*Seeing the crowds, he went up on the mountain, and when he sat down his disciples came to him.* [2]*And he opened his mouth and taught them. . . .*

OVERVIEW: Why did the Lord ascend the mount to deliver his teaching? That he might give the heavenly commandments to his disciples, leaving the earthly and seeking the sublime (CHROMATIUS); that he might bring the people with him to a higher life (JEROME); that the highest teaching of the Father and the Son might be made known (AUGUSTINE); to show us that whoever teaches God's way of justice must embody his own teaching from the heights of spiritual virtue. Hence whoever today wishes to learn the mysteries of truth must go up to the mountain of the church (ANONYMOUS). Jesus taught them according to their readiness to hear, both by his silence and by his speech (CHRYSOSTOM). The severity of the law was first given by Moses on the mountain, but the people were forbidden to draw close. Now with Jesus, all are invited to draw near to him to hear of the gift of the gospel (CHROMATIUS).

5:1 Jesus Ascends the Mountain

BRINGING THE GREAT CROWD TO A HIGHER POINT. JEROME: The Lord went up the mountain that he might bring the crowds with him to higher things. The crowds were unable to go up, however, and he was followed by the disciples to whom he spoke, not standing but sitting together. For they were unable to understand this brilliant man in his majesty. Many of the simple believers literally believed that he taught the Beatitudes and other things on the Mount of Olives, but this is not really true.[1] From the events that went before and followed, the place in Galilee has been shown to be what we believe is either Mount Tabor or some other high mountain. After he finished speaking, the Evangelist says, "Now when he had entered Capernaum." COMMENTARY ON MATTHEW 1.5.1.[2]

ASCENT TO THE HEIGHTS. CHROMATIUS: From the low and humble to the high and exalted places, the Lord, ready to instruct his disciples, went up the mountain—specifically to the Mount of Olives—so that according to the very meaning of this word, he might present the gift of his divine mercy. The Lord went up the mountain that he might give the precepts of the heavenly commandments to his disciples, leaving the earthly and seeking the sublime things as though already placed on high. He went up that he might now give the divine gift of the long-promised blessing, according to what David had once declared: "For indeed he who gave the law will give blessings." TRACTATE ON MATTHEW 17.1.1-2.[3]

THE MOUNT OF MOSES AND THE SERMON ON THE MOUNT. AUGUSTINE: If we ask what the mountain signifies, it is rightly understood to point toward the gospel's higher righteousness. The precepts given to the Hebrews were lower. Yet, through his holy prophets and servants and in accordance with a most orderly arrangement of circumstance, the same God gave the lower precepts to a people to whom it was fitting to be bound by fear. Through his Son he gave the

---

[1]The localization of the mountain here rejected by Jerome must have been widespread. We also find it in Chromatius's interpretation of this passage. [2]CCL 77:23-24. [3]CCL 9a:268.

higher precepts to a people to whom it is fitting to be set free by love. Sermon on the Mount 1.1.2.[4]

Embodied Speech from the Heights of Spiritual Virtue. Anonymous: Wasn't he able to teach right there where the people were? He went up on the mountain for two specific reasons. First, that he might fulfill the prophecy of Isaiah, who said, "Go up to a high mountain, O Zion, herald of good tidings."[5] Next, that he might show the mystery of love. For his ascent signifies the height of virtue. He therefore went up the mountain to show us that whoever teaches and whoever hears God's way of justice must stand on the height of spiritual virtues. The one who teaches must himself be an example of his words, so he may teach more by his works than his words, as the apostle says to Timothy: "Set the believers an example."[6] The one who walks in the valley of earthly life, however, treads on obscure pathways and speaks high-flown words: He does not teach anyone but chastens himself. For no one can stand in the valley and speak from a mountain. Speak from where you take your stand. Take your stand from where you are speaking. Incomplete Work on Matthew, Homily 9.[7]

Looking Toward the Church as the Mighty Mountain. Anonymous: The church is called a mountain. It is pictured in Scripture as the "mountain of God, a mighty mountain."[8] Christ therefore went up the mountain to reveal there the mysteries of truth to his disciples. He showed that whoever wishes to learn the mysteries of truth ought to go up the mountain of the church—not to just any mountain, but to the mighty mountain. For there are mountains of heretics that are not mighty but swollen. On these mountains are revealed not the mysteries of truth but lies that fly in the face of the truth. That is why the Holy Spirit scolds those who go up such mountains when he says through the prophet: "Why do you look with envy, O swollen mountains?"[9] Heretical assemblies are called swollen because their heart is swollen like fat.[10] Incomplete Work on Matthew, Homily 9.[11]

All Are Invited to Come. Chromatius: And that he might more openly show the grace of the apostles and the author of this very great blessing, he added, "They shall walk from strength to strength; God shall look down upon Zion."[12] That is to say, the Son of God, who gave blessings to the apostles on Zion. On this mountain he also gave his apostles a blessing. He is the One who had once handed down the Mosaic law on Mt. Sinai, showing that he was the author of both laws. . . . When the law was first given on the mountain, the people were forbidden to draw close. But now, as the Lord was teaching on the mountain, no one is forbidden. Rather, all are invited that they may hear, because there is severity in the law and grace in the gospel. In the former case, terror is instilled in the unbelievers. In the latter case, a gift of blessings is poured out on the believers. Tractate on Matthew 17.1.3-4.[13]

5:2 Jesus Teaches His Disciples

According to Their Readiness to Hear. Chrysostom: And for what reason is the clause added, "He opened his mouth"? To inform you that in his very silence he gave instruction, and not only when he spoke. At one time he taught by "opening his mouth," while at another by the works that he did.[14] But when you hear that he taught them, do not think of him as discussing matters with his disciples only, but rather with the entire group through his teaching to them. For since the crowd was just like any crowd

---

[4]PL 34:1231; FC 11:20*. Like Moses, Jesus delivers the new law from a mountain. Both are given by the same Lawgiver, the first to bind by fear, the second to set free by love. [5]Is 40:9. [6]1 Tim 4:12. [7]PG 56:679. [8]Ps 68:15 (67:15 LXX). [9]Ps 68:16 (67:16 LXX). [10]Ps 119:70 (118:70 LXX). They swell beyond the limits of revealed teaching. [11]PG 56:680. [12]Ps 84:7 (83:7 LXX). [13]CCL 9a:268-69. [14]His speech was not only through words but also actions.

always is, including as it did those who live on a very low level, he withdrew the group of his disciples and addressed his teaching to them, but in his conversation with them he also provided for the rest, who were at this point very far from being ready to hear his sayings on self-denial

without being offended. THE GOSPEL OF MATTHEW, HOMILY 15.1.[15]

---

[15]PG 57:223; cf. NPNF 1 10:91**. The general public was not yet ready to discern the meaning of Jesus' teaching. Later they will be taught by the disciples.

5:3-12 THE BEATITUDES

[3]*"Blessed are the poor in spirit, for theirs is the kingdom of heaven.*
[4]*"Blessed are those who mourn, for they shall be comforted.*
[5]*"Blessed are the meek, for they shall inherit the earth.*
[6]*"Blessed are those who hunger and thirst for righteousness, for they shall be satisfied.*
[7]*"Blessed are the merciful, for they shall obtain mercy.*
[8]*"Blessed are the pure in heart, for they shall see God.*
[9]*"Blessed are the peacemakers, for they shall be called sons of God.*
[10]*"Blessed are those who are persecuted for righteousness' sake, for theirs is the kingdom of heaven.*
[11]*"Blessed are you when men revile you and persecute you and utter all kinds of evil against you falsely on my account.* [12]*Rejoice and be glad, for your reward is great in heaven, for so men persecuted the prophets who were before you."*

OVERVIEW: One is said to be poor in spirit when one has repented and become humbled like a child (ANONYMOUS). When the prophets announced that God would choose a humbled people who would stand in awe of his words, they anticipated the leading Beatitude: humility of spirit (HILARY). Those are truly blessed who, having spurned the riches of the world, become rich in God (CHROMATIUS). The kingdom is the most fitting life for those who are already practicing virtue. On account of the Holy Spirit these blessed ones are poor by willing freely to be so (JEROME).

Those who mourn are comforted by cessation of the pain of mourning (ANONYMOUS). Mourning in this case does not refer to mourning over death but over sin (JEROME, CHRYSOSTOM).

Those who mourn over the sins of the whole world are especially blessed (CHROMATIUS, ANONYMOUS).

Imbued with the gospel, the meek imitate the gentleness of the Lord (CHROMATIUS). The meek are those who are more content to endure an offense than to commit one (ANONYMOUS). The blessing of the meek is not merely figurative but real. The meek will be blessed in this world and in the world to come (AUGUSTINE, CHRYSOSTOM). As long as this present life is in this corrupted state, it is the land of the dead, subject to vanity; but once it has been liberated from the slavery of corruption to the freedom of the glory of God's children, it becomes the land of the living (ANONYMOUS).

To hunger and thirst for righteousness is to desire God's righteousness alone (ANONYMOUS) and to do nothing else but think of righteousness and search for it (CHROMATIUS). The passion of thirst and the heat and burning of long-suffering are implied in the metaphor of thirsting for righteousness (APOLLINARIS). The thirst for righteousness produces true wealth, which does not fear poverty or tremble at hunger (CHRYSOSTOM). To behold God is the end by which we are to be perfected, not the end by which we come to nothing (AUGUSTINE). The epitome of virtue is the good unmingled with any lesser good, hence the good of God himself (ORIGEN). The reward from God is much greater than that received from others for any human acts of goodness (CHRYSOSTOM). When you hear the voice of a beggar, remember that before God you yourself are a beggar. As you treat your beggar, so will God treat his (AUGUSTINE). One who is truly merciful will show mercy even to one's own enemies (ANONYMOUS).

The pure of heart are those who have gotten rid of sin, cleansed themselves of all the pollution of the flesh and pleased God through works that grow from faith and from the practice of justice (CHROMATIUS). Whoever acts justly and intends so with the mind sees God, for human justice is like God's justice (ANONYMOUS). Unless your heart is pure, you will not be permitted to see what cannot be seen unless the heart be pure. Nothing can satisfy one who would not be satisfied with God (AUGUSTINE).

Peace is present where faith gleams, hope is strengthened and charity is kindled (AUGUSTINE). Christ himself is our peace (ANONYMOUS). The peacemakers are those who guard the peace of the church under the unity of the apostolic teaching (CHROMATIUS). Contentiousness is overcome in this kingdom of peace, where all things are so well ordered inwardly and outwardly that everything that is common to humanity and to the beasts is spontaneously governed by that which is distinctive to humanity, namely, empathic understanding and reason

(AUGUSTINE). The peacemaker is one who demonstrates the harmony of the Scriptures, where others only see a contradiction (CYRIL OF ALEXANDRIA). Those who embody peace within themselves express the reign of God (AUGUSTINE).

Those who undergo persecution for the sake of justice are given grace to endure the hardship without anxiety (AUGUSTINE). In being unjustly reviled, they will receive their blessed reward in heaven (ANONYMOUS). The blessedness of persecution for righteousness' sake is best exemplified by the apostles and with them all those who for the sake of justice are persecuted (CHROMATIUS). One may be persecuted for righteousness' sake not only at the hands of alien peoples but also at the hands of one's own people (ANONYMOUS).

In every Beatitude the blessed are receiving the kingdom of heaven (CHRYSOSTOM). Taking into account the reward of glory, the faithful remain ready to endure every form of suffering that they may be fit partners in God's glory (CHROMATIUS). One who desires what is in heaven does not fear reproaches on earth. So weigh earthly disturbance against heavenly glory (ANONYMOUS).

5:3 The Poor in Spirit

YOU WHO ARE POOR IN SPIRIT. ANONYMOUS: Although the Evangelist Luke explains in part the same Beatitudes, the Beatitudes in Matthew must be considered more complete. The former were spoken on a level plain, whereas the latter were expounded on a mountain. The former were low-key in nature, whereas the latter were well-rounded and more directly addressed to the apostles themselves. The reason for this difference we outlined earlier.[1] Luke simply said "you

---

[1]The interpretation of Luke here is not extant. This author points out the difference between the two accounts and deduces that Jesus preached the Beatitudes twice, in a more complete form for the more mature disciples (Matthew) and a less complete form for the less mature crowds (Luke).

poor,"[2] whereas Matthew said "you poor in spirit." One who is poor in spirit and humble of heart has a meek spirit and does not think great things of himself. On the other hand, one who imagines himself to be rich in spirit will imagine great things of himself. He is proud and does not fulfill the commandment of Christ that "unless you turn and become like children, you will never enter the kingdom of heaven."[3] Only one who has repented and become like a child is poor in spirit. INCOMPLETE WORK ON MATTHEW, HOMILY 9.[4]

PERFECT BLESSEDNESS IS HUMILITY OF SPIRIT. HILARY: "Blessed are the poor in spirit, for theirs is the kingdom of heaven." The Lord taught by way of example that the glory of human ambition must be left behind when he said, "The Lord your God shall you adore and him only shall you serve."[5] And when he announced through the prophets that he would choose a people humble and in awe of his words,[6] he introduced the perfect Beatitude as humility of spirit. Therefore he defines those who are inspired as people aware that they are in possession of the heavenly kingdom.... Nothing belongs to anyone as being properly one's own, but all have the same things by the gift of a single parent. They have been given the first things needed to come into life and have been supplied with the means to use them. ON MATTHEW 4.2.[7]

THE BLESSED POOR, RICH IN GOD. CHROMATIUS: We know many poor people, indeed, who are not merely poor but blessed. For the necessity of poverty does not produce blessedness in each of us, but a devout trust sustained through poverty does. Some, having no worldly resources, continue to sin and remain without faith in God. Clearly we cannot call these people blessed. We must inquire just who are these blessed of whom the Lord says, "Blessed are the poor in spirit, for theirs is the kingdom of heaven." Jesus means that those persons are

truly blessed who, having spurned the riches and resources of the world to become rich in God, desire to be poor in the world. Indeed, such people seem to be poor in the sight of the world, but they are rich in God, needy in the world but wealthy in Christ. TRACTATE ON MATTHEW 17.2.1-2.[8]

FREE HUMILITY, NOT FORCED POVERTY, IS BLESSED. JEROME: This is what we read elsewhere: "He shall save the humble in spirit."[9] But do not imagine that poverty is bred by necessity. For he added "in spirit" so you would understand blessedness to be humility and not poverty. "Blessed are the poor in spirit," who on account of the Holy Spirit are poor by willing freely to be so. Hence, concerning this type of poor, the Savior also speaks through Isaiah: "The Lord has anointed me to preach good tidings to the poor."[10] COMMENTARY ON MATTHEW 1.5.3.[11]

THE KINGDOM IS FITTING FOR THOSE WHO PRACTICE VIRTUE. ANONYMOUS: What does it mean that theirs is the kingdom of heaven? Is not the kingdom fitted for those who practice virtue? Even as the road to hell is lined with all the vices, and especially pride, all the virtues lead toward the kingdom of heaven, and especially humility. For the root of all evil is pride, and the root of all good is humility.[12] It is only fitting that one who exalts himself shall be humbled, and one who humbles himself shall be exalted. INCOMPLETE WORK ON MATTHEW, HOMILY 9.[13]

5:4 Those Who Mourn

MOURNING UNREPENTED SIN. JEROME: The mourning discussed here does not concern the common natural law of the dead but rather their

[2]Lk 6:20. [3]Mt 18:3. [4]PG 56:680. [5]Mt 4:10. [6]See Is 66:2. [7]SC 254:120-22. [8]CCL 9a:269. [9]Ps 34:18 (33:18 LXX). [10]Is 61:1. [11]CCL 77:24. [12]Cf. Lk 14:11. [13]PG 56:680-81.

sins and vices. Thus Samuel grieved over Saul,[14] and the Lord repented that he had made Saul king over Israel.[15] Also Paul the apostle says that he wept and mourned over those who, after committing fornication and impure deeds, did not feel the need of repentance.[16] Commentary on Matthew 1.5.4.[17]

Mourning the Sins of the World. Chromatius: As with Jesus' earlier teaching on the poor, here too he speaks of those who mourn. The blessed of whom he speaks are not those bereaving the death of a spouse or the loss of cherished servants. Rather, he is speaking of those blessed persons who . . . do not cease to mourn over the iniquity of the world or the offenses of sinners with a pious, duty-bound sentiment. To those who mourn righteously, therefore, they will receive, and not undeservedly, the consolation of eternal rejoicing promised by the Lord. Tractate on Matthew 17.3.1-2.[18]

A Greater Blessedness. Anonymous: Those who mourn their own sins are indeed blessed, but blessed in a less wonderful way than those who mourn the sins of others. Those who mourn the sins of others are less likely to have sins of their own to mourn. These are the ones who should be called teachers. They are with the Lord on the mountain. Incomplete Work on Matthew, Homily 9.[19]

Intense Grief over Sin. Chrysostom: He calls blessed even those who mourn. Their sorrow is of a special kind. He did not designate them simply as sad but as intensely grieving. Therefore he did not say "they that sorrow" but "they that mourn." This Beatitude is designed to draw believers toward a Christian disposition. Those who grieve for someone else—their child or wife or any other lost relation—have no fondness for gain or pleasure during the period of their sorrow. They do not aim at glory. They are not provoked by insults nor led captive by envy nor beset by any other passion. Their grief alone occupies the whole of their attention. The Gospel of Matthew, Homily 15.3.[20]

Mourners to Be Comforted. Anonymous: Those who mourn receive comfort when the pain of mourning ceases. Those who mourn over their own sins and have obtained forgiveness shall be comforted in this world. Those who mourn over the sins of others will be comforted in the future age to come. As long as they are in the world, not knowing the outcomes of God's providence and not fully understanding those who have fallen under the sway of the devil's influence, they mourn over all sinners, even those who without evil intention yet do evil. They see all sinners as buffeted by the devil. They clearly see that God's own cannot perish and those who perish are not of God. No one can escape from the hands of God. Once their mourning has ended, however, they shall be comforted. Without further suffering, they shall rejoice in their blessedness. Incomplete Work on Matthew, Homily 9.[21]

5:5 The Meek

Imitating the Lord's Meekness. Chromatius: The meek are those who are gentle, humble and unassuming, simple in faith and patient in the face of every affront. Imbued with the precepts of the gospel, they imitate the meekness of the Lord, who says, "Learn from me, for I am meek and humble of heart."[22] Moses found the greatest favor with God because he was meek. It was written about him: "And Moses was the meekest of all people on earth."[23] Furthermore, we read in David's psalm: "Be mindful, O Lord, of David and his great meekness."[24] Tractate on Matthew 17.4.1-2.[25]

---

[14]1 Sam 15:11. [15]1 Sam 15:35. [16]2 Cor 12:21. [17]CCL 77:24-25. [18]CCL 9a:271. [19]PG 56:681. [20] PG 57:225-26; NPNF 1 10:93**. [21]PG 56:681. [22]Mt 11:29. [23]Num 12:3. [24]Ps 132:1 (131:1 LXX). [25]CCL 9a:272.

ENDURING OFFENSES. ANONYMOUS: A gentle person neither provokes evil nor is provoked by evil. Charges of sin do not prevail against such persons insofar as they are not the cause of sin. The meek one is more content to endure an offense than to commit one. For unless one is unafraid of being offended, one cannot be without sin. For even as weeds are never lacking in a field, provokers are never lacking in the world. Therefore that person is truly gentle who, when he or she has been offended, neither does evil nor even thinks of doing it. INCOMPLETE WORK ON MATTHEW, HOMILY 9.[26]

A PRESENT BLESSING. CHRYSOSTOM: Tell me, what kind of earth is referred to here? Some say a figurative earth, but this is not what he is talking about.[27] For nowhere in Scripture do we find any mention of an earth that is merely figurative. But what can this Beatitude mean? Jesus holds out a prize perceptible to the senses, even as Paul also does. For even when Moses had said, "Honor your father and your mother," he added, "For so shall you live long upon the earth."[28] And Jesus himself says again to the thief, "Today you shall be with me in paradise."[29] Today! In this way he does not speak only of future blessings but also of present ones. THE GOSPEL OF MATTHEW, HOMILY 15.3.[30]

A PERPETUAL INHERITANCE. AUGUSTINE: "Inherit the earth," I believe, means the land promised in the psalm:[31] "Thou art my hope, my portion in the land of the living."[32] It signifies the solidity and stability of a perpetual inheritance. The soul because of its good disposition is at rest as though in its own place, like a body on the earth, and is fed with its own food there, like a body from the earth. This is the peaceful life of the saints. The meek are those who submit to wickedness and do not resist evil but overcome evil with good.[33] Let the haughty therefore quarrel and contend for earthly and temporal things. But "blessed are the meek, for they shall inherit the land." This is the land from which they can-

not be expelled. SERMON ON THE MOUNT 1.2.4.[34]

ETERNAL BEINGS WILL INHERIT AN ETERNAL LAND. ANONYMOUS: The psalmist wrote, "I believe that I shall see the goodness of the Lord in the land of the living."[35] But some say that as long as this land is in this corrupted state, it is the land of the dead, for it is subject to the worthless and empty. But once it has been liberated from the slavery of corruption to the freedom of the glory of God's children, it becomes the land of the living, so that immortals inherit immortality. According to another commentator, it is a sort of heaven in which the saints are about to live; hence it is called the land of the living. As to our lower region, it is earth; but as to the heaven above, it is called the land of the living. Others say that our body is on earth and as long as it is subject to death, it is the land of the dead. When the body has been transformed, however, and made to conform with the body of Christ's glory, it will dwell in the land of the living. Eternal beings will inherit it as an eternal land, and spiritual beings and saints as a spiritual and holy land. INCOMPLETE WORK ON MATTHEW, HOMILY 9.[36]

5:6 Those Who Hunger and Thirst for Righteousness

GOD IS THE TRUE VIRTUE. ORIGEN: But if I must utilize a bold explanation indeed, I think that perhaps it was through the word that is measured by virtue and justice that the Lord

---

[26]PG 56:681. [27]Chrysostom argues against interpretations of the earth, particularly those of Alexandrian character (Origen), which he considers excessively spiritualistic. [28]Eph 6:2-3. [29]Lk 23:43. [30]PG 57:226; NPNF 1 10:93**. The blessing of the meek is not merely figurative but earthly. The meek will be blessed in this present world and in the world to come. [31]Addressed to God. [32]Ps 142:5 (141:5 LXX). [33]Rom 12:21. [34]PL 34:1232; FC 11:22; NPNF 1 10:93. The land the meek shall inherit is a land from which they cannot be expelled. [35]Ps 27:13 (26:13 LXX). [36]PG 56:681-82. The land of the living that the meek will inherit is the perpetual inheritance of eternal life with God.

presents himself to the desire of the hearers. He was born as wisdom from God for us, and as justice and sanctification and redemption.[37] He is "the bread that comes down from heaven"[38] and "living water,"[39] for which the great David himself thirsted. He said in one of his psalms, "My soul has thirsted for you, even for the living God; when shall I come and appear before the face of God?"[40] . . . "I shall behold your face in righteousness; I shall be satisfied in beholding your glory."[41] This then, in my estimation, is the true virtue, the good unmingled with any lesser good, that is, God, the virtue that covers the heavens, as Habakkuk relates.[42] FRAGMENT 83.[43]

THE PASSIONATE LONGING FOR JUSTICE. CHROMATIUS: He taught that we must seek after righteousness with earnest desire, not with fainthearted energy. Indeed, he calls those persons blessed who in their search for righteousness virtually burn with passionate longing in their hunger and thirst. For if each one of us really hungers and thirsts for righteousness with eager desire, we can do nothing else but think and seek after righteousness. It is necessary that we eagerly desire that for which we hunger and thirst. TRACTATE ON MATTHEW 17.5.1.[44]

TRANSFERING DESIRE TO A NEW OBJECT. CHRYSOSTOM: Note how drastically he expresses it. For Jesus does not say, "Blessed are those who cling to righteousness," but "Blessed are those who hunger and thirst after righteousness"—not in a superficial way but pursuing it with their entire desire. By contrast, the most characteristic feature of covetousness is a strong desire with which we are not so hungry for food and drink as for more and more things. Jesus urged us to transfer this desire to a new object, freedom from covetousness. THE GOSPEL OF MATTHEW, HOMILY 15.4.[45]

THIRSTING FOR RIGHTEOUSNESS. APOLLINARIS: When Luke mentions these blessed ones, he calls them simply those "who hun-

ger."[46] But Matthew here defines them as those who willingly and from a longing for the good abstain from fleshly pleasures. Both of them speak in a similar way. Whoever longs for the righteousness of God has found what is truly desirable. But the yearning for righteousness is not satisfied by analogy to the appetite alone. For brotherhood in justice is desired not merely as food. That is only half the total picture. But now he has also represented this yearning as analogous to thirst for something to drink. By the passion of thirst he intends to indicate the heat and burning of intense longing. He says that such a person "will be filled." But such fulfillment does not produce a turning away but rather an intensification of the desire. FRAGMENT 11.[47]

THE DOCILE HEART. ANONYMOUS: To hunger and thirst for righteousness is to desire God's own righteousness. People should hear and do God's righteousness, not as though they hear or do it unwillingly but from their heart's desire. Every good that is not done out of this sort of love for righteousness is not pleasing to God. Hence the Lord, through John, does not simply call everyone to drink, but only those who are thirsty, saying, "If anyone thirst, let that one come to me and drink."[48] Similarly it was not for nothing that he spoke of those who "hunger and thirst for righteousness." Whoever hungers for righteousness wants to live actively according to God's righteousness; this is proper for the person with a good heart. One who thirsts for righteousness wants to acquire the knowledge of God that one can gain only by studying the Scriptures. This is fitting for the person with an attentive heart. "For they shall be satisfied." They are filled with the abundance of God's reward. Greater are the rewards of God than even the most avid desires of the saints. INCOM-

---

[37]1 Cor 1:30. [38]Jn 6:50. [39]Jn 4:10-11. [40]Ps 42:2 (41:2 LXX). [41]Ps 17:15 (16:15 LXX). [42]Hab 3:3. [43]GCS 41.1:49. [44]CCL 9a:273. [45]PG 57:227; NPNF 1 10:94**. [46]Lk 6:21. [47]MKGK 4. [48]Jn 7:37.

PLETE WORK ON MATTHEW, HOMILY 9.[49]

THE PROMISE OF FULFILLMENT. CHROMATIUS: Rightly then the One who is the heavenly bread and the fountain of living waters promises in return to those who thus hunger and thirst the fullness of perpetual refreshment: "Blessed are those who hunger and thirst for righteousness, for they shall be satisfied." This indeed is that righteousness of faith that comes from God and Christ, of which the apostle says, "The righteousness of God through faith in Jesus Christ in all and upon all who believe in him."[50] TRACTATE ON MATTHEW 17.5.2.[51]

THEY SHALL BE FILLED. CHRYSOSTOM: Then he designates the prize, again by analogy with things sensible, saying, "for they shall be filled." Thus, because it is commonly thought that the rich are made wealthy through their own greed, Jesus says in effect: "No, it is just the opposite. For it is righteousness that produces true wealth. Thus so long as you act righteously, you do not fear poverty or tremble at hunger. Rather those who extort are those who lose all, while one who is in love with righteousness possesses all other goods in safety." If those who do not covet enjoy such great abundance, how much more will they be ready to offer to others what they have. THE GOSPEL OF MATTHEW, HOMILY 15.4.[52]

5:7 The Merciful

BLESSED BY THE LORD OF COMPASSION. CHROMATIUS: By a great number of witnesses indeed, just as many in the Old Testament as the New, we are called by the Lord to show compassion. But as a shortcut to faith we deem enough and more than enough what the Lord himself in the passage at hand expresses with his own voice, saying, "Blessed are the compassionate, for God will have compassion for them." The Lord of compassion says that the compassionate are blessed. No one can obtain

God's compassion unless that one is also compassionate. In another passage he said, "Be compassionate, just as your Father who is in the heavens is compassionate."[53] TRACTATE ON MATTHEW 17.6.1-2.[54]

THE REWARD OF COMPASSION. CHRYSOSTOM: Jesus speaks here not only of those who show mercy by giving worldly goods but also of those who demonstrate mercy in their actions. There are many ways to show mercy. The commandment is broad in its implications. What reward can people expect if they obey the commandment? "They obtain mercy."

The reward at first glance appears to be an equal reimbursement, but actually the reward from God is much greater than human acts of goodness. For whereas we ourselves are showing mercy as human beings, we are obtaining mercy from the God of all. Human mercy and God's mercy are not the same thing. As wide as the interval is between corrupted and perfect goodness, so far is human mercy distinguished from divine mercy. THE GOSPEL OF MATTHEW, HOMILY 15.4.[55]

AS BEGGARS IN GOD'S PRESENCE. AUGUSTINE: Hear what follows: "Blessed are the compassionate, for God will have compassion on them." Do this, and it will be done to you. Do it in regard to another that it might be done in regard to you. For you may overflow yet remain in need. You may overflow with temporal things but remain in need of eternal life. You hear the voice of a beggar, but before God you are yourself a beggar. Someone is begging from you, while you yourself are begging. As you treat your beggar, so will God treat his. You who are empty are being filled. Out of your fullness fill an empty person in need, so that your own

---

[49]PG 56:682. [50]Rom 3:22. [51]CCL 9a:273. [52]PG 57:227; NPNF 1 10:94**. [53]Lk 6:36. [54]CCL 9a:274; PG 57:227; NPNF 1 10:94**. God's mercy infinitely exceeds the best of our merciful actions. [55]PG 57:227; NPNF 1 10:94.

emptiness may be again filled by the fullness of God. SERMON 53.5.[56]

MERCY TOWARD ENEMIES. ANONYMOUS: The kind of compassion referred to here is not simply giving alms to the poor or orphan or widow. This kind of compassion is often found even among those who hardly know God. But that person is truly compassionate who shows compassion even to his own enemy and treats the enemy well. For it is written, "Love your enemies, and treat well those who hate you."[57] Remember that God too sends his rain and asks his sun to rise not only over the grateful but also over the ungrateful.[58] So Jesus calls us to "be compassionate, just as your Father is compassionate."[59] Such a person is truly blessed, for if in fact he hasn't sinned, which is difficult for us all, God's grace helps him along in increasing his sense of justice. So he prays, "Forgive me my debts, just as I too forgive my debtors." INCOMPLETE WORK ON MATTHEW, HOMILY 9.[60]

5:8 The Pure in Heart

THE PROMISE OF SEEING GOD. CHRYSOSTOM: Note that the reward is spiritual. Those he here calls "pure" are either those who have so fully filled their lives with goodness that they are practically unaware of evil within themselves, or he may be referring to those who live a moderate, simple life, or there is nothing that we need so much in order to behold God as a self-controlled life. In the same vein Paul wrote, "Pursue peace with everyone and the holiness without which no one will see the Lord."[61] He is here speaking of such sight as it is possible for one to have.[62] For there are many who show mercy, who refuse to rob others and who are not covetous but who still may remain entangled in sins like fornication and licentiousness. Jesus adds these words to indicate that the former virtues do not suffice in and of themselves. Paul, writing to the Corinthians, bore witness concerning the Macedonians, who were rich not only in alms-

giving but also in the rest of the virtues. For having spoken of the generous spirit they demonstrated toward their own possessions, Paul says, "They gave themselves to the Lord and to us."[63] THE GOSPEL OF MATTHEW, HOMILY 15.4.[64]

WHAT ONLY THE PURE HEART CAN BEHOLD. AUGUSTINE: Mark well what follows. When the text says "blessed are the pure in heart," it refers to those who have been made clean within, for they shall see God. To behold God is the end and purpose of all our loving activity. But it is the end by which we are to be perfected, not the end by which we come to nothing. Note that food is finished in a different way than a garment is finished. Food is finished when it is consumed in the eating. A garment is finished when it is completed in the weaving. Both are finished, but the former's finish means destruction; the latter's, perfection. Whatever we do, whatever good deeds we perform, whatever we strive to accomplish, whatever we laudably yearn for, whatever we blamelessly desire, we shall no longer be seeking any of those things when we reach the vision of God. Indeed, what would one search for when one has God before one's eyes? Or what would satisfy one who would not be satisfied with God? Yes, we wish to see God. Who does not have this desire? We strive to see God. We are on fire with the desire of seeing God. But pay attention to the saying, "Blessed are the pure of heart, for they shall see God." Provide yourself with this means of seeing God. Let me speak concretely: Why would you, while your eyes are bleary, desire to see a sunrise? Let the eyes be sound, and that light will be full of joy. If your eyes are blind, that light itself will be a torment. Unless your heart is pure, you will not be permitted to see what

---

[56]PL 38:366; FC 11:213-14. As we are beggars before God, we should treat beggars as we would be treated. [57]Lk 6:27. [58]Mt 5:45. [59]Lk 6:36. [60]PG 56:682. [61]Heb 12:14. [62]Not of that which is beyond our finitude. [63]2 Cor 8:5. [64]PG 57:227-28; NPNF 1 10:94**.

cannot be seen unless the heart be pure. SER-
MON 53.6.[65]

SEEING GOD FACE TO FACE. CHROMATIUS: The
pure of heart are those who have gotten rid of
sin's filth, have cleansed themselves of all the
pollution of the flesh and have pleased God
through works of faith and justice. As David testifies in a psalm, "Who will climb up the Lord's
mountain, or who will stand in his holy place?
The one with innocent hands and a pure heart,
who has not received his soul in vain."[66] And
David, rightly knowing that God can be seen
only with a pure heart, prays as follows in the
psalm, "Create in me a clean heart, O God, and
renew a right spirit within me."[67] So the Lord
shows that it is pure-hearted people like this
who are blessed. They are those who, living by
faith in God with a pure mind and unstained
conscience, will win the right to see the God of
glory in the heavenly kingdom to come, "no
longer in a mirror and in riddles, but face to
face," as the apostle has said.[68] TRACTATE ON
MATTHEW 17.6.3-4.[69]

SEEING GOD IN CREATION. APOLLINARIS: He
calls "pure of heart" here those who have
acquired virtue in general. Showing the inade-
quacy of what he had said before, he adds "for
they shall see God." Why then is it said that "no
one has seen God at any time"?[70] We maintain
that he is seen and understood by reason. Either
we may see God through the holy Scriptures
with the eyes of the understanding, or again,
through the wisdom visible in the universe it is
possible to see, in a conjectural sort of way, him
who made it. God is seen in the same way that
in objects made by human beings, the maker of a
given work is, after a certain manner, seen by
the intellect. But what is seen is not the nature
of the artificer but only his or her artistic skill.
So also, whoever sees God by looking at the creation gains an impression not of the essence but
of the wisdom of the One who has made all
things. Therefore the Lord tells the truth when

proclaiming that God is seen by the pure in
heart, while at the same time the Scripture does
not lie when it asserts that God has not been
seen nor can be seen. FRAGMENT 13.[71]

**SEEING GOD IN THIS AGE AND IN THE AGE TO
COME.** ANONYMOUS: "Blessed are those with a
pure heart, for they will see God." There are two
ways of seeing God: in this age and in the age to
come. In this age, as has been written, "He who
sees me sees my Father, too."[72] For they have a
pure heart who not only do no evil and intend
no evil but who also always do and intend everything good. For it is possible now and then to do
good but not to intend it. Those who do so may
do good, but not on account of God. And God
does not reward such good, for the good
rewarded by God isn't the one that is merely
done but the one that is well done. Moreover, a
person who does good on account of God no
doubt also intends the good. So whoever acts
entirely justly and intends so with his mind sees
God, for justice is the likeness of God. For God
is just. So, to the extent that anybody has torn
himself from evils and done good things, to that
extent he also sees God, either dimly or clearly,
or slightly or to a greater degree, or partly or
completely, or now and then or always, or in
accordance with human possibility. In this very
way, a person too who acts and intends in an evil
way sees the devil, for every evil is the symbol of
the devil. In that age, however, those pure in
heart in this way will see God face to face, no
longer in a mirror darkly,[73] as is the case here.
INCOMPLETE WORK ON MATTHEW, HOMILY 9.[74]

5:9 The Peacemakers

GUARDING THE PEACE OF THE CHURCH.
CHROMATIUS: The peacemakers are those who,
standing apart from the stumbling block of

---

[65]PL 38:366; FC 11:214. [66]Ps 24:3-4 (23:3-4 LXX). [67]Ps 51:10
(50:10 LXX). [68]1 Cor 13:12. [69]CCL 9a:274-75. [70]Jn 1:18. [71]MKGK
5. [72]Jn 14:9. [73]1 Cor 13:12. [74]PG 56:682.

disagreement and discord, guard the affection of fraternal love and the peace of the church under the unity of the universal faith. And the Lord in the Gospel particularly urges his disciples to guard this peace, saying, "I give you my peace; I leave you my peace."[75] David earlier testified that the Lord would give this peace to his church, saying, "I will listen to what the Lord speaks in me, for he will pronounce his peace to his people and upon his holy ones and to those who turn to him."[76] TRACTATE ON MATTHEW 17.7.1-2.[77]

WHERE PEACE IS. AUGUSTINE: There is in the inner person a kind of daily quarrel; a praise-worthy battle acts to keep what is better from being overcome by what is worse. The struggle is to keep desire from conquering the mind and to keep lust from conquering wisdom. This is the steadfast peace that you ought to develop in yourself, that what is better in you may be in charge of what is worse. The better part in you, moreover, is that part in which God's image is found. This is called the mind, the intellect. There faith burns, there hope is strengthened, there charity is kindled. SERMON 53A.12.[78]

THE PEACEMAKER. CYRIL OF ALEXANDRIA: The peacemaker is the one who demonstrates the harmony of the Scriptures, where others see only a contradiction: the Old with the New, the law with the prophets, Gospel with Gospel.[79] Accordingly, having imitated the Son of God, "he shall be called a son," having by his work grasped of the "spirit of adoption."[80] FRAGMENT 38.[81]

CHRIST IS OUR PEACE. ANONYMOUS: Peace is the only begotten God, of whom the apostle says, "For he himself is our peace." So people who cherish peace are children of peace. But some may be thought to be peacemakers who make peace with their enemies but remain heedless of evils within. They are never reconciled in heart with their own internal enemies, yet they

are willing to make peace with others. They are parodies of peace rather than lovers of peace. For that peace is blessed which is set in the heart, not that which is set in words. Do you want to know who is truly a peacemaker? Hear the prophet, who says, "Keep your tongue from evil, and let your lips not speak deceit. Do not let your tongue utter an evil expression."[82] INCOMPLETE WORK ON MATTHEW, HOMILY 9.[83]

THE BLESSINGS OF PEACE. CHRYSOSTOM: Here he not only responds that they should not feud and become hateful to one another, but he is also looking for something else and something more, that we bring together others who are feuding. And again he promises a spiritual reward. What kind of reward is it? "That they themselves shall be called sons of God." For in fact this was the crucial work of the Only Begotten: to bring together things divided and to reconcile the alienated. THE GOSPEL OF MATTHEW, HOMILY 15.4.[84]

AN EXPRESSION OF THE COMING REIGN OF GOD. AUGUSTINE: Where there is no contention, there is perfect peace. And that is why the children of God are peacemakers, because nothing can finally stand against God. In this way the children possess a likeness to God the Father. And those who calm their passions and subject them to reason, to mind and spirit, and who keep their carnal lusts under control engender peace within themselves. Thereby they themselves become the kingdom of God. In this kingdom all things are so well ordered that everything in humanity that is common to us

---

[75]Jn 14:27. [76]Ps 85:8 (84:8 LXX). [77]CCL 9a:275. [78]MA 1:633; WSA 3 3:83. [79]For Cyril the peacemaker is the one able to stress the unity and harmony of the Scriptures. Cyril takes aim at the heretics (Gnostics, Marcionites and Manichaeans) who divided the Old Testament from the New, but he also challenges those people (particularly pagan polemicists such as Porphyry and Julian) who pointed out contradictions between books of the Scriptures or Gospels. [80]Rom 8:15. [81]MKGK 164-65. [82]Ps 34:13-14 (33:13-14 LXX). [83]PG 56:682. [84]PG 57:228; cf. NPNF 1 10:94-95. God's saving work is peacemaking.

and to the beasts is spontaneously governed by that which is chief and preeminent in humanity, namely, the reasoning mind. This preeminent human faculty is itself subject to a still higher power, which is Truth itself, the only begotten Son of God. SERMON ON THE MOUNT 1.2.9.[85]

5:10 Those Who Are Persecuted

PERSECUTION FOR RIGHTEOUSNESS' SAKE. CHROMATIUS: Not without reason did the Lord previously mention hungering and thirsting for justice. He instructs us so to thirst in our desire for justice that for its sake we should despise the world's persecutions, the punishments of the body and death itself. The martyrs above all are the epitome of those who for the righteousness of faith and the name of Christ endure persecution in this world. To them a great hope is promised, namely, the possession of the kingdom of heaven. The apostles were chief examples of this blessedness, and with them all the just people who for the sake of righteousness were afflicted with various persecutions. Due to their faith they have come into the heavenly realms. TRACTATE ON MATTHEW 17.8.1-2.[86]

THREE CROSSES. AUGUSTINE: "For the sake of justice." This addition clearly distinguishes the martyr from the robber. For the robber too in return for evil deeds suffers at the law's hand and doesn't ask for a prize or garland but instead pays the due penalty. It is not the penalty as such but the basis for the penalty that makes the martyr. Let us first choose the right reason, and then let us endure the penalty without anxiety.

There were three crosses in a single place when Christ suffered: he himself was in the middle, and at his two sides were two robbers. Look at the penalty: it is similar for all three. Yet one of the robbers found paradise on the cross. The man in the middle, judging, condemns the proud man and receives the humble man. That piece of wood served as a judgment seat for Christ. He who judges, who is able to make the judgment correctly, says to the robber who confessed: "Truly I tell you, today you will be with me in paradise."[87] For the robber was humbling himself. Note what he had so simply said, "Remember me, Lord, when you come to your kingdom."[88] The implication: I know my evil deeds. May I continually be crucified until you come. And because everybody who lowers himself shall be lifted up, Christ immediately expressed his thought and showed his mercy. SERMON 53A.13.[89]

ON PERSECUTION BY YOUR OWN PEOPLE. ANONYMOUS: We are not to suppose that this refers only to those who suffer persecution from alien nations for not worshiping idols. This refers also to those who are blessed for not abandoning the truth when they suffer persecution from heretics.[90] They too suffer for the sake of righteousness. While the heathen nations deny Christ, the heretics deny Christ's truth. Those who deny Christ's truth deny Christ himself. For Christ is the truth. And so the heretics, who undertake persecution not on account of Christ but on account of Christ's supposed truth, while they at first sight seem to be Christians, in fact are heathen in their mode of justice. If such people persecute you, you are blessed in the same way as John the Baptist was blessed under persecution. For John was killed neither because he was heathen nor because of heresy but on moral grounds, because he kept reproaching Herod for his adultery. In fact, all the prophets were killed by their own people, not by heathen kings. If, however, it is true that the prophets are martyrs, there is no doubt that a person who suffers something for God's cause today, even if one suffers it at the hands of one's own people, receives an eternal reward. INCOMPLETE WORK ON MATTHEW, HOMILY 9.[91]

---

[85]PL 34:1233; FC 11:23-24. [86]CCL 9a:276-77. [87]Lk 23:43. [88]Lk 23:42. [89]MA 1:634; WSA 3 3:83-84. [90]Supposed Christians who deny the apostolic witness. [91]PG 56:683.

5:11 *Those Who Are Reviled*

FALSELY ON CHRIST'S ACCOUNT. CHRYSOS-TOM: But to keep you from supposing that being slandered of itself makes people blessed, he has added two qualifications: first, that it happens for Christ's sake, and second, that what is said be false. Do not expect to be blessed if you are being reviled for something evil, and what is being said is true. THE GOSPEL OF MATTHEW, HOMILY 15.4.[92]

WHEN PEOPLE REVILE YOU. ANONYMOUS: He has just been speaking about enduring persecution. Now it is as if someone were asking God: God, what if we are not enduring persecution for your sake or for the sake of justice? What if we are facing the reproach and the evil talk of wicked people? You will be blessed, Jesus says, "not only if you endure persecution but also if others utter all kinds of evil against you falsely on my account." Many people become our enemies because of our belief in God, but they do not persecute us openly. Maybe they do not have the power to persecute.[93] Nevertheless they go all about and slander us and say deplorable things about us. The Scripture says, "You will be blessed when people revile you and persecute you and utter all kinds of evil against you falsely on my account." So your reward does not end the moment you have given a glass of water compassionately. If somebody wrongs us, even with a single, slight word, your soul will not be lacking a reward. INCOMPLETE WORK ON MATTHEW, HOMILY 9.[94]

5:12 *Rejoice, for Your Reward Is Great*

ENDURING PERSECUTION. CHROMATIUS: Not only should we patiently endure all the horrible treacheries of the persecutors that can be contrived in a time of persecution for Christ's name against the just, or the various reproaches that can be heaped upon us, or the punishments that can be applied to the body, but we should even welcome them with exultation because of the coming glory. For he says, "Rejoice in that day and exult; I tell you this, because your reward is great in heaven." How glorious is the endurance of this persecution, the reward for which the Lord says is in heaven! And so, taking into account the reward of the proposed glory, we should be ready with devout faith for every endurance of suffering, so that we may be ready to be made partners in the prophets' glory. TRACTATE ON MATTHEW 17.9.2-3.[95]

THE CONTEXT OF THE KINGDOM OF HEAVEN. CHRYSOSTOM: Look then at the reward again: "for your reward is great in heaven." And don't be discouraged if you don't hear the kingdom of heaven granted with every single Beatitude. For even if Jesus names the rewards differently, he still puts all of them in the kingdom of heaven. For in fact he says, "Those who mourn will be comforted, and those who show mercy will receive mercy, and those pure in heart will see God, and the peacemakers will be called sons of God." In all these things the blessed One does nothing but hint at the kingdom of heaven. For people who enjoy these things will certainly reach the kingdom of heaven. So do not suppose that the reward of the kingdom of heaven belongs only to the poor in spirit. It also belongs to those who hunger for justice, and to the meek and to all these blessed others without exception. For he set his blessing upon all these things to keep you from expecting something belonging to this material world. For if one wore a prize or garland for things that are to be dissolved together with the present life, things that flit away faster than a shadow, would that one be blessed? THE GOSPEL OF MATTHEW, HOMILY 15.5.[96]

---

[92]PG 57:228; NPNF 1 10:95. [93]The author writes at a time when Christianity has become the state religion. Consequently, by *persecution* he means the hostility still shown by pagans toward the Christian religion, which only in exceptional cases exhibited itself in acts of open violence. [94]PG 56:683-84. [95]CCL 9a:277. [96]PG 57:228; NPNF 1 10:95.

WEIGH EARTHLY DISTURBANCE AGAINST HEAVENLY GLORY. ANONYMOUS: Weigh earthly shame against heavenly glory, and see whether what you suffer on earth is not much lighter than what you expect in heaven. But perhaps you may say, "Who can be joyful when reviled? Who can not only endure being reviled but rejoice in it with a great soul?" The answer is, only one who does not delight in empty glory. One who desires what is in heaven does not fear reproaches on earth. He does not care about what people say about him but rather how God judges him. But one who rejoices in the praise of others and how much they praise him is saddened when he receives no praise. He feels sad at others' reproaches. But a person who is not lifted up by others' praise is not lowered by their reproach. Wherever any one seeks his own glory, just there he also fears reproach. A person who constantly seeks glory on earth constantly fears troubles on earth. But a person who seeks glory only with God fears no disturbance except for God's judgment. A soldier endures the danger of war so long as he hopes for the spoils of victory. So how much more should you who are waiting for the reward of the heavenly kingdom have no fear of the world's reproaches. INCOMPLETE WORK ON MATTHEW, HOMILY 9.[97]

[97]PG 56:684.

5:13-16 SALT AND LIGHT

[13]*"You are the salt of the earth; but if salt has lost its taste, how shall its saltness be restored? It is no longer good for anything except to be thrown out and trodden under foot by men.*

[14]*"You are the light of the world. A city set on a hill cannot be hid.* [15]*Nor do men light a lamp and put it under a bushel, but on a stand, and it gives light to all in the house.* [16]*Let your light so shine before men, that they may see your good works and give glory to your Father who is in heaven."*

OVERVIEW: As salt preserves meat from decaying, so also do Christ's disciples have a preservative effect (ORIGEN). The disciples must not lose their delightful taste (HILARY, CHROMATIUS). Those who have been educated for heavenly wisdom ought to remain steadfast so as not to be made tasteless by the devil's treachery (CHROMATIUS). They are called to restore to the whole created order its original succulence, which has degenerated into rottenness (CHRYSOSTOM). Jesus calls salt the frame of mind that is filled with the apostolic word. When it has been sowed in our souls, it allows the word of wisdom to dwell in us (CYRIL OF ALEXANDRIA). It is only as they become salt, penetrating the taste and texture of the world, that they refract God's illumination of the world through the light of his Truth (CHRYSOSTOM). Jesus' disciples are called the light of the world because they are illumined by One who is the true and eternal light (CHROMATIUS, CHRYSOSTOM). The worldly are less like lamps than buckets (THEODORE of MOPSUESTIA), lacking in God, empty from above but full from below (CHRYSOSTOM). The leader of the church should be equipped with the widest range of virtues (ANONYMOUS).

5:13 *The Salt of the Earth*

SALT PRESERVES FOODS. ORIGEN: Salt is useful for so many purposes in human life! What need is there to speak about this? Now is the proper time to say why Jesus' disciples are compared with salt. Salt preserves meats from decaying into stench and worms. It makes them edible for a longer period. They would not last through time and be found useful without salt. So also Christ's disciples, standing in the way of the stench that comes from the sins of idolatry and fornication, support and hold together this whole earthly realm. FRAGMENT 91.[1]

RESISTANCE TO CORRUPTION. HILARY: The salt of the earth, I suppose, seems at first like nothing special. So what did Jesus mean when he called the apostles the "salt of the earth"? We must look for the words' appropriate meaning. Both the apostles' task and the nature of salt itself will reveal this. The element of water and the element of fire are combined and united in salt. So ordinary salt, made for the use of the human race, imparts resistance to corruption to the meats on which it is sprinkled. And, of course, it is very apt to add the sensation of hidden flavor. Likewise the apostles are the preachers of surprising heavenly things and eternity. Like sowers, they sow immortality on all bodies on which their discourse has been sprinkled. They are perfected by the baptism of water and fire. So those who are to be salted with the power of gospel teaching have rightly been called the "salt of the earth." They are right now being preserved to the end. ON MATTHEW 4.10.[2]

THE WORD SOWN IN OUR SOULS. CYRIL OF ALEXANDRIA: He calls "salt" the frame of mind that is filled with the apostolic word, which is full of understanding. When it has been sown in our souls, it allows the word of wisdom to dwell in us. It has been compared with salt because of salt's good taste and delightfulness. For without salt neither bread nor fish is edible. So too without the apostles' understanding and instruction, every soul is dull and unwholesome and unpleasant to God. FRAGMENT 41.[3]

DO NOT LOSE YOUR DELIGHTFUL TASTE. HILARY: Jesus calls the faithful the "salt of the earth." He warns them to persist in the strength of the power handed over to them. Otherwise, losing their own taste, they are unable to make anything else tasty. Deprived of salt's taste, they are unable to make what is rotten edible. He warns them lest, cast forth from the church storerooms, they be trampled underfoot by the feet of passersby—the very feet of those they should have served with salt. ON MATTHEW 4.10.[4]

RESTORING THE TASTINESS OF THE CREATED ORDER. CHRYSOSTOM: It is as a matter of absolute necessity that he commands all this. Why must you be salt? Jesus says in effect: "You are accountable not only for your own life but also for that of the entire world. I am sending you not to one or two cities, nor to ten or twenty, nor even to one nation, as I sent the prophets. Rather, I am sending you to the entire earth, across the seas, to the whole world, to a world fallen into an evil state." For by saying, "You are the salt of the earth," Jesus signifies that all human nature itself has "lost its taste,"[5] having become rotten through sin. For this reason, you see, he requires from his disciples those character traits that are most necessary and useful for the benefit of all. THE GOSPEL OF MATTHEW, HOMILY 15.6.[6]

GOOD FOR NOTHING. CHROMATIUS: He shows that those who have been educated for the faith and in heavenly wisdom ought to remain faithful and steadfast and not "lose their taste." If they forsake the faith and divine wisdom, they

---

[1]GCS 41.1:52; cf. *Letter to Diognetus* 6. [2]SC 254:126-28. [3]MKGK 165. [4]SC 254:128. [5]Mt 5:13. [6]PG 57:231; NPNF 1 10:97**.

either plunge headlong into heresy or return to the folly of unbelievers. And so Jesus says, "But if the salt loses its flavor, with what will it be seasoned?" For people of this sort, made tasteless by the devil's treachery and having lost the grace of faith, are good for nothing. Though they once might have seasoned nonbelievers still foreign to the faith with the word of divine preaching, they instead showed themselves useless. Judas Iscariot deteriorated into this sort of useless salt. After he had rejected divine wisdom, having changed from an apostle into an apostate, he not only did not help others. He became wretched and useless even to himself. TRACTATE ON MATTHEW 18.4.1-2.[7]

5:14 *The Light of the World*

ILLUMINED BY CHRIST. CHROMATIUS: The Lord has already called his disciples the "salt of the earth" because they seasoned with divine wisdom the hearts of the human race which had been made tasteless by the devil. Now he also calls them the "light of the world." For, illumined by his very own self who is the true and eternal light, they too become light within the darkness. For since he himself is the sun of righteousness, he rightly also calls his disciples "light of the world." Through them, as if through shining rays, he poured the light of his knowledge on the entire world. For by showing the light of truth, the Lord's disciples made the darkness of error flee from people's hearts. TRACTATE ON MATTHEW 19.1.1-2.[8]

FIRST SALT, THEN LIGHT. CHRYSOSTOM: You are the light of the world—not of a single nation nor of twenty cities but of the entire inhabited earth. You are like a light for the mind, far better than any particular sunbeam. Similarly, you are spiritual salt. First you are salt. Then you are light. The metaphors of salt and light drive home the great benefit of these stinging words and the profit of this rigorous discipline, how it binds and does not permit us to become dissolute in our behavior. THE GOSPEL OF MATTHEW, HOMILY 15.7.[9]

CHRIST UNITES US IN ONE COMMONWEALTH. HILARY: He calls the flesh he has assumed a city. For as a city consists in a variety and multitude of inhabitants, so by virtue of his assumed body he contains in himself a certain union of the entire human race. Thus he becomes a city by our union in him, and we through union with his flesh are the community of the city. Therefore he cannot be hidden. Situated on God's lofty height, he is held up to all in admiration of his good works as deserving of contemplation and understanding.

But a lamp is not to be lit and hidden under a bushel. For what benefit is derived from keeping light enclosed? Thus the lamp of Christ must not be hidden under a bushel. . . . Hung on the wood of the cross, it sheds everlasting light on all those who dwell in the church. ON MATTHEW 4.12-13.[10]

DO NOT FENCE IN GOODNESS. CHRYSOSTOM: The person characterized by humility, gentleness, mercy and righteousness does not build a fence around good deeds. Rather, that one ensures that these good fountains overflow for the benefit of others. One who is pure in heart and a peacemaker, even when persecuted for the sake of truth, orders his way of life for the common good. THE GOSPEL OF MATTHEW, HOMILY 15.7.[11]

THE HOLY CITY. ANONYMOUS: What is this city? It is the church of the holy people, of which the prophet says, "Glorious things of you are spoken, city of our King."[12] Moreover, all the faithful are its citizens, of whom the apostle says, "You are fellow citizens with the saints and are part of God's household."[13] INCOMPLETE WORK ON MATTHEW, HOMILY 10.[14]

---

[7]CCL 9a:282. [8]CCL 9a:285. [9]PG 57:232; NPNF 1 10:97-98. [10]SC 254:130; cf. SC 254:126-28. [11]PG 57:231; NPNF 1 10:97**. [12]Ps 87:3 (86:3 LXX). [13]Eph 2:19. [14]PG 56:686.

5:15 *Lighting a Lamp*

THE LIGHTERS OF THE LAMP. ANONYMOUS: This city has been set upon a mountain. The city refers to the apostles, the prophets and other teachers who have been instructed in Christ. For Christ is the mountain, of whom Daniel says, "Look, the rock has been hewn without hands and has become a large mountain and has taken possession of the whole earth."[15]

Now through another comparison he wants to show why Christ himself makes his saints manifest. He does not want them to be hidden: "Neither do people light a lamp in order to put it under a bucket, but they do so to put it on a lampstand, so that it will give light to all the people in the house." Who are the lighters of this lamp? The Father and the Son. What is that lamp? The divine word, of which it has been said, "Your word is a lamp for my feet and a light for my path."[16] The lamp of the word sheds light so that the way might be manifest, that it might give light to those who are in the house, either the house of the church or of the world. What is this lampstand? The church, which bears the word of life. So Paul too speaks of those "among whom you shine, like lightgivers in the world containing the word of life."[17] So too every person in the church, possessing the word of God, is called a lampstand. But worldly people are more like bushel buckets, lacking both God and everything that is of God. INCOMPLETE WORK ON MATTHEW, HOMILY 10.[18]

HIDING THE LAMP UNDER A BUCKET. THEODORE OF MOPSUESTIA: So, what does the Savior mean by the "bucket" under which some people put the lamp? Here by "bucket" he means vice, and by "lamp," virtue. People who intend to perform some illicit act walk in darkness, avoiding, if possible, the light. FRAGMENT 26.[19]

5:16 *Letting Your Light Shine*

THE BODY SERVICE TO THE LIGHT. AUGUS-

TINE: That person places the lamp under a bushel who obscures and conceals the light of good teaching with earthbound interests. Rather, one should place the truth up high "on the lampstand." That indicates the light that shines as a result of bodily service, so that it is presented to believers through their embodied ministry. In this way our voices and tongues and other operations of the body are conveyed into good works by those who are learning. SERMON ON THE MOUNT 1.6.17.[20]

GOOD WORKS TO GLORIFY GOD. AUGUSTINE: Of course, the very words of the gospel are self-explanatory. While they feed the hearts of those who knock, they do not hinder the shouts of those who hunger. One must look deeply into the human heart to see in what direction it is turned and on what point its gaze is fixed. Suppose someone desires that his good work be seen by others. Suppose he regards his glory and profit according to the estimation of others and seeks to be elevated in the sight of others. By doing so he fulfills neither of the commands that the Lord has given in this text. For he has sought to practice his justice before the eyes of others, in order to be seen by them. Therefore his light has not caused others to give glory to the Father who is in heaven. He did not wish to have glory rendered to God but to himself. He did not love the will of God but sought advantage for himself. Of such the apostle says, "For they all seek their own interests, not those of Jesus Christ."[21] The saying "Let your light so shine before others that they may see your good works" is incomplete. He immediately adds the reason why this should be done: "that they may give glory to your Father who is in heaven." This means that even though one is seen by others in doing good works, in one's conscience one ought to have the simple intention of glori-

---

[15]Dan 2:34-35. [16]Ps 119:105 (118:105 LXX). [17]Phil 2:15-16. [18]PG 56:686. [19]MKGK 105. [20]PL 34:1238; FC 11:35**. [21]Phil 2:21.

fying God. It is only for the sake of God's glory that we should allow our good works to become known. SERMON 54.3.[22]

TEACHING AND PRACTICING. ANONYMOUS: "Even so let your light shine before others, in order that they may see your good works and give glory to your Father in heaven." That is to say, so shine and teach, not only that people may hear your words but also that they may see your good works. Let those you illumine by the light of your words be seasoned by the salt of your works. For the one who teaches and practices what he teaches, teaches truly. But one who does not practice what he teaches does not teach anyone but casts a bad light on himself. And it is better to practice and not to teach than to teach and not to practice. Because one who practices, though he may keep silent, corrects some people by his example. But one who teaches and does not practice not only corrects no one but even scandalizes many. For who is not tempted to sin when he sees the teachers of goodness committing sins? Therefore the Lord is magnified through those teachers who teach and practice. He is blasphemed through those who teach and do not practice. INCOMPLETE WORK ON MATTHEW, HOMILY 10.[23]

LET YOUR LIGHT SHINE. ANONYMOUS: The church leader should be equipped with all the virtues. He should be poor, so that he can chastise greed with a free voice. He should always be someone who sighs at inordinate pleasure, whether in himself or in others. He is ready to confront those who do not hesitate before they sin and those who do not feel sorry for having sinned after they sin. So let him sigh and lament. Let him show thereby that this world is difficult and dangerous for the faithful. He should be somebody who hungers and thirsts for justice, so that he might have the strength confidently to arouse by God's Word those who are lazy in good works. He knows how to use the whip of rebuke, but more by his example than by his voice. He should be gentle. He rules the church more by mercy than by punishment. He desires more to be loved than feared. He should be merciful to others but severe with himself. He sets on the scales a heavy weight of justice for himself but for others a light weight. He should be pure of heart. He does not entangle himself in earthly affairs, but more so he does not even think of them. INCOMPLETE WORK ON MATTHEW, HOMILY 10.[24]

---

[22]PL 38:373; FC 11:229-30*. The good works of faith are done with the intention of glorifying God alone. [23]PG 56:687. [24]PG 56:684-85.

5:17-20 THE NEW SPIRIT AND THE OLD LAW

[17]*"Think not that I have come to abolish the law and the prophets; I have come not to abolish them but to fulfil them.* [18]*For truly, I say to you, till heaven and earth pass away, not an iota, not a dot, will pass from the law until all is accomplished.* [19]*Whoever then relaxes one of the least of these commandments and teaches men so, shall be called least in the kingdom of heaven; but he who does them and teaches them shall be called great in the kingdom of heaven.* [20]*For I tell you, unless your righteousness exceeds that of the scribes and Pharisees, you will never enter the kingdom of heaven."*

OVERVIEW: Jesus fulfilled the law (HILARY, ANONYMOUS) when he completed by his passion the once prefigured mystery of the paschal meal (CHROMATIUS). Those things considered least important by the unfaithful are not insignificant before God (ORIGEN, CHROMATIUS, ANONYMOUS). The law is summed up in the gospel (JEROME). Those called least in the kingdom are those who misunderstand God's commands (CHRYSOSTOM), who teach but do not follow the Lord's commands (ANONYMOUS). Whoever sets aside one of the least of the commandments of the law should expect to be set aside as an inventor of laws opposed to God (CYRIL OF ALEXANDRIA). The scribes and Pharisees were less concerned with faith in the divine promise than with human praise (CHROMATIUS). Teachers' learning, even if tainted by a small sin, demotes them from the highest degree. It does not profit them to teach a righteousness that they undermine by the slightest fault (JEROME). After the coming of Christ we are favored with a greater strength than law as such (CHRYSOSTOM).

5:17 Fulfilling the Law and the Prophets

JESUS' PASSION FULFILLED THE LAW. CHROMATIUS: The Son of God, who is the author of the law and the prophets, did not come to abolish the law or the prophets. He gave the people the law that was to be handed down through Moses, and he imbued the prophets with the Holy Spirit for the preaching of the things to come. Therefore he said, "I have come not to abolish the law and the prophets but to fulfill them."
He fulfilled the law and the prophets in this way: He brought to pass those things that had been written about him in the law and the prophets. Hence, when he drank the vinegar offered him on the cross, he said, "It is finished,"[1] evidently to show that everything written about him in the law and the prophets had been completed, even including the drinking of vinegar.

He fulfilled the law at any rate when he completed by the sacrament of his passion the once prefigured mystery of the paschal meal. Consequently the apostle says, "For Christ our paschal lamb has been sacrificed."[2] TRACTATE ON MATTHEW 20.1.1-2.[3]

FULFILLING EVEN THE LEAST OF THE COMMANDMENTS. CHROMATIUS: While it is sinful to abolish the least of the commandments, all the more so the great and most important ones. Hence the Holy Spirit affirms through Solomon: "Whoever despises the little things shall gradually die."[4]

Consequently nothing in the divine commandments must be abolished, nothing altered. Everything must be preserved and taught faithfully and devotedly that the glory of the heavenly kingdom may not be lost. Indeed, those things considered least important and small by the unfaithful or by worldly people are not small before God but necessary. For the Lord taught the commandments and did them.[5]

Even small things point to the great future of the kingdom of heaven. For this reason, not only words but also deeds are important; and you should not only teach, but what you teach, you should do. TRACTATE ON MATTHEW 20.2.1-3.[6]

NOT TO ABOLISH. ANONYMOUS: For two reasons Christ says that he did not come to abolish the law but to fulfill it. First, so he might persuade his disciples, whom he had instructed to excel in all good works, to follow his own example. Even as he fulfilled every law, they too must eagerly fulfill even the least part of the law. Second, because Jesus worked on the sabbath and touched lepers, other Jews accused him of attempting to abolish the law. Or at least so it seemed. He needed to respond to these false accusations. He said, "Do not think that I have come to abolish the law or the prophets. I have

---

[1]Jn 19:30. [2]1 Cor 5:7. [3]CCL 9a:291. [4]Sir 19:1. [5]Cf. Mt 5:19. [6]CCL 9a:292.

not come to abolish but to fulfill." The Law and the Prophets are both in force. They prophesy concerning Christ and constitute the law of living. Christ fulfilled them both. INCOMPLETE WORK ON MATTHEW, HOMILY 10.[7]

5:18 Until All Is Accomplished

THE ONE DOT. ORIGEN: But the "one dot" is not only the iota of the Greeks but also that which among the Hebrews is called the yod. And the "one iota" or "one dot" can symbolically be said to be Jesus, since the beginning of his name is written not only by Greeks with an iota but also by Hebrews with a yod. So Jesus will be the one dot, the Word of God in the law which does not pass from the law until all is accomplished. But the iota might also be (as he himself says) the Ten Commandments of the law, for everything else passes away, but these do not pass away. But neither does Jesus pass away; if he "falls to the ground"[8] he does so willingly, in order to bear much fruit. Again, the "one iota" or "one dot" has mastery over things both in heaven and on earth.[9] FRAGMENT 99.[10]

LAW SUMMED UP IN THE GOSPEL. JEROME: We are promised a new heaven and a new earth, which the Lord God will make. If new ones are to be created, the old ones will therefore pass away. As for what follows, "Not one iota, not a dot, shall be lost from the law until all is accomplished," this literally shows that even what is considered least important in the law is full of spiritual sacraments, and it is all summed up in the gospel. COMMENTARY ON MATTHEW 1.5.18.[11]

LAW FULFILLED THROUGH GRACE. CHROMATIUS: He fulfilled the law at the time by completing the sacrifices of the law and all the examples prefigured in himself . . . by accepting a body. Certainly he fulfilled the law at the time he confirmed with evangelical grace the precepts of the law he had given. He proceeds to demonstrate he had come to fulfill the law: "Until heaven and

earth pass away, not one iota, not a dot, shall be lost from the law until all is accomplished." Therefore we know from Christ's teaching how true and divine is the preaching of the law. The Lord reveals that not a single iota or a dot will be lost. TRACTATE ON MATTHEW 20.1.3-4.[12]

NOT ONE IOTA. ANONYMOUS: A man aware of what he has said does not leave hollow words behind. So how could divine words ever remain hollow? God punishes a man if he does not do what God teaches him. How could Christ not actually fulfill what was spoken through the prophets? Therefore he fulfilled the law even in its least requirements. INCOMPLETE WORK ON MATTHEW, HOMILY 10.[13]

5:19 Who Is Great in the Kingdom of Heaven

BEYOND THE LAW. HILARY: With a beautiful introduction Christ moves beyond the work of the law. He does not intend to abolish it but to enhance it by fulfilling it. He declares that his apostles will not be able to enter heaven unless their righteousness exceeds that of the Pharisees. Therefore he bypasses what is laid down in the law, not for the sake of abolishing it, but for the sake of fulfilling it. ON MATTHEW 4.16.[14]

LEAST IN THE KINGDOM. CHRYSOSTOM: For what reason then does he call some of these commandments "least," though they are so magnificent and lofty? Jesus spoke this way because he was about to introduce his own teaching as a new law. As he humbles himself and speaks of himself with great modesty, so he refers to his own teaching in the same manner. In this way Jesus teaches us to practice humility in everything. And besides, since some suspected his teaching to be a new departure, he temporarily taught it in a more reserved way.

[7]PG 56:687. [8]Jn 12:24. [9]Lit.,"above and below." [10]GCS 41.1:56. [11]CCL 77:27. [12]CCL 9a:291. [13]PG 56:688. [14]SC 254:134.

But when you hear "least in the kingdom of heaven," you are to think of nothing but hell and punishment. For it was his practice to speak not only of the joy the kingdom brings but also of the time of the resurrection and the fearful event of the second coming. Think of one who calls a brother a fool. That one transgresses only one commandment, maybe even the slightest one, and falls into hell. Compare that one with another who breaks all the commandments and instigates others to break them. Do both have the same relation to the kingdom? This is not the argument Jesus is making. Rather, he means that one who transgresses only one of the commands will on the final day be the least—that is, cast out—and last, and will fall into hell. THE GOSPEL OF MATTHEW, HOMILY 16.[15]

SETTING ASIDE THE LEAST OF THE COMMANDMENTS. CYRIL OF ALEXANDRIA: Whoever sets aside "one of the least of the commandments" of the law is set aside by God as God's enemy and as an inventor of laws opposed to God. And now out of the law of the gospel that one receives the retribution which, under the ancient law, was not defined. For this reason Christ fittingly says, "I am not come to destroy but to fulfill." For that which then was lacking, here is made full.[16] It is said in the law: "Stand in the presence of the elderly"[17] and "If you see the beast of your enemy fallen under its load, go help him lift it up."[18] If anyone transgressed these commandments, there was no retribution specified under the law. So Christ makes up this lack when he says that in the kingdom of heaven such a person will be treated with scorn. FRAGMENT 48.[19]

5:20 Righteousness Exceeding That of the Scribes and Pharisees

THE FAULTS OF THE TEACHER TAINT THE TEACHING. JEROME: He therefore rebukes the Pharisees, who showed contempt for God's

commandments and set up their own traditions, for their teaching among the people is of no value if they destroy even a small part of what is in the law. We can understand this in another sense, namely, that a teacher's learning, even if tainted by a small sin, demotes him from the highest place. It does not profit him to teach a righteousness that he undermines by the slightest fault. The Beatitude is perfected if what you teach with your words you practice with your works. COMMENTARY ON MATTHEW 1.5.18.[20]

EXCEEDING THE RIGHTEOUSNESS OF THE SCRIBES. CHRYSOSTOM: Jesus speaks of righteousness here as virtue in its fullness. In speaking of Job, Jesus said, "He was a blameless man, righteous."[21] According to the same meaning of the word, Paul even called that person righteous for whom, as he said, no law is laid down: "For the law is not made for a righteous person."[22] One might find "righteous" in many other passages rendered as "virtuous in general."

But I urge you to observe how grace has abounded under the new covenant. Jesus desires to have his prospective disciples considered as greater than the teachers under the old covenant. For by "scribes and Pharisees" here he meant the upright, not the lawbreakers. If they were not acting in a commendable fashion, he would not have spoken of them as righteous. Nor would he have compared the unreal to the real.

Note how Jesus also in this passage commends the old law. He does so by comparing it with the new, a comparison that implies that it is of the same family, so to speak. More or less, it does share many family resemblances. He does not find fault with the old law but in fact makes it more strict. Had it been evil, Jesus would not have accentuated it. Instead, he would have discarded it.

If the law is so commendable, how is it not

---

[15]PG 57:243; NPNF 1 10:106**. [16]Or supplied. Note that the Greek verbs are active, not passive. [17]Lev 19:32. [18]Ex 23:5. [19]MKGK 167. [20]CCL 77:27. [21]Job 1:1 LXX. [22]1 Tim 1:9.

adequate to bring us into the kingdom? After the coming of Christ we are favored with a greater strength than law as such. Those who are adopted as children are bound to strive for greater things. THE GOSPEL OF MATTHEW, HOMILY 16.4.[23]

SMUGNESS OF THE PHARISEES. CHROMATIUS: He finds fault with the righteousness of the scribes and Pharisees, for they were not concerned with faith in the divine promise but with human praise and worldly glory. We have an example of this in the puffed-up and proud Pharisee who seemed to prefer the merits of his own righteousness and shamelessly made himself conspicuous in God's sight with his smugness and complacent words.

The scribes and Pharisees therefore stressed the appearance of righteousness, not that they might please God but that they might seek the fame of human glory and acquire earthly gain and material comforts. Hence the Lord urges us to give priority to the works of heavenly righteousness and the merits of faith over that detestable righteousness of human praise. TRACTATE ON MATTHEW 20.3.1-2.[24]

LEAST IN THE KINGDOM DISTINGUISHED FROM ENTERING THE KINGDOM. ANONYMOUS: The righteousness of the scribes and Pharisees is found in the commandments of Moses, whereas the fulfillment of those commandments is found in the commandments of Christ. So this is what he says: Unless a person, in addition to the commandments of the law, fulfills these precepts of mine that people may believe to be unimportant, he shall not enter the kingdom of heaven. The former may free a person from pun-

ishment imposed on transgressors of the law, but they do not bring a person into the kingdom. The latter free a person from punishment and introduce him into the kingdom. On this point of abolishing and not keeping the least of these commandments, he says about the lawbreaker: "Whoever does away with one of these least commandments shall be called least in the kingdom of heaven," meaning that even if that person is least he is still in the kingdom. But why does he say concerning the nonobservant person that unless the righteousness of the Christian exceeds that of the scribes and Pharisees, that one shall not enter the kingdom of heaven? For whoever does not enter the kingdom of heaven will be outside the kingdom. On this, note that to be least in the kingdom is the same as not entering the kingdom. For to be someone in the kingdom is not the same as to reign with Christ but only to be among Christ's people. It is as though he said, He who does not keep the law though he teaches it will indeed be among the Christians, but he will be the least Christian, or with the least of the Christians. But he who enters the kingdom will share in the kingdom with Christ, as is said elsewhere about the good servant: "Enter into the joy of your master";[25] that is to say, rejoice together with your Lord. Hence that person who does not enter the kingdom of heaven will certainly not possess the glory of the kingdom of heaven with Christ, though he will be in the kingdom, that is, counted among those over whom Christ the king of heaven reigns. INCOMPLETE WORK ON MATTHEW, HOMILY 11.[26]

---

[23]PG 57:244; NPNF 1 10:107**. [24]CCL 9a:293. [25]Mt 25:21. [26]PG 56:689.

5:21-26 THE FIRST EXAMPLE OF THE NEW SPIRIT: ANGER AND RECONCILIATION

[21]*"You have heard that it was said to the men of old, 'You shall not kill; and whoever kills shall be liable to judgment.'* [22]*But I say to you that every one who is angry with his brother[i] shall be liable to judgment; whoever insults[j] his brother shall be liable to the council, and whoever says, 'You fool!' shall be liable to the hell[k] of fire.* [23]*So if you are offering your gift at the altar, and there remember that your brother has something against you,* [24]*leave your gift there before the altar and go; first be reconciled to your brother, and then come and offer your gift.* [25]*Make friends quickly with your accuser, while you are going with him to court, lest your accuser hand you over to the judge, and the judge to the guard, and you be put in prison;* [26]*truly, I say to you, you will never get out till you have paid the last penny."*

i Other ancient authorities insert *without cause*   j Greek *says Raca to* (an obscure term of abuse)   k Greek *Gehenna*

OVERVIEW: Christ's commandment contains the law, but the law does not contain Christ's commandment (ANONYMOUS). While the old law commands us not to murder, the gospel commands us not to get angry without reason, that we may remove every root of sin from our hearts (CHROMATIUS). It is as though Jesus were saying to a lethargic student, "You have spent enough time on these lessons. It is now time to press on to lessons higher than these" (CHRYSOSTOM).

One who reproaches someone who is filled with the Holy Spirit as empty-headed becomes liable to the council of holy men (HILARY). God, who looks at a person's intentions, brings the one who is guilty of ridiculing his brother to the council of the holy, because ridicule aimed at one person redounds to the insulting of all (CHRYSOLOGUS). If no human being can tame the tongue, we must look to God who will tame it (AUGUSTINE). When the Lord himself justly terms as fools people who are in no way righteous, he does this not out of anger but for the sake of truth (THEODORE OF MOPSUESTIA).

A gift offered to God is not acceptable unless the giver puts aside his or her anger and becomes reconciled to the brother (CHROMATIUS). One

who hates is akin to a murderer (THEODORE OF HERACLEA). Jesus does not even receive the sacrifice of worship without the sacrifice of love. Not before or later but precisely while the very gift is lying there, when the sacrifice is already beginning, he sends you to be reconciled to your brother (CHRYSOSTOM). One who does not love one's brother does not love the Lord (CYRIL OF ALEXANDRIA). Let brotherly peace come first, before one approaches the altar (JEROME, AUGUSTINE). You be the first to ask pardon (ANONYMOUS). If you do not make peace with your opponent and you both die and go before Christ the judge, you will be quickly handed over to punishment (ANONYMOUS). When you ignore conscience you put yourself at grave risk (ORIGEN). The accuser is the Holy Spirit through conscience (CHROMATIUS). So do not delay settling with others until you are thrown into some enormous conflict (CHRYSOSTOM, JEROME). Cut off the intent to sin before you act to sin (ORIGEN).

5:21 The Ancient Commandment Against Killing

IT WAS SAID TO THE PEOPLE OF OLD. CHRYsostom: It was he himself who also gave those laws, but in an indirect manner. If on the one hand he had said, "You have heard that I said to those of ancient times," the saying would have been hard for his present hearers to believe and would have been a roadblock for their understanding. If on the other hand, after Jesus said, "You have heard that it was said to those of ancient times by my Father," he had added, "But I say," he still would have seemed to be taking yet more on himself.

So he simply states the commandment, attempting to make only one point: to demonstrate that at the right time he had come to clarify this requirement. For by the words "it was said to those of ancient times" he pointed out the length of time since they had received this commandment. He did this to shame those hearers who were still reluctant to advance to the higher levels of his teachings. Jesus spoke much like a teacher to a lazy student: "Don't you know how much time you have spent learning syllables?" He also covertly intimates this through his use of the expression "those of ancient times." For the future, Jesus summons his hearers to a loftier order of instruction. It is as though he had said, "You have spent enough time on these lessons. It is now time to press on to lessons higher than these."

It is fitting that Jesus does not disturb the order of the commandments but begins with the earlier ones, those with which the law began, to point to the harmony between them. THE GOSPEL OF MATTHEW, HOMILY 16.5.[1]

THE DEEPER MEANING OF THE LAW. CHROMATIUS: This is what the Lord said: "I have not come to abolish the law but to fulfill it." In other words, to accentuate what was considered least; that is to say, to reform for the better the precepts of the law.

For this reason the holy apostle says, "Do we, then, overthrow the law by this faith? By no means! On the contrary, we uphold the law.". . . The law commands us not to murder.

The gospel commands us not to get angry without reason, that we may remove every root of sin from our hearts, because anger can even lead to homicide. TRACTATE ON MATTHEW 21.1.1-2.[2]

CHRIST CONTAINS THE LAW. ANONYMOUS: This fulfilling of the law, depending on the circumstances, fell naturally into place. As Christ did and taught these things, he fulfilled the law—he did not do away with it. For Christ's commandment is not contrary to the law but broader than the law. Christ's commandment contains the law, but the law does not contain Christ's commandment. Therefore whoever fulfills the commandments of Christ implicitly fulfills the commandments of the law. For one who does not get angry is much less capable of killing. But one who fulfills what the law commands does not completely fulfill what Christ commands. Often a person will not kill because of the fear of reprisal, but he will get angry. Do you see then that the fulfilled law has the benefit of not being abolished? Consequently, without these commandments of Christ the commandments of the law cannot stand. For if the freedom to get angry is allowed, there are grounds for committing murder. For murder is generated by anger. Take away the anger, and there will be no murder. Therefore whoever gets angry without cause commits murder with respect to the will, even if he does not actually do so out of fear of reprisal. The remorse may not be the same as if he had committed the deed, but such a sin matches the one who gets angry. Thus John in his canonical epistle says, "Everyone who hates his brother without cause is a murderer."[3] Consider the wisdom of Christ. Wanting to show that he is the God who once spoke in the law and who now commands by grace, he placed that commandment before all others in the law. And now he placed it at the beginning of his commandments. It was first written in the law: "You

[1]PG 57:245; NPNF 1 10:108. [2]CCL 9a:295. [3]1 Jn 3:15.

shall not murder."[4] He immediately begins with murder, so that through a harmony between commandments he is found to be the author of the law and of grace. "Everyone who is angry with his brother without cause shall be liable to judgment."[5] Therefore whoever gets angry with cause will not be liable. For if there is no anger, teaching will be of no use, nor will judgments be necessary, nor will criminal actions have to be held in restraint. Therefore just anger is the mother of discipline. Those who get angry with cause not only do not sin, but, unless they get angry, they do sin. Moreover, irrational patience sows the seeds of vice, nurtures negligence and encourages not only the wicked but also the good to do evil. Although a wicked person may be rebuked, he is not made to change his ways; but a good person, unless he is rebuked, will come to ruin because evil rather than good prevails in his body. Anger with cause is not anger but judgment. Incomplete Work on Matthew, Homily 11.[6]

5:22 Liable to Judgment

CHARGING EMPTY-HEADEDNESS. HILARY: "Whoever says to his brother, 'Raca,' shall be liable to the council."[7] One who reproaches with empty-headedness someone who is filled with the Holy Spirit becomes liable to the council of holy men and is to expiate this outrage against the Holy Spirit through punishment handed down by the holy judges. "Whoever says, 'You fool!' shall be liable to the hell of fire.". . . Thus whatever the law has not condemned as to a person's works, the faith of the Gospels castigates because of one's readiness simply to use insulting words. On Matthew 4.17.[8]

TAMING THE TONGUE. AUGUSTINE: What are we to do? "Whoever says, 'You fool!' shall be liable to the hell of fire." But "no human being can tame the tongue." Will everyone therefore go to the hell of fire? By no means. "Lord, you have become our refuge from generation to genera-

tion."[9] Your wrath is just. You send no one to hell unjustly. "Where shall I go from your spirit? or where shall I flee from your presence,"[10] unless to you? Thus let us understand, my dearly beloved, that if no human being can tame the tongue, we must take refuge in God, who will tame it. Does your own human nature prevent you from taming your tongue? "No human being can tame the tongue."[11]

Consider this analogy from the animals that we tame. A horse does not tame itself; a camel does not tame itself; an elephant does not tame itself; a snake does not tame itself; a lion does not tame itself. So too a man does not tame himself. In order to tame a horse, an ox, a camel, an elephant, a lion and a snake, a human being is required. Therefore God should be required in order for a human being to be tamed. Sermon 55.2.[12]

PUT ASIDE ANGER. CHROMATIUS: How greatly the Lord esteems fraternal love we know from this, for he makes clear that a gift offered to God is not acceptable unless the giver of a gift to his brother puts aside his anger and becomes reconciled to him.

Furthermore, we learn that the gifts offered by Cain were rejected by God. He failed to observe charity toward his brother and harbored anger in his heart. Hence, not without good reason does the Lord in the Gospel indicate in many places the prime necessity of fraternal charity when he says, "A new commandment I give you, that you love one another."[13]

And again: "By this will all men know that you are my disciples, if you have love for one another."[14] Rightly so, the Lord also spoke through Zechariah: "Render true judgments, show kindness and mercy each to his brother."[15] Through David he likewise declared: "Refrain

---

[4]Ex 20:13. [5]Mt 5:22. [6]PG 56:689-90. [7]"Raca" is an insult referring to empty-headedness. [8]SC 254:136. [9]Ps 90:1 (89:1 LXX). [10]Ps 139:7 (138:7 LXX). [11]Jas 3:8. [12]PL 38:375; FC 11:234*. It takes God to tame the tongue, which humans cannot tame. [13]Jn 13:34. [14]Jn 13:35. [15]Zech 8:16-17.

from anger, and forsake wrath!"[16] TRACTATE ON MATTHEW 21.3.1-3.[17]

WITH AIRS OF SUPERIORITY. THEODORE OF HERACLEA: He has said two things: "Whoever says, 'Raca,' and whoever says, 'You fool,'" referring foolishness to the soul, and "despicable" to things of the body. By this he describes one who assumes an air of superiority, exalts himself over his brothers in the faith. Such a one hates them and turns away from them or looks down upon them with disgust or, frequently, passes them by as not worthy of a single look. He derives this sense of superiority from advantages of either body or soul and, on this account, looks down on his brothers as inferior to him. Such a person, Jesus says, is not considered by me as immune from condemnation. For the one who hates is akin to a murderer; such a person ought especially to have had love for these others on account of their shared faith, even though their common human nature should have been reason enough to unite them in friendship. FRAGMENT 27.[18]

TO RIDICULE A BELIEVER IS TO RIDICULE GOD'S WISDOM. PETER CHRYSOLOGUS: "Whoever says to his brother, 'Raca,' shall be liable to the council." The word *raca*, my brothers, is not simply an expression but the visceral reaction of a ridiculer as well as an insult. It usually manifests itself by a sidelong glance or a flaring of the nostrils or a rattle in the throat, so that one's will concocts insults and the extent of the harm done is unknown. But God, who looks at a person's intentions, sees his desires and judges his feelings, brings the one who is guilty of ridiculing his brother to the council of the holy, because ridicule aimed at one person redounds to the insulting of everyone; the condition of one limb spreads to the body, and the suffering of the body goes up to the head. Thus, as to what a ridiculer has inflicted on his brother, he will realize and regret in the heavenly council that his insight reached up to God.

"Whoever says, 'You fool!' shall be liable to the hell of fire." What the angry man concealed in his heart, what the ridiculer held in his throat, the backbiter has put into words. Thus the expressed insult will be reckoned with in the fire of hell. The judgment for hidden faults depends on the Savior's decision, so that based on an examination of causes a just judgment is rendered. Clearly then a manifest crime will produce a punishment. But someone may ask, "Just how great is the force of a word, that whoever says to his brother, 'You fool!' will be accorded severe punishment?" Very great, my brothers, very great, for Christ is in your brother, and Christ is the wisdom of God. Therefore whoever says to his brother "You fool!" has ridiculed God's wisdom. SERMONS 177.6-7.[19]

TRUTH MAY SPEAK OF FOOLS. THEODORE OF MOPSUESTIA: In speaking of the judgment and of the council and of the Gehenna of fire, Jesus refers to one and the same punishment. He does not indicate various things through the difference of the words, nor some different chastisement. But if it is not permissible to call somebody a fool, why does the Lord himself employ the expression *fools*?[20] It is not fitting to call one's particular brother a fool, for such a word issues from anger and not from righteousness. It is even more impious when it is spoken against someone who is holy. But the Lord justly terms as fools people who are in no way righteous and in no way what he is. He does this not out of anger but for the sake of truth. Again, Gehenna is the place of eternal and infernal punishment. FRAGMENT 28.[21]

5:23 Offering Your Gift at the Altar

THERE REMEMBER YOUR BROTHER. CHRYSOSTOM: What goodness! What all-surpassing love

---

[16]Ps 37:8 (36:8 LXX). [17]CCL 9a:297-98. [18]MKGK 64. [19]CCL 24b:1076-77. [20]E.g., Mt 23:17, 19. [21]MKGK 106.

is shown to humanity! Showing no regard for the honor rightfully his, he calls us to pour forth love toward our neighbor. He explains that he did not speak his earlier threatening words out of hatred or desire to punish but from the most tender affection. For what can be more gentle than these words? "Interrupt the service you are offering me," he says, "so that your love may continue. To be reconciled to your brother is to offer sacrifice to me." Yes, this is the reason Jesus did not say "after the offering" or "before the offering." Rather, precisely while the very gift is lying there, when the sacrifice is already beginning, he sends you at that precise time to be reconciled to your brother. Neither after removing nor before presenting the gift, but precisely while it lies before you, you are to run to your brother.

What is his motivation in making such an immediate command? It seems to me he has two ends in mind toward which he is hinting and preparing. First, as I have previously said, he desires to show how highly he values love and considers it to be the greatest sacrifice. So he does not even receive the sacrifice of worship without the sacrifice of love. Next, he is imposing such a necessity for reconciliation that it admits of no excuse. The person who has been commanded not to offer sacrifice to God before one is reconciled will hurry to the one who has been grieved and eradicate the enmity between the two. He does so that his sacrifice may not lie unconsecrated. The Gospel of Matthew, Homily 16.9.[22]

Loving the Wounded Brother. Cyril of Alexandria: The statement "if you should bring your gift" shows that this is conceived as a means of salvation and as an escape from punishment for sinners. For this God invented repentance. One will avert punishment, however, who tends to the feelings of another who has been wounded. But one who does not love his brother does not love the Lord. Hence it is fitting that whoever bears hard feelings toward

his brother is not accepted, since he does not approach the Lord in truth.[23] Fragment 50.[24]

5:24 First Reconcile with Your Brother

Cutting Off the Intent to Sin. Origen: To give assent to sin is already a completed evil, even if someone does not actually commit the deed. And by this saying our Savior, hurling us away from the cause of sins, endeavors to cut sin off completely. For when this intention is not present in our souls, neither shall the action accompany it. Fragment 103.[25]

Let Brotherly Peace Come First. Jerome: He did not say, "If you have anything against your brother" but "If your brother has anything against you," so that a greater need for reconciliation is imposed on you. As long as we are unable to make peace with our brother, I do not know whether we may offer our gifts to God. Commentary on Matthew 1.5.23.[26]

Leave Your Gift Before the Altar. Augustine: In the spiritual sense therefore we may understand faith as an altar in the inner temple of God, to which the visible altar symbolically points. Whatever gift we offer to God—whether it be prophecy, or doctrine, or prayer, or a hymn, or a psalm, or whatever other spiritual gifts of this kind may come to mind—cannot be acceptable to God unless it is held up by sincere faith and firmly and immovably fixed on it, so that our words may be pure and undefiled. Sermon on the Mount 1.10.27.[27]

Be First to Ask Pardon. Anonymous: Do not counter with "He offended me; I didn't offend him. He ought to square up with me, and not I

[22]PG 57:250; NPNF 1 10:112**. [23]Lit., whoever is in the brother's grief. The ambiguity here is whether the ill feeling is to be ascribed to "whoever" or to the "brother." [24]MKGK 168. [25]GCS 41.1:58. [26]CCL 77:28. [27]PL 34:42; FC 11:45*. The altar before which we are to leave our gifts and go first to be reconciled to our neighbor is the altar of faith within the inner temple of our own relation to God.

with him." If for the sake of your salvation the Lord orders you to make friends, though you are the one who has been more offended, you must apologize, that you may have double credit: first, because you have been offended and, second, because you were the first to apologize. For if you have offended someone and then ask pardon of him, the Lord will forgive you for your offense because you were the first to ask pardon. You will have no reward, however, if you are found to be the guilty person and have asked pardon. But if one has done wrong by you and you are the first to apologize, you will have a great reward. Hurry therefore to be the first one to make friends. Otherwise, if you should delay, he may be the first to apologize and may snatch from your hands the reward of love. If he has offended you and asked your pardon, your friendship is fruitless. For what righteousness do you have before the Lord if you receive an apology and are thereby placated? Certainly the Lord does not want you to grovel for forgiveness, but he orders you to be the first to apologize. INCOMPLETE WORK ON MATTHEW, HOMILY 11.[28]

5:25 Make Friends with Your Accuser

DO NOT IGNORE CONSCIENCE. ORIGEN: In this life, this way traveled by all, you do well to accept and not ignore the suggestions of the conscience. But if you are inconsiderate and negligent in this life, conscience itself, assuming the role of a prosecutor, will accuse you before the judge. Conscience will subject to the juryman's decision, and you will be handed over to incurable punishments. Such things you would not have suffered, if along the way you had in fact acquired goodwill toward your accuser, accepting his reproaches as offered out of goodwill. For this also the divine Evangelist John says in his letter: "If our conscience does not condemn us, we have confidence before God."[29] FRAGMENT 102.[30]

MAKE FRIENDS QUICKLY. CHRYSOSTOM: Hav-

ing mentioned first the judgment, then the council, then hell, and having spoken of his own sacrifice, Jesus then adds, "Come to terms quickly with your accuser while you are on the way to court." That is, don't be saying, "What if I am the injured party? What if I have been plundered and dragged before the tribunal?" Even this kind of circumstance fails to qualify as an excuse or occasion for refusing to be reconciled. Jesus commands us even in these circumstances not to be at enmity with others. Then, since this command was so significant, he illustrates his counsel with examples drawn from daily affairs. Less intelligent people, after all, are more apt to respond to present realities than future ones. "What is that you are saying?" he asks. "So your adversary is stronger and has wronged you? He will wrong you even more if you don't make it right and he ends up taking you to court. In the former case, by giving up some money, you keep yourself free. Once a judge has passed sentence, however, you will be thrown in jail and pay a stiff fine. If you stay out of court, you will reap two benefits. First, you won't have to suffer anything painful. Second, the good you end up doing will be your own doing and not something you have been forced to do. But if you refuse to be convinced by these words, you are wronging yourself more than your opponent." THE GOSPEL OF MATTHEW, HOMILY 16.10.[31]

THE HOLY SPIRIT ACCUSES. CHROMATIUS: Others, who seem to have a more complete explanation, believe that the opponent here must be understood as the Holy Spirit, who opposes the vices and desires of the flesh. As the apostle points out, "The flesh lusts against the Spirit, and the Spirit against the flesh; for these are opposed to each other, so that you do not do what you would."[32]

---

[28]PG 56:692. [29]1 Jn 3:21. [30]GCS 41.1:58. [31]PG 57:252; NPNF 1 10:113**. Be ready for final judgment by settling unreconciled disputes here and now. [32]Gal 5:17.

The Spirit indeed desires heavenly things; the flesh lusts after earthly things. The Spirit rejoices over spiritual gifts; the flesh is attracted to bodily vices. Concerning this the apostle says, "Do not grieve the Holy Spirit of God, with whom you have been sealed for the day of redemption."[33] Therefore, the Lord instructs us to listen to this adversary of sin and human error, upholding those things that are righteous and holy. We should obey him in all things while we are with him on the way, in the caravan of this present life. By doing so we will have peace and perpetual fellowship with him. TRACTATE ON MATTHEW 22.3.1-2.[34]

DO NOT WAIT TO MAKE PEACE. ANONYMOUS: The Lord makes haste, that we may hasten to make friends with our enemies as long as we live in this life. This life common to all people is a casual life, through which both the good and the wicked pass. God knows the danger if either enemy should die before peace is made. Even if they wanted to make peace, they are unable to, since they have been separated by death. But if in the course of this life you do not make peace with your opponent whom you have offended and you should both die and go before Christ the judge, he will deliver you up to Christ, accusing you of guilt in his court, and the judge will hand you over to the guard (the angel of cruel punishments), and the latter will send you to the prison of hell. But if you had made peace in this world, you could have obtained pardon of the most serious act, as is written: "Charity covers a multitude of sins."[35] Once you have been convicted and put in prison, punishment will be exacted from you not only for your serious sins but also for the idle words you spoke. For instance, if you said "Raca" to someone, your opponent will hand you over to the judge, even if he was the first one to apologize. As Solomon says, "If your enemy is hungry, give him bread to eat . . . for you will heap coals of fire on his head."[36] What does it mean to "heap coals of fire" if not to make him more accountable to

God? If someone does good to his enemy, therefore, he will make him more culpable before God. Hence he who is the first to apologize to his enemy makes him guilty before God. INCOMPLETE WORK ON MATTHEW, HOMILY 11.[37]

5:26 *You Will Remain in Prison*

YOU WILL NEVER GET OUT. JEROME: From what precedes and follows, we are given to understand that our Lord and Savior exhorts us to peace and harmony while we are pilgrims in this world. As the apostle says, "Strive for peace with all persons." For in the previous section Jesus said, "If you are offering your gift and there remember that your brother has something against you," he immediately goes on to say "make friends" or come to terms with "your opponent," and so forth. Then he orders, "Love your enemies and bless those who hate you and pray for those who persecute you."[38] This is clear from the explanation that follows. Many people, however, have a confused idea of the flesh and the soul or the soul and the spirit.[39] They wonder: How is the flesh to be sent to prison if the soul is at odds with it, for the soul and the flesh must be united and the flesh can do nothing unless the mind gives the order? And how can the Holy Spirit dwelling in us turn over to a judge the opposing flesh or soul when he himself is the judge? The epistle of Peter says, "Our adversary the devil prowls around like a roaring lion."[40] Some interpret that the adversary is the devil. Then they draw the odd conclusion that they are being counseled by the Savior that as far as possible we should be kind toward the devil who is the enemy and avenger. Nor should we make him suffer for us—though he offers incentives to vice to us who sin through our own will—by

---

[33]Eph 4:30. [34]CCL 9a:301. [35]1 Pet 4:8. [36]Prov 25:21-22; Rom 12:20. [37]PG 56:693. [38]Mt 5:44. [39]The interpretation rejected here by Jerome has an Origenist flavor. Perhaps he read it in the portion of Origen's *Commentary on Matthew* that is no longer extant, which he drew on extensively. [40]1 Pet 5:8.

consenting to have him who is the great troublemaker suffer punishment also for our sake. They say that each saint should be benevolent to this demonic adversary by not making him suffer torments on his account. Thus some people rashly reason that individuals make a covenant with the devil in baptism by saying, "I relinquish to you, Satan, your splendors and your vices and your world steeped in wickedness." If we therefore keep that covenant, we will be benevolent and obliging toward our adversary and by no means deserving of imprisonment. COMMENTARY ON MATTHEW 1.5.25.[41]

PAYMENT FOR SIN. JEROME: But the Lord says that if we have transgressed any of the things we pledged to the devil, we shall be handed over to the judge and the guard. We shall be put in prison and not be released until we have paid back the last farthing. A farthing is a type of coin consisting of two mites. On this point, the poor widow in one Gospel is said to have put a farthing into the treasury; in another Gospel, two mites.[42] There is no discrepancy here, for one farthing contains two mites. So this is what he says: You will not come out of prison until you have paid for the least of your sins. COMMENTARY ON MATTHEW 1.5.25.[43]

THE LAST FARTHING. AUGUSTINE: But, with regard to paying the last farthing, the expression can be quite reasonably understood as the equivalent of saying that nothing is left unpunished—just as in ordinary parlance we use the expression "to the very dregs" when we wish to declare that something is so completely consumed that nothing is left. Or it can be understood in the sense that earthly sins could be designated by the last fourth or the earth is found to be the fourth and the last part of the distinct elements of this world. This assumes that you begin from the heavens, count the air second, the water third and the earth fourth. For this reason the expression "until you have paid the last penny" can be rightly understood as meaning until you have expiated earthly sins. For the sinner has also heard the expression "Earth you are, and to the earth you shall return."[44] SERMON ON THE MOUNT 1.11.30.[45]

---

[41]CCL 77:29-30. [42]This clarification is pointless. In citing from memory Jerome has forgotten that whereas Luke 21:2 has only "two mites," Mark 12:42 has "two mites, which make a farthing." [43]CCL 77:30. [44]Gen 3:19. [45]PL 34:1243-44; FC 11:47-48*. The last farthing may mean either that nothing is left unpunished, or, since the last farthing or the "last fourth" may refer to the earth as the last of the four elements (heavens or fire, air, water, earth), the phrase may mean until all earthly sins are expiated.

5:27-32 THE SECOND AND THIRD EXAMPLES: LUST, ADULTERY AND DIVORCE

[27]"You have heard that it was said, 'You shall not commit adultery.' [28]But I say to you that every one who looks at a woman lustfully has already committed adultery with her in his heart. [29]If your right eye causes you to sin, pluck it out and throw it away; it is better that you lose one of your members than that your whole body be thrown into hell.[k] [30]And if your right hand causes you to sin, cut it off and throw it away; it is better that you lose one of your members than that your whole body go into hell.[k]

[31]"It was also said, 'Whoever divorces his wife, let him give her a certificate of divorce.' [32]But I say to you that every one who divorces his wife, except on the ground of unchastity, makes her an adulteress; and whoever marries a divorced woman commits adultery."

k Greek *Gehenna*

OVERVIEW: As anger is the mother of murder, lust is the mother of adultery (ANONYMOUS, CHROMATIUS). The soul was created to have its own authority and thus is free. It is able to avoid anger, if it so wishes. It can choose not to lust, if it so wishes. God does not address his commands merely to the flesh, as if detached from the soul (ANONYMOUS). Once one has kindled the flame of lust, even when the object of lust is absent, the one who lusts is forming continually images of prohibited actions (CHRYSOSTOM). The member of the body as such is not the subject of chastisement but the will and the voluntary motivation that underlies the impulse of the will (HILARY). What is best in us may soon devolve into a vice (JEROME). Insofar as the eye symbolizes, for example, an unworthy bishop, who through his disreputable faith becomes a scandal to the church, Christ advises that he be plucked out, lest the people be held to account for his sins (CHROMATIUS). It is common to think analogically of the right hand as the will of the soul and the left hand as the will of the body (ANONYMOUS). If your spiritual advisor or minister or right hand becomes a stumbling block or leads to evil, cut off the relationship (AUGUSTINE). One should not spare even things thought most necessary if through them any harmful activity threatens to come about (APOLLINARIS).

Our Lord orders that chaste wedlock be preserved by indissoluble law, showing that the law of marriage was first instituted by Christ himself (CHROMATIUS). A Christian man must not only not defile himself, but he must not give others an occasion to defile themselves (ANONYMOUS). The divorcing husband makes the wife an adulteress (CHRYSOSTOM, THEODORE OF HERACLEA). She remains his body, since they are one flesh (THEODORE OF MOPSUESTIA).

5:27-28 Committing Adultery

ADULTERY ALREADY. CHRYSOSTOM: For he did not simply say "whoever shall desire," since it is possible for one to desire even when sitting alone in the mountains. Rather, Jesus said, "whoever looks with lust," that is, one who thinks about another solely for the purpose of lusting, who, under no compulsion, allows the wild beast to intrude upon his thoughts when they are calm. This intrusion no longer comes from nature but from self-indulgence. The ancient Scripture corrects this from the first, saying, "Don't gaze upon another's beauty."[1] And then, so that no one should say, if I gaze but am not taken captive, he punishes the look, lest through a false security you should some time fall into sin. "What then," one may say, "if I should look, and desire indeed, but do no evil?" Even so you find your place among the adulterers. For the Lawgiver has pronounced it, and you must not question further. For when you look once, twice or three times, you will perhaps have power to refrain; but if you make this your habitual practice, kindling the furnace within you, you will assuredly be overcome. Your human nature is no different from that of other people. If we see a child holding a knife, though we don't see him hurt, we spank him and forbid him to ever do so again. In the same way, God removes the licentious look even before the act, lest at any time you should fall in act also. For he who has once kindled the flame, even when the woman whom he has beheld is absent, is forming continually within

[1]Sir 9:8.

108

himself images of shameful things. The images often lead even to the concrete act. Hence Christ takes away even that embrace which is in the heart only. THE GOSPEL OF MATTHEW, HOMILY 17.2.[2]

THE FUEL OF ADULTERY. CHROMATIUS: Because adultery is a serious sin and in order to uproot it, lest our conscience be defiled, he forbade even lust, which is the fuel of adultery. According to the words of blessed James in his epistle, "Lust when it has conceived gives birth to sin; and sin when it is full-grown brings forth death."[3] The Holy Spirit speaks concerning this to David: "Happy shall he be who takes your little ones and dashes them against the rock."[4] The symbolism here is that the blessed and truly evangelical person roots out the desires and lust of the flesh arising from human weakness. He does this immediately before they grow, at the onset, through faith in Christ who has been described as a rock.[5] TRACTATE ON MATTHEW 23.1.6-7.[6]

GOD'S COMMAND ADDRESSES THE WILLING SOUL. ANONYMOUS: Those who care little for their souls do not look sufficiently into their hearts. They do not consider it a sin to get angry with their neighbors without cause and do not think it a sin to lust after a woman who belongs to another provided they do not follow up their lust. But it is a great sin among those who fear God and hold their hearts in high regard. And it is a great sin before God, who looks not only at one's actions but also at one's heart. With the inwardness of this commandment the law is not abolished but fulfilled, and without it the Lord's commandment would be untenable.

Every act of adultery arises from lust. Therefore how can adultery be restrained under the commandment of the law, unless the force of lust has been nipped in the bud under Christ's commandment? For just as anger is the mother of murder, lust is the mother of adultery. Consequently one who gets angry at his brother with-

out cause kills him in his heart, even though he does not actually kill him. It is still murder in the sight of God, who does not regard the action more than the disposition.

So too the man who lusts after a woman who belongs to another has already committed adultery with her in his heart, though he has not had relations with her for whatever restraining reason. He is still an adulterer before God, who looks more at the will than the act. For the overt act of adultery may have been lacking, but not the will. Even those who are unaware of the deeper mystery of human nature can agree on this much: Every carnal nature is subject to these passions. No one, not even a saint, can possibly detach himself from the temptation to anger or lust. Yet they go on to imagine that Christ, as though commanding an impossible thing, is setting up a trap to make people culpable. Anyone who commands impossible things sows occasions of offense and lays grounds for punishment.

This leads us to a reflection on the division between the wills of the soul and the body. We have two natures in us: the flesh and the soul. We thus indeed have two wills, that of the soul and that of the flesh. We may thus say we also have two angers, the anger of the soul and the anger of the flesh. Similarly we might speak of having a lust of the soul and a lust of the flesh. The flesh may come under the compulsion of getting angry and feeling lust, despite its will, since it was not created to have its own authority. It is not now under its own authority, as though created with it, but under the law of sin. For the flesh has been sold into the slavery of sin. That is why the apostle says, "For the mind that is set on the flesh is hostile to God; it does not submit to God's law, indeed it cannot."[7] But the soul was created to be its own authority, according to the law of God's

---

[2]PG 57:256; NPNF 1 10:116-17**. It is like playing with fire to choose to kindle the furnaces of lust within you by gazing upon another's beauty.   [3]Jas 1:15.   [4]Ps 137:9 (136:9 LXX).   [5]Cf. 1 Cor 10:4.   [6]CCL 9a:305.   [7]Rom 8:7.

righteousness. For that reason, the soul is able not to get angry, if it so wishes, and not to lust, if it so wishes. Thus when we get angry and feel the force of lust, if we are dissatisfied with ourselves and are quick to suppress either our anger or our lust, it is clear that our flesh alone is getting angry or lusting but not our soul. But if we become self-satisfied in these things and decide to give vent to any anger or lust we feel, then our soul as well gets angry and lusts at the same time as the flesh. Therefore, since God knows that the nature of the flesh is not subject to him, God does not bother to command the flesh as such, as if it stood alone. What knowing person then will give a command to someone who, despite good intentions, is unable to obey? Rather, God speaks to the soul, which is able to obey him in all things and which, despite an angry and lustful flesh, is able not to get angry and not to be consumed with lust. INCOMPLETE WORK ON MATTHEW, HOMILY 12.[8]

5:29 Pluck Out Causes to Sin

THE MEMBER NOT THE CAUSE OF SIN. HILARY: As the degree of innocence increases, faith becomes more advanced. For we are advised to be free not only from our own particular faults but also from those things that affect us outwardly. For is it not because of sin that the bodily members were condemned in the first place? The right eye is no less sinister than the left. It is pointless to chastise a foot that is unaware of lust and thus involves no grounds for punishment. But our members indeed do differ from each other while we are all one body. We are here being advised to pluck out inordinate loves or friendships if they are the occasion that leads us further into wrongdoing. We would do well to not even have the benefit of a member, like an eye or a foot, if it furnishes the avenue by which one is drawn by excessive affections into a partnership with hell. Even the cutting away of a member might be beneficial if the heart (figuratively speaking) were also able to be cut away.

But if the impulse of the heart is left unchanged, the cutting away of a member would be pointless. ON MATTHEW 4.21.[9]

THE GIST OF THE HYPERBOLE. APOLLINARIS: He speaks about the numbers of the body but employs hyperbole. It is not that one should literally "cut off one's members." Rather, one is called to mortify them and render them useless for sin, as the apostle has said.[10] One should not spare even things thought most necessary, if through them any bad activity threatens to occur. FRAGMENT 23.[11]

THE ANALOGY OF THE EYE. JEROME: Since Jesus spoke before about lust for a woman, he now rightly refers to an unruly thought or feeling as an eye. By the right hand and other members of the body the onset of the will and emotions is suggested. Thus what we conceive in the mind we might complete with an act. Hence we must be aware that what is best in us may soon devolve into a vice. If your right eye and your right hand are an occasion of sin to you, how much more is this true of the left members. If your soul begins to slip, how much more the body, which has a greater tendency to sin. In other words, in the right eye and the right hand of one's siblings and wife and children and relatives and neighbors, an emotion is indicated. If we perceive they are an obstacle to us in contemplating the true light, we must cut off those parts. Otherwise, in our desire to profit from others, we may perish for all eternity. Hence it is said concerning the high priest whose soul is dedicated to the worship of God: "He shall not defile himself for mother and father and children."[12] That is, he shall have affection only for the One to whose worship he is dedicated. COMMENTARY ON MATTHEW 1.5.29.[13]

---

[8]PG 56:693-94. [9]SC 254:140. [10]Cf. Col 3:5; 1 Cor 9:27. [11]MKGK 8. [12]Lev 21:11. [13]CCL 77:31-32.

REMOVING AN UNWORTHY BISHOP. CHROMA-TIUS: But since the body has been mentioned, this can be understood more properly of the body of the church. In this body the eye, like a precious member, is recognized as the bishop who enlightens the entire body by the light of a divine commandment. The passage properly applies here: "If your right eye is an occasion of sin to you, pluck it out and cast it from you; for it is better for you that one of your members should perish than your whole body should be thrown into hell." Hence, if this type of eye—symbolizing an unworthy bishop—through his disreputable faith and base dealings becomes a scandal to the church, Christ advises that he be plucked out, lest the people be held accountable for his sins.

For it is written that "a little leaven leavens the whole lump."[14] And again: "Keep yourself from every kind of evil."[15] The hand is understood to signify a priest who, because of his disreputable faith or life, becomes a scandal to God's people. The Lord orders that he be cut away, that is, removed, lest the church become defiled by his sin. For the church, according to the apostle, ought to be holy and spotless. TRACTATE ON MATTHEW 23.3.1-2.[16]

5:30 Losing a Member, Saving the Body

ON REJECTING BAD COUNSEL. AUGUSTINE: In this connection, I can think of no more fitting example than that of a dearly beloved friend, for that which we ardently love is certainly that which we may rightly call a member. And we may rightly call this member a counselor, for he is, as it were, an eye that shows the way, and because he is on the right side, we may rightly call him a counselor in divine matters. In this way, a friend on the left side is indeed a counselor, but a counselor in earthly matters, which pertain to the needs of the body. However, it would be superfluous to talk about him insofar as he may be an occasion of sin, since not even the friend on the right side is to be spared. But a counselor in

divine matters is actually a stumbling block if, under the guise of religion and doctrine, he is trying to lead us into some pernicious belief. Let the right hand therefore be understood as a beloved helper and minister in divine works. For, just as contemplation is properly represented by the word *eye*, so action is rightly represented by the word *hand*. In this way, the left hand signifies the works that are necessary for this life and body. SERMON ON THE MOUNT 1.13.38.[17]

THINK OF THE RIGHT HAND AS THE WILL OF THE SOUL. ANONYMOUS: I believe that all these things [the eye and the hand and the foot] are spoken of in reference to the soul, as we said before. He speaks of the soul as an eye; that is, a mind through which the soul sees. On this he says in another place: "If your eye, is sound, your whole body will be full of light."[18] This carnal eye without the soul is not an eye. It is the mirror of that interior eye: the mind. The body has its own mind, even as it has its own soul, according to the apostle's words on the mind of the soul: "Therefore I myself with my mind serve the law of God but with my flesh the law of sin."[19] Concerning the mind of the body, he says, "Puffed up by his mere human mind, such a one is not united to the Head."[20] Likewise concerning the hand or the foot. He may be thinking of a person's right hand as the will of the soul but the left hand as the will of the body. This bodily hand is not a literal hand but the organ of that hand. For unless the will moves it, whether for good or for evil, it is not moved at all. Thus a person's right hand is the will of the soul, but the left hand is the will of the body. Hence the parts of the soul are referred to as "right" and the parts of the body as "left," for the soul was created with its own authority, which gives it a tendency either to good or to evil. It was also

---

[14]1 Cor 5:6. [15]Cf. 1 Cor 5:13. [16]CCL 9a:306-7. [17]PL 34:1248; FC 11:57*. If your spiritual advisor or minister or right hand becomes a stumbling block or leads to evil, cut off the relationship. [18]Mt 6:22. [19]Rom 7:25. [20]Col 2:18-19.

created under the law of righteousness, that it might see what is right, hear what is right and act and walk accordingly. The parts of the body are referred to as "left," since the flesh was not created with its own authority that it might tend to either good or to evil. It has become prone to evil under the law of sin, and it cannot see or hear or do what is right. Thus all holy people are referred to as "right" but sinners as "left." Incomplete Work on Matthew, Homily 12.[21]

5:31 Divorcing One's Wife

Let No One Put Asunder What God Has Joined. Chromatius: In all things our Lord and Savior reforms for the better the justice of the ancient law. Indeed, it seems that long ago a license for divorce was granted by Moses on tenuous grounds to the Jewish people who were living licentiously and serving their pleasures. This was due not to the system of law but to the unbridled pleasure of a carnal people unable to uphold the righteousness of the law according to rigorous standards.

This concession was allowed, according to what the Lord himself said in another place in his reply to the inquiring Sadducees. For when they asked why Moses had allowed a bill of divorce to be given, the Lord answered, "Moses, by reason of the hardness of your hearts, permitted you to put away your wives, but it was not so from the beginning."[22] And now, not without good reason does our Lord and Savior, with that license removed, restore the precepts of his former constitution. For he orders that chaste wedlock be preserved by indissoluble law, showing that the law of marriage was first instituted by himself. For he said, "What therefore God has joined together, let no one put asunder."[23] Tractate on Matthew 24.1.1-3.[24]

Four Injustices Simultaneously Committed in Divorce. Anonymous: When he spoke about someone who gets angry without cause and who is consumed with lust, he deftly intro-

duced the commandment about putting away wives. For if he who gets angry with his brother without cause is liable to judgment, how will that person not be liable who, without the sin of fornication, so hates his wife that he puts her away? But you say, "My wife has a lot of faults." So what? Are you without fault? If we must bear the weaknesses of strangers according to the apostle, "Bear one another's burdens, and so you will fulfill the law of Christ,"[25] how much more must we bear those of wives? If a man looks with lust at a woman, he commits adultery with her in his heart. How will that person not be held to account for adultery who puts away his wife and gives her occasion to commit adulteries, so that she too commits adultery with another and he with her? For a Christian must both remain undefiled and not give others an occasion to defile themselves. Otherwise their wrongdoing redounds to the sin of him who becomes the cause of sin for others. Note also that whoever gives a certificate of divorce according to the law commits four injustices at the same time. First, as far as God is concerned, there is a killing that is occuring.[26] Second, the man has put aside a woman who has not committed fornication. Third, he has made an adulteress out of her. Fourth, if he takes her back again, he still commits adultery. None of these injustices are committed, however, when Christ's commandment has been kept. Incomplete Work on Matthew, Homily 12.[27]

5:32 Making a Woman an Adulteress

He Makes Her an Adulteress. Chrysostom: How can one who is meek and a peacemaker and poor in spirit and merciful cast out his wife? How can one who reconciles be alienated from her that is his own? . . . Even in this case he makes one exception: "for the cause of

---

[21]PG 56:695. [22]Mt 19:8. [23]Mt 19:6; Mk 10:9. [24]CCL 9a:309. [25]Gal 6:2. [26]A murder is taking place, the death of a relationship. [27]PG 56:697.

fornication." One who does not look with unchaste eyes upon another woman will certainly not commit fornication. By not committing fornication he will give no occasion that they should become alienated. Thus you see Jesus presses his point without reserve and builds up this fear as a bulwark, urging on the husband great danger, who if he does cast her out, makes himself accountable for her adultery. THE GOSPEL OF MATTHEW, HOMILY 17.4.[28]

DISSOLVING A MARRIAGE. THEODORE OF HERACLEA: Through these things he clearly teaches that it is not unreasonable divorce which dissolves a marriage in God's sight. Rather, irresponsible action dissolves a marriage, even if the divorce is legal. For the whole teaching of Christ judges things according to one's disposition.[29] FRAGMENT 34.[30]

SHE REMAINS HIS BODY. THEODORE OF MOPSUESTIA: He has mixed his statement about divorce with one concerning fornication, for men who turn away from their own spouses out of a desire for intercourse with other women have committed adultery. The same applies to women. Thus he does not allow the divorced woman to remarry. The man she lives with must pay the penalties of an adulterer. For even if, to all appearances, she is separated from her husband, in spiritual reality she remains his body. At the beginning, she was joined and fitted by God to her husband as "one flesh."[31] For the same reason, neither is the man able to marry another woman. FRAGMENT 33.[32]

---

[28]PG 57:260; NPNF 1 10:119**. [29]Or intention. [30]MKGK 66. [31]Gen 2:24. [32]MKGK 107.

5:33-48 THE FOURTH, FIFTH AND SIXTH EXAMPLES: OATHS, REVENGE AND LOVE

[33]*"Again you have heard that it was said to the men of old, 'You shall not swear falsely, but shall perform to the Lord what you have sworn.'* [34]*But I say to you, Do not swear at all, either by heaven, for it is the throne of God,* [35]*or by the earth, for it is his footstool, or by Jerusalem, for it is the city of the great King.* [36]*And do not swear by your head, for you cannot make one hair white or black.* [37]*Let what you say be simply 'Yes' or 'No'; anything more than this comes from evil.*[1]

[38]*"You have heard that it was said, 'An eye for an eye and a tooth for a tooth.'* [39]*But I say to you, Do not resist one who is evil. But if any one strikes you on the right cheek, turn to him the other also;* [40]*and if any one would sue you and take your coat, let him have your cloak as well;* [41]*and if any one forces you to go one mile, go with him two miles.* [42]*Give to him who begs from you, and do not refuse him who would borrow from you.*

[43]*"You have heard that it was said, 'You shall love your neighbor and hate your enemy.'* [44]*But I say to you, Love your enemies and pray for those who persecute you,* [45]*so that you may be sons*

of your Father who is in heaven; for he makes his sun rise on the evil and on the good, and sends rain on the just and on the unjust. [46]*For if you love those who love you, what reward have you? Do not even the tax collectors do the same?* [47]*And if you salute only your brethren, what more are you doing than others? Do not even the Gentiles do the same?* [48]*You, therefore, must be perfect, as your heavenly Father is perfect."*

l Or *the evil one*

OVERVIEW: The law prescribes that no one swear falsely, but according to the gospel one must not swear at all (CHROMATIUS). Those who are living in the simplicity of faith have no need for the formality of an oath (HILARY). If your opponents believed that you would swear truthfully, they would never compel you to swear (ANONYMOUS). Do not make an idol of creation by swearing an oath to some creaturely being (CYRIL OF ALEXANDRIA). One who swears by earthly elements makes implicit reference to the One who is the author of all these things (CHROMATIUS). Refer all glory to God (CHRYSOSTOM).

If we begin with the law's mandate to return evil for evil to everyone, we are all made evil and the foundation of the law itself is dissolved (ANONYMOUS). Rather, we resist evil by surrendering ourselves to suffer wrongfully (CHRYSOSTOM). The Lord wishes that the hope of our faith, extending into eternity, be tested by these challenges, so that the very toleration of a hidden injury should be a witness of our future judgment (HILARY). Turning the other cheek scandalizes those who do not understand the reasonings of faith (ORIGEN). If a tempter initiates a lawsuit for the testing of our faith and desires to rob us of the things that are ours, the Lord orders us to offer willingly not only the things that the person seeks unjustly but even those the tempter does not demand (CHROMATIUS). Like Joseph, flee without your coat to the covering of a higher justice (ANONYMOUS). You will win full freedom from unworthy passions by possessing all things in common and by going the second mile out of mercy (CHRYSOSTOM).

Going the second mile may also have a spiritual meaning: that of going with one who believes in the Father, the first mile, yet with whom you must be patient in traveling the second mile to belief in the Son and Spirit (CHROMATIUS). The rich person is less likely to be tested through physical suffering than to be tested and proved in generosity (ANONYMOUS). Freely give as you have freely received (JEROME). Whether, Jesus says, it be a friend or an enemy, a believer or an unbeliever, do good to the person in need (THEODORE OF HERACLEA).

Christ commanded us to love our enemies not so much for our enemies as for us: not because enemies are fit to merit love but because it is not fitting that we hate anyone (ANONYMOUS). Christ does not command impossibilities (THEODORE OF HERACLEA). If you hate your enemy, you have hurt yourself more in the spirit than you have hurt him in the flesh (ANONYMOUS). Adoption denotes the character of our vocation to the eternal inheritance as joint heirs with Christ by a spiritual regeneration (AUGUSTINE). One who loves an enemy loves not for one's own sake but on account of God; hence that person has a great treasure (ANONYMOUS).

The spiritual meaning of the sun as representing truth is grounded in the literal meaning of the sun as light. The spiritual meaning of the rain as the watering by the teaching of the truth is grounded in the literal meaning of rain as refreshment (AUGUSTINE). God is more content that sinners should enjoy his benefits though they don't deserve them than that the just should be robbed of benefits against their deserving (ANONYMOUS). We are called to be models for the just and the unjust of the imitation of Christ, who distributes equally the sun and the rain by his coming in baptism and by the sacraments of the Spirit (HILARY).

5:33 Not Swearing Falsely

FAITH NEEDS NO OATH. HILARY: The law had prescribed a penalty for false swearing, so that the ritual of an oath might hold false testimony in check.... But faith removes the need for using an oath. It establishes in truth the dealings of our life. Once the inclination to deceive has been checked, it enjoins simplicity in speaking and hearing.... Therefore those who are living in the simplicity of faith have no need for the ritual of an oath. With such people, what is, always is, and what is not, is not. For this reason, their every word and deed are always truthful. ON MATTHEW 4.23.[1]

PERJURY GENERATED BY OATHS. ANONYMOUS: Here is the fourth commandment, which is considered the least one[2] by those self-assured persons who think that truthful swearing is not a sin and that the commandment of the law cannot stand without it. Now, unless an oath is forbidden, we cannot put a stop to perjury, for perjury is generated by oaths. For there is no one who frequently swears who does not at times commit perjury. Because of this, Solomon warns, "Do not accustom your mouth to an oath; there is much misfortune in it."[3] For even as the one who is accustomed to speaking often finds it necessary to say inappropriate things ... one who makes it a habit to swear on suitable occasions, drawn along by custom, frequently and even unwillingly will swear also in superfluous matters. Now, as with any custom, when we want to do something we do it; and when we do not want to do it, we refrain from doing it. And Solomon teaches us that God's judgment is against those who swear: "A man who swears much shall not ward off the blight from his house."[4] If therefore the blight will not depart

from those who swear frequently, how will it depart from those who swear occasionally? Tell me, my friend, what do you gain by swearing? For if your opponent believed that you would swear truthfully, he would never compel you to swear. But since he believes that you may commit perjury, he compels you to swear. INCOMPLETE WORK ON MATTHEW, HOMILY 12.[5]

5:34 Do Not Swear by Heaven

SWEARING OATHS INAPPROPRIATE. CHROMATIUS: By the grace of gospel teaching, the law given by Moses acquired an advantage. The law prescribes that one must not swear falsely; but according to the gospel one must not swear at all. The Holy Spirit had seen fit to order this through Solomon when he said, "Do not accustom your mouth to oaths."[6] And again: "Even as a well-chastised servant is not deterred from envy, whoever swears and does business will not be purged from sin."[7] Therefore it is absolutely inappropriate for us to swear. What need is there for us to swear when we are not allowed to lie at all and our words must always be true and trustworthy, so much so that they may be taken as an oath? On this, the Lord not only forbids us to swear falsely but even to swear, lest we appear to tell the truth only when we swear and lest (while we should be truthful in our every word) we think it is all right to lie when we do not take an oath. For this is the purpose of an oath: Everyone who swears, swears to the fact what he is saying is true. Therefore the Lord does not want a gap between our oath and our ordinary speech. Even as there must be no faithlessness in an oath, in our words there must be no lie. For both false swearing and lying are punished with divine judgment, as the Scripture says: "The

---

[1]SC 254:142. [2]In the Gospel text the prohibition of oath taking is of a general nature, not addressed specifically to the greedy. The clarification here results from Jesus' previous prohibitions of violence and concupiscence. The author here prefers to associate this new prohibition with a specific sin as well. [3]Sir 23:9. [4]Sir 23:11. [5]PG 56:697. [6]Sir 23:9. [7]Cf. Sir 23:11.

mouth that lies kills the soul."[8] So whoever speaks the truth swears, for it is written: "A faithful witness will not lie."[9] TRACTATE ON MATTHEW 24.2.2-4.[10]

5:35 Do Not Swear by Earth

DO NOT DEIFY CREATION. CYRIL OF ALEXANDRIA: For this reason Jesus prohibits us from swearing by heaven or by the earth. This is in order that we should not give to creation an honor surpassing creation. Do not deify creation. Those who swear, he says, "swear by the greater," as the apostle has said.[11] And he also forbids swearing by Jerusalem. For the earthly Jerusalem is a type of the Jerusalem above,[12] and God swears only by himself, that is, by his own glory.[13] Wherefore, since the similarity transcends us, we are obliged to swear neither by ourselves nor by our own glory, for we are not free like God but are subject to God's authority. FRAGMENT 63.[14]

5:36 Do Not Swear by Your Head

DO NOT SWEAR BY EARTHLY ELEMENTS. CHROMATIUS: These words of the Lord whereby he forbids us to swear by these different elements invite a double explanation.

First, he wanted to draw us away from the use of oaths and the customs of human error, lest each of us through swearing by these elements accord a creature the honor of divine veneration or believe one has impunity in swearing falsely if one swears by the elements of the world. . . . It can also be explained in this way: When one swears by heaven and earth, one swears by him who made heaven and earth, as the Lord himself declared elsewhere: "He who swears by the altar swears by it and by all things that are on it; and he who swears by the temple swears by it and by him who dwells in it."[15] Jesus goes on to say, "nor by Jerusalem," for it is the city of the great King, that is, the symbol of Christ's body, which is the spiritual and heavenly church. "Neither shall

you swear," he says, "by your head," for according to the apostle, "the head of every man is Christ."[16] Therefore the one who swears by these things makes reference to him who is the author of all these things. TRACTATE ON MATTHEW 24.3.1-4.[17]

5:37 Unadorned Speech

A SIMPLE YES OR NO. CHRYSOSTOM: He has prohibited anyone from swearing by his head, for in doing so one would be worshiping himself. Rather, Jesus intends to refer all glory to God, signifiying that human beings are not finally masters of themselves. Oaths made by the head are thus discredited. For if no one would relinquish his own child to another, how much more will God refuse to relinquish his own work to you? For though it be your head, yet it remains the property of another. For he did not say, "You cannot make one hair grow" but "You cannot make one hair white or black" or change its quality.

What is it then that exceeds a simple yes or no? It is the oath, not the perjury. For lying is openly acknowledged to be wrong, and no one needs to learn that it is of the Adversary. It is not an excess but a deficiency. An excess, though, means something more, something over and above the statement itself. This is the nature of an oath.

Someone might then object: If the evil one is the source of all oaths, how could they have found a place in God's law? Well, we could say much the same thing about Jesus' teaching on divorce. How is divorce now accounted adultery, particularly when divorce was permitted by Moses? What can we reply? The precepts Moses uttered at that time accounted for the weakness of those who were receiving the laws.

---

[8]Wis 1:11. [9]Prov 14:5. [10]CCL 9a:310-11. [11]Heb 6:16: "Men indeed swear by a greater than themselves, and in all their disputes an oath is final for confirmation." [12]Gal 4:26. [13]Heb 6:13; cf. Is 45:23; Jer 22:5. [14]MKGK 172. [15]Mt 23:20-22. [16]1 Cor 11:3. [17]CCL 9a:311-12.

Just as a lisp is unworthy of a philosopher, so the scent of burnt offerings is unworthy of God. Our understanding of the principles of virtue has advanced beyond the time of Moses. Therefore divorce is now seen to be adultery and the necessity of an oath to be from the evil one. If the earlier laws had been devilish from the first, they would never have resulted in such goodness. Had Moses' laws not been forerunners, Jesus' teaching would not have been so easily received. Don't require a present excellence from past laws, when their usefulness has now been surpassed. Still, if you wish to retain them, even now they demonstrate their virtue. They show their virtue most of all through the fault we discover by their aid. The faults we now see commend them most to us. For had they not brought us up well and prepared us for the reception of the greater precepts, they would not have appeared as good.

It is similar with the breast of the mother; when it has fulfilled its task, it dismisses the child to a more mature diet and after that appears useless. Thus the mother who once viewed it as necessary for the baby now taunts with ten thousand mockeries the child's need for the breast. Breastfeeding is over. In the same way, Christ says that the ancient laws are from the evil one, not to indicate that the old law is of the devil but in order that he might with great earnestness lead them away from their ancient poverty. THE GOSPEL OF MATTHEW, HOMILY 17.5-6.[18]

5:38 An Eye for an Eye

DO NOT RETURN EVIL FOR EVIL. ANONYMOUS: A law prescribing an eye for an eye, a tooth for a tooth, has this foundation: Each will spare the other as long as one fears for one's own limbs. It was thereby imagined that no evil person would be found. But woe to the earth for its failures! For as long as we live in this world, over which the devil rules, slanderers, fighters and persecutors will necessarily abound. If therefore we begin, according to the mandate of the law, to return evil for evil to everyone, we are all made evil, the foundation of the law is dissolved, and what results? While the law wanted to make the evil good, it also made the good evil. If, however, following the mandate of Christ, we do not resist evil, then even if the evil ones are not harmed, still the good will remain good. Thus through the mandate of Christ, the mandate of the law is also filled. For one who fulfills the mandate of the law does not at the same time fulfill that of Christ; but one who fulfills the mandate of Christ at the same time fulfills that of the law. INCOMPLETE WORK ON MATTHEW, HOMILY 12.[19]

5:39 Turn the Other Cheek

OFFER THE OTHER CHEEK. ORIGEN: Jesus' words regarding turning the other cheek concern more than simply long-suffering. For it is against nature to be so arrogant as to hit the other person. The one therefore who is "ready to give an answer" to every malicious person "concerning the faith that is in him"[20] will not offer resistance. The spiritual meaning is this: To one who strikes him upon the right cheek—that is, against the rational doctrines—the believer will offer also the ethical ones. This will scandalize those who do not understand the reasonings of faith. They will cease from their accusations, since they will be ashamed and continue progress in divine things. FRAGMENT 108.[21]

TOLERATE A HIDDEN INJURY AS A WITNESS TO FUTURE JUDGMENT. HILARY: The Lord wishes that the hope of our faith, extending into eternity, be tested by these things, so that the very toleration of a hidden injury should be a witness of our future judgment. The law used to hold unfaithful Israel within a boundary of fear and contained the desire for injury by the threat of injury returned. Faith, however, does not per-

---

[18]PG 57:261-62; NPNF 1 10:120-21**. [19]PG 56:699. [20]1 Pet 3:15. [21]GCS 41.1:60.

mit resentment for injuries, nor does it wish for revenge. . . . There is in the judgment of God a greater consolation for those who have suffered injury and a punishment more dreadful than injuries returned. Therefore the Gospels not only warn us away from iniquities but also drive out the latent desire for vengeance. For if we have received a blow, we ought to offer the other cheek. . . . The Lord who accompanies us on our journey offers his own cheek to slaps and his shoulders to whips, to the increase of his glory. ON MATTHEW 4.25.[22]

RESIST NOT EVIL. CHRYSOSTOM: For this reason Jesus has also added, "But I say to you, do not resist the evil one." He did not say "do not resist your brother" but "the evil one"! We are authorized to dare to act in the presence of evil through Christ's influence. In this way he relaxes and secretly removes most of our anger against the aggressor by transferring the censure to another.

"What then?" one asks. "Should we not resist the evil one at all?" Indeed we should, but not in this way. Rather, as Jesus has commanded, we resist by surrendering ourselves to suffer wrongfully. In this way you shall prevail over him. For one fire is not quenched by another, but fire by water. THE GOSPEL OF MATTHEW, HOMILY 18.1.[23]

5:40 Give Your Coat and Cloak

BE REMOVED FROM EVERY LAWSUIT. CHROMATIUS: Beyond the tolerance of physical injury, the Lord wants us also to have contempt for things of this world and to be so far removed from every lawsuit or contest of judgment. If by chance a slanderer or tempter comes forward to initiate a lawsuit for the sake of testing our faith and desires to rob us of the things which are ours, the Lord orders us to offer willingly not only the things that the person goes after unjustly but even those not demanded. TRACTATE ON MATTHEW 25.2.1.[24]

JOSEPH'S FLIGHT. ANONYMOUS: Just as Joseph lost his cloak in the hand of the prostitute and fled dressed with a better cloak,[25] so throw your cloak into the hands of the slanderer and flee with the better covering of justice. If not, while you want to reclaim the clothes of the body, you may squander the most precious clothing of the soul. If the unbelievers see you, a Christian, repay injuries with worse injuries by worldly means and hammer earthly judgments against a lawless plunderer even to the destruction of your soul, how should they believe in reality of the hope of the heavenly kingdom that Christians preach? For they who hope for heavenly things easily spurn earthly things. Yet I doubt that those who strongly embrace worldly things believe firmly in heavenly promises. INCOMPLETE WORK ON MATTHEW, HOMILY 12.[26]

5:41 Go a Second Mile

THE SECOND MILE. CHRYSOSTOM: Do you grasp the excellence of a Christian disposition? After you give your coat and your cloak, even if your enemy should wish to subject your naked body to hardships and labors, not even then, Jesus says, must you forbid him. For he would have us possess all things in common, both our bodies and our goods, as with them that are in need, so with them that insult us. For the latter response comes from a courageous spirit, the former from mercy. Because of this, Jesus said, "If any one shall compel you to go one mile, go with him two." Again he leads you to higher ground and commands you to manifest the same type of aspiration. For if the lesser things he spoke of at the beginning receive such great blessings, consider what sort of reward awaits those who duly perform these and what they become even before we hear of receiving

---

[22]SC 254:144-46. [23]PG 57:265; NPNF 1 10:124**. One whose life is hid in Christ resists evil in a most surprising manner by surrendering oneself to suffer wrongfully. [24]CCL 9a:315. [25]Joseph the patriarch fleeing the immodest wife of Potiphar (Gen 39:6-23). [26]PG 56:700.

rewards. You are winning full freedom from unworthy passions in a human and passible body. THE GOSPEL OF MATTHEW, HOMILY 18.3.[27]

A MISSIONAL INTERPRETATION OF THE SECOND MILE. CHROMATIUS: Some believe that this section, "He who is pressed into service for one mile, let him go with that man as far as another two," is to be understood spiritually in this fashion: If a nonbeliever, or one who has not yet followed the knowledge of the truth, makes mention of the one God the Father, the founder of all things, as if coming to God by the way of the law, go with that one the second mile. That is, after his profession of God the Father, lead this same person, by the way of truth, to the knowledge of the Son and the Holy Spirit, showing that one is to believe not only in the Father but also in the Son and the Holy Spirit. TRACTATE ON MATTHEW 25.3.2.[28]

5:42 Give to One Who Begs

FREELY GIVE. JEROME: If we think that only this is all that is taught about almsgiving, then there are many poor to whom it cannot apply. And even the wealthy can give forever, if they are always giving. For the sake of goodness, therefore, this doctrine of almsgiving was given to the apostles: that they who have freely received should freely give.[29] Money of that sort is never lacking. As much as is given, by that much it is increased, and though the fountain water drench the fields below, it never runs dry. COMMENTARY ON MATTHEW 1.5.42.[30]

CONSTRAINTS ON IRRESPONSIBLE GIVING. THEODORE OF HERACLEA: In giving us these directives so that their sense might be diligently examined, he did not intend us to take them according to the bare sound of the words. For he does not command to give to everyone who asks without exception, even if one has nothing to give, for that is impossible. Nor does he instruct

us, if we have plenty, to give to someone who asks with a bad motive. For the donation then goes for evil things, as when someone asks for the sake of lust and intemperance and not for real need, and the person who gives merely provides fuel for such intemperance. For why is it said concerning the apostles that "distribution was made to each as any had need"?[31] This tells us that they gave not so much to those who simply asked but that they provided for others on the basis of need. And do not forget about the verse that says, "A man is acceptable according to what he has, not according to what he does not have,"[32] and "not so that others should be relieved and you burdened."[33] FRAGMENT 37.[34]

THE RICH AND THE POOR. ANONYMOUS: All these mandates suit the character of the poor person. But who knocks out the tooth of the rich and powerful? Let the rich not knock out the tooth of the poor! Who tries to steal the tunic of the rich and powerful with lies? Let the rich not steal the tunic of the poor with lies! Who presses the rich and powerful into service? Let the rich not press the poor into service! If such is the case, the rich person is fruitless. And how might that one fulfill the justice of the law and of grace, that he might become a perfect servant of God? How? If anyone seeks a loan from him, let him give it. It is the law that you do not take from another, even if you do not give what is yours. It is grace, however, that you do not take from another and you give what is yours. Therefore whoever gives a loan fulfills both the law and grace. For he who gives freely of his own, would he then take the goods of another? The rich man therefore cannot be tested or proved through physical suffering. No one will likely do him violence; rather, he is tested and proved by generosity. INCOMPLETE WORK ON MATTHEW, HOMILY 12.[35]

---

[27]PG 57:268; NPNF 1 10:125-26**. [28]CCL 9a:316. [29]Cf. Mt 10:8. [30]CCL 77:34. [31]Acts 4:35. [32]2 Cor 8:12. [33]2 Cor 8:13. [34]MKGK 66-67. [35]PG 56:701.

5:43 *Hating an Enemy*

THE OLD LAW. THEODORE OF HERACLEA: Whether, he says, it be a friend or an enemy, a believer or an unbeliever, do good to the person in need. Do not follow the Jewish law that focuses repayment primarily on friends. For this reason, when they were urging the Lord to heal the son of the royal officer, they said to him, "He is worthy to have you do this for him," because "he has even built us our synagogue."[36] FRAGMENT 38.[37]

YOU TEAR YOURSELF APART BY HATING. ANONYMOUS: We have seen how murder is born from anger and adultery from desire. In the same way, the hatred of an enemy is destroyed by the love of friendship. Suppose you have viewed a man as an enemy, yet after a while he has been swayed by your benevolence. You will then love him as a friend. I think that Christ ordered these things not so much for our enemies as for us: not because enemies are fit to be loved by others but because we are not fit to hate anyone. For hatred is the prodigy of dark places. Wherever it resides, it sullies the beauty of sound sense. Therefore not only does Christ order us to love our enemies for the sake of cherishing them but also for the sake of driving away from ourselves what is bad for us. The Mosaic law does not speak about physically hurting your enemy but about hating your enemy. But if you merely hate him, you have hurt yourself more in the spirit than you have hurt him in the flesh. Perhaps you don't harm him at all by hating him. But you surely tear yourself apart. If then you are benevolent to an enemy, you have rather spared yourself than him. And if you do him a kindness, you benefit yourself more than him. INCOMPLETE WORK ON MATTHEW, HOMILY 13.[38]

5:44 *Loving and Praying for Enemies*

CHRIST DOES NOT COMMAND IMPOSSIBILITIES. THEODORE OF HERACLEA: The law of the Lord transcends both the law of nature and the law revealed to Moses. For the things that are impossible with humans are possible with God.[39] But Christ does not legislate impossibilities, as Stephen showed at the time of his passion, when he bent his knees and prayed for those who were stoning him.[40] Similarly Paul, who had suffered so many things at the hands of the Jews, also prays for them.[41] Therefore the infrequency of these things shows that they are not impossible. For most people, though, they are difficult to accomplish owing to their unwillingness to strive to reach the summit of virtue. FRAGMENT 40.[42]

PRAY FOR THOSE WHO PERSECUTE YOU. CHRYSOSTOM: For neither did Christ simply command to love but to pray. Do you see how many steps he has ascended and how he has set us on the very summit of virtue? Mark it, numbering from the beginning. A first step is not to begin with injustice. A second, after one has begun, is not to vindicate oneself by retaliating in kind. A third, to refuse to respond in kind to the one who is injuring us but to remain tranquil. A fourth, even to offer up one's self to suffer wrongfully. A fifth, to give up even more than the wrongdoer wishes to take. A sixth, to refuse to hate one who has wronged us. A seventh, even to love such a one. An eighth, even to do good to that one. A ninth, to entreat God himself on our enemy's behalf. Do you perceive how elevated is a Christian disposition? Hence its reward is also glorious. THE GOSPEL OF MATTHEW, HOMILY 18.4.[43]

5:45 *Imitating the Father*

THE EVIL AND THE GOOD. THEODORE OF HERACLEA: The imitator of God and Christ makes the sun of his word and the brightness of his righteousness to shine on both evil and good

---

[36]Lk 7:4-5. [37]*MKGK* 67. [38]PG 56:702. [39]Lk 18:27. [40]Acts 7:60. [41]1 Cor 4:12. [42]*MKGK* 68. [43]PG 57:269; NPNF 1 10:126**.

people, and the rain from his mouth falls upon both the righteous and the sinful. FRAGMENT 42.[44]

JOINT HEIRS WITH CHRIST BY ADOPTION. AUGUSTINE: With regard to what immediately follows, namely, "That you may be children of your Father who is in heaven," it is to be understood in the sense in which John also speaks when he says, "He gave them the power of becoming children of God."[45] For there is One who is the Son by nature, and he absolutely knows no sin. But since we have received the power to become sons, we are made sons insofar as we fulfill the precepts that have been given by the Son. "Adoption" is the term used by the apostle to denote the character of our vocation to the eternal inheritance, in order to be joint heirs with Christ. By spiritual regeneration we therefore become sons and are adopted into the kingdom of God, not as aliens but as his creatures and offspring. SERMON ON THE MOUNT 1.23.78.[46]

A SPIRITUAL INTERPRETATION OF SUN AND RAIN. AUGUSTINE: Since he calls us to the adoption as sons through the only begotten Son himself, he calls us to his own likeness. For, as the Lord at once adds, "He makes his sun to rise on the good and the evil and sends rain on the just and the unjust." Now, if you would understand the expression "his sun" to mean not the sun that is visible to bodily eyes but his wisdom, to which the following expressions refer—"he is the brightness of eternal light"[47] and also "The sun of justice is risen upon me,"[48] as well as "But to you that fear the name of the Lord, the sun of justice shall arise"[49]—then you must also understand the rain as a watering by the teaching of truth, because that teaching has become manifest to the good and to the evil. But you may prefer to understand it as the sun that is manifest to the bodily eyes of beasts as well as people and to understand the rain as the showers that produce the fruits that God has given us for the perfec-

tion of the body. I believe this to be surely the more probable meaning, since the other "sun" does not rise except on the good and the holy, for this is the very thing that the unjust bewail in the book that is called the Wisdom of Solomon: "And the sun [of understanding] has not risen upon us."[50] And the spiritual rain refreshes only the good, for the vine signifies the bad of whom it is said, "I will command my clouds not to rain upon it."[51] SERMON ON THE MOUNT 1.23. 79.[52]

THE DESTINY OF THE JUST AND THE UNJUST NOT SEPARATED. ANONYMOUS: He put it carefully when he said "over the just and the unjust," not "over the unjust as over the just,"[53] because God puts all good things on the earth, not on account of all people but on account of the few holy ones. He is more content that sinners should enjoy the benefits of God against their deserving than that the just should be robbed of his benefits against their deserving. Likewise, when the Lord is irritated by sinners, he sends his punishment not on account of the good but only on account of the sinners; nevertheless it touches the just in equal measure with the sinners. For as in prosperity he does not separate the sinners from the just, so he does not separate the just from the sinners in hard times. He does not separate the sinners from the just in prosperity, lest, being separated, they should

---

[44]*MKGK* 68. [45]Jn 1:12. [46]PL 34:1268; FC 11:105-6*. We embody our sonship and daughterhood by living as if we were receiving our eternal inheritance, which is enabled by our spiritual regeneration. [47]Wis 7:26. [48]See Breviary, Response 8, Festival of the Blessed Virgin Mary; cf. FC 11:106 n. 4. [49]Mal 4:2. [50]Wis 5:6. [51]Is 5:6. [52]PL 34:1268-69; FC 11:106-7. The spiritual meanings of sun and rain are grounded in and constrained by their literal meanings. The spiritual meaning of sun as truth is grounded in the literal meaning of the sun as light. The spiritual meaning of the rain as the watering by the teaching of the truth must be grounded in the literal meaning of rain as refreshment. [53]If indeed the scriptural text recorded that God brought down rain on the unjust and the just alike, one could deduce that God grants gifts indiscriminately. The author here, however, is convinced that God grants gifts to the good and punishment to the evil, though sometimes the evil are involved in the gifts and the good in the punishments.

know themselves to be cast down and despair. He does not separate the just from the sinners in hard times, lest, being separated, they should know themselves to be chosen and boast. Above all, prosperity should not benefit the evil but rather hurt them, nor should difficult times harm the good but rather benefit them. INCOMPLETE WORK ON MATTHEW, HOMILY 13.[54]

5:46-47 What Reward Have You?

THE PERFECTION OF LOVING THE ENEMY. ANONYMOUS: He who loves his friends loves them for his own sake, not on account of God, and therefore he has no treasure. The loving itself delights him. However, he who loves his enemy loves not for his own sake but on account of God. Hence he has great treasure, because he goes against his own instincts. For where labor sows the seed, there it reaps the fruit. "Be ye therefore perfect, just as your Father is perfect." He who loves his friend does not in fact sin but does not work justice. It is half a good that one depart from evil and not pursue good. It is perfect, however, that one not only flee evil but also accomplish good. So he said, "Be perfect," so that you might both love your friends on account of shunning evil and love your enemies on account of possessing justice. The former frees us from punishment; the latter leads us into glory. For a representative of God is not perfect who does not resemble God through his or her works. INCOMPLETE WORK ON MATTHEW, HOMILY 13.[55]

5:48 Perfect as the Heavenly Father Is Perfect

ALL THINGS ARE PERFECTED BY GOODNESS. HILARY: Matthew concludes, "All things are perfected by goodness." The law used to demand that your neighbor be loved and allowed hatred against an enemy. Faith, rather, requires that enemies be cherished. It breaks the tendency we have to be peevish and urges us to bear life's difficulties calmly. Faith not only deters anger from turning into revenge but even softens it into love for the injurer. It is merely human to love those who love you, and it is common to cherish those who cherish you. Therefore Christ calls us into the life of heirs of God and to be models for the just and the unjust of the imitation of Christ. He distributes the sun and the rain through his coming in baptism and by the sacraments of the Spirit. Thus he has prepared us for the perfect life through this concord of public goodness, because we must imitate our perfect Father in heaven. ON MATTHEW 4.27.[56]

THE LAW OF GOSPEL LOVE. CHROMATIUS: The Lord has shown that we cannot have the good work of perfect love if we love only those from whom in turn we know the return of mutual love will be paid in kind. For we know that love of this sort is common even to nonbelievers and sinners. Hence the Lord wishes us to overcome the common law of human love by the law of gospel love, so that we may show the affection of our love not only toward those who love us but even toward our enemies.... Thus we may imitate the example of true piety and our Father's goodness. TRACTATE ON MATTHEW 21.2.1.[57]

---

[54]PG 56:703-4. [55]PG 56:703. [56]SC 254:146-48. [57]CCL 9a:320.

6:1-4 GIVING TO THE NEEDY

[1]*"Beware of practicing your piety before men in order to be seen by them; for then you will have no reward from your Father who is in heaven.*

[2]*"Thus, when you give alms, sound no trumpet before you, as the hypocrites do in the synagogues and in the streets, that they may be praised by men. Truly, I say to you, they have received their reward.* [3]*But when you give alms, do not let your left hand know what your right hand is doing,* [4]*so that your alms may be in secret; and your Father who sees in secret will reward you."*

OVERVIEW: Since egotism and virtue are directly opposed to each other, they can never happily coexist in the soul (ORIGEN). Alms may be given to be seen or not seen, depending upon inward intent (CHRYSOSTOM). One who acts to be seen by others not only fails to enter heaven but also earns pitiably little on earth (ANONYMOUS). We should not broadcast what we do, because it is not the mark of a devout mind to do any of the works of God in order to anticipate the glory of human praise (CHROMATIUS). Those who perform acts of kindness when others are present function like trumpets for their own goodness (ANONYMOUS). The pursuit of human praise will receive only that reward it seeks from other people (HILARY). Your quiet giving should be concealed from the very hands that give (CHRYSOSTOM). The right hand is not to know the left in giving alms (CHROMATIUS). Every good thing becomes more pleasing when hidden by us but revealed by God (ANONYMOUS). The praise of another need not even be sought by one who acts uprightly (AUGUSTINE).

6:1 Beware of Public Piety

AS FIRE TO WATER, SO IS EGOTISM TO VIRTUE. ORIGEN: Just as water always conflicts with fire and fire with water and such things can never dwell together simultaneously, so likewise egotism and virtue are opposed to each other and can never easily coexist in one and the same soul. Therefore egotism is to be expelled from our souls, and we must abide in Christ's commandments. FRAGMENT 114.[1]

THE FALSE PIETY THAT ATTEMPTS TO BE SEEN. CHRYSOSTOM: When Jesus warned, "Beware of practicing your piety before men," he then added pointedly, "to be seen by them." On first glance it seems as if the same thing were being repeated, but if you were carefully to pay attention, you will note a careful distinction. Alms may be given in the presence of others primarily to be seen by them, or they may be given in the presence of others but not to be seen, or they may be openly given in order to be seen but still not be seen, or they may be given quietly and still be seen. He is not focusing simply on the outward act done but the inward intent. THE GOSPEL OF MATTHEW, HOMILY 19.2.[2]

REMOVING CARE FOR THE PRESENT. HILARY: He removes all concern for things of the present and bids those thunderstruck by the hope of the future to pursue neither the favor of others by parading their virtue nor religious boasting through an outpouring of public prayer. Rather, the fruit of good works is to be contained within

---

[1]GCS 41.1:61. [2]PG 57:274; NPNF 1 10:131**. God sees the inward intent of good works.

the knowledge of faith, because the pursuit of human praise will receive only that reward which it looks for from people, while to yearn for God's approval is to pursue a reward longed for patiently. ON MATTHEW 4.28.[3]

NO REWARD FROM YOUR FATHER. ANONYMOUS: You who have offered nothing to God, what do you expect to receive from God? Everything done on account of God is given to God and received by God. But what is done to be seen by others is poured into the wind.... What is human praise but the sound of the whistling winds? ... Those who act on account of others, to be praised by them, have wasted their energy. What sort of wisdom is it to put on a show and to prepare empty speeches? Those who do so scorn the treasure of God waiting in eternity in heaven, preferring fleeting human words. It is better to do nothing than to act to be seen. For those who do nothing, even if they do not enter heaven, at least squander nothing on earth. But those who act to be seen by others not only fail to enter heaven but also earn pitiably little on earth. INCOMPLETE WORK ON MATTHEW, HOMILY 13.[4]

6:2 Sounding No Trumpet

AGAINST BROADCASTING GOOD ACTS. CHROMATIUS: Earlier Jesus taught that the work of justice is to be done not for the sake of humans but for the sake of God. Now we are also instructed that we should not blow the trumpet when we perform acts of charity. That is, we should not broadcast what we do, because it is not the mark of a devout mind to do any of the works of God in order to anticipate the glory of human praise. Many people, you see, make a donation for the use of the poor in order to reap from the gesture the human praise and the renown of their contemporaries. The Lord shows that they have received the reward of their work in this age. For as long as they seek the glory of this age, they lose the reward of the

future promise. TRACTATE ON MATTHEW 26.4.2.[5]

TRUMPETING ONE'S OWN GOODNESS. ANONYMOUS: Every act or speech through which one boasts in good works is like a trumpet. Consider one who performs an act of kindness when he sees someone present but does not do so when no one is there. He is like a trumpet, because through this act his boasting is broadcast. Likewise, consider one who performs an act of kindness when someone asks him to do so but does not do it when no one asks. This bad habit is a trumpet. Again, consider one who gives something of value to an upper-class person, should he see one, a person who is able to reciprocate. But to the lowly and to the poor chained by sufferings, he gives nothing. This too is a trumpet, even if he acted in secret, as long as he did it to seem praiseworthy (first, because he did it; second, because he did it secretly). The very act of concealment trumpets his charity. Whatever this man did, thanks to which he stands out or desires to stand out ... that is a trumpet. The very act of kindness, although it actually happened, trumpets itself. Therefore it is not so much the place or the act, but rather the intention, that is to be kept secret. INCOMPLETE WORK ON MATTHEW, HOMILY 13.[6]

6:3 Right and Left Hands

NOT LITERAL HANDS. CHRYSOSTOM: Jesus is not talking about literal left and right hands. Rather, he speaks spiritually with intentional exaggeration. "If it is possible," he says, "for you to remain unaware, let this be your goal. The result, if it be possible, is that your giving be concealed from the very hands that serve." It is not, as some say, that we should hide it from wrong-headed people, for he has commanded here that it should be concealed from all. THE

---

[3]SC 254:148. [4]PG 56:706. [5]CCL 9a:321. [6]PG 56:707.

GOSPEL OF MATTHEW, HOMILY 19.2.[7]

ALMS NOT FOR BOASTING. CHROMATIUS:
Here the Lord is not speaking literally of the
hands of the human body. Hands as such cannot
know, having the senses neither of seeing nor or
language. Rather, "on the right hand" means
righteous deeds and "on the left" signifies sinful
deeds or persons. Thus we read it written in the
book of Kings that "hand" means people when it
says, "Do I not have ten hands in Israel?"[8]—that
is, ten tribes of Israel. Therefore, there is no
doubt that "on the right hand" means "the just"
and "on the left" means "sinners," according to
what Solomon related: "The Lord acknowledges
the divisions on the right; the perverse are those
who are on the left."[9] The Lord makes very plain
the meaning of this "right" and "left" in the Gospel when he declares that the just are to be
placed at the right, the sinners on the left.[10] If
something is to be accomplished according to
the teaching of the Lord, then the right hand of
the just must not know what the left is doing.
That is, in order to labor religiously and faithfully, we should not boast in the sight of sinners
and unfaithful people. TRACTATE ON MATTHEW
26.5.2-4.[11]

6:4 Alms Given in Secret

ALMSGIVING IN SECRET. AUGUSTINE: A hypocrite is one who pretends to be something one is
not. This person pretends to be righteous yet
shows no evidence of righteousness. All attention is focused on how one is being perceived or
praised by others. Even pretenders may receive
this praise precisely while they are deceiving
those to whom they seem to be good. But they
receive no reward from God the searcher of the
heart—only reproach for their deceit. They may
have a human reward, but from God they hear,
"Depart from me, you workers of deceit. You

may speak my name, but you do not do my
works."[12] So you receive your reward with others, you have received the glory of others—so
what? If you do good for the express purpose of
having human glory, what good have you? The
praise of others need not even be sought by one
who acts rightly. We ought to follow one who
acts rightly, profiting by imitating what we
praise. SERMON ON THE MOUNT 2.2.5.[13]

**GOD WILL REVEAL GOOD WORKS IN DUE
TIME. ANONYMOUS:** Understand that he means
the secret place of the heart rather than a location. For the Lord dwells in the recesses of your
heart, not in a particular secret place. Remember that the Lord does not wish us to act in
secret in order that our work may be invisible.
Elsewhere he says, "Let your light shine so that
others may see your good works and may glorify
your Father who is in heaven."[14] But it is the
Lord who in due time will reveal. Every good
thing becomes more pleasing when it is hidden
by us but revealed by God. If you display yourself, there are few who will praise you, and few
will understand, even if you should appear humble. The one who does understand this will
lament you rather than praise you. If, on the
other hand, God reveals you, no one will find
fault, except perhaps an evil person, to whom a
good person is displeasing. For it is impossible
that the Lord would ignore the good work of a
good person done in secret. God will make such
a one known in this age and boast in him in the
future, because the glory comes from God.
INCOMPLETE WORK ON MATTHEW, HOMILY 13.[15]

---

[7]PG 57:275; NPNF 1 10:131**. [8]2 Sam 19:43. [9]cf. Eccles 10:2;
Prov 4:27. [10]Mt 25:33. [11]CCL 9a:322. [12]Mt 7:21-23. [13]PL
34:1271-72; NPNF 1 6:35**; ACW 5:95-96. In the presence of God
it is pointless to focus on how one is being perceived. Hypocrisy is
rejected by the One who sees through our deceptions. The praise of
others need not even be sought by one who acts rightly. [14]Mt 5:16.
[15]PG 56:708.

6:5-8 PRINCIPLES OF PRAYER

[5]*"And when you pray, you must not be like the hypocrites; for they love to stand and pray in the synagogues and at the street corners, that they may be seen by men. Truly, I say to you, they have received their reward.* [6]*But when you pray, go into your room and shut the door and pray to your Father who is in secret; and your Father who sees in secret will reward you.*

[7]*"And in praying do not heap up empty phrases as the Gentiles do; for they think that they will be heard for their many words.* [8]*Do not be like them, for your Father knows what you need before you ask him."*

OVERVIEW: When you pray, set aside all turmoil, as if you were being joined by choirs of angels and singing with the seraphim (CHRYSOSTOM). As soon as sincere prayer issues from the mouth, the angels take it up in their hands and bring it before God (ANONYMOUS). One who is earnestly offering a supplication looks exclusively to the One who has the power to grant the request, letting all other claims recede (CHRYSOSTOM). The hypocrites' reward comes from those from whom they most desire to receive it (CHRYSOSTOM). They sell an empty form of religion, and they buy an empty word of praise (ANONYMOUS). It is not to human beings that they are praying but to God, who is present everywhere, who hears even before they speak and who knows already the secrets of the heart (CHRYSOSTOM). Anna, Daniel, Cornelius and Jonah are biblical prototypes of those who fulfilled the precepts of this Gospel teaching, who prayed in secret and were heard by the Lord (CHROMATIUS). The soul enters the interior center of the self when it prays. It thinks of nothing except for what it prays and to whom it prays, closing the doorway of its bodily senses, so that it may shut outside all external thoughts and cares (ANONYMOUS). We pray not to inform God or instruct God but to ask earnestly, to become intimate with God, to be humbled and reminded of our sins (CHRYSOSTOM). Pagan priests spend a long time summoning something that has no ears to hear (ANONYMOUS). We are called and invited to be honest before God about our actual, urgent needs (CHRYSOSTOM). The contrite publican, asking forgiveness for his sins, came away more justified than the wordy, self-elevating Pharisee (CHROMATIUS). We do not pray to demand from God what we want but that it may please him to bestow what we need (ANONYMOUS).

6:5 When You Pray

PRAY WITH THE ANGELS. CHRYSOSTOM: When you pray, it is as if you were entering into a palace—not a palace on earth, but far more awesome, a palace in heaven. When you enter there, you do so with complete attentiveness and fitting respect. For in the houses of kings all turmoil is set aside, and silence reigns. Yet here you are being joined by choirs of angels. You are in communion with archangels and singing with the seraphim, who sing with great awe their spiritual hymns and sacred songs to God, the Lord of all. So when you are praying, mingle with these voices, patterning yourself according to their mystical order. It is not to human beings that you are praying but to God, who is present everywhere, who hears even before you speak and who knows already the secrets of the heart. If you pray to this One, you shall receive a great reward. "For your Father who sees in secret shall reward you openly." He did not merely say he would give it to you but reward you, as if he himself had made a pledge to you and so honored you with a great honor. Because God himself is hidden, your prayer should be hidden. The Gospel of Matthew, Homily 19.3.[1]

Departing with Empty Hands. Chrysostom: While pretending to pray to God, the hypocrites are looking around for human praise. The elaborate garb they wear is laughable, and hardly that of a sincere supplicant. One who is earnestly offering a supplication looks exclusively to the One who has the power to grant the request and lets all other claims recede. But if you leave behind the one you are petitioning and immediately go wandering about looking everywhere for others' approval, you will depart with empty hands. The Gospel of Matthew, Homily 19.2.[2]

Open the Storehouse of Prayer. Anonymous: Our talk is about prayer, which alone the soul offers to God from its depths. It is a kind of spiritual wealth. All acts of justice which a person does, that person does according to his capability and brings them forth from the store of his capacity. Prayer alone he speaks according to his faith and brings forth from the store of his faith. Do you want to know how precious prayer is? No act of outward justice is compared with incense: only prayer is. As is shown in the Revelation of John, the great angel proceeds before the visage of the altar, holding in his hand a censer of the fragrances of incense, and it is said to him, "These are the prayers of the holy ones."[3] Just as well-blended incense delights the worshipful person, so the prayer of the just person is sweet before God. Do you wish to know its dignity? As soon as it issues from the mouth, the angels take it up in their hands and bring it before God, just as the archangel said to Tobias: "I am he who has brought your prayer before God."[4] Incomplete Work on Matthew, Homily 13.[5]

The Hypocrites Have Received Their Reward. Chrysostom: Your inner will cannot be hid. This is why Jesus did not say, "They shall not receive a reward" but "They have received their reward"—already! Their reward comes from those from whom they themselves most desire to get it. God does not desire this. For God preferred to bestow upon humanity the grace that comes only from himself. Those who seek their reward from people cannot receive another reward from the One for whom they have sought nothing. The Gospel of Matthew, Homily 19.2.[6]

Selling and Buying. Anonymous: Wherever each one sows his seed, there he reaps; and what he sows, that too he reaps. The hypocrites pray on account of others, not on account of God. Thus they are praised by others, not God. Deceitfully they pray, and even then they are not really praying. Deceitfully they are praised, though they are not really praiseworthy. They sell an empty form of religion, and they buy an empty word of praise. Just as the prayer of these people does not please God, neither does the praise of others adorn them. For what is placed in a word lasts as long as the word is spoken; when the word has ended, the benefit that was placed in the word also has ended. Incomplete Work on Matthew, Homily 13.[7]

6:6 *Where You Pray*

The Bedroom of Our Hearts. Hilary: We are asked to pray with the bedroom door closed, as it were, and we are taught to pour out our prayer in every place. The saints' prayers were undertaken in the presence of wild animals, in prisons, in flames, from the depths of the sea

---

[1]PG 57:277; NPNF 1 10:133**. The fitting approach to prayer is awe in the presence of God. [2]PG 57:276; NPNF 1 10:132**. The reward of hypocrites comes from those from whom they most want to receive it: not God but human auditors. [3]Rev 8:3; 5:8. [4]Tob 12:12. [5]PG 56:708-9. [6]PG 57:276; NPNF 1 10:132**. [7]PG 56:709.

and the belly of the beast. Hence we are admonished not to enter the recesses of our homes but the bedroom of our hearts. With the office of our minds closed, we pray to God not with many words but with our conscience, for every act is superior to the words of speakers. On Matthew 5.1.[8]

Entering the Inner Chamber. Augustine: Enter into your inner chamber. Do not let the door stand open to the boisterous, through whom the things that are outside profanely rush in and assail the inner self. Sermon on the Mount 2.3.11.[9]

Cleansing the Heart. Augustine: Outside the inner chamber are all things in time and space, which knock on the door. Through our bodily senses they clamor to interrupt our prayer, so that prayer is invaded with a crowd of vain phantoms. This is why you must shut the door. The senses of the body are resisted, that the spirit of prayer may be directed to the Father. This occurs in the inmost heart, where prayer is offered to the Father in secret. There "your Father who sees in secret will reward you." This is a fitting conclusion to good counsel, not merely calling us to pray but also showing us how, not merely calling us to give alms but also showing the right spirit for doing so. The instruction is to cleanse the heart. Nothing cleanses the heart but the undivided and single-minded striving after eternal life from the pure love of wisdom alone. Sermon on the Mount 2.3.11.[10]

Shutting Out All External Cares. Anonymous: These things are better understood in a spiritual sense, as spoken about the soul. "Room" is the heart, or the inner, that is, spiritual intellect. It has been written, "That which you say in your hearts, also grieve for in private."[11] The doorway is the exterior, bodily sense through which all things, good and bad, enter upon the soul. So also in the Canticle, Wisdom speaks in the person of the church:

"Lo, my beloved knocks at the door, 'Open to me, my sister, my dearest.' "[12] Christ too knocks at the door of the Christian, entering the heart either through the divine Scriptures or good thoughts. The one who receives them opens oneself to Christ. The one who sends them away shuts the door. For this reason Jesus orders that the soul enter the inward understanding when it prays, so that it thinks of nothing except for what it prays and to whom it prays. Thus it closes the doorway of its bodily sense, so that it may shut outside all external thoughts and cares. Incomplete Work on Matthew, Homily 13.[13]

Examples of Praying in Secret. Chromatius: We find in the books of Kings that very holy woman Hannah fulfilling the precepts of this Gospel teaching. For while praying without uttering a sound, in her heart and in the sight of God, she poured out her desire in her prayers. She was immediately found worthy to be heard by the Lord.[14] In the same way the Lord granted to Daniel, who always prayed in secret with three servants, to understand the interpretations of his dream and the secrets of revelation.[15] Cornelius too, not yet instructed in the precepts of the gospel, prayed secretly and faithfully in his room and was found worthy to hear the voice of the angel speaking.[16] What should we say of Jonah, who, not only in his room but trapped in the stomach of the whale, deserved so greatly to be heard through his prayers that from the depths of the sea and from the belly of so great a beast he escaped unharmed and alive?[17] Tractate on Matthew 27.1.4-5.[18]

6:7 No Empty Phrases

---

[8]SC 254:150. [9]PL 34:1274; NPNF 1 6:37**; ACW 5:101. The door to external temporal and physical attractions must be shut so that full attentiveness can be given to God, by cleansing the inmost heart. [10]PL 34:1274; NPNF 1 6:37**; ACW 5:101. [11]Ps 4:4 . [12]Song 5:2. [13]PG 56:709-10. [14]1 Sam 1:13-17. [15]Dan 1:17. [16]Acts 10:1-4. [17]Jon 2:1-11. [18]CCL 9a:325-26.

AVOID AN ABUNDANCE OF WORDS. CHROMA-TIUS: Nonbelievers think that they can more easily obtain from the Lord what they require by using many words, but the Lord does not expect this from us. Rather, he wants us to send up our prayers not with wordy speech but with faith that comes from the heart. By doing so we command the merits of justice to him. He surely knows better all the things of which we have need and before we speak is aware of everything that we are going to request. TRACTATE ON MATTHEW 27.2.1-2.[19]

PAGAN PRIESTS SUMMON IDOLS THAT CANNOT HEAR. ANONYMOUS: Let us note carefully the gods to whom the pagans pray, that we may understand how not to pray. They pray to demons, who may hear but are not able to heed. They are not even able to supply evil things, unless God permits it. They pray to dead kings, Jove, Mercury, and others, whose crimes are more manifest than their names. They were not able to help, even while they lived. They pray to insensate idols, who are not able to hear nor to give responses. Understandably then their priests spend a long time summoning where there is no one to hear. When the priests of Baal called on their gods through immolated sacrifices, Elijah said in mockery, "Shout, shout strongly: perhaps your gods are sleeping."[20] In the same way the person who prolongs his prayer with a lot of talk rails at God, as if he were sleeping. INCOMPLETE WORK ON MATTHEW, HOMILY 13.[21]

HOW TO PRAY. CHRYSOSTOM: By the example of the importunate widow who prevailed with the pitiless and cruel ruler by persevering in her requests,[22] we are shown how to pray. We hear the insistent voice of the friend who came late at night and roused the sleeper from his bed,[23] not for friendship's sake but out of his urgent need. By these examples Jesus called us continually to make earnest supplication to the Father. He did

not ask us to compose a prayer of ten thousand phrases and so come to him and merely repeat it. He warned against those who "think that they shall be heard for their loquacity." "For your Father knows what you need before you ask him." But if he already knows what we need, why do we pray? Not to inform God or instruct him but to beseech him closely, to be made intimate with him, by continuance in supplication; to be humbled; to be reminded of our sins. THE GOSPEL OF MATTHEW, HOMILY 19.4.[24]

THE WORDY AND THE SIMPLE PRAYER. CHRO-MATIUS: We have an example of just how great a distance there is between the wordy and the humble and simple prayer in the story of the Pharisee and the publican. The prayer of the Pharisee vaunting himself in his abundance of words was rejected. The humble and contrite publican, on the other hand, asking forgiveness for his sins, came away more justified than the self-boasting Pharisee. In this we find fulfilled what was written: "The prayer of the humble penetrates the clouds,"[25] reaching God who is ready to hear the request of the one who prays. TRACTATE ON MATTHEW 27.2.3.[26]

6:8 Your Father Knows Your Needs

BEFORE YOU ASK. ANONYMOUS: Your Father knows what is necessary for you before you ask him. If he knows what we want ahead of time, then we do not pray to demand from God what we want but that it may please him to bestow what we need. God is to be conciliated, not taught; a long prayer is not needful for him but a genuine spirit. INCOMPLETE WORK ON MATTHEW, HOMILY 13.[27]

[19]CCL 9a:326. [20]1 Kings 18:27. [21]PG 56:710. [22]Lk 18:1-8. [23]Lk 11:5. [24]PG 57:278; NPNF 1 10:133**. We are called and invited to be honest before God about our actual, urgent needs, so as to bring us into intimate communion with God. [25]Sir 35:21. [26]CCL 9a:326-27. [27]PG 56:710-11.

6:9-15 THE LORD'S PRAYER

> ^{9}*"Pray then like this:*
>   *Our Father who art in heaven,*
>   *Hallowed be thy name.*
> ^{10}*Thy kingdom come,*
>   *Thy will be done,*
>   *On earth as it is in heaven.*
> ^{11}*Give us this day our daily bread;*^{m}
> ^{12}*And forgive us our debts,*
>   *As we also have forgiven our debtors;*
> ^{13}*And lead us not into temptation,*
>   *But deliver us from evil."*^{n}
> ^{14}*For if you forgive men their trespasses, your heavenly Father also will forgive you;* ^{15}*but if you do not forgive men their trespasses, neither will your Father forgive your trespasses."*

m Or *our bread for the morrow*   n Or *the evil one.* Other authorities, some ancient, add, in some form, *For thine is the kingdom and the power and the glory, for ever. Amen.*

OVERVIEW: To address God as Father is the privilege of belief in the Son (TERTULLIAN, ORIGEN), a privilege we receive and learn about from the one who mothers our faith, namely, the church (TERTULLIAN). Do not think of heaven in simplistic spatial metaphors, as if the birds are nearer to God than we (AUGUSTINE). By saying "our Father who art in heaven" we are both adoring God and expressing our faith (TERTULLIAN). God wishes to be called Father, that he may give us great confidence in seeking him (ANONYMOUS). God who is incomparably holy is not made more holy by our prayer; rather, we pray that his holy name may daily be made holy in us (CYPRIAN). To pray to hallow his name is to pray that we may be enabled to live so blamelessly that through us all may glorify God (CHRYSOSTOM).

People who pray for the coming of the kingdom of God rightly pray that the kingdom of God might be established in themselves (ORIGEN) and that God might reign in us (CYPRIAN). The citizens of this kingdom live already in it, as in a well-ordered city where God already reigns (ORIGEN). All are equal in God's presence, whether king or pauper (CHRYSOSTOM). Christ is the kingdom of God, whose advent we crave to be quickly manifested to us (CYPRIAN). The kingdom of God, though already present on the earth, is as yet unrecognized by those who remain ignorant of it (AUGUSTINE). God is intrinsically and by nature Lord, but he does not compel obedience. Hence he does not coercively reign over all, so not all people are in his kingdom, because not all do his will (ANONYMOUS). The prayer for God's will to be done does not imply that anyone could prevent the fulfillment of God's will or that he needs our prayer to accomplish his will (TERTULLIAN). Even as one cannot do good without God's help, neither does God will to do good in someone unless that one wills to let him do good (ANONYMOUS).

We pray that our bread be given to us daily. This means that we who daily receive the Eucharist for the food of salvation may not be separated by sin from Christ's body (CYPRIAN).

When we receive bread daily we partake of the divine nature. This is the bread that nourishes our essential humanity (ORIGEN). This daily bread is given to supply just enough for one day (CHRYSOSTOM). Yet this supersubstantial bread (*maar*) also means "for tomorrow," for eternity, and implies a bread that is not reducible to physical substances (JEROME).

Since we sin daily, we are commanded to ask pardon for sins daily (CYPRIAN). If baptism remits all sin, we nonetheless continue to pray for forgiveness for continuing sins after baptism (CHRYSOSTOM). We will not receive forgiveness unless we have first forgiven others (AUGUSTINE, ANONYMOUS). Evil is not from God's will in creation but from the free choice of creatures (CHRYSOSTOM). We pray not only that old sins will be forgiven but that new sins will be resisted (TERTULLIAN). We are more like God in the act of forgiveness than at any other moment. To forgive is to be like God. (CHRYSOSTOM). This prayer for forgiveness belongs to believers who call God Father, who discover daily forgiveness within the nurturing pedagogy of the church (CHRYSOSTOM). This petition assumes that we are ready to forgive those who ask our pardon, since we too want to be forgiven by our most generous Father with respect to those who seek pardon from us (AUGUSTINE). One who says he or she forgives but does not forgive will not be forgiven (ANONYMOUS). A decisive covenant with God is implied in forgiving as we have been forgiven, so important that its neglect places in question the fulfillment of all the previous petitions (AUGUSTINE).

The devil is not evil by nature, for evil is not something derived from any nature as created but what has been added to nature by choice (CHRYSOSTOM). The brief petition to be delivered from evil summarizes and comprehends all our petitions to God (CYPRIAN). The first three petitions pertain to eternal life: hallowing God's name, praying for the coming kingdom and the complete fulfillment of the will of God (AUGUSTINE). The last four petitions pertain to tempo-

ral life: daily bread, forgiveness of sins, struggle against temptations, deliverance from evil (AUGUSTINE).

6:9 Approaching Our Heavenly Father

SHOWING BELIEF. TERTULLIAN: Prayer begins with a demonstration of our belief in God and a blessed act of faith at the moment when we say, "Father, who art in heaven." For we are thereby both adoring God and demonstrating our faith, and this form of address is the result. It is written, "To those who believe in God he gave the power to be called the children of God."[1] ON PRAYER 2.1.[2]

THE CHURCH IS THE MOTHER OF FAITH. TERTULLIAN: Our Lord so frequently spoke to us of God as Father. He even taught us to call none on earth father,[3] but only the one we have in heaven.[4] Therefore, when we pray to the Father, we are following this command. Blessed are they who recognize their Father! Remember the reproach made against Israel, when the Spirit calls heaven and earth to witness, saying, "I have begotten sons and they have not known me."[5] In addressing him as Father we are also naming him God, so as to combine in a single term both filial love and power. Addressing the Father, the Son is also being addressed, for Christ said, "I and the Father are one." Nor is Mother Church passed over without mention, for the mother is recognized in the Son and the Father, as it is within the church that we learn the meaning of the terms *Father* and *Son*. ON PRAYER 2.2-6.[6]

THE PRIVILEGE OF CALLING GOD ABBA. ORIGEN: According to the apostle, "as long as the heir has not reached his majority, he differs little from a servant, though he be lord of all. He

---

[1]Jn 1:12. [2]CCL 1:258; FC 40:159**; ANF 3:682**. [3]In the same voice that we say *Abba*. [4]Mt 23:9. [5]Is 1:2. [6]CCL 1:258; FC 40:159-60**; ANF 3:682**. To address God as Father is the privilege of belief in the Son, a privilege we receive and learn about from the one who mothers our faith, namely, the church.

remains under tutors and governors until the time of his maturity appointed by his father."[7] But the "fullness of time"[8] consists in our Lord Jesus Christ coming among us, when those who desire it receive adoption as sons, as Paul says in these words: "For you have not received the spirit of bondage in fear, but you have received the spirit of adoption as sons, whereby we cry, 'Abba! Father!'"[9] ON PRAYER 22.2.[10]

APPROACHING GOD WITH GREAT CONFIDENCE. ANONYMOUS: He wishes himself to be called Father rather than Lord, so that he may give us great confidence in seeking him and great hope in beseeching him. Servants do not always demand what they want nor even always seek with a good conscience things that are righteous. Frequently servants do not consider what pertains to the benefit of their master but to their own benefit. Hence they do not always deserve to be heard. Sons, however, always make petition because they seek with good conscience what is righteous. They do not consider first what is for their own good but what is for the good of their father. Hence they always deserve to be heard. If you believe yourself to be a son of God, seek those things that are advantageous for you to receive and that it behooves him to bestow. However, if you always seek from him carnal and earthly things, you are setting yourself a difficult or impossible task. How would those things benefit you who don't have them, which everywhere he admonishes you to scorn if you did have them? INCOMPLETE WORK ON MATTHEW, HOMILY 14.[11]

THE LIMITS OF SPATIAL METAPHORS. AUGUSTINE: Let the new people, therefore, who are called to an eternal inheritance freely employ the word of the New Testament and say, "Our Father who art in heaven," that is, the place where holiness and justice reign. For God is not contained spatially. The heavens may be in a sense "higher" created bodies of the world, even while remaining created, and so cannot exist apart from some spatial location. But do not think of this spatially, as if the birds are nearer to God than we. It is not written that "the Lord is closer to tall people" or "nearer to those who live on higher hills." For it is written, "The Lord is near to the broken-hearted and saves the crushed in spirit,"[12] namely, close to those who are humble. SERMON ON THE MOUNT 2.5.17.[13]

IN HEAVEN ALL INEQUITIES ARE OVERCOME. CHRYSOSTOM: This at once takes away hatred, quells pride, casts out envy and brings in the mother of all good things, charity. By inward prayer the inequality of human things is thwarted. It shows how nearly equal are the king and the poor person in all those matters that are most indispensable and of greatest weight. Behind those closed doors before God, we are all equals. THE GOSPEL OF MATTHEW, HOMILY 19.4.[14]

GOD IS NOT MADE HOLY BY DEGREES. CYPRIAN: We pray "Hallowed be thy name," not that we wish that God may be made holy by our prayers but that his name may be hallowed in us. But by whom is God made holy, since he himself is incomparably holy? It is because he commands us, "Be holy, even as I am holy,"[15] that we ask and entreat that we who were sanctified in baptism may continue in that which we have begun to be. And this we pray for daily, for we have need of daily sanctification, that we who daily fall away may wash out our sins by continual sanctification.[16] TREATISES, ON THE LORD'S PRAYER 12.[17]

---

[7]Gal 4:2. [8]Gal 4:4. [9]Rom 8:15. [10]GCS 3:347; ACW 19:73-74*. It is the distinct privilege of those who believe in God the Son to address God as Father in the same way he did. [11]PG 56:711. [12]Ps 34:18 (33:18 LXX). [13]PL 34:1276-77; NPNF 1 6:39**; ACW 5:106. The spatial metaphors are only partially useful in speaking of both God's almightiness and nearness yet limited by finite perceptions. [14]PG 57:278; NPNF 1 10:134*. [15]1 Pet 1:16; cf. Lev 20:7. [16]When we pray to be holy even as God is holy, we are following his command by asking that the sanctification begun in our baptism may continue. [17]CCL 3a:96; ANF 5:450*.

GLORIFYING HIS NAME. CHRYSOSTOM: The prayer to hallow God's name corresponds with what Jesus has previously taught: "Let your light so shine before others that they may see your good works and glorify your Father who is in heaven,"[18] just as the seraphim too, giving glory, sang "Holy, holy, holy."[19] So "hallowed" means "glorified." In effect he is saying, "Enable us to live so purely that through us all may glorify you." It points us again to mature self-control, that we may present to all a life so irreprehensible that every one of those who observe may offer to the Lord the praise due to him for this. THE GOSPEL OF MATTHEW, HOMILY 19.4.[20]

6:10 God's Kingdom and Will

CHRIST REIGNS IN THE MATURING SOUL. ORIGEN: The kingdom of God, according to the word of our Lord and Savior, "comes not with observation"; and "neither shall they say, Behold here, or behold there"—but "the kingdom of God is within us"[21] (for "the word is very near to us,"[22] in our mouths and in our hearts). So one who prays for the coming of the kingdom of God rightly prays that the kingdom of God might be established in himself, that it might bear fruit and be perfected in himself. Every saint, being ruled by God as king and obedient to the spiritual laws of God, as it were, dwells within this kingdom as in a well-ordered city. The Father is present to such a one, and Christ reigns with the Father in the soul that is maturing. This is in accord with the promise that "we will come to him and make our abode with him."[23] ON PRAYER 25.1.[24]

THE KINGDOM IS CHRIST'S OWN COMING. CYPRIAN: We ask that the kingdom of God may come to us, even as we also ask that his name may be sanctified in us. But when was it ever the case that God did not reign? Or when did that kingdom begin with him who both always has been and never ceases to be? We are here praying that our kingdom, which has been promised us by God, may come, the very kingdom

acquired by the blood and passion of Christ. We pray that we who now are his subjects in the world may hereafter reign with Christ when he reigns. For this he himself promises when he says, "Come, you blessed of my Father, receive the kingdom that has been prepared for you from the beginning of the world."[25] Christ himself, dearest beloved, is the kingdom of God, whom we day by day desire to come, whose advent we crave to be quickly manifested to us. For since he is himself the resurrection, since in him we rise again, so also the kingdom of God may be understood to be himself, since in him we shall reign. TREATISES, ON THE LORD'S PRAYER 13.[26]

MAY THE KINGDOM BE FULLY MANIFESTED. AUGUSTINE: The expression "thy kingdom come" is not to be thought of as if God were not now reigning.[27] But some might get the strange impression that "come" implies "for the first time upon the earth"—as if to imply that God were not even now really reigning upon earth! Or that God had not always reigned upon the earth from the foundation of the world! "Come," therefore, is to be understood in the sense of "manifested to humanity." Just as light that is present is absent to the blind or to those who shut their eyes, so the kingdom of God, though it never departs from the earth, yet is absent to those who know nothing about it. To none, however, will ignorance of God's kingdom be permitted when his Only Begotten comes from heaven. Then he will be recognizable not only by the intellect but visibly as the Man of the Lord to judge the living and the dead. SERMON ON THE MOUNT 2.6.20.[28]

---

[18]Mt 5:16. [19]Is 6:3; Rev 4:8. [20]PG 57:279; NPNF 1 10:134*. [21]Lk 17:20-21. [22]Deut 30:14. [23]Jn 14:23. [24]GCS 3:356-57; ACW 19:84-85. [25]Mt 25:34. [26]CCL 3a:97; ANF 5:450-51**. The kingdom for which we pray is Christ's own coming. His kingdom is eternal and not locked into temporal categories. [27]Augustine is here asking: Does the prayer imply that God's reign has not yet begun or is not present? [28]PL 34:1278; ACW 5:109**; NPNF 1 6:40. The kingdom of God, though already present on the earth, is as yet unrecognized by those who remain ignorant of it.

Not All Are in God's Kingdom. Anonymous: The kingdom of God is called the retribution or the tribulation, which the just receive according to the reward of their justice or sinners according to the guilt of their sinning. The saints too are called the kingdom of God, as it is written, "And they will gather the weeds out of his kingdom,"[29] that is, out of the Christian people. The kingdom of God is also called justice, as it is said, "The kingdom of God will be taken away from you and will be given to the nation that does his work."[30] For all these things, there is one interpretation. It is one thing to be a king and another thing to rule. Understand, God is naturally a king, but he does not reign in all. Not all people are his kingdom because not all do his will. Among evil people God does not reign, but the devil—it is his will they do. Incomplete Work on Matthew, Homily 14.[31]

Whether God Needs Our Prayer to Accomplish His Will. Tertullian: When we pray "thy will be done on earth as it is in heaven," we do not imply that anyone could prevent the fulfillment of God's will or that he needs our prayer to accomplish his will. Rather, we pray that his will be done in all. Think of heaven and earth as a picture of our very selves, spirit and flesh. The sense of the petition is the same, namely, that in us (as spirit and flesh, as heaven and earth combined) the will of God may be done on earth as it is in heaven. Now, what does God will more than that we ourselves walk according to his ways? We ask therefore that he supply us with the energy of his own will and the capacity to do it, that we may be saved, both in heaven and on earth. The sum of his will is the salvation of those whom he has adopted. On Prayer 4.1-2.[32]

That All May Do God's Will. Augustine: We pray that God's will may be accomplished in sinners also, even as it is accomplished in the saints and the just. This can be taken in two ways. First, we are to pray even for our enemies. For what else shall we call those in spite of whose will the Christian and Catholic name still spreads? According to this understanding the petition, "thy will be done on earth as it is in heaven," is intended to convey the following meaning: As the righteous do your will, let sinners do it also, so they may be converted. Second, the interpretation may be taken in the sense that "your will be done on earth as it is in heaven" is to be understood as a petition for the final rendering of his just due to every person. This will be done at the last judgment, when the lambs will be separated from the goats. Sermon on the Mount 2.6.22.[33]

Human Good Is Accomplished Only with God's Help. Anonymous: Notice how carefully Jesus spoke. He did not say, "Father, hallow thy name among us, bring thy kingdom upon us, do thy will among us," lest God should seem to hallow himself among people or want to bring his kingdom among those he wishes or to do his will among those he wishes; and thus God would show partiality toward certain people. Nor did he say, "Let us hallow thy name, let us receive thy kingdom, let us do thy will, in heaven and on earth," lest it seem that only people are hallowing God or receiving his kingdom or doing his will. Rather, he spoke moderately and impersonally; in other words, "Let it be hallowed, let it come, let it be done," that he might show the necessary work of both persons, for humans consider God necessary and God considers human willing necessary for the doing of justice. For even as people cannot do good without God's help, neither does God will to do good in people unless they will to let him. Incom-

---

[29]Mt 13:41. [30]Mt 21:43. [31]PG 56:711. [32]CCL 1:259; FC 40:161-62**; ANF 3:682**. If we think of heaven and earth as a figure of our very selves, spirit and flesh, we are praying here that in us (as spirit and flesh, as heaven and earth blended) the will of God may be done. [33]PL 34:1279; FC 11:130**; NPNF 1 6:41; ACW 5:110, 15:3, 46. To pray that God's will be done on earth as in heaven requires that we pray that it may be done also in sinners, and finally by all wills, that justice shall be rendered to all.

plete Work on Matthew, Homily 14.[34]

6:11 *Asking for Our Daily Bread*

The Bread That Essentially Nourishes Our True Humanity. Origen: Since some understand from this that we are commanded to pray for material bread, it will be well to refute their error here and to establish the truth about the *epiousios* (supersubstantial)[35] bread. We must ask them how it could be that he who commanded us to ask for great and heavenly favors should command us to intercede with the Father for what is small and of the earth, as if he had forgotten—so they would have it—what he had taught. For the bread that is given to our flesh is neither heavenly, nor is the request for it a great request.

We, on our part, following the Master himself who teaches us about the bread, shall treat the matter explicitly. In the Gospel according to John he says to those who had come to Capernaum seeking for him: "Amen, amen, I say to you, you seek me, not because you have seen miracles but because you did eat of the loaves and were filled."[36] One who has eaten of the bread blessed by Jesus and is filled with it tries all the more to understand the Son of God more perfectly and hastens to him. Hence his admirable command: "Labor not for the meat that perishes but for that which endures to life everlasting, which the Son of Man will give you."[37] . . . The "true bread" is that which nourishes the true humanity, the person created after the image of God. On Prayer 27.2.[38]

Daily Eucharist in Union with Christ. Cyprian: "Daily bread" may be understood both spiritually and simply, because both meanings help us to understand salvation. For Christ is the bread of life; and this bread is not the bread of all, but it is our bread. And as we say "our Father," because he is the father of those who understand and believe, so too we say "our bread," because Christ is the bread of us who

touch his body. Now we ask that this bread be given to us today, lest we who are in Christ and receive his Eucharist daily as the food of salvation should be separated from Christ's body through some grave offense that prohibits us from receiving the heavenly bread. For according to his words: "I am the living bread that came down from heaven; if anyone eats of this bread, he will live forever; and the bread that I shall give is my flesh for the life of the world."[39] Treatises, On the Lord's Prayer 18.[40]

Bread for Eternity. Jerome: In the Gospel the term used by the Hebrews to denote supersubstantial bread is *maar.* I found that it means "for tomorrow," so that the meaning is "Give us this day our bread" for tomorrow, that is, the future.[41] We can also understand supersubstantial bread in another sense: bread that is above all substances and surpasses all creatures. Commentary on Matthew 1.6.11.[42]

Necessary Food for One Day. Chrysostom: What is daily bread? Just enough for one day. Here Jesus is speaking to people who have natural needs of the flesh, who are subject to the necessities of nature. He does not pretend that we are angels. He condescends to the infirmity of our nature in giving us his commands. The severity of nature does not permit you to go without food. So for the maturing of your life, he says, I require necessary food, not a complete

---

[34]PG 56:712. [35]Although it is unlikely that the adjective *epiousios* was coined *ex novo* by the Evangelists, it is true that in all of Greek literature the term appears only here and in a parallel passage in Luke. Origen links it to the root of *ousia* "essence, substance," and he builds his interpretation on this connection. In passage 6, on the other hand, he connects it more plausibly to the root of the verb *hiēmi* "to go." The difficulty here posed by Origen continues to interest modern scholars, as is widely known. [36]Jn 6:26. [37]Jn 6:27. [38]GCS 3:363-64; ACW 19:92-93. The bread is that which nourishes true humanity created in God's image. [39]Jn 6:51. [40]CCL 3a:101; ANF 5:452*. We call it our bread because Christ is the bread of those who are in Eucharistic union with his body. [41]The explanation of *epiousios* suggested by Jerome, returning to the Aramaic text of the Lord's Prayer, is also accepted by some modern scholars. [42]CCL 77:37.

freedom from natural necessities. But note how even in things that are bodily, spiritual correlations abound. For it is not for riches or frills that we pray. It is not for wastefulness or extravagant clothing that we pray, but only for bread. And only for bread on a daily basis, so as not to "worry about tomorrow."[43] THE GOSPEL OF MATTHEW, HOMILY 19.5.[44]

6:12 Forgiving Debts and Debtors

ASKING PARDON DAILY. CYPRIAN: How necessary, providential and expedient it is for us to be reminded that we are sinners and must ask pardon for our sins. And while we ask for God's forgiveness, our minds retain an awareness of those sins! Lest anyone become complacent and suffer the fate of flattering himself, he is instructed and reminded that he sins daily, while he is ordered to ask pardon for his sins. Thus John advises us in his epistle, "If we say that we have no sin, we deceive ourselves, and the truth is not in us. If we acknowledge our sins, the Lord is faithful and just to forgive us our sins."[45] In his epistle there is a twofold connection. We must ask pardon for our sins and obtain forgiveness when we ask pardon. Moreover, he said that the Lord is faithful in pardoning sins and loyal to his promise, for he who taught us to ask forgiveness for our trespasses and sins promised paternal mercy and subsequent pardon. He added and clearly imparted a law that binds us by a definite condition and guarantee. We shall be pardoned for our trespasses as we forgive those who trespass against us, knowing that we cannot obtain pardon for our sins unless we give equal pardon to those who sin against us. In this regard he says in another place: "With what measure you measure, it shall be measured to you."[46] And the servant who, after his every offense has been forgiven by the Lord, is unwilling to forgive his fellow servant shall be sent to prison. Because he was unwilling to pardon his fellow servant, he forfeited what the Lord had pardoned him.[47] TREATISES, ON THE LORD'S PRAYER 22-23.[48]

PRAYING DAILY FOR FORGIVENESS. CHRYSOSTOM: This prayer for forgiveness belongs to believers. For the uninitiated could not call God Father. We discover forgiveness within the nurturing pedagogy of the church. If then the prayer belongs to believers and they pray, entreating that sins may be forgiven them, it is clear that even after baptism the profit of repentance is not taken away.[49] If he had not meant to signify this, why would he have instructed us to pray for forgiveness? He asks us to bring our sins to remembrance and ask for forgiveness, and he teaches us how to obtain remission. He makes the way uncomplicated. By this rule of supplication it is clear that it is possible even after the font of baptism that our offenses may still be washed away. He thereby persuades us to be modest, commands us to forgive others, sets us free from vengeful obsessions, promises pardon, and holds before us good hopes and a high view of the unspeakable mercy of God. THE GOSPEL OF MATTHEW, HOMILY 19.5.[50]

FORGIVE THOSE WHO ASK YOUR PARDON. AUGUSTINE: It is certainly a bargain to be reckoned with when we say, "Forgive us our trespasses as we forgive those who trespass against us." We can be sure that we have violated that rule if we do not forgive those who ask our pardon, since we too want to be forgiven by our most generous Father with respect to those who seek pardon from us. Now, as to that commandment by which we are ordered to pray for our enemies,[51] we are not ordered to pray for those who seek forgiveness. For such persons are not enemies. In no way, however, can someone really say that he is praying for a person he does not

---

[43]Mt 6:34. [44]PG 57:280; NPNF 1 10:135**. [45]1 Jn 1:8-9. [46]Mt 7:2. [47]Mt 18:23-35. [48]CCL 3a:104; FC 36:146-47*; ANF 5:453. [49]Since we sin daily, to avoid self-deception, we are called to pray daily for our sins. Lest anyone think oneself innocent and so perish all the more, the faithful pray every day for forgiveness. [50]PG 57:280-81; NPNF 10:135-36**. Even after baptism the profit of repentance is not taken away, and our offenses may still be washed away. [51]Mt 5:44.

know. Therefore it must be said that we should forgive all sins committed against us if we want the Father to forgive what we have committed. SERMON ON THE MOUNT 2.8.29.[52]

YOU WILL NOT OUTSMART GOD. ANONYMOUS: With what assurance does that person pray who harbors animosity toward someone who has offended him? Even as he lies when he prays and says, "I forgive" and does not forgive, so too he seeks pardon from God, but he will not be pardoned. Therefore, if that person who has been offended prays to God without assurance unless he pardons the very person who offended him, how do you think that person prays who not only has been offended by another but himself offends and oppresses others through injustice? But many people who are unwilling to forgive those who sin against them avoid saying this prayer. They are ill-advised, first, because the one who does not pray as Christ taught is not Christ's disciple; second, because the Father does not graciously hear a prayer that the Son has not recommended. For the Father knows the words and meaning of his Son, and he does not accept what the human mind has devised but what the wisdom of Christ has expressed. Therefore you may indeed say a prayer, but you may not outsmart and deceive God. And you will not receive forgiveness unless you yourself have first forgiven. INCOMPLETE WORK ON MATTHEW, HOMILY 14.[53]

6:13 Deliverance from Evil

NEW SINS MUST BE RESISTED. TERTULLIAN: To complete the prayer that was so well arranged, Christ added that we should pray not only that our sins be forgiven but also that they be resisted completely: "Lead us not into temptation," that is, do not allow us to be led by the tempter. God forbid that our Lord should seem to be the tempter, as if he were not aware of one's faith or were eager to upset it! That weakness and spitefulness belongs to the devil. For

even in the case of Abraham, God had ordered the sacrifice of his son not to tempt his faith but to prove it. In him he might illustrate that which he was later to teach, that no one should hold loved ones dearer than God. . . . The disciples were so tempted to desert their Lord that they indulged in sleep instead of prayer. Therefore the phrase that balances and interprets "lead us not into temptation" is "but deliver us from evil." ON PRAYER 8.1-3, 5-6.[54]

WHETHER THE DEVIL IS EVIL BY NATURE. CHRYSOSTOM: Jesus here calls the devil "the wicked one," commanding us to wage against him a war that knows no truce. Yet he is not evil by nature, for evil is not something derived from any nature as created but is what has been added to nature by choice. The devil is the prototypically evil one, because of the excess of his evil choices and because he who in no respect was injured by us wages against us an implacable war. Thus we do not pray "deliver us from the wicked ones" in the plural but "from the wicked one." THE GOSPEL OF MATTHEW, HOMILY 19.6.[55]

THE RECAPITULATION OF ALL PREVIOUS PETITIONS. CYPRIAN: After all those things, in the prayer's summation there occurs a little clause concluding all our petitions and prayer in succinct fashion. For at the very last we state "but deliver us from evil," understanding the phrase to mean all adversities that the enemy undertakes against us in this world. There can be strong and faithful protection against these adversities if God delivers us, if, as we pray and implore, he furnishes us his aid. Moreover, when we say "deliver us from evil," nothing remains for which we should ask still further. When once we seek God's protection against evil, having obtained this, we stand secure and

---

[52]PL 34:1282; FC 11:137-38. [53]PG 56:714. [54]CCL 1:262; FC 40:166-67. [55]PG 57:282; NPNF 1 10:136**. Evil is not from God's will in creating but from the free choice of creatures. The devil is wicked not by nature but by choice. Hence evil is not an intrinsic aspect of God's creation.

safe against all the works of the devil and of the world. For what fear, indeed, is there with regard to the world for one who has God as protector in the world? Treatises, On the Lord's Prayer 27.[56]

THE ORDERING OF THE SEVEN PETITIONS. Augustine: We must consider and carefully set forth the respective and distinctive notes of those seven petitions. While our present life is passing away like time, our hope is fixed on the life eternal, and while we cannot reach the eternal without first passing through the present life, eternal things are first in importance. In addition, the fulfillment of the first three petitions has its beginning in the life that begins and ends in this world. For the hallowing of God's name began with the advent of the Lord's humility; and the coming of his kingdom—the coming in which he will appear in brightness—will be made manifest not after the end of the world but at the ending of the world; and the perfect fulfilling of God's will on earth as in heaven—whether you take the words *heaven* and *earth* to mean the righteous and the sinful, or the spirit and the flesh, or the Lord and the church, or all of these together—will be fully achieved through the full attainment of our blessedness, and therefore at the ending of the world. But all three will continue for all eternity; for the hallowing of God's name will continue forever, and of his kingdom there is no end, and there is the promise of everlasting life for our blessedness. Therefore these three things will continue, completely fulfilled, in the life that is promised to us.

It seems to me that our remaining four petitions pertain to the needs of this temporal life. The first of them is "give us this day our daily bread"; the mere fact that it is called a "daily" bread shows that it pertains to the present time, the time which the Lord has called "today." This is equally clear, no matter what significance one may attach to the expression "daily bread"; that is to say, whether we take it as signifying spiritual bread or the bread that is visible either in the sacrament or in our earthly food. Of course, this opinion does not imply that spiritual food is not everlasting. What the Scriptures call daily food is offered to the soul in the sound of human speech or in some kind of sign that is confined to time. There will be none of these things when everyone will be "taught of God"[57] and will be imbibing the ineffable light of truth through mind alone but not imparting it through any bodily actions. Perhaps that is the very reason why this nourishment is called food rather than drink. For just as food must be broken up and chewed before it can become nourishment for the body, so also is the soul nourished by the Scriptures when it has uncovered and digested their inner meaning. But whatever is taken in the form of drink is not changed as it flows into the body. Therefore truth is called food as long as it is referred to as daily bread; when there will be no need of breaking it, so to speak, and chewing it, then it will be in the form of drink. This will be the case when there will be no need of discussing and discoursing, when nothing will be needed but a drink of pure and crystal truth.

In this life we are both receiving and granting forgiveness of sins, and this is the second of those four petitions. But in eternity there will be no forgiving of sins, because there will be no sins to be forgiven. Temptations make this life troublesome, but there will be no temptations after the fulfillment of the promise, "You will hide them in the secret of your presence."[58] Of course, the evil from which we wish to be delivered is an evil that is present with us in this life, and it is during this life that we wish to be delivered from it. For through God's justice we have by our own faults made this life mortal, and through the mercy of God we are being delivered from that mortality. Sermon on the Mount 2.10.36-37.[59]

6:14-15 *Forgiving Trespasses*

---

[56]CCL 3a:107; FC 36:150-51. The brief petition to be delivered from evil summarizes and comprehends all our petitions to God.   [57]Is 54:13.   [58]Ps 31:20 (30:20 LXX).   [59]PL 34:1285-86; FC 11:144-46.

READINESS TO FORGIVE. CHRYSOSTOM: Nothing makes us so like God as our readiness to forgive the wicked and wrongdoer. For it is God who has made "the sun to shine on the evil and on the good."[60]

For this same reason again in every one of the clauses Jesus commands us to make our prayers together in one voice, saying, "our Father," and "thy will be done in earth as it is in heaven," and "give us the bread, and forgive us our debts," and "lead us not into temptation," and "deliver us." So everywhere he is teaching us to use this plural word that we may not retain so much as a vestige of resentment against our neighbor.

How great a reproof then must they deserve, who, after all this, still do not forgive and even ask God's vengeance on their enemies. In doing so they diametrically transgress this command. Meanwhile Christ is seeking in every way possible to hinder our conflicts with one another. For since love is the root of all that is good, by removing from all quarters whatever mars it he brings us together and cements us to each other. For there is not one, not a single one, whether father or mother or friend, who loves us as much as the God who created us. THE GOSPEL OF MATTHEW, HOMILY 19.7.[61]

THE CONSEQUENCE OF FAILURE TO FORGIVE. AUGUSTINE: And certainly we should not heedlessly neglect to call attention to the fact that of all the pronouncements in which the Lord has ordered us to pray, he has deliberately attached a very special commendation to the pronouncement that deals with the forgiving of sins. In this pronouncement he wished us to be merciful because that is the only prescribed means of avoiding miseries. Indeed, in no other petition do we pray in such a manner as to make a kind of covenant with the Lord, for we say, "Forgive us as we also forgive." If we default in this covenant, the whole petition is fruitless, for he says, "For if you forgive men their trespasses, your heavenly Father also will forgive you; but if you do not forgive men their trespasses, neither will your Father forgive your trespasses."[62] SERMON ON THE MOUNT 2.11.39.[63]

---

[60]Mt 5:45. [61]PG 57:283; NPNF 1 10:137**. Why is the plural "our" preferred to the singular "my"? We are more like God in the act of forgiveness than at any other moment. To forgive is to be like God. His forgiving act is toward us in the plural, all humanity. Hence we are to forgive all who are indebted to us, as we have all been forgiven our indebtedness. [62]Mt 6:14-15. [63]PL 34:1287; FC 11:148.

6:16-23 FASTING, TREASURES IN HEAVEN AND THE LIGHT OF THE BODY

[16]*"And when you fast, do not look dismal, like the hypocrites, for they disfigure their faces that their fasting may be seen by men. Truly, I say to you, they have received their reward.* [17]*But when you fast, anoint your head and wash your face,* [18]*that your fasting may not be seen by men but by your Father who is in secret; and your Father who sees in secret will reward you.*

[19]*"Do not lay up for yourselves treasures on earth, where moth and rust° consume and where thieves break in and steal,* [20]*but lay up for yourselves treasures in heaven, where neither moth nor rust° consumes and where thieves do not break in and steal.* [21]*For where your treasure is, there will your heart be also.*

^{22}*"The eye is the lamp of the body. So, if your eye is sound, your whole body will be full of light;* ^{23}*but if your eye is not sound, your whole body will be full of darkness. If then the light in you is darkness, how great is the darkness!"*

o Or *worm*

OVERVIEW: Gradually the Sermon on the Mount is leading into more demanding matters. Voluntary poverty could not be adequately dealt with until pride had been treated (CHRYSOSTOM). Pride can appear not only in the pomp of worldly wealth but even in the garment of sackcloth, where it is all the more dangerous because it is a deception under the pretense of service to God (AUGUSTINE). Some Christians compete with hypocrites in looking dismal while fasting. They do better to fast in secret (CHRYSOSTOM). Fix your treasure and your heart on that which will abide forever rather than on something that will pass away (AUGUSTINE).

All he has said about prayer and fasting prepares the way for the Lord's discourse on contempt for riches (CHRYSOSTOM). Some treasures corrupt. A thing becomes defiled if it is mixed with a baser substance, even though that other substance is not vile in its own nature. Fix your treasure and your heart on that which will abide forever (AUGUSTINE). As in bodily health it is our aim to keep the eye healthy, so also it should be our aim to keep the mind sound in relation to the soul. What the mind is to the soul, that the eye is to the body—its illuminator. As when the eye is blinded, the ability of the other members is diminished, so also when the mind is depraved the soul is vulnerable to countless evils (CHRYSOSTOM). The expression "whole body" designates all those works that the Lord reproves and orders us to put to death (AUGUSTINE). He calls mammon "a master," not because of its own nature but on account of the wretchedness of those who bow down before it (CHRYSOSTOM).

The love of money wounds the center of your vitality, your soul, your very life, and may overthrow your salvation. In relation to God's providence, all things about which we are anxious

will pass away (CHRYSOSTOM). The kingdom of God is the end to be sought above all things. When you perform any good deed, think about its eternal consequence and pay no heed to the temporal (AUGUSTINE). The intrinsic value of life is not comparable to any temporal or physical reality. The Lord shows how great is the value set upon personal existence (CHRYSOSTOM). There is a difference between a good that ought to be sought as an end and a value that ought to be seen as a means. If one's intention is pure, then unfailingly all our works are good works, because they are performed in accordance with that intention. Cleanse the intention of your heart from all duplicity. Seek the Lord in simplicity of heart (AUGUSTINE).

6:16 No Dismal Faces

LOOKING DISMAL. CHRYSOSTOM: In this spectacle we not only imitate the hypocrites, but also we far outdo them. We sigh loudly and complain bitterly. I know some, well—actually I know many—who, even while neglecting to fast, yet still wear the garments of those who fast. They cloak themselves with a false exoneration worse than their actual sin.

"I do this," they say, "so that I might not offend the many [who are expecting me to fast]." What are you saying? The divine law commands this [fasting], and yet you say you are causing "offense" by obeying? If you practice the inward fast you cause offense, but if you do not fast inwardly [but make a show of fasting outwardly], then quite the opposite, you are not causing offense—is there anything more foolish than this? Why don't you stop being worse than the hypocrites [you criticize], doubling your own hypocrisy, and instead consider to what extremes this great evil leads? Do you feel any shame now, as we look at the emphasis [of the passage] before us? For Jesus not only says that they put on appearnaces, but he levels [an even more] vehement attack against them when he says, "They disfigure their faces." THE GOSPEL OF MATTHEW, HOMILY 20.1.[1]

VOLUNTARY POVERTY. CHRYSOSTOM: It is only after he has cast out the demon of empty conceit, and not before, that he opportunely introduces his discourse on voluntary poverty. For nothing so trains people to be fond of riches as a fondness for glory. This is what motivates those who have herds of slaves, swarms of eunuchs, horses with decorations of gold, silver tables, and all the rest of it. It makes them all the more ridiculous. All these do not satisfy any wants or increase any pleasures. They only make a show before others. THE GOSPEL OF MATTHEW, HOMILY 20.2.[2]

6:17-18 Fasting Seen by the Father

THE PRETENSE OF DIVINE SERVICE. AUGUSTINE: Vainglory can find a place not only in the splendor and pomp of worldly wealth but even in the sordid garment of sackcloth as well. It is then all the more dangerous because it is a deception under the pretense of service to God. When one dazzles by immoderate adornment of the body and its raiment or by the splendor of whatever else one may possess, by that very fact one is easily shown to desire ostentacious display. This person deceives nobody by a crafty semblance of holiness. But if, through extraordinary squalor and shabbiness, one is attracting others' attention to one's manner of professing Christianity, and if one is doing this of choice and not merely enduring it through necessity, then one may determine by one's other works whether one is doing it through an indifference toward needless adornment or through ambition of some kind. Indeed, the Lord has forewarned us to beware of wolves in sheep's clothing: "By their fruits you shall

know them."[3] Trials of one kind or another that cause these people to lose the very advantages they have gained through their dress or claimed to deny what they sought to gain by it will inevitably reveal whether it is a case of a wolf under a sheep's skin or a sheep under its own. But just as sheep ought not to change their skin even though wolves sometimes hide themselves beneath it, so a Christian ought not try to delight the eyes of others by needless adornment just because pretenders very often assume that scanty garb which necessity demands and assume it for the purpose of deceiving those who are less aware. SERMON ON THE MOUNT 2.12.41.[4]

6:19 Treasures on Earth

PREPARATION FOR THE DISCOURSE ON RICHES. CHRYSOSTOM: Previously he had only said that we must show mercy. Here he also points out how great is the mercy we must show. He says, "Don't store up treasure." It would have been impossible to introduce his discourse on disdain for riches without much preparation. So he broke the discourse up into small portions. Having readied the hearer's mind, he brings up the tougher subject in a way that is plausible. THE GOSPEL OF MATTHEW, HOMILY 20.2.[5]

TREASURES THAT CORRUPT. AUGUSTINE: If someone does something with the intent of gaining earthly profit, that one's heart is upon the earth. How can a heart be clean while it is wallowing in the mud? On the other hand, if it be fastened upon heaven it will be clean, for whatever is heavenly is unpolluted. A thing becomes defiled if it is mixed with a baser substance, even though that other substance be not vile in its own nature. Gold, for example, is debased by pure silver if mixed with it. So also is our mind defiled by a desire for the things of earth, although the earth

---

[1]PG 57:285-87; NPNF 1 10:140**. Fast in secret. [2]PG 57:288-89; NPNF 1 10:141-42**. [3]Mt 7:16. [4]PL 34:1287; FC 11:149-50. [5]PG 57:289; NPNF 1 10:142**.

itself is pure in its own class and in its own order. SERMON ON THE MOUNT 2.13.44.[6]

6:20 Treasures in Heaven

TREASURES THAT ABIDE. AUGUSTINE: Let us not think that in this text the word *heaven* signifies the universe of heavenly bodies, for the word *earth* includes every kind of body, for one ought to disregard the whole world when laying up treasure in heaven. Therefore the reference is to that heaven of which it is said, "The heaven of heaven is the Lord's."[7] Moreover, since we ought to fix our treasure and our heart on that which will abide forever and not on something which will pass away, the heaven here mentioned means the spiritual firmament, for "heaven and earth will pass away." SERMON ON THE MOUNT 2.13.44.[8]

6:22-23 Light and Darkness

AS MIND IS TO SOUL, THE EYE IS TO THE BODY. CHRYSOSTOM: Now Christ leads us to an analogy more within the reach of our senses, that we may not be confused. He has already spoken of the mind as enslaved in captivity. Now he shifts his attention to the eye and to lessons on outward things lying directly before our eyes, so that we might grasp it easily and that we may learn from the body what we did not learn from the mind. For what the mind is to the soul, the eye is to the body. THE GOSPEL OF MATTHEW, HOMILY 20.3.[9]

SEEKING THE RIGHT INTENTION. AUGUSTINE: We know that all our works are pure and pleasing in the sight of God if they are performed with a single heart. This means that they are performed out of charity and with an intention that is fixed on heaven. For "love is the fulfillment of the law."[10] Therefore in this passage we ought to understand the eye as the intention with which we perform all our actions. If this intention is pure and upright and directing its

gaze where it ought to be directed, then unfailingly all our works are good works, because they are performed in accordance with that intention. And by the expression "whole body," Christ designated all those works that he reproves and that he commands us to put to death. For the apostle also designates certain works as our "members." "Therefore," Paul writes, "mortify your members which are on earth: fornication, uncleanness, covetousness,"[11] and all other such things. SERMON ON THE MOUNT 2.13.45.[12]

WHEN UNDERSTANDING IS QUENCHED. CHRYSOSTOM: If your eyes were completely blind, would you choose to wear gold and silk? Wouldn't you consider your sound health to be more desirable than mere externals? For if you should lose your health or waste it, all the rest of your life would be unhappily affected. For just as when the eyes are blinded, some of the ability of the other members is diminished, their light being quenched, so also when the mind is depraved, your life will be filled with countless evils. As therefore in the body it is our aim to keep the eye sound, so also it should be our aim to keep the mind sound in relation to the soul. But if we destroy this, which ought to give light to the rest, by what means are we to see clearly any more? For as he who destroys the spring may also dry up the river, so he who has quenched the understanding may have confounded all his actions in this life. So it is said, "If the light that is in you be darkness, how great is the darkness?"[13] For when the pilot is drowned, when the candle is put out, when the general is taken prisoner, what sort of hope will remain for those that are under his command? THE GOSPEL OF MATTHEW, HOMILY 20.3.[14]

---

[6]PL 34:1289; FC 11:152-53. [7]Ps 115:16 (113:16 LXX). [8]PL 34:1289; FC 11:153. [9]PG 57:290-91; NPNF 1 10:143**. [10]Rom 13:10. [11]Col 3:5. [12]PL 34:1289; FC 11:153-54. [13]Mt 6:23. [14]PG 57:291; NPNF 1 10:143**.

6:24-34 GOD AND POSSESSIONS

[24]"No one can serve two masters; for either he will hate the one and love the other, or he will be devoted to the one and despise the other. You cannot serve God and mammon.[x]

[25]"Therefore I tell you, do not be anxious about your life, what you shall eat or what you shall drink, nor about your body, what you shall put on. Is not life more than food, and the body more than clothing? [26]Look at the birds of the air: they neither sow nor reap nor gather into barns, and yet your heavenly Father feeds them. Are you not of more value than they? [27]And which of you by being anxious can add one cubit to his span of life?[p] [28]And why are you anxious about clothing? Consider the lilies of the field, how they grow; they neither toil nor spin; [29]yet I tell you, even Solomon in all his glory was not arrayed like one of these. [30]But if God so clothes the grass of the field, which today is alive and tomorrow is thrown into the oven, will he not much more clothe you, O men of little faith? [31]Therefore do not be anxious, saying, 'What shall we eat?' or 'What shall we drink?' or 'What shall we wear?' [32]For the Gentiles seek all these things; and your heavenly Father knows that you need them all. [33]But seek first his kingdom and his righteousness, and all these things shall be yours as well.

[34]"Therefore do not be anxious about tomorrow, for tomorrow will be anxious for itself. Let the day's own trouble be sufficient for the day.

x *Mammon is a Semitic word for money or riches*   p *Or to his stature*

OVERVIEW: The hurt one receives from the love of mammon results in the loss of more than riches. Rather, the wound occurs at the center of our vitality. It casts us away from the God who made us and cares for us and loves us. By serving this harshest master, one falls away from the highest blessing of being God's servant (CHRYSOSTOM). Cleanse the intention of the heart from all duplicity (AUGUSTINE). In the light of God's providence, none of our cares, anxieties or toils will ever come to anything, but all will utterly pass away. The accelerating emphasis is upon the great value set upon our humanity and the concern God shows for us personally (CHRYSOSTOM). In saying "seek first," Christ clearly shows the difference between ends and means. Our final good is therefore the kingdom of God and his justice (AUGUSTINE). When the need for food and clothing is pressing, these things will be provided by the Father, who knows when the faithful need them (AUGUSTINE).

6:24 God and Mammon

SERVING TWO MASTERS. CHRYSOSTOM: Now Jesus calls mammon here "a master," not because of its own nature but on account of the wretchedness of those who bow themselves beneath it.[1] So also he calls the stomach a god,[2] not from the dignity of such a mistress but from the wretchedness of those enslaved. To have mammon for your master is already worse itself than any later punishment and enough retribution before the punishment for any one trapped in it. For what condemned criminals can be so wretched as

---

[1]According to a line of reasoning dating back to Clement of Alexandria, Chrysostom explains that riches are not evil in their very nature but in the evil use to which they are put, which causes humankind so much unhappiness.   [2]Phil 3:19.

143

those who, once having God for their Lord, do from that mild rule desert to this grievous obsession for money? Even in this life such idolatry trails immense harm in its path, with losses unspeakable. Think of the lawsuits! The harrassments, the strife and toil and blinding of the soul! More grievous, one falls away thereby from the highest blessing—to be God's servant. THE GOSPEL OF MATTHEW, HOMILY 21.2.[3]

CLEANSING AWAY DUPLICITY. AUGUSTINE: "He will be devoted to one and disregard the other." He does not say that one will hate the other, for scarcely anyone's conscience could hate God.[4] But one disregards God—that is to say, one does not fear God but presumes on his goodness. From this negligent and tormented confidence, the Holy Spirit recalls us when he says through the prophet: "Son, do not add sin to sin; and do not say, 'The mercy of God is great.'"[5] Note when Paul says, "Do you not know that God's kindness is meant to lead you to repentance?"[6] For whose mercy can be accounted as great as the mercy of him who forgives all, if they convert to him? He makes the wild olive a partaker of the fatness of the original olive tree. At the same time, whose severity can be accounted as great as the severity of him who has not spared the natural branches but has broken them off because of unbelief?[7] Therefore, whoever wishes to love God and to beware of offending him, let such a one cleanse the upright intention of his heart from all duplicity. In this way, he will "think of the Lord in goodness and seek him in simplicity of heart."[8] SERMON ON THE MOUNT 2.14.48.[9]

6:25 Do Not Be Anxious

TAKE NO THOUGHT ABOUT YOUR LIFE. CHRYSOSTOM: Note that he did not simply say, "Don't be anxious for your life," but he added the reason and so commanded this. After having said, "You cannot serve God and mammon," he added, "Therefore I say to you, don't worry."

Therefore? Why therefore? Because of the unspeakable loss. For the hurt you receive is not in riches only; rather, the wound is in the most vital parts, in the subversion of your salvation, casting you as it does away from the God who made you, cares for you and loves you. "Therefore I tell you, do not be anxious about your life." Only after Jesus has shown the hurt to be unspeakable, then and not before does he make the instruction stricter. He not only asks us to cast away what we have but also forbids us to take thought even for the food we need, saying, "Take no thought for your life, what you shall eat," not because the soul needs food, for it is incorporeal. He spoke figuratively. For though the soul as such needs no food, it cannot endure to remain in the body unless the body is fed. THE GOSPEL OF MATTHEW, HOMILY 21.2.[10]

6:26 The Birds of the Air

MORE AND LESS IMPORTANT. AUGUSTINE: These examples are not to be analyzed like allegories. We must not inquire about the allegorical significance of the birds of the air or the lilies of the field. These examples are proposed so that more important things may be suggested from things of less importance. SERMON ON THE MOUNT 2.15.52.[11]

6:27-30 Lilies of the Field

GOD'S PROVIDENCE AND OUR ANXIETIES. CHRYSOSTOM: Do you see how Jesus clarifies what has been obscure by comparing it to what is self-evident? Can you add one cubit, or even the slightest measure, to your bodily life span by worrying about it? Can you by being anxious about food add moments to your life? Hence it is clear that it is not our diligence but

---

[3]PG 57:296; NPNF 1 10:147**. [4]Note *Retractations* 1.19.8. [5]Sir 5:5-6. [6]Rom 2:4. [7]Rom 11:17-22. [8]Wis 1:1. [9]PL 34:1290-91; FC 11:156*. [10]PG 57:296-97; NPNF 1 10:148**. [11]PL 34:1291-92; FC 11:159.

the providence of God, even where we seem to be active, that finally accompanies everything. In the light of God's providence, none of our cares, anxieties, toils or any other such things will ever come to anything, but all will utterly pass away. THE GOSPEL OF MATTHEW, HOMILY 21.3.[12]

THE VALUE OF LIFE. CHRYSOSTOM: Note the acceleration of images: just when the lilies are decked out, he no longer calls them lilies but "grass of the field."[13] He then points further to their vulnerable condition by saying "which are here today." Then he does not merely say "and not tomorrow" but rather more callously "cast into the oven." These creatures are not merely "clothed" but "so clothed" in this way as to be later brought to nothing. Do you see how Jesus everywhere abounds in amplifications and intensifications? And he does so in order to press his points home. So then he adds, "Will he not much more clothe you?" The force of the emphasis is on "you" to indicate covertly how great is the value set upon your personal existence and the concern God shows for you in particular. It is as though he were saying, "You, to whom he gave a soul, for whom he fashioned a body, for whose sake he made everything in creation, for whose sake he sent prophets, and gave the law, and wrought those innumerable good works, and for whose sake he gave up his only begotten Son." THE GOSPEL OF MATTHEW, HOMILY 22.1.[14]

BALANCING COUNSEL AND REPROOF. CHRYSOSTOM: It is not until he has clearly revealed his affection that he proceeds also to reprove them, saying, "O you of little faith." For this is the quality of a wise counselor. He balances counsel and reproof, that he may awaken persons all the more to the force of his words. THE GOSPEL OF MATTHEW, HOMILY 22.1.[15]

6:31-33 *Seeking God's Kingdom and Righteousness*

ENDS AND MEANS. AUGUSTINE: At first he makes it abundantly clear that these things are not to be sought as if they were for us the kind of blessings for the sake of which we ought to make all our actions good actions but that they are necessities nevertheless. Then Jesus says, "Seek first his kingdom and his righteousness, and all these things shall be yours as well." In this sentence he clearly shows the difference between a good that ought to be sought as an end and a value that ought to be seen as a means. Our final good is therefore the kingdom of God and his justice. We ought to seek this good and fix our aim upon it. Let us perform all our actions for the sake of it. Yet, since we are waging war in this life in order to be able to reach that kingdom and since this life cannot be maintained unless those necessities are supplied, he says, "These things shall be given you besides, but seek you first the kingdom of God and his justice." SERMON ON THE MOUNT 2.16.53.[16]

SEEK FIRST. AUGUSTINE: When he said that the one is to be sought first, Jesus clearly intimates that the other is to be sought later—not that it is to be sought at a later time but that it is to be sought as a thing of secondary importance. He showed that the one is to be sought as our good, that the other is to be sought as something needful for us, but that the needful is to be sought for the sake of the good. SERMON ON THE MOUNT 2.16.53.[17]

6:34 *Each Day's Trouble Sufficient*

PAYING NO HEED TO TEMPORAL THINGS. AUGUSTINE: With a single heart, therefore, and exclusively for the sake of the kingdom of heaven, we ought to do good to all. And in this well-doing we ought not to think about temporal rewards, either exclusively or conjointly with

---

[12]PG 57:298; NPNF 1 10:149**. [13]Mt 6:30. [14]PG 57:299; NPNF 1 10:150**. [15]PG 57:299-300; NPNF 1 10:150-51**. [16]PL 34:1292; FC 11:159-60*. [17]PL 34:1292; FC 11:160*.

the kingdom of God. For it is with reference to all these temporal things that the Lord used the word *tomorrow* when he said, "Do not think about tomorrow." For that word is not used except in the realm of time, where the future succeeds the past. Therefore, when we perform any good deed, let us think about eternal things and pay no heed to the temporal. Then our deed will be not only good but also perfect. "For tomorrow," he says, "will have anxieties of its own." By this he means that you are to take food or drink or clothing when it is fitting that you do so. When the need for them is pressing, these things will be at hand; our Father knows that we need all these things. "For sufficient for the day," he says, "is its own evil." In other words, when the need is urgent, we have sufficient reason for using these things. I suppose that this necessity is called evil because it partakes of the nature of punishment for us since it is part of the frailty and mortality that we have merited by committing sin. To this penalty of temporal necessity, therefore, do not add something more troublesome. SERMON ON THE MOUNT 2.167.56.[18]

---

[18]PL 34:1294; FC 11:164-65*.

7:1-6 ON JUDGING

[1]*"Judge not, that you be not judged.* [2]*For with the judgment you pronounce you will be judged, and the measure you give will be the measure you get.* [3]*Why do you see the speck that is in your brother's eye, but do not notice the log that is in your own eye?* [4]*Or how can you say to your brother, 'Let me take the speck out of your eye,' when there is the log in your own eye?* [5]*You hypocrite, first take the log out of your own eye, and then you will see clearly to take the speck out of your brother's eye.*

[6]*"Do not give dogs what is holy; and do not throw your pearls before swine, lest they trample them under foot and turn to attack you."*

OVERVIEW: Some sins rush to judgment in consciousness, while others remain hidden until the last day. We do well not to pass judgment on hidden things until the Lord comes, who will bring to light the hidden things of darkness (AUGUSTINE). Jesus does not thereby forbid judging altogether but commands that one first take the plank out of one's eye and that one may then set right the issues relating to others (CHRYSOSTOM). One had best not pretend to counsel another when one has the same fault unexamined (AUGUSTINE). Be careful not to offer precious things to those who, like hungry dogs, may be prone to rush in and tear them apart. It is better that one make a search for what is concealed than assault or despise what is revealed, or like swine, trample upon the truth (AUGUSTINE).

7:1-2 Judge Not

THE RUSH TO JUDGMENT. AUGUSTINE: This carries the same intent as another passage, "Pass no judgment before the time, until the Lord comes, who will both bring to light the hidden things of darkness and reveal the thoughts of the heart; and then everyone will have his praise from God."[1] Some actions are indifferent, and, since we do not know with what intention they are performed, it would be rash for any to pass judgment on them and most rash to condemn them. The time for judging these actions will come later, when the Lord "will bring to light the hidden things of darkness and reveal the thoughts of the heart." And in another passage the same apostle also says, "Some sins are manifest even before the judgment, but some sins afterward."[2] When it is clear with what intention they are committed, he calls them manifest sins, and these sins precede judgment. This means that if judgment follows them at once, it will not be rash judgment. But concealed sins follow judgment, because not even these will remain hidden in their proper time. And this is to be understood about good works as well, for he thus continues: "In like manner also the good works are manifest, and whatever things are otherwise cannot be hidden."[3] On things that are manifest, therefore, let us pass judgment, but with regard to hidden things, let us leave the judgment to God. For whether the works themselves be bad or good, they cannot remain hidden when the time comes for them to be revealed. SERMON ON THE MOUNT 2.18.60.[4]

7:3-5 Logs and Specks

THE LOG IN YOUR OWN EYE. CHRYSOSTOM: Here Christ wants to show the great outrage he has toward people who do such things. For wherever he wants to show that the sin is great and that the punishment and anger for it is great, he begins with an open rebuke. For example, to show that he was provoked to anger he said to the man who was demanding the hundred silver coins, "Wicked slave, I forgave you all that debt."[5] In the same way also here he says, "Hypocrite." For the verdict that one's brother needs a splinter taken from his eye does not come from concern but from contempt for hu-

manity. Even while one is putting on a mask of love toward others, one is actually performing a deed of consummate evil by inflicting numerous criticisms and accusations on close companions, thereby usurping the rank of teacher when one is not even worthy to be a disciple. For this reason he called this one "hypocrite."

So then, you who are so spiteful as to see even the little faulty details in others, how have you become so careless with your own affairs that you avoid your own major faults? "First remove the plank from your eye." You see that Jesus does not forbid judging but commands that one first remove the plank from one's own eye. One may then set right the issues relating to others. For each person knows his own affairs better than others know them. And each one sees major faults easier than smaller ones. And each one loves oneself more than one's neighbor. So if you are really motivated by genuine concern, I urge you to show this concern for yourself first, because your own sin is both more certain and greater. THE GOSPEL OF MATTHEW, HOMILY 23.2.[6]

SEEING THE SPECK IN ANOTHER'S EYE. AUGUSTINE: The word *hypocrite* is aptly employed here, since the denouncing of evils is best viewed as a matter only for upright persons of goodwill. When the wicked engage in it, they are like impersonators, masqueraders, hiding their real selves behind a mask, while they portray another's character through the mask. The word *hypocrites* in fact signifies pretenders. Hence we ought especially to avoid that meddlesome class of pretenders who under the pretense of seeking advice undertake the censure of all kinds of vices. They are often moved by hatred and malice.

Rather, whenever necessity compels one to reprove or rebuke another, we ought to proceed with godly discernment and caution. First

---

[1] Cor 4:5. [2] 1 Tim 5:24. [3] 1 Tim 5:25. [4] PL 34:1297; FC 11:170-71. [5] Mt 18:32. [6] PG 57:309-10; NPNF 1 10:158.

of all, let us consider whether the other fault is such as we ourselves have never had or whether it is one that we have overcome. Then, if we have never had such a fault, let us remember that we are human and could have had it. But if we have had it and are rid of it now, let us remember our common frailty, in order that mercy, not hatred, may lead us to the giving of correction and admonition. In this way, whether the admonition occasions the amendment or the worsening of the one for whose sake we are offering it (for the result cannot be foreseen), we ourselves shall be made safe through singleness of eye. But if on reflection we find that we ourselves have the same fault as the one we are about to reprove, let us neither correct nor rebuke that one. Rather, let us bemoan the fault ourselves and induce that person to a similar concern, without asking him to submit to our correction. SERMON ON THE MOUNT 2.19.64.[7]

7:6 Pearls Before Swine

UNREADINESS TO RECEIVE GODLY TEACHING. AUGUSTINE: Now in this precept we are forbidden to give a holy thing to dogs or to cast pearls before swine. We must diligently seek to determine the gravity of these words: holy, pearls, dogs and swine. A holy thing is whatever it would be impious to profane or tear apart. Even a fruitless attempt to do so makes one already guilty of such impiety, though the holy thing may by its very nature remain inviolable and indestructible. Pearls signify all spiritual things that are worthy of being highly prized. Because these things lie hidden in secret, it is as though they were being drawn up from the deep. Because they are found in the wrappings of allegories, it is as though they were contained within shells that have been opened.[8] It is clear therefore that one and the same thing can be called both a holy thing and a pearl. It can be called a holy thing because it ought not to be destroyed and a pearl because it ought not to be despised.

One tries to destroy what one does not wish to leave intact. One despises what is deemed worthless, as if beneath him. Hence, whatever is despised is said to be trampled under foot. You know that dogs rush madly to tear apart whatever they attack, leaving nothing intact. Hence the Lord says, "Do not give to dogs what is holy." For although the holy thing itself cannot be shattered or destroyed but remains intact and unharmed, what must be considered is the desire of those who resist the truth with the utmost violence and bitterness. They do everything in their power to destroy what is holy, as if its destruction were possible. Although swine—unlike dogs—do not attack by biting, they befoul a thing by trampling all over it. Therefore "do not cast your pearls before swine, lest they trample them under their feet and turn and attack you." Thus we may rightly understand that these words (dogs and swine) are now used to designate respectively those who assail the truth and those who resist it.

By saying "lest they turn and tear you apart" Jesus does not say, "Lest they tear apart the pearls themselves." For by trampling on the pearls even when they turn around to hear something further, they lacerate[9] the one who cast the pearls they have already trampled upon. Of course, it would not be easy to find anything that would please one who would trample on pearls. Who could please one who despises divine truth revealed at such great cost? But I do not see how anyone who tries to teach such people will not themselves be torn apart by indignation and disgust, for both dogs and swine are unclean animals.[10] Therefore we must be careful not to reveal anything to one who cannot bear it, for it is better that one make a search for what is concealed than assail or despise what is

---

[7]PL 34:1298-99; FC 11:174-75*. [8]The interpretive task, therefore, is to crack through the shell of the language to its inner spiritual meaning. [9]Cut the feet of. [10]Liturgically speaking, they are not ready to enter into the temple.

revealed. Indeed, it is only through hatred or contempt that people refuse to accept truths of manifest importance. Hence for one reason some are called dogs, and for the other reason some are called swine. SERMON ON THE MOUNT 2.20.68-69.[11]

---

[11]PL 34:1300; FC 11:177-78*.

7:7-12 GOD'S ANSWERING OF PRAYER

[7]*"Ask, and it will be given you; seek, and you will find; knock, and it will be opened to you.* [8]*For every one who asks receives, and he who seeks finds, and to him who knocks it will be opened.* [9]*Or what man of you, if his son asks him for bread, will give him a stone?* [10]*Or if he asks for a fish, will give him a serpent?* [11]*If you then, who are evil, know how to give good gifts to your children, how much more will your Father who is in heaven give good things to those who ask him!* [12]*So whatever you wish that men would do to you, do so to them; for this is the law and the prophets."*

OVERVIEW: The door is not opened except to one who knocks in the form of asking and seeking (AUGUSTINE). To knock is to approach God with intensity and passion (CHRYSOSTOM). Since we who are evil know how to give good gifts, God who is incomparably good will know all the better how to give good gifts to us when we, like children, ask (AUGUSTINE). Since you know what you wish others to do for you, it is clear what you ought to do for others (CHRYSOSTOM). This way of stating the central maxim of the Christian life does not contradict the other ways of stating the maxim as encompassing the love of God and one's neighbor. People cannot serve another with a single heart unless they render that service in such a way that they look for no temporal advantage, which they cannot do unless motivated by the love of God (AUGUSTINE). Hence virtue is defined in accordance with our nature, so that we all know within ourselves what our duties are and can never again find refuge in ignorance (CHRYSOSTOM).

7:7-8 Ask, Seek, Knock

ASKING, SEEKING AND KNOCKING. AUGUSTINE: But when the precept was given that a holy thing should not be given to dogs and that pearls should not be cast before swine, questions abound. Mindful of our own ignorance and frailty and hearing it prescribed that we are not to give away something that we have not yet received,[1] we might therefore ask, "What holy thing do you forbid me to give to dogs, and what pearls do you forbid me to cast before swine? For I do not see that I have as yet received them." Most aptly, then, did the Lord go on to say, "Ask, and it shall be given you; seek and you shall find; knock, and it shall be opened to you. For everyone who asks, receives; and one who seeks,

---

[1]One who has not yet fully received and appropriated scriptural teaching is not yet prepared to give it away or offer it to another. The blessed life calls for doing the truth oneself before one offers it as a teaching for others.

finds; and to one who knocks, it shall be opened." The asking refers to obtaining soundness and strength of mind through prayer, in order that we may be able to fulfill the precepts that are being given. The seeking refers to finding truth. For the blessed life is made up of acting and knowing. Action requires a store of strength, while contemplation requires the manifestation of truths. Of these two, we are to ask for the first and we are to seek for the other in order that the one may be given and that the other may be found. In this life, however, knowledge consists in knowing the way toward that blessedness rather than in possessing it. But when anyone has found the true way, that one will arrive at that possession. As for you, it is to one who knocks that the door is opened. In order that these three things—the asking, the seeking and the knocking—may be illustrated by an example, let us consider the case of one who is unable to walk because of weak limbs. Of course, such a one must first be healed and strengthened for walking. Hence the Lord said, "Ask." SERMON ON THE MOUNT 2.21.71-72.[2]

KNOCK, AND IT WILL BE OPENED. CHRYSOSTOM: However, Jesus did not simply command us to ask but to ask with great concern and concentration—for this is the meaning of the word he used for "seek." For those who are seeking put aside everything else from their minds. They become concerned only with the thing that they are seeking and pay no attention at all to the circumstances. Even those who are looking for gold or servants that have been lost understand what I am saying. So this is what he meant by seeking. But by knocking Jesus meant that we approach God with intensity and passion. Therefore, O mortal, do not give up. Do not show less eagerness for virtue than desire for possessions. For you frequently sought possessions but did not find them. Nevertheless, although you knew that you could not guarantee that you would find them, you used every means of searching for them. Yet even though in this case you have a

promise that you surely will receive, you do not even demonstrate the smallest fraction of that same eagerness. But if you do not receive immediately, do not despair in this way. For it is because of this that Jesus said "knock" to show that even if he does not open the door immediately we should remain at the door knocking. THE GOSPEL OF MATTHEW, Homily 23.4.[3]

7:9-11 Giving Good Gifts

OUR GIFTS TO OUR CHILDREN AND GOD'S GIFTS TO US. AUGUSTINE: But how do evil people give good gifts? Those whom he here calls evil are sinners. As such they are still lovers of this world. It is in accordance with their notion of good that their gifts are to be called good. Their gifts are called good, that is, because the givers consider them good. Although these things are good in the order of nature, they are nevertheless temporal things pertaining to the infirmities of life. Moreover, whenever an evil person bestows them, he is not giving what is his own, for "the earth and the fullness thereof is the Lord's.... Who made heaven and earth, the sea, and all things that are in them."[4] So even we who are evil know how to give what is asked. How much more confidence ought we to have that God will give us good things when we ask. God will not deceive us by giving us one thing rather than another when we ask of him. Even we do not deceive our children. And whatever good gifts we bestow, we give what is God's and not our own. SERMON ON THE MOUNT 2.21.73.[5]

7:12 How to Treat Others

---

[2]PL 34:1302; FC 11:181-83*. To ask is to pray for soundness of mind. To seek is to look for ways to embody the truth. To knock is to take action to embody the truth. [3]PG 57:312; NPNF 1 10:160. [4]Ps 24:1; 146:6 (23:1; 145:6 LXX). [5]PL 34:1303; FC 11:183-84. We who are drenched in the history of sin still know something about how to give good things to our children. We do not deceive them. In giving, we give to them what is God's, not our own. Since we who are evil know how to give these good gifts, would not God who is good know all the better how to give good gifts to us when we, like children, ask?

WHATEVER YOU WISH OTHERS WOULD DO
TO YOU. CHRYSOSTOM: In this statement Jesus
briefly sums up all that is required. He shows that
the definition of virtue is short and easy and
known already to all. And he did not merely say,
"Whatever things that you want," but "Therefore[6]
whatever things that you want." For he did not
add this word *therefore* in its straightforward sense,
but rather he used it with a deeper meaning. He is
saying, "If you want to be heard, do these things in
addition to those about which I have already spoken." What are these additional things? "Whatever
are those things that you want people to do to
you." Do you see how this shows that our wishes
imply careful regulation of our behavior? Note
that he did not say, "Whatever things that you
want God to do for you, do these things to your
neighbor." Thus you cannot say, "How is that even
possible? He is God and I am a human being!"
Instead, Jesus said, "Whatever things that you
want your fellow servant to do, you yourself also
perform for your neighbor." What is less of a burden than this? What is more just? Then the praise
is exceedingly great: "For this is the law and the
prophets." From this it is clear that virtue is
defined in accordance with our nature. So we all
know within ourselves what our duties are. We
cannot ever again find refuge in ignorance. THE
GOSPEL OF MATTHEW, HOMILY 23.5.[7]

WHETHER LOVE OF GOD IS IMPLIED IN THE
COMMAND. AUGUSTINE: Elsewhere Jesus says
that there are two precepts on which the whole
law and the prophets depend.[8] The present precept seems to concern only the love of neighbor
and not the love of God as well. Of course, if he
had said, "All things whatever you wish to have
done to you,[9] do you also those things," he would
then have embraced those two precepts in the one
maxim, for it would be readily understood that
everyone would wish to be loved by both God
and other persons. So, when someone would be
given that one precept—when he would be
required to do whatever he would wish to have
done to him—then he would of course implicitly

be given the other precept as well: that he should
love both God and neighbor. But it would seem
that the present maxim means nothing more than
"You shall love your neighbor as yourself,"[10] for it
seems very expressly restricted to persons, since
it reads, "Whatever you wish that people would
do to you, do so to them." However, we must pay
close attention to his further observation on this
point, for Jesus goes on to say, "This is the law
and the prophets." In the case of the previously
mentioned two precepts, he did not say merely
that "the law and the prophets depend on them."
He said that "the whole law and the prophets
depend" on them, for that is the sum of prophecy.
But by omitting the word *whole* in the present
instance, he seems to reserve a place for the other
precept—the precept that pertains to the love of
God. At any rate, the present instruction is one
that was most apt for the occasion when he was
expounding the precepts that pertain to singleness of heart. For there might be reason to fear
that a person may have a double heart toward
another, since the matters of the heart are hidden.
But there is hardly anyone who would wish that
others would deal double-heartedly with oneself.
It is impossible for one to render service single-
heartedly to another unless one renders it in such
a way that one looks for no temporal advantage
from it. And one cannot do this unless one is
motivated by the kind of intention that we have
sufficiently discussed earlier, when we were
speaking about the eye that is single. SERMON ON
THE MOUNT 2.22.75.[11]

---

[6]"So" in the RSV text. [7]PG 57:314; NPNF 1 10:161-62. You know
what you wish others to do for you. Hence it is clear what you ought to
do for others. [8]"Love God with all your heart, soul, mind and
strength, and your neighbor as yourself" (Mt 22:37-38; see also vv. 39-
40). [9]Not by human beings only but also by God. [10]Mt 22:39. [11]PL
34:1304; FC 11:185-86**. Does this limited way of stating the maxim
stand in tension with the other twofold (love of God and others) way
of stating the maxim? This way of stating the maxim as pertaining primarily to human relationship does not contradict the other ways of
stating the maxim as encompassing the love of God and the neighbor.
No one can serve another with a single heart unless one renders that
service in such a way that one looks for no temporal advantage, which
one cannot do unless motivated by the love of God.

7:13-20 THE NARROW GATE

[13]"Enter by the narrow gate; for the gate is wide and the way is easy,[q] that leads to destruction, and those who enter by it are many. [14]For the gate is narrow and the way is hard, that leads to life, and those who find it are few.

[15]"Beware of false prophets, who come to you in sheep's clothing but inwardly are ravenous wolves. [16]You will know them by their fruits. Are grapes gathered from thorns, or figs from thistles? [17]So, every sound tree bears good fruit, but the bad tree bears evil fruit. [18]A sound tree cannot bear evil fruit, nor can a bad tree bear good fruit. [19]Every tree that does not bear good fruit is cut down and thrown into the fire. [20]Thus you will know them by their fruits."

q Other ancient authorities read for the way is wide and easy

OVERVIEW: Few from among Israel were saved (ORIGEN). The temporary nature of the toils on the way is contrasted with the eternal nature of the victor's crowns, so as to become a continuing encouragement to the traveler on the way (CHRYSOSTOM). Those who spurn the easy yoke of faith view the way that leads to life as demanding and the entry gate narrow (AUGUSTINE). The ancient adversary is forever introducing deception as if it is true, so Jesus warns the faithful to carefully distinguish truth from deception, as symbolized by wolves. So do not look to the mask but to the behavioral fruits of those who patiently pursue the narrow way (CHRYSOSTOM). A bad person cannot perform good works, nor can a good person perform bad works (AUGUSTINE). Jesus both protects the faithful that they may not be easily deluded and deters those who would teach evil things (THEODORE OF MOPSUESTIA). The Lord does not say that for the wicked there is no way to change or that the good cannot fall away but that so long as one is living in wickedness, one will not be able to bear good fruit (CHRYSOSTOM).

7:13-14 Narrow and Wide Gates

THE YOKE IS EASY. AUGUSTINE: He says this not because the Lord's yoke is rough or his burden heavy but because there are a few who wish their labors to end. They do not put their full trust in the Lord when he cries, "Come to me, all you who labor, and I will give you rest. Take my yoke upon you, and learn from me, for I am meek and humble of heart. . . . For my yoke is easy, and my burden light."[1] Hence the humble and the meek of heart are named at the very beginning of this sermon. But because there are many who spurn this smooth yoke and this light burden, it comes to pass that the way that leads to life is demanding and the entry gate is narrow. SERMON ON THE MOUNT 2.23.77.[2]

THE ROAD THAT LEADS TO LIFE. CHRYSOSTOM: Remember that later Jesus would say, "My yoke is easy, and my burden is light."[3] And here he implies the same thing.[4] Does it not seem inconsistent then to say here that the good road is narrow and constricted? Pay attention. He has made it clear the burden[5] is very light, easy and agreeable. "But how," one may say, "is the narrow and constricted road easy?" Because it is both a

---

[1]Mt 11:28-30. [2]PL 34:1304-5; FC 11:187-88*. It is not because the Lord's yoke, his command itself, is heavy but because so few are willing to put their trust in the Lord in meekness that the way seems so narrow. [3]Mt 11:30. [4]For he has just said that you already clearly know the requirement of God, to do unto others as you would have them do unto you. [5]As enabled by grace.

gate and a road. The other road is, of course, both a gate and a road, but on that way there is nothing that is enduring. All things on that way are temporary, both things pleasant and painful.[6] THE GOSPEL OF MATTHEW, HOMILY 23.5.[7]

AN ETERNAL CROWN. CHRYSOSTOM: It is not only on the way that the things of excellence become easy. In the end they become even more agreeable. For it is not just the passing away of toil and sweating but also the anticipated arrival at a pleasant destination that is sufficient to encourage the traveler. For this road ends in life! The result is that both the temporary nature of the toils and the eternal nature of the victor's crowns, combined with the fact that these toils come first and the victor's crowns come afterward, become a hearty encouragement. THE GOSPEL OF MATTHEW, HOMILY 23.5.[8]

7:15 False Prophets

BEWARE OF FALSE PROPHETS. CHRYSOSTOM: Jesus reminded them of what happened to their ancestors who were attracted to false prophets. The same dangers are now faced as those that occurred in earlier days. He reminded them of the experience of their ancestors so that they would not despair at the multitude of troubles that would mount up on this way that is narrow and constricted. He reminded them that it is necessary to walk in a way that goes contrary to the common opinion. One must guard oneself not only against pigs and dogs but those other, more elusive creatures: the wolves. They were going to face inward anxieties as well as outward difficulties, but they are not to despair. "Therefore do not be thrown into confusion," Jesus says in effect, "for nothing will happen that is new or strange. Remember that the ancient adversary is forever introducing deception as if true." THE GOSPEL OF MATTHEW, HOMILY 23.6.[9]

WOLVES IN SHEEP'S CLOTHING. CHRYSOSTOM: Notice that along with the dogs and pigs there is

another form of ambush and plotting that causes far more trouble than that of dogs or pigs. For the dogs and pigs do not hide their nature. They are obvious. But the movements of wolves are hidden in shadows. Hence he commanded that one should not only avoid the dogs and pigs but also that one should continuously and carefully look out for wolves, because one cannot see them the moment they attack. For this reason he says, "Watch out!"—to make his hearers more careful to distinguish deception from truth. THE GOSPEL OF MATTHEW, HOMILY 23.6.[10]

7:16 Grapes Not Harvested from Thistles

BY THEIR FRUITS. CHRYSOSTOM: It does not seem to me that "false prophets" here refers to the heretics but rather to persons who live morally corrupt lives while wearing a mask of virtue. They are usually called frauds by most people. For this reason Jesus continued by saying, "By their fruits you will know them." For it is possible to find some virtuous persons living among heretics. But among the corrupted of whom I speak it is in no way possible. "So what difference does it make," Jesus says in effect, "if even among these false prophets some do put on a hypocritical show of virtue? Certainly they will soon be detected easily." The nature of this road upon which he commanded us to walk is toilsome and hard. The hypocrite would seldom choose to toil but would prefer only to make a show. For this very reason the hypocrite is easily detected. When Jesus notes that "there are few who find it," he distinguishes these from those who do not find the way yet pretend to find it.

---

[6]Whether it is easy or hard, wide or narrow, long or short, temporally viewed, the faithful are still being given a pathway and a gate leading to eternal life. [7]PG 57:314; NPNF 1 10:162. [8]PG 57:314; NPNF 1 10:162. The shortness of the temporal road and the greatness of the eternal gate make the road easy, even if for a short time narrow and hard. [9]PG 57:315; NPNF 1 10:163. [10]PG 57:315; NPNF 1 10:163. The wolves are hypocrites who pretend to be virtuous but are constantly bearing the bad fruits of their inward corruption.

So do not look to the mask but to the behavioral fruits of those who pursue the narrow way. THE GOSPEL OF MATTHEW, HOMILY 23.6.[11]

7:17 Good Fruit from Good Trees

THE SOUND TREE BEARS GOOD FRUIT. CHRYSOSTOM: Even though Jesus seems to make virtually the same point a second time,[12] it is hardly redundant. For in the second time around he prevents anyone from concluding, "The evil tree bears evil fruit, but it also bears good fruit, so as to make it difficult to recognize an evil tree, because the crop is of two kinds." No. Jesus says, "This is not so. For the evil tree bears only evil fruits and would never[13] bear good fruits. So also it is the same way with the opposite kind of tree."

What then? Is there no such thing as a good person who becomes corrupt? Or a corrupt person who becomes good? Isn't life full of many examples of such reversals? But the Messiah is not saying that the evil person is incapable of changing or that the good person will never fail in anything. But he is saying that so long as a person is living in a degenerate way, he will not be able to generate good fruit. For he may indeed change to virtue, being evil, but while continuing in wickedness, he will not bear good fruit.

What then? Did not David, even though good, bear evil fruit? No, because he did not bear evil fruit while remaining good but while being changed. For if indeed he had remained continually good as he had been, he would not have produced the bad fruit. For it surely was not while abiding in the habits of excellence that he had the audacity to do the very things that he had the audacity to do. THE GOSPEL OF MATTHEW, HOMILY 23.7.[14]

7:18 Good and Bad Trees

IDENTIFYING FRAUD BY ITS RESULTS. CHRYSOSTOM: Jesus also said these things to shut the mouths of those who say nothing but slander and to reign in the lips of those who speak maliciously. For many are suspicious of good people because so many others are evil, but Jesus by this saying has deprived them of all excuse. For on this premise one would not even be able to say, "I am deceived and was misled." For he has provided you a rule by which accurately to identify the frauds by their deeds. He has also commanded you to proceed on the basis of practices and not to mix up all cases at random. THE GOSPEL OF MATTHEW, HOMILY 23.7.[15]

7:19 Bad Trees Cut Down

ROTTEN TREES. THEODORE OF MOPSUESTIA: Others maintain that these things are said with reference to teachers of foreign doctrines[16] and to people who mingle lies with the truth. Just as one cannot gather evil fruit from a tree that produces good fruit, neither can one gather grapes or figs from one that bears thorns; similarly, from an evil mindset, one does not hear good words, nor would you expect evil teaching to come from a pious teacher. But in protecting the others so that they may not be easily deluded, Jesus at the same time deters those who would attempt to teach evil things. For, he says, "every tree that does not bear good fruit is cut down and cast into the fire." Just as fruitless trees are thrown into the fire, so human beings who do not bear the fruits of religion with their mouths will consequently receive punishment. FRAGMENT 38.[17]

WHETHER SOULS CAN CHANGE FOR BETTER OR WORSE. AUGUSTINE: On this point, one must carefully avoid the error of those who think that they find in these two trees a reason for believing that there are two natures and that

---

[11]PG 57:315-16. [12]In v. 18 as in v. 17. [13]As an evil tree. [14]PG 57:316; NPNF 1 10:163-64. [15]PG 57:316-17; NPNF 1 10:164. Christ does not say that for the wicked there is no way to change or that the good cannot fall away but that so long as one is living in wickedness, one will not be able to bear good fruit. [16]Cf. 1 Tim 1:3. [17]MKGK 108.

one of them belongs to the nature of God but that the other neither belongs to God nor depends on him.[18] This error has been rather fully discussed in other books, and if that is not sufficient it will receive still further treatment later. But we must now show that these two trees furnish no argument in support of it. First of all, in this similitude the Lord is speaking about two kinds of persons. This is so obvious that if anyone will but read the passages in the context of those that precede and follow it, he will be amazed at the blindness of those who would misinterpret it impersonally. Again, they fix their attention on the saying, "A good tree cannot bear bad fruit, nor can a bad tree bear good fruit," and then they think that an evil soul cannot be changed into a better or a good soul into a worse. As though, in truth, the saying were "A good tree cannot become a bad tree, nor

a bad tree become a good tree!" But what has been said is that "a good tree cannot bear bad fruit, and a bad tree cannot bear good fruit." The tree, of course, is the soul itself—that is, the person—and the fruits are the person's works. So a bad person cannot perform good works, nor can a good person perform bad works. SERMON ON THE MOUNT 2.24.79.[19]

[18]The adversaries mentioned here by Augustine are the Manichaeans, who admitted two opposing natures—one good and one evil, respectively the work of the supreme God and the Power of Darkness. In order to create a scriptural foundation for their dualistic doctrine, the Manichaeans (like the Gnostics before them) made use of this passage of the Gospel, from which they derived the existence of an evil nature independent from the evil use of free will by rational beings. [19]PL 34:1305; FC 11:189-90*. The saying does not imply that an evil soul cannot be changed into a better soul. The implication is that the soul itself in its goodness or badness produces either good or bad fruit. So, a bad person cannot perform good works, nor can a good person perform bad works.

7:21-29 HEARERS AND DOERS OF THE WORD

[21]"Not every one who says to me, 'Lord, Lord,' shall enter the kingdom of heaven, but he who does the will of my Father who is in heaven. [22]On that day many will say to me, 'Lord, Lord, did we not prophesy in your name, and cast out demons in your name, and do many mighty works in your name?' [23]And then will I declare to them, 'I never knew you; depart from me, you evildoers.'

[24]"Every one then who hears these words of mine and does them will be like a wise man who built his house upon the rock; [25]and the rain fell, and the floods came, and the winds blew and beat upon that house, but it did not fall, because it had been founded on the rock. [26]And every one who hears these words of mine and does not do them will be like a foolish man who built his house upon the sand; [27]and the rain fell, and the floods came, and the winds blew and beat against that house, and it fell; and great was the fall of it."

[28]And when Jesus finished these sayings, the crowds were astonished at his teaching, [29]for he taught them as one who had authority, and not as their scribes.

OVERVIEW: Jesus implied here that to do his Father's will is to do his will, there being no other will of the Son than the will of the Father (CHRYSOSTOM). God knows those whom he loves and loves those who single-mindedly believe in him and do the things that please him (Cyril of Alexandria). When the storm is most violent, the upheavals the greatest and the temptations continuing, such a person is not shaken even slightly (Chrysostom). This is the way the Lord builds his church—upon the rock, with steadfastness and strength, so the gates of hell shall not prevail against it (Origen). Those who do evil cannot claim God as cause of their own wickedness and stupidity. They make themselves like fools when they withdraw from that which proceeds according to nature (Cyril of Alexandria). When Jesus spoke he did not refer to someone else but showed that he was the One who had the authority to decide (Chrysostom).

7:21 Doing the Will of the Heavenly Father

The Will of the Father. Chrysostom: He said "whoever does the will of my Father" shall enter, not whoever does my will. Why? Nothing is insufficient if they do the will of the Father. What he did say was itself a very difficult thing to accept in view of their weakness. He implied that to do his Father's will is to do his will. There is no other willing of the Son than the will of the Father. This may apply in particular to those who commit themselves in detail to legal rules[1] yet take little thought for the actual embodiment of their better intentions. Elsewhere Paul confronts them directly when he says, "Consider this. You bear the name Jew, rely on the law, boast in God and know the will of God,"[2] but in all this you derive no benefit as long as the actual fruits of good living are not present. The Gospel of Matthew, Homily 24.1.[3]

7:22-23 Depart from Me, Evildoers

I Never Knew You. Cyril of Alexandria: There may be some who, in the beginning, believed rightly and assiduously labored at vir-

tue. They may have even worked miracles and prophesied and cast out demons. And yet later they are found turning aside to evil, to self-assertive deception and desire. Of these Jesus remarks that he "never knew them." He ranks them as equivalent to those who were never known by him at all. Even if they at the outset had lived virtuously, they ended up condemned. God knows those whom he loves, and he loves those who single-mindedly believe in him and do the things that please him. Fragment 88.[4]

7:24 Building on Rock

Living with Security. Chrysostom: Whereas his teaching has up to now largely focused on the future kingdom, its unspeakable rewards and its consolations, now he shifts his focus to the present life, its current fruits and how great is the strength of virtue within it. What then is its strength? It is living with security, not being easily overcome by any of life's terrors and standing above all those who treat others maliciously. What could be as good as this? For not even the one who wears the royal crown would be able to furnish this for himself. But one who pursues the way of excellence can have this stability, for that one alone is possessed of this equilibrium in full abundance. In the crashing surf of the present circumstances such a one experiences a calm sea. This is amazing. It is when the storm is violent, the upheaval great and the temptations continual that such a person is not shaken in the slightest. This is not a way of living that applies to fair weather only. For he says, "The rain came down, the floods came, the winds blew, and they beat against that house. And it did not fall because it was founded upon the rock."

In referring to rain, floods and winds Jesus is speaking about all those human circumstances and misfortunes, such as false accusations,

---

[1]The Mosaic law. [2]Rom 2:17-18, slightly modified. [3]PG 57:321; NPNF 1 10:167. [4]MKGK 180.

plots, bereavements, deaths, loss of family members, insults from others, and all the horrid things in life about which one could speak. Jesus says that a soul that pursues the way of excellence does not give in to any of these potential disasters. And the cause of this is that this soul has been founded upon the rock.

Now "rock" refers to the reliability of Jesus' teaching. For his commands are stronger than any rock. They place one quite above all the human waves of life. For the one who guards these commands with care will excel not only over human beings when treated maliciously but even over the demons themselves in their plots. THE GOSPEL OF MATTHEW, HOMILY 24.2.[5]

7:25 A Solid House

PERSECUTIONS ACCOMPLISH NOTHING. ORIGEN: "For neither death nor life nor angels nor other things can separate us from the love of Christ."[6] Neither can the flooding of rivers, as in the lands of Egypt and Assyria, do harm. Only those are harmed who build on sand, who practice the wisdom of the world.[7] The winds that blow are like the false prophets. All these, coming together in one place, "beat upon" the house. If it is founded on rock, they do no harm. "The way of a snake upon a rock" is not to be found.[8] But in the form of temptations and persecutions, which may mount into a flood, they beat upon even the one who seems to be well-founded. The house falls if it does not have Christ as its basis and foundation. But the truly wise person builds one's house "upon a rock." This is the way the Lord builds his church—upon the rock, with steadfastness and strength. This is why "the gates of hell shall not prevail against it."[9] All the persecutions that fall upon that house accomplish nothing. The house is founded upon the rock. FRAGMENT 153.[10]

7:26 Building on Sand

PUNISHMENT INSTEAD OF BENEFIT. CHRYSOS-

TOM: And he was right in calling this one a fool, because what could be more brainless than building a house on the sand? For such a one endures the work of building but deprives oneself of the fruit of one's labor and of relaxation, experiencing punishment instead of benefit. For it is surely clear to everyone that even those who follow a wicked path have to sweat in labor. Even the robber, the adulterer and the false accuser have to work and strain so that they can bring their evil to completion. But they not only reap no benefit at all from these labors but also experience much loss. For Paul was implying this when he said, "The one who sows to one's flesh will reap corruption from one's flesh."[11] Who are these persons who build on the sand? Those who are given up to fornication, debauchery, drunkenness and anger—they are building on sand. THE GOSPEL OF MATTHEW, HOMILY 24.3.[12]

7:27 Great Was Its Fall

THE FLOODS CAME. CYRIL OF ALEXANDRIA: Spiritually understood, the one who rightly hears the word is contrasted with the builder who builds his house on sand. In time of temptation the house falls down. The onslaught of evil wind covers it with silt, and troubled waters flood into the soul. From this turbid flood stream of iniquity the house is shaken to its foundations. This should rouse us to become aware of the danger that comes in final judgment. Those who hear the Lord's words are like a wise man building on rock. Those who do not follow the Lord's words are likened to a foolish

---

[5]PG 57:323; NPNF 1 10:169. The gospel's way of excellence enables greater stability in the present, even amid life's hazards, than power or fortune can command. [6]Rom 8:38-39. [7]The rivers of Egypt and Assyria symbolize the wisdom of the world, an enemy of Christ. The sons of Abraham who build precariously on the sand are the Jews, based on the connection of the sand in Matthew 7:26 to the sand in Genesis 22:17; the descendants of Abraham would be as numerous as the grains of sand on the seashore. [8]Prov 30:19. [9]Mt 16:18. [10]GCS 41.1:76. [11]Gal 6:8, slightly modified. [12]PG 57:325; NPNF 1 10:170.

man building on sand. One who practices virtue is made thoroughly able "through Christ who strengthens him."[13] We receive everything from God who puts things right. From him comes wisdom and insight and union with all that is good. The bad person cannot claim God as cause of his own wickedness and stupidity. He makes himself like the fool when he withdraws from that which proceeds according to nature. He then turns toward what is unnatural. FRAGMENT 89.[14]

7:28-29 Teaching with Authority

LOVE AND AUTHORITY. CHRYSOSTOM: Surely it was logical that they were in pain over the heavy weight of what he had said. They were stunned by the soaring level of the requirements that he had made. But now the strength of the one teaching was so great that he seized many of them and threw them into great amazement. Because of their pleasure in what he said, Jesus

finally persuaded them not to leave as he finished speaking. For not even after he went down from the mountain did the hearers leave, but even then the whole audience followed him because of the great love that was shown in what he had said. But most of all they were astounded at his authority. For when he said these things, he did not refer to another, as even the prophet Moses did, but everywhere he showed that he himself was the One who had the authority to decide. For even when he was establishing laws Jesus continually added, "But I say to you."[15] And when he was reminding them of the final day of judgment, he showed that he himself is the One who will bring justice, both through the punishments and through the honors. This is what made such a commotion among them. THE GOSPEL OF MATTHEW, HOMILY 25.1.[16]

---

[13]Phil 4:13. [14]MKGK 180. [15]Mt 5:22, 28, 32, 34, 39, 44. [16]PG 57:327; NPNF 1 10:171-72.

8:1-4 HEALING THE LEPER

[1]*When he came down from the mountain, great crowds followed him;* [2]*and behold, a leper came to him and knelt before him, saying, "Lord, if you will, you can make me clean."* [3]*And he stretched out his hand and touched him, saying, "I will; be clean." And immediately his leprosy was cleansed.* [4]*And Jesus said to him, "See that you say nothing to any one; but go, show yourself to the priest, and offer the gift that Moses commanded, for a proof to the people."*[r]

r Greek *to them*

OVERVIEW: The leper knew that if the Lord willed, he could cleanse him. He was not reproved for making this assumption. Rather, Jesus confirmed the assumption about his own glory and authority that lay hidden underneath the leper's question (CHRYSOSTOM). We are here taught that the whole person has been trans-

formed in contemplation, action and behavior when touched by divine things (CYRIL OF ALEXANDRIA). The leper when cleansed was not to entrust the recognition of his cleansing to private judgment but to show himself to the priests, who could bear witness that Jesus did not transgress the law (CHRYSOSTOM).

8:1 Descending the Mountain

WHEN HE CAME DOWN. CHRYSOSTOM: When Jesus came down from the mountain, a leper came to him and said, "Lord, if you will, you can make me clean." How respectful was the understanding and faith of the leper in drawing near. For he did not interrupt the teaching or break into the gathering. He waited for the proper time and approached him only after "he came down." THE GOSPEL OF MATTHEW, HOMILY 25.1.[1]

8:2 A Leper Asks for Cleansing

LORD, IF YOU WILL, YOU CAN. CHRYSOSTOM: With great fervor before Jesus' knees, the leper pleaded with him[2] with sincere faith. He discerned who Jesus was. He did not state conditionally, "If you request it of God" or "If you pray for me." Rather, he said simply, "If you will, you can make me clean." He did not pray, "Lord, cleanse me." Rather, he leaves everything to the Lord and makes his own recovery depend entirely on him. Thus he testified that all authority belongs to him.

One might ask, "What if the leper had been mistaken in this assumption?" If he had been mistaken, wouldn't it have been fitting for the Lord to reprove him and set him straight? But did he do this? No. Quite to the contrary, Jesus established and confirmed exactly what he had said. THE GOSPEL OF MATTHEW, HOMILY 25.1.[3]

8:3 Immediate Healing

JESUS' AUTHORITY TO HEAL. CHRYSOSTOM: Jesus did not say, "Be clean," but rather responded to the leper's assumption, saying, "I will. Be clean." This left no doubt as to whether the leper's assumption was correct. Jesus simply approved it.

The apostles would speak from an entirely different assumption when they later said to the amazed crowd, "Why do you stare at us as though by our own power or piety we have made him walk?"[4] The Lord, who often spoke with modesty, obscuring his own glory, speaks here in a way so as to establish the opinion of those who were amazed at his authority: "I will. Be clean." Many and great were the signs that he would offer, but only here has he uttered this distinctive word about his own authority. Jesus confirmed the assumption with respect to his authority by purposely adding, "I will." The important thing was not that he said this but that he responded approvingly to what was being said and confirmed it. The cleansing followed immediately. THE GOSPEL OF MATTHEW, HOMILY 25.1.[5]

8:4 Going to the Priest

PRIESTLY CORROBORATION. CHRYSOSTOM: It was an ancient law that the leper when cleansed should not entrust the recognition of his cleansing to private judgment but should show himself to the priest. By this means it would be confirmed in his own eyes, and he could then be numbered among the clean. For if the priest had not corroborated it, he would have remained outside the camp among the unclean. THE GOSPEL OF MATTHEW, HOMILY 25.3.[6]

LET THE AUTHORITIES JUDGE. CHRYSOSTOM: Jesus did not imply that showing the healing to the priest was something he needed. Rather, he temporarily remits him to the law. This stopped every mouth. He did this lest others might claim that Jesus had arrogated to himself the priest's honor. He performed the miracle himself, yet he entrusted its examination to the authorities and caused them to sit as judges of his own miracles. He was saying in effect: "I am so far from struggling against Moses or the priests that I even guide those cleansed to submit themselves to the

---

[1]PG 57:328; NPNF 1 10:172**. [2]Mk 1:40. [3]PG 57:328; NPNF 1 10:172**. [4]Acts 3:12. [5]PG 57:328; NPNF 1 10:172**. [6]PG 57:330; NPNF 1 10:173**.

priests." THE GOSPEL OF MATTHEW, HOMILY 25.3.[7]

THE GIFT THAT MOSES COMMANDED. CYRIL OF ALEXANDRIA: What then was the gift that was to be brought by the leper according to the law? "Two small birds,"[8] one of which the priest killed "over running water." Taking "cedar wood and broken scarlet and hyssop" and the living bird, he dipped them "in the blood of the slain bird, over running water." He anointed the right ear, hand and foot of the leper who was cleansed.[9] He sent the living bird outside the city, "into the open field."[10] Observe, therefore, how perfectly Christ depicts these things for us. By the living bird you may understand the living, heavenly Word. By the blood of the slain bird, you should understand the blood of our suffering Lord, for whom we say that he suffered "in the flesh," rather than "in his own body." The cedar is a wood not prone to rot. The incorruptible flesh, the body of Christ, "did not see corruption."[11] Hyssop symbolizes the effervescence, activity and power of the Spirit. Scarlet intends the confession of the covenant made with blood. The running water signifies the life-creating gift of baptism. . . . Through this baptism, whoever

has become a leper through sin may be cleansed. The sending of the living bird outside of the city teaches us to abandon this world, as did Christ in his ascension into heaven. Having thus come into the presence of God the Father, he makes intercession for all of us, and we therefore shall be cleansed. By the anointing of the leper's right ear, hand and foot, we are taught that we must be, in contemplation and in action and in our way of life, in touch with divine things. FRAGMENT 93.[12]

JESUS DOES NOT TRANSGRESS THE LAW. CHRYSOSTOM: What is meant by "a proof to the people"? It was for their reproof, or as a demonstration or for accusation if they should prove fickle. For since the religious professionals would call him a deceiver and imposter and persecute him as an adversary of God and transgressor of the law, he was prepared to say, "You shall bear witness to me that I am not a transgressor of the law." THE GOSPEL OF MATTHEW, HOMILY 25.3.[13]

---

[7]PG 57:330; NPNF 1 10:173-74**. [8]Lev 14:1-7. [9]Cf. Lev 14:14. [10]Lev 14:7. [11]Acts 2:31. [12]MKGK 181-82. [13]PG 57:330; NPNF 1 10:174**.

8:5-13 THE CENTURION'S SERVANT HEALED

[5]*As he entered Caperna-um, a centurion came forward to him, beseeching him* [6]*and saying, "Lord, my servant is lying paralyzed at home, in terrible distress."* [7]*And he said to him, "I will come and heal him."* [8]*But the centurion answered him, "Lord, I am not worthy to have you come under my roof; but only say the word, and my servant will be healed.* [9]*For I am a man under authority, with soldiers under me; and I say to one, 'Go,' and he goes, and to another, 'Come,' and he comes, and to my slave, 'Do this,' and he does it."* [10]*When Jesus heard him, he marveled, and said to those who followed him, "Truly, I say to you, not even[s] in Israel have I found such faith.* [11]*I tell you, many will come from east and west and sit at table with Abraham, Isaac, and Jacob in the kingdom of heaven,* [12]*while the sons of the kingdom will be thrown into the outer*

darkness; there men will weep and gnash their teeth." [13]*And to the centurion Jesus said, "Go; be it done for you as you have believed." And the servant was healed at that very moment.*

s Other ancient authorities read *with no one*

OVERVIEW: The Lord's purpose in coming to the centurion's house was not merely to enter into his house but into his heart (AUGUSTINE). The centurion had grasped what Martha had not, that Jesus himself is the One who answers prayer. He fully expected the healing of his servant (CHRYSOSTOM). It was not those who first received the law and prophets who were destined to sit at table with Abraham but those who in spirit willingly belonged to the household of faith. The only nation that beheld and directly knew Jesus crucified him. The other nations of the world, as seen prototypically in the case of the centurion, would come to hear and believe with great faith (AUGUSTINE). The centurion perceived the authority of Jesus by analogy with his understanding of his own authority to command (THEODORE OF MOPSUESTIA). Faith is given by God but born and preserved in the freedom that God gives humanity as a likeness to himself (IRENAEUS).

8:5 A Centurion Beseeches Jesus

THE CENTURION EXPECTED THE HEALING. CHRYSOSTOM: Some argue that the centurion, by his description, implied the reason why he had not brought his servant to Jesus, saying, "Lord, my servant is lying paralyzed at home, in terrible distress," as though he was at his last gasp, or even, as Luke said, he was "at the point of death."[1] In my opinion, however, the reason he had not brought him in was itself a sign of his great faith, even much greater than those who let the patient down through the roof.[2] Because the centurion knew for certain that even a mere command was enough for raising the servant up, he thought it unnecessary to bring him. THE GOSPEL OF MATTHEW, HOMILY 26.1.[3]

8:6 In Distress

MY SERVANT. THEODORE OF MOPSUESTIA: He uses the word *boy*[4] here to indicate his house servant. Luke shows this clearly, calling him his "slave" or "servant."[5] FRAGMENT 41A.[6]

8:7 I Will Come to Your House

JESUS' OFFER. CHRYSOSTOM: What did Jesus do? Something he had never done before. While on previous occasions he had responded to the wish of his supplicants, in this case he rather springs actively toward it. He offers not only to heal him but also to come to his house. By this we learn of the centurion's excellent faith. For if he had not made this offer but rather had said, "Go your way, let your servant be healed," we would not have known these things. THE GOSPEL OF MATTHEW, HOMILY 26.1.[7]

8:8 The Centurion Pleads Unworthiness

LORD, I AM NOT WORTHY. AUGUSTINE: When the Lord promised to go to the centurion's house to heal his servant, the centurion answered, "Lord, I am not worthy to have you come under my roof; but only say the word, and my servant will be healed." By viewing himself as unworthy, he showed himself worthy for Christ to come not merely into his house but also into his heart. He would not have said this with such great faith and humility if he had not already welcomed in his heart the One who came into his house. It would have been no great joy for the Lord Jesus to enter into his house and not to

---

[1]Lk 7:2. [2]Lk 5:19. [3]PG 57:333; NPNF 1 10:176**. [4]Theodore's explanation comes from the fact that *pais* could mean either son or servant (cf. RSV). [5]See Lk 7:2-10. [6]MKGK 109. [7]PG 57:333; NPNF 1 10:176**.

enter his heart. For the Master of humility both by word and example sat down also in the house of a certain proud Pharisee, Simon, and though he sat down in his house, there was no place in his heart. For in his heart the Son of Man could not lay his head.[8] SERMON 62.1.[9]

MY SERVANT WILL BE HEALED. CHRYSOSTOM: It is curious that when Martha, who was very dear to Jesus, said, "I know that whatever you ask from God, God will give it to you,"[10] far from being praised, she was rebuked and corrected by the Lord as not having spoken quite fittingly.... For Jesus was teaching her that he himself is the fountain of all good things, the resurrection and the life, as if to say, "I do not wait to receive active power but have it already in myself." THE GOSPEL OF MATTHEW, HOMILY 26.2.[11]

8:9 One Under Authority

A MAN UNDER AUTHORITY. THEODORE OF MOPSUESTIA: It was a sign of the centurion's intelligence that merely by thinking to himself about what was likely, he believed such things about Christ. For he says, "I also am a man. But nevertheless I am the lord over those I have received authority to rule. Therefore it is nothing strange if you, who have received authority from God, should be able to command illnesses to depart by a mere word." The centurion did not approach Jesus as one who is Son of God and Lord of the whole creation (for at that time, before the crucifixion, this was not yet known even by the disciples). Rather, he came to him as to a man who, because of his virtues, had received from God some greater-than-human authority. This is why he says, "For I also am a man." For since he had said to him, "say the word," and this might seem proper to God only, he rightly adds the statement, "for I also am a man," as though to say, "It is nothing surprising if you, a man who has received authority from God, should be able to do this thing, since I

myself, a man like you, receive subjects and am set over them to command them as I will." FRAGMENT 41A.[12]

8:10 Such Faith Not Found in Israel

THE EFFECT OF HIGH EXPECTATIONS. CHRYSOSTOM: Jesus is found marveling at the centurion. He turns his attention to him and honors him with the gift of the kingdom. He calls others to the same zeal. THE GOSPEL OF MATTHEW, HOMILY 26.2.[13]

NOT EVEN IN ISRAEL. AUGUSTINE: Now this man was a Gentile—he was, after all, a centurion. The Jewish nation already had troops of the Roman Empire among them. This man was in command of troops there, to the extent that a centurion could be in command. He was under authority, and he had authority. As a subordinate, he was obedient; as having subordinates, commanding.... Even if the Lord did not enter bodily into this man's house, yet he was already so present in majesty that he healed his faith and his servant. Yet the same Lord had appeared in bodily presence among his own covenant people. He was not born in some other country. He did not suffer or walk or endure his human sufferings or do wonders in some other nation. None of all this took place in other nations. Yet through the centurion the prophecy was fulfilled that was spoken of him: "A people whom I have not known has served me." And how did the centurion know him? By "obeying me with the hearing of the ear."[14] SERMON 62.2.[15]

8:11-12 Sitting at Table with the Patriarchs

MANY WILL SIT AT TABLE WITH ABRAHAM.

---

[8]Mt 8:20. [9]PL 38:415; NPNF 1 6:298** (Sermon 12). [10]Jn 11:22. [11]PG 57:334-35; NPNF 1 10:177**. [12]MKGK 109-10. [13]PG 57:335; NPNF 1 10:177**. [14]Ps 18:43-44 (17:43-44 LXX). [15]PL 38:416; NPNF 1 6:299** (Sermon 12); WSA 3 3:157-58.

AUGUSTINE: Note how what you have heard in the Gospel as something to come has by now already happened. Jesus commends the centurion's faith, whose flesh was alien but whose spirit was of the household of faith. It was to him that he said, "Many will come from east and west and sit at table with Abraham, Isaac and Jacob in the kingdom of heaven, while the sons of the kingdom will be thrown into the outer darkness." What sons of what kingdom? He is speaking of the people of the covenant, who received the law. To them the prophets were sent. To them was given the temple and the priesthood. They had celebrated the anticipations of things to come. Yet those things of which they would celebrate in figures they did not acknowledge in actual presence. This is why they shall "be thrown into the outer darkness; there men will weep and gnash their teeth."[16] Odd, isn't it? That they would be sent away, while the Christians would be called from the east and the west to the heavenly banquet to sit down with Abraham and Isaac and Jacob, whose bread is righteousness and whose cup is wisdom. SERMON 62.6.[17]

8:13 The Servant Healed

AS YOU BELIEVED. IRENAEUS: There is no coercion with God. He has a good will toward us continually. He gives reliable counsel to humans and angels (who also are rational beings), to whom he has given the power of choice. Those who yield obedience therefore possess what is good freely and justly. It is given by God but preserved by themselves. . . . The human spirit is possessed of free will from the beginning, and God is possessed of free will, in whose likeness humanity was created. Humanity is advised to hold fast to the good and thereby be responsive to God. This refers not only to works but faith as well. God preserved the human will free and under his own self-control . . . as is shown in Jesus' word to the centurion: "Go. Be it done for you as you have believed." AGAINST HERESIES 3.37.1, 4-5.[18]

---

[16]Mt 8:11-12. [17]PL 38:417; NPNF 1 6:300** (Sermon 12); cf. *WSA* 3 3:158-59. [18]ANF 1:518-20*.

8:14-17 FULFILLING PROPHECY: HEALINGS AND EXORCISMS

[14]*And when Jesus entered Peter's house, he saw his mother-in-law lying sick with a fever;* [15]*he touched her hand, and the fever left her, and she rose and served him.* [16]*That evening they brought to him many who were possessed with demons; and he cast out the spirits with a word, and healed all who were sick.* [17]*This was to fulfil what was spoken by the prophet Isaiah, "He took our infirmities and bore our diseases."*

OVERVIEW: Jesus entered the tiny quarters of a fisherman to offer the grace of healing (CHRYSOSTOM). Well into the evening he continued to heal (CYRIL OF ALEXANDRIA). The sum of all diseases, even death itself, has its root and foundation in sin, which Jesus was forgiving (CHRYSOSTOM). This was to show that it was not in his activity alone but in his passion, his willingness to suffer, that Christ became the source of healing to humanity (Apollinaris). Constantly Jesus taught the disciples that the common good is to be preferred to private interest (Chrysostom).

8:14-15 Healing Peter's Mother-in-Law

THE ILLNESS OF PETER'S MOTHER-IN-LAW. CHRYSOSTOM: Though his wife's mother had apparently been at home lying ill and sick of a fever, Peter did not press him to come to his house but waited first for his teaching to be finished and for many others to be healed. Only then did he seek him out. This suggests that from the beginning the disciples were careful not to put their private concerns above the common good. . . . Jesus entered of his own accord to Peter's house to offer grace to his disciple. Think of what sort of houses these fishermen must have lived in. He did not hesitate to enter these tiny quarters, thereby teaching us all to trample pride underfoot. THE GOSPEL OF MATTHEW, HOMILY 27.1.[1]

8:16 Healings and Exorcisms

THAT EVENING. CYRIL OF ALEXANDRIA: Why didn't anyone bring them by day? Maybe it was out of respect for the scribes and Pharisees, or like Nicodemus, from embarrassment at their infirmities. Maybe it was because the sick people had no one to carry them to Jesus. FRAGMENT 95.[2]

8:17 Taking Our Infirmities and Bearing Our Diseases

HE TOOK OUR INFIRMITIES. CHRYSOSTOM: Do you see how the multitude by this time was growing in faith? For even when the evening was descending, they continued to bring their sick to him. Though the time was limited, they did not even think of going home. Note that the Evangelist did not specify how great a multitude of per-

sons were healed. He did not mention them one by one but in one word spanned an unspeakable sea of miracles, lest the spectacle's greatness drive us again to curiosity or doubt that even so many with such varied diseases should be delivered and healed by him in one brief moment of time. Rather, he calls upon the prophet to attest what was happening. Once again this indicates the abundance of scriptural demonstrations we have that point to his identity. Isaiah had prophesied of just these things when he said, "Surely he has borne our griefs and carried our sorrows."[3] Note that Isaiah did not say that he merely did away with our infirmities but that he himself *bore* them. Here Isaiah seems to be speaking of our sins being carried by him, in harmony with John, who said, "Behold the Lamb of God who takes away the sin of the world."[4] How does the Evangelist correlate infirmities and sins? He is either recollecting the Isaiah passage in its plain, historical sense, or he is pointing to the fact that most of our diseases arise from sins of our souls. For if the sum of all diseases, even death itself, has its root and foundation from sin, how much more is this true of most of our bodily diseases? THE GOSPEL OF MATTHEW, HOMILY 27.1.[5]

HUMANITY HEALED THROUGH JESUS' SUFFERING. APOLLINARIS: In this saying Isaiah pointed toward the cross. But why was this saying employed by the Evangelist at this point when he was speaking of his healings?[6] This was to show that it was not in his activity alone but in his passion, his willingness to suffer, that Christ became the source of healing to humanity. By the indignities he endured and by his own death he prepared life for all humanity. He subdued those who were evilly disposed against themselves. FRAGMENT 37.[7]

---

[1]PG 57:343-44; NPNF 1 10:184-85**. [2]MKGK 182-83. [3]Is 53:4. [4]Jn 1:29. [5]PG 57:345; NPNF 1 10:185**. That he actively bore our sins is more than that he merely took them away from us. [6]The question derives from the natural application of Isaiah's prophecy to Jesus' passion, though here the Evangelist applies it to Jesus' healings. [7]MKGK 11.

8:18-22 THE NATURE OF DISCIPLESHIP

[18]*Now when Jesus saw great crowds around him, he gave orders to go over to the other side.* [19]*And a scribe came up and said to him, "Teacher, I will follow you wherever you go."* [20]*And Jesus said to him, "Foxes have holes, and birds of the air have nests; but the Son of man has nowhere to lay his head."* [21]*Another of the disciples said to him, "Lord, let me first go and bury my father."* [22]*But Jesus said to him, "Follow me, and leave the dead to bury their own dead."*

OVERVIEW: To his own disciples Jesus revealed God's future mysteries more deeply than in the things that were spoken to the crowds only in parables (CYRIL OF ALEXANDRIA). Jesus enabled his hearers to see better into their own weak, proud motivations (CHRYSOSTOM). By his quiet miracles, Jesus taught them freedom from ostentation (TERTULLIAN, CHRYSOSTOM). Pride is all too prone to make premature confession, while human frailty is slow to follow through thoroughly (MAXIMUS OF TURIN). Those who like foxes desire to hide their sins while stealing the fruits of others lack the grace of confession (MAXIMUS OF TURIN). He does not openly convict his interrogators who were up to mischief but rather replies to their secret thoughts, leaving it to themselves to realize they are convicted (CHRYSOSTOM). The worship of God requires putting God before all other things we think of as precious, even the ties of the family (CYRIL OF ALEXANDRIA). Put to death what is earthly in you, as if you would cut off gangrenous flesh (ORIGEN). Jesus was not commanding sons and daughters to think lightly of the honor due to parents but rather signifying that nothing ought to be more urgent to us than the affairs of the kingdom of heaven. Do not let anything take first place over service to the coming reign of heaven (CHRYSOSTOM).

8:18 Going to the Other Side

TRAINING IN SELF-CONSTRAINT. CHRYSOS-

TOM: Note once again his freedom from superficialities. He charged the devils not to disclose his identity.[1] He commanded the multitudes to depart. In doing so, he was training all his followers in self-constraint and teaching them to do nothing for display. At the same time he was silencing the envy of his detractors. He thereby showed that he was not a healer of bodies only but also of souls, and a teacher of forbearance. He demonstrated this by first healing their diseases and then by teaching them not to do anything merely for vanity's sake. The crowds meanwhile were clinging to him, loving him, marveling at him, desiring to be with him. For who would want to depart from one who performed such miracles? Who would not long to linger there, even if it were only to glimpse his face and the mouth that was saying such things? THE GOSPEL OF MATTHEW, HOMILY 27.2.[2]

CROSSING OVER TO DEEPER LIFE IN THE SPIRIT. CYRIL OF ALEXANDRIA: But it is only to the disciples that Jesus "gave orders to cross over to the other side," lest, from the crowds pressing about him, his disciples should be prevented from hearing those very teachings that were most appropriate for them. To the disciples he revealed God's future mysteries more deeply than in the things that were spoken to the crowds only "in parables." Only the disciples had left behind all present goods and followed him

---

[1]As in Mk 1:34; Lk 4:41. [2]PG 57:345-46; NPNF 1 10:185-86**.

through love of learning. He commands them to cross over from temporary things to eternal things, from the earthly to the heavenly, from the carnal to the spiritual. FRAGMENT 97.[3]

8:19 A Scribe Promises to Follow Jesus

REVEALING THE HEART. CHRYSOSTOM: He does not openly convict those who were up to mischief. He replies to their secret thoughts, leaving it to themselves only to know they are convicted. . . . These were not the words of one who was turning his back on the scribe but rather of one who was making clear to the scribe his own proud disposition, even while yet permitting him, if he were willing to proceed, to follow him. After the scribe had heard Jesus' convicting response and had been proven to be wholly unready for it, he did not then proceed to say, "I am ready to follow you." Similarly there are many other places where Christ made this sort of subtle response. THE GOSPEL OF MATTHEW, HOMILY 27.2.[4]

THE PREMATURE CONFESSION. MAXIMUS OF TURIN: The scribe's declaration is prompt indeed, but proud. The Lord was on his way toward his final suffering, descent into hell and ascent into heaven. Is human frailty really prepared to follow him "wherever he goes"? This is more a foolish presumption than a confession of faith. Later the Lord would say to the apostle Peter, when he thought that he would follow the Savior in every circumstance: "Where I am going you are not able to follow me now."[5] And when Peter obstinately insisted and said that death would not separate him from [Jesus], he heard that he would deny the Lord three times. In this he was censured, as it were, for his pride. Thus the one who promised, while confessing Christ, that he would not be separated from him by death is cut off from fellowship with him by a little maidservant's question. SERMONS 41.3.[6]

8:20 Nowhere to Lay His Head

FOLLOW THE LORD'S PATTERN OF HUMILITY. TERTULLIAN: Joseph and Daniel served as slaves, but you are the slaves of no one, insofar as you share in those who serve Christ, who has freed you from the captivity of the world. You act after the Lord's pattern. He walked in humility and obscurity. He had no definite home. "The Son of Man has nowhere to lay his head." He is unadorned as to dress. He exercised no right of power even over his own followers. In short, though conscious of his own kingdom, he shrank back from being made a king. ON IDOLATRY 18.4-5.[7]

LIVING LIKE A FOX. MAXIMUS OF TURIN: Every Christian who wishes to hide his sins is spiritually a fox. For just as the fox lives in a hidden place because of its deceit, so also the sinner conceals himself in dens, guarding silence because of his knowledge of his sins. Just as the fox does not dare to manifest the deceitfulness of its deeds in the midst of society, so also the sinner is ashamed to confess the wickedness of his life in the midst of the church. One is a fox who sets up a snare for his neighbor, who daily strives to nibble away at others' property, steal their fruits and devour their animals and—what is common in our day—seize swine like wolves and not only chickens, as the foxes do. Although he is strong enough to live by his own labor, he prefers to take pillage like the madness of a wild beast. SERMONS 41.4.[8]

8:21 A Disciple Asks to Bury His Father

PUTTING GOD FIRST, EVEN BEFORE FAMILY. CYRIL OF ALEXANDRIA: In this place the question is raised as to whether the honor due God does not take precedence over the duty to honor one's parents. When the two conflict, it is necessary to hold to the one and despise the other,[9]

---

[3]MKGK 183. [4]PG 57:346-47; NPNF 1 10:186**. [5]Jn 13:36. [6]CCL 23:165; ACW 50:102. [7]CCL 2:1119; ANF 3:72-73*. [8]CCL 23:166; ACW 50:103*. [9]See Mt 6:24.

especially if honoring parents gets in the way of pleasing God. The worship of God requires putting God before all other things we think of as precious. In this way we will not, like Cain, be found relegating secondary things to God. In a similar way, the old law prohibited the priests from drawing near to dead bodies and commanded them to keep away even from services for their own family and not to succumb to excessive fleshly sympathy.[10] But while the law taught through shadows, Christ teaches in a way wholly transparent and undisguised. Whoever wishes to serve God must not let any ties of kinship become an excuse, on grounds of preoccupation, for not following Christ. Christ himself, for the benefit of those who were with him, even slighted his own mother and brothers, saying, "Who is my mother, and who are my brothers?" and "Such a one is my mother."[11] FRAGMENT 98.[12]

8:22 Let the Dead Bury the Dead

PUT TO DEATH WHAT IS EARTHLY IN YOU. ORIGEN: The statement "Let the dead bury their dead" implies spiritually: Waste no more time on dead things. You are to "put to death therefore what is earthly in you: immorality, impurity, passion, evil desire and covetousness, which is idolatry."[13] These things therefore are dead. Cast them away from you. Cut them off as you would cut off gangrenous flesh to prevent the contamination of the whole body, so that you may not hear it said, "Leave the dead[14] to bury their dead."[15] But to some it seems abnormal and contradictory that the Savior does not allow the disciple to bury his father. It seems inhumane. But Jesus does not in fact forbid people from burying the dead, but rather he puts before this the preaching of the kingdom of heaven, which makes people alive.[16] As for bury-

ing the body, there were many people who could have done this. FRAGMENT 161.[17]

FIRST THINGS FIRST. CHRYSOSTOM: Mark well the difference between the scribe who earlier had impudently blurted out, "I will follow you wherever you go" and the other one who was asking to do a sacred duty when he said, "Permit me first to go [bury my father]." Yet Jesus did not permit him, saying, "Follow me, and leave the dead to bury their own dead." In both cases, Jesus was paying attention strictly to their inward intention. But one may ask, "Why was the latter not permitted?" Because on the one hand, there were plenty of others who could fulfill that duty. The dead person was not going to remain actually unburied. On the other hand, it appears that it was not fit for this particular person to be taken away from the more urgent matters required of him. . . . Was it not then, one may ask, extreme ingratitude to be absent from the burial of one's own father? If indeed he did so out of negligence, it would have been ingratitude. But his departure would not have been considered fitting if it required interrupting a more urgent order of responsibility. So Jesus resisted him, not as if he were commanding him to think lightly of the honor due to parents, but signifying that nothing ought to be to us more urgent than the affairs of the kingdom of heaven. We ought with all diligence to cling to these and not to put them off in the slightest, though our engagements be exceedingly indispensable and pressing. THE GOSPEL OF MATTHEW, HOMILY 27.3.[18]

---

[10]Lev 21:11. [11]Mt 12:48, 50. [12]MKGK 183-84. [13]Col 3:5. [14]Or those who bear in themselves deadening sin. [15]Mt 8:22. [16]Lk 9:60. [17]GCS 41.1:80. [18]PG 57:347-48; NPNF 1 10:187**. Do not let anything take first place over service to the coming reign of heaven.

8:23-27 CALMING THE STORM

²³*And when he got into the boat, his disciples followed him.* ²⁴*And behold, there arose a great storm on the sea, so that the boat was being swamped by the waves; but he was asleep.* ²⁵*And they went and woke him, saying, "Save, Lord; we are perishing."* ²⁶*And he said to them, "Why are you afraid, O men of little faith?" Then he rose and rebuked the winds and the sea; and there was a great calm.* ²⁷*And the men marveled, saying, "What sort of man is this, that even winds and sea obey him?"*

OVERVIEW: Jesus took with him those whom he was training to be champions of the gospel, coaching them against despair (CHRYSOSTOM). Jesus remained asleep in the boat until the apex of the storm, when the pilot's skill is most sorely tested (PETER CHRYSOLOGUS). Only then did the disciples appeal in terror to the very master of the elements (PETER CHRYSOLOGUS). He slept to give occasion for their timidity. He permitted the storm that they might understand their deliverer. His sleeping made it evident that he was a man. His calming of the seas declared him God (CHRYSOSTOM). So Christ today calms the waves surrounding the vessel of the church, so as to provide an anticipatory signal that he will finally calm the crisis of shipwreck of the whole of fallen human history (PETER CHRYSOLOGUS).

8:23 Getting into the Boat

COACHING AGAINST DESPAIR. CHRYSOSTOM: He took the disciples with him, not for nothing and not merely to face an absurd hazard but in order to permit them to witness the miracle that was to take place on the sea. For like a superb trainer, he was gradually coaching and fitting them for endurance. He had two objectives in mind. He wanted to teach them to remain undismayed amid dangers and modest in honors. So, to prevent them from thinking too much of themselves, having sent away the multitude, he kept them near him but permitted them

to be tossed with a tempest. By doing so he disciplined them to bear trials patiently. His former miracles were indeed great, but this one contained a unique kind of discipline of exceptional importance. For it was a sign akin to that of old.[1] To do this, he took his disciples with him by himself. He permitted others to see his other miracles, but when trials and terrors were rising, he took with him none but those he was training to be champions of the gospel. THE GOSPEL OF MATTHEW, HOMILY 28.1.[2]

8:24 A Storm Arises

THE HEIGHT OF THE STORM TESTS THE PILOT'S SKILL. PETER CHRYSOLOGUS: The sea offered its heaving back for Christ to walk upon. Now it leveled its crests to a plain, checked its swelling and bound up its billows. It provided rocklike firmness, so he could walk across the waterway. Why did the seas heave so, and toss and pitch, even as if threatening its Creator? And why did Christ himself, who knows all the future, seem so unaware of the present that he gave no thought to the onrushing storm, the moment of its height and the time of its peril? While all the rest were awake, he alone was fast asleep even with utter doom threatening both himself and his dear ones. Why? It is not a calm

---

[1]He is pointing to the miracle of Moses in the dividing of the Red Sea, which he later explains. [2]PG 57:349-50; NPNF 1 10:189**.

sky, beloved, but the storm which tests a pilot's skill. When the breeze is mild even the poorest sailor can manage the ship. But in the crosswinds of a tempest, we want the best pilot with all his skill. SERMONS 20.1.[3]

WHY DOES HE SLEEP? CHRYSOSTOM: He sleeps to give occasion for their timidity and to make their perception of what was happening more distinct. . . . He permits the storm, that by their deliverance they might attain to a clearer perception of that benefit. THE GOSPEL OF MATTHEW, HOMILY 28.1.[4]

8:25 We Are Perishing

THE MASTER OF THE ELEMENTS. PETER CHRYSOLOGUS: The disciples' efforts as seamen had failed, as they could see. The seas attempted to spend their fury against them, and the waves were ready to swallow them. The twisting winds had conspired against them. So they ran in fear to the very Pilot of the world, the Ruler of the universe, the Master of the elements. They begged him to check the billows, banish the danger, save them in their despair. SERMONS 20.1.[5]

8:26 Jesus Rebukes the Elements

WHY ARE YOU AFRAID? CHRYSOSTOM: It is not in the presence of the multitudes that he corrects their "little faith." He calls them apart to correct them. Before the tempest of the waters he stills the tempests in their souls. He admonishes them, "Why are you so fearful, O you who have little faith?" He instructs them concerning how human fear emerges out of weakness of mind, not out of the actual approach of threatening trials. Their awakening him was a sign of their lack of a right understanding of who he was. They knew his power to rebuke when he was awake, but his power to rebuke when asleep they had not yet grasped. Even after so many other miracles their impressions of him were still confused. This is why he remarked that

they were still without understanding. THE GOSPEL OF MATTHEW, HOMILY 28.1.[6]

MEN OF LITTLE FAITH. CYRIL OF ALEXANDRIA: The exclamation "save us" is commendable, since it shows faith. But to say "we are perishing" brings a charge of littleness of faith against those who were in deep distress. They indeed put their hope in Christ who was sailing with them. They were not totally faithless but were at that point "of little faith," since in their danger they did not take courage from the fact of Christ's being with them. FRAGMENT 99.[7]

A GREAT CALM. PETER CHRYSOLOGUS: Christ gets into the vessel of his church, always ready to calm the waves of the world. He leads those who believe in him through safe sailing to the heavenly homeland and makes those whom he made to share in his humanity citizens of his land. Christ does not need the vessel, therefore, but the vessel needs Christ. Without the heavenly helmsman the vessel of the church is unable to sail over the sea of the world and, against critical odds, arrive at the heavenly harbor. SERMONS 50.2.[8]

8:27 The Disciples Marvel

WHAT SORT OF MAN? CHRYSOSTOM: How did they know he was a man? They could see him sleeping. He commanded a ship. So why were they so perplexed about his humanity, saying, "What manner of man is this?" His sleeping showed he was a man. His calming of the seas declared him God. THE GOSPEL OF MATTHEW, HOMILY 28.1.[9]

EVEN THE WINDS OBEY HIM. PETER CHRYSOLOGUS: Finally it was by Christ's mere command that he controlled the sea, struck back the

---

[3]CCL 24:116-17; FC 17:61-62*. [4]PG 57:351; NPNF 1 10:190. [5]CCL 24:117; FC 17:62*. [6]PG 57:351; NPNF 1 10:190. [7]MKGK 184. [8]CCL 24:277-78. [9]PG 57:351-52; NPNF 1 10:190**.

winds, stopped the whirlwinds, brought back the calm. Then those who were crossing the sea perceived, believed and acknowledged that he is the very Creator of all. SERMONS 20.1.[10]

[10]CCL 24:117; FC 17:62*.

8:28-34 THE GADARENE DEMONIACS

[28]*And when he came to the other side, to the country of the Gadarenes,[t] two demoniacs met him, coming out of the tombs, so fierce that no one could pass that way.* [29]*And behold, they cried out, "What have you to do with us, O Son of God? Have you come here to torment us before the time?"* [30]*Now a herd of many swine was feeding at some distance from them.* [31]*And the demons begged him, "If you cast us out, send us away into the herd of swine."* [32]*And he said to them, "Go." So they came out and went into the swine; and behold, the whole herd rushed down the steep bank into the sea, and perished in the waters.* [33]*The herdsmen fled, and going into the city they told everything, and what had happened to the demoniacs.* [34]*And behold, all the city came out to meet Jesus; and when they saw him, they begged him to leave their neighborhood.*

t Other ancient authorities read *Gergesenes*; some, *Gerasenes*

OVERVIEW: Those possessed by demons were being held in captivity to idolatry. They were living apart from the worshiping community (CHROMATIUS). The demons claimed that the Son of God had come in an untimely way (CYRIL OF ALEXANDRIA). Plunging from the sky, they are commanded to enter into the swine (PETER CHRYSOLOGUS), which are a ready residence for the demons (CHROMATIUS). The demons entered the swine to show how savage they have become against humans who by their vices have permitted their intrusion into human freedom (PETER CHRYSOLOGUS). They begged Jesus to leave their neighborhood. Even they knew they were unworthy of the Lord's presence (JEROME). The Holy Spirit will not enter a perverse soul or dwell in a body enslaved to sin (CHROMATIUS).

8:28-29 Two Demoniacs Come from the Tombs

THE OTHER SIDE. CHROMATIUS: The "other side" must first be understood according to its plain sense. Yet according to an allegorical interpretation, the demoniacs who met the Lord in the country of the Gerasenes, that is, the country of the Gentiles, might be understood to have the appearance of the descendants of Ham and Japheth, Noah's two sons, as distinguished from the Jewish people, who take their origin from Shem the firstborn son of Noah. Or they might be understood as all of those held captive by the devil in the error of idolatry. They are burdened by the chains of their offenses and the fetters of their sins. They were not living in the town, that is, in the covenant community where the law and the divine precepts were in force. Rather, they dwell in the tombs, worshiping idols and venerating the memories of potentates or images of the dead. TRACTATE ON MATTHEW 43.4.[1]

[1]CCL 9a:407-8.

THE DEMONS CRIED OUT. CYRIL OF ALEXANDRIA: The divine nature of the only begotten Son was already scorching the demons in unspeakable flames. Christ was shutting up the fiercest demons in blocked roads. He was undoing the devil's tyranny. "You have come before the time," they cried out. For they knew from the Scriptures that Christ was going to come and would judge them. Treating the incarnation as if it had happened at the wrong time, they pled that he had come in an untimely way. This misrepresentation is not surprising. In their deceptiveness, they did not hesitate to say even this. Yet, although they know that vengeance is to fall upon them, they still say haughtily, "What have you to do with us?" They know that the final Judge in fact has a score to settle with them, inasmuch as they had broken his commandments. FRAGMENT 101.[2]

THE DEMONS' PLEA. CHRYSOSTOM: For [the demons] said, "Did you come here to torment us before the time?" You see, they could not deny that they had sinned, but they demanded that they not suffer their punishment before the time. Because [Jesus] had caught them in the act of perpetrating those horrors so incurable and lawless and deforming and punishing his creature in every way, and because their crimes were so excessive they supposed that [Jesus] would not delay in punishing them, they besought and entreated him. They who had not even endured bands of iron came bound. And they who ran about the mountains went forth into the plain. And they who hindered all others from passing stood still at the sight of [Jesus] blocking the way. THE GOSPEL OF MATTHEW, HOMILY 28.2.[3]

8:30 *The Herd of Swine*

AT SOME DISTANCE. CHROMATIUS: The swine to which the demons fled symbolize the unfaithful and unclean people who, feeding at some distance by the sea, were living according to the sins of the world. Thus the swine showed themselves to be a ready residence for the demons. Living nearby this worldly sea they are steeped in error and inordinate desire. This made it easy for them to be overcome by the demons. TRACTATE ON MATTHEW 43.5.[4]

8:31 *The Demons Possess the Swine*

FROM HEAVEN TO TOMBS TO FILTH. PETER CHRYSOLOGUS: Slaves ask for suitable indignities: "Send us into the swine." Foulness begs to be sent from the tombs into the swine, so that it does not think of getting rid of its bad odors but of changing odors. "Send us into the swine." Plunging from the sky, they seek filth. After living in the upper world, they look for the sloughs of pigs. "Send us into the herd." A herd is sent into the herd, so that a gang of demons is brought forth, and it seems that two men have caused what a great number of pigs could not endure. SERMONS 16.7.[5]

8:32 *The Swine Destroyed*

WHY THE DEMONS ENTERED THE SWINE. PETER CHRYSOLOGUS: "He said to them, 'Go!'" The foul-smelling animals are delivered up, not at the will of the demons but to show how savage the demons can become against humans. They ardently seek to destroy and dispossess all that is, acts, moves and lives. They seek the death of people. The ancient enmity of deep-rooted wrath and malice is in store for the human race. Demons do not give up easily unless they are forcibly overcome. They are doing the harm they are ordered to do. Therefore the foul-smelling animals are delivered up that it may be made clear to the demons that they have permission to enter the swine but not to enter humans. It is by our vices that we empower them to do harm. Similarly, by our power of faith we tread on the necks of demons.

---

[2]*MKGK 184-85.* [3]PG 57:352-53; NPNF 1 10:191*. [4]CCL 9a:408. [5]CCL 24:101.

They become subject to us under Christ who is triumphant. Sermons 16.8.[6]

8:33 The Herdsmen Tell What Happened

The Flight of Idolaters. Chromatius: The herdsmen fled at the sight of the divine power and reported to the town what had happened. The people entreated the Lord to depart from their district. This may symbolize the leaders of the Jews or the priests of idols, who, dispensing the food of their errors to unclean and unfaithful people, are feeding them like swine to perpetual death. Tractate on Matthew 43.5.[7]

The Migration of Heretical Teaching. Chromatius: Or this may be understood in another way, for there may be more than one spiritual meaning,[8] namely, we can look upon these two demoniacs in a larger sense as two [Gentile] peoples (as we noted before)[9] who by the word and grace of Christ were freed from the bond of the demons. Perhaps we may interpret the swine as heretics who, driven from the community of believers, are known to have migrated. If so, the herdsmen could be viewed as architects of heresies and teachers of falsehood who are feeding these heretical swine as it were with the foul and unclean food of disreputable teachings, feeding them not for life but for death. For these wayward teachers are feeding them, not the heavenly bread nor the food of a wholesome life but the most foul and unclean teachings of falsehood. Tractate on Matthew 43.6.[10]

8:34 They Begged Jesus to Leave

Unworthy of the Lord's Presence. Jerome: They entreat him to leave their district, not out of pride on their part (as many believe) but out of humility. They judge themselves unworthy of the Lord's presence, just as Peter after the catch of fish fell before the Savior's knees and said, "Depart from me, for I am a sinful man, O Lord." Commentary on Matthew 1.8.34.[11]

Begging the Lord to Leave. Chromatius: The town from which they came to meet the Lord, asking him to leave their district, represents the synagogue, which did not want to receive the Lord and Savior of the human race even after witnessing his divine power. He therefore returned to his own town. Because he was rejected by the synagogue, he came to his church, which is properly called the city of Christ. On seeing him, the Gerasenes entreated the Lord to depart from their district. Such people are also found among us. Out of faithlessness they compel the Lord and Savior of the world to depart from the district of their hearts, for according to Scripture, "the Holy Spirit will not enter a perverse soul or dwell in a body enslaved to sin."[12] Tractate on Matthew 43.7.[13]

---

[6]CCL 24:101. [7]CCL 9a:408-9. [8]Following Origen, Chromatius points out that while the literal meaning of a scriptural passage is unique, more than one spiritual (i.e., allegorical) interpretation can be found for it. [9]Descendants of Ham and Japheth (see 8:28 above). [10]CCL 9a:409. [11]CCL 77:53. [12]Wis 1:4. [13]CCL 9a:409-10.

9:1-8 JESUS HEALS A CRIPPLED MAN

---

[1]*And getting into a boat he crossed over and came to his own city.* [2]*And behold, they brought to him a paralytic, lying on his bed; and when Jesus saw their faith he said to the paralytic,*

"Take heart, my son; your sins are forgiven." ³*And behold, some of the scribes said to themselves, "This man is blaspheming."* ⁴*But Jesus, knowing[u] their thoughts, said, "Why do you think evil in your hearts?* ⁵*For which is easier, to say, 'Your sins are forgiven,' or to say, 'Rise and walk'?* ⁶*But that you may know that the Son of man has authority on earth to forgive sins"—he then said to the paralytic—"Rise, take up your bed and go home."* ⁷*And he rose and went home.* ⁸*When the crowds saw it, they were afraid, and they glorified God, who had given such authority to men.*

u Other ancient authorities read *seeing*

OVERVIEW: Jesus' own city was Nazareth (JE-ROME), yet even though he was Lord and Savior of the world, the people he was helping preferred that he go away (CHROMATIUS). The healing of the body points beyond itself to the healing of the soul (CHRYSOSTOM). It was the faith of the paralytic's friends, not the paralytic, that Jesus recognized (JEROME). The physician does not waste time probing into the senseless wishes of one who is irrationally delirious; rather the physician urgently listens to the patient's friends (PETER CHRYSOLOGUS). Jesus first granted remission of sins and then showed his ability to restore health; with the taking up of the pallet, he made it clear that bodies would be free from infirmity and suffering. Finally, with the paralytic's return to his home, Jesus showed that believers must be given back the way to paradise (HILARY). Whether the sins of the paralytic were forgiven, only he who could forgive them would know for sure (JEROME). With the same majesty and power by which Jesus perceived the thoughts of the scribes, he is able to forgive people their sins (JEROME). Christ thereby shows here that he is truly God and equal to the One by whom he is begotten (CHRYSOSTOM, HILARY). The sins of Adam are forgiven in Christ (HILARY).

9:1 Jesus Came to His Own City

HIS OWN CITY. JEROME: We should understand his town as none other than Nazareth, for he was called a Nazarean. COMMENTARY ON

MATTHEW 1.9.2.[1]

WE PREFER HIM TO GO AWAY. CHROMATIUS: On seeing him, the Gerasenes entreated the Lord to depart from their district. Such people are also to be found among us. Out of faithlessness they compel the Lord and Savior of the world to depart from the district of their hearts. According to Scripture, "The Holy Spirit will not enter a perverse soul or dwell in a body enslaved to sin."[2] TRACTATE ON MATTHEW 43.7.[3]

9:2 They Brought Him a Paralytic

THE FAITH OF THE PARALYTIC'S FRIENDS. JEROME: They brought to him, as we said before, a second paralytic lying on a pallet because he was unable to enter. "And Jesus, seeing" not the "faith" of him who was brought forward but of those who were bringing him forward, said to the paralytic, "Take heart, my son, your sins are forgiven you." O wonderful humility! He addresses as "son" this abject and infirm paralytic with disjointed members whom the priests did not stoop to touch. A son, indeed, because his sins are forgiven him. In line with the biblical metaphor,[4] a soul lying in its body with all the strength of its members gone is brought for healing to the perfect Doctor, the Lord. If the

---

[1]CCL 77:54. [2]Wis 1:4. [3]CCL 9a:409-10. [4]The term *tropologia* originally meant an allegorical interpretation in general. From the late fourth century, however, it came to mean specifically a moral allegory, as in this example from Jerome.

soul is healed through his mercy, it will receive strength enough to immediately take up its pallet. COMMENTARY ON MATTHEW 1.9.2.[5]

JESUS SAW THEIR FAITH. PETER CHRYSOLOGUS: Note in this regard, my brothers, that God does not inquire into the wants of those who are deliriously ill. He does not wait to see the faith of the ignorant or probe the senseless wishes of the sick. Yet he does not refuse to *help* the faith of another, so that by grace alone he confers whatever is proper of the divine will. In fact, my brothers, when does a doctor ever inquire into or examine the wishes of those who are ailing, for a patient is prone to be of a contrary mind in his wishes and demands? SERMONS 50.4.[6]

YOUR SINS ARE FORGIVEN. HILARY: Now in the narrative of the paralytic a number of people are brought forward for healing. Jesus' words of healing are worthy of reflection. The paralytic is not told, "Be healed." He is not told, "Rise and walk." But he is told, "Take heart, my son; your sins are forgiven you." The paralytic is a descendent of the original man, Adam. In one person, Christ, all the sins of Adam are forgiven. In this case the person to be healed is brought forward by ministering angels. In this case, too, he is called a son, because he is God's first work. The sins of his soul are forgiven him, and pardon of the first transgression is granted. We do not believe the paralytic committed any sin [that resulted in his illness], especially since the Lord said elsewhere that blindness from birth had not been contracted from someone's sin or that of his parents.[7] ON MATTHEW 8.5.[8]

9:3-4 The Scribes Doubt Jesus

WHY DO YOU THINK EVIL IN YOUR HEARTS? JEROME: We read in the prophet the words of God: "It is I who cleanse you from all your iniquities."[9] Consequently the scribes, because they were judgmental in construing the words of God, accused him of blasphemy. But the Lord,

reading their thoughts, shows himself to be God who knows the hidden things of the heart. He breaks his silence: "With the same majesty and power by which I perceive your thoughts, I am able to forgive their sins; see for yourselves what the paralytic has received." COMMENTARY ON MATTHEW 1.9.3.[10]

KNOWING THEIR THOUGHTS. CHRYSOSTOM: Only God could know what is in another's mind. That Jesus has this knowledge is attested from many evidences. Jesus shows here that he is truly God and equal to the One by whom he is begotten. He does this by revealing and making clear to them what they were thinking. Indeed, some were debating within themselves the very issue of whether Jesus is nothing less than God. But because they were afraid of the crowd, they did not dare to bring their opinion out into the open. He revealed their thoughts while showing great restraint when he said, "Why do you ponder evil thoughts in your hearts?"

And surely if there was any cause to be annoyed it would have been felt by the suffering paralytic, because it seemed that he had been almost completely bypassed. Imagine him complaining, as if he were thinking: "I came to receive healing, but now you are talking about my sins being forgiven. How do you know this? Why do you change the subject?" But in fact the paralytic now says nothing of the sort. Rather, he gives himself over to the authority of the One who heals.

But those who are malicious and all too full of themselves are always plotting against the good works of others. Therefore he chides them but does so in all fairness, as if to say, "For if you disbelieved in my first statement and thought that it was boasting, consider that I am adding something else to it: the revelation of your secrets." THE GOSPEL OF MATTHEW, HOMILY 29.2.[11]

---

[5]CCL 77:54. [6]CCL 24:279-80. [7]See Jn 9:1-3. [8]SC 254:198-200. [9]Is 43:25. [10]CCL 77:54. [11]PG 57:359-60; NPNF 1 10:196-97.

9:5 Power to Forgive Sins

RISE AND WALK. JEROME: It is easier said than done. Whether the sins of the paralytic were forgiven, only he who forgave them knew for sure. "Arise and walk": both he who arose and those who saw him arise were able to vouch for this. Hence there is a bodily sign in order to demonstrate a spiritual sign, though its impact is to curb the imperfections of body and soul. And we are given an understanding of sin and many bodily weaknesses to come. Perhaps, too, sins are forgiven first, so that with the causes of infirmity removed health may be restored. COMMENTARY ON MATTHEW 1.9.5.[12]

9:6 Rise and Walk

TAKE YOUR PALLET AND GO HOME. HILARY: Furthermore, so it could be understood that he was in a body and that he could forgive sins and restore health to bodies, Jesus said, "That you may know that the Son of Man has power on earth to forgive sins," then he said to the paralytic, "Arise, take up your pallet." He could have simply said "Arise," but since the reason for doing every work had to be explained, he added, "Take up your pallet and go home." First he granted remission of sins; next he showed his ability to restore health. Then, with the taking up of the pallet, he made it clear that bodies would be free from infirmity and suffering; lastly, with the paralytic's return to his home, he showed that believers are being given back the way to paradise from which Adam, the parent of all, who became profligate from the stain of sin, had proceeded. ON MATTHEW 8.7.[13]

9:7-8 The Crowds Glorify God

THEY MARVELED AND GLORIFIED GOD. CHRYSOSTOM: Do you see how he is shown to be Creator of both souls and bodies? He heals the paralysis in both soul and body. The healing of

the soul is made evident through the healing of the body, even while the body still remains a creature crawling on the ground. The crowds were slow to recognize who he was: "When the crowds saw it, they were afraid, and they glorified God, who had given such authority to humans." . . . He proceeded by his daily actions to arouse them and lift up their thinking. It would have been no small thing for him to be thought greater than all others, as having come from God. If they had established this adequately in their own minds, they would have known in due order that he was indeed the Son of God.[14]

But they did not grasp these things clearly. Because of this they did not come close to recognizing who he was. For again they were saying, "This man is not from God! How can this man be from God?" Their minds churned over these statements continuously. THE GOSPEL OF MATTHEW, HOMILY 29.2.[15]

THEY WERE AFRAID. HILARY: Admiration and not fear had to accomplish this work, but even now the order of the mystery remains. To add a glimpse of the future to the truth of the present, the crowds fear the Lord's words and actions. It is frightful to face death without having one's sins forgiven by Christ, for no one returns to the eternal home unless forgiveness of sins has been granted. "And they honored God who had given so much power to humans." Everything is concluded in proper order, and with the cessation of desperate fear, honor is rendered to God for giving so much power to humans. But this was due to Christ alone, to whom it was normal to share the Father's very essence. No wonder then that he could do these things—for the power of God is not limited. Otherwise praise would have come from

---

[12]CCL 77:54-55. [13]SC 254:200-202. [14]The healing of the paralytic brought the crowds to a better understanding of Jesus. Nevertheless they classified Jesus with "human beings" (9:8), leaving him still open to the charge of blasphemy (9:3). [15]PG 57:360-61; NPNF 1 10:197*.

the man healed and not from the many. But the reason here for honor offered to God is this: Power was given through God's Word to humanity for the remission of sins, the resur-

rection of bodies and the return to heaven. ON MATTHEW 8.8.[16]

---

[16]SC 254:202.

9:9-13 JESUS CALLS MATTHEW

[9]*As Jesus passed on from there, he saw a man called Matthew sitting at the tax office; and he said to him, "Follow me." And he rose and followed him.*

[10]*And as he sat at table*[v] *in the house, behold, many tax collectors and sinners came and sat down with Jesus and his disciples.* [11]*And when the Pharisees saw this, they said to his disciples, "Why does your teacher eat with tax collectors and sinners?"* [12]*But when he heard it, he said, "Those who are well have no need of a physician, but those who are sick.* [13]*Go and learn what this means, 'I desire mercy, and not sacrifice.' For I came not to call the righteous, but sinners."*

v Greek *reclined*

OVERVIEW: Matthew was changed suddenly from a publican to an apostle (JEROME). Though he was immersed in worldly affairs, Matthew was freely chosen by the Lord, who knows the hidden recesses of the heart (CHROMATIUS). Jesus, acquainted with our inmost hearts, knows when each one of us is ready to respond most fully (CHRYSOSTOM). As they sat at table, through dining, conviviality and pleasant conversation, Jesus sought the return of the sinner, who was overwhelmed by the sheer presence of God (PETER CHRYSOLOGUS). The Lord went to the banquet of sinners to offer spiritual food to his hosts (JEROME). He gave aid to the sick, but those who believed they were healthy saw no need for a cure. The law of ritual sacrifices was unable to provide help, but health was in store for all in the granting of mercy (HILARY). Matthew presented a heavenly feast to all who would come by faith as publicans and sinners to the knowledge of Christ (CHROMATIUS). Like a physician, Jesus healed souls as the need

emerged, on any occasion where people were hurting. He associated with the sick of soul because that was essential if he was to bring healing to them (CHRYSOSTOM).

9:9 Matthew Chosen

SITTING AT THE TAX OFFICE. CHRYSOSTOM: Why did Jesus not call Matthew at the same time as he called Peter and John and the rest? He came to each one at a particular time when he knew that they would respond to him. He came at a different time to call Matthew when he was assured that Matthew would surrender to his call. Similarly, he called Paul at a different time when he was vulnerable, after the resurrection, something like a hunter going after his quarry. For he who is acquainted with our inmost hearts and knows the secrets of our minds knows when each one of us is ready to respond fully. Therefore he did not call them all together at the beginning, when Matthew was still in a hardened condition. Rather, only after countless miracles, after his fame was spread abroad, did he call Matthew. He knew Matthew had been softened for full responsiveness.

We may admire, incidentally, the self-effacing temperament of Matthew, for we note how he does not disguise his own former life. In his account he freely adds his own name and his own bad profession, while the other Gospel writers had generously protected him under another name.[1] But why did Matthew himself indicate precisely that he was "sitting at the tax office"? To point to the power of the One who called him, underscoring that he was being actively drawn away from the midst of the very evils in which he was presently engaged and that he had not already abandoned his wicked business as a tax gatherer. THE GOSPEL OF MATTHEW, HOMILY 30.1.[2]

CHANGED FROM PUBLICAN TO APOSTLE. JEROME: Out of respect and deference, the other Evangelists were unwilling to call him by the common name of Matthew but said Levi.[3] So Matthew went by a double name in accordance with what Solomon noted: "An accuser is righteous at the beginning of his words." And in another place: "Tell your sins, and you will be justified."[4] Matthew also calls himself a publican to show his readers that no one must despair of salvation if he has changed for the better, for he was suddenly changed from a publican to an apostle. COMMENTARY ON MATTHEW 1.9.9.[5]

HE DID NOT DELAY. CHROMATIUS: The Lord, about to give salvation to all sinners believing in him, willingly chose Matthew the former publican. The gift of his esteem for Matthew stands as an example for our salvation. Every sinner must be chosen by God and can receive the grace of eternal salvation if one is not without a religious mind and a devout heart. So Matthew was chosen willingly by God. And though he is immersed in worldly affairs, because of his sin-

cere religious devotion he is judged worthy to be called forth by the Lord ("Follow me"), who by virtue of his divine nature knows the hidden recesses of the heart. From what follows, we know that Matthew was accepted by the Lord not by reason of his status but of his faith and devotion. As soon as the Lord says to him, "Follow me," he does not linger or delay, but thereupon "he arose and followed him." TRACTATE ON MATTHEW 45.1.[6]

9:10 Sinners Sat with Jesus and His Disciples

MANY TAX COLLECTORS CAME. CHRYSOSTOM: Now the tax collectors came together because they were of the same trade as Matthew was. For he took pride in the visit of the Messiah and invited them all together. The Messiah applied every form of healing. Not only while he was engaging in a formal discussion or healing or refuting his enemies, but even at breakfast he used to restore persons who were in bad condition. By means of these practices he taught us that every moment and every action can offer benefit to us.

Certainly the dishes Matthew set before him at that time had come from unrighteousness and covetousness. But Christ did not ask to be excused from participating in them, because the gain to be derived from it was going to be great. Rather, he shared the same roof and the same table with people who had erred in their manner of acquiring such things. For such is the nature of the physician. If he did not put up with the decay of the persons who are sick, he would not set them free from their sickness. Certainly Jesus got a bad reputation from this action, by eating with Matthew, by eating in his house and by eating with many tax collec-

---

[1]Mk 2:14; Lk 5:27. [2]PG 57:361-62; NPNF 1 10:198-99**. [3]In parallel passages in Mark (Mk 2:14) and Luke (Lk 5:27), the person addressed by Jesus is called Levi. The explanation provided here by Jerome—that the person had two names—is the one usually proposed by the ancient exegetes and is accepted by many modern scholars. [4]Is 43:26. [5]CCL 77:55. [6]CCL 9a:417.

tors. This is why you see them criticizing him with this: "Behold a man who is gluttonous and drinks a lot of wine, a friend of tax collectors and sinners." The Gospel of Matthew, Homily 30.2.[7]

Jesus' Majesty Covered As He Sat at Table. Peter Chrysologus: Jesus' sitting at table has more significance for Matthew than just dining.[8] Jesus will be feasting not on food but on the return of sinners. He will call them back through feasting, collegiality and human affection, enjoying himself with their pleasant conversation while reclining at table. He knew that if they recognized him as a powerful judge they would be shattered by the terror of his majesty and overwhelmed by the sheer presence of God unveiled (*nuda*). Thus, veiled in a human body he was able to communicate with humans. He who wanted to assist the guilty hides the fact that he was a judge. He who did not deny dignity to faithful servants conceals his lordship. He who desired the weak to be embraced by a parent's love covers his majesty. Sermons 29:4.[9]

9:11 The Pharisees Question the Disciples

Why Eat with Sinners? Hilary: The Jews were seething with envy that the Lord was spending time with publicans and sinners. He declared to them that the words of the law were being concealed under a cloak of faithlessness. He gave aid to the sick and medicine to those in need. For those who believed they were healthy, however, no cure was necessary. But in order for them to understand that none of his followers were healthy, he advised them to learn the meaning of "I desire mercy, and not sacrifice."[10] In other words, the law linked to the ritual of sacrifices was unable to give help, but health was in store for all in the granting of mercy. "For I have not come to call the righteous, but sinners to repentance." He had come for all. So why does Jesus say that he did not come for the right-

eous? . . . No one is righteous by reason of the law. He therefore showed the emptiness of boasting about the law, because with sacrifices imposed on the sick for their health, mercy was needed for all things set down in the law. For if righteousness came from the law, forgiveness through grace would not be necessary. On Matthew 9.2.[11]

The Heavenly Feast at Matthew's House. Chromatius: According to the allegorical or mystical account, Matthew's house is his mind, which Christ entered through Matthew's faith in his grace. He is viewed as having truly "sat at table" there, for this same Matthew deserved to be the writer of this Gospel. Describing the Lord's deeds and power, he presented a heavenly feast not only to the Lord and his disciples but also to all believers who, coming as publicans and sinners to the knowledge of Christ, deserved being included in so great a feast. In effect, Matthew's house can be viewed as a church comprising publicans and sinners. He presents to all the leaders there the feast of his faith and preaching, with the Lord and his disciples seated at table. Tractate on Matthew 45.5.[12]

9:12-13 Calling Sinners, Not the Righteous

Attending the Banquet of Sinners. Jerome: The Lord went to the banquet of sinners that he might have an opportunity to teach and to offer spiritual food to his hosts. In effect, when he is mentioned as frequently going out to attend feasts, nothing is said other than what he did there and taught there. Thus, we see both the Lord's humility in reaching out to sinners and the force of his teaching in converting penitents. What follows: "I desire mercy, and not sacrifice" and "I came not to call the righteous

---

[7]PG 57:363-64; NPNF 1 10:199-200. [8]*Simma (sigma)* is a rare term meaning, among other things, "dining room, triclinium." [9]CCL 24:171. [10]Hos 6:6. [11]SC 254:204-6. [12]CCL 9a:420.

but sinners" (as he cites testimony from the prophet) challenged the scribes and Pharisees, who considered themselves righteous and shunned both publicans and sinners. Commen-

tary on Matthew 1.9.13.[13]

[13]CCL 77:56.

9:14-17 THE QUESTION ABOUT FASTING

[14]Then the disciples of John came to him, saying, "Why do we and the Pharisees fast,[w] but your disciples do not fast?" [15]And Jesus said to them, "Can the wedding guests mourn as long as the bridegroom is with them? The days will come, when the bridegroom is taken away from them, and then they will fast. [16]And no one puts a piece of unshrunk cloth on an old garment, for the patch tears away from the garment, and a worse tear is made. [17]Neither is new wine put into old wineskins; if it is, the skins burst, and the wine is spilled, and the skins are destroyed; but new wine is put into fresh wineskins, and so both are preserved."

w Other ancient authorities add much or often

Overview: When fasting is fraught with heavy words, displayed with pale faces, advertised to a fault and designed to please human but not divine eyes, it is not in harmony with the joy of the coming kingdom (Peter Chrysologus). The reason the disciples did not fast was not because of gluttony but because of the dispensations of providence that were then occurring (Chrysostom). Jesus said there was no need for his disciples to fast as long as the bridegroom is with them. This points to the joy of his presence (Hilary). Since Jesus was the expected messianic bridegroom proclaimed by John the Baptist, the children of the marriage, the disciples, were called at this time to assist the groom in the festivities (Severus). The old garments and wineskins denote the scribes and Pharisees, while the patch of shrunk cloth and the new wine signify the gospel. The Jews could not assimilate Jesus' teaching without challenging their whole system of law (Jerome). The fabric of the old law was worn away by Judaic zealousness, split

apart by schools of thought and depleted by impure actions. The cloth of the gospel is not part of the tear but the beginning of the weave. (Peter Chrysologus).

9:14 John's Disciples Ask About Fasting

No Need to Fast in the Presence of the Bridegroom. Hilary: The Pharisees and John's disciples were fasting, and the apostles were not. But Jesus answered them in a spiritual way and indicated to John's disciples that he was a bridegroom. John taught that all hope in life lay in Christ. While he was still preaching, however, his disciples could not be received by the Lord. Up until the time of John, the law and the prophets prevailed, and unless the law came to an end, none of them would subscribe to faith in the gospel. The fact that he said there was no need for his disciples to fast as long as the bridegroom is with them illustrates the joy of his presence and the sacrament of the holy food, which no one need be without while he is present, that is, bearing Christ in the light of the mind. But once he is gone, Jesus says that they will fast, for all those who do not believe that Christ has risen will not have the food of life. By faith in the resurrection, the sacrament of the heavenly bread is received. Whoever is without Christ will be forsaken, fasting from the food of life. On Matthew 9.3.[1]

Why Do Your Disciples Not Fast? Chrysostom: The reason the disciples did not fast was not because of gluttony but because of the dispensations of providence in fulfilling prophecy. At this point he uses the statement about his suffering to lay a foundation for a later time. In this way Jesus instructs the disciples in his controversies with others and is already training them to get practice in things that seem to be daunting. To make this statement directly to the disciples at this point would have been burdensome and depressing. Indeed, in places where Jesus spoke about such things after this it did disturb them. But because it was said to others in this case, its effect was much less depressing to the disciples.[2]

Now it was likely that the disciples of John the Baptist were also thinking highly of themselves as a result of John's suffering. Because of this Jesus also put down this inflated conceit through what he said. Nevertheless he did not yet introduce the topic of the resurrection. For it was not yet the right time. For the topic that Jesus did introduce, that he who was thought to be human would die, was only natural. But the topic of his resurrection was beyond the natural. The Gospel of Matthew, Homily 30.4.[3]

The Law of Fasting and the Will to Fast. Peter Chrysologus: What did John's disciples have in common with the Pharisees if not a bond of ill will uniting those whom discipline had separated? In this case jealousy loses its bearings: Accustomed to separating people, it united them. The Jews were not disposed to

esteem Moses less than the Lord, and John's disciples were by no means willing to prefer Christ to John. Thus they grumbled in common spite against Christ. "Why do we and the Pharisees often fast, whereas your disciples do not fast?" Why? Because with you, fasting is a matter of the law and not of the will. Fasting does not reflect the one who fasts but the one who orders the fast. And what is the fruit of fasting to you who fast unwillingly? Sermons 31.2.[4]

9:15 Not Fasting While the Bridegroom Is Present

Question on Fasting. Severus: When John's disciples approached . . . they questioned him even while he was at table, in the manner of a physician with the publicans: "Why do we and the Pharisees often fast, whereas your disciples do not fast?"[5] Do you see how the same jealousy motivates and provokes birds of a feather and is made keen by the cruel goad of envy? On the one hand, it set the Pharisees, who boasted about being teachers, against the Teacher. For that reason they also said, "Why does your teacher eat with tax collectors and sinners?"[6] On the other hand, envy set John's disciples against Christ's disciples. That is why they also said, "How come your disciples do not fast?" Cathedral Sermons, Homily 92.[7]

Not Time to Mourn. Severus: It is with the words of John, your own teacher, whom you esteem so highly, that I answer you. Keep it in mind, and you will have the answer to your question. When John bore witness concerning me, he said, "He who has the bride is the bridegroom."[8] So, if I am the bridegroom and you don't make a liar out of your own teacher, you know in advance that it is important for my dis-

---

[1]SC 254:206. [2]Jesus accomplished a number of different goals by addressing his statements in this passage to the disciples of John the Baptist instead of to his own disciples. [3]PG 57:367; NPNF 1 10:202*. [4]CCL 24:179. [5]Mt 9:14. [6]Mt 9:11. [7]PO 25:33. [8]Jn 3:29.

ciples, while they are the children of the marriage . . . to be gay and joyful and not to become upset or miserable over fasting. In certain respects, fasting is a source of annoyance and can also be arduous for those without a mature disposition. CATHEDRAL SERMONS, HOMILY 92.[9]

9:16 New Cloth on Old Garments

DO NOT TEAR THE GARMENT BY PREMATURE PATCHING. CHRYSOSTOM: Once again Jesus constructs his argument with illustrations from common life. And what he says is something like this: "The disciples have not yet become strong. They still need a lot of help at a level they can understand. They have not yet been regenerated by the Spirit. At this time there is no need to dump on them a load of commandments while they are still in this learning period." He therefore proceeded gradually to set maxims and precepts for his disciples within the times of their step-by-step maturing, as they were better prepared to receive them. This was to teach them later to deal very gently with others, when the time would come that they would be taking this message to the whole world and receiving as disciples all sorts of persons. THE GOSPEL OF MATTHEW, HOMILY 30.4.[10]

THE BEGINNING OF A NEW WEAVE. PETER CHRYSOLOGUS: He says that the fabric of the old law was worn away by Judaic zealousness, corrupted by the senses, split apart by factions and

worn out by impure actions. The shrunk cloth of the gospel he calls a garment. But make note of the cloth, not simply the tear but the beginning of the weave. First of all, the fabric of Christ's royal garment was woven out of wool that came from a lamb: "The Lamb of God who takes away the sins of the world."[11] The royal vestment was a woven vestment, which the blood of his passion tinged with purple splendor. SERMONS 31.4.[12]

9:17 New Wine in Old Wineskins

PUT NEW WINE IN FRESH WINESKINS. JEROME: What he is saying is this: Until a person has been reborn and, having put aside the old person, puts on the new person because of my passion, he cannot observe right fasting and the precepts of temperance. Otherwise, through undue austerity one may lose even the faith one seems to possess. Christ gave two examples: the garment and the old and new wineskins. The old ones denote the scribes and Pharisees. The patch of shrunk cloth and the new wine signify the gospel precepts, which the Jews cannot observe, else a worse tear is made. COMMENTARY ON MATTHEW 1.9.17.[13]

---

[9]PO 25:34. [10]PG 57:367; NPNF 1 10:202*. In this text Jesus provided his disciples with an illustration of the need to accommodate themselves to the limited abilities of new disciples. [11]Jn 1:29. [12]CCL 24:180. [13]CCL 77:58.

9:18-26 THE DYING GIRL AND THE WOMAN WHO TOUCHED JESUS' CLOAK

[18]*While he was thus speaking to them, behold, a ruler came in and knelt before him, saying, "My daughter has just died; but come and lay your hand on her, and she will live." [19]And Jesus rose and followed him, with his disciples. [20]And behold, a woman who had suffered from a hem-*

orrhage for twelve years came up behind him and touched the fringe of his garment; [21]for she said to herself, "If I only touch his garment, I shall be made well." [22]Jesus turned, and seeing her he said, "Take heart, daughter; your faith has made you well." And instantly the woman was made well. [23]And when Jesus came to the ruler's house, and saw the flute players, and the crowd making a tumult, [24]he said, "Depart; for the girl is not dead but sleeping." And they laughed at him. [25]But when the crowd had been put outside, he went in and took her by the hand, and the girl arose. [26]And the report of this went through all that district.

OVERVIEW: Note how the two stories interweave: Wholeness is conferred on one who is sick, while life is restored to another who is dead (HILARY). Whether the girl was still breathing or dead was unclear and debated by the Fathers (CHRYSOSTOM, PETER CHRYSOLOGUS). God can sooner restore life-giving warmth to limbs frozen in death than people can infuse vigor in bodies immersed in sleep (PETER CHRYSOLOGUS). The woman approached the Lord not in her home or in the town from which she was excluded but while the Lord was walking by, so that in the course of going to one woman, another was cured (JEROME). In the synagogue ruler we perceive a figure of the prophets and the apostle Peter, through whom the calling of the Gentiles was first made known (CHROMATIUS). The daughter of the synagogue ruler signifies the Jewish people, whereas the bleeding woman can also signify the church of the Gentiles (AUGUSTINE). When Jesus subdued the woman's hemorrhage, it was another sign of his knowledge of all things. He put an end to her fear. He gave her no cause to be stung by her conscience. Jesus made her faith an exhibit to all. And he indirectly admonished the ruler of the synagogue by what he says to the woman (CHRYSOSTOM). There are interlacing themes in all these narratives: the urgent petition of the father, the faith of the woman, the gathering of the crowd in the house, the shouting of the two blind men and the bringing of the deaf and dumb demoniac (HILARY).

THE NARRATIVES INTERWEAVE. HILARY: The prayers of the ruler, the faith of the woman, the gathering of the crowd in the house and the shouting of the two blind men, as well as the bringing of the deaf and dumb demoniac ... are all interrelated. The ruler here is understood to be the law. He prays to the Lord for the people. The law has nourished them on Christ in the expectation of his foretold coming, and he restores life to the dead girl. Now we do not read of any ruler who was a believer. Hence the person of this praying ruler may rightly be taken as a model of the law. The Lord promised to help him, and he made good on his promise. ON MATTHEW 9.5.[1]

LAY YOUR HAND ON HER. CHRYSOSTOM: His action overpowered his speech. This caused the jaws of his critics to drop all the further. In this case, the one who came running was himself a ruler of his synagogue! And the crisis was appalling. For the child was his only daughter, only twelve years old, in the very flower of her life. It was especially for this reason that he raised her up and did so immediately.

Luke says that people came who said, "Do not bother the teacher any longer, because she has already died."[2] Because of this we will say that Matthew's statement, "She has just now died," came from one who was making a guess based on the time that had elapsed since he had started on his journey. Another possibility is that the man was overstating the misfortune. For it is the

9:18-19 A Synagogue Ruler Comes to Jesus

[1]SC 254:208. [2]Lk 8:49, slightly modified.

habit among people who are in need to exaggerate their personal problems and to say a little more than what actually is the case. They do this to get a response more effectively from those with whom they are pleading their cause.[3]

But note the ruler's insensitivity,[4] how he abruptly requires of Christ two things, both his actual presence and the laying on of his hands. This, by the way, is a clue that he might have left her still breathing. Similarly you will recall Naaman the Syrian imploring the prophet: "I thought that he would surely come out to me and stand and call in the name of the Lord his God, wave his hand over the spot and cure me of my leprosy."[5] For those who are more or less dull of temper tend more to require sight and sensible signs. THE GOSPEL OF MATTHEW, HOMILY 31.1.[6]

9:20 A Woman Suffering from a Hemorrhage

THE RULER'S DAUGHTER AND THE HEMORRHAGING WOMAN. JEROME: The Gospel according to Luke says that the ruler's daughter was twelve years old. Note also that the woman concerned, who was from the Gentiles, began to get sick at a place believed to be in a Jewish district.[7] Except by way of contrast between physical conditions, the girl's ailment is not indicated. As for the woman who had a hemorrhage, she approached the Lord not in her home or in the town (because according to the law she was excluded from towns) but while the Lord was walking by, so that in the course of going to one woman, another was cured. The apostles say in this regard, "It was necessary that the word of God should be spoken first to you. Since you judge yourselves unworthy of eternal life, behold, we turn to the Gentiles." COMMENTARY ON MATTHEW 1.9.20.[8]

9:21 Touching Jesus' Garment

SHE TOUCHED THE FRINGE OF HIS GARMENT.

CHRYSOSTOM: Why did she not approach him openly? Was she ashamed on account of her continuing menstrual period? Did she consider herself unclean? If the menstruous woman had been declared ritually unclean,[9] she surely would have had these reservations. For in terms of Mosaic law her flow of blood was regarded as uncleanness.[10] For this reason she remained hidden. She concealed herself. In this respect she had not yet understood his ministry; otherwise she would not have thought it necessary to remain concealed. THE GOSPEL OF MATTHEW, HOMILY 31.1.[11]

9:22 Daughter, Your Faith Has Made You Well

MAKING THE WOMAN VISIBLE. CHRYSOSTOM: So what did Messiah do? He did not let her go unnoticed but led her into the center of attention and made her visible. He had many reasons for doing this.

Some might imagine that "he did this merely for love of glory—otherwise why would he not allow her to remain concealed?" But what are they proposing who might say this? That he should keep her silent, that he should ignore her need, and thereby pass up miracles too numerous to mention, all because he is in love with

---

[3]Chrysostom reconciles the differences between the accounts of Matthew and Luke. He adds an indictment against people who need physical demonstrations for their faith to be effective. [4]Chrysostom is rather combative in what he says about the leader of the synagogue because he may see in him a paradigm for the leaders of the synagogues of his own time. In Chrysostom's day, synagogues were not necessarily led by individuals from any one group but were becoming increasingly dominated by ideas from the later rabbis, who were the ideological descendants of the Pharisees. This is why Chrysostom implies an identification between the leader of the synagogue and the Pharisees. [5]2 Kings 5:11 LXX. [6]PG 57:369-70; NPNF 1 10:205**. [7]The hemorrhaging woman, symbolic of the Gentiles, had been ill for twelve years, the age of the ruler's dying daughter—symbolic of the Jews. When the Jews began to believe in God, the pagans became spiritually ill. [8]CCL 77:59. [9]By a priest. [10]Lev 15:25: "When a woman has a discharge of blood for many days at a time other than her monthly period or has a discharge that continues beyond her period, she will be unclean as long as she has the discharge." [11]PG 57:371; NPNF 1 10:205-6**.

glory? What an unholy thought, inspired by the most unholy one of all.

What then is his intention in bringing her forward? First, Jesus puts an end to her fear. He does not want her to remain trapped in dread. He gives no cause for her conscience to be harmed, as if she had stolen the gift. Second, he corrects her assumption that she has no right to be seen. Third, he makes her faith an exhibit to all. He encourages the others to emulate her faith. Fourth, his subduing the fountains of her hemorrhage was another sign of his knowledge of all things. And finally, do you remember the ruler of the synagogue? He was at the point of despair, of utter ruin. Jesus is indirectly admonishing him by what he says to the woman. The Gospel of Matthew, Homily 31.2.[12]

The Ironies Unfold. Hilary: As the woman is healed, the crowd of sinners is made whole. At first it seemed more appropriate to follow the law of cleanliness. But a more pristine wholeness is restored to publicans and sinners in the appearance of the woman. Thus, upon meeting the Lord as he was passing by, she believed firmly that by touching his garment she would be healed of her flow of blood. Dressed in shabby clothes and defiled by the uncleanness of her interior affliction, in her faith she hastens to touch the tassel of his cloak. In the midst of the apostles she sought to touch the gift of the Holy Spirit as it was coming from Christ's body. She is suddenly healed. . . . The Lord praised her faith and constancy, because what had been prepared for Israel, the common people of the Gentiles were now claiming for themselves. On Matthew 9.6.[13]

The Church of the Gentiles Touches the Lord. Augustine: The daughter of the synagogue ruler signifies the Jewish people, whereas the woman signifies the church of the Gentiles. The Lord Christ, born of the Jews in the flesh, was presented to those Jews in the flesh. But he sent others to the Gentiles; he did not go himself. His bodily and visible community ties were in Judea. Therefore the apostle says, "For I say that Christ has been a minister of the circumcision in order to show God's fidelity in confirming the promises made to our fathers."[14] It was said to Abraham, "By your descendants shall all the nations of the earth bless themselves,"[15] "that the Gentiles might glorify God for his mercy."[16] Therefore Christ was sent to the Jews. He went to restore life to the daughter of the synagogue ruler. The woman appears on the scene, and she is healed. She is healed first in faith, being practically ignored by the Savior, for he said, "Who touched me?"[17] Here we have an ignoring attitude by God and faith in the mystery by her. It means something when someone who cannot ignore, ignores. And what does it mean? It points to the healed church of the Gentiles, the bodily presence of which is not seen by Christ, whose voice is heard in the psalm: "People whom I had not known served me. As soon as they heard of me they obeyed me."[18] The world heard and it believed. The Jewish people saw and at first they crucified. But later they too came to him. Also the Jews will believe—but at the end of the world. Sermons 63b.[19]

9:23-24 Not Dead but Sleeping

Death and Sleep. Peter Chrysologus: Christ reaches the house and sees the girl who appears to be dead. In order to move faithless hearts to faith, he says that the ruler's daughter is sleeping and is not dead. Ostensibly it is not easier to rise from death than to rise from sleep. So he says, "The girl is asleep, not dead." With God, indeed, death is sleep, for God can bring a dead person back to life sooner than a sleeping person can be wakened from sleep by humans; and God can sooner restore life-giving warmth

---

[12]PG 57:371-72; NPNF 1 10:206**. [13]SC 254:210. [14]Rom 15:8. [15]Gen 22:18. [16]Rom 15:9. [17]Mk 5:30. [18]Ps 18:43-44 (17:43-44 LXX). [19]MA 1:611-12; WSA 3 3:180-81.

to limbs frozen in death than humans can infuse vigor in bodies immersed in sleep. Hear the words of the apostle: "In a moment, in the twinkling of an eye the dead shall rise."[20] Because the blessed apostle was unable to refer to the speed of the resurrection in words, he opted for examples. How could he touch upon rapidity when divine power anticipates rapidity itself? And how does time enter the picture when something eternal is given outside of time? Even as time applies to temporality, so does eternity exclude time. SERMONS 34.5.[21]

9:25-26 The Ruler's Daughter Raised

THE UNRULY CROWD PUT OUTSIDE. CHROMATIUS: In the flute players and bustling onlookers who laughed to scorn the Lord who said, "The girl is asleep, not dead," we see an example of the synagogue rulers and the onlookers of Jewish people who, when they heard that the hope of eternal life had been promised by the Son of God to the Gentiles, held up to ridicule and contempt this great grace of the Lord. Not unjustly did the Lord order them to be sent outside. He showed that incredulous and unbelieving people of this kind are to be excluded from the promise of eternal life or from God's kingdom by him who is the Author of life and the Lord of the heavenly kingdom. TRACTATE ON MATTHEW 47.7.[22]

THE GIRL AROSE. CHROMATIUS: In the synagogue ruler we perceive a figure of the prophets or apostles, especially Peter, by whom the calling of the Gentiles was first heard; that is, the girl represented all those holy people who pleased God, not through the works of the law but through the righteousness of faith....

Moreover, for us to understand that the entire mystery of our salvation is prefigured in this girl; after she was raised from the dead, as Luke reports, the Lord directs her to eat something. Evidently the order of our faith and salvation is here shown. For when each believer among us is freed in baptism from perpetual death and comes back to life upon acceptance of the gift of the Holy Spirit, it is necessary that the person also be directed to eat that heavenly bread about which the Lord says, "Unless you eat the flesh of the Son of Man and drink his blood, you have no life in you."[23] TRACTATE ON MATTHEW 47.6-7.[24]

[20]1 Cor 15:52. [21]CCL 24:198-99. [22]CCL 9a:434. [23]Jn 6:53. [24]CCL 9a:433-34.

9:27-34 TWO BLIND MEN AND A MAN WHO COULD NOT TALK

[27]And as Jesus passed on from there, two blind men followed him, crying aloud, "Have mercy on us, Son of David." [28]When he entered the house, the blind men came to him; and Jesus said to them, "Do you believe that I am able to do this?" They said to him, "Yes, Lord." [29]Then he touched their eyes, saying, "According to your faith be it done to you." [30]And their eyes were opened. And Jesus sternly charged them, "See that no one knows it." [31]But they went away and spread his fame through all that district.

[32]*As they were going away, behold, a dumb demoniac was brought to him.* [33]*And when the demon had been cast out, the dumb man spoke; and the crowds marveled, saying, "Never was anything like this seen in Israel."* [34]*But the Pharisees said, "He casts out demons by the prince of demons."*[a]

a Other ancient authorities omit this verse

OVERVIEW: The blind men saw because they believed; they did not believe because they saw (HILARY). Bereft of the light of faith and covered by the veil of the law, they were being held in the gloom of blindness, but their sight was restored as soon as they expressed their faith in the Son of God (CHROMATIUS). What death and disability demonstrated in the previous cases, blindness demonstrated in this case (JEROME). Their eyes having been ruined, these men received faith by hearing alone. Ironically, however, now having sight to witness to what was happening, they were commanded to say nothing. Yet they spread the word everywhere (CHRYSOSTOM).

The demoniac had no tongue to speak for himself, no way to ask on his own behalf, so he was brought to Jesus. As his tongue was chained, so was his soul (CHRYSOSTOM). Just as the blind men received light, so too was this man's tongue healed (JEROME). The series of miracles occur in a proper order; the devil having been first cast out, the other bodily benefits follow suit. With the folly of all superstitions put to flight by the knowledge of God, sight and hearing and words of healing are offered (HILARY). The Pharisees continued to disparage Jesus' works, contradicting themselves unashamedly (CHRYSOSTOM).

9:27 Two Blind Men Ask for Mercy

THEY SAW BECAUSE THEY BELIEVED. HILARY: At that point, two blind men follow the Lord as he was passing by. But if they could not see, how could the blind men know of the Lord's departure as well as his name? Moreover, they called him "Son of David" and asked to be made well. In the two blind men, the entire earlier prefiguration[1] is complete. The ruler's daughter seems to be from these people, namely, the Pharisees and John's disciples, who already made common cause in testing the Lord. To these unknowing persons the law gave evidence as to the one from whom they sought a cure. It indicated to them that their Savior in the flesh was of the line of David. It also introduced light to the minds of those who were blind from past sins. They could not see Christ but were told about him. The Lord showed them that faith should not be expected as a result of health but health should be expected because of faith. The blind men saw because they believed; they did not believe because they saw. From this we understand that what is requested must be predicated on faith and that faith must not be exercised because of what has been obtained. If they should believe, he offers them sight. And he charges the believers to be silent, for it was exclusively the task of the *apostles* to preach. ON MATTHEW 9.9.[2]

BEREFT OF THE LIGHT OF FAITH. CHROMATIUS: According to one allegorical interpretation, these two blind men symbolize the two kingdoms into which the Jews were divided (after Solomon's death, between Rehoboam and Jeroboam). According to another interpretation, we might consider the people of the Jews and the people of the Gentiles as being prefigured in these two blind men. But this would not be appropriate. For would it be possible for the people of the Gentiles, before being enlightened, to declare Christ to be the Son of David,

[1]Of the previous narratives. [2]SC 254:212-14.

for they had not heard of the law or the prophets? For that reason, more properly it is understood concerning these two blind men that they did know from the law and the prophets that Christ is the Son of David. Both were blind, therefore, through their own unfaithfulness, for they were not yet able to see the true light, the only Son of God who was foretold in the law and the prophets. Bereft of the light of faith and covered by the veil of the law, they were being held in the gloom of blindness, according to the blessed apostle who says, "To this day whenever Moses is read a veil lies over their minds; but when one turns to the Lord the veil is removed."[3] And again: "For to this day, when they read the old covenant, that same veil remains unlifted, because only through Christ is it taken away."[4] Therefore sight was restored to these blind men as soon as they expressed their faith in the Son of God. This shows that whoever from these two peoples should believe that the Son of God came to save humankind would receive knowledge of the true light as soon as the blindness of error is removed. TRACTATE ON MATTHEW 48.2.[5]

9:28 Do You Believe?

WHEN THEY ENTERED HIS HOUSE. JEROME: As the Lord Jesus was passing on from the ruler's house and proceeding to his own (as we read above): "And getting into a boat he crossed over and came to his own city,"[6] suddenly "two blind men cried out and said, 'Have pity on us, Son of David!'" They are not healed along the route, as they might expect, but only after he reached his house. They approach him and go inside. First, their faith is discussed that they may receive the light of true faith. Another sign is added to the first sign we mentioned about the ruler's daughter and the woman with a hemorrhage, so that what death and disability demonstrated in the one case, blindness demonstrated in the other. Both men were blind at the time the Lord was passing through this world on

the way to his house. Unless they had exclaimed "Have pity on us, Son of David!" and in answer to Jesus' question "Do you believe that I can do this to you?" affirmed "Yes, Lord," they would not have received the pristine light. COMMENTARY ON MATTHEW 1.9.27.[7]

9:29 Healed According to Their Faith

JESUS QUESTIONS THEM. CHRYSOSTOM: For what purpose did it happen that, while they are crying out, he delays and questions them further? Here again Jesus is teaching us utterly to resist the glory that comes from the crowd. There was a house nearby. He led them into the house to heal them there in private. Then he charged them to tell no one. THE GOSPEL OF MATTHEW, HOMILY 32.1.[8]

9:30 Silence Commanded

TELL NO ONE. CHRYSOSTOM: This command to silence is itself no light charge against the religious leadership. The eyes of these two men had been ruined. They then received faith by hearing alone. They themselves could now see this miracle. Ironically, however, having now sight to witness to what was happening, they were commanded to say nothing. You can hear their earnestness in their loud cries, in their pleading simply for mercy and in their supplications. So they called him Son of David, because that name was above all thought to be honorable, the name that the prophets called those whom they wished most to commend and declare great. THE GOSPEL OF MATTHEW, HOMILY 32.1.[9]

9:31 They Spread His Fame

THEY REVEALED WHAT JESUS HAD DONE. CHRYSOSTOM: The blind men did not follow his

---

[3]2 Cor 3:15-16. [4]2 Cor 3:14. [5]CCL 9a:437. [6]Mt 9:1. [7]CCL 77:60-61. [8]PG 57:377; NPNF 1 10:210**. [9]PG 57:377; NPNF 1 10:210-11**.

instruction but immediately became preachers and evangelists. Though asked to hide what had been done, they revealed it. Remember that elsewhere he had said to a different hearer, "Return to your home and declare how much God has done for you."[10] This does not run contrary to what he says here but complementary to it. For it teaches us that we should say nothing about ourselves. In fact, it even teaches that we should prevent those who want to praise us from doing so. But it also teaches that if the glory would be offered up to God, not only should we not prevent this but we should even command that it be done.[11] THE GOSPEL OF MATTHEW, HOMILY 32.1.[12]

9:32 A Demoniac Brought to Jesus

A DEMONIAC. CHRYSOSTOM: For the condition was not a natural one but was the scheme of a demon.[13] It is also for this reason that the man needs others to lead him to Jesus. For he could not make a request by himself, because he was unable to speak; and he also could not petition others, because the demon had bound his tongue and along with his tongue had shackled his soul. Because of this Jesus did not even demand faith from him but immediately corrected the man's disorder. For it says, "After the demon had been cast out, the mute person spoke."

"And the crowds were amazed, saying, 'It has never been seen this way in Israel.'" This statement especially bothered the Pharisees, because the crowds placed Jesus before everyone else—not merely before people who lived at that time but even before all who had ever lived. And they put him first, not because he was healing people but because he healed easily; he healed quickly; he healed countless cases of disease; he healed diseases that were incurable. Hence the people reacted in this way. THE GOSPEL OF MATTHEW, HOMILY 32.1.[14]

HIS TONGUE LOOSENED. JEROME: What is called in Greek *kophos* is more commonly known

as deaf rather than dumb, but the Scriptures indiscriminately use *kophos* to mean dumb or deaf. Spiritually, just as the blind men receive light, so too the dumb man's tongue is loosened that he may speak and give glory to him whom he once rejected. COMMENTARY ON MATTHEW 1.9.33.[15]

9:33 Nothing Like This Seen in Israel

THE PROPER ORDER OF THE SEQUENCE OF MIRACLES. HILARY: In the deaf and dumb and demoniac appear the need of the Gentiles for a complete healing. Beleaguered on all sides by misfortune, they were associated with all types of the body's infirmities. And in this regard a proper order of things is observed. For the devil is first cast out; then the other bodily benefits follow suit. With the folly of all superstitions put to flight by the knowledge of God, sight and hearing and words of healing are introduced. The declaration of the onlookers followed their admiration over what took place: "Never has the like been seen in Israel." Indeed, he whom the law could not help was made well by the power of the Word, and the deaf and dumb man spoke the praises of God. Deliverance has been given to the Gentiles. All the towns and all the villages are enlightened by the power and presence of Christ, and the people are freed from every impairment of the timeless malady. ON MATTHEW 9.10.[16]

THE CROWDS MARVELED. CHRYSOSTOM: The affliction of the dumb demoniac was not natural. It was the work of the evil spirit. So it was that the demoniac was "brought to him." For he

---

[10]Lk 8:39; cf. Mk 5:19. [11]The command to let no one know about the healing of the blind men provides an example of humility but does not forbid us from giving glory to God when God acts on our behalf. [12]PG 57:378; NPNF 1 10:211**. [13]Jesus treated diseases caused by a demon in a way different from normal diseases. Various features of his healings also set him apart from others who healed. His exorcisms, healings and other activities demonstrated his true origin. [14]PG 57:378; NPNF 1 10:211. [15]CCL 77:61-62. [16]SC 254:214.

had no tongue to speak for himself, no way to ask on his own behalf, being speechless. He could not petition another, since the evil spirit had bound his tongue. And as his tongue was fettered, so was his soul.

This is why Jesus did not require a confession of faith from him. He straightway healed the disease. "And when the demon had been cast out, the dumb man spoke; and the crowds marveled, saying, 'Never was anything like this seen in Israel.' " THE GOSPEL OF MATTHEW, HOMILY 32.1.[17]

9:34 Cast Out by the Prince of Demons?

THE PHARISAIC COMPLAINT. CHRYSOSTOM: Now this healing especially vexed the Pharisees. They were disturbed that Jesus was being exalted above all others, not only those who are but all who had ever been. For he did what he did so easily and quickly. He cured diseases innumerable and otherwise incurable. The crowd exalted him. But the Pharisees continued to disparage his works, contradicting themselves unashamedly. Such a thing is wickedness—which finds itself desperately saying, "He casts out demons by the prince of demons."

What could be more absurd than this! For in the first place, as he also says later on, it is impossible for demons to cast out demons.[18] For it is a demon's custom to clap in applause at the activities of his own kind, not oppose them. Second, not only did he himself cast out demons, but he also purified lepers, raised dead people, reined in the sea, canceled sins, proclaimed the kingdom and approached the Father. Demons would never choose to do these things and would not ever be able to accomplish them. THE GOSPEL OF MATTHEW, HOMILY 32.2.[19]

---

[17]PG 57:378; NPNF 1 10:211**. [18]Mt 12:25-26. [19]PG 57:378; NPNF 1 10:211-12**.

9:35-38 THE NEED FOR LABORERS IN THE HARVEST

[35]*And Jesus went about all the cities and villages, teaching in their synagogues and preaching the gospel of the kingdom, and healing every disease and every infirmity.* [36]*When he saw the crowds, he had compassion for them, because they were harassed and helpless, like sheep without a shepherd.* [37]*Then he said to his disciples, "The harvest is plentiful, but the laborers are few;* [38]*pray therefore the Lord of the harvest to send out laborers into his harvest."*

OVERVIEW: Jesus went about in all the cities, in the countryside and in the synagogues, instructing all to respond to those who attacked him not in kind but with ever greater benevolence (CHRYSOSTOM). He had compassion on them because there was no shepherd to help them reap the abundance that the Holy Spirit was providing for them. No matter how much the harvest is gathered, it abounds all the more in fruitfulness (HILARY). The potential believers are many, the well-prepared apostolic leaders are few (JEROME). Jesus himself is the Lord of the harvest (CHRYSOSTOM).

9:35 Jesus Goes About Preaching and Healing

IN ALL THE CITIES AND VILLAGES. CHRYSOS-TOM: Jesus not only refrained from punishing his detractors for their insensitivity, but he did not even give them a simple rebuke. This gives further evidence of his meekness and refutes their malicious talk. He exhibits further proof of his glory by the signs that were to follow and the refutations that would become more explicit. For these reasons he went about in all the cities, in the countryside and in the synagogues, instructing all to respond to those who attacked him, not with fresh vilification but with ever greater benevolence. So do good to your companions not for their sake alone but for God's sake. Whatever they may do, do not cease doing them good. Your reward will be greater. When you are vilified, if you quit doing good, you signify that you are seeking the praise of others, not the praise of God.

For this reason Christ was sent to teach us that he came simply to do good. He did not wait for the sick to come to him. He himself hurried to them, bearing them a twofold blessing: the gospel of the reign of God and the healing of their diseases. And for this he went everywhere, not overlooking the slightest village. THE GOSPEL OF MATTHEW, HOMILY 32.3.[1]

9:36 Sheep Without a Shepherd

HE HAD COMPASSION FOR THE PEOPLE. HILARY: No instigator had stirred up the crowds. They were not harassed and helpless because of some mishap or disturbance. So why is Jesus so moved with compassion for these people? Clearly the Lord has pity on these people held in the sway of an unclean spirit and burdened by the law, because no shepherd was about to restore to them the guardianship of the Holy Spirit. The fruit of this gift was indeed potentially abundant but not yet harvested by anyone. The bounty of the Spirit overwhelms the multitude of those who take hold of it. For no matter how much it is gathered by everyone, it abounds in fruitfulness. And because it is

good to have many people through whom he is served, he orders his disciples to pray to the Lord of the harvest to send forth as many laborers as possible into the harvest. He prays that God may bestow an abundance of reapers to take hold of what the gift of the Holy Spirit was preparing. Through prayer and exhortation, God pours out this gift upon us. ON MATTHEW 10.2.[2]

9:37 The Harvest and the Laborers

THE LABORERS ARE FEW. JEROME: An abundant harvest signified the multitude of people. The few laborers signified the dearth of teachers. He commands them to ask the Lord of the harvest to send out laborers into his harvest. These are the laborers of whom the psalmist speaks: "May those who sow in tears reap with shouts of joy! He that goes forth weeping, bearing the seed for sowing, shall come home with shouts of joy, bringing his sheaves with him."[3] And that I may speak in broader terms: an abundant harvest represents all the believing multitude. The few laborers imply the apostles and their imitators who are sent to the harvest. COMMENTARY ON MATTHEW 1.9.37.[4]

9:38 Asking for Laborers

THE LORD OF THE HARVEST. CHRYSOSTOM: He shows how great the gift is when he says, "Ask from the Lord of the harvest." And in an inconspicuous manner Jesus indicates that he himself is the one who holds this authority. Then to signify how promising is the harvest, Jesus calls them to "pray therefore the Lord of the harvest." In doing so he indirectly declares this lordship to be his own prerogative. For after having said, "pray therefore the Lord of the harvest" when they had not made any request or prayer, he himself at once appoints them,

[1]PG 57:378-79; NPNF 1 10:212**. [2]SC 254:216-18. [3]Ps 126:5-6 (125:5-6 LXX). [4]CCL 77:63.

reminding them also of the sayings of John,[5] about the threshing floor, the separation of the husks from the kernels of grain, the husks that are left over, and of the One who is winnowing. From this it is clear that he himself is the farmer, he himself is the Lord of the harvest, he himself is the master of the prophets. For if he sent them to gather the harvest, it is clear that they do not harvest what belongs to someone else. Instead, they harvest the things that he sowed through the prophets. In calling their ministry a harvest, he was encouraging them but also empowering them to this ministry. THE GOSPEL OF MATTHEW, HOMILY 32.1-2.[6]

---

[5]Mt 3:12. [6]PG 57:379-80; NPNF 1 10:213**.

10:1-4 THE CHOOSING OF THE TWELVE

[1]*And he called to him his twelve disciples and gave them authority over unclean spirits, to cast them out, and to heal every disease and every infirmity.* [2]*The names of the twelve apostles are these: first, Simon, who is called Peter, and Andrew his brother; James the son of Zebedee, and John his brother;* [3]*Philip and Bartholomew; Thomas and Matthew the tax collector; James the son of Alphaeus, and Thaddaeus;*[x] [4]*Simon the Cananaean, and Judas Iscariot, who betrayed him.*

x Other ancient authorities read *Lebbaeus* or *Lebbaeus called Thaddaeus*

OVERVIEW: Jesus chose the lowly and despised to carry out his mission. Four were fishermen, two were publicans, and one was a traitor (CHRYSOSTOM). Even as he had healed every disease and every infirmity, he empowered his apostles so to heal (JEROME). Only after they had seen the dead raised, the sea rebuked, devils expelled, the legs of a paralytic brought to life, sins remitted, lepers cleansed, and had received a sufficient proof of his power both by deeds and words did he send them out (CHRYSOSTOM). Many of the names of the apostles had layered levels of meaning (JEROME).

10:1 Jesus Calls Twelve Disciples

THE EMPOWERMENT OF THE APOSTLES. JEROME: The kind and merciful Lord and Master does not begrudge his followers and disciples their powers. Even as he had healed every disease and every infirmity, he empowered his apostles to heal every disease and every infirmity. But there is a great gap between having and granting, between giving and receiving. Whatever he does, he does in the power of the Lord. Whatever they do, they display their own weakness and the power of the Lord, saying, "In the name of Jesus, arise and walk." It must be noted, further, that the power to work miracles is granted to the apostles even to the twelfth man. COMMENTARY ON MATTHEW 1.10.1.[1]

PREPARING DISCIPLES FOR FUTURE DANGERS. CHRYSOSTOM: If the Spirit had not yet

---

[1]CCL 77:63.

been given, since Jesus had not yet been glorified, how then did the disciples cast out the unclean spirits? They did this by his own command, by the Son's authority.[2]

Note the careful timing of their mission. They were not sent out at the beginning of their walk with him. They were not sent out until they had sufficiently benefited by following him daily. It was only after they had seen the dead raised, the sea rebuked, devils expelled, the legs of a paralytic brought to life, sins remitted, lepers cleansed, and had received a sufficient proof of his power both by deeds and words—only then did he send them out. And he did not send them out unprepared to do dangerous deeds, for as yet there was no danger in Palestine. They had only to stand against verbal abuse. However, Jesus still warned them of larger perils to come, preparing them for what was future. THE GOSPEL OF MATTHEW, HOMILY 32.3.[3]

10:2-4 The Names of the Apostles

LOWLY FISHERMEN AND DESPISED PUBLICANS CHOSEN. CHRYSOSTOM: "Now the names of the twelve apostles are these; first, Simon, who is called Peter." There was also another Simon, the Canaanite, Judas Iscariot, Judas the brother of James, James the son of Alphaeus, and James the son of Zebedee. Mark lists them according to their dignity. After the two leaders, Jesus then numbers Andrew. Matthew, however, lists them without this kind of distinction. He even places Thomas before himself, as one who was much less significant.

Let us observe the order of the list of disciples from the beginning: "First, Simon, who is called Peter, and Andrew his brother." Even this is no small praise. One he named from the excellence of his character and the other from his relation to the first. Then, "James the son of Zebedee, and John his brother." Do you note that he does not arrange them according to their dignity? For John seems to me to be greater, not only than the others but even than his brother. After this,

when he had said, "Philip, and Bartholomew," he added, "Thomas, and Matthew the publican." (Luke lists them in the opposite order.) Next, "James the son of Alphaeus," to distinguish him from James the son of Zebedee. Then after mentioning "Lebbaeus, whose surname was Thaddaeus," and "Simon" Zelotes, whom he calls also "the Canaanite," he comes finally to the traitor. He described him as a betrayer, not as if he were viewed as enemy or adversary but as one writing a history. He does not say "the abominable, the utterly despicable one" but simply named him from his city, "Judas Iscariot." He does so because there was also another Judas, "Lebbaeus, whose surname was Thaddaeus," who Luke identifies as the brother of James, writing, "Judas the brother of James." Therefore to distinguish him from this man, the text simply reads, "Judas Iscariot, who betrayed him." Matthew is not ashamed to speak of his betrayal. There was no attempt to disguise things that might seem to be matters of reproach. At the very top of the list is the unlearned Peter. Now see what happens: "These twelve," it is said, "Jesus sent!"

What kind of people were these? Fishermen and publicans. Indeed, four of them were lowly fishermen and two were publicans—Matthew and James—and one was even a traitor. These "he sent!" THE GOSPEL OF MATTHEW, HOMILY 32.3.[4]

THE HIDDEN MEANING OF THE NAMES. JEROME: The order in which the apostles were divided and the distinction of each one were given by him who plumbs the depths of the heart. The first to be recorded is Simon called Peter (to distinguish him from the other Simon, who is called the Cananaean from the village of Cana in Galilee, where the Lord turned the water into wine). He also calls James the son of Zebedee because he is followed by another James, the son of Al-

---

[2]The disciples have the power to drive away impure spirits, even before having received the Holy Spirit at Pentecost, because they act in the name of Christ. [3]PG 57:380; NPNF 1 10:213**. [4]PG 57:380-81; NPNF 1 10:213-14**. Jesus chose the lowly and despised to carry out his mission.

phaeus. And he associates the apostles by pairs. He joins Peter and Andrew as brothers not so much in the flesh as in the spirit; James and John, who left behind their natural father and followed the true Father; Philip and Bartholomew, Thomas and Matthew the publican. The other Evangelists, in listing the names, put Matthew first and then Thomas; nor do they mention the name *publican*, lest in recalling his former way of life they seem to insult the Evangelist. But Matthew, as we said before, places himself after Thomas and calls himself a publican so that "where sin abounded, grace has abounded even more."[5]

Simon the Cananaean is the one whom another Evangelist calls the Zealot. In fact, Cana interpreted means "zeal." Church history relates that the apostle Thaddaeus was sent to Edessa, Abgarum in the region of Osroene. The person whom Luke the Evangelist calls Jude the brother of James, elsewhere called Lebbaeus, which interpreted means "little heart," is believed to have been referred to by three names. Simon Peter and the sons of Zebedee (called sons of thunder) were named for their strength of mind and great faith. Judas Iscariot took his name either from his hometown or from the tribe of Issachar. By a certain prophecy he was born in condemnation of himself, for Issachar interpreted means "reward," as to signify the price of the traitor. COMMENTARY ON MATTHEW 1.10.2.[6]

[5]Rom 5:20. [6]CCL 77:63-64.

10:5-15 THE MISSION AND INSTRUCTION OF THE TWELVE

[5]*These twelve Jesus sent out, charging them, "Go nowhere among the Gentiles, and enter no town of the Samaritans, [6]but go rather to the lost sheep of the house of Israel. [7]And preach as you go, saying, 'The kingdom of heaven is at hand.' [8]Heal the sick, raise the dead, cleanse lepers, cast out demons. You received without paying, give without pay. [9]Take no gold, nor silver, nor copper in your belts, [10]no bag for your journey, nor two tunics, nor sandals, nor a staff; for the laborer deserves his food. [11]And whatever town or village you enter, find out who is worthy in it, and stay with him until you depart. [12]As you enter the house, salute it. [13]And if the house is worthy, let your peace come upon it; but if it is not worthy, let your peace return to you. [14]And if any one will not receive you or listen to your words, shake off the dust from your feet as you leave that house or town. [15]Truly, I say to you, it shall be more tolerable on the day of judgment for the land of Sodom and Gomorrah than for that town.'"*

OVERVIEW: The command to "go nowhere among the Gentiles" was given before the resurrection, whereas the command to "go to all the world" was given after the resurrection (JEROME). They were being sent first to the lost sheep of the house of Israel, who raged against them with the tongues and jaws of wolves and vipers (HILARY). Jesus wished to offer the proclamation of the coming kingdom first to the Jews, and only then would it be offered to the

193

Gentiles (GREGORY THE GREAT). The radical obedience of the apostles exhibits their greatness (CHRYSOSTOM). The deeds of the apostles make their words even more credible (JEROME). Whatever impairment Adam's body had received from his encounter with Satan, Jesus empowered the disciples to wipe away through their sharing in his power (HILARY). We are to leave all things behind as we enter upon holy ground (JEROME). All treasure on earth is detrimental for this journey. The garment of Christ is all we will ever need (HILARY). You will be given food in due season insofar as you are worthy of it; you will be worthy of it if you ask for nothing beyond mere necessities (CHRYSOSTOM). Inquire in each town as to who is worthy, and stay with them (HILARY). History teaches us the radical precariousness of all political systems. Their ruins teach us that they are not to be loved (GREGORY THE GREAT).

10:5 These Twelve Jesus Sent Out

AVOID THE UNENLIGHTENED. HILARY: They are warned to avoid the ways of the Gentiles, not because they were never going to be sent for the salvation of the Gentiles, but because they were to avoid the works and lifestyle of the unenlightened Gentiles. They were forbidden to enter the towns of the Samaritans. Yet, did he not cure the Samaritan woman? They were warned, moreover, not to go into the assemblies of heretics.[1] For heterodoxy does not differ at all from unenlightenment. Therefore they were being sent to the lost sheep of the house of Israel, who raged against him with the tongues and jaws of wolves and vipers. At any rate, the law was due to receive the special benefit of the gospel. The less excuse Israel had for its ungodly behavior, the more zeal it might have in heeding the warning. ON MATTHEW 10.3.[2]

GO NOWHERE AMONG THE GENTILES. JEROME: This passage is not contrary to the command given later: "Go, therefore, and make dis-

ciples of all nations, baptizing them in the name of the Father, and of the Son and of the Holy Spirit." The former command was given before the resurrection and the latter after the resurrection. It was necessary to announce Christ's first coming to the Jews, lest they have a good excuse for saying that the Lord rejected them because he had sent the apostles to the Gentiles and the Samaritans. In line with the metaphor, we who call ourselves Christians are advised not to walk in the ways of the Gentiles and heretics, for they have not only a separate religion but also a separate way of life. COMMENTARY ON MATTHEW 1.10.5-6.[3]

10:6 The Lost Sheep of Israel

THE HOUSE OF ISRAEL. GREGORY THE GREAT: Isn't it clear to all, dearly beloved, that our Redeemer came into the world for the salvation of the Gentiles? Yet when we behold Samaritans called daily to the faith, what did he mean when he sent his disciples to preach and said, "Go nowhere among the Gentiles, and enter no town of the Samaritans, but go rather to the lost sheep of the house of Israel"? He wished that the proclamation be offered first to the Jews alone. Then it would be offered to the Gentiles. This conclusion we draw from the actual outcome of history. When the former were called but refused to be converted, the holy preachers would turn to the calling of the Gentiles as outsiders. So what happened to the Jews by way of example proved to be an increase of grace for the Gentiles. For there were at that time some from among the Jews who were to be called and some from among the Gentiles who were not to be called. FORTY GOSPEL HOMILIES 4.1.[4]

10:7 Preach the Kingdom of Heaven

---

[1]The Samaritans named in the Gospels are symbolic of heretics. [2]SC 254:218. [3]CCL 77:65. [4]PL 76:1089; CS 123* (Homily 17). So the resistance to grace among the Jews would ultimately open the door to an increase of grace among the Gentiles.

PREACH AS YOU GO. CHRYSOSTOM: Do you perceive the unparalleled magnificence of their ministry? Do you comprehend the dignity of the apostles? They are not authorized to speak of things perceivable by the senses. They do not repeat what Moses said or the prophets before them. Rather, they spoke of new and strange things. Moses and the prophets spoke of temporal promises of an earthly land. The apostles proclaimed the kingdom of heaven and all that this implies.

Not only does the loftiness of their message characterize them as greater, but so does the lowly nature of their obedience. They were not reluctant nor irresolute, like those who came before. Instead, warned as they were of perils, wars and intolerable evils, they receive his commands with simple obedience. They immediately became heralds of the coming kingdom. THE GOSPEL OF MATTHEW, HOMILY 32.4.[5]

THE KINGDOM OF HEAVEN IS AT HAND. GREGORY THE GREAT: But let us hear what the preachers were commanded when they were sent out: "Go and preach," saying, "The kingdom of heaven is at hand." Even if the gospel were to be silent, dearly beloved, the world now proclaims this message. Its ruins are its words. Struck by so many blows, it has fallen from its glory. It is as if the world itself reveals to us now that another kingdom is near, which will succeed it. It is abhorred by the very people who loved it. Its own ruins preach that it should not be loved.

If someone's house were shaken and threatened with ruin, whoever lived in it would flee. The one who loved it when it was standing would hasten to leave it as soon as possible when it was falling. Therefore if the world is falling, and we embrace it by loving it, we are choosing rather to be overwhelmed than to live in it. Nothing separates us from its ruin insofar as our love binds us by our attachment to it.

It is easy now, when we see everything heading for destruction, to disengage our minds from love of the world. But then it was very difficult,

because the disciples were sent to preach the unseen kingdom of heaven at the very time when everyone far and wide could see the kingdoms of earth flourishing. FORTY GOSPEL HOMILIES 4.2.[6]

10:8 Give Without Pay

THE GIFT OF POWER. HILARY: All the power possessed by the Lord is bestowed upon the apostles! Those who were prefigured in the image and likeness of God in Adam have now received the perfect image and likeness of Christ. They have been given powers in no way different from those of the Lord. Those once earthbound now become heaven-centered. They will proclaim that the kingdom of heaven is at hand, that the image and likeness of God are now appropriated in the company of truth, so that all the holy ones who have been made heirs of heaven may reign with the Lord. Let them cure the sick, raise the dead, cleanse the lepers and cast out devils. Whatever impairment Adam's body had incurred from being goaded on by Satan, let the apostles wipe away through their sharing in the Lord's power. And that they may fully obtain the likeness of God according to the prophecy in Genesis,[7] they are ordered to give freely what they freely have received.[8] Thus a gift freely bestowed should be freely dispensed. ON MATTHEW 10.4.[9]

SIGNS CONFIRMING THE PROMISES. JEROME: Lest anyone hold as unworthy of belief these

---

[5]PG 57:381; NPNF 1 10:214**. [6]PL 76:1090; CS 123:121-22* (Homily 17). The world currently teaches us of its own vulnerability. Roman history, Gregory argued, is confirming the radical precariousness of human systems, which themselves are implicitly pointing toward the coming reign of God. [7]Gen 1:26-27. According to one interpretation, widespread in antiquity and here accepted by Hilary, the likeness to God indicates a level of perfection superior to that of an image. Thus humans would have been created merely after the image of God, to progress in stages—thanks to their merits—until they resemble God. Other exegetes, however—including Augustine—recognize no difference between the image and the likeness of God. [8]Mt 10:8. [9]SC 254:218-20.

rough men bereft of eloquence, unschooled and unlettered, as they promise the kingdom of heaven, Jesus empowered them to cure the sick, cleanse the lepers and cast out devils. Many signs would confirm the promises made. And because spiritual gifts are defiled if connected with rewards, Jesus adds a condemnation of avarice: "Freely you have received, freely give." I, your Lord and Master, have given this to you without cost, and you should give, lest the grace of the gospel be corrupted. COMMENTARY ON MATTHEW 1.10.7-8.[10]

10:9 Take No Money

TAKE NO COPPER IN YOUR BELTS. JEROME: Consequently he gave this order to the preachers of truth to whom he had said before: "Freely you have received, freely give." If they truly declare that they do not receive payment, the possession of gold, silver and money is superfluous. For if they were to have gold and silver, it would seem they were preaching not for the sake of humanity's salvation but for the sake of their own financial gain. "No copper in your belts." One who cuts off riches nearly cuts off what is necessary for life. Thus as the apostles and teachers of true religion taught that all things were governed by providence, they show they are not concerned about what tomorrow will bring. COMMENTARY ON MATTHEW 1.10.8.[11]

10:10 Take No Supplies

TAKE NO BAG FOR YOUR JOURNEY. HILARY: They are forbidden to keep gold, silver or money in their belts, to carry a wallet for their journey, to keep two tunics, or sandals, or to take a staff in hand. The laborer deserves his food. Does it not cause envy, as I believe, to carry money in one's belt? And what does the forbidden possession of gold, silver and copper in one's belt signify? The belt is the equipment of the ministry, and the sash helps one to work efficiently. Therefore we are warned about any-

thing in our ministry that is of monetary value, nor should the possession of gold, silver and copper become necessary for our apostolic mission. "Take no wallet for your journey." Leave behind any concern for worldly goods. All treasure on earth is detrimental, for where our treasure is, there our heart will be.[12] "Nor two tunics." The garment of Christ is all we will ever need. And, because of the depravity of our mind, we should not put on any other garment, either of a heretical sect or of the law. "Nor sandals." Are frail humans capable of going barefoot? On holy ground covered with thorns and briars, as God said to Moses,[13] we are urged to stand firm with bare feet and to have no other footwear for our journey than what we have received from Christ. "Nor staff in hand," that is, the possession of external power, or unworthily holding a staff from the root of Jesse—for whatever else it may be, it will not be the staff of Christ. Rather, we are to be equipped for our journey in the world with every higher level of language, grace, travel fare, clothes, footwear and power. Following these directions, we shall be found worthy of our reward; that is, through observance of them, we will receive the reward of heavenly hope. ON MATTHEW 10.5.[14]

TAKE NO STAFF. JEROME: "Nor staff." Why do we who have the Lord as our help seek the aid of a walking stick? And since he had sent the apostles out to preach somewhat divested and ill equipped and the teachers seemed to be in difficult straits, he tempered the severity of his command with the following sentence: "The laborer deserves his living." However, Jesus said, accept by way of food and clothing whatever you need. Jesus' teaching is reflected in Paul's words: "Having sufficient food and clothing, with these let us be content."[15] And in another place: "Let one who is instructed in the word share all good things with the teacher,"[16] so that the disciples

---

[10]CCL 77:65. [11]CCL 77:66. [12]Mt 6:21. [13]Ex 3:5. [14]SC 254:220-22. [15]1 Tim 6:8. [16]Gal 6:6.

of those who have a healthy fear of the demonic will make them sharers of their own material goods, not because of greediness but genuine need. We said this by way of interpretation. According to another scriptural interpretation,[17] teachers may not possess gold or silver or money in their belts. Gold is often understood to mean feeling, silver to mean speech and copper to mean voice. We are not allowed to accept these things from others but to possess them as given by the Lord. Nor are we allowed to accept the teachings of heretics and philosophers and false doctrine or to be burdened by the cares of the world or to be two-faced or to have our feet bound by deadly chains. But we are to be divested of everything as we advance on holy ground. We are not to have a staff that is changed into a snake[18] or to lean upon the flesh for any support. A staff or walking stick of this kind is a reed: If you press on it just a little, it will break and will pierce your hand. COMMENTARY ON MATTHEW 1.10.10.[19]

ASKING ONLY FOR NECESSITIES. CHRYSOSTOM: By saying "the laborer deserves his food," Jesus is not implying that every door will be opened to you. Rather, this saying requires great prudence. It will profit you both with respect to your reputation and for meeting your needs. His meaning is that you will be given food in due season insofar as you are worthy of it. And you will be worthy of it if you ask for nothing beyond mere necessities. THE GOSPEL OF MATTHEW, HOMILY 32.5.[20]

10:11 Find Out Who Is Worthy

WHO IS WORTHY. JEROME: Entering a new town, the apostles were unable to know what kind of persons they were meeting. Therefore a host must be chosen according to his reputation and the judgment of his neighbors. Otherwise the dignity of the message preached might be tainted by the ill repute of the recipient. Since they must preach to all, only one host is to be chosen; and they are not to bestow favor on persons with whom they stay but to receive it. COMMENTARY ON MATTHEW 1.10.11.[21]

STAY THERE UNTIL YOU DEPART. CHRYSOSTOM: You are intentionally to seek out honorable persons. You are not then to move from house to house, looking constantly for better fare, which would vex those who would be receiving you and give you the reputation of gluttony and self-indulgence. This seems evident in his saying, "And whatever town or village you enter, find out who is worthy in it, and stay with him until you depart." THE GOSPEL OF MATTHEW, HOMILY 32.5.[22]

10:12-13 Worthy or Unworthy Houses

IF IT IS WORTHY. HILARY: These things really baffle the mind. For if the apostles are not to submit to hospitality unless they first inquire who is worthy, how will the house later be found unworthy? And what if the host does not listen to their words and does not receive them? Either there is no fear of this in the well-intentioned person, or, if he is found unworthy, there is no point in sharing his dwelling. And what good will it do to inquire who is worthy if respect and punishment are advised regarding an unworthy host? But the Lord instructs them to desire no part of the home and hospitality of those who either reproach Christ or turn a deaf ear to him. In each town they are to inquire who in the house is worthy, that is, if the church and Christ are inhabitants there, and not to move on to anywhere else if the house is worthy and the host well-intentioned.

There would be many Jews with a great affection for the law who, although they might

---

[17]In the Alexandrian exegetical terminology, *anagōgē* indicates the spiritual meaning of the sacred text, arrived at by raising the interpretation above the literal level of the text normally—though not always—through the use of allegory. [18]Ex 4:3. [19]CCL 77:66-67. [20]PG 57:383; NPNF 1 10:215**. [21]CCL 77:66-67. [22]PG 57:383; NPNF 1 10:215**.

believe in Christ out of admiration for his works, still lingered in the works of the law. And others, curious to explore the freedom that is in Christ, would pretend they were going over to the gospel from the law. Many others, too, would be led into heresy out of a misguided understanding. And since all those who deceive and flatter their listeners in this way claim they have the catholic truth, he forewarned his apostles that they must inquire whether the person they are to dwell with is worthy. And since naïve persons might go along with the ideas of the host through deceptive words, one must make cautious use of a house that was called worthy, that is, the church that is called catholic. He directs that it should be saluted peaceably, so that peace is spoken rather than given. For thus he instructed them: "Salute it, saying, 'Peace to this house.'" Hence their peaceful greeting is in words and must be tendered as a gesture. Furthermore, he said that peace itself, which is the very heart of compassion, ought not to come to that house unless it is worthy. If that house is not found worthy, the homage of heavenly peace must be withheld. ON MATTHEW 10.7-9.[23]

10:14-15 If They Will Not Receive You

SHAKE THE DUST OFF YOUR FEET. CHRYSOSTOM: You be the first to show respect. Do not wait to be saluted by others. But this is not a mere salutation; it is also a blessing. For "if the house is worthy, let your peace come upon it." But if they treat you with insolence, their first reproach will be to not receive the benefit of your peace, and the last will be that they will suffer the doom of Sodom. You are to seek out the houses of those who are worthy. If you shake the dust off your feet, you are showing either that you have not been received and heard or that you are attesting to them the long journey you have traveled for their sake. THE GOSPEL OF MATTHEW, HOMILY 32.5.[24]

[23]SC 254:224-26. [24]PG 57:383; NPNF 1 10:216**.

10:16-25 WARNING OF COMING PERSECUTIONS

[16]"Behold, I send you out as sheep in the midst of wolves; so be wise as serpents and innocent as doves. [17]Beware of men; for they will deliver you up to councils, and flog you in their synagogues, [18]and you will be dragged before governors and kings for my sake, to bear testimony before them and the Gentiles. [19]When they deliver you up, do not be anxious how you are to speak or what you are to say; for what you are to say will be given to you in that hour; [20]for it is not you who speak, but the Spirit of your Father speaking through you. [21]Brother will deliver up brother to death, and the father his child, and children will rise against parents and have them put to death; [22]and you will be hated by all for my name's sake. But he who endures to the end will be saved. [23]When they persecute you in one town, flee to the next; for truly, I say to you, you will not have gone through all the towns of Israel, before the Son of man comes.

[24]"A disciple is not above his teacher, nor a servant[y] above his master; [25]it is enough for the

disciple to be like his teacher, and the servant[y] *like his master. If they have called the master of the house Be-elzebul, how much more will they malign those of his household."*

y Or *slave*

OVERVIEW: Jesus sends the disciples out with only one coat, barefooted, without a staff, without clothing or provisions, to accentuate his unspeakable power. He is exhibiting the gentleness of sheep, even while they are going out among wolves (CHRYSOSTOM, ANONYMOUS). Whatever fearful things they were to face, the more would they be given grace to face them (CHRYSOSTOM). Wherever the apostles pray they will be persecuted by civil authorities who believe they are serving God. The One who sustains them in peace will help them all the more in conflict (ANONYMOUS). When Christ has been attested before the authorities by the words of the martyrs amid the tortures of savage persecutors, the way will be open for the Gentiles to believe in him, though they remain stubborn (HILARY).

Jesus was preparing the disciples for what was to occur throughout the whole world. They are being taught a new kind of warfare. Both governors and the governed will betray them (CHRYSOSTOM). Never think back on previous deeds. Think about the end (ANONYMOUS). Knowledge of things to come is helpful for acquiring tolerance, especially if our own will to endure has been anticipated by the Lord's example (HILARY). The believer should not fear persecution but should turn away from it, as did the apostles in Jerusalem (JEROME). The Christian message will pass quickly from Israel to the Gentiles under the conditions of persecution. When it has been proclaimed to all the Gentiles, the Son will return and Israel will be reclaimed (HILARY). The disciple is like the master by the grace of adoption, not by nature (THEODORE OF MOPSUESTIA).

10:16 Wise as Serpents, Harmless as Doves

SHEEP IN THE MIDST OF WOLVES. ANONYMOUS: But let us consider this. Why did he say,

on the one hand, "like sheep" and, on the other hand, did he not say "like wolves" but simply "wolves"? If he had called the former "sheep" for the sole reason of their gentleness, since by nature they were human indeed but sheep by gentleness, certainly he would have called the latter "wolves," for they too, though like wolves in cruelty, by nature were human. For this reason, therefore, he called the former "sheep" but called the latter not "like wolves" but fully "wolves," since people, who are God's creatures, though they may be good, always have in them something evil according to the flesh. And one is called a sheep insofar as one is good; yet *like* a sheep, however, insofar as one is not fully good. For one who does not know God can have nothing good in himself. So one is referred to as a "wolf," not "like a wolf," because he has nothing good in himself and does not know God in himself. INCOMPLETE WORK ON MATTHEW, HOMILY 24.[1]

10:17 Councils and Synagogues

THEY WILL FLOG YOU. CHRYSOSTOM: Again he is preparing them for this new sort of combat. They are to suffer wrong and willingly permit others to inflict punishment upon them. This is meant to teach them that the victory is in suffering evil for the sake of good. By this means their eternal trophies are being prepared. He does not instruct them to fight and resist those who would persecute them. All he promises them is that they will suffer with him the utmost ills. THE GOSPEL OF MATTHEW, HOMILY 33.2.[2]

10:18 Dragged Before Rulers

---

[1]PG 56:756-57. [2]PG 57:391; NPNF 1 10:221**.

Bear Testimony for My Sake. Chrysostom: Some may object, saying, "How then will others come to faith, when they see on our account children being slain by their fathers, and brothers killing brothers, and all things filled with abominations?" How could this sort of warfare work out? Will not we be treated as though we were destructive demons? As though we were a plague and pests to be driven out from every quarter? Won't they see that the earth is filled with the blood of kinsmen fighting kinsmen? Even so our sole purpose is to bring peace into their houses, even amid so much conflict. And this peace is beautiful. Suppose there had been some great number of us, not merely twelve! Suppose we had been wise and skilled in rhetoric, trained orators rather than "unlearned and ignorant." What would have come of our proclamation? Suppose we had been kings, in possession of armies and an abundance of wealth? Would we have been thereby more persuasive in proclaiming this kingdom of peace? When we despise our own safety, why do they pay all the more attention to us?

But they were not thinking or saying these things. They were not putting Jesus' commands to some pragmatic test. Rather, they simply yielded and obeyed. And this obedience did not come from their own moral excellence as such but rather itself was a gift of grace from their teacher. Whatever fearful things they were to face, the more so would they be given grace to face them.

He said, "Truly, I say to you, it shall be more tolerable on the day of judgment for the land of Sodom and Gomorrah than for that town." And again he warned shortly after this, "And you will be dragged before governors and kings for my sake, to bear testimony before them and the Gentiles." This is no small exhortation, that we should both suffer these things because of Christ and serve as a reproof to humans. The Gospel of Matthew, Homily 33.3.[3]

10:19 What You Are to Say

A New Sort of Warfare. Chrysostom: He is teaching them a new sort of warfare. He sends them out exposed, with only one coat, barefoot and without a staff, without clothing or provisions. The manner of their battle array is entirely unimpressive. He calls them to allow themselves to be totally supported by the generosity of such as receive them. All this is to accentuate his unspeakable power. Then, to press this reverse strategy to its limits, he tells them to exhibit the gentleness of sheep, even though they are going out among wolves, and not simply toward the wolves but trustfully moving right into the midst of the wolves. The Gospel of Matthew, Homily 33.1.[4]

Offered as a Sacrifice. Anonymous: "For they will deliver you up to councils, and scourge you in their synagogues."[5] As though for the greater glory of God, they will whip you in their synagogues. Where there are prayers and praises and readings or sacrifices, there they will punish the apostles as though offering to God a sacrifice. In fact, the suffering of the apostles was a sacrifice to God, not as wages paid to the Jews but as their own crown. For the Jews, however, it marked their downfall. Incomplete Work on Matthew, Homily 24.[6]

10:20 The Spirit Speaking in You

Your Father Speaks Through You in Every Age. Augustine: To be sure, we heard in that reading, "But when they deliver you up, do not be anxious how or what you are to speak . . . for it is not you who are speaking but the Spirit of your Father who speaks through you." And he says in another place: "Behold, I am with you always, even to the end of the world."[7] Does this mean that the people who heard those words of the Lord would be here until the end of the world? The Lord was referring, rather, not

---

[3]PG 57:391; NPNF 1 10:221-22**. [4]PG 57:389; NPNF 1 10:219-20. [5]Mt 10:17; Mk 13:9. [6]PG 56:758. [7]Mt 28:20.

only to those about to depart from this life but also to the others, including us and those who would come after us in this life. He saw everyone in his single body, and the words he spoke, "I am with you even to the end of the world," were heard by them and by us too. And if we did not hear them then in our knowledge, we heard them in his foreknowledge. Therefore, safe as sheep among the wolves, let us keep the commandments of him who directs us. And let us be "innocent as doves but cautious as snakes."[8] Innocent as doves that we may not harm anyone; cautious as snakes that we may be careful of letting anyone harm us. SERMON 64A.2.[9]

IT IS NOT YOU WHO SPEAKS. ANONYMOUS: For the greater consolation of the apostles, he did not say, "The Spirit of your Father who speaks in you" but "who speaks." He meant that neither then nor now can they do or speak anything without the Spirit of God. It is as though he said to them, "You see me hungry, and you believe that I am the heavenly bread. You see me thirsty, and you believe that I am the spring of water welling up to eternal life.[10] You believe in me and declare that I speak the truth. How are we to understand this human faculty that sees one thing and believes another and then professes that belief? So, if now at a time when there is no danger, my grace is at work in you, how much more will it be in you when persecution comes? For he who sustains you in peace will help you all the more in war." INCOMPLETE WORK ON MATTHEW, HOMILY 24.[11]

10:21 Relatives Will Rise Against Each Other

CHILDREN WILL RISE AGAINST PARENTS. HILARY: This entire saying of the Lord refers to the Jews and the heretics: "Brother will deliver up brother to death, and the father his child, and children will rise against parents." The family in a single house will disagree among themselves. This means that whereas the people were formerly united (for the "people" is meant under the names of parents and relatives), we will now be exposed to vicious hatred. We will be offered up to earthly judges and kings, who attempt to secure either our silence or our cooperation. For we are to bear testimony to these people and to the Gentiles, and after that testimony has been borne, our persecutors will be deprived of the excuse that they are ignorant of divine things. When Christ has been prophesied by the words of the martyrs amid the tortures of savage persecutors, the way will be open for the Gentiles to believe in him, though they remain stubborn. ON MATTHEW 10.12.[12]

THOSE YOU TRUSTED WILL BETRAY YOU. ANONYMOUS: He therefore told them to be wary of people as though of the worst kind of evils. Now if he had not said this in finding fault with people, it would have been sufficient for him to say, "Beware, for they will betray you." But now he adds "Beware of men," for he intends to show that of all evils human beings are the worst. In fact, if you compare them with the wild animals, you will find that they are the worst. For though an animal may show cruelty, its cruelty falls short of human cruelty since an animal is irrational. When a person, who is rational, is cruel, it is not easy to escape his or her cruelty. If you compare a human with a snake, you will find that a human is worse than a snake. Even though a snake is venomous, it is afraid of people. If it can take them by surprise, it will bite them; but if it cannot, it will flee. People are venomous like a snake, but they do not have a snake's fear. Therefore, as long as a person has the time, he lies in wait like a snake. If he comes upon his prey, he will lunge forward like a wild animal. The moment a snake is threatened, it becomes deadly; but if it is not threatened, it slithers away. People, even when not threatened, fly into a rage; and they rage even more against

---

[8]Mt 10:16. [9]MA 1:311-12; WSA 3 3:189. [10]Jn 4:14. [11]PG 56:759. [12]SC 254:230.

those who have not threatened them. In short, every wild animal has a peculiar evil of its own, whereas humanity has within its will every evil. INCOMPLETE WORK ON MATTHEW, HOMILY 24.[13]

10:22 Hated but Enduring to the End

HATED BY ALL. CHRYSOSTOM: The courts of justice will go against you. Kings will assail you, as will governors, the synagogues of the Jews and the magistrates of the Gentiles. Both rulers and ruled will combat you. He was preparing them not only for what was to befall them in Palestine but also throughout the world. For they were soon to be sent to the Gentiles with this same proclamation. In doing so they would find that the whole world opposes them. In this spiritual warfare all that dwell upon the earth, all peoples, tyrants and kings, will be arrayed against them. THE GOSPEL OF MATTHEW, HOMILY 33.3.[14]

ENDURING TO THE END. ANONYMOUS: "But the one who endures to the end will be saved." This is said because many begin but few reach the end. There is always pleasure in the beginning, but the end is the time of testing. For no one can endure with God to the end without becoming a person who belongs to God by means of grace. Everything done because of the flesh is mortal. The body is itself impermanent. But what is done because of God is eternal, just as God is eternal. What is glorious is not to begin something good but to reach the end in a good way. Hence the very essence of a good life is a good death. Firmness of heart can reach the end. Fleshly desire often starts some good thing but cannot reach the end except by the grace of God. So then, now that you have turned to God and begun to serve God and do the works of righteousness, never think back on your previous deeds. Think about your end. The contemplation of our previous good service leads to pride, but the contemplation of our end leads to

holy reverence. This is the meaning of "the one who endures to the end will be saved." INCOMPLETE WORK ON MATTHEW, HOMILY 24.[15]

10:23 Flee Persecution

THE FLIGHT OF THE GOSPEL. HILARY: He then tells them to flee out of one city into another. This means that his message would first go beyond the borders of Judea and pass into Greece. Then the messengers would be harassed and the various apostles would suffer among the cities of Greece. At last the message would be established among all the Gentiles. He also wished to indicate that the Gentiles would believe in the apostles' preaching but that Israel alone would not believe until his own return. For this reason he said, "You will not have gone through all the towns of Israel before the Son of Man comes," that is, after the conversion of all of the Gentiles. Israel will be left, and when he comes in splendor, it will fill out the number of the holy and be established in the church. ON MATTHEW 10.14.[16]

DO NOT FEAR PERSECUTION. JEROME: This should be read as referring to the time when the apostles were sent forth to preach. It was properly said to them: "Go nowhere among the Gentiles, and enter no town of the Samaritans,"[17] because they should not fear persecution but should turn away from it. We see that this is what the believers did in the first days. When persecution began in Jerusalem, they scattered throughout all Judea. Their time of trial thus became a seedbed for the good news.

On the spiritual level we propose this symbolic interpretation. When we are persecuted in one city—that is, in one book or passage in Scripture—we will flee to other cities, that is, to other books. No matter how menacing the persecutor may be, he must come before the judg-

---

[13]PG 56:758. [14]PG 57:391; NPNF 1 10:221**. [15]PG 56:760. [16]SC 254:232. [17]Mt 10:5.

ment seat of the Savior. Victory is not to be granted to our opponents before we have done this. COMMENTARY ON MATTHEW 1.10.23.[18]

FROM ONE TOWN TO THE NEXT. CYRIL OF ALEXANDRIA: Jesus commands his disciples to flee from one town to the next, and from that one to another. In saying this he is not telling his disciples to be cowardly. He is telling them not to cast themselves into dangers and die at once, for that would be a loss to those who otherwise will benefit from the teaching. FRAGMENT 120.[19]

BEFORE THE SON OF MAN COMES. THEODORE OF HERACLEA: His coming is not described as a manifest one at the end of our life. His coming will appear as spiritual guidance and help for those who are persecuted from time to time for the sake of God. FRAGMENT 68.[20]

10:24 A Disciple Not Above the Teacher

LIKE THE TEACHER. THEODORE OF MOPSUESTIA: It is truly said that a disciple is not above his teacher according to his nature. For he who is made like his teacher by adoption can never go beyond his nature, but to be made like his teacher is the highest end he can reach. It is also for this reason that Jesus says there is only one teacher, and that teacher is himself. For the teachers among humans are more like routinely stamped images of teachers than like true ones, as each of them teaches what he himself takes for granted. One will make more progress if one is reconciled to the good that has already been given. FRAGMENT 53.[21]

10:25 The Servant Like the Master

OUR LORD'S EXAMPLE. HILARY: Knowledge of things to come is very edifying for acquiring tolerance, especially if our own will to endure has been molded by another's example. Our Lord, who is eternal light and the leader of all believ-

ers and the founder of immortality, sent consolations in advance to his disciples for the sufferings they would endure. This was so that no disciple would think himself above his teacher or above the Lord, when in reality he is a servant. For some call the master of the house by a demon's name out of their ill will. If we were indeed equal to our Lord or to the circumstances of his sufferings, how much more would they commit every sort of injury and insult on those of his household who have more fully entered the realm of glory? ON MATTHEW 10.15.[22]

CALLING THE MASTER BEELZEBUL. CHRYSOSTOM: What Christ is saying to the faithful is, I am now already sharing with you the same stigma you are presently suffering. That is sufficient for your encouragement. I, your Master and Lord, have felt the same grief you now feel. And if that distresses you further, remember this: that even from this foreboding you will soon be freed. For why do you now grieve? Are you troubled that someone is calling you a deceiver or a liar? So what? Wait a little while. In time you will be seen as benefactors of the world and champions of faith. For time reveals whatever is concealed. Time will refute their false accusations and make your good intent known. For as historic events unfold, a larger design will be recognized. Everyone will finally grasp the real state of the case and not merely the frail words used to describe it. Then your adversaries will be revealed as false accusers, liars and slanderers. With time lengthening to reveal and proclaim your innocence, you will shine brighter than the sun. Your voice will in time be heard more clearly than a trumpet. Your good intent will be attested by all. So do not let what is now being said demoralize you. Rather, let the hope of the good things to come raise you up. For the true story of your testimony cannot

---

[18]CCL 77:69-70. [19]MKGK 192. [20]MKGK 75. [21]MKGK 114. [22]SC 254:234.

be suppressed forever. THE GOSPEL OF MATTHEW, HOMILY 34.1.[23]

THE RELATION BETWEEN MASTER AND SERVANT. CHRYSOSTOM: Observe how he reveals that he is the Lord and God and Creator of all things. What does it mean that "a disciple is not above his teacher, nor a servant above his master"? As long as one is a disciple or a servant, one is not ready to receive honor. So do not speak to me of what is lacking in the Master. Learn your arguments from all that is sufficient about him. Jesus does not say "how much more will they malign his servants?" but instead "how much more will they malign those of his household?" This demonstrates his close relationship with them. In another place Christ says, "I no longer call you my slaves; you are my friends."[24] Moreover, he does not say "if they are insolent to the master of the house and accuse him." Instead, he includes the exact form their insolence took, namely, that they called him Beelzebul. THE GOSPEL OF MATTHEW, HOMILY 34.1.[25]

---

[23]PG 57:399; NPNF 1 10:227**. Since time discovers all things concealed, be assured that the truth will ultimately be vindicated. [24]Jn 15:15. [25]PG 57:398-99; NPNF 1 10:227.

10:26-31 THE ONE TO FEAR

[26]"So have no fear of them; for nothing is covered that will not be revealed, or hidden that will not be known. [27]What I tell you in the dark, utter in the light; and what you hear whispered, proclaim upon the housetops. [28]And do not fear those who kill the body but cannot kill the soul; rather fear him who can destroy both soul and body in hell.[z] [29]Are not two sparrows sold for a penny? And not one of them will fall to the ground without your Father's will. [30]But even the hairs of your head are all numbered. [31]Fear not, therefore; you are of more value than many sparrows."

z Greek Gehenna

OVERVIEW: We are not to fear our persecutors' threats or stratagems, because the day of judgment will reveal that these all were empty (HILARY). Although the mystery has been hidden from the ages, it is now made manifest to all (ANONYMOUS). In contrast with Jesus' quiet tone of voice, the disciples would soon be making a proclamation with a boldness of speech that was to be conferred upon them (CHRYSOSTOM). Those things that were once said in the darkness are now preached in the light (HILARY). What Jesus teaches through the indirect communication of parables, the apostles are proclaiming openly (ANONYMOUS). Jesus was restraining himself, looking toward a more appropriate time for public speech (EUSEBIUS OF EMESA). Do not grieve over death, but sin (THEODORE OF MOPSUESTIA, AUGUSTINE). The body is dead without the soul, and the soul is dead without God (AUGUSTINE).

Some things happen because of God's direct will, but some happen merely with his permissive consent (ORIGEN). When persons sell themselves for the sake of an insignificant sin, it is like two sparrows being sold for a penny. Yet whatever is sold sinfully, Christ can buy back and redeem (HILARY). The sparrows do not fall apart from the will of God, who intends even these to serve a useful purpose (APOLLINARIS). If God is not ignorant of anything that happens in creation and if God loves us more truly than the best human father, then we need not be afraid (CHRYSOSTOM).

10:26 *Having No Fear*

REVEALED IN JUDGMENT. HILARY: This refers to the day of judgment, which will make known the hidden conscience of our will and reveal to public knowledge those things that now seem obscure. Jesus is admonishing us, therefore, that we are not to fear our persecutors' threats or stratagems or power, because the day of judgment will reveal that these all were nothing and empty. ON MATTHEW 10.16.[1]

10:27 *Uttered in the Light*

WHAT YOU HEAR IN THE DARK. HILARY: We do not take this to mean that the Lord was accustomed to preach at night and to transmit his teaching in the dark. Rather, to those who are carnal, everything he said is darkness, and to unbelievers his word is night.... Therefore Jesus commands that those things which were said in the darkness should be preached in the light. In this way the things he secretly whispered into their ears will be heard from the housetops, from on high, through those who speak as heralds. ON MATTHEW 10.17.[2]

WHAT YOU HEAR WHISPERED. CHRYSOSTOM: The point is not that Jesus was literally whispering into their ears or speaking in physical darkness. Rather, he was here pressing a strong figure of speech. He was conversing with them quietly and alone in a small corner of Palestine. In contrast with this tone of voice, they would soon be preaching with a boldness of speech that

would in due time be conferred upon them. The metaphor of whispering in the ear in a dark place, in this present quietness, is contrasted with what is to come. For they were soon to be commissioned to speak not to one or two or three cities but to the whole world. They would soon be traversing land and sea, amid inhabited countries and across deserts, addressing both princes and tribes, philosophers and orators, telling it like it is with an open face and with all boldness of speech. THE GOSPEL OF MATTHEW, HOMILY 34.2.[3]

PUBLIC SPEECH AT THE APPROPRIATE TIME. EUSEBIUS OF EMESA: But someone may ask, "If it is good to speak in the light, why did he himself speak in darkness? And if it is good to preach from the housetops, why did he himself quietly speak into their ears?" He keeps quiet because it is timely, but he instructs the disciples to proclaim and preach his words. He is not afraid—it is, rather, for ignorant people to fear the Lord Jesus. He is carefully managing his speech, much like a steward manages money. At times he keeps silent and at other appropriate times he speaks openly. HOMILY 27.3.[4]

BEYOND THE ENIGMA OF PARABLES. ANONYMOUS: What is the meaning of "What I tell you in the dark, utter in the light; and what you hear whispered, proclaim upon the housetops"? This refers to the darkness of the Jewish people, as is written elsewhere: "The light shines in the darkness, and the darkness has not overcome it."[5] The "darkness" means that they have not been capable of recognizing the true light. And so the Lord was proclaiming that whatever he had said among the Jews would have to be made manifest in the church.... To return to our passage, "What I tell you in the dark, utter in the light; and what you hear whispered, proclaim upon the housetops." This means, "What I am now

[1]SC 254:234. [2]SC 254:234-36. [3]PG 57:399-400; NPNF 1 10:227-28**. [4]SSL 27:196. [5]Jn 1:5.

telling you through the enigma of parables, you are hereafter to say openly." INCOMPLETE WORK ON MATTHEW, HOMILY 25.[6]

No Place Where Christ Will Not Be Known. ANONYMOUS: He now reveals to them what will be the outcome of their preaching, because their preaching was going to have a glorious result. "Here I am," he says. "I am the light hidden in the shadows, God concealed in a man, exaltation in humility. So although this mystery was hidden from the ages, it will now be made manifest to all through you, so that the prophecy I spoke will be fulfilled: 'Its rising is from the end of the heavens, and its circuit to the end of them; and there is nothing hid from its heat.'"[7] For there is no place where the sun is not seen and its heat is not felt. In the same way there will be no place where Christ is not known and his divine nature is not understood. In this way all humankind will be divided into two groups: the unbelievers who will have no excuse and will be punished, and believers. INCOMPLETE WORK ON MATTHEW, HOMILY 25.[8]

10:28 Fear the One Who Can Kill Body and Soul

Do Not Fear Those Who Kill the Body. ANONYMOUS: "Do not fear those who kill the body." The essence of the human is not the body, but the soul. It is the soul alone that God made in his own image and the soul that he loves. For the sake of the soul he even created the world. Our enemies are jealous of the soul and persecute the soul. For the sake of the soul even the Son of God came into the world. But the body is the garment of the soul, as the apostle says: "For while we are still in this body, we sigh with anxiety; not that we would be unclothed but that we would be further clothed, so that what is mortal may be swallowed up by life."[9] If a madman destroyed someone's garment that is worn over the body, his victim would think of him as the inflicter of an injury, but there would be no

harm to the victim's nature. In the same way if unbelievers murder the body that is worn over the soul, the soul is grieved by the murder, but there is no harm to the soul's nature. . . . What do you mean that the soul perishes? Was not the soul created to be immortal? "Death" can mean not only the snuffing out of the body but also torment. Thus Paul says, "Every day I die for your glory, which I possess in Jesus Christ."[10] And John says this in Revelation: "Blessed and holy is the one who shares in the first resurrection! Over such the second death has no power."[11] For the second death is fire and sulphur. You can see therefore that by "damnation of the soul" he does not mean the disappearance of the soul but the torture of the soul in hell, which is the second death. INCOMPLETE WORK ON MATTHEW, HOMILY 25.[12]

Do Not Bewail Death, but Sin. AUGUSTINE: The gospel is life. Impiety and infidelity are the death of the soul. So then, if the soul can die, how then is it yet immortal? Because there is always a dimension of life in the soul that can never be extinguished. And how does it die? Not in ceasing to be life but by losing its proper life. For the soul is both life to something else, and it has it own proper life. Consider the order of the creatures. The soul is the life of the body. God is the life of the soul. As the life that is the soul is present with the body, that the body may not die, so the life of the soul (God) ought to be with the soul that it may not die.

How does the body die? By the departure of the soul. I say, by the departure of the soul the body dies, and it lies there as a mere carcass, what was a little before a lively, not a contemptible, object. There are in it still its several members, the eyes and ears. But these are merely the windows of the house; its inhabitant is gone. Those who bewail the dead cry in vain at the windows of the house. There is no one there within it to hear.

---

[6]PG 56:761. [7]Ps 19:6 (18:6 LXX). [8]PG 56:760. [9]2 Cor 5:4. [10]1 Cor 15:31. [11]Rev 20:6. [12]PG 56:762-64.

... Why is the body dead? Because the soul, its life, is gone. But at what point is the soul itself dead? When God, its life, has forsaken it.... This then we can know and hold for certain: the body is dead without the soul, and the soul is dead without God. Every one without God has a dead soul. You who bewail the dead rather should bewail sin. Bewail ungodliness. Bewail disbelief. SERMON 65.5-7.[13]

DESTROYED IN HELL. THEODORE OF MOPSUESTIA: When Jesus says "hell," he is emphasizing that punishment there is eternal. By "hell" he means the condemnation awaiting those who receive recompense according to their life.

His choice of words shows that there is a great difference between the two things. He first says "kill" but next says "destroy," and from destruction there is no longer any salvation. FRAGMENT 56.[14]

10:29 A Sparrow's Fall

WITHOUT YOUR FATHER'S WILL. ORIGEN: In this passage, Jesus demonstrates his foresight in all things. The word *without* refers not to will but to foreknowledge. Some things happen because of his direct will, but some happen merely with his approval and consent. And so on the literal level, he is showing the subtlety of his foresight and his previous knowledge of events.

On the spiritual level,[15] however, a sparrow falls to the ground when it looks at what is below it and falls to earth, ensnared by the vices of the flesh, given up "to dishonorable passions."[16] It loses its freedom together with its honor. For a sparrow is either borne always upward, or else it comes to rest by alighting on mountains or hills (the hills are metaphors for Scripture). And such a person is one who has been raised aloft by the Word but has his mind on earthly concerns. FRAGMENT 212.[17]

CHRIST BUYS BACK WHAT IS SOLD. HILARY: What is sold is the body and soul. It is a sin to

sell them to anyone, because Christ redeems from sin and is the Redeemer of body and soul. So when persons sell themselves for the sake of an insignificant sin, it is like two sparrows being sold for a penny. They were born for flying and to be carried to heaven on spiritual wings, but they are overtaken by the price of their immediate pleasures, and by such actions they trade away all their eternal treasures for the sake of temporal luxury. ON MATTHEW 10.18.[18]

THE SPARROW'S FALL KNOWN BY GOD. APOLLINARIS: However, you must know that the story of the sparrows is figurative, since foresight in matters like these makes no difference at all to God. As the apostle said, "Is it for oxen that God is concerned?"[19] It is for the sake of humanity that he has foresight of sparrows, which he gives to us for our use. The "penny" is symbolic of something seemingly worthless. FRAGMENT 55.[20]

10:30-31 Of More Value Than Many Sparrows

FEAR NOT. CHRYSOSTOM: What do you see in creation of less value than a tiny sparrow? But even the sparrow will not fall without God's knowledge. Jesus does not mean that the sparrow falls by God's direct will because it is unworthy but that nothing that occurs is hidden from God. If then God is not ignorant of anything that happens in creation, and if God loves us more truly than the best human father, and if God loves us so as to have numbered our very hairs, then we need not be afraid. Jesus said this not to indicate that God literally has a number placed on the very hairs of our head but rather to show that God has perfect knowledge of

---

[13]PL 38:428-30; NPNF 1 6:307** (Sermon 15). [14]MKGK 114-15. [15]*Rhetos* signifies the literal interpretation of the text, while *noetos* signifies the spiritual, here expressed through allegory. [16]Rom 1:26. [17]GCS 41.1:101-2. [18]SC 254:236-38. [19]1 Cor 9:9. [20]MKGK 16.

everything about us and providentially cares for everything about us. Therefore, if God both knows all things that happen to us and is able to save us and willing to do so, then whatever we may be suffering, we need not think that God has forsaken us in our suffering. For it is not God's will to keep us wholly separated from that which elicits dread but rather to persuade us not to make an idol out of whatever we dread. It is this, more than anything else, that constitutes deliverance from dread. "Therefore, don't be afraid. You are of more value than many spar-

rows." Don't you see that God views your fear with more concern than the lives of many sparrows? He already knows the secrets of your heart. Hence Jesus adds, "Do not fear." For even if that which you dread prevails, it prevails only over your body; this is the limited part of yourself, which nature will surely take in due time and bring to an end. THE GOSPEL OF MATTHEW, HOMILY 34.2-3.[21]

---

[21]PG 57:400-401; NPNF 1 10:228-29**.

10:32-42 CONFESSING AND REJECTING CHRIST

[32]*So every one who acknowledges me before men, I also will acknowledge before my Father who is in heaven;* [33]*but whoever denies me before men, I also will deny before my Father who is in heaven.*

[34]*"Do not think that I have come to bring peace on earth; I have not come to bring peace, but a sword.* [35]*For I have come to set a man against his father, and a daughter against her mother, and a daughter-in-law against her mother-in-law;* [36]*and a man's foes will be those of his own household.* [37]*He who loves father or mother more than me is not worthy of me; and he who loves son or daughter more than me is not worthy of me;* [38]*and he who does not take his cross and follow me is not worthy of me.* [39]*He who finds his life will lose it, and he who loses his life for my sake will find it.*

[40]*"He who receives you receives me, and he who receives me receives him who sent me.* [41]*He who receives a prophet because he is a prophet shall receive a prophet's reward, and he who receives a righteous man because he is a righteous man shall receive a righteous man's reward.* [42]*And whoever gives to one of these little ones even a cup of cold water because he is a disciple, truly, I say to you, he shall not lose his reward."*

OVERVIEW: Confession by the lips is worth nothing without faith of the heart, and faith of the heart is worth nothing without confession by the lips (ANONYMOUS). The whole world is becoming divided against itself for the sake of faith in Christ. A necessary conflict has been

sent to break a peace that is evil (JEROME). This is peace: when the cancer is cut away. The incurable part must be surgically removed. Only in this way does the military commander preserve the peace: by cutting off those in rebellion (CHRYSOSTOM). The only true and lasting peace is found in God's righteousness (APOLLINARIS). At times God brings a creative disunity to our earthly lives in order to break an evil unity (ANONYMOUS). There are times when conflict is necessary between the believer and the unbeliever (EUSEBIUS OF EMESA).

Love your father, your mother, your sons, but love them ordinately in relation to your love of God (JEROME). Jesus bids parents not to attempt what is impossible by assuming that their love of their children can be rightly compared with their love toward God (CHRYSOSTOM). Say to your parents, "I will love you in Christ, not in stead of Christ. You will be with me in him, but I will not be with you without him" (AUGUSTINE).

It is better to die for God's sake and live eternally than to live for the sake of human interests alone and suffer eternal death (ANONYMOUS). We are unworthy of Christ if we do not take up our cross, by which we suffer, die, are buried and resurrected together with him (HILARY). How great is the impairment to those who love their own lives in an exaggerated way. How great is the blessing to those who are ready to give up their lives for a well-ordered love (CHRYSOSTOM). Christ comes to us in the office of a mediator, as one who comes from God (HILARY). Whatever reward there is for the traveler, one who receives that traveler for God's sake will have the same reward (ANONYMOUS). One who receives the apostles who preach the Father, Son and Spirit receives the fullness of deity itself (THEODORE OF HERACLEA). One who has properly extracted the meaning of the apostle's writing and has not misunderstood it is receiving the apostle as well as Christ, who speaks and dwells in the apostle (ORIGEN).

10:32 Acknowledged Before the Heavenly Father

WHO ACKNOWLEDGES ME. APOLLINARIS: The prize is superior insofar as it comes from God. It is not the same thing to acknowledge in a human manner and to be acknowledged in God's man-

ner. . . . The believer then must acknowledge God with both heart and mouth. "For one believes with one's heart and so is justified, and one confesses with his one's lips and so is saved."[1] FRAGMENT 56.[2]

10:33 Denied Before the Father

WHOEVER DENIES ME. CHRYSOSTOM: The Son does not here speak soothing words but rather speaks of the consequences of denial. Note carefully: It is not by some power within yourself that you make your confession but by the help of grace from above. But if you deny me, the Son, he is saying, then I will deny you in the presence of the Father. Someone may then object: "How then am I to be blamed if God, forsaking me, denies me?" The answer is, Your being forsaken is the fault of you yourself, the forsaken person, not of God.

"But why," you object, "should I need to confess faith with my mouth if I confess faith in my mind?" No, we must confess with our mouths in order that we may be steadily trained to speak boldly. It is only through this more abundant love and determination that we will be raised on high.

In this way Jesus addresses himself to each one of us personally. He is not here addressing his original disciples only but every one of us who follows after his disciples in accord with their witness to him. One who learns this lesson will teach it in boldness to others, prepared to suffer all things easily and with a ready mind. This is why so many have come to have faith in the witness of the apostles to this Word. THE GOSPEL OF MATTHEW, HOMILY 34.3.[3]

FAITH OF THE HEART AND CONFESSION OF THE LIPS. ANONYMOUS: He does not say, "Every one who acknowledges me in his own heart" but "before others."[4] If one does not

---

[1]Rom 10:10. [2]*MKGK 16.* [3]PG 57:401-2; NPNF 1 10:229**. [4]Mt 10:32.

acknowledge him before others, it does one no good to believe in Christ in one's heart. For it is impossible that one who denies with one's lips can believe in one's heart. For the root of confession is the heart's faith. Confession is thus the fruit of faith. As long as a root is living, it must produce either branches or leaves, and if the plant does not produce these, we know beyond a doubt that its root is withered in the ground. In the same way, as long as the faith of the heart is healthy, it always sows the seeds of confession with the lips. But if there is no acknowledgment with the lips, you should know beyond a doubt that the faith of the heart has already withered away. For the apostle says, "For one believes with one's heart and so is justified, and one confesses with one's lips and so is saved."[5] And so confession by the lips is worth nothing without faith of the heart, and faith of the heart is worth nothing without confession by the lips. If it benefits you to believe with the heart without confessing before others, does it also benefit an infidel to confess Christ deceitfully, even though he does not believe in his heart? If it results in no benefit to an unbeliever to confess without faith in the same way, it will not benefit you to believe without confessing. INCOMPLETE WORK ON MATTHEW, HOMILY 25.[6]

10:34 Not Peace but a Sword

HOW PEACE REQUIRES A SWORD. CHRYSOSTOM: What sort of peace is it that Jesus asks them to pronounce upon entering each house? And what kind of peace is it of which the angels sing, "Glory to God in the highest and on earth peace"? And if Jesus came not to bring peace, why did all the prophets publish peace as good news? Because this more than anything is peace: when the disease is removed. This is peace: when the cancer is cut away. Only with such radical surgery is it possible for heaven to be reunited to earth. Only in this way does the physician preserve the healthy tissue of the body. The incurable part must be amputated.

Only in this way does the military commander preserve the peace: by cutting off those in rebellion. Thus it was also in the case of the tower of Babel, that their evil peace was ended by their good discord. Peace therefore was accomplished. THE GOSPEL OF MATTHEW, HOMILY 35.1.[7]

GOD'S BATTLE AGAINST A CHEAP PEACE. APOLLINARIS: The unbelievers' disagreement with the believers will produce a distinction. Now since the unbelievers think that peacemaking is their proper duty, they say, "Do not believe that it is best under all circumstances to be saved, for you owe it as a duty to be at peace with all." But there are some who are preparing for battle against our peace, and you should not let their false peace rule. For the only true concord is according to God . . . and this above all is peace. FRAGMENT 57.[8]

GOOD PEACE VERSUS BAD PEACE. ANONYMOUS: There is a good peace and there is an evil peace. There is a good peace among good, faithful and just people. . . . For faith is born through the word of God, but it is preserved through peace and nourished by love, as the apostle says: "It is faith which works through love."[9] But faith devoid of love can produce none of the fruit of good works. And so if the faithful should be separated by any disagreement, that is an evil conflict, as the Lord has said: "No house divided against itself will stand."[10] And if the brotherhood is divided, it will consume itself, as the apostle has said: "But if you bite and devour one another, take heed that you are not consumed by one another."[11] On the other hand, there is an evil peace among unbelievers and iniquitous people. Among them is a single sinfulness, and so there is a common agreement to sin. For unbelief and iniquity are born through the encouragement of a demon, but they are preserved through peace. And so if at any time the

---

[5]Rom 10:10. [6]PG 56:766. [7]PG 57:405; NPNF 1 10:232**. [8]*MKGK* 17. [9]Gal 5:6. [10]Mt 12:25. [11]Gal 5:15.

unfaithful and iniquitous are divided against each other, that is a good conflict. For when there is peace among good people, faith and justice are established, but unbelief and injustice lie dormant. But when conflict arrives, faith and justice sink down while unbelief and injustice rise up anew. In the same way, when there is peace among iniquitous people, injustice and unbelief are established but faith and justice lie dormant. And when harmony arrives, unbelief and injustice sink down while faith and justice rise up. In this way then God brought a good disunity to the earth in order to break an evil unity. All people used to be together as if they lived in a single house of disbelief—all people, the good and the evil together, for some were in evil because they pursued evil, and others remained in evil out of ignorance of the good. But God brought a sword of disunity among them, which was the word of truth. Concerning this, the apostle says, "For the word of God is living and active, sharper than any two-edged sword, piercing to the division of soul and spirit, of joints and marrow, and discerning the thoughts and intentions of the heart."[12] INCOMPLETE WORK ON MATTHEW, HOMILY 26.[13]

10:35 Relatives Set Against One Another

FAITH MAY SEVER ONE FROM ONE'S FAMILY. HILARY: And so when we are renewed by the water of baptism through the power of the Word, we are separated from the sins and ancestors of our origin; we are cut away from the inordinate love of father and mother as if by an incision from God's sword, and we are divided from them. And as we shed our former self with its sins and unfaithfulness and are made new by the Spirit in mind and body, we will necessarily detest the habits of our old, inborn way of life. ON MATTHEW 10.24.[14]

NECESSARY STRIFE. EUSEBIUS OF EMESA: The Lord himself proclaims peace, which is why the apostle Paul also admonishes peace and says,

"For he is our peace."[15] This means, of course, the peace of those who believe and receive. But in what way does he not bring peace to the earth? When the daughter believed and the father remained an unbeliever, "what has a believer in common with an unbeliever?"[16] For the proclamation of peace caused a division. With a believing son and an unbelieving father there is necessarily strife. The peace that was proclaimed itself caused a division: a good division! For it is in peace that we are saved. HOMILY 26.[17]

10:36 Foes in the Household

IN ONE'S OWN HOUSEHOLD. JEROME: He had said previously, "What I tell you in the dark, declare in the light; and what you hear whispered, proclaim upon the housetops."[18] He now explains what follows after this proclamation. The whole world is divided against itself for the sake of faith in Christ. Every house contains both unbelievers and believers. And a necessary conflict has been sent to break an evil peace. It is written in Genesis that God did a similar thing to the rebellious people who streamed out of the east and rushed to build a tower, by which they meant to reach the heights of heaven. God divided their languages.[19] For this same reason David prays in the psalm, "O God, scatter the peoples who delight in war."[20] COMMENTARY ON MATTHEW 1.10.34.[21]

10:37 Not Worthy of Me

FAMILIAL LOYALTY AND LOVE OF GOD. JEROME: For he had previously said, "I have not come to bring peace but a sword."[22] He adds that he has divided people against father and mother and relatives, so that no one will place familial loyalty before religion. He says, "He who loves

[12]Heb 4:12. [13]PG 56:767-68. [14]SC 254:244-46. [15]Eph 2:14. [16]2 Cor 6:15. [17]SSL 27:188. [18]Mt 10:27. [19]Gen 11:9. [20]Ps 68:30 (67:30 LXX). [21]CCL 77:73-74. [22]Mt 10:34.

father or mother more than me is not worthy of me."[23] We also read in the Song of Songs, "He established love in me."[24] We must preserve this order in all our relations. Love your father, your mother, your sons. If a time comes when love for a parent and for the children of God are in conflict and both cannot be maintained, then forthright rejection of your family may be a higher form of familial loyalty in relation to God. COMMENTARY ON MATTHEW 1.10.37.[25]

WHETHER LOVE OF PARENTS IS COMPARABLE TO THE LOVE OF GOD. CHRYSOSTOM: He said this to bring fathers to greater gentleness and children to greater freedom, just at the point where love might be most tempted to hinder them. He bids parents not to attempt what is impossible by assuming that their love of their children can be rightly compared with their love toward God. He instructs the children not to attempt what is impossible by seeking to make their love of parents greater than their love of God.

Then lest his hearers should become riled or count this saying as too demanding, see how he turns the argument even further in a more drastic direction. For after saying "who hates not father and mother," he even adds, "and his own life!" So do not compare love of God merely with love of parents, brothers and sisters and wife. If you are serious, compare it with the love of your very life. For nothing is dearer to you than your life. Yet if you are also not ready to give up this love, in all things you must bear the opposite lot. THE GOSPEL OF MATTHEW, HOMILY 35.2.[26]

LOVE YOUR FAMILY IN CHRIST. AUGUSTINE: Let a father say, "Love me." Let a mother say, "Love me." To these words I will say, "Be silent." But isn't what they are asking for just? Shouldn't I give back what I have received? The father says, "I fathered you." The mother says, "I bore you." The father says, "I educated you." The mother says, "I fed you." . . . Let us answer our father and mother when they justly say "love us." Let us answer, "I will love you in Christ, not instead of Christ. You will be with me in him, but I will not be with you without him." "But we don't care for Christ," they say. "And I care for Christ more than I care for you. Should I obey the ones who raised me and lose the One who created me?" SERMON 65A.5.[27]

10:38 Taking One's Cross

READINESS TO DIE. ANONYMOUS: The man who bears his own cross is one who, if necessary, is ready to face any danger for the sake of God, up to and including death, rather than abandon Christ. He is ready to be tortured any day, because of his way of life. Even if he does not suffer anything as great as death, he will still receive mercy. For it is the intention that is rewarded, not the deed. Intentions come from our free choice, but a deed is accomplished only through the grace of God. "He who finds his life will lose it."[28] It is better to die for God's sake and live eternally than to live for the sake of human interests and suffer eternal death. He died for us, although he was incapable of dying unless he wished to. How much more ought we to die for him, we who are mortal even if we do not wish to be? If our Lord died for his servants without even a reward, it is more than equitable that a servant should die for the Lord and be rewarded besides. INCOMPLETE WORK ON MATTHEW, HOMILY 26.[29]

10:39 Finding and Losing Life

ONE WHO LOSES LIFE WILL FIND IT. HILARY: Here the stated doctrine and its meaning run along the same course. After he commands us to abandon everything that is most valuable in earthly life, he adds, "He who does not take up

---

[23]Mt 10:37. [24]Song 2:4. [25]CCL 77:74. [26]PG 57:407; NPNF 1 10:233**. [27]RB 86:43; WSA 3 3:200. [28]Mt 10:39; Mk 8:35; Jn 12:25. [29]PG 56:769.

his cross and follow me is not worthy of me." This is because those who belong to Christ have crucified their bodies with their sinful practices and pleasures. We are unworthy of Christ if we do not take up our own cross, by which we suffer, die and are buried and resurrected together with him. Only by this pledge of faith in the Spirit will he triumph in new life in us.

"He who finds his life will lose it, and he who loses his life for my sake will find it."[30] This obviously means that through the power of the Word and separation from our old vices, we will receive spiritual profit in death and a fine exacted against our life. Therefore we must accept death in the reformation of our life. We are to fashion our vicious selves on the model of our Lord's cross, and we are to cling to an open profession of glory, even against persecutors and with disregard of things present. ON MATTHEW 10.25-26.[31]

APPROPRIATE LOVE. CHRYSOSTOM: See how great is the impairment to those who have an exaggerated love for their own life. And how great is the blessing to those who are ready to give up their lives for a well-ordered love! So he bids his disciples to be willing to give up parents, children, natural relationships, kinships, the world and even their own lives. How onerous are these injunctions! But then he immediately sets forth the greater blessings of rightly ordered love. Thus these instructions, Jesus says, are so far from harming that they in fact are of greatest benefit. It is their opposites that injure. He then counsels them, as he so often does, in accord with the very desires that they already possess. Why should you be willing to give up your life? Only because you love it inordinately. So for the very reason of loving it ordinately, you will scorn loving it inordinately, and so it will be to your advantage to the highest degree. You will then in the truest sense love your life.

Jesus does not reason in this way only in the case of the love of parents or children. He teaches the same with regard to your very life,

which is nearest to you of all. THE GOSPEL OF MATTHEW, HOMILY 35.2.[32]

ONE WHO FINDS LIFE WILL LOSE IT. CYRIL OF ALEXANDRIA: Here Jesus calls the departure of life from the body the "loss of life," speaking figuratively. "He who finds his life"[33] refers to anyone who too highly values transitory existence and as it were sells it at a profit. He will face the hands of death when he is sent to unremittable punishment and death. FRAGMENT 128.[34]

10:40 Whoever Receives You

THE MEDIATOR. HILARY: "He who receives a prophet because he is a prophet shall receive a prophet's reward."[35] He who receives a prophet receives him who dwells in the prophet, and he becomes worthy of a prophet's reward by receiving the prophet because he is a prophet. And a like reward is allotted for receiving a righteous person. One who does this becomes righteous by honoring righteousness. In this way righteousness is attained through faith, taking on mercy as its duty. This happens when someone receives a righteous person and becomes a prophet himself by reason of his own reverence. He will receive the honor due to a righteous person and a prophet. ON MATTHEW 10.28.[36]

10:41 Receiving One's Reward

RECEIVING A RIGHTEOUS PERSON'S REWARD. ORIGEN: This passage has a deeper[37] meaning. One who has properly extracted the meaning of the apostle's writing, and has not misunderstood it is receiving the apostle as well as Christ who speaks and dwells in the apostle and is the source of the apostle's teaching. And since the divine mind of the Father is also in the Son, one

[30]Mt 10:39; Mk 8:35; Jn 12:25. [31]SC 254:246-48. [32]PG 57:407-8; NPNF 1 10:234**. [33]Mt 10:39; Mk 8:35; Jn 12:25. [34]MKGK 194. [35]Mt 10:41. [36]SC 254:250. [37]Or mystical.

who receives the word "of wisdom"[38] and everything that is Christ is receiving God the Father of all things. The first part refers mystically to the new covenant, the last part to the old covenant. And if one believes that the prophets spoke wisely, not from their own understanding but because they were moved by the Holy Spirit, when one receives the meaning in them he possesses the prophetic Spirit and quite reasonably receives a prophet's reward. And if one who understands righteousness and unrighteousness (and does not live unrighteously himself) receives a righteous person, that one is not only hospitable but righteous in addition. That one receives a righteous person's reward. FRAGMENT 218.[39]

RECEIVE THE RIGHTEOUS. THEODORE OF HERACLEA: The one who receives people sent by anyone gladly honors the one who sent them, and vice versa. Or alternately: the one who receives the apostles who preach the Trinity receives "the fullness of deity"[40] itself. And I think it likely that even in our days we receive them in spirit, if we receive their counsels with an open mind. FRAGMENT 72.[41]

RECEIVE THE TRAVELING PROPHET. ANONYMOUS: By the word *prophet* he means to signify all preachers of Christ, and by "righteous man" he means every Christian person. For not only teachers may wander from city to city because of persecution but so may all righteous Christians who believe in Christ. And so "because he is a prophet" means "as a prophet of Christ." And "because he is a righteous man" means a righteous servant of Christ. Now, two things must happen if this good deed is to have its reward. You must both receive a Christian and receive that one as a Christian, whether a minister or a lay believer. But you will not receive the reward of a Christian if you do not receive a Christian, nor will you receive a reward if you receive a Christian but do not receive that one as a Christian. Thus what is the meaning of "He who

receives a prophet because he is a prophet shall receive a prophet's reward, and he who receives a righteous man because he is a righteous man shall receive a righteous man's reward"? This means that whatever reward there is for the traveler, the one who receives that traveler for God's sake will have the same reward. And so these two are made equal, both the one who suffers for God's sake and the other who gives refreshment for God's sake. INCOMPLETE WORK ON MATTHEW, HOMILY 26.[42]

10:42 A Cup of Cold Water

GIVING A CUP OF COLD WATER. HILARY: He teaches that no deed of a good conscience is useless. It is no crime for a believer to have hope that transcends another's unbelief. For he foresaw that there would be many who glory merely in the name of apostleship but whose every action proves they are unworthy. They deceive and lie perpetually. And yet when we grant these people the favors that are due them because of their mere appearance of religiosity, he does not withhold from us the reward of doing his work and of hope. For even if they are the very least, that is, the worst sinners of all—for nothing is smaller than the "least"—nonetheless he decrees that we have duties toward them. These duties are light but not useless. They are represented by the phrase "cold water." For honor is to be paid not to the sins of the individual but to his status as a disciple. He grants his reward to the faith of the one who gives, not to the deceitfulness of the one who receives. ON MATTHEW 10.29.[43]

OVERCOMING EVASIONS. JEROME: Jesus said, "He who receives you receives me." But there are many false prophets and false preachers who perhaps make this doctrine difficult. He has also cured this stumbling block by saying, "He who

---

[38]1 Cor 2:4; 12:8. [39]GCS 41.1:104. [40]Col 2:9. [41]*MKGK* 76. [42]PG 56:770. [43]SC 254:250-52.

receives a righteous man because he is a righteous man will receive a righteous man's reward."[44] Then again, someone may object and say, "I am prevented by poverty. My own lack prevents me from acting as a host." Jesus eliminated this excuse, too, by the easily fulfilled command that we should offer a cup of cold water with our whole heart. He said "cold water" rather than "hot water" so that we could not object because of our poverty or lack of fuel for hot water. As I have mentioned before, the apostle gave a similar instruction to the Galatians: "Let the one who is taught the word share all good things with the one who teaches."[45] He admonishes disciples to give refreshment to their teachers because before he had specified this, it was possible for anyone to plead poverty and avoid the instruction. He clears up this important doubt when he says, "God is not mocked, for whatever a man sows, that he will also reap."[46] Paul means "If you plead poverty but know in your conscience that the case is otherwise, your excuse accomplishes nothing. You can disobey my admonitions, but be warned that you will reap exactly what you have sown." COMMENTARY ON MATTHEW 1.10.40-42.[47]

---

[44]Mt 10:41. [45]Gal 6:6. [46]Gal 6:7. [47]CCL 77:75-76.

11:1-19 MESSENGERS FROM JOHN THE BAPTIST; JESUS SPEAKS OF JOHN

[1]And when Jesus had finished instructing his twelve disciples, he went on from there to teach and preach in their cities.

[2]Now when John heard in prison about the deeds of the Christ, he sent word by his disciples [3]and said to him, "Are you he who is to come, or shall we look for another?" [4]And Jesus answered them, "Go and tell John what you hear and see: [5]the blind receive their sight and the lame walk, lepers are cleansed and the deaf hear, and the dead are raised up, and the poor have good news preached to them. [6]And blessed is he who takes no offense at me."

[7]As they went away, Jesus began to speak to the crowds concerning John: "What did you go out into the wilderness to behold? A reed shaken by the wind? [8]Why then did you go out? To see a man[a] clothed in soft raiment? Behold, those who wear soft raiment are in kings' houses. [9]Why then did you go out? To see a prophet?[b] Yes, I tell you, and more than a prophet. [10]This is he of whom it is written,

'Behold, I send my messenger before thy face,
who shall prepare thy way before thee.'

[11]Truly, I say to you, among those born of women there has risen no one greater than John the Baptist; yet he who is least in the kingdom of heaven is greater than he. [12]From the days of John the Baptist until now the kingdom of heaven has suffered violence,[c] and men of violence take it by force. [13]For all the prophets and the law prophesied until John; [14]and if you are willing to accept it, he is Elijah who is to come. [15]He who has ears to hear,[d] let him hear.

^{16}*"But to what shall I compare this generation? It is like children sitting in the market places and calling to their playmates,*

^{17}*'We piped to you, and you did not dance;*
we wailed, and you did not mourn.'

^{18}*For John came neither eating nor drinking, and they say, 'He has a demon';* ^{19}*the Son of man came eating and drinking, and they say, 'Behold, a glutton and a drunkard, a friend of tax collectors and sinners!' Yet wisdom is justified by her deeds."*^{e}

a *Or What then did you go out to see? A man* . . .   b *Other ancient authorities read What then did you go out to see? A prophet?*   c *Or has been coming violently*   d *Other ancient authorities omit to hear*   e *Other ancient authorities read children* (Lk 7.35)

OVERVIEW: After commissioning the apostles, Jesus proceeded to separate himself from them, to give them room and opportunity to do what he had called them to do (CHRYSOSTOM). When John was about to be killed by Herod, he sent his disciples to Christ, intending that when they met him, they would believe in him (JEROME, HILARY). Why did John send his disciples to ask a question he was already able to answer (GREGORY THE GREAT)? It is hardly conceivable that John was ignorant about the Christ (THEODORE OF MOPSUESTIA). Was it that John was rather asking more specifically about whether he was destined to precede Jesus in his ministry into the nether world (GREGORY THE GREAT)? Anyone who is to know Christ must know him personally (THEODORE OF MOPSUESTIA).

The Fathers offered various spiritual interpretations of this passage. As the law had announced Christ, predicted the forgiveness of sins and promised the kingdom of heaven, so John thoroughly accomplished all of this work. When the law's embodiment was oppressed in prison, he sent a mission out to behold the good news (HILARY). Jesus answered nothing directly concerning his identity but left them to discern it from the miracles (CHRYSOSTOM). Jesus replied to John's disciples: "You will be blessed if you take no offense at me" (ANONYMOUS). Jesus defended John, signifying that he had not fallen away from his former confidence, nor had he changed his mind (CHRYSOSTOM). Remember that you did not go out into the wilderness to see a man like a reed who is blown about by

every wind, so irresolute that he cannot make up his mind about what he previously predicted (JEROME). John is not a reed bending with each slight breeze of approval or rumor (GREGORY THE GREAT, ANONYMOUS). John had already borne witness to Christ and in so doing received more from Christ than he gave. When John glorified Christ, he conferred human praise upon him; but Christ conferred divine glory on John (ANONYMOUS). John is described as a messenger or an angel (JEROME). One is angelic who with his human nature passes into angelic holiness and attains by the grace of God what is not his by nature. Insofar as John was a man and yet called an angel, he was more glorious than if he had been an angel both in name and nature (ANONYMOUS). Having said that he is greater than a prophet, Jesus signified in what way he is greater. In being so very near the One who was to come (CHRYSOSTOM), John attested the One who was born from a woman yet existed prior to the woman (ANONYMOUS). Any saint present with God in heaven is greater than one who remains in the battle (JEROME). Compared with all born of women, John is the greatest, but compared with those who partake of the Spirit in the kingdom of heaven, John will be found to be the least (THEODORE OF MOPSUESTIA).

The glory pledged to Israel by the patriarchs, which the prophets announced and Christ offered, is now being seized and carried off by the Gentiles (HILARY). Some continue to seek to force their way into heaven by the merit of their works (JEROME). In saying that people of violence would try to take the kingdom by force, Jesus is thinking of a kind of Jewish legalism that did not believe in the way of Christ but also stood in others' way (CYRIL OF ALEXANDRIA). "The days of John" are understood not chronologically in reference to time but in reference to the state of the soul in readiness to hear the divine Scripture (ORIGEN). John the Baptist is called Elijah because he came in the spirit and goodness of Elijah and had the same grace and power of the Holy Spirit (JEROME, APOLLINARIS, THEODORE OF MOPSUESTIA). Just as when some children are dancing and others are singing a dirge, so the Jews underwent such an experience. They accepted neither the vigor of John nor the freedom of Christ (CYRIL OF ALEXANDRIA, JEROME).

11:1 Instructing the Disciples

HE WENT ON FROM THERE. CHRYSOSTOM: After Jesus commissioned the apostles, he proceeded to separate himself from them, to give them room and opportunity to do what he had called them to do. For while he was present with them and healing others, no one would be inclined to approach them. THE GOSPEL OF MATTHEW, HOMILY 36.1.[1]

11:2 John Sends His Disciples to Jesus

JOHN REPRESENTS THE ACCOMPLISHED LAW, NOW IMPRISONED. HILARY: A fuller spiritual meaning is to be found in these actions, which were being accomplished in and through John. Here we behold the efficient power of John's embodied action and also the grace manifest in John. As announced in prophecy: the law rose up and took shape in John.[2] For the law announced Christ, predicted the forgiveness of sins and promised the kingdom of heaven. John thoroughly accomplished all this work that belonged to the law. Therefore when the law (i.e., John) was inactive, oppressed as it was by the sins of the common people and held in

chains by the vicious habits of the nation, so that Christ could not be perceived, the law (represented by John) was confined by chains and the prison. But the law (i.e., John) sent others to behold the good news. In this way unbelief would be confronted with the accomplished truth of what had been prophesied. By this means the part of the law that had been chained[3] by the misdeeds of sinners would now be freed through the understanding of the good news freely expressed. ON MATTHEW 11.2.[4]

JOHN SENT WORD BY HIS DISCIPLES. THEODORE OF MOPSUESTIA: About this text, some will argue, "When John sent his disciples, he was neither ignorant himself nor did he mean for them to learn, which seems clear to anyone who has entered to a certain extent into the meaning of the holy Scriptures." But this is foolish, because when John was about to die and join the departed, he sent them to ask whether he was the one who was to come and free those who had been vanquished by death.[5] In this way the good news was delivered to his disciples as well.[6] John had already said, "Behold, the Lamb of God, who takes away the sin of the world."[7] He already knew very well that the Messiah would offer his suffering up to God for the sake of all humanity. Certainly, if John indeed knew that Jesus was the Christ, he was not ignorant of the Christ. On the contrary, he knew exactly what benefits were to come to humanity through him. John might seem to be telling different people different things in different contexts. Isn't it true that John had so much knowledge about Christ that he said a great deal about him to various people? Isn't it true that in accordance with the

---

[1]PG 57:413; NPNF 1 10:238*. [2]Mt 3:3; cf. Is 40:3. [3]As John was now in chains in prison. [4]SC 254:252-54. [5]The descent into hell is perhaps implied. [6]According to one interpretation found in Origen and Gregory the Great, among others (cf. D. Sheerin, *Vigilae Christianae* 30 [1976]: 1ff.), John the Baptist announced the coming of Christ even in hell. Theodore, along with Chrysostom and others, repeats this interpretation merely to deny and confute it. [7]Jn 1:29.

greater part of what John had said in his own testimony, he recognized Jesus as the deliverer of good news? It is hardly conceivable that John was ignorant about the Christ but now was guessing and wanted to find out for sure from him. That would be inconsistent. And who would, in the attempt to discover something so great, send along his disciples as if they were competent in themselves to teach and witness?

There is another point being made here. The present life is the time when we must conduct ourselves responsibly. After death there is judgment and punishment. However, Christ's death did not universally redeem the sins of all those who had already died. For when it is said that the bronze gates and iron bars were shattered, this is said because the body of Christ then appeared immortal for the first time and death was shown to be defeated. What does this mean, then? Were all people unrighteous before the coming of Christ? Not at all. Before Christ it was enough to refrain from idolatry and to worship the one true God in order to be saved. But now that alone is not enough. We must also know Christ personally. And so we must not imagine that someone will confess to Christ in hell, where even if all repent, no one is comforted. FRAGMENT 57.[8]

11:3 Shall We Look for Another?

ARE YOU HE WHO IS TO COME? JEROME: John asks this not because he is ignorant[9] but to guide others who are ignorant and to say to them, "Behold, the Lamb of God, who takes away the sin of the world!"[10] And he had heard the voice of the Father saying, "This is my beloved Son, with whom I am well pleased."[11] Rather, it is the same sort of question as when the Savior asked where Lazarus was buried. The people only meant to show him the tomb, but he wanted them to be brought to faith and see the dead man return to life. Similarly, when John was about to be killed by Herod, he sent his disciples to Christ, intending that when they met him,

the disciples would observe his appearance and powers and believe in him, and they would tell this to their teacher when he questioned them. COMMENTARY ON MATTHEW 2.11.3.[12]

FORERUNNER EVEN INTO HELL. GREGORY THE GREAT: It seems almost as if John did not know the one he had pointed out, as if he did not know whether he was the same person he had proclaimed by prophesying, by baptizing, by pointing him out!

We can resolve this question more quickly if we reflect on the time and order of the events. For when John is standing beside the river Jordan, he declares that this is the Redeemer of the world. But when he has been thrown into jail, he asks whether they were to look for another or whether he had come. This is not because he doubts that he is the Redeemer of the world. John now wants to know whether he who had personally come into the world would also descend personally into the courts of hell. For John had preceded Christ into the world and announced him there. He was now dying and preceding him to the nether world. This is the context in which he asks, "Are you he who is to come, or shall we look for another?" But if he had spoken more fully he might have said, "Since you thought it worthy of yourself to be born for humanity, say whether you will also think it worthy of yourself to die for humanity. In this way I, who have been the herald of your birth, will also be the herald of your death. I will announce your arrival in the nether world as the One who is to come, just as I have already announced it on earth." FORTY GOSPEL HOMILIES 6.1.[13]

---

[8]*MKGK* 115. [9]These words of John the Baptist suggest that he was unsure of the identity of Jesus, but in the Gospel of John he immediately demonstrates his knowledge of Christ's superiority. In the following passages various interpretations are proposed that aim to resolve this difficulty. [10]Jn 1:29. [11]Mt 3:17. [12]CCL 77:77. [13]PL 76:1095-96; CS 123:28-29** (Homily 5). Why did John send his disciples to ask a question he was already able to answer? John was rather asking more specifically about whether he was destined to precede Jesus in his ministry into the nether world.

11:4-5 *Jesus Responds to John*

WHAT YOU SEE AND HEAR. ANONYMOUS: And then consider whether their words are at one with their feelings. Now as it first appears, John asks Christ through his disciples, "Are you he who is to come, or shall we look for another?"[14] John was actually saying to his disciples, "Go, look, and believe; for this is none other than he who was to come." Similarly, as it first appears, Christ answered John by saying, "Go and tell John this: the blind receive their sight and the deaf hear; and blessed is he who takes no offense at me."[15] He was actually saying to John's disciples, "Look here, see and understand that the blind receive their sight and the deaf hear; and you will be blessed if you take no offense at me."

What then is the meaning of "what you see and hear"? As Luke says, the Lord knew that these disciples would come from John. And at that time, he was preparing a worthy meal for a multitude of guests, good people. In this way, even though Christ was silent, his works would tell of him,[16] for those who had been cured were thanking him. Some said, "We never saw anything like this in Israel."[17] And others said, "God has visited his people with goodness."[18] Others said, "Glory be to God, who has given such authority to humans."[19] And so the disciples of John would feast their eyes and ears, seeing the miracles of healing and hearing the voices of those who thanked him; or at least seeing miracles done by him and hearing his teaching; or at the very least seeing the good health of those who had been sick and hearing the testimony of those from whom demons had been cast out. INCOMPLETE WORK ON MATTHEW, HOMILY 27.[20]

11:6 *One Who Takes No Offense*

THE POOR RECEIVE GOOD NEWS. HILARY: And when the Lord had shown forth all of himself in miraculous works, in giving sight to the blind, the power of walking to the lame, cleans-ing to the lepers, hearing to the deaf, voices to the mute, life to the dead and preaching to the poor, he said, "Blessed is the one who takes no offense at me." Now, had anything really been done through Christ that would cause John to take offense? Not in the least. For John himself also spent his time in his own teaching and work. However, one ought to look to a higher meaning that is both powerful and fitting. What does it mean that the poor have good news preached to them? Poor people are those who have abandoned their lives, who have taken up his cross and followed, who have been made humble in spirit. For such the kingdom of heaven is prepared. Because all experiences of this kind come together in the Lord and because his cross was to be a source of offense to many, he declared that people are blessed if their faith is not threatened by a cross or death or burial. ON MATTHEW 11.3.[21]

BLESSED IS ONE WHO TAKES NO OFFENSE. CHRYSOSTOM: Jesus knew the mind of John who sent them, for he knew, as God knows, our inner thoughts. There he was, actively healing the blind, lame, and many others. He healed not to teach John, who was already convinced, but those who had come to him doubting. Having healed them he said, "Go and tell John what you hear and see: the blind receive their sight and the lame walk, lepers are cleansed and the deaf hear, and the dead are raised up, and the poor have good news preached to them." And then he added pointedly, "And blessed is the one who takes no offense at me." By saying this Jesus implied that he knew even his questioners' unuttered thoughts. For if he had said simply "I am he," this would have fallen short of overcoming their unstated sense of being offended. And it would have given fuel to some Jews who were already saying to him, "You bear record of yourself."[22] Hence he answered nothing directly con-

---

[14]Mt 11:3. [15]Mt 11:4-6. [16]Lk 7:20-21. [17]Mt 9:33; Mk 2:12. [18]Lk 7:16. [19]Mt 9:8. [20]PG 56:772-73. [21]SC 254:254. [22]Jn 8:13.

cerning his identity but left them to learn of it from the miracles, freeing what he taught from suspicion and making it plainer. Then Jesus gently chided them for being silently offended in him. He made their case for them, leaving it to their own conscience alone to judge, calling no witness of his reprimand other than they themselves who knew what they had been thinking. For it was of their own inward offense that he was thinking when he said, "Blessed is the one who takes no offense at me." In this way Christ drew them all the more closely to himself. THE GOSPEL OF MATTHEW, HOMILY 36.2.[23]

11:7 Jesus Speaks About John

AS THEY WENT AWAY. CHRYSOSTOM: Why "as they went away"? That he might not seem to be flattering John. And in correcting John's disciples, Jesus does not broadcast their suspicion. He merely provides a remedy for the thoughts that were mentally disturbing them. This made it clear to them that he knew the secrets of all. For he did not say, as he might have to the other religious leaders, "Why are you thinking evil?" For if John's disciples had doubt in their minds it was not out of wickedness but out of ignorance. So Jesus does not rebuke them but merely corrects their understanding. He then defends John, signifying that he had not fallen away from his former confidence, nor had he changed his mind. For John was not a man easily swayed and fickle but steadfast and sure. He was far from being such as to betray the things committed to him. THE GOSPEL OF MATTHEW, HOMILY 37.1.[24]

THE WEAKNESS OF THE REED. GREGORY THE GREAT: He did not expect assent to this but denial. As soon as a slight breeze blows on a reed it bends away. What does the reed represent if not an unspiritual soul? As soon as it is touched by praise or slander, it turns in every direction. If a slight breeze of commendation comes from someone's mouth, it is cheerful and proud, and it bends completely, so to speak, toward being pleasant. But if a gust of slander comes from the source from which the breeze of praise was coming, it is quickly turned in the opposite direction, toward raving anger. John was no reed, shaken by the wind. No one's pleasant attitude made him agreeable, and no one's anger made him bitter. FORTY GOSPEL HOMILIES 6.2.[25]

11:8 Why Did You Go Out?

SOFT RAIMENT BELONGS IN KINGS' HOUSES. JEROME: If the Lord had intended a higher meaning unfavorable to John, as many imagine that he did, in saying "Blessed is the one who takes no offense at me," why does he now speak about John with highest praise? Because the crowd that was present did not know the inner purpose of John's question. They thought John doubted Christ, although he himself had prophesied about him. Now the crowd learns that John asked not on his own behalf but on that of his disciples. "Why did you go out into the wilderness?" To see a man like a reed who is blown about by every wind, a man so irresolute that he cannot make up his mind about what he himself previously predicted? Or else, perhaps he is pricked by the goad of his envy for me, and his preaching runs after an empty fame, and he covets the money he may get by it? But why should this man desire wealth for abundance of feasting? He feeds on locusts and wild honey. Or wealth to wear soft clothes? His clothes are made of camel's hair. But people who are flatterers, and run after money, and covet wealth, and overflow with luxury and wear soft clothes—such people live in the palaces of kings. Thus it is shown that the austere way of life and the strict preaching must avoid the halls of kings

---

[23]PG 57:415; NPNF 1 10:239-40**. [24]PG 57:419; NPNF 1 10:243**. [25]PL 76:1096; CS 123:30* (Homily 5). John's preaching of repentance was not shaped by what he thought other people would think of him.

and turn away from the palaces of the luxurious. COMMENTARY ON MATTHEW 2.11.6.[26]

A MAN CLOTHED IN SOFT RAIMENT. ANONYMOUS: "What did you go out into the wilderness to behold? A man clothed in soft raiment?" A lover of present pleasure who gladly made use of the earthly goods of the present. Didn't you see that his garment was of camels' hair, and he wore a leather girdle around his waist? And his food was locusts and wild honey. Thus by the testimony of his own way of life, Jesus condemned the world and its goods; yet he remained steadfastly in the world. However, he entered the world not in order to remain in it himself but to challenge the idolatry of the world's riches. Jesus was born in the world, but he turned aside from the goods of the world. Again, although he was born in the world, he did not remain in it as a sinner; instead, in converting sinners to righteousness, he freed them from the world. For this wicked world has many pleasures with which to seduce people. INCOMPLETE WORK ON MATTHEW, HOMILY 27.[27]

11:9 More Than a Prophet

THE TASK OF A PROPHET. ANONYMOUS: "Yes, I tell you, and more than a prophet." Now, it is the task of a prophet to foretell Christ. But was it also the task of a prophet to recognize God while he was still implanted in the womb? It is the task of a prophet to receive prophecy in exchange for a worthy way of life and faith. But was it the task of a prophet to be made a prophet before being made a man and before receiving any reward? It is the task of a prophet to receive blessing from God. But is it the task of a prophet to confer the blessing of baptism on God? It is the task of a prophet to speak of Christ before his time. But is it the task of a prophet to stand face to face with Christ and point him out with his finger? It is the task of a prophet to give prophecies about God. But is it

the task of a prophet that God should make prophecies about the prophet himself, as when he says, "Behold, I send my messenger before your face?"[28]

"This is he of whom it is written, 'Behold, I send my messenger before your face.'"[29] He now begins to tell the reasons why the blessed John was more than a prophet—from such a One John did deserve praise. Now John had borne witness to Christ, "Behold, the Lamb of God."[30] But he received more from Christ than he gave. For when John glorified Christ, he conferred human praise on him; but Christ conferred divine glory on John. For John spoke of Christ as a Lamb, but when Christ foretold John he spoke of him as an angel. And John did not praise Christ in full measure, for Christ not only took away the sin of the world but also granted eternal life to the world. But Christ exalted John higher than he appeared; John was a man, but Christ called him an angel. INCOMPLETE WORK ON MATTHEW, HOMILY 27.[31]

11:10 A Messenger to Prepare the Way

I SEND MY MESSENGER BEFORE YOUR FACE. JEROME: John is greater than the other prophets for this reason: the other prophets predicted to John that someone was to come, but John pointed out with his finger that he had indeed come, saying, "Behold, the Lamb of God, who takes away the sins of the world."[32] And he reached not only the rank of a prophet but even to that of Baptist, by baptizing his Lord. This heightened his significance. He thereby fulfilled the prophecy of Malachi in which an angel is foretold.[33] John belonged to the order of the angels not by nature but by the importance of his task. It means he was the messenger who would announce the coming of the Lord. COMMENTARY ON MATTHEW 2.11.9.[34]

---

[26]CCL 77:78-79. [27]PG 56:773-74. [28]Lk 7:27. [29]Mt 11:10; Mal 3:1. [30]Jn 1:29. [31]PG 56:774. [32]Jn 1:29. [33]Mal 3:1. [34]CCL 77:79.

221

HOW JOHN IS GREATER THAN A PROPHET.
CHRYSOSTOM: But suppose someone might say, "What if John had one opinion earlier but later changed his mind?" This is why Jesus spoke further about his garments, his imprisonment and his role in prophecy. Having said that he is greater than a prophet, Jesus signifies also in what way he is greater. And in what is he greater? In being so very near the One who was to come. For "behold, I send," he says, "my messenger before your face," which means in proximity to Messiah. For as with kings, those who ride near the chariot are more illustrious than the rest, just so John also appears in his course near the advent itself. THE GOSPEL OF MATTHEW, HOMILY 37.2.[35]

MY MESSENGER WILL PREPARE THE WAY.
ANONYMOUS: Listen now and learn the real meaning of this. If it is not too bold to say so, I believe that insofar as John was a man and yet was called an angel because of his strength and his merit, he was more glorious than if he had been an angel both in name and nature. If an angel is called an angel, that is not so much a tribute to his merit as merely fitting to his nature. A man is miraculous, however, if with his human nature he passes into angelic holiness and attains by the grace of God what is not his by nature. INCOMPLETE WORK ON MATTHEW, HOMILY 27.[36]

11:11 The Least in the Kingdom Greater Than John

AMONG THOSE BORN OF WOMEN. ANONYMOUS: It is one thing to be generically the son of a woman, another thing to be [in Paul's sense] a man "born of woman."[37] A man such as John who is the son of a woman was born in a woman and had his origin in the woman and did not exist prior to the woman. But the unique man "born of woman" is not necessarily born initially in the woman. Christ, as we know, was a man "born of woman," but as to what is being said here, John—the man spoken of—is the son of a

woman. Christ was "born of woman" and yet existed prior to the woman. Therefore every son of a woman is born of a woman, but not every man born of a woman is the son of a woman. And thus Paul did not say that Jesus was "among the sons of women" because that would mix him in with the generic category of all sons.

Moreover, the Scripture does not say that John was greater than the other saints but that "no one greater than John has arisen." The text makes him equal to the others, not superior. However, righteousness is so deep that no one can be perfect in it except God alone. I think that in God's own keen judgment, each of the saints may be viewed individually as greater or lesser. From this we conclude that if no one is greater than John, he is therefore greater than them all. INCOMPLETE WORK ON MATTHEW, HOMILY 27.[38]

THE LEAST IN THE KINGDOM. THEODORE OF MOPSUESTIA: If John is being judged against other people according to being born from a woman, he will be found to be the greatest of them all. He alone was filled with the Holy Spirit inside his mother's womb, so that he "leaped,"[39] and his mother prophesied because she partook in this as well. But if John is judged in relation to those who are to partake of the Spirit in the kingdom of heaven, Jesus says, he will be found to be least. Thus Jesus says that John by no means partakes of such great grace as those who will be reborn into immortality after Jesus' resurrection from the dead and that John will experience physical death. At that time, however, the Spirit's abundance toward people will be so great that no one who has partaken of even the least part of it can afterward fall into death. FRAGMENT 59.[40]

ALREADY SERVING GOD IN HEAVEN. JEROME: "Yet he who is least in the kingdom of heaven is

---

[35]PG 57:420-21; NPNF 1 10:244**. [36]PG 56:774. [37]Gal 4:4. [38]PG 56:775. [39]Lk 1:41. [40]MKGK 116.

greater than he." Now, many would like to interpret this with reference to the Savior, as meaning that the one lesser in age is the greater in worth. However, let us interpret it simply to mean that every saint who is already with God is greater than anyone who remains expectant, as yet in the battle. For it is one thing to possess the crown of victory, another to be still fighting in the ranks. Some conclude that the very newest angel who serves God in heaven is greater than any one, even the best, who dwells on the earth still in expectation. COMMENTARY ON MATTHEW 2.11.11.[41]

JESUS IS THE KINGDOM. ORIGEN: The kingdom of heaven is Jesus the Christ himself, who exhorts all people to repentance and draws them to himself by love. FRAGMENT 226.[42]

11:12 The Kingdom Suffers Violence

THE KINGDOM OF HEAVEN. HILARY: What violence? People did not believe in John the Baptist. The works of Christ were held to be of no importance. His torment on the cross was a stumbling block. "Until now" prophecy has been dormant. But now the law is fulfilled. Every prediction is finished. The spirit of Elijah is sent in advance through John's words. Christ is proclaimed to some and acknowledged by others. He is born for some and loved by others. The violent irony is that his own people rejected him, while strangers accepted him. His own people speak ill of him, while his enemies embrace him. The act of adoption offers an inheritance, while the family rejects it. Sons refuse to accept their father's last will, while the slaves of the household receive it. This is what is meant by the phrase "the kingdom of heaven suffers violence." Earlier expectations are being torn apart. The glory that was pledged to Israel by the patriarchs, which was announced by the prophets and which was offered by Christ, is now being seized and carried off by the Gentiles, through their faith. ON MATTHEW 11.7.[43]

11:13 All the Law and the Prophets

FROM THE DAYS OF JOHN UNTIL NOW. ORIGEN: "The days of John" and of Jesus are understood not in reference to time but in reference to the state of the soul of the hearer of the divine Scripture. And the word now marks out clearly the days of Jesus, which the psalm points to in this way: "In his days righteousness shall arise, and there will be an abundance of peace till the time when he is taken away."[44] One who has been previously taught comes to the beginning of Jesus' discourses and still makes progress in introductory things by way of that road that appears to be rugged and steep. One thereby "takes by force" the kingdom of heaven, which "suffers violence." The expression "suffers violence" is not to be taken in an active sense but a passive, as if to say "it has been taken."[45] But if the perfect Word, when he receives someone who was awaiting freedom under the law and prophetic schoolmasters and housekeepers, bestows on such a one his father's inheritance freely, then fittingly it is said that "all the prophets and the law prophesied until John." FRAGMENT 227.[46]

ALL THE PROPHETS AND THE LAW. JEROME: This should not exclude the prophets who came after John the Baptist, for we read in the Acts of the Apostles that Agabus and Philip's four young unmarried daughters uttered prophecies.[47] But insofar as the law and prophets of the Scriptures looked toward the future, they prophesied about our Lord. So when it is written, "All the prophets and the law up to the time of John have prophesied,"[48] the time of Christ is made known as those previous voices had said it would come. Then John showed he had come. COMMENTARY ON MATTHEW 2.11.13.[49]

---

[41]CCL 77:80. [42]GCS 41.1:107. [43]SC 254:260. [44]Ps 72:7 (71:7 LXX); the LXX has "the moon" for "he." [45]Origen's observation reveals the uncertainty as to whether the verb biazetai should be understood in the active or the passive, which he himself contends and is the normal modern interpretation. [46]GCS 41.1:108. [47]Acts 21:8-11. [48]Mt 11:13. [49]CCL 77:80-81.

11:14 *Elijah Who Is to Come*

HE IS ELIJAH. APOLLINARIS: He called John Elijah because of Elijah's power and spirit. And since this statement of Jesus was obscure, he left the understanding of it for those capable of perceiving its meaning. But the angel Gabriel also said this about John: "And he shall go before him in the spirit and power of Elijah,"[50] showing that he was the same as Elijah, even if, as a visible human being, he was other than Elijah. FRAGMENTS 62-63.[51]

A NEW STATE. THEODORE OF MOPSUESTIA: Jesus is in effect saying: Just as Elijah will come toward the end of this present age preaching about my imminent appearance from heaven, in the same way this one[52] has spread the good news of my coming,[53] bringing an end to the old things.[54] My coming is something new, a type of the state of things that is about to occur. FRAGMENT 61.[55]

HE CAME IN THE SPIRIT OF ELIJAH. JEROME: So John the Baptist is called Elijah, not in accordance with foolish philosophers and certain heretics who introduce the topic of metempsychosis (transmigration of souls)[56] but because, according to other evidence of the gospel, he came in the spirit and goodness of Elijah and had either the same grace or power of the Holy Spirit. The austerity of their life and firm resolve were equally strong in Elijah and in John. Both lived in the desert. The former girded himself with a belt of skins, and the latter had a similar belt. The former was forced to flee because he accused Ahab and Jezebel of the sin of impiety in their lives. John was beheaded because he accused Herod and Herodias of unlawful marriage. There are those who think therefore that John is called Elijah because, just as Elijah would lead the way in the second coming of our Savior (according to Malachi) and would announce that the Judge was coming, so John acted at the first coming and because each was a

messenger either of the first or second coming of our Lord. COMMENTARY ON MATTHEW 2.11.15.[57]

11:15 *Ears to Hear*

LET PEOPLE HEAR. CHRYSOSTOM: Jesus did not stop even at this praise of John but said, "He is Elijah who is to come." Then he added, to underscore the need for deeper understanding, "He who has ears to hear, let him hear." Jesus said this to stir them up to inquire further. By this they were awakened so that everything might be plain and clear. Thus no one could claim that Jesus was unapproachable or that they did not dare ask him questions. For they were asking all sorts of questions and testing him in many small matters. Even when their mouths were stopped a thousand times, they did not turn away from him. For if they did not hesitate to inquire of him about these common things, they surely would be inquiring about indispensable things in whatever way they wanted to learn. In this way he himself was encouraging them and drawing them on to ask such questions. THE GOSPEL OF MATTHEW, HOMILY 37.3.[58]

11:16 *Like Children in the Marketplace*

A METAPHOR OF THE GENERATION. JEROME: The comparison of children sitting in the marketplace, shouting and saying to their peers, "We sang for you and you did not dance, we lamented and you did not mourn" is made with that generation of Jews in mind. Recall the Scripture that says, "To what will I compare this generation? It is like the children sitting in the marketplace," and the rest. We are not offered a

---

[50]Lk 1:17. [51]*MKGK* 18. [52]John the Baptist. [53]In the time of Christ it was a common belief among the Jews that Elijah would return to earth to announce the coming of the Messiah before the end of the world. [54]Putting a conclusion to the things of the old covenant. [55]*MKGK* 116. [56]As though the soul of Elijah had occupied the body of John the Baptist. [57]CCL 77:81-82. [58]PG 57:422; NPNF 1 10:245-46**.

complete understanding or a shared interpretation of allegory. But whatever we say about children should be related to their comparison with "this generation." Those children who are sitting in the marketplace are the ones of whom the prophet Isaiah speaks: "Behold, I and my children, whom God has given me."[59] And also the psalm: "The testimony of God is faithful, giving wisdom to children."[60] And elsewhere: "Out of the mouth of babies and sucklings you have achieved glory."[61] So those children sat in the marketplace or in the *agora*, which is described in Greek more plainly as where there are many items for sale. Because the Jews did not want to listen, the children not only spoke but shouted to them, at the top of their voices: "We sang to you, and you did not dance." We challenged you to do good deeds at the sound of our song and to dance to our flute, just as David danced before the ark of the Lord, and you did not want to. "We lamented" and we challenged you to seek repentance, and you did not want to do even this, rejecting both proclamations, which were an exhortation as much to goodness as to repentance after committing a sin. It is no wonder you have despised the dual path to salvation since you scorned poverty and wealth alike. If you are pleased with poverty, why did John displease you? If wealth pleases you, why did the Son of Man displease you? You called one of these a man with a demon, the other a glutton and a drunkard. Therefore, because you did not want to accept either teaching, "wisdom has been vindicated by her children," that is, the direction and teaching of God. I, who am the glory of God and the wisdom of God, have been acknowledged to have acted justly by my sons, the apostles, to whom my Father unveiled what he had hidden from wise, experienced people. COMMENTARY ON MATTHEW 2.11.16.[62]

11:17 Piping but No Dancing

THE DISSONANCE OF DANCING AND LAMENTING. CYRIL OF ALEXANDRIA: When some children are dancing and others are singing a dirge, their purpose does not agree. Both sides find fault with their friends for not being in harmony with them. So the Jews underwent such an experience when they accepted neither the gloominess of John the Baptist nor the freedom of Christ. They did not receive help one way or another. It was fitting for John as a lowly servant to deaden the passions of the body through very hardy training, and for Christ by the power of his Godhead freely to mortify the sensations of the body and the innate practice of the flesh, and to do so without reliance on strenuous ascetic labors. Nevertheless John, "while he was preaching the baptism of repentance,"[63] offered himself as a model for those who were obliged to lament, whereas the Lord "who was preaching the kingdom of heaven"[64] similarly displayed radiant freedom in himself. In this way Jesus outlined for the faithful indescribable joy and an untroubled life. The sweetness of the kingdom of heaven is like a flute. The pain of Gehenna is like a dirge. FRAGMENTS 142-43.[65]

11:18-19 Wisdom Known by Its Deeds

CAUSE DISTINGUISHED FROM EFFECT. HILARY: "Wisdom has been vindicated by her children."[66] Those who resist the kingdom of heaven tear apart heaven itself in attempting to justify themselves. The action of Wisdom is just, because she has transferred her gift from the obstinate and faithless to the faithful and obedient covenant people. However, it is useful in this place to consider carefully the virtue of the remark "Wisdom has been proved right by her actions," which Jesus certainly said about himself. For Jesus is Wisdom itself not because of his acts of power but by his very nature.[67]

---

[59]Is 8:18. [60]Ps 19:7 (18:7 LXX). [61]Ps 8:2. [62]CCL 77:82-83. [63]Mk 1:4; Lk 3:3. [64]Mt 4:23; 9:35; 24:14. [65]MKGK 198. [66]Mt 11:19; cf. Lk 7:35. [67]Christ, as the Son of God preexisting the incarnation, is by nature—in addition to the Logos—the divine Wisdom. Thus the cosmological function of the Old Testament Wisdom of Proverbs 8 (cf. 1 Cor 1:24) applies to him.

Everything has capability, but capability is demonstrated in actions. Thus an act of goodness is not the same as goodness itself, just as an effect is distinguishable from its cause. ON MATTHEW 9.9.[68]

JOHN CAME, AND THE SON CAME. THEODORE OF MOPSUESTIA: Those who were looking for the truth, he says, accepted the leadership of John and of Christ. It changed their lives. They managed this wisdom for the benefit of those who were searching. He calls the things that have happened wisely, wisdom. The Jews did not believe in Christ, either through the fasting and ascetic life of John or through the submissive mode of life and providential citizenship of Christ the Lord himself. Still, he who fulfilled everything wisely by neglecting none of those

things that contributed to their profit and salvation was judged harshly by them. And no longer hereafter could they accuse him, because Jesus fulfilled all his promises and did not leave behind for them a shadow either of unkindness or of ingratitude. FRAGMENT 62.[69]

THE LIVING WISDOM. THEODORE OF HERACLEA: Christ himself was judged by those who believed in him to be the living, foundational wisdom, who managed everything justly. Although he was treated spitefully by the unbelieving Jews, he did not stop speaking kindly to the Jews and calling them to be his children. FRAGMENT 77.[70]

---

[68]SC 254:262. [69]MKGK 117. [70]MKGK 77.

11:20-24 THE UNBELIEVING TOWNS

[20]*Then he began to upbraid the cities where most of his mighty works had been done, because they did not repent.* [21]*"Woe to you, Chorazin! woe to you, Beth-saida! for if the mighty works done in you had been done in Tyre and Sidon, they would have repented long ago in sackcloth and ashes.* [22]*But I tell you, it shall be more tolerable on the day of judgment for Tyre and Sidon than for you.* [23]*And you, Caperna-um, will you be exalted to heaven? You shall be brought down to Hades. For if the mighty works done in you had been done in Sodom, it would have remained until this day.* [24]*But I tell you that it shall be more tolerable on the day of judgment for the land of Sodom than for you."*

OVERVIEW: At Bethsaida and Capernaum the mute praised the Lord with their voices, the blind saw, the deaf heard, the lame ran about, the dead came alive, yet such great miracles did not produce any enduring disposition to faith (HILARY) or even repentance (JEROME). These cities were found to be not only as bad as other current cities but as bad as any that ever existed

(CHRYSOSTOM). Because of those miracles Jesus said that Capernaum had been raised up to heaven, but because of their lack of faith their fall to hell was all the more dramatic. Similar miracles might have happened in Tyre and Sidon, or even in Sodom and Gomorrah, if they had come to repent (THEODORE OF HERACLEA). Jesus spoke harshly so as to use every possible means to reclaim them to repentance (CHRYSOS-TOM).

11:20-22 Woes Pronounced on the Towns

EVEN AFTER MIRACLES THEY DID NOT REPENT. JEROME: Our Savior laments Chorazin and Bethsaida, cities of Galilee, because after such great miracles and acts of goodness they did not repent. Even Tyre and Sidon, cities that surrendered to idolatry and other vices, are preferred to them. Tyre and Sidon are preferred for the reason that although they trampled down the law, still Chorazin and Bethsaida, after they transgressed natural and written law, cared little for the miracles that were performed among them. If we ask where it is written that our Lord performed miracles in Chorazin and Bethsaida, we read above: "And he went around to all the towns and villages, curing every infirmity" and the rest. Thus among the other towns and villages it must be judged that the Lord performed miracles in Chorazin and Bethsaida as well. COMMENTARY ON MATTHEW 2.11.22.[1]

11:23 Mighty Works Done

EXALTED TO HEAVEN? JEROME: This means one of two things. You will sink to hell for the reason that you most arrogantly opposed my prophecy. Or, although you have received so much privilege in being raised to heaven by my kind generosity, by my miracles and by my acts of goodness, even then you will be battered by a greater punishment because you did not care to believe them. COMMENTARY ON MATTHEW 2.11.23.[2]

BROUGHT DOWN TO HADES. THEODORE OF HERACLEA: Many were the miracles Jesus performed in the city of Capernaum. For this reason it was all the more necessary that those who dwelled there should believe. This city was for a time "lifted up unto heaven" on account of the miracles. But on account of the sin and unbelief of its inhabitants, an even more dreadful fall occurred, and they were "brought down to Hades." Christ was the steward. When the time was right, the Word became incarnate and performed miracles. He chastised Gentiles and Jews proportionately. Tyre and Sidon transgressed only natural law, but the Jews, who disobeyed Christ, transgressed the law of Moses and the prophets. Jesus said this even more sternly when he wished to point out that their wickedness was greater by comparison. For, if not these things, then other things might have happened in Tyre and Sidon, and even in Sodom and Gomorrah, if they had come to repentance. But, as I said, he presents this comparison in order more forcefully to demonstrate their wickedness. FRAGMENT 78.[3]

11:24 On the Day of Judgment

THEIR INSENSITIVITY. HILARY: The curse of disobedience is distinguished from the blessing of obedience. It was necessary for the Jews to be admonished. The ill will of their faithlessness is highlighted by the extraordinary grace of his works there. The Jews were censured by the example of the faithful, to whom salvation came entirely from faith. But these cities displayed no change whatever at Jesus' actions.

At Bethsaida and Capernaum the mute praised the Lord with their voices, the blind saw, the deaf heard, the lame ran about, and the dead came alive, yet astonishment at such great miracles did not produce any disposition for faith. Hearing about the deeds alone ought to have called them to awe and to faith. Yet this unresponsiveness is found not only in the small sins of Tyre and Sidon but also with the great sins of Sodom and Gomorrah. The desire for belief would perhaps have come closer to them if these remarkable acts of virtue had really touched them. ON MATTHEW 11.10.[4]

---

[1]CCL 77:84. [2]CCL 77:84. [3]MKGK 77-78. [4]SC 254:264-66.

DOES THE FAULT LIE IN THE PREACHER? JE-ROME: The wise reader may inquire and say, "If Tyre, Sidon and Sodom could repent at the admonishment of our Savior and at his wonderful miracles, they are not to blame because they did not at first believe. But the fault of silence rests in the one who did not want to preach even to those who were likely to repent."

To this charge the response is easy and clear: We do not fathom the decisions of God. We do not know the secrets of his singular acts of dispensation. . . . Chorazin and Bethsaida were condemned because they did not want to believe in our Lord even when he was with them in person. Meanwhile Tyre and Sidon were pardoned because they believed the apostles. So do not try to fathom the precise time or place when you may expect the salvation of the believers. It was unexpectedly in Capernaum, a very beautiful town, that unbelieving Jerusalem was condemned. To this city there was an ironic reply in Ezekiel: "Sodom has been vindicated on account of you."[5] COMMENTARY ON MATTHEW 2.11.23.[6]

MORE TOLERABLE FOR SODOM. CHRYSOSTOM: It is not for nothing that Jesus mentions Sodom along with the others. He does this to heighten the charge against these cities. This stood as proof of their very great recalcitrance. For they were found to be as bad not only as other cities that currently existed but also as bad as any that ever existed! Thus elsewhere Jesus also makes incriminating comparisons, censuring them by the Ninevites and the queen of the south. In those cases, however, the comparison was with those who did seek to do right, and in these cases with those who had grossly ignored God's coming. Ezekiel anticipated this intensity of expression when he condemned Jerusalem: "You have justified your sisters in all your sins."[7] These were cities where Jesus was prone to linger as a favored place. And not even at this does he hold back his speech. He makes their dread even more intense by saying that they would suffer things more grievous than Sodom and Tyre. Jesus alarmed them when he used every possible means to reclaim them to repentance. THE GOSPEL OF MATTHEW, HOMILY 37.4.[8]

---

[5]Ezek 16:52. [6]CCL 77:85. [7]Ezek 16:51. [8]PG 57:424-25; NPNF 1 10:247**.

11:25-30 COME TO ME AND REST

[25]*At that time Jesus declared, "I thank thee, Father, Lord of heaven and earth, that thou hast hidden these things from the wise and understanding and revealed them to babes;* [26]*yea, Father, for such was thy gracious will.*[f] [27]*All things have been delivered to me by my Father; and no one knows the Son except the Father, and no one knows the Father except the Son and any one to whom the Son chooses to reveal him.* [28]*Come to me, all who labor and are heavy laden, and I will give you rest.* [29]*Take my yoke upon you, and learn from me; for I am gentle and lowly in heart, and you will find rest for your souls.* [30]*For my yoke is easy, and my burden is light."*

f Or *so it was well-pleasing before thee*

OVERVIEW: All creation is encompassed in the two terms "heaven and earth" (AUGUSTINE). The Arians object that because Christ renders thanks to the Father, he is less than the Father.

228

To this the apostolic tradition answers that nothing prevents the consubstantial Son from accepting and praising his own Father, saving the world beneath heaven through him (CYRIL OF ALEXANDRIA). The Son here glorifies the Father, who had foreseen the trajectory of the Word from the Jews to the Gentiles (ORIGEN). Jesus called the scribes and Pharisees wise though they did not really possess wisdom but only that which appeared to be wisdom, because of their cleverness with words. He called fishermen, unskilled in evil, to be the children to whom he revealed his Word (THEODORE OF HERACLEA, EPIPHANIUS THE LATIN). We are not to attempt to plumb the depths of the mystery of the motivations of the divine will (ANONYMOUS). We can, however, know the Father by knowing the Son (HILARY). Here the Son shows that his nature is ineffable and inconceivable, like the Father's. For only the divine nature of the Trinity comprehends itself. Only the Father knows his own Son, and only the divine child recognizes the eternal One by whom he has been begotten. Only God the Holy Spirit understands the deep things of God in the intercommunication of the Father and the Son (CYRIL OF ALEXANDRIA, CHRYSOSTOM).

What do we learn from him whose yoke we take? Go deep, descend low, become lowly of heart, build a deep foundation for excellence (AUGUSTINE). As the Maker and Lord of all, he spoke to the weary Jews who did not have the strength to bear the yoke of the law. He spoke to idolaters heavy laden and oppressed by the devil and weighed down by the multitude of their sins (CLEMENT OF ALEXANDRIA). It is a pleasing weight that strengthens even more those who carry it. We do not bear grace; grace bears us (ANONYMOUS).

11:25 Things Hidden from the Wise

REVEALED TO THE GENTILES. ORIGEN: Jesus praises and glorifies the Father, who had foreseen the entire trajectory of the Word first to the Jews and then to the Gentiles. Our Lord here gives thanks to his Father, the Lord of heaven and earth, for his mission in becoming incarnate in the form of a servant. He speaks about the Father's good pleasure now to hide this mystery about himself from Israel, which might be expected to be wise, and to reveal it to the Gentiles, who were until now without understanding. It is thereby demonstrated that God did not forget to fulfill his purpose, nor did Christ's coming fail in its appointed end. These things indeed have happened, God knowing them beforehand and having commanded beforehand the repentance of grace. The justice of God's good pleasure is here passed over in silence, but elsewhere it is clearly displayed. God's good will is not irrational. People do not fail to attain knowledge and wisdom about it for any reason other than their own deficiencies. FRAGMENT 239.[1]

LORD OF HEAVEN AND EARTH. AUGUSTINE: Jesus says, "My Father, Lord of heaven and earth," Father of him through whom all things were made. Surely all creation is embraced by these two nouns *heaven* and *earth*. Therefore the first book of God's Scripture says, "In the beginning God made heaven and earth."[2] And "my help is from the Lord, who made heaven and earth."[3] By the name of heaven is understood whatever is in heaven, and by the name of earth is understood whatever is on earth. Thus, by mentioning these two parts of creation no aspect of creation is overlooked, since the created object is either here or there. Moreover, when the Son speaks to his Father his confession, Jesus admonishes us that confession is owed to God not for our sins alone. For very often when it is heard in the Scriptures, "You shall confess to the Lord," many who hear this beat their breasts in remorse. They do not recall

[1]GCS 41.1:112; cf. Origen *Fragments from Commentaries on the Gospel of Matthew* 301, Apollinaris *Fragment* 66, in MKGK 19. [2]Gen 1:1. [3]Ps 121:2 (120:2 LXX).

that the term *confession* means anything else except their accustomed use when they show repentance, confessing their sins and awaiting their just deserts from God, not because they deserve to suffer but because God deems it worthy to act mercifully. But if there were not confession in the act of praise, Jesus would not say, "I confess to you, Father," since he had no sin to confess. It is said in another book of the Scripture: "You shall confess to the Lord" and say in your confession that "all the works of the Lord are very good." This is certainly a confession of praise and not of fault. SERMON 68.2.[4]

I THANK YOU, FATHER. CYRIL OF ALEXANDRIA: He employs the phrase "I confess you" in accordance with human custom. Instead of saying "I acknowledge you," he brings in the phrase "I glorify you."[5] For it is customary in the divinely inspired Scripture for the word *confession* to be taken in some such a sense. It is written, "Let the people give thanks," Lord, "to your great name, because it is formidable and holy."[6] And again, "I will give thanks to you, Lord, with all my heart."[7]

But those who are perverted in mind say, "Look here, if he renders thanks to the Father, how then is he not less than the Father?" To this objection one who knows how to guard the doctrines of truth might say, "My good man, what prevents the consubstantial Son from accepting and praising his own Father, who through him saves what is under heaven? If you believe because of this confession that he is in a lesser position than the Father, look also at what comes next. Jesus acknowledges and calls his Father Lord of heaven and earth. For he confesses him as 'Lord of heaven and earth' and at the same time he calls upon him as 'Father.' But the Son of God who is ruler of all is in every way with him the Lord and Master of all, not as one worse or differing in substance, but as God from God. He is crowned with equal renown, having substantially with him equality in everything whatsoever." FRAGMENT 145.[8]

GRACE REVEALED TO THOSE SIMPLE AT EVIL. THEODORE OF HERACLEA: Jesus called the Jews wise, either because they were entrusted with the oracles of God or because they were evildoers and wise at doing evil, but he called the apostles children. He called the scribes and Pharisees wise, though they did not really possess wisdom but only what appeared to be wisdom because of their cleverness with words. He called the fishermen, who were unskilled in evil, children. In this way, the grace of God was clearly manifested as Jesus made himself known to simple men. . . . And even if it was Christ himself who, for the most part, did these things, nevertheless, by giving thanks for them as things done by the Father, he shows that they share a common will and gives thanks for God's love for us in the things by which we have received benefit. FRAGMENT 80.[9]

REVEALED TO BABES. EPIPHANIUS THE LATIN: And he revealed these things to children. To which children? Not those who are children in age but to those who are children in respect to sin and wickedness. To them Jesus revealed how to seek the blessings of paradise and the things to come in the kingdom of heaven, because thus it was well pleasing before God that "they should come from the east and the west and that they should lie down with Abraham, Isaac and Jacob in the kingdom of heaven; but that the sons of this worldly kingdom should be cast into the outer darkness, where there will be weeping and gnashing of teeth."[10] INTERPRETATION OF THE GOSPELS 26.[11]

11:26 The Father's Gracious Will

PLEASING TO GOD. ANONYMOUS: He does not say why it was thus pleasing to him but only

---

[4]MA 1:356-57; WSA 3 3:222-23. [5]Cyril indicates that *exomologeisthai* is here used not in its normal sense of "to confess, admit, acknowledge" but in the sense of "to glorify." [6]Ps 99:3 (98:3 LXX). [7]Ps 9:1; 111:1 (9:1; 110:1 LXX). [8]MKGK 199. [9]MKGK 78-79. [10]Mt 8:11-12. [11]PL Supp 3:865.

gives thanks to the Father, because it was thus pleasing to him. So also you should never discuss God's designs, what he did in his works or why he did so. But in whatever way God so wished to arrange his own creation, let thanksgiving be sufficient for you as evidence in regard to the very nature of God. God does nothing without reason and justice. He created you not for his own examination but for his own honor. God did not want you to be a judge of his own actions but a servant of his commands. It is characteristic of a good master to foresee everything that concerns the benefit of the servant. Moreover, it is characteristic of a good servant to work faithfully and not to discuss the master's actions. INCOMPLETE WORK ON MATTHEW, HOMILY 28.[12]

11:27 Knowing the Father by the Son

ALL THINGS DELIVERED TO ME BY MY FATHER. JEROME: The Father entrusts. The Son receives. What is entrusted? All things have been entrusted to the Son, but this does not mean cosmically heaven and earth and the elements and the rest of nature which God himself made and established. Rather, it refers personally to the people who have access to the Father through the Son and who were formerly rebellious but afterward began to know God. COMMENTARY ON MATTHEW 2.11.27.[13]

NO ONE KNOWS THE FATHER EXCEPT THE SON. HILARY: So that it might not be supposed that anything in him is less than what is in God,[14] Jesus said that everything was entrusted to him by his Father, that he alone was known to his Father and that his Father was known to him alone or to one to whom he himself had wished to reveal his Father. By this revelation Jesus showed that the same essence of both Father and Son existed in their knowledge of each other. One who could know the Son would also know the Father in his Son, because everything was handed down to him from the Father. More-

over, nothing else was handed down than what was known to the Father in the Son alone, but the things that belonged to the Father were known to be revealed in the Son alone. Thus in this mystery of mutual knowledge it is understood that nothing else existed in the Son than what was known to be in the Father. ON MATTHEW 11.12.[15]

ANYONE TO WHOM THE SON CHOOSES TO REVEAL HIM. CHRYSOSTOM: This may seem to the uninitiated quite disconnected with the passage that went before, but the two stand in full accord. Having said "all things have been delivered to me by my Father," he adds, "and no one knows the Son except the Father, and no one knows the Father except the Son and any one to whom the Son chooses to reveal him." In this he is quietly signifying his great privilege of knowing the Father and being of the same substance with him, he being the only One who knows the Father so intimately. . . .

Note the timing and context in which he said this. It was just after he had worked miracles and the disciples of John had received proofs of his might by his works. He then thanks the Father that "that you have hidden these things from the wise and understanding and revealed them to babes." THE GOSPEL OF MATTHEW, HOMILY 38.2.[16]

EVERYTHING HANDED DOWN FROM THE FATHER. CYRIL OF ALEXANDRIA: The one who sees the Son, who has the image of the Father in himself, sees the Father himself. . . . These things are to be understood in a manner befitting to God. He said, "Everything has been handed down to me" so that he might not seem to be a member of a different species or inferior to the Father. Jesus added this in order to show that his nature is ineffable and inconceivable, like the Father's. For only the divine nature of

---

[12]PG 56:777. [13]CCL 77:86. [14]On Christ as image (= revealer) see Col 1:15. [15]SC 254:266. [16]PG 57:430; NPNF 1 10:252**.

the Trinity comprehends itself. Only the Father knows his own Son, the fruit of his own substance. Only the divine Son recognizes the One by whom he has been begotten. Only the Holy Spirit knows the deep things of God, the thought of the Father and the Son. Fragment 148.[17]

11:28-29 Rest for Your Souls

LEARN FROM MY LOWLINESS. AUGUSTINE: You are to "take my yoke upon you, and learn from me."[18] You are not learning from me how to refashion the fabric of the world, nor to create all things visible and invisible, nor to work miracles and raise the dead. Rather, you are simply learning of me: "that I am meek and lowly in heart." If you wish to reach high, then begin at the lowest level. If you are trying to construct some mighty edifice in height, you will begin with the lowest foundation. This is humility. However great the mass of the building you may wish to design or erect, the taller the building is to be, the deeper you will dig the foundation. The building in the course of its erection rises up high, but he who digs its foundation must first go down very low. So then, you see even a building is low before it is high and the tower is raised only after humiliation. SERMON 69.2.[19]

YOU WILL FIND REST. CYRIL OF ALEXANDRIA: Stand apart from the inclination to love sin and to love the flesh. Turn to deeds worthy of praise. Draw near to me, so that you may become sharers of the divine nature and partakers of the Holy Spirit. Jesus called everyone, not only the people of Israel. As the Maker and Lord of all, he spoke to the weary Jews who did not have the strength to bear the yoke of the law. He spoke to idolaters heavy laden and oppressed by the devil and weighed down by the multitude of their sins. To Jews he said, "Obtain the profit of my coming to you. Bow down to the truth. Acknowledge your Advocate and Lord. I set you free from bondage under the law, bondage in

which you endured a great deal of toil and hardship, unable to accomplish it easily and accumulating for yourselves a very great burden of sins." FRAGMENT 149.[20]

11:30 An Easy Yoke, a Light Burden

MY BURDEN IS LIGHT. APOLLINARIS: If the yoke is easy and the burden light, why did he call "the way" "narrow"? It is narrow to the careless, for to the zealous the Lord's tasks are light. For even if they involve bodily suffering for a little while, yet the one who is now nourished with good hopes is the devout one who easily bears these pains. FRAGMENT 67.[21]

HOW CHRIST'S YOKE DIFFERS FROM THAT OF MOSES. THEODORE OF MOPSUESTIA: How is it then that he himself demands a high degree of strictness? He answers, "You have not yet had experience of things that are mine, and for this reason you think this way. But if you would take up my yoke and would believe in those things I give, you would find the greatest difference between the things that are from me and those that are from Moses. From me there is great, patient endurance and kindness. Seeing such a weight of sins—murders and self-love and things more unnamable than these—I am long-suffering and bear with those who do these things, not despising them but waiting for them to repent. If ever they should repent and change their ways, I immediately forgive them, not remembering their former acts. But the law of Moses is not like this. When you sin, it immediately punishes the sinner. It knows no repentance. It promises no remission. When I make demands about the covenant, I am not so much preoccupied with investigating the things that happened. For me, it is enough that a soul choose what is good with a genuine resolution. But the law goes overboard, both adding more

---

[17]MKGK 200. [18]Mt 11:29. [19]PL 38:441; NPNF 1 6:315** (Sermon 19). [20]MKGK 201. [21]MKGK 19.

punishments to the smaller ones and cursing the transgressors. Therefore my yoke is good on account of forgiveness, and my burden is light because it is not a collection of customs and various observances but decisions of the soul." FRAGMENT 67.[22]

WHAT MAKES THE YOKE EASY. EPIPHANIUS THE LATIN: Therefore let everyone who wants life and desires to see good days put down the yoke of iniquity and malice. The prophet says, "Let us burst their bonds and thrust their yoke from us."[23] For unless one throws behind the yoke of iniquity, that is, the spark of all vices, one cannot take up the agreeable and light yoke of Christ. But if the yoke of Christ is so agreeable and light, how is it that divine religion seems so harsh and bitter to some people? It is bitter to some because the heart that has been tainted by earthly desires cannot love heavenly things. It has not yet come to Christ, so that it can take up his yoke and learn that he is gentle and humble of heart. Hence we observe, my dearest friends, from the teaching of our Lord,

that unless a person is gentle and humble of heart, he or she cannot bear the yoke of Christ. INTERPRETATION OF THE GOSPELS 26.[24]

GRACE BEARS US. ANONYMOUS: "My yoke is easy and my burden light."... The prophet says this about the burden of sinners: "Because my iniquities lie on top of my head, so they have also placed a heavy burden on me."[25]..."Place my yoke upon you, and learn from me that I am gentle and humble of heart." Oh, what a very pleasing weight that strengthens even more those who carry it! For the weight of earthly masters gradually destroys the strength of their servants, but the weight of Christ rather helps the one who bears it, because we do not bear grace; grace bears us. It is not for us to help grace, but rather grace has been given to aid us. INCOMPLETE WORK ON MATTHEW, HOMILY 29.[26]

---

[22]MKGK 118. [23]Ps 2:3. [24]PL Supp 3:865-66. [25]Ps 38:4 (37:4 LXX). [26]PG 56:780.

12:1-8 THE QUESTION ABOUT THE SABBATH

[1]At that time Jesus went through the grainfields on the sabbath; his disciples were hungry, and they began to pluck heads of grain and to eat. [2]But when the Pharisees saw it, they said to him, "Look, your disciples are doing what is not lawful to do on the sabbath." [3]He said to them, "Have you not read what David did, when he was hungry, and those who were with him: [4]how he entered the house of God and ate the bread of the Presence, which it was not lawful for him to eat nor for those who were with him, but only for the priests? [5]Or have you not read in the law how on the sabbath the priests in the temple profane the sabbath, and are guiltless? [6]I tell you, something greater than the temple is here. [7]And if you had known what this means, 'I desire mercy, and not sacrifice,' you would not have condemned the guiltless. [8]For the Son of man is lord of the sabbath."

OVERVIEW: The sabbath was given to remind humanity that God the Creator rested from labor, and so should we (THEODORE OF HERACLEA). Christ did not attempt to repeal the sabbath law, but rather he greatly magnified the sabbath. With Christ came the time for everyone to be trained by a higher requirement (CHRYSOSTOM, HILARY). He never broke the law without adequate cause and always gave a reasonable justification. His purpose in eating grain on the sabbath was to bring the old law to transformation, yet not in a defiant manner (CHRYSOSTOM). The Pharisees remained quiet when nothing great was happening, but when they saw miracles of healing, they were offended (CYRIL OF ALEXANDRIA). Yet they themselves had violated the sabbath by immolating victims in the temple (JEROME). Jesus concluded something more decisive: the deed of plucking grain on the sabbath is no sin at all. The messianic Lawgiver was overriding the presumed law. This reversal was occurring in a particular time and place and by those with a special calling: in the temple, on the sabbath, by priests (CHRYSOSTOM). Jesus clearly revealed that he himself was the temple (HILARY).

12:1 The Disciples Pick Grain on the Sabbath

THROUGH THE GRAINFIELDS. HILARY: We must first point out the beginning of this passage: "At that time Jesus went through the standing grain." This is set at the time he gave thanks to God the Father for having given salvation to the people. The same meaning is given to what went before (his thanksgiving) and what came after (his walking in the fields). Note the relationships. Spiritually viewed, the land is the world, the sabbath is the day of rest, and the crop is the effect of future believers upon the harvest. Therefore, having gone out to a field on the sabbath, the day of rest under God's law, he proceeded into this world, to visiting the crop, the sown field of the human race. And since

hunger is the craving for human salvation, the disciples hasten to pluck off the ears of corn, namely, the holy people, to get their fill of salvation. But the grain is not yet ready for human consumption. Rather, the crop upholds faith in the events to come. The added power of words completes the sacrament that implies both hunger and fullness. ON MATTHEW 12.2.[1]

HIS DISCIPLES WERE HUNGRY. CHRYSOSTOM: How could he who foreknew all things be unaware of the consequences of this action, unless it had been his will that the sabbath law had to be reinterpreted? That was his will indeed, but not in a simple sense. He never broke the law without adequate cause, and always by giving a reasonable justification. His purpose in doing so was to bring the old law to an end, yet not in a defiant manner. There are indeed occasions in which he repeals the old law directly and without any fanfare, as when he anointed the eyes of the blind man with clay, and as when he said, "My Father is still working, and I also am working."[2] He does this to glorify his own Father and to soothe the enmity of the Jews. His appeal is to the necessity of nature in this case, since his disciples were hungry. THE GOSPEL OF MATTHEW, HOMILY 39.1.[3]

12:2 Not Lawful on the Sabbath

THE PHARISEES SAW IT. CYRIL OF ALEXANDRIA: For where nothing great or noble happens, the Pharisees remain quiet. But where they see certain people being healed, they are more offended than anyone else. In this way they are the enemies of humanity's salvation and without understanding of the sacred writings. If the new covenant announced of old by Jeremiah differs from the first covenant, it ought by all means to make use not of old laws but of new ones. But the Pharisees, not willing to comprehend this, lay snares for the holy apostles and

---

[1]SC 254:270. [2]Jn 5:17 NRSV. [3]PG 57:433-34; NPNF 1 10:255**.

say about them to Christ: "Look here, we see those you've schooled opposing themselves to the stipulations of the law. For where the law commands everyone to rest on the sabbath and to touch no manner of work, your disciples pluck ears of wheat with their hands." But tell me, O Pharisee, when you have set the sabbath table for yourself, don't even you break the bread? Why then do you blame others? FRAGMENT 152.[4]

12:3-4 The Bread of the Presence

DAVID ATE THE BREAD OF THE PRESENCE. JEROME: To put down the chicanery of the Pharisees it is recorded in ancient history that David was fleeing from Saul and came to Nob.[5] Having been received by Ahimelech the priest, he asked him for food. Since Ahimelech had no common bread at hand, he gave David some holy bread, which only priests and Levites could lawfully eat. The priest asked whether the young men had kept themselves from women, and he received the answer "since yesterday and the day before."[6] He did not hesitate to give the bread, having thought it better, remembering that the prophet says, "I desire mercy and not sacrifice."[7] In view of the danger of hunger, Ahimelech judged it better to help people than to offer sacrifice to God. The slain victim pleasing to God is the salvation of humankind. If David is holy and the priest Ahimelech is not offensive to you, but they have broken both commandments of the law with a probable excuse—in this case, hunger—why do you not find acceptable the same hunger in the apostles that you find acceptable in others? However, in this there is a great difference: the disciples plucked grain on the sabbath, whereas David ate the levitical bread. . . . Note that neither David nor his young men accepted the loaves of the presence until they replied that they had kept themselves from women. COMMENTARY ON MATTHEW 2.14.4.[8]

12:5 The Priests in the Temple

PRIESTS GUILTLESS. CHRYSOSTOM: Do not reply that one does not free oneself from blame by noting that someone else is committing the same offense. Or that if the offender has no blame, his act becomes a rule for others to plead.

Jesus was not satisfied with such reasoning. Instead, he concludes something more decisive: the deed itself in this case is no sin at all! This more than anything was the sign of a glorious victory: For here the Giver of the law was overriding the law.[9] This victory occurs in a particular place, the temple, and on a particular day, the sabbath. One might even point to several levels of legal reversal, pertaining to the work that is done; it is done by priests, and more so, that it elicits no charges. For they remain guiltless.

Do you see how many levels of argument Jesus is making in stating this case? They are "in the temple." The persons involved are "priests." The time is "the sabbath." The act itself is "profane." Note that he does not say gently that they "break" the sabbath law but more grievously that they "profane" it. Yet in all this they not only escape punishment but are free from blame, being "guiltless."

So do not treat the example of the priests in the same way as the example of David. For David's case occurred only once, and was not done by a priest, and occurred due to an explicit need, and so was deserving of excuse. But the example of the priests was done repeatedly, every sabbath, was done by priests, and was done in the temple, and it too was of necessity. They were acquitted of charges not by special pleading or indulgence but on reasonable grounds according to the principles of justice. THE GOSPEL OF MATTHEW, HOMILY 39.2.[10]

HOW THE PRIESTS PROFANE THE TEMPLE. JEROME: You falsely accuse my disciples, Jesus says, for plucking ears of grain while passing

---

[4]MKGK 201-2. [5]1 Sam 21:1-9. [6]1 Sam 21:5. [7]Hos 6:6. [8]CCL 77:88. [9]The Lawgiver was overriding a particular interpretation of the law. [10]PG 57:435; NPNF 1 10:256**.

through the standing fields. They did this because of their pangs of hunger. But you must violate the sabbath by immolating victims in the temple, slaughtering bulls and burning holocausts on a heap of firewood and, according to the testimony of the other Gospel, circumcising children on the sabbath.[11] Thus, while you wish to observe the one law, you dishonor the sabbath. But God's commands do not contradict each other. COMMENTARY ON MATTHEW 2.12.5.[12]

12:6 Greater Than the Temple

CHRIST IS THE TEMPLE. HILARY: Christ also reminded them of another prophecy so that they might learn that all things that were spoken of previously were accomplished in him through the law, that the priests in the temple broke the sabbath without offense, clearly revealing that Jesus himself was the temple. In him salvation was given to the Gentiles through the teaching of the apostles, while the people who were bound by the law wandered about faithlessly, so that he himself might be greater than the sabbath. Evangelical faith lived in Christ transcends the law. ON MATTHEW 12.4.[13]

12:7 Not Condemning the Guiltless

IF YOU HAD KNOWN. HILARY: In order to show that this appearance of his work anticipated all the power of things to come, he added, "If you understood what the saying means: 'I want mercy, not sacrifice,' you would never have condemned the blameless." The business of our salvation lies not in sacrifice but in mercy. When law is made void, we are saved by the goodness of God. If they had understood the grace of this statement, they would never have condemned the blameless. They would not have condemned the apostles whom they were going to accuse falsely, out of envy, of transgressing the law. When the ancient practice of sacrifices was stopped, the strangeness of mercy became more clearly known. Had this

been known, they would not have thought that the Lord of the sabbath was confined by the law of the sabbath. ON MATTHEW 12.5.[14]

MERCY, NOT SACRIFICE. CHRYSOSTOM: The faithful are more than priests. For the Lord of the temple himself has come to them. The Truth personally has arrived, not merely the image of the truth. So he could say, "I tell you, something greater than the temple is here!"

Nevertheless, great as the sayings were which they heard, they made no reply, for they were inattentive to the coming salvation of humanity. Then, because it might otherwise seem harsh to his hearers, Jesus quickly drew a veil over his discourse, giving it a lenient turn, yet even then conveying a sharp admonition: "If you had known what this means, 'I desire mercy, and not sacrifice,' you would not have condemned the guiltless." Do you see once again how his speech is inclined toward leniency, yet showing the priests themselves to be in need of leniency? THE GOSPEL OF MATTHEW, HOMILY 39.2.[15]

12:8 The Lord of the Sabbath

THE LAW OF THE SABBATH. CHRYSOSTOM: Doubtless he speaks of himself when he mentions the "Lord of the sabbath." Mark relates a complementary saying about our common human nature, that "the sabbath was made for humans, not humans for the sabbath.[16]

Why then should someone who gathered sticks on the sabbath be censured? The law that was established earlier could not be scorned without jeopardizing the law to be given later.

The sabbath did confer many benefits, great blessings in the earlier dispensation. It made people more gentle toward those close to them. It guided them toward being more sympathetic. It located them temporally within God's creation and providence, as Ezekiel knew.[17] The

---

[11]Jn 7:22-23. [12]CCL 77:89. [13]SC 254:272. [14]SC 254:272. [15]PG 57:436; NPNF 1 10:256-57**. [16]Mk 2:27. [17]Ezek 20:19-20.

sabbath trained Israel by degrees to abstain from evil and disposed them to listen to the things of the Spirit.

They would have stretched the law out of shape if, when he was giving the law of the sabbath, Jesus had said, "You can work on the sabbath, but just do good works, do nothing evil." This would have brought out the worst in them. So he restrained them from doing any works at all on the sabbath. And even this stricter prohibition did not keep them in line. But he himself, in the very act of giving the law of the sabbath, gave them a veiled sign of things to come. For by saying, "You must do no work, except what shall be done for your life,"[18] he indicated that the intent of the law was to have them refrain from evil works only, not all works. Even in the temple, much went on during the sabbath, and with great diligence and double toil. Thus even by this very shadowy saying Jesus was secretly opening the truth to them.

Did Christ then attempt to repeal a law so beneficial as the sabbath law? Far from it. Rather, he greatly magnified the sabbath. For with Christ came the time for everyone to be trained by a higher requirement. THE GOSPEL OF MATTHEW, HOMILY 39.3.[19]

WHY THE SABBATH WAS GIVEN. THEODORE OF HERACLEA: You will also thus observe that knowing God is more necessary than resting on the sabbath. The sabbath was given to the Jews when, in Egypt, they were turned toward idolatry. And the sabbath was given for this reason: so that they would not call the world uncreated and outside the sphere of providence, but that they would acknowledge that God is both the One who planned it and that it is he himself who made the world in six days and on the seventh day rested. When God commanded them to do no work on the sabbath, it was to remind them of this. Subsequently, the fact that God is the Maker of the universe has become known to all, and so much of the detailed sabbath law has become superficial. If these extreme arguments about the sabbath were truly useful, they would have been applied not only to human beings but even to the sun and moon. Imagine that the very sun would cease working its benefits to us on the sabbath day. No. This commandment has been given to human beings, even from the foundation of the world. FRAGMENT 84.[20]

---

[18]Ex 12:16. [19]PG 57:436-37; NPNF 1 10:257**. [20]MKGK 79-80.

12:9-14 THE MAN WITH A PARALYZED HAND

[9]*And he went on from there, and entered their synagogue.* [10]*And behold, there was a man with a withered hand. And they asked him, "Is it lawful to heal on the sabbath?" so that they might accuse him.* [11]*He said to them, "What man of you, if he has one sheep and it falls into a pit on the sabbath, will not lay hold of it and lift it out?* [12]*Of how much more value is a man than a sheep! So it is lawful to do good on the sabbath."* [13]*Then he said to the man, "Stretch out your hand." And the man stretched it out, and it was restored, whole like the other.* [14]*But the Pharisees went out and took counsel against him, how to destroy him.*

OVERVIEW: The Pharisees challenged Jesus within the synagogue, in the case of the man with a withered hand. Symbolically they were bringing to the Savior the barrenness of their own hands, since having a withered hand signified unfruitfulness (ORIGEN). Jesus' desire was to heal first their bitterness before he healed the withered hand. But even in his attempts to offer them healing, both by what he said and did, their malady proved all the more intractable (CHRYSOSTOM). The hand was restored to the same condition as the other hand, making it a partner in the service of the apostles in their duty of preaching salvation (HILARY).

12:9 Entering the Synagogue

THE BARRENNESS OF THEIR OWN HANDS. ORIGEN: The spiritual sense of the expression "he went on from there" can be understood in this way: When he establishes a new covenant and the sabbath no longer is in force, then he goes over or departs to another place. For this reason they accuse him and his disciples, not outside but within the synagogue. Their offenses are thereby increased to the brim. They brought to the Savior the barrenness of their hands. For having a withered hand indicated unfruitfulness. But that which is unfruitful is coming near to being reversed. FRAGMENT 249.[1]

12:10 The Pharisees Seek to Accuse Jesus

THEIR BITTERNESS INTRACTABLE. CHRYSOSTOM: "Is it allowed" to heal on the sabbath? He knew their love of wealth. He knew that they were all the more taken up with love of things than persons. And indeed the other Evangelist[2] said that Jesus also scrutinized them as he asked this question, that by his very glance he might win them over, but they did not become softened. While in other cases he healed manually by the laying on of his hands, in this case he only speaks and gazes. But nothing would make them more gentle. Rather, even while the man was

being healed, their condition was becoming worse. Jesus' desire was to heal first their bitterness before he healed the withered hand. But even in his various attempts to offer them healing, both by what he said and did, their malady proved all the more intractable. THE GOSPEL OF MATTHEW, HOMILY 40.1.[3]

12:11-12 Lawful to Do Good on the Sabbath

DOING GOOD ALLOWED ON THE SABBATH. CHRYSOSTOM: Again on the sabbath he performed a healing, defending himself on behalf of the disciples' activities. The Lukan Gospel writer says "that he made the man stand in the middle"[4] and asked them if it was allowed to do good on the sabbath. Note well the Lord's goodness of heart. He made him stand in the middle so that he might bend them to his vision, so that by being overcome by the sight they might reject wickedness and in pitying the man they might cease from their savage behavior. But the wild and misanthropic men chose rather to distract Christ from his teaching than to see this man saved. . . . Thus the other Gospel writers say that Jesus asked questions, but this author says that he was asked questions. "And they questioned him: 'Is it allowed to heal on the sabbath?' so that they might accuse him." It is likely that both events happened. For since they were brutal and saw that [Jesus] would come at any rate to heal him, they were eager to preoccupy him with questions, resolving to hinder him. Therefore they asked, "Is it allowed to heal on the sabbath?" not so that they might learn but "so that they might bring charges against him." And indeed the act was sufficient if they wished to prosecute him. But through his words they wished to find an excuse for prosecution by preparing beforehand for themselves an abundance of arguments. . . . "And he made the man stand

---

[1]GCS 41.1:116. [2]The recourse to parallel passages in the other Gospels (here Mk 3:3; Lk 6:8) permits Chrysostom to deepen the interpretation of Matthew. [3]PG 57:440; NPNF 1 10:259-60**. [4]Lk 6:8.

in the middle,"[5] not because Jesus feared them but because he was eager to help them and to draw them toward his mercy. THE GOSPEL OF MATTHEW, HOMILY 40.1.[6]

12:13 The Man's Hand Healed

IT WAS RESTORED. HILARY: Such healing is rightly attributed to our Lord. After his return from the cornfield from which his apostles had gotten the produce, he went to the synagogue. From there Jesus intended to acquire laborers for his own harvest. Many of them afterwards lived with the apostles. Many were healed, as in the case of the maimed man.[7] Yet the leaders of the synagogue did not believe in the grace of salvation. The use of the man's hand had atrophied. That function of his body had withered, by which he was able to do or share in certain tasks. So the Lord ordered him to stretch out his hand, and it was restored to him as the other one was. His whole cure rested on the word of the healer alone. The hand was restored to the same condition as the other hand. It was made a partner in the service of the apostles in their duty of granting salvation. ON MATTHEW 12.7.[8]

12:14 The Pharisees Take Counsel

THEY SOUGHT TO DESTROY HIM. JEROME: Envy is responsible for the fact that they set a trap for our Lord. What had he done to incite the Pharisees to kill him? Certainly it was because the man had stretched out his hand. Who of the Pharisees did not stretch out his hand on the sabbath day when he was carrying food, when he was offering a drinking cup or performing the other actions that are necessary for nourishment? So if stretching forth one's

hand and lifting up food or drink on the sabbath are not offenses, why should they make this accusation? They themselves are found guilty of doing the same, especially since that stonecutter had not carried anything of the sort that they had but had only stretched out his hand at the order of our Lord. COMMENTARY ON MATTHEW 2.12.14.[9]

VEHEMENT DETRACTORS. CHRYSOSTOM: By this he makes clear that deluded souls are not even persuaded by miracles. And he shows how his disciples also had been wrongly blamed by them without cause. Note how vehement his detractors have suddenly grown, and this happens especially when they see others benefiting from his ministry! When they see someone delivered either from disease or iniquity, then that immediately cues them to further find fault. They become like wild beasts. According to this pattern they repeatedly demeaned him, as when he was about to save the prostitute, and again when he was eating with publicans, and now again, when they saw the withered hand restored.[10]

Note carefully how he does not cease in his tender care for the infirm yet softens the envy of his adversaries. Hence "great multitudes followed him, and he healed them all; and he charged those that were healed that they should make him known to no one." But the multitudes seemed more ready to admire him and trail after him than to change their decadent ways. THE GOSPEL OF MATTHEW, HOMILY 40.2.[11]

---

[5]Lk 6:8. [6]PG 57:439; NPNF 1 10:259**. [7]As is his habit, Hilary connects the interpretations of adjacent passages of the Gospel: the healing of the man with the withered hand illustrates the preceding episode, the ears of corn harvested on the sabbath. [8]SC 254:274. [9]CCL 77:90-91. [10]Mt 12:9-14. [11]PG 57:440; NPNF 1 10:260**.

12:15-21 GOD'S CHOSEN SERVANT

[15]*Jesus, aware of this, withdrew from there. And many followed him, and he healed them all,* [16]*and ordered them not to make him known.* [17]*This was to fulfil what was spoken by the prophet Isaiah:*

[8]*"Behold, my servant whom I have chosen,*
my beloved with whom my soul is well pleased.
I will put my Spirit upon him,
and he shall proclaim justice to the Gentiles.
[19]*He will not wrangle or cry aloud,*
nor will any one hear his voice in the streets;
[20]*he will not break a bruised reed*
or quench a smoldering wick,
till he brings justice to victory;
[21]*and in his name will the Gentiles hope."*

OVERVIEW: Jesus came to the lost sheep of the house of Israel, but they were not ready to receive their own Shepherd. Upon hearing that they had taken counsel to destroy him, he withdrew, not fearing their judgment but to dispel evil (ORIGEN). By ordering the miracle to be kept secret he refused to boast about himself (HILARY). It is not as an adversary that Christ transcends the law, as if he were an enemy of the Lawgiver, but as though he were of one mind with the Lawgiver. The prophets foretold his travels and changes of place and the intent with which he would act (CHRYSOSTOM). Jesus was loved by God and was pleasing in his Father's will. The Spirit of God was upon him (HILARY). He taught by his way of life not to scream or to show off but to lead a public life of respect with virtuous actions (APOLLINARIS). Jesus bore with his opposition patiently, so as not to reduce them to utter oblivion on account of their weakness, until he had fulfilled the purpose of his mission (THEODORE OF HERACLEA).

12:15 Jesus Withdraws

AWARE OF THEIR INTENT. ORIGEN: To the extent that one draws near to Jesus, one does not hold counsel,[1] for no counselor of evil things draws near to Jesus. But when others go out, departing from Jesus, they hold counsel to destroy Jesus, to destroy the Light, the good Way, the Life, the Treasure, the Pearl, Love itself and Peace. If anyone destroys these, he is called a "son of destruction." But "Jesus, aware of this, withdrew from there." He had no reason to remain around the sons of destruction. They sought to destroy him, but we, who were not seeking, have found him. This recalls the words of the prophet: "I am found by those who do not seek for me; I have been made manifest to those who were not asking after me."[2] For he came "to the lost sheep of the house of Israel" who had forgotten their own Shepherd. So Jesus withdraws, not fearing their judgment but to dispel evil. And, lest anyone should suppose that it was through fear that he had withdrawn, Jesus

---

[1]Origen interprets the physical departure of the Pharisees from Jesus as a symbol of their spiritual departure from him. [2]Is 65:1.

healed everyone, displaying his almighty power. But, as one who does what is fitting, without pride, he sent them away, telling them not to publicize this. FRAGMENT 252.[3]

12:16 Jesus Orders Silence About Healings

WHY HE ORDERED SILENCE. HILARY: He ordered those whom he healed to be silent. Was it silence about the healing that he ordered? Not at all. For the salvation that was given to each one was its own testimony. But by ordering it to be kept secret Jesus also shunned boasting about himself. It was better that knowledge of him remains in himself. So he admonished them to remain silent about him. The observance of silence springs from that about which one must keep silent. ON MATTHEW 12.9.[4]

12:17 The Son Fulfills Isaiah's Prophecy

ISAIAH'S FOREKNOWLEDGE OF CHRIST'S HIDDEN INTENTIONS. CHRYSOSTOM: Then so that you might not be troubled at the events and their strange frenzy, Jesus reminded them of the prophet who had predicted them. For so great was the accuracy of the prophets that they did not omit even these little matters. But they foretold his travels, changes of place and the intent with which he would act, that we might learn that they spoke by the Spirit. If human secrets cannot be easily discerned, how much more difficult it is to discern Christ's purpose, except when the Spirit reveals it to us. THE GOSPEL OF MATTHEW, HOMILY 40.2.[5]

12:18 The Chosen Servant

I SHALL PUT MY SPIRIT ON HIM. JEROME: Through Isaiah the prophet the person of the Father states this: "I shall put my Spirit upon him." The Spirit is not placed upon the Word of God nor upon the only begotten Son who proceeds from the Father but upon the One about whom it is said, "Here is my Son."[6]

COMMENTARY ON MATTHEW 2.12.18.[7]

12:19 He Will Not Lift His Voice

NO ONE WILL HEAR HIS VOICE IN THE STREETS. APOLLINARIS: Those who teach "in the streets" do this,[8] not for the sake of helping anyone but out of egotism and to hoodwink the gullible. The result of this is that everyone views them with suspicion and they fail to reach the goal of their teaching. Thus the Savior taught us these lessons not only by word. His way of life also taught us not to scream nor to show off but to lead a public life in respect to virtuous actions. For a talkative disposition would be most harmful for us. It is the opposite that is most useful and beneficial. FRAGMENT 71.[9]

HE WILL NOT CRY ALOUD. CHRYSOSTOM: The prophet celebrated in advance both the Savior's meekness right alongside his unspeakable power. Thereby he opened to the Gentiles a great and effective door. Isaiah also foretold the ills that were to overtake the Jews. He foreknew the Son's oneness with the Father: "Israel is my chosen, my soul has accepted him; I have put my Spirit upon him."[10] For it is not as an adversary that Christ transcends the law, as if he were an enemy of the Lawgiver, but as though he were of one mind with the Lawgiver and held to the very same purposes. Then, proclaiming the Lord's meekness, Isaiah said, "He shall not cry nor lift up his voice."[11] For his desire indeed was to enable healing in their presence. But since they pushed him away, he did not contend any further against their opposition. THE GOSPEL OF MATTHEW, HOMILY 40.2.[12]

---

[3]GCS 41.1:117. [4]SC 254:274-76. [5]PG 57:440; NPNF 1 10:260**. It is clear that Isaiah spoke by the Spirit because he foreknew even the Messiah's inner intentions. [6]Cf. Is 42:1. [7]CCL 77:91. [8]Wrangle and cry aloud. [9]MKGK 20. [10]Is 42:1 LXX. The Hebrew text is translated "Behold my servant, whom I have chosen, my beloved with whom my soul is well pleased. I will put my Spirit upon him, and he shall proclaim justice to the Gentiles." [11]Is 42:2 LXX. [12]PG 57:440-41; NPNF 1 10:260**.

12:20-21 *Hope for the Gentiles*

IN HIS NAME WILL THE GENTILES HOPE.
HILARY: But even amid this desire to keep silent about himself, the purpose of Jesus' words was fulfilled through Isaiah. About his prophecy I now give you the following important reminder: Jesus was loved by God and was pleasing in his Father's will. The Spirit of God was upon him. Judgment was made known to the Gentiles by him. The reed that was crushed was not broken, and the smoking wick was not extinguished. This means that the frail, shaken bodies of the Gentiles were not worn out but rather preserved to salvation. The meager flame only smoking now on the wick was not extinguished. The spirit of Israel was not removed from the rest of the ancient story of grace. The capability of restoring all the light exists in the time of repentance. But that was appointed within the statutes of a fixed time, "till he brings justice to victory." When the power of death was removed, he would bring judgment at the return of his splendor to the Gentiles who would believe in his name through faith. ON MATTHEW 12.10.[13]

HE BORE WITH THEM PATIENTLY. THEODORE OF HERACLEA: He did not eagerly contend with the folly of the rulers, nor did he scream and provoke them to anger against himself. Rather, with gentleness Jesus withdrew slowly so that he might not, in confuting them, cause them to be destroyed while they were still weak in soul like "a bruised reed" or like "smoking flax," that is, very close to being snuffed out. He bore with them patiently, so as not to reduce them to utter oblivion on account of their weakness, until he had fulfilled the purpose of his dispensation, that is, to bring judgment to a full end. By this dispensation all the nations would come to believe. FRAGMENT 85.[14]

THE SMOLDERING WICK. JEROME: The one who does not stretch out a hand to a sinner and does not carry a brother's load breaks the crushed reed. And the one who despises the small spark of faith in children extinguishes the smoking wick. Christ did neither of these. He came for this purpose: to save those who were perishing. COMMENTARY ON MATTHEW 2.12.20.[15]

HE WILL NOT BREAK A CRUSHED REED.
CHRYSOSTOM: And showing both his strength and their weakness, Jesus said, "He will not break a crushed reed."[16] For in fact it was easy enough for God to break them all to pieces like a reed, and not just any reed but one already crushed. "And he will not quench a smoldering wick."[17] By this he points to their anger that had been kindled and his might that is able to put down their anger and to quench it easily. By this is signified his great mildness.

What then? Shall these things always be? And will Christ endure perpetually those who form such frantic plots against him? Far from it. When he has performed his saving action, then he shall also execute its corresponding purposes. Isaiah declared this by saying both that "he shall bring forth justice to victory"[18] and "in his name shall the Gentiles trust."[19] Paul similarly instructed us to "take every thought captive to obey Christ, being ready to punish every disobedience, when your obedience is complete."[20]

But what is meant by "he shall bring forth justice to victory"?[21] When Christ has completely fulfilled his own part, then, we are told, he will also bring down upon unbelievers his final judgment, when he has left them no contradicting arguments, however shameless, when they will then believe in his wondrous glory. For he knows how to say that justice is a judgment. But his dispensation will not be confined merely to the punishment of unbelievers. He will also proceed to win to himself the nations of the world, so he added, "and in his name will the Gentiles

---

[13]SC 254:276. [14]MKGK 80. [15]CCL 77:91. [16]Is 42:3a LXX. [17]Is 42:3b LXX. [18]Is 42:3c LXX. [19]Is 42:4b LXX. [20]2 Cor 10:6. [21]Is 42:3c LXX.

hope."[22] Then, to inform us that this too is proceeding according to the purpose of the Father from the beginning, the prophet has given us this assurance together with what he has just said: "this is my beloved in whom my soul is well pleased."[23] For it was very clear that the beloved committed these actions according to the purpose of the one who loved him. THE GOSPEL OF MATTHEW, HOMILY 40.2.[24]

---

[22]Mt 12:21. [23]Mt 12:18. [24]PG 57:441; NPNF 1 10:260-61**. God's saving action will at the same time bring judgment upon unbelievers and offer opportunity for all the nations to believe.

12:22-32 JESUS AND THE BINDING OF THE RULER OF THE DEMONS

[22]*Then a blind and dumb demoniac was brought to him, and he healed him, so that the dumb man spoke and saw.* [23]*And all the people were amazed, and said, "Can this be the Son of David?"* [24]*But when the Pharisees heard it they said, "It is only by Be-elzebul, the prince of demons, that this man casts out demons."* [25]*Knowing their thoughts, he said to them, "Every kingdom divided against itself is laid waste, and no city or house divided against itself will stand;* [26]*and if Satan casts out Satan, he is divided against himself; how then will his kingdom stand?* [27]*And if I cast out demons by Be-elzebul, by whom do your sons cast them out? Therefore they shall be your judges.* [28]*But if it is by the Spirit of God that I cast out demons, then the kingdom of God has come upon you.* [29]*Or how can one enter a strong man's house and plunder his goods, unless he first binds the strong man? Then indeed he may plunder his house.* [30]*He who is not with me is against me, and he who does not gather with me scatters.* [31]*Therefore I tell you, every sin and blasphemy will be forgiven men, but the blasphemy against the Spirit will not be forgiven.* [32]*And whoever says a word against the Son of man will be forgiven; but whoever speaks against the Holy Spirit will not be forgiven, either in this age or in the age to come."*

OVERVIEW: The blind, mute man neither saw nor spoke. Symbolically viewed, he neither recognized his Maker nor gave thanks to him (ANONYMOUS). Yet in his healing he spoke to praise God through his faith, and in seeing he saw Christ as the light shining through the eyes of his heart (EPIPHANIUS THE LATIN). The Pharisees, however, who were not ignorant of the truth of the matter, spoke lies about Christ with the evil intent to turn people away from their faith (ANONYMOUS). They claimed that all this power of his against demons came from Beelzebub, prince of demons (HILARY). If the charge is that Jesus is Satan, then Satan would be casting out Satan, and thus the premise of the charge would be faulty. It is not plausible that one would be said to stand by that which was likely to cause one to fall (CHRYSOSTOM).

The house divided against itself may be understood as Jerusalem, where the people of the law oppose the fulfillment of the law in Christ (HILARY). The devil's kingdom cannot stand divided against itself (Augustine). We ought rather to follow that kingdom that cannot be divided—the heavenly and eternal one, the spiritual city of Jerusalem, the true house of God that no hostile power ever has been or will be able to overcome (Chromatius). If "I by the finger of God cast out the devils," the inference is that the Son of God has appeared (Chrysostom, Jerome, Anonymous) by the power of the Spirit of God (Apollinaris).

Human history has become the possession of demons, having been brought by evil under the devil's authority as prince of demons (Theodore of Mopsuestia). Jesus calls the devil "strong," not as though he were so by his original created nature but as signifying his tyranny over us, which he obtained through our own voluntary indolence (Cyril of Alexandria). The demons could not have been plundered unless the devil was first overcome. This is what is now happening: Christ is making the devil's arts useless (Chrysostom). It is proper of the devil to scatter to destruction and of Christ to gather to salvation. Here the Lord anticipates the future ravages of the divided church due to heresies (Chromatius). If anyone does not help Christ build, that person is not with Christ but against him. Though he is able to help Christ, he does not (Anonymous).

It follows that nothing is so beyond the pale of forgiveness as to deny Christ. This is to forsake the nature of the Spirit of the Father residing in him. Any insult aimed at Christ is aimed at God, because God is in Christ and Christ is in God (Hilary, Chrysostom, Severus). This is the blasphemy that will not be forgiven: persistent and ongoing impenitence that continues absolutely to resist the Holy Spirit even after baptism (Augustine).

12:22 A Blind, Mute Demoniac Healed

Reprise. Hilary: The healing of the blind, mute, demon-possessed man follows. It was not without reason that, although he had said that all the multitudes were healed together, now a blind, mute man possessed by a demon was offered to him so that the same order of understanding might follow without any ambiguity. The Pharisees accused the apostles of plucking ears of corn, that is, of prematurely gathering the people of their age. But in his presence mercy was praised over sacrifice. A man with a withered hand was offered up in a synagogue and was cured. Yet not only were these deeds not useful in converting Israel, but the Pharisees even entered into a plan of murder. So it was necessary that the salvation of the Gentiles happen after these events in the dramatic definitive form of a single person. A blind, mute man who was the dwelling place of a demon was being prepared as one fit for God, that he might behold God in Christ and might praise the works of Christ by his acknowledgment of God. The crowd was stunned at the accomplishment of this deed. But the Pharisees' envy grew worse. These great deeds of his surpassed their human weakness. Shamefully they escaped any acknowledgment of this deed of God, covering it over with the greater crime of their own treachery. They did this so that they could say that all this power of his against demons came from Beelzebub, prince of demons. They could not suppose that these were the achievements of a man. On Matthew 12.11.[1]

The Man Neither Saw Nor Spoke. Anonymous: When Jesus left the synagogue . . . then the whole world was offered to him in one man. He was a blind, mute man who neither saw nor spoke. Symbolically he neither recognized his Maker nor gave thanks to him. What was visibly done in the case of one man therefore could be understood to have significance for everyone. For really, if the Lord had not turned Judea aside, all the Gentiles would still be blind and mute in the power of the devil. Incomplete Work on Matthew, Homily 29.[2]

---

[1]SC 254:276-78. [2]PG 56:781.

Christ Healed His Sight and Speech.
Epiphanius the Latin: The entire population
of the Gentiles was blind, sitting in darkness
and in the shadow of death. They could not see
Christ with the eyes of their hearts blinded.
This was because they did not know the law and
could not praise God. They were possessed by a
demon, because after such great idolatry and
hunger for the demonic, they were led captive as
it were by an unclean spirit. "Then a blind and
dumb demoniac was brought to him." By whom
was he offered if not by the apostles, who
quickly brought all the Gentiles who were
attacked by the devil to bring offering to God?
Jesus cured him in their presence, "in such a way
that he might speak and might see." He spoke
because he praised God through his faith. He
saw Christ because light shined on the eyes of
his heart. He was healed because, now by leaving behind his mad idolatry and his various mis-
takes, he was faithfully serving the Lord.
Interpretation of the Gospels 24.[3]

12:23-24 By Whose Power Was the Man Healed?

The People Were Amazed. Anonymous:
How precise he was in saying "they were
stunned," because they did not yet know who
Jesus was. No one can really judge another's
work unless one understands the character of
the one who is performing the work. For example, if a student of some master creates a great
work, we marvel because the student who was
appointed such a task by him could accomplish
it. But if the master himself has done it, we are
not very amazed. For what is the great accomplishment, that a highly trained master created a
great work? So also whatever deed God has
done, it is less than his ability. For that reason,
when the Son of God does a miracle, it must call
forth faith, not astonishment. Do you want to
know why they did not recognize him and so
were astounded? Hear what they say: "Can this
be the Son of David?" If they had recognized

him rightly, they would never have merely said,
"This is the Son of David." They would have
said, "This is the Son of God."

When the Pharisees heard this, they said,
"This man does not cast out demons except by
the power of Beelzebub, prince of demons." Let
us look at this. Did the Pharisees say this, or
did they think it? The reason for the question
comes from the Gospel writer since he does
say, "When the Pharisees heard this, they
spoke." In the next passage, however, the following is said: "Jesus, knowing their
thoughts"—and he did not say, hearing their
words. So who knew what? Perhaps some
spoke out loud, but they spoke from evil
thoughts. For people frequently say what is not
true about someone, but they do not speak
with an evil intent to disparage him. Instead,
they speak not knowing the truth of the matter. The Pharisees, however, who were not
ignorant of the truth of the matter, spoke lies
about Christ with the evil intent to turn people
from their faith in Christ by means of their dis-
paraging talk. They saw that the crowd was
stunned and was saying, "Isn't this the Son of
David?" These were the words of the people
who were coming to faith. So the Pharisees,
who were roused to jealousy, attempted to prevent people from believing in Jesus after seeing
his miracle by saying, "Why are you moved by
great astonishment? Why do you speak unnec-
essarily, and ask whether he is the Son of
David? We recognize clearly that this man does
not cast out demons except through Beelzebub,
prince of demons." They said this, not ignorant
of the truth of the matter. They very well knew
that the power of Satan does not work a miracle of this kind. Incomplete Work on Matthew, Homily 29.[4]

12:25 A Kingdom Divided

Jesus Recognizes Their Motives. Anony-

[3]PL Supp 3:861. [4]PG 56:781.

MOUS: "But Jesus, knowing their thoughts, spoke to them." Yet indeed, as the discussion plainly shows, the Pharisees did not say this but thought it. Moreover, since their wickedness was concealed, what harm could they do to the glory of Christ? None. For the man who thinks evil destroys himself. He does not destroy another. But look at Christ's mercy. If the Pharisees had said this openly and Jesus had responded to them, perhaps we would say that he thus responded to their words in order to confound their wickedness. Now, however, it is clear that he answered them thus not to confound their wickedness but to heal their wounded conscience. Jesus hoped that when they saw their own thoughts expressed in his words, they would understand that it was not simply a man who perceived the content of their hearts. INCOMPLETE WORK ON MATTHEW, HOMILY 29.[5]

THE DESTRUCTIVE DIVISION IS WITHIN JERUSALEM. HILARY: The law comes from God. The promise of the kingdom of Israel comes from the law, and the announcement of Christ's birth and arrival come from the law. If the kingdom of the law is divided against itself, it will of necessity be abandoned. Every power is pulled down by division, and the strength of a kingdom separated from itself is destroyed. Thus the kingdom of Israel has fallen from the law when the people of the law oppose the fulfillment of the law in Christ. "But both a city and a house divided against themselves will not stand." The dwelling of a city is the same principle as that of a kingdom. But this city of Jerusalem is always viewed in contrast to the boastful tyranny of the nations. Now after Jerusalem had been inflamed against the Lord by the madness of its people and after the crowd of the faithful had put his apostles to flight, then it will not stand because of the division of those who are leaving. And so, what directly follows this division is the order for that city's destruction. ON MATTHEW 12.13-14.[6]

THE HOUSE DIVIDED. CHROMATIUS: The Lord declared that a kingdom or city or house divided against itself could not stand. This was said in reference to the kingdom that the Jews themselves occupied under the rule of Jeroboam, the servant of Solomon, which was judged as abandoned before being divided. The Jews would lose entirely the city of Jerusalem, to which Samaria had been hostile. They would lose the dwelling place of God's temple against which golden calves and the house of idols had been erected. He showed them that they ought rather to follow that kingdom that cannot be divided—that is, the heavenly and eternal one. The spiritual city of Jerusalem always remains fixed and immovable. No hostile power ever has been or will be able to overcome the true house of God. That house which is protected by the Son of God is quite safe. TRACTATE ON MATTHEW 49.5.[7]

12:26 How Will Satan Stand?

THE DEVIL'S KINGDOM CANNOT STAND DIVIDED. AUGUSTINE: In saying this, he wanted it to be understood from their confession that they had chosen to live in him by not believing in the kingdom of the devil and that the devil could not stand divided against himself. So let the Pharisees choose what they want. If Satan could not cast out Satan, they could find nothing to say against the Lord. But if Satan can cast out Satan, let them look out for themselves all the more and let them abandon his kingdom because it cannot stand divided against itself. SERMON 71.1.[8]

THE INCONSISTENCY IMPLIED. CHRYSOSTOM: The wars abroad are not so ruinous as the civil wars. As with civil wars, so wars happen inside the body. In all things it is the same, but in this case Jesus takes his illustration from the public

---

[5]PG 56:781. [6]SC 254:278-80. [7]CCL 9a:443. [8]PL 38:445; NPNF 1 6:318 (Sermon 21).

sphere, for what is more powerful on earth than a kingdom? Nothing. But nevertheless it perishes if divided against itself. And what would you say of a city, similarly, if it were to break down by its own weight? What great blame would fall on those who carry the burden of its affairs! And what of a house? Whether it is a small matter or a great one, it perishes when it revolts against itself. Furthermore, if I am possessed by a demon and through it cast out demons, there is dissent and strife between demons, and they rise up against one another. And if they rise up against one another, their strength is destroyed. "For if Satan casts out Satan"—note that he did not say "demons," implying that there was a great deal of harmony in them toward each other. Rather, he said hierarchically, "If Satan casts out Satan, he is then divided against himself." But if he is divided, he is becoming weaker and being ruined. And if he is ruined, how can he cast out another? Do you see how great is the joke[9] of the accusation, how great the folly, the inconsistency? It is not plausible that one would be said to stand by that which was likely to cause one to fall. THE GOSPEL OF MATTHEW, HOMILY 41.1.[10]

12:27 They Shall Judge You

A MATTER OF ATTRIBUTION. JEROME: If they were exorcists casting out devils by invoking God's name, he intimates by clever questioning that they should declare the work to be of the Holy Spirit. He goes on to say, "If the casting out of devils by your [the Pharisees'] children is attributed to God and not to devils, how come the same work does not have the same cause?" Therefore "they shall be your judges," not by authority but by comparison. While they attribute to God the casting out of devils, you attribute it to Beelzebub the prince of devils. But it was said about the apostles (and this we should bear in mind), they will be the judges of those children, for they will sit on twelve thrones judging the twelve tribes of

Israel. COMMENTARY ON MATTHEW 2.12.27.[11]

BY WHOM DO YOUR SONS CAST OUT DEMONS? ANONYMOUS: Jesus called his disciples apostles,[12] who were among those he recently sent to preach, giving them power to cast out unclean spirits.[13] In their belief, they told him, "Lord, even the demons have been subject to us in your name."[14] In whose name have they been casting out devils? If they have been casting them out in my name with the words "In the name of Jesus Christ I order you to go out of him," it is true, because I do not cast out demons in the name of Beelzebub. In fact, whoever it is that casts out demons by Beelzebub, his name cannot be so awesome and revered that others could cast out demons in his name. "Therefore they shall be your judges." When? "When they shall sit on twelve thrones, judging the twelve tribes of Israel."[15] Then the Pharisees will undoubtedly say in judgment of me: "Therefore we do not believe you as you were casting out devils, because we thought you were casting out devils in Beelzebub." The children of faith will answer you back: "If you were to take a good look and see that we were casting out devils in his name, you would realize that the spirit of Beelzebub is not with him in whose name such mighty works are being done." INCOMPLETE WORK ON MATTHEW, HOMILY 29.[16]

12:28 The Kingdom of God Has Come on You

THE SPIRIT OF GOD. APOLLINARIS: Again, his ability "to cast out demons" in the Spirit was something which, as man, he had been made able to do, according to the divine economy.[17] And if the work of the Spirit is the kingdom of

[9]Or absurdity. [10]PG 57:446; NPNF 1 10:264-65**. [11]CCL 77:92-93. [12]Mt 10:2. [13]Mt 10:8. [14]Lk 10:17. [15]Mt 19:28. [16]PG 56:784. [17]*Oikonomia* indicates the divine project involving the incarnation of Christ. The following observation of Apollinaris is addressed to those who at his time denied the divinity of the Holy Spirit (Macedonians, Pneumatomachians).

God, we should in no way regard the Spirit as something added to the Godhead, as if brought in from the servile creation in order to prepare for the divine kingdom. FRAGMENT 72.[18]

PERSONALLY TO YOU. CHRYSOSTOM: To cast out demons is a work of the highest power and not of any ordinary power. For Matthew said, "If it is by the Spirit of God that I cast out demons," just as Luke said, "If I by the finger of God cast out the demons."[19] The inference then might seem to be that if this is so, then quite obviously the Son of God has appeared. This, however, he did not quite say directly but in a reserved way so as not to provoke them. He dimly intimates it by saying "then the kingdom of God has come upon you." Do you grasp this wisdom? His presence was quietly shining forth precisely through the very things to which they were assigning blame. Then, to conciliate them, Jesus said not simply "the kingdom is come" but in a personal sense "to you." It is as though he had said, "Good things have come specifically to you, so why then do you feel so displeased that you are being wonderfully blessed? Why do you make war against your own salvation? This is that very time which the prophets long ago foretold. This is the sign of that advent which was expected by them. Even these things now are being accomplished by divine power. You yourselves know that they are happening. That is a fact. But that they are being accomplished by divine power, you do not realize, so the deeds themselves cry out. It is impossible that Satan should be the stronger power now, for he must of necessity be weaker. For it cannot be that one who is weak can, as though strong, cast out the strong man, the devil." In speaking thus Jesus at the same time pointed to the power of charity and the vulnerability of contentious divisiveness. THE GOSPEL OF MATTHEW, HOMILY 41.2.[20]

12:29 Binding the Strong Man

CHRIST PREVAILS OVER SATAN. CHRYSOSTOM: See how the reverse is confirmed contrary to what his adversaries were trying to establish. They wanted to show that it was not by his own power that Jesus cast out demons. But he instead proved that he held in bondage with all authority not only the demonic powers but even their foremost leader. Christ prevails over Satan by his own power, and thus over the demonic forces. This is evident from the events reported. Satan is the prince of demons and they only subjects. If so, how could they have been plundered unless he were first overcome and made to bow down?

And here Jesus' saying seems to me to encompass a prophecy. For not only, I suppose, are the evil spirits the possessions of the devil but also the human beings that are doing Satan's works. Therefore he intends not only to cast out devils but also to drive away error from the world. He is putting down all sorceries and making the devil's arts useless. THE GOSPEL OF MATTHEW, HOMILY 41.3.[21]

ENTERING THE STRONG MAN'S HOUSE. CYRIL OF ALEXANDRIA: He calls the devil strong, not as though he were so by his created nature but as signifying his tyranny over us, which he has obtained through our own indolence. The Son says, in effect, "I will despoil him, not by allowing him to have human beings as worshipers but by changing their belief so that they might come to acknowledge God. In that case, how then could he become my ally? For is he fighting against himself." FRAGMENT 155.[22]

PLUNDERING THE DEVIL'S HOUSE. THEODORE OF MOPSUESTIA: Jesus here compares the earth with a house and human beings with vessels or possessions. Human beings have become possessions of demons and of the devil, having by evil means been brought under his authority.

---

[18]MKGK 20-21. [19]Lk 11:20. [20]PG 57:447; NPNF 1 10:265**. [21]PG 57:448; NPNF 1 10:266**. The demonic powers could not have been overcome unless their leader, the strong man, Satan, were first bound up. This Christ did. [22]MKGK 202.

Thus it was impossible for the demons' own possessions to be taken away unless the demons were first weakened and bound with chains. FRAGMENT 68.[23]

12:30 One Not with Jesus Is Against Him

ONE WHO DOES NOT GATHER WITH ME SCATTERS. CHROMATIUS: And rightly Jesus adds, "He who is not with me is against me. And he who does not gather with me scatters." By this he meant that his work is one thing and the devil's work another. For the devil is the enemy of human well being. It is proper for the devil to scatter to utter destruction and for Christ to gather to salvation. Hence it is clear that one who is against the Lord cannot be with the Lord. Therefore, although the Lord seems to be repudiating those Pharisees who, unwilling to gather with Christ, have remained the Lord's enemies and adversaries, he speaks also of all heretics and schismatics. Drawing impious conclusions against the church or the Lord by way of unorthodox teachings or schismatic beliefs, they aim to tear asunder and ravage the incorrupt body of the church and the unity of peace and faith. They are oblivious to Solomon's words: "He who splits a log is endangered by it."[24] Clearly those who cause separation in the church shall run the risk of eternal death. TRACTATE ON MATTHEW 50.2.[25]

ONE WHO IS NOT WITH ME. ANONYMOUS: "He who is not with me is against me." The will of the devil—what is it? Only evil. And my will—what is it? Only good. Notice, then, since I am not with the devil, I am against the devil. For even as good is not with evil but always against evil, so too they are not with each other but against each other; and their will and their work are at odds. The devil speaks of fornication; I speak of purity. Thus he turns away the pure and gathers the licentious, whereas I turn away the licentious and gather the pure. He teaches discord, and I teach peace. He gathers

the quarrelsome and disturbed, and I the like-minded and gentle. Notice, then, that I do not gather with him, but I scatter. He says less that he may signify more. If he who is not with me is against me, how much more will he who is against me be not with me? He is not with me because he does not do the things that I do. He is against me because he acts contrary to me. Since I build, if anyone does not help me, even if he does not destroy, he is not with me but against me, for though he is able to help me, he does not. But if he manages to destroy, how much more is he against me! INCOMPLETE WORK ON MATTHEW, HOMILY 29.[26]

12:31 All Sins Forgiven but One

EVERY BLASPHEMY WILL BE FORGIVEN—EXCEPT. HILARY: He condemns in no uncertain terms the thinking of the Pharisees and their intellectual bedfellows. He promises forgiveness of all sins and denies pardon for blasphemy against the Spirit. For although other words and deeds may be treated with liberal forgiveness, there is no mercy if God is denied in Christ. For whatever sins one may commit, he extends the benevolence of his repeated admonition. All kinds of sins are to be forgiven, but blasphemy against the Holy Spirit shall not be forgiven. For what is so beyond the pale of forgiveness as to deny Christ since he is of God? To forsake Christ is to forsake the nature of the Spirit of the Father residing in him. For Jesus fulfills every work in the Spirit of God, is himself the kingdom of heaven, and in him God is reconciling the world to himself. Therefore any blasphemy aimed at Christ is aimed at God, because God is in Christ and Christ is in God. ON MATTHEW 12.17.[27]

BLASPHEMY AGAINST THE HOLY SPIRIT. CHRYSOSTOM: What is Jesus saying at this

---

[23]MKGK 119. [24]Eccles 10:9. [25]CCL 9a:446-47. [26]PG 56:786. [27]SC 254:282-84.

point? He is saying, "You have spoken many things against me. You have called me a deceiver and an adversary of God. These things I forgive you upon your repentance. There will be no penalty exacted. But blasphemy against the Spirit shall not be forgiven, not even to those who repent." But how could this be right? For even this was forgiven upon repentance. Many at least of those who said these words believed afterward, and all was forgiven them. What is it then that Christ was implying? That this sin is above all things inexcusable. Why so? Because they might have been ignorant of Jesus and who he might be, but of the Spirit they could not be ignorant due to their own previous experience. For the prophets had spoken by the Spirit. The Old Testament as a whole had an exalted understanding of the Holy Spirit. What he says, then, is this: "So be it—you may be offended at me, because of the humanity I have assumed. But you cannot say the same of the Holy Spirit.[28] You cannot claim not to know the Spirit. Therefore your blasphemy has no excuse, and you will suffer the consequences both here and hereafter." THE GOSPEL OF MATTHEW, HOMILY 41.3.[29]

IT WILL BE FORGIVEN. SEVERUS: Therefore, no matter what they say in blasphemy—even against the Son of Man when they were scandalized under the economy of law according to the flesh, as I pointed out—our Lord makes it clear they will be forgiven on the excuse of their ignorance of the mystery, his self-abasement and humility shown as a man. That is why Jesus said, "It will be forgiven humans"[30] and did not say "you." What he was saying in effect was "It is to those who do not know the depth of my dispensation that I offer forgiveness." But in their blasphemy they heaped insults against the divine signs he manifested and the many miracles he worked through the Spirit who was in him and who is of the same essence (*ousia*). They exclaimed, "He casts out demons by the prince of demons."[31] Those insults—since they smack of blasphemy against the Holy Spirit and

(because of the facts themselves) what is proper of God, with no room for excuse—Christ says they shall not be forgiven. They could not use ignorance as a pretext for their defense. CATHEDRAL SERMONS, HOMILY 98.[32]

12:32 Blasphemy Against the Spirit

CONTINUING IMPENITENCE AFTER BAPTISM. AUGUSTINE: Against this unmerited gift,[33] against this free grace of God, the impenitent heart may continue to murmur. So it is unrepentance that is a blasphemy against the Spirit.[34] It is not forgiven either in this world or in the next. Think of a person whose sins are entirely forgiven in faithful baptism and whom the church has welcomed.[35] This is the very church commissioned to remit sin, in which whatever sins it remits are promised to be truly remitted. You are speaking a very evil, utterly graceless word against the Holy Spirit, you are speaking it in thought or out loud, if when the patience of God is beckoning you to repentance, you harden your impenitent heart. By doing so you store up wrath for yourself on the day of wrath and of the revelation of the just judgment of God, who will render to us all according to our works.[36] This is the impenitence that is called both by the name of blasphemy and speaking against the Holy Spirit, which will never be forgiven. This is the

---

[28]The words of Jesus regarding sins against the Son of Man and against the Holy Spirit (the former remissible and the latter irremissible) posed a great challenge to the ancient exegetes. The most common interpretation holds the Son of God to be the humanity of Christ and the Holy Spirit his divine nature or the divine nature in general. [29]PG 57: 449; NPNF 1 10:266-67**. [30]Mt 12:31. [31]Mt 9:34. [32]PO 25:154-55*. [33]Of the Holy Spirit, for previously Augustine has been speaking in this sermon about perfect love as the gift of the Holy Spirit, by which sins are cast out, and the people of God gathered together in unity. The unclean spirit struggles against this gift. NPNF 1 6:324-25. [34]Augustine takes exception to the interpretation of Chrysostom (see note 28). By irremissible sin Jesus means the desperation caused by the refusal of repentance. In fact, Augustine believes, every sin is remissible. Thus the only irremissible sin occurs when a person despairing of salvation does not repent, thereby remaining in the grasp of sin. [35]To the Lord's table. [36]Rom 2:4-6.

flagrant impenitence against which both the herald[37] and the Judge[38] cried out when they proclaimed: "Repent, for the kingdom of heaven is near."[39] It is the same impenitence against which the Lord opened his mouth to preach the gospel. He preached against it when he foretold that the gospel itself was to be preached in the whole world; when he said to the disciples after rising from the dead that it was necessary for the Christ to suffer and to rise again from the dead on the third day; and for repentance and the for-

giveness of sins to be preached in his name throughout all nations, beginning from Jerusalem.[40] Yes, this refusal to repent has absolutely no forgiveness, neither in this age nor in the age to come, because repentance obtains forgiveness in this world in preparation for the next. SERMON 71.12.20.[41]

---

[37]John the Baptist. [38]Jesus Christ. [39]Mt 3:2; 4:17. [40]Lk 24:46-47. [41]PL 38:455-56; *WSA* 3 3:258**; NPNF 1 6:325 (Sermon 21).

12:33-37 A TREE AND ITS FRUIT

[33]*"Either make the tree good, and its fruit good; or make the tree bad, and its fruit bad; for the tree is known by its fruit. [34]You brood of vipers! how can you speak good, when you are evil? For out of the abundance of the heart the mouth speaks. [35]The good man out of his good treasure brings forth good, and the evil man out of his evil treasure brings forth evil. [36]I tell you, on the day of judgment men will render account for every careless word they utter; [37]for by your words you will be justified, and by your words you will be condemned."*

OVERVIEW: One needs only to examine the fruit to discover what kind of tree it is. Having no fault to find with Jesus' works, the fruit, the Pharisees passed the opposite judgment upon the tree, himself. They called him a demoniac, which, as anyone can see, is self-evidently reckless. For a good tree cannot bring forth evil fruit (CHRYSOSTOM). In saying "make the tree bad and its fruit bad," Jesus did not command us to do so but warned us to guard against those who think they are able, though they remain bad, to speak good things or to do good works (AUGUSTINE). The wicked have little business quoting Scripture and no moral right to twist it. An account must be rendered to God for every idle, careless and useless word (HILARY). Jesus calls them a "brood of vipers" because they prided themselves on their forefathers but had no advantage

thereby (CHRYSOSTOM).

It is not surprising that they can utter nothing good, for words follow the disposition of the soul (THEODORE OF MOPSUESTIA). The hidden fountain behind wicked words is the corrupted heart (CHRYSOSTOM). On the day of judgment each person must render an account of his or her words (JEROME, THEODORE OF HERACLEA). Those who watch how they speak need not fear judgment (CHRYSOSTOM).

12:33 Trees Are Known by Their Fruit

EITHER-OR. HILARY: Though spoken in the present, Jesus' words would be borne out in the future. For in the present he refutes the Jews. They could see that the works of Christ were beyond human power, but they were unwilling to declare them as works of God. In saying this Jesus anticipates the future of numerous perversions of faith, especially of those who would divest the Lord of the dignity and union with the Father's nature and so plunge into heresy. They then wander aimlessly in the arena between those who act with the excuse of ignorance and those who live in the knowledge of truth. . . .

Through a tree's inherent vitality, fruitfulness abounds. Therefore either the tree must be made good with good fruit or made bad with bad fruit, because by its fruit the tree is known. The meaning is not that a bad tree, according to the nature of trees, can constitute what is good or be good in its branches if it is bad. Rather, it is that Christ must either be left behind as useless or held onto as good because of the usefulness of good fruit. ON MATTHEW 12.18.[1]

KNOWN BY ITS FRUIT. CHRYSOSTOM: This accusation[2] is against common reason, straining against all the other congruities in these circumstances. They brought no direct charge against his deeds but only against the one who did them. It is shameless to interpret maliciously. Even more so it is shameless to make up charges contrary to what everyone could see was happening.

Yet note how free Jesus is from contentiousness. For he did not simply say "Make the tree good and its fruit good." Rather, he silenced them completely, demonstrating his own considerateness and their insolence, by saying in effect: So you are determined to find fault with my deeds. I do not quarrel with this. But I want you to be aware of how inconsistent and contradictory are your charges. For in this way your motives are transparent. You persist against what is all too clear to everyone else. In this way your malice is disclosed.

Truly the distinction between trees is shown by their fruit. It is not that the fruit is known by the tree, for one need only to examine the fruit alone to find what kind of tree it is. But what if it is argued that the tree is incongruous with the

fruit? Nonetheless the fruit is what makes the tree known. His implication: It would be more consistent if you either found fault with my deeds or praised them, so that I could meet these charges openly. But having no fault to find with my works, the fruit, you pass the opposite judgment upon the tree, me. You call me a demoniac, which, as anyone can see, is self-evidently reckless. For a good tree cannot bring forth evil fruit. THE GOSPEL OF MATTHEW, HOMILY 42.1.[3]

MAKE THE TREE GOOD. AUGUSTINE: When he says, "Make the tree good and its fruit good," this is not a friendly admonition but a clear command to be obeyed. And when Jesus says, "Make the tree bad and its fruit bad," he does not command you to do so, but he warns you to guard against it. He is referring to those who think they are able, though they are bad, to speak good things or to do good works. This the Lord Jesus says they cannot do. For a person must first be changed in order for his works to be changed. But if a person remains in an evil state, that one cannot do good works. If he abides in what is good, he will not be found producing evil works. SERMONS ON NEW TESTAMENT LESSONS 72.1.1.[4]

12:34 One Speaks from the Abundance of the Heart

ONE WHO IS EVIL CANNOT SPEAK GOOD. HILARY: He taught that a corrupt outlook on life arises out of a corrupted nature. He taught

---

[1]SC 254:284-86. [2]From the Pharisees, Mt 12:24: "It is only by Beelzebul, the prince of demons, that this man casts out demons." [3]PG 57:451; NPNF 1 10:268-69**. [4]PL 38:467; NPNF 1 6:332 (Sermon 22). In opposing those who imagined they could do good works even while remaining inwardly corrupt, Jesus admonished them to be wary lest the fruit of good works become warped by an inwardly corrupted nature. In doing so he directed them by precept categorically to make the tree (the will) good. The moral status of the requirement to avoid evil is an admonition, while the moral status of the precept to "make the tree good" is an intrinsic necessity for anyone who seeks to do good.

that from an evil storehouse nothing can come but what is evil. An account must be rendered to God for every idle, careless and useless word. We are to be condemned or justified by the words we speak. The mercy or the judgment we receive shall depend on the inward conviction we have about the Lord of heavenly glory. ON MATTHEW 12.19.[5]

YOU BROOD OF VIPERS. CHRYSOSTOM: "If you are an evil tree, you cannot produce good fruit. I am not surprised at what you are saying. For being both ill bred and ill conceived, you have acquired an evil way of speaking." See how precisely, and without any room for exception, Jesus defines their indictment. In a single phrase he uses their own arguments to demonstrate his point and to underscore his indictment. He calls them a "brood of vipers" because they prided themselves on their forefathers. To signify that they had no advantage thereby, Christ first throws out their exalted claims about their relation to Abraham and then assigns them to forefathers of similar disposition. He thus stripped them of their illusions. THE GOSPEL OF MATTHEW, HOMILY 42.1.[6]

DISPOSITION OF THE SOUL. THEODORE OF MOPSUESTIA: "O worst of men," he says, "you have not shrunk from any wickedness of vipers. So it is not surprising that you utter nothing good. For words follow the disposition of the soul. How can you speak good, when you are evil?" FRAGMENT 70.[7]

12:35 Good and Evil Treasures

THE FOUNTAIN BEHIND WICKED WORDS. CHRYSOSTOM: When wickedness is overflowing within, its words will pour out of one's mouth. So when you hear someone speaking wicked words, do not suppose only so much wickedness to be in that one as the words display, but suspect the fountain to be much more abundant. For that which is spoken outwardly is the super-

abundance of that which is within. THE GOSPEL OF MATTHEW, HOMILY 42.1.[8]

GOOD OR BAD BY CHOICE. CYRIL OF ALEXANDRIA: When he says "treasure," Christ refers to the multitude of motives that lie in the soul. It is not by nature that people are good or bad but by their own choice.[9] He makes this plain in his remark to the Pharisees: It is possible for one and the same person at one time to become good, at another time evil, for "a good man speaks out of the abundance of his heart," and likewise for the bad. FRAGMENT 158.[10]

12:36 Rendering an Account

EVERY CARELESS WORD. JEROME: This, too, goes with what was said before, and the meaning is that on the day of judgment each person must render an account of his or her words. If an idle word which by no means edifies the listeners is not without harm to the speaker, how much more will you Pharisees, who criticize the works of the Holy Spirit and say that I cast out devils by Beelzebub the prince of devils, have to render an account of your criticism? An idle word is what is spoken without benefit to the speaker and the listener. We overlook serious things and utter frivolous things and tell old wives' tales. One who acts like a buffoon and makes mouths drop with boisterous laughter and who utters disgraceful things—that person shall be held to account, not for an idle word but a slanderous word. COMMENTARY ON MATTHEW 2.12.36.[11]

12:37 Judged by One's Words

CONDEMNED BY YOUR OWN WORDS. THEODORE OF HERACLEA: If we are called to account "for every careless word," how much more will

---

[5]SC 254:288. [6]PG 57:451-52; NPNF 1 10:269**. [7]MKGK 119. [8]PG 57:452; NPNF 1 10:269. [9]Cyril refers to Gnostics and Manichaeans, who identified humanity as good or evil according to nature, not free choice. [10]MKGK 203. [11]CCL 77:96.

those who have blasphemed against the Spirit of the only begotten Son receive a more bitter punishment on the day of judgment. And if, Christ says, someone merely utters a slander against someone else, that one will by no means escape judgment. If they will give an account concerning an idle word, how much more so concerning a work. FRAGMENTS 88-89.[12]

CAREFUL OF WORDS. CHRYSOSTOM: Do you see how far the Judge is from being vindictive? How favorable the account required? For it is not upon what someone else has spoken of you but from what you have yourself spoken. From this will the Judge give his sentence. This is the fairest of all procedures. It rests wholly with you to speak or not to speak.

So it is not those who are slandered but the slanderers who have cause to tremble and be anxious. Those slandered are not constrained to answer for themselves concerning the evil things said of them. But the slanderers will answer for the evil they have spoken. And over these words danger hangs. So persons censured should be without anxiety, not being required to give account of the evil others have said. But the censurers have cause to be in anxiety and to tremble, as being subject themselves to be dragged before the judgment seat. Hence slander is indeed a diabolical snare, and a sin containing no pleasure but only harm. . . .

So the plotter first destroys himself. One who walks on fire burns himself up. One who smites others bruises himself. One who kicks against the goads draws blood from himself. THE GOSPEL OF MATTHEW, HOMILY 42.2.[13]

---

[12]MKGK 81. [13]PG 57:453; NPNF 1 10:270.

12:38-42 THE DEMAND FOR A SIGN FROM HEAVEN

[38]*Then some of the scribes and Pharisees said to him, "Teacher, we wish to see a sign from you." [39]But he answered them, "An evil and adulterous generation seeks for a sign; but no sign shall be given to it except the sign of the prophet Jonah. [40]For as Jonah was three days and three nights in the belly of the whale, so will the Son of man be three days and three nights in the heart of the earth. [41]The men of Nineveh will arise at the judgment with this generation and condemn it; for they repented at the preaching of Jonah, and behold, something greater than Jonah is here. [42]The queen of the South will arise at the judgment with this generation and condemn it; for she came from the ends of the earth to hear the wisdom of Solomon, and behold, something greater than Solomon is here.*

OVERVIEW: The Pharisees imagined that Jesus was not in control of his passions and that he could be at one moment moved to anger and in the next moment manipulated by flattery (CHRYSOSTOM). To seek from the Son of God a sign of his divinity was nothing else than to disbelieve his words, as if he is speaking falsely about himself unless he backs up his words with signs (ANONYMOUS). Those who wish to know the Son of God through a demonstration of signs but not through faith will remain trapped in their disbelief, falling on the stumbling block of his death, which is the sign of Jonah (Anonymous). The three days of his death and resurrection refer to the end of Friday, all of Saturday and the beginning of Sunday of the passion week (Theodore of Heraclea). Jonah prefigured the Son of Man (Augustine), and the people of Nineveh prefigured the believers (Anonymous). Yet there are many limitations in the analogy between Jonah and Jesus (Chrysostom, Cyril of Alexandria). The church fulfills the type of the queen of the south, providing not gifts of perishable things but faith, the incense of knowledge, the outpouring of an offering, the sweat of the virtues and the blood of martyrdom (Origen, Augustine). Yet there remain many limits to this analogy as well (Anonymous).

12:38 Jesus Rejects the Demand for a Sign

Flattering the Teacher. Chrysostom: *Then.* When? Just when they ought to be kneeling before him, to admire, to be amazed and give way, then they refuse to cease from their wickedness. And note their words too, teeming with flattery and dissimulation. For they tried to draw him out in their deceptive way. First they insult, then they flatter him; now calling him a demoniac, now again Master, both out of an evil mind. No more self-contradictory words were ever spoken.

This is why he rebukes them severely. Note that when they were questioning him roughly and insulting him, Jesus reasoned with them gently. But when they were flattering him he reproached them with greater severity. They imagine that he is in control of neither passion and that he can be at one moment moved to anger and in the next moment softened by flattery. The Gospel of Matthew, Homily 43.1.[1]

Their Perversity. Anonymous: When the demoniac had been healed, some of the Jewish bystanders blasphemed the Lord, saying, "This

man does not cast out devils except by Beelzebub, the prince of devils." And others tempted him, saying, "Teacher, we wish to see you give a sign from heaven." The form of those expressions may be different indeed, but they have a common perversity. To ascribe to the devil the works of the Son of God is to blaspheme the Son of God or the Holy Spirit. Likewise, to seek from the Son of God a sign of his divinity is to insult the Son of God, because to seek from him a sign of his divinity is nothing else but to disbelieve the words of him who is speaking, as it were, false things about himself unless he backs up his words with overt signs. Incomplete Work on Matthew, Homily 30.[2]

We Wish to See a Sign. Cyril of Alexandria: They say the miracles he has performed are from devils. He only conjures up imaginary images on the earth. So come then, by your power: perform a miracle from heaven. For another Evangelist says clearly that they wanted Jesus to perform a sign from heaven as an action befitting his divine power.[3] They said this, blinded in their minds, as though Jesus were unable to do anything befitting God. For to open the eyes of the blind and to raise the dead and to rebuke the winds and the sea—all these miracles could be accomplished only by a divine power. Fragment 160.[4]

12:39 No Sign Except the Sign of Jonah

An Evil and Adulterous Generation. Origen: That generation was evil, on account of the influence that had come to be in it from the evil one. It was adulterous because it had left her natural husband—the word or law of truth—and had come to be wedded to a lie. The law which is "in the members" of our flesh wars against "the law of the mind."[5] It is an adulterer of the soul. Every opposing power, when it has

---

[1]PG 57:457; NPNF 1 10:273. [2]PG 56:787. [3]Mk 8:11; Lk 11:16; Mt 16:1. [4]MKGK 204. [5]Rom 7:23.

intercourse with the soul unfaithfully—the soul that has as its bridegroom the Word of God—causes the soul to commit adultery. FRAGMENT 274.[6]

A WISH FOR A SIGN. ANONYMOUS: Do you wish to see a sign? Where were you when the devil, chastised by me not with a whip but with a word, cried out, "What are we to do with you, Jesus of Nazareth? Have you come here to torment us before the time? We know that you are the Son of God."[7] The devils became aware of my power, and how is it that you have failed to see the sign of my works? Where were you when the blind seated by the wayside cried out, "Jesus, Son of David, have mercy on us,"[8] that we may see? INCOMPLETE WORK ON MATTHEW, HOMILY 30.[9]

THE SIGN OF JONAH. ANONYMOUS: What is the sign of Jonah? The stumbling block of the cross. So it is not the disputers of knowledge who will be saved but those who believe true teaching. For the cross of Christ is indeed a stumbling block to those who dispute knowledge but salvation to those who believe. Paul testifies to this: "But we, for our part, preach the crucified Christ—to the Jews indeed a stumbling block and to the Gentiles foolishness, but to those who are called, both Jews and Greeks, Christ, the power of God and the wisdom of God."[10] Why do the Jews seek signs and the Greeks seek wisdom? God pointed to the sign of the stumbling block of the cross to both the Jews and the Greeks. Thus those who wish to find Christ not through faith but through wisdom will perish on the stumbling block of foolishness. Those who wish to know the Son of God not through faith but through a demonstration of signs will remain trapped in their disbelief, falling on the stumbling block of his death. It is no small wonder that the Jews, considering the death of Christ, thought he was merely a man, when even Christians—as they purport to be but really are not—because of his death are reluc-

tant to declare the only begotten, the crucified, as incomparable majesty. INCOMPLETE WORK ON MATTHEW, HOMILY 30.[11]

12:40 Three Days and Three Nights

THE THREE DAYS OF JESUS' DEATH AND RESURRECTION. THEODORE OF HERACLEA: Christ says he will spend "three days and three nights in the heart of the earth." He is referring to the end of Friday, all of Saturday and the beginning of Sunday [of the passion week], in keeping with the way people understood the beginning and ending of days. For we too commemorate the third day of those who have died, not when three days and three nights, completed in equal measure, have gone by. But we reckon as a single, complete day that day on which the person died, regardless of what hour the death occurred. We count as another day that on which we take our leave of the departed in hymns before the tombs. Following this same kind of sequence, then, the Lord announced that he would spend a full three days and nights under the earth. A clear indication of this is the fact that the women arrived at that very time, in order to fulfill those things that the law prescribed to be done for the dead upon the third day. FRAGMENT 90.[12]

JONAH PREFIGURED THE SON OF MAN. AUGUSTINE: The Savior pointed out that Jonah the prophet, who having been tossed into the sea was caught in the belly of the whale and emerged on the third day, prefigured the Son of Man who would suffer and rise on the third day. The Jewish people were censured in comparison with the Ninevites, for the Ninevites, to whom Jonah the prophet had been sent by way of reproof, placated God's wrath by repenting and gained his mercy. "And behold," he said, "something greater than Jonah is here,"[13] the Lord

---

[6]GCS 41.1:123. [7]Mt 8:29. [8]Mt 20:30. [9]PG 56:788. [10]1 Cor 1:23-24. [11]PG 56:788. [12]*MKGK* 81-82. [13]Mt 12:41; Lk 11:32.

Jesus implying himself. The Ninevites heard the servant and amended their ways; the Jews heard the Lord and not only did they not amend their ways but moreover they killed him. SERMON 72A.1.[14]

CHRIST FORETOLD BY THE PROPHETS. ANONYMOUS: In the mystery of this analogy, Jonah was considered to have been a prophet through Christ. Through Jonah, Christ was shown to be the Son of God. What do I mean by this? Unless Christ had come into the world and fulfilled those things foretold by the prophets, it would not have been certain that these men were prophets. For those who are said to foretell the future are considered to be seers only when the things they foretold have come to pass. Thus Christ was indeed born after the prophets. Before that, however, he accorded the prophets a distinction, and later he accepted it from them. Christ therefore showed them to be prophets by his deeds, because they showed him to be the Son of God by their words. INCOMPLETE WORK ON MATTHEW, HOMILY 30.[15]

12:41 One Greater Than Jonah

DIFFERENCES BETWEEN JONAH AND JESUS. CHRYSOSTOM: For Jonah was a servant, but I am the Master; and he came forth from the great fish, but I rose from death. He proclaimed destruction, but I am come preaching the good tidings of the kingdom. The Ninevites indeed believed without a sign, but I have exhibited many signs. They heard nothing more than those words, but I have made it impossible to deny the truth. The Ninevites came to be ministered to, but I, the very Master and Lord of all, have come not threatening, not demanding an account, but bringing pardon. They were barbarians, but these—the faithful—have conversed with unnumbered prophets. And of Jonah nothing had been prophesied in advance, but of me everything was foretold, and all the facts have agreed with their words. And Jonah

indeed, when he was to go forth, instead ran away that he might not be ridiculed. But I, knowing that I am both to be crucified and mocked, have come nonetheless. While Jonah did not endure so much as to be reproached for those who were saved, I underwent even death, and that the most shameful death, and after this I sent others again. And Jonah was a strange sort of person and an alien to the Ninevites, and unknown; but I a kinsman after the flesh and of the same forefathers. THE GOSPEL OF MATTHEW, HOMILY 43.2.[16]

THE LIMITATIONS OF THE ANALOGY. CYRIL OF ALEXANDRIA: If Jonah then is taken as a type of Christ, he is not so taken in every respect[17]—he was sent to preach to the Ninevites, but he sought to flee from the presence of God.[18] And he is seen to shrink from going to the east. The Son also was sent from God the Father to preach to the nations, but he was not unwilling to assume this ministry.

The prophet appeals to those sailing with him to throw him into the sea,[19] then he was swallowed by a great fish, then after three days he was given back up and afterwards went to Nineveh and fulfilled his ministry. But he was embittered beyond measure when God took pity upon the Ninevites. Christ willingly submitted to death, he remained in the heart of the earth, he came back to life and afterward went up to Galilee and commanded that the preaching to the Gentiles should begin. But he was not grieved to see that those who were called to acknowledge the truth were being saved.

Thus just as bees in the field, when flitting about the flowers, always gather up what is useful for the provision of the hives, so we also, when searching in the divinely inspired Scrip-

---

[14]MA 1:155-56; WSA 3 3:281. [15]PG 56:788. [16]PG 57:459; NPNF 1 10:274. [17]Jonah is a symbolic and prophetic prefiguration of Christ only for certain of his acts, such as his three-day sojourn in the stomach of the great fish (symbolic of Christ's three days in the tomb), not for others mentioned here by Cyril. [18]Jon 1:2-3. [19]Jon 1:12.

tures, need always to be collecting and collating what is perfect for explicating Christ's mysteries and to interpret the Word fully without cause for rebuke. FRAGMENT 162.[20]

THE PEOPLE OF NINEVEH. ANONYMOUS: "The people of Nineveh will arise at the judgment with this generation and condemn it." For they received the prophet, whereas the Jews rejected Christ, the Lord of the prophets. Nineveh, not having been instructed by the law or the prophets or admonished by the apostles, turned to the Lord, knowing their sins. The latter, having been imbued with so many commandments of the law and the prophets, turned away from the Lord. The former, who had turned to being the people of the devil, within three days became the people of God. The latter, who had always appeared to be the people of God, within three days after Christ was crucified became the people of Satan. The Ninevites, not knowing who the person was and hearing incredible things, might have sought from him the signs and wonders of their conversion, that by those things the worthy person of the preacher and the incontestable truth of his words might be shown. But hearing nothing of those things and seeing nothing, they were saved by faith alone. The Jews, however, saw heavenly nature working so many signs in witness. Yet not only did they turn a deaf ear to him, but they conspired to bring about his death. The Ninevites, repenting with great sorrow and remorse, received the forgiveness of their sins. But the Jews did not want to accept the forgiveness of sins offered them, because they thought that the gifts and the calling of the Messiah would be offered without repentance. INCOMPLETE WORK ON MATTHEW, HOMILY 30.[21]

12:42 One Greater Than Solomon

FROM THE ENDS OF THE EARTH. ORIGEN: The church of the Gentiles, which in truth is gathered "from the ends of the earth," fulfills the place of the queen of the south, not providing gifts in "perishable things, silver" and spices, but faith, the incense of knowledge, the outpouring of an offering, the sweat of the virtues and the blood of martyrdom. For with such gifts the true Solomon is pleased, who is Christ, "our peace."[22] For "Solomon" is interpreted as "peaceful." FRAGMENT 277.[23]

GREATER THAN SOLOMON. AUGUSTINE: It was nothing strange for Christ to be more than Jonah and to be more than Solomon, for he is the Lord and they are the servants. But who are those who looked askance at the presence of the Lord, whereas foreigners listened to his servants? SERMON 72A.1.[24]

THE QUEEN OF THE SOUTH. ANONYMOUS: "The queen of the south will rise up in the judgment with this generation and will condemn it." Although she was gentle and a woman, she was not deterred by the weakness of her sex from completing so long a journey. For the desire of wisdom gave strength to her weakness. But these men and priests, whose task it was to love wisdom, showed contempt for the wisdom placed on their lap before their very eyes. She hastened to Solomon. The Pharisees withdrew from God. She came to him that she might hear his unadorned words just once. They, seeing the very works of his divinity that day, blasphemed him. She, merely hearing of Solomon's repute, desired to see him. They, witnessing the truth of Christ, walked away. She offered many gifts so as to hear him. But they did not want to receive the rewards of the kingdom of heaven in order to believe. INCOMPLETE WORK ON MATTHEW, HOMILY 30.[25]

---

[20]MKGK 205. [21]PG 56:789. [22]Eph 2:14. [23]GCS 41.1:124. [24]MA 1:56; WSA 3 3:281. [25]PG 56:789.

12:43-50 RETURN OF AN EVIL SPIRIT; JESUS' MOTHER AND BROTHERS

[43]*"When the unclean spirit has gone out of a man, he passes through waterless places seeking rest, but he finds none.* [44]*Then he says, 'I will return to my house from which I came.' And when he comes he finds it empty, swept, and put in order.* [45]*Then he goes and brings with him seven other spirits more evil than himself, and they enter and dwell there; and the last state of that man becomes worse than the first. So shall it be also with this evil generation."*

[46]*While he was still speaking to the people, behold, his mother and his brothers stood outside, asking to speak to him.*[g] [48]*But he replied to the man who told him, "Who is my mother, and who are my brothers?"* [49]*And stretching out his hand toward his disciples, he said, "Here are my mother and my brothers!* [50]*For whoever does the will of my Father in heaven is my brother, and sister, and mother."*

g Other ancient authorities insert verse 47, *Some one told him, "Your mother and your brothers are standing outside, asking to speak to you"*

OVERVIEW: What happens when someone who has once believed now disbelieves? The demons may again take up their abode there with a vengeance (CYRIL OF ALEXANDRIA). The seven good spirits are the spirit of wisdom and understanding, counsel and strength, knowledge and true godliness, and reverence toward God. Arrayed against these are the sevenfold evil spirits: the spirit of stupidity and error, the spirit of foolhardiness and cowardice, the spirit of ignorance and impiety and the spirit of pride contrary to the fear of God (AUGUSTINE).

To refute Christ's words, the devil slyly introduced Christ's relatives in the flesh. By focusing attention on them he sought to draw attention away from Christ's divinity (ANONYMOUS). When Jesus said, "Whoever does the will of my Father is my brother," he was not speaking in contempt of his family but in order to show that he valued more highly closeness of soul than of the body (THEODORE OF MOPSUESTIA, GREGORY THE GREAT). It is greater for Mary to have been a believing disciple of Christ than the mother of Christ (AUGUSTINE).

12:43-44 Seeking Rest but Not Finding It

THROUGH WATERLESS PLACES. HILARY: The law which was given later intervened, casting out the unclean spirit dwelling in the hearts of the elect people. It kept that spirit away as if it were surrounding the people with its protective power. Going out from there, the spirit wandered among the nations in the deserts and arid places, leaving behind its old home, so that it might rest in these places until the day of judgment and not in a troubled dwelling [as Israel provided].

But when God's grace was imparted afresh to the nations, flowing as a living fountain through the cleansing water [of baptism], there was no place for the spirit to continue living among them, and indeed he had no rest with them. After reconsidering its present situation, the spirit believed the best thing to do was to return to the house from which it had come. That house, having been cleaned out through the law, decorated with the proclamation of the prophets and finally prepared by the coming of Christ, was found to be vacant. The custodian of the law had left—because the whole law [was valid] until John—and those living there did not receive Christ.

Also, there was no inhabitant in the dwelling, and it had been left unguarded. Because of the concern of those who were living there before, the place had been kept clean and adorned for the incoming dweller. Then seven spirits even more evil entered in—as many as there were the gifts of grace offered by Christ which God's all-embracing wisdom had placed there with a sevenfold glory.[1] In this way the possession of wicked spirits was as great as the possession of grace would have been. Thus "the last state of that man becomes worse than the first," because the unclean spirit left the house for fear of the law but now returns with a vengeance because of the grace that was rejected. On Matthew 12:22-23.[2]

12:45 The Last State Worse Than the First

Seven Other Spirits. Augustine: When there is forgiveness of sins through the sacraments, the house is cleaned; but the Holy Spirit must be a necessary inhabitant. And the Holy Spirit inhabits only those who are humble of heart, for God says, "Upon whom will my Spirit rest?" And he answers the question: "Upon the one who is humble and quiet and who fears my word."[3] Therefore, when he is the inhabitant, he fills up, rules, acts, deters from evil, inspires one to do good and tempers justice with sweetness, so that one may do good with the love of an upright heart and not with the fear of punishment.

But once that unclean spirit that made you evil has gone out of you, that is, from your mind, when your sins have been forgiven, it roams through dry places in search of a resting place. Finding none, the unclean spirit returns to his house, where he finds everything clean and in order. Then he takes with him seven other spirits more evil than himself; and the last state of that person becomes worse than the first. He takes

with him seven other spirits. What is meant by "seven other spirits"? Is the unclean spirit itself sevenfold? What does this mean? By seven the whole group is signified.[4] The whole spirit went away, the whole spirit came back; and would that only one spirit returned! What does it mean: "He takes with him seven other spirits"? Those spirits you did not have when you were evil, you will have unexpectedly when you are good. Listen carefully while I explain as best I can. By a sevenfold operation the Holy Spirit is committed to our care, so that we may have the "spirit of wisdom and understanding, counsel and fortitude, knowledge and true godliness, and fear of God."[5] Arrayed on the opposite side of this sevenfold good is the sevenfold evil: the spirit of stupidity and error, the spirit of foolhardiness and cowardice, the spirit of ignorance and impiety, and the spirit of pride against the fear of God. These are seven evil spirits. What are the seven other spirits even more evil? The seven other spirits even more evil are found in hypocrisy. One evil spirit is the spirit of stupidity, the other worse evil is the pretense of wisdom. The evil spirit of error, the other worse evil, is the pretense of truth. The evil spirit of foolhardiness, the other worse evil, is the pretense of counsel. The evil spirit of cowardice, the other worse evil, is the pretense of fortitude. The evil spirit of ignorance, the other worse evil, is the pretense of knowledge. The evil spirit of impiety, the other worse evil, is the pretense of piety. The evil spirit of pride, the other worse evil, is the pretense of fear. Seven were intolerable. Who will tolerate fourteen? Necessarily, therefore, when the pretense of truth is added to malice, the last state of that person becomes worse than the first. Sermon 72A.2.[6]

The Souls of the Lawless. Cyril of Alexandria: This is said with good reason. For

---

[1]The gifts of the spirit to come prophesied in Isaiah 11:2-3 LXX. [2]SC 254:292. [3]Is 66:1. [4]This is the usual symbolic meaning of the number seven, insofar as God completed the creation of the world in seven days. [5]Is 11:2-3. [6]MA 1:156-57; WSA 3 3:282-83.

when someone who has once been freed from evils loses self-control, he suffers a much worse fall than previously. For this reason "he passes through waterless places seeking rest." This indicates how thoroughly the demons' stratagem has taken hold of such a person—completely and absolutely. There are many reasons why such a person should have kept himself under control before it is too late. He has already suffered. He has been redeemed. The threat of a worse future punishment should be constraining. But none of these reasons has prevailed to make them better.

Now remember how the evil spirit inhabited the people when they were in Egypt, how they lived according to Egyptian customs and laws and became filled with all kinds of uncleanness. When they had been delivered by Moses and had received the law as a guide calling them to the light of true divine knowledge, the wicked and unclean spirit left them. But what happens when someone who has believed now disbelieves? The demons again take up their abode there with a vengeance. For just as the Holy Spirit, when he sees a person's heart desisting from all uncleanness, abides and dwells and rests in that one, so also the unclean spirit likes to take lodging in the souls of the lawless. FRAGMENT 163.[7]

12:46-48 Who Is My Family?

FAMILY RELATIONSHIPS. APOLLINARIS: That "his brothers" did not yet believe in him we learn from John,[8] while from Mark[9] we have also heard something else: for his own family tried to lay hands on him, as though he were beside himself.[10] On account of their frame of mind, the Lord does not often mention them as his own family. He points instead to those who are obedient. To believers he applies all the terms of family relationship, those, namely, who had been joined to him in the kindred fellowship of obedience. Even if temporarily he had a quarrel with Mary, as Simeon had foretold when he had said "a sword shall pierce through your own

soul," she overcame these things, as was fitting, and the Lord graciously made mention of her at his passion and entrusted her to the beloved disciple.[11] FRAGMENT 75.[12]

12:49 The Disciples Are Jesus' Brothers

WHO IS MY MOTHER? AUGUSTINE: Is it not true that the Virgin Mary did the Father's will, she who believed in faith, conceived in faith and was chosen so that, through her, salvation could be born for us among humans and was begotten by Christ before Christ was begotten in her? Holy Mary carried out, plainly and clearly, the Father's will. Therefore it is greater for Mary to have been a disciple of Christ than the mother of Christ. Indeed, it is greater and better to have been the disciple of Christ than the mother of Christ. Mary was therefore blessed because, even before she gave birth, she bore the Master in her womb.... Mary is holy and Mary is blessed, but the church is greater than the Virgin Mary. And why? Because Mary is a part of the church, a holy limb, an extraordinary limb, an outstanding limb, but she is only a limb of the whole body. If she is but a part of the whole body, greater indeed is the body than a limb. Christ is the head, and Christ is the entire head and body. What shall I say? We have a divine head. We have God as our head. SERMON 72A.7.[13]

MY MOTHER AND MY BROTHERS. ANONYMOUS: The devil observed that Christ was persuading the people that he was the Son of God. He was saying, "Behold, something greater than Jonah is here,"[14] and "Behold, something greater than Solomon is here."[15] The devil feared that if he who was considered only a man was acknowledged to be the Son of God, the devil would be

---

[7]MKGK 205-6. [8]Jn 7:5. [9]p. 238 n.2. Here too the recourse to parallel passages in the other Gospels (Mk 3:31; Jn 7:5) allows sharper clarification of the passage in question, in this case the hostility expressed toward Jesus by his relatives. [10]Mk 3:21. [11]Jn 19:27. [12]MKGK 22-23. [13]MA 1:162-63; WSA 3 3:287-88. [14]Mt 12:41. [15]Mt 12:42.

abandoned by all. To refute Christ's words, the devil slyly introduced Christ's own relatives in the flesh. By focusing attention on them, he hoped to obscure the nature of Christ's divinity. Thus someone came forward, the devil's advocate as it were, who with human speech spoke diabolical words, saying, "Behold, your mother and your brothers are standing outside, asking to speak to you." He seemed to be saying, "Why are you boasting, Jesus, about how you came down from heaven, you who have roots on earth? "Behold, your mother and your brothers are standing outside." He thus implied that he who has been brought forth by humans cannot be the Son of God. You cannot conceal the one who has been exposed by nature. Then Jesus looked at him who appeared to be a man but who was really the devil speaking. "And who is my mother and who are my brothers?" I have no relatives in this world, I who created the world before its very foundation. I do not know a beginning in the flesh (as Photinus believed),[16] I who was with God already at the beginning. What you see in me as merely a man is only my garment, not my [theandric] nature.

"And stretching out his hand toward his disciples, he said, 'Here are my mother and my brothers.'" Without denigrating the process of birth or being ashamed of embodiment as a human, Jesus gave that answer. He wanted to show that the spiritual [God-human] relationship must take precedence over the merely carnal relationship. INCOMPLETE WORK ON MATTHEW, HOMILY 30.[17]

12:50 *The Will of My Father in Heaven*

WHOEVER DOES THE WILL OF MY FATHER. THEODORE OF MOPSUESTIA: He said these things, not in contempt of his mother and his brothers, but in order to show that he values more highly closeness of soul than any blood relation of body. For it was necessary to say this, both for those who thought that it was more important for him to interact with his own family, as well as for the instruction of those who were present. For just as he himself says to the disciples, "he who loves father or mother more than me is not worthy of me,"[18] in the same way, I think, Jesus sets a higher value on his disciples than on his "mother and brothers." FRAGMENT 71.[19]

MY MOTHER THROUGH FAITH. GREGORY THE GREAT: If someone can become the brother of the Lord by coming to faith, we must ask how one can become also his mother. We must realize that the one who is Christ's brother and sister by believing becomes his mother by preaching. It is as though one brings forth the Lord and infuses him in the hearts of one's listeners. And that person becomes his mother if through one's voice the love of the Lord is generated in the mind of his neighbor. FORTY GOSPEL HOMILIES 3.2.[20]

---

[16]Photinus of Sirmium, a heretic of the fourth century, denied the personal existence of Christ as Logos, the Son of God prior to the incarnation. [17]PG 56:791. [18]Mt 10:37. [19]*MKGK* 119-20. [20]PL 76:1086; CS 123:5-6 (Homily 1).

13:1-9 THE PARABLE OF THE SOWER

[1]*That same day Jesus went out of the house and sat beside the sea.* [2]*And great crowds gathered about him, so that he got into a boat and sat there; and the whole crowd stood on the beach.* [3]*And he told them many things in parables, saying: "A sower went out to sow.* [4]*And as he sowed,*

some seeds fell along the path, and the birds came and devoured them. ⁵Other seeds fell on rocky ground, where they had not much soil, and immediately they sprang up, since they had no depth of soil, ⁶but when the sun rose they were scorched; and since they had no root they withered away. ⁷Other seeds fell upon thorns, and the thorns grew up and choked them. ⁸Other seeds fell on good soil and brought forth grain, some a hundredfold, some sixty, some thirty. ⁹He who has ears,ᵇ let him hear."

h Other ancient authorities add here and in verse 43 *to hear*

OVERVIEW: Jesus sat by the seaside of this world so the crowds might gather about him (JEROME) face to face (CHRYSOSTOM) to hear him speak in parables (HILARY). This is so his identity as the Anointed One might become manifest (CYRIL OF ALEXANDRIA). He mixes what is clear with what is obscure, so that through the things the hearers understand they may be drawn to the knowledge of the things they do not understand (HILARY). In speaking of the sower, Jesus was engaged in the act of sowing (JEROME). He did not go where he had not been before, nor did he abandon the place he had left, because God is everywhere (ANONYMOUS).

The ground along the path is life according to this world, the path of those who know everything that is of the world and nothing that is of God. A word sown in you is best cultivated and not choked away if you cultivate it by listening carefully to the Scriptures and the traditions of the doctors (ANONYMOUS). The farmer might be laughed at for sowing on rock. But in the case of the free, rational soul, the conditions for reception must be rightly prepared. Had it been impossible, this sower would not have sown. And if the preparation did not take place, this is no fault of the sower but of the souls who are unwilling to be changed (CHRYSOSTOM). The desire for riches suffocates the word and does not allow it to yield fruit (ANONYMOUS). Those who have in themselves a hardened mind do not receive the divine seed but become a well-trodden way for the unclean spirits (CYRIL OF ALEXANDRIA).

13:1 *Jesus Sits Beside the Sea*

HE WENT OUT OF THE HOUSE. ORIGEN: When Jesus then is with the multitudes, he is not in his house, for the multitudes are outside of the house, and it is an act that springs from his love of humanity to leave the house and to go away to those who are not able to come to him. COMMENTARY ON MATTHEW 10.1.[1]

FACE TO FACE. CHRYSOSTOM: It was not without a purpose that he "sat beside the sea." The Gospel writer has expressed this in a hidden manner. The purpose of Jesus' doing this was to order his listeners in a precise way. He wanted to see them all face to face. He left no one at a disadvantage at his back. THE GOSPEL OF MATTHEW, HOMILY 44.2.[2]

13:2 *He Preaches to a Great Crowd*

AT A DISTANCE FROM THE WORD. HILARY: There is a reason why the Lord was sitting in the boat and the crowds were standing outside like simple followers: he was about to speak in parables. Jesus was therefore indicating that those who were outside the church were at a distance from being able to grasp his words of truth. For the boat symbolizes the church, and those who lie barren and fruitless outside like grains of sand are unable to understand the word of life put forward and preached. ON MATTHEW 13.1.[3]

---

[1]GCS 40:1-2; ANF 9:414. [2]PG 57:467; NPNF 1 10:280. [3]SC 254:294-96.

He Got into a Boat. Jerome: The people were unable to enter Jesus' house, nor could they be present when the apostles heard the mysteries. For that reason the compassionate and merciful Lord goes out of the house. He sits by the seaside of this world so the crowds may gather about him and hear along the shore what they were not entitled to hear inside. "So that he got into a boat and sat down. And all the crowds stood on the shore." Jesus was in the boat as it was being buffeted here and there by the waves of the sea. Secure in his majesty, he made the boat approach the land. And the people, sensing no danger or insurmountable odds, stood in rapt attention on the shore to hear his words. Commentary on Matthew 2.13.2.[4]

13:3 Teaching in Parables

Many Things in Parables. Chrysostom: "He told them many things in parables." He had not done this on the mount.[5] Here he wove into his discourse many parables. For on the mount were multitudes only, and a simple people. But here are also scribes and Pharisees. The Gospel of Matthew, Homily 44.2.[6]

Different Parables for Different Hearers. Jerome: The crowd is not of a single mentality, for each person has a different frame of mind. He therefore speaks to them in many parables so they may receive different teachings depending on their frame of mind. Further, it should be noted that he did not speak everything to them in parables, but many things. For if he spoke everything to them in parables, the people would go away without gaining anything. Jesus mixes what is clear with what is obscure, so that through the things they understand they may be drawn toward the knowledge of the things they do not understand. Commentary on Matthew 2.13.3.[7]

Flagging the Hearer's Attention. Chry-

sostom: But note carefully what kind of parable he began with. Note the order in which Matthew put them. Which parable does he speak first? That which it was most necessary to speak first, that which makes the hearer more attentive. For because Jesus was going to talk with them in hidden sayings, he dramatically catches the attention of his hearers by his first parable. The Gospel of Matthew, Homily 44.2.[8]

Sowing Among Crowds. Jerome: He was indoors, staying at the house, where he spoke to the disciples about that which is holy. He who sows the word of God then went out of his house that he might sow among the crowds. This means that the sower who sows is the Son of God the Father, sowing the word among the ordinary people. Note too that this is the first parable that was given with an interpretation. Furthermore, whenever the Lord speaks to his disciples and answers their questions indoors, he sows words that give us to understand nothing more or less or other than what he has accurately explained. Commentary on Matthew 2.13.3.[9]

The One Prophesied to Speak Parables. Cyril of Alexandria: For this reason Jesus speaks in parables, in order that through them he should show that he is the One who was prophesied. Concerning [him] David said, "I will open my mouth in parables,"[10] and again, "and there will be a man who shall hide his words, and he will be hidden as though carried away by the waves of the sea."[11] Fragment 164.[12]

He Went Out. Anonymous: "The sower went forth to sow," not simply going from place

[4]CCL 77:101. [5]Cf. Mt 5:1 (the Sermon on the Mount). [6]PG 57:467; NPNF 1 10:281. [7]CCL 77:101-2. [8]PG 57:467; NPNF 1 10:281. [9]CCL 77:102. [10]Ps 78:2 (77:2 LXX). [11]Is 32:2. [12]MKGK 206.

to place but with a deliberate design. He did not go where he had not been before, nor did he abandon the place he had left, because God is everywhere. He did not go beyond his presence because God is everywhere. Rather, he went out because God is present where his righteousness is honored. Where his righteousness is not present, neither is God fully received. Those who are within his righteousness are found inside, and those who are not within his righteousness are found outside. Therefore, as long as God was in heaven where all are righteous, he was inside. Coming forth into the fallen world, however, which was completely outside God's righteousness, he went outside in order to bring it inside. Therefore, since all nations, disdaining God's righteousness, were living under the power of the devil, he went forth outside in order to sow righteousness in the world, where it had been absent before on account of their sins. "The sower went out to sow." It was not sufficient for him to say, "He went out to sow," but he added, "The sower went out to sow" to point out that he was not a new sower and was not doing this work for the first time. It was just like God to do this. He has always been sowing. Indeed, from the beginning of the human race it was natural for God to sow the seeds of knowledge. He is the One who, through Moses, sowed among the people the seeds of the commandments of the law. He is the One who, speaking through the prophets, sowed not only the remedies of things present but also the knowledge of things future. He went out, so that in a human body and through himself, he might sow his divine commandments. INCOMPLETE WORK ON MATTHEW, HOMILY 31.[13]

13:4 Sowing Along the Path

ALONG THE PATH. ANONYMOUS: "Some seeds fell by the path." What is this path? It is the world into which all are born and pass through. It is a path, a pilgrimage and a passing to all who come from God and hasten to God. As the prophet said, "I am your passing guest, a sojourner, like all my fathers."[14] So even as the wayfarer is not concerned about anything along the way except for what he really needs, so too humans in their passage through the world must not be concerned about anything except for that which they really need. What is found along the path? People living according to this world, who know everything that is of the world and nothing that is of God. But day and night their minds and appetites are concerned with eating well and drinking well and cultivating the sordidness of the body. From these things all evils arise. INCOMPLETE WORK ON MATTHEW, HOMILY 31.[15]

THE BIRDS CAME AND DEVOURED THEM. CYRIL OF ALEXANDRIA: Let us look, as from a broader perspective, at what it means to be on the road. In a way, every road is hardened and foolish on account of the fact that it lies beneath everyone's feet. No kind of seed finds there enough depth of soil for a covering. Instead, it lies on the surface and is ready to be snatched up by the birds that come by. Therefore those who have in themselves a mind hardened and, as it were, packed tight do not receive the divine seed but become a well-trodden way for the unclean spirits. These are what is here meant by "the birds of the heaven." But "heaven" we understand to mean this air, in which the spirits of wickedness move about, by whom, again, the good seed is snatched up and destroyed. Then what are those upon the rock? They are those people who do not take much care of the faith they have in themselves. They have not set their minds to understand the touchstone of the mystery.[16] The reverence these people have toward God is shallow and rootless. It is in times of ease and fair weather that they practice Christianity, when it involves none of the painful trials of winter. They will not preserve their faith in this way, if in times of tumultuous

---

[13]PG 56:792. [14]Ps 39:12 (38:12 LXX). [15]PG 56:792. [16]Of communion with Christ.

persecution their soul is not prepared for the struggle. FRAGMENT 168.[17]

13:5-6 Falling on Rocky Ground

ON ROCKY GROUND. ANONYMOUS: The seeds of the word that are lying on rocky ground are snatched away by fleeting devils. Tell me, whose fault is it? That of the devils who snatch away the seeds or that of the careless souls who do not bury them in the furrows of their hearts? I believe the fault is not that of the snatching devils. The thief who breaks through the wall enters the secret part of the house. But since he is stationed in a position outside, how can the thief be blameworthy so to speak? Thus also the devil, were he able to enter the innermost recesses of your heart to snatch the word away from you against your will, would indeed be blameworthy. But now what has been neglected and held in contempt by you, he snatches away. INCOMPLETE WORK ON MATTHEW, HOMILY 31.[18]

THEY WITHERED AWAY. ANONYMOUS: "And other seeds fell upon rocky ground." A rock has two properties of nature: strength and hardness. Therefore a man is said to be a rock either because of the constancy of his faith or because of the hardness of his heart. The prophet says in this regard, "I will take out of them the heart of stone."[19] What then is the ground? It is the sin nature that remains in the soul of the faithful who are still drawn toward the flesh. For many have a good mind according to nature, but some do not have a faithful mind. Their mind is from God, but their soul is from the divided will. There are people who, if you speak to them about the glory of the saints or the blessedness of the heavenly kingdom, immediately become joyful and take delight in listening. Being wise according to nature, they readily accept the word. But you who are not content to give alms from your possessions, how will you be able to sustain the loss of your material things when hard times or persecutions strike in the light of

God's word? You will become unsettled. INCOMPLETE WORK ON MATTHEW, HOMILY 31.[20]

13:7 Falling on Thorns

HOW THE WORD IS CULTIVATED. ANONYMOUS: "Other seeds fell among thorns." First, I would like to say how a word sown in you is cultivated, as you may well understand, and how it is choked by your neighbors. You cultivate it by listening carefully to the Scriptures and the traditions of the doctors. In this way the word of God is strengthened in you, grows and gladdens you, for thus it is with everything according to your belief. INCOMPLETE WORK ON MATTHEW, HOMILY 31.[21]

HOW THE WORD IS CHOKED. ANONYMOUS: You must realize that the pursuit of wealth holds you back from attending church services to hear the Scriptures and the traditions of the doctors and be fed on the word that you have received. Though you approach with your body, you do not approach with your mind. Though you listen with your ears, you do not listen with your heart. Your heart lies entirely in those things you are concerned about. The desire for wealth does not permit you to do good works. Further, why does it permit you to lend what you own at interest, and what compels you to aggrandize yourself on another person's property? Likewise, if the word of God is jeopardized because you desire wealth or fear to lose what you have or wish to acquire what you do not have, you do not openly profess the truth of your faith. Do you see how the concern and desire for riches suffocate the word and do not allow it to yield fruit? INCOMPLETE WORK ON MATTHEW, HOMILY 31.[22]

---

[17]*MKGK* 207-8. [18]PG 56:793. [19]Ezek 36:26. [20]PG 56:793. [21]PG 56:794. [22]PG 56:795. Note that "the traditions of the doctors" on Scripture were included in church services at this time as a means of nurture in the Word.

13:8-9 *Bringing Forth Grain*

Receptivity of the Soil Varies. Chrysostom: A fourth part is saved. But even here all are not alike. There are great differences.

Now these things Jesus said, showing that he preached to all without grudging. For the sower makes no distinction in the land submitted to him but simply and indifferently casts his seed. So he himself too makes no distinction of rich and poor, of wise and unwise, of slothful or diligent, of brave or cowardly. He plants his seed among all, fulfilling his part. Although foreknowing the results, it is within his power to say, "What ought I to have done that I have not done?"[23] And the prophets speak of the people as of a vine: "For my beloved had a vineyard"[24] and "He brought a vine out of Egypt."[25] His concern is with sowing the seed. What is this illustrating? That obedience now will be quick and easier and will presently yield its fruit.

But when you hear once again that "the sower went forth to sow," do not think of it as a needless repetition. For the sower frequently goes forth for some other act also, either to plough, or to cut out the evil herbs, or to pluck up thorns, or to attend to some such matter. But now he is going forth to sow.

Now tell me how the greater part of the seed was lost? Not through the sower but through the ground that received it. The soul was unreceptive.

Note that Jesus does not say: The careless received some seed and lost it, the rich received other seed and choked it, and the superficial received some seed and betrayed it. It is not his intention to rebuke them severely, lest he should cast them into despair. Christ leaves the reproof to the conscience of his hearers. Remember also in the parable of the net that much was gathered in that was unprofitable.[26]

But he speaks this parable as if to anoint his disciples and to teach them that they are not to be despondent even though those lost may be more than those who receive the word. It was

with this same ease that the Lord himself continued to sow, even he who fully foreknew the outcomes.

But why would it be reasonable to sow among thorns or on rocks or on the pathway? With regard to the seeds and the earth it cannot sound very reasonable. But in the case of human souls and their instructions, it is praiseworthy and greatly to be honored. For the farmer might be laughed at for doing this, since it is impossible for a rock to bear fruit. It is not likely that the path will become anything but a path or the thorns anything but thorns. But with respect to the rational soul, this is not so predictable. For here there is such a thing as the rock changing and becoming rich land. Here it is possible that the wayside might no longer be trampled upon or lie open to all who pass by but that it may become a fertile field. In the case of the soul, the thorns may be destroyed and the seed enjoy full security. For had it been impossible, this sower would not have sown. And if the reversal did not take place in all, this is no fault of the sower but of the souls who are unwilling to be changed. He has done his part. If they betrayed what they received of him, he is blameless, the exhibitor of such love to humanity.

But mark this carefully: there is more than one road to destruction. There are differing ones, and wide apart from one another. For they who are like the wayside are the coarse-minded and indifferent and careless; but those on the rock such as fail from willed weakness only. The Gospel of Matthew, Homily 44.4-5.[27]

Some a Hundredfold, Some Sixty, Some Thirty. Anonymous: "Some upon good soil." Good soil stands for those who abstain from deceitful wealth and who do good as far as they are able. They yield fruit thirtyfold. If they show contempt for all their goods and undertake to serve God, they have sixtyfold. And if they are

---

[23]Is 5:4. [24]Is 5:1. [25]Ps 80:8 (79:8 LXX). [26]Mt 13:47-50. [27]PG 57:467-68; NPNF 1 10:281-82.

afflicted by a bodily infirmity and put up with it patiently, they have a hundredfold, and the ground is good.

One who yields thirtyfold, that is, who does no evil but does good to the extent one can, this is indeed thirtyfold. One does not yield completely. One who yields sixtyfold is not fully able to show contempt for all one's goods and fast regularly all one's life, or live in celibacy, or suffer bodily deprivations. That would be sixtyfold. Therefore the Lord says to his apostles, who are capable of sixtyfold: "Sell what you have and give alms."[28] But upon those incapable of sixtyfold he enjoins thirtyfold, saying, "Give to everyone who asks of you, and do not turn away from the one who asks for a loan."[29] Likewise, the one who is capable of sixtyfold cannot completely attain a hundredfold. How many are those who are able to give up their goods, suffer the loss of their possessions, live in celibacy, suffer bodily deprivations and yet do not have the heart to sustain a hundredfold? INCOMPLETE WORK ON MATTHEW, HOMILY 31.[30]

---

[28]Lk 12:33. [29]Lk 6:30. [30]PG 56:795.

13:10-17 THE PURPOSE OF THE PARABLES

[10]Then the disciples came and said to him, "Why do you speak to them in parables?" [11]And he answered them, "To you it has been given to know the secrets of the kingdom of heaven, but to them it has not been given. [12]For to him who has will more be given, and he will have abundance; but from him who has not, even what he has will be taken away. [13]This is why I speak to them in parables, because seeing they do not see, and hearing they do not hear, nor do they understand. [14]With them indeed is fulfilled the prophecy of Isaiah which says:
'You shall indeed hear but never understand,
    and you shall indeed see but never perceive.
[15]For this people's heart has grown dull,
    and their ears are heavy of hearing,
    and their eyes they have closed,
lest they should perceive with their eyes,
    and hear with their ears,
and understand with their heart,
    and turn for me to heal them.'
[16]But blessed are your eyes, for they see, and your ears, for they hear. [17]Truly, I say to you, many prophets and righteous men longed to see what you see, and did not see it, and to hear what you hear, and did not hear it."

OVERVIEW: The gentle disposition of the disciples is seen in their inquiry into the purpose of parables (CHRYSOSTOM). All rational souls are given a chance to understand the difference between good and evil. Yet not all receive the grace of knowing the mysteries of the kingdom. It is not the fault of God who does not give but of persons who do not ask or work that they may be ready to receive the kingdom (ANONYMOUS).

In people who are teachable and well disposed for receiving, the Holy Spirit will make his dwelling, increasing in them his gifts. But in those who have acquired only a tiny spark of light and have been negligent even with that, the little that they formerly had is quenched and is taken from them (CYRIL OF ALEXANDRIA). When people have zeal and eagerness, God will give everything sufficient for their needs. But if they have a zero level of responsiveness, God's gifts are blocked by the recipients. Even what they seemed to have is being taken away from them. Here it is not so much God taking something away from them as it is their unreadiness to receive these gifts (CHRYSOSTOM). That person does not receive who brings emptiness to God (ANONYMOUS).

Jesus spoke in parables to make invisible things seen and to avoid harsh language (THEODORE OF MOPSUESTIA). It was not because Christ was speaking in parables that seeing they did not see (ANONYMOUS). Gospel faith receives a perfect gift, because it enriches with new fruit those things that have been begun. But once it is rejected, even the help of one's former means of support may be taken away (HILARY).

13:10 The Disciples Ask About Parables

THE DISCIPLES GENTLY CAME AND ASKED. CHRYSOSTOM: We have good cause to admire the disciples. Longing as they do to learn, they know when they ought to ask. They do not ask in the presence of the crowd. Matthew shows this by saying, "And they came." But to show that this is not a conjecture, Mark has expressed it more distinctly by saying that "they came to him privately."[1] This is what his brothers and his mother should have done. It would have been better if his family had not called him out and made a scene.

But mark the disciples' gentle affection, how they have much regard for the others and how they seek the other's good first and then their own. "For why," they ask, "do you speak to them in parables?" They did not say, "Why do you speak to us in parables?" On other occasions as well we can see their kindness in their human relationships, as when they said, "Send the multitude away"[2] and "Do you know that they were offended?"[3] THE GOSPEL OF MATTHEW, HOMILY 45.1.[4]

THE REQUEST IN THE BOAT. JEROME: The question may be raised as to how the disciples came up to Jesus when he was sitting in the boat. Perhaps we should understand by this that they had gotten into the boat with him a short while before and were now standing there asking him to interpret the parable. COMMENTARY ON MATTHEW 2.13.10.[5]

13:11 The Secrets of Heaven

THE GENERAL KNOWLEDGE OF GOOD AND EVIL. ANONYMOUS: "To you it is given to know the mysteries of the kingdom of heaven." In light of these words some might put the blame on God for their own negligence, saying: "It isn't my fault if I don't know what God has not given me to know." And they don't say this dolefully, because they do not understand anything about God. Rather, they are only seeking an excuse for their sins. The psalm says concerning them: "Incline not my heart to any evil, to finding excuses for my wicked deeds in company with those who work iniquity."[6] Therefore let us speak more clearly on this point. Every intellect is from the Holy Spirit and is a God-given grace. It is one thing that God has given his grace to all humanity. It is another thing to refine this by saying that the grace he gives is not given to all people irrespective of their responses but to those who

---

[1]Mk 4:10. [2]Lk 9:12. [3]Mt 15:12. [4]PG 58:471; NPNF 1 10:284. [5]CCL 77:103. [6]Ps 141:4 (140:4 LXX).

are more worthy and excellent and fit to be chosen.

Notice how Jesus says, "To you it is given to know the mysteries of the kingdom of heaven."[7] He did not say "to you it is given" to someone who has no knowledge whatever of good and evil. All rational souls are given a chance to understand the difference between good and evil. Yet not all have the grace of knowing the mysteries of the kingdom. It is not the fault of God who does not give, because this general rational knowledge is available, but of the person who does not ask or make haste or work in order to be ready to receive the kingdom. If you pursue this general knowledge of good and evil—that is, if you make good use of what you can know—you will be ready to receive the special knowledge of knowing the mystery. But if you have hidden that general knowledge in the ground, that is meant to supply nature's needs, how will you merit the special knowledge that is meant as a reward for good will or works? INCOMPLETE WORK ON MATTHEW, HOMILY 31.[8]

13:12 Having Abundance

ACCORDING TO RESPONSIVENESS. CHRYSOSTOM: Although the saying is quite obscure, it indicates unspeakable justice. For what Christ is saying is something like this: When anyone has zeal and eagerness, there will be given to him on God's part all things sufficient for his needs. But if he lacks any responsiveness and is not ready to contribute his own share, neither are God's gifts bestowed. In that case even "what he seems to have," so Jesus says, "shall be taken away from him." Here it is not so much God taking something away from him as it is his own unreadiness to receive these gifts.

We ourselves do this all the time. When we see someone listening carelessly and when with much effort we cannot persuade him to listen at all, then it remains for us to be silent. For if we continue, even his carelessness is aggravated. But for someone who is striving to learn, we lead

on and pour in much. THE GOSPEL OF MATTHEW, HOMILY 45.1.[9]

WHEN THE SPARK IS NEGLECTED. CYRIL OF ALEXANDRIA: In people who are teachable and well disposed for receiving the divine words the Holy Spirit will make his abode, increasing in them his gifts. But in those who have acquired only a tiny spark of light and have been negligent even with that, even the little that they formerly had becomes utterly quenched and is taken from them. This is what some Jews have experienced, who received a light from the law but gained no increase from it. When the Truth arrived, they became dim-sighted toward it; even what they had has been taken away. FRAGMENT 165.[10]

EVEN WHAT ONE HAS WILL BE TAKEN AWAY. ANONYMOUS: It is certainly possible for something to be added to someone who has. But it is impossible to take away from him who does not have. How are we to understand this? If something is taken away from him who does not have and yet he does not have anything to begin with, what is taken away from him? Here is how we should understand this. He who has a mind and does not do justice with it pertaining to God's glory but rather occupies it with earthly things, of him we say: having he does not have. For though he has a mind and can see, he is said to be blind. That person does not have who brings nothing to God. INCOMPLETE WORK ON MATTHEW, HOMILY 31.[11]

13:13 Not Seeing, Hearing or Understanding

WHY I SPEAK IN PARABLES. THEODORE OF

---

[7]These words of Jesus and the remainder of his address could easily have been interpreted in a predestinationist or even Manichaean sense (cf. pp. 155 n. 18, 253 n. 9.) Consequently Catholic exegetes interpreted them in such a way as to show that for better or worse, each person remains the master of his or her destiny. [8]PG 56:796-97. [9]PG 58:471-72; NPNF 1 10:285. [10]MKGK 206. [11]PG 56:797.

MOPSUESTIA: It was frequently his habit to make use of parables for at least two reasons: either because he would be speaking about things unseen, so as, by the parable, to make invisible things seen, so far as this was possible. Or it was because of the unworthiness of the hearers, when nothing beneficial would come to them from the things that were said. But there was another, third cause for parables. Frequently, when he was saying something by way of refutation, he would by means of a parable temper the harshness of the refutations for the sake of the hearers, as when he tells the parable of the vineyard and says that "he will miserably destroy those evil men" and "will rent out his vineyard to others."[12] In saying these things to the Pharisees, Jesus clearly avoided harsh language. FRAGMENT 73.[13]

THEY DO NOT SEE. ANONYMOUS: If Jesus had said, "I will speak to them in parables so that seeing they may not see," it might be thought to not be the fault of those Jews who did not understand but of Christ who spoke in such a way that they did not understand. But now he says, "This is why I speak to them in parables, because seeing they do not see." You must understand therefore it is not the fault of Christ who is unwilling to speak clearly but of those who while hearing are unwilling to hear. It was not because Christ was speaking in parables that they did not see but because of their way of seeing. Therefore Christ spoke to them in parables. Behold, they saw the wonders of Moses. Did they not truly see? If they did truly see, they certainly would have also feared God the worker of miracles. Behold, they heard the Teacher of the law. Did they not truly hear? If they did truly hear him, they certainly would have lived according to the law and believed in him about whom the law prophesied. They saw also the wonderful things, but seeing they did not really see. If they had seen them, they would also have profited by them. It is easier for those who see to know what they saw than for those who hear

to understand what they heard. How did it happen that those who heard of the wonderful revelation of God did not see and know them? Because the Jews seeing were accustomed not to see and hearing not to hear; therefore God did not give them the eyes of faith to see Christ's divine miracles or to hear his living words. INCOMPLETE WORK ON MATTHEW, HOMILY 31.[14]

13:14 Seeing but Not Perceiving

YOU SHALL SEE BUT NEVER PERCEIVE. CHRYSOSTOM: After this, lest any one should suppose his words to be a mere accusation and lest people should say, "Being our enemy he is bringing these charges and calumnies against us," Jesus introduces the prophet Isaiah. The prophet pronounced the same judgment as Jesus himself: "With them indeed is fulfilled the prophecy of Isaiah, which says, 'You shall indeed hear but never understand, and you shall indeed see but never perceive.'" So it is the prophet himself who accuses them with the same precise point. He did not say "You see not" but "You shall indeed see but never perceive." He did not say "You do not hear" but "You shall indeed hear but never understand." So they first inflicted the loss on themselves, by stopping their ears, by closing their eyes, by making their heart fat. For they not only failed to hear but also "heard heavily," and they did this, he said, "lest they should turn for me to heal them." Thus he described their aggravated wickedness and their determined defection from him. But he said this to draw them closer to him, and to provoke them and to signify that if they would convert he would heal them. It is much as if one should say, "He would not look at me, and I thank him; for if he had given me even a glance, I would straightway have given in." He spoke in this way to signify how he would wish to have been reconciled. He implied that both their conversion was possible

---

[12]Mt 21:41. [13]MKGK 120. [14]PG 56:798.

and that upon their repentance they might be saved. It was not for his own glory alone, but for their salvation, that he was doing all things.

For if it had not been his will that they should hear and be saved, he would have remained silent and would not have spoken in parables. But now in this very manner he stirs them up, even by speaking under a veil. "For God does not will the death of the sinner but that he should turn to him and live."[15] THE GOSPEL OF MATTHEW, HOMILY 45.1-2.[16]

13:15 Hearts Grown Dull

THEIR EARS REFUSE TO HEAR. HILARY: Faith perceives the mysteries of the kingdom. A person will make progress in those things he has been immersed in and will abound with an increase in that progress. But in those things he has not been immersed in, even that which he has shall be taken away from him. In other words, he suffers the loss of the law from the loss of his faith. Lacking faith, the people of the law lost even the efficacy of the law. Therefore, gospel faith receives a perfect gift, because it enriches with new fruit those things that have been undertaken. But once it is rejected, even the help of one's former means of support is taken away. ON MATTHEW 13.2.[17]

THOSE UNWILLING TO HEAR. JEROME: He gives reasons why seeing they do not see and hearing they do not hear. He says, "The heart of this people has been hardened . . . and with their ears they have been hard of hearing." And lest we think that their hardness of heart and hearing are natural and not voluntary, Jesus alludes to the fault of the will and says, "They have closed their eyes, lest at any time they see with their eyes, and hear with their ears, and understand with their mind, and be converted, and I heal them."[18] Therefore with closed eyes they who are unwilling to perceive the truth hear in parables and in riddles. COMMENTARY ON MATTHEW 2.13-15.[19]

LEST THEY SHOULD TURN. CYRIL OF ALEXANDRIA: To say "lest at any time they should turn and I should heal them" points to a hardened intractability. . . . For he speaks in this way in order to save them, since [otherwise] he ought rather to have said nothing but have been silent, except that it is not for his own glory's sake but for their salvation that Jesus does everything. FRAGMENT 166.[20]

13:16 Hearing and Seeing

BLESSED ARE YOUR EARS. CYRIL OF ALEXANDRIA: He blesses them, accordingly, as hearers of the Son's voice and as having been made ready to see him, through whom and in whom they saw, intellectually, the nature of God and the Father. Of these things the saints of old were accounted worthy, those, namely, who most completely possess a joy in good things. FRAGMENT 167.[21]

13:17 What the Prophets Longed For

THE PROPHETS LONGED TO SEE WHAT YOU SEE. HILARY: He teaches the blessedness of the apostolic times to those whose eyes and ears are fortunate to look upon and hear the salvation of God. These are the prophets and the righteous who have longed to see and hear the fulfillment of the expected times. They share in the joy of that expectation reserved for the apostles. ON MATTHEW 13.3.[22]

THEIR EARS ARE HEAVY OF HEARING. CHRYSOSTOM: Do you see that what has been given them is a free gift? Yet they would not have been blessed unless they had cooperated with the gift with well doing of their own. Do not tell me this is spoken obscurely. Those who did not hear might have come and asked him for further clarification, as the disciples did. But they did not

---

[15]Ezek 18:23. [16]PG 58:472-73; NPNF 1 10:285. [17]SC 254:296. [18]Mt 13:15. [19]CCL 77:103-4. [20]MKGK 207. [21]MKGK 207. [22]SC 254:296.

will to do so, being careless and apathetic. Why do I say that they did not will to do this? They were doing the very opposite, not only disbelieving, not only not listening, but even waging war. They were disposed to be very bitter against all he said. So Jesus brings before them the charge of the prophet: "Their ears were unwilling to hear."

But the hearers were not like this, and this is why they were blessed. In yet another way he assures them again, saying, "Many prophets and righteous people longed to see what you see and did not see it, and to hear what you hear and did not hear it," that is, hear of my coming, my miracles, my voice, my teaching. Here he compares the hearers to the nonhearers. He affirms the hearers as blessed not only because they have seen what the prophets did not see but even what those of old desired to see but did not. For they indeed beheld by faith only, but these were beholding by sight too, and much more distinctly.

Do you see once again how Christ connects the old dispensation with the new, signifying that those of old not only knew the things to come but also greatly desired them? But had they pertained to some strange and opposing God, they would never have desired them. THE GOSPEL OF MATTHEW, HOMILY 45.2.[23]

MANY PROPHETS. JEROME: It seems that what he said elsewhere runs counter to this point: "Abraham desired to see my day. He saw it and rejoiced."[24] He did not say all the prophets and righteous people desired to see what you see, but many. Among many it may be that some see and some do not see, although in our interpretation we seem to be making a distinction between the merits of the saints. Therefore Abraham saw dimly as though in a mirror, but you now have and hold your Lord and question him freely and eat with him. COMMENTARY ON MATTHEW 2.13.17.[25]

---

[23]PG 58:473-74; NPNF 1 10:285-86. [24]Jn 8:56. [25]CCL 77:104.

13:18-23 JESUS EXPLAINS THE PARABLE OF THE SOWER

[18]*"Hear then the parable of the sower.* [19]*When any one hears the word of the kingdom and does not understand it, the evil one comes and snatches away what is sown in his heart; this is what was sown along the path.* [20]*As for what was sown on rocky ground, this is he who hears the word and immediately receives it with joy;* [21]*yet he has no root in himself, but endures for a while, and when tribulation or persecution arises on account of the word, immediately he falls away.*[i] [22]*As for what was sown among thorns, this is he who hears the word, but the cares of the world and the delight in riches choke the word, and it proves unfruitful.* [23]*As for what was sown on good soil, this is he who hears the word and understands it; he indeed bears fruit, and yields, in one case a hundredfold, in another sixty, and in another thirty."*

i Or *stumbles*

OVERVIEW: If the seed of the one who is dense is snatched away, the seed of intellect ought to be taken up and covered in the ground of memory (ORIGEN). The diversity of soils stands for the diversity of the souls of believers (JEROME). One suffers from worldly cares when one does not rejuvenate one's own soil but receives the word without paying attention (ORIGEN). Riches are enticing indeed, promising one thing and producing another. On bad ground there are three diverse situations: by the path, upon rocky ground and among thorns. So too on good ground there are three types: fruit of one hundredfold, sixtyfold and thirtyfold (JEROME).

13:18-19 The Path and Lack of Understanding

WHAT IS SOWN IN THE HEART. JEROME: "The wicked one comes and snatches away what has been sown in his heart." The wicked one snatches away the good seed. You must also understand that it was sown in the heart. The diversity of soils stands for the diversity of the souls of believers. "And when trouble and persecution come because of the word, he at once falls away." Notice what was said: "He at once falls away." Hence there is some distance between the one who is constrained by many troubles and sufferings to deny Christ and the one who in the face of persecution immediately falls away and succumbs. COMMENTARY ON MATTHEW 2.13.19-21.[1]

13:20-21 The Rocky Ground and Lack of Endurance

BY THE WAYSIDE. ORIGEN: Not all the Gospel writers use the same terms in reporting this parable. Matthew wrote of "the evil one," Mark of "Satan," and Luke of "the devil."[2] The phrases "by the wayside" and "in the path" are not quite the same thing. Weigh in the allusion of the statement "I am the way."[3] Both Matthew and Mark say, most felicitously, that the word was sowed "on stony ground," not upon a "stone."

Now to all that which is "by the wayside," the words "those who do not understand" apply. But to the good ground these words apply: "This is he who hears the word and understands it." Perhaps then those seeds that fall "on stony ground" and those that fall "among thorns" fall between the people without knowledge and those who understand. This then is an exhortation to meditate diligently upon the faculty of perception. If the seed of the one who is dense is snatched away, the seed of intellect ought to be taken up and covered in the ground of memory, so that it may spread forth roots and may not be found naked or snatched away by the spirits of wickedness. FRAGMENT 291.[4]

13:22 The Thorns and the Cares of the World

THE DELIGHT IN RICHES. ORIGEN: "The deceitfulness of riches chokes," and so does the speech of heretics. The rich are liars, contrasted with "the poor, righteous person," who is poor in speech and knowledge but righteous in life. The "care of all the churches" of which the apostle speaks[5] is distinguished from the "care of this world."[6] One suffers from these worldly cares when one does not rejuvenate one's own soil but receives the word without paying attention and sprouts up thorns, with which the earth was cursed because of the disobedience of Adam. He heard of the "thorns and thistles it shall produce for you,"[7] "whose end is to be burned."[8] For these are not sown but spring forth of themselves. They "choke the word" of God through troubles and whims. One who knows truly both understands and bears fruit. But if anyone seems to understand without bearing fruit, one does not understand. If one seems to bear fruit without understanding, one does not bear fruit. This displays the variety of levels of virtue spoken of in the text: "sixtyfold and thirtyfold and a hun-

---

[1]CCL 77:105. [2]Mt 13:19; Mk 4:15; Lk 8:12. [3]Jn 14:6. [4]GCS 41.1:129-30. [5]2 Cor 11:28. [6]Cf. 2 Cor 7:10. [7]Gen 3:18. [8]Heb 6:8.

dredfold." Virtue's strictness is not exhibited by everyone to the same degree. Some care less about it, some more. FRAGMENTS 294-95.[9]

SOWN AMONG THORNS. JEROME: "The seed sown among the thorns is the person who listens to the word, but the anxiety of the world and the deceitfulness of riches choke the word, and it is made fruitless." This reminds us of the words spoken to Adam: "You shall eat your bread among thorns and thistles."[10] This mystically signifies that those who give themselves over to the pleasures and cares of this world eat the heavenly bread and true food among thorns. Hence the Lord fittingly added, "The deceitfulness of riches chokes the word." Riches are enticing indeed, promising one thing and doing another. The possession of riches is uncertain. They are borne from place to place. Unpredictably they either desert the haves or gorge the have-nots. The Lord also states that it is difficult for the rich to enter the kingdom of heaven, for riches choke the word of God and weaken the force of the virtues. COMMENTARY ON MATTHEW 2.13.22.[11]

13:23 The Good Soil

DIFFERENCES OF LIGHT AMONG THE RIGHTEOUS. ORIGEN: Daniel, knowing that the intelligent are the light of the world and that the multitudes of the righteous differ in glory, seems to have said this, "And the intelligent shall shine as the brightness of the firmament, and from among the multitudes of the righteous as the stars for ever and ever."[12] And in the passage, "There is one glory of the sun, and another glory of the moon, and another glory of the stars. For one star differs from another star in glory: so also is the resurrection of the dead,"[13] the apostle says the same thing as Daniel, taking this thought from his prophecy. COMMENTARY ON MATTHEW 10.3.[14]

THREE TYPES OF RESULTS. JEROME: "And the one sown upon good ground is he who hears the word, understands it and bears fruit." Even as on bad ground there were three diverse situations (by the path, upon rocky ground and among thorns), so too on good ground the diversity is of three types: fruit of one hundredfold, sixtyfold and thirtyfold. Both in one and the other there is a change that takes place in the will, not in the nature itself. In both the unbelievers and believers it is the heart that receives the seed. "The wicked one comes," he says, "and snatches away what has been sown in his heart." In the second and third cases, he says, "That is he who hears the word." In the explanation of the good ground, he is the one who hears the word. First we must listen, then understand; after understanding, we must bear the fruits of good teaching and yield fruit either one hundredfold, sixtyfold or thirtyfold. COMMENTARY ON MATTHEW 2.13.23.[15]

---

[9]GCS 41.1:131-32. [10]Gen 3:18. [11]CCL 77:105. [12]Dan 12:3. [13]1 Cor 15:41-42. [14]GCS 40:3; ANF 9:415. [15]CCL 77:105-6.

13:24-30 THE PARABLE OF THE WEEDS AMONG THE WHEAT

²⁴Another parable he put before them, saying, "The kingdom of heaven may be compared to a man who sowed good seed in his field; ²⁵but while men were sleeping, his enemy came and sowed weeds among the wheat, and went away. ²⁶So when the plants came up and bore grain, then the weeds appeared also. ²⁷And the servantsʲ of the householder came and said to him, 'Sir, did you not sow good seed in your field? How then has it weeds?' ²⁸He said to them, 'An enemy has done this.' The servantsʲ said to him, 'Then do you want us to go and gather them?' ²⁹But he said, 'No; lest in gathering the weeds you root up the wheat along with them. ³⁰Let both grow together until the harvest; and at harvest time I will tell the reapers, Gather the weeds first and bind them in bundles to be burned, but gather the wheat into my barn.' "

j Or *slaves*

OVERVIEW: The good seed are taken to be the children of the kingdom, because whatever good things are sown in the human soul, these are the offspring of the kingdom of God (ORIGEN). The devil sows weeds among sleeping people, among those who through negligence are overcome by their infidelity as in a kind of lethargy (CHROMATIUS). The householder ordered his servants to put up with the weeds and not to separate them now (AUGUSTINE). A separation would occur on the last day (ORIGEN, CHROMATIUS). We should not be quick to judge. What is doubtful should be left to God's judgment when the day of judgment comes (JEROME). The angels and servants of the Word will gather from the kingdom of Christ all things that cause a stumbling block to souls, which they will scatter and burn (ORIGEN).

13:24 Sowing Good Seed

GOOD SEED. ORIGEN: Consider now, if in addition to what we have already recounted, you can otherwise take the good seed to be the children of the kingdom, because whatever good things are sown in the human soul, these are the off-spring of the kingdom of God. They have been sown by God the Word who was in the beginning with God.[1] Wholesome words about anything are children of the kingdom. COMMENTARY ON MATTHEW 10.2.[2]

THE SOWER OF GOOD SEEDS. CHROMATIUS: The Lord clearly points out that he is the sower of good seeds. He does not cease to sow in this world as in a field. God's word is like good seed in the hearts of people, so that each of us according to the seeds sown in us by God may bear spiritual and heavenly fruit. TRACTATE ON MATTHEW 51.1.[3]

13:25 Sowing Bad Seed

WHEN PEOPLE ARE ASLEEP. ORIGEN: But while people are asleep they do not act according to the command of Jesus, "Watch and pray that you enter not into temptation."[4] At that point the devil on the watch sows what are called tares—that is, evil opinions—over and among the good seeds that are from the Word.

[1]Jn 1:2. [2]GCS 40:2; ANF 9:414. [3]CCL 9a:450. [4]Mt 26:41.

According to this the whole world might be called a field, and not the church of God only. For the Son of Man sowed the good seed throughout the entire world, but the wicked one sowed tares—that is, evil words—which, springing from wickedness, are children of the evil one. COMMENTARY ON MATTHEW 10.2.[5]

13:26 Grain and Weeds

THE WEEDS APPEARED. CHROMATIUS: The Lord points out that our foe the devil sows the weeds of his wickedness and malice to choke the seed of God in us. Thus he says, "But while men were asleep, his enemy came and sowed weeds among the wheat and went away." The Lord indicates that the devil sows weeds among sleeping people— that is, among those who through negligence are overcome by their infidelity as in a kind of lethargy and fall asleep amid the divine injunctions. The apostle says concerning them: "For they who sleep, sleep at night, and they who are drunk, are drunk at night. Therefore let us not sleep as do the rest, but let us be wakeful and sober."[6]

Those foolish virgins about whom we read in the Gospel, weighed down by their lethargy and infidelity, not having taken oil for their vessels, were unable to go forth and meet the bridegroom.[7] Hence it is always uppermost in the mind of this devil—the enemy of the human race—to sow weeds among the wheat.

But he who awaits the Lord faithfully, once the sleep of infidelity has been banished from him, will not be bothered by this nighttime sower. . . . According to the Lord's interpretation, the good seed represents the children of the kingdom and the weeds represent the wicked children. TRACTATE ON MATTHEW 51.1.1-2.[8]

13:27 The Servants Come to the Householder

WHY WEEDS? AUGUSTINE: The Lord then explained for us what he had said. See what we choose to be in his field. See which of the two we will be at harvest time. The field is the world, and the church is spread throughout the world. Let the one who is wheat persevere until the harvest; let those who are weeds be changed into wheat. There is this difference between people and real grain and real weeds, for what was grain in the field is grain and what were weeds are weeds. But in the Lord's field, which is the church, at times what was grain turns into weeds and at times what were weeds turn into grain; and no one knows what they will be tomorrow. SERMON 73A.1.[9]

13:28 Gathering the Weeds?

WARNING AGAINST SOWING WEEDS. JEROME: As I said before, we must adapt our faith to those things that the Lord explained. Those things which he did not mention and which he left to our intelligence will be briefly touched on here. Think of those who were asleep as signifying the teachers of the different churches. Think of the householder's servants as none other than the angels who daily look upon the Father's face. Think of the enemy who sowed the weeds as the devil because he wanted to be a god. COMMENTARY ON MATTHEW 2.13.37.[10]

13:29 Rooting Up Grain by Mistake

DO NOT ROOT UP THE WHEAT. AUGUSTINE: The workers of the householder wanted to go and gather up the weeds, but they were not allowed to do so. Though they indeed wanted to gather them up, they were not allowed to separate the weeds. They did what they were suited for and left it to the angels to do the separation. At first they were unwilling to leave the separation of the weeds up to the angels. But the householder, who knew them all and saw that a

---

[5]GCS 40:2; ANF 9:414. [6]1 Thess 5:6-7. [7]Mt 25:1-13. [8]CCL 9a:450-51. [9]MA 1:249; WSA 3 3:295. [10]CCL 77:111-12.

separation was necessary, ordered them to put up with the weeds and not to separate them. In answer to their words, "Do you want us to go and gather them up?" he replied, "No, lest in gathering the weeds you root up the wheat along with them." "Therefore, Lord, will the weeds also be with us in the barn?" "At harvest time I will say to the reapers, 'Gather up first the weeds, and bind them in bundles to burn. Allow what you do not have with you in the barn to grow in the field.'" SERMON 73A.I.[11]

13:30 *Separated at the Harvest*

UNTIL THE HARVEST. JEROME: The words the Lord spoke—"Lest gathering the weeds you root up the wheat along with them"—leave room for repentance. We are advised not to be quick in cutting off a fellow believer, for it may happen that one who has been corrupted today by evil may recover his senses tomorrow by sound teaching and abide by the truth. And that which follows, "Let both grow together until the harvest," seems to be contrary to the other precept: "Put away evil from your midst," whereby there must be no fellowship with those who are called believers but who are adulterers and fornicators. If uprooting is forbidden and patience must be kept until harvest time, how are some people to be removed from our midst? Between wheat and weeds there is something called darnel, when the plant is in its early growth and there is no stalk yet. It looks like an ear of corn, and the difference between them is hardly noticeable. The Lord therefore advises us that we should not be quick to judge what is doubtful but should leave judgment up to God. So when the day of judgment comes, he may not cast out from the body of saints those who are suspected of misdeeds but those who are obviously guilty. As to his words that the bundles of weeds are to be consigned to the fire and the wheat is to be gathered in the barn, it is clear that all heretics and hypocrites are to be burned in the fires of

hell. But the holy ones, who are called wheat, are to be gathered up in barns—that is to say, heavenly mansions. COMMENTARY ON MATTHEW 2.13.29-30.[12]

LET THEM GROW TOGETHER. CHROMATIUS: But when the servants of the householder, namely, on the part of the apostles, ask the Lord whether they should separate the weeds from the wheat, he allowed them both to grow together until the harvest—that is, until the end of time. He clearly indicated that he would send reapers at that time, namely, angels, so that, once they have separated the wheat from the weeds—that is, once the holy ones have been separated from the wicked—they may gather the righteous in heavenly kingdoms, like wheat in barns. All the wicked and sinners will burn amid the punishments of hell like weeds in the fire, where the Lord declares they will forever weep and grind their teeth, saying, "There shall be weeping and grinding of teeth."[13] And when the Lord says there will be weeping and grinding of teeth, he is undoubtedly pointing to the future resurrection not only of the soul (as certain heretics would have it) but also of the body. Indeed, weeping and grinding of teeth are properly so-called punishments of the body. Therefore the gravity of the error that has a hold on heretics of this type can be seen from these words of the Lord, for they do not believe in the future resurrection of the body. TRACTATE ON MATTHEW 51.1.2.[14]

AT HARVEST TIME. ORIGEN: And at the end of things, which is called "the consummation of the age,"[15] there will of necessity be a harvest, in order that the angels of God who have been appointed for this work may gather up the bad opinions that have grown upon the soul, and overturning them may give them over to fire which is said to burn, that they may be con-

---

[11]MA 1:249; WSA 3 3:296. [12]CCL 77:112. [13]Mt 13:42. [14]CCL 9a:451. [15]Mt 13:39.

sumed. And so the angels and servants of the Word will gather from Christ's entire kingdom all things that cause a stumbling block to souls and their reasonings that create iniquity, which they will scatter and cast into the burning furnace of fire. Then those who become conscious that they have received the seeds of the evil one in themselves, because of their having been asleep, shall wail and, as it were, be angry with themselves. This is the "gnashing of teeth."[16] Similarly it is said in the Psalms, "They gnashed me with their teeth."[17] Then above all "shall the righteous shine," no longer differently as at the first but all "as one sun in the kingdom of their Father."[18] Then, as if to indi-cate that there was indeed a hidden meaning, perhaps in all that is concerned with the expla-nation of the parable, maybe most of all in the saying "Then shall the righteous shine as the sun in the kingdom of their Father," the Savior adds, "He that has ears to hear, let him hear."[19] The Lord thereby teaches those who are atten-tive that in the exposition, the parable has been set forth with such perfect clearness that it can be understood by the novice. COMMENTARY ON MATTHEW 10.2.[20]

---

[16]Mt 13:42. [17]Ps 35:16 (34:16 LXX). [18]Mt 13:43. [19]Mt 13:43. [20]GCS 40:2-3; ANF 9:414-15.

13:31-43 THE PARABLES OF THE MUSTARD SEED AND THE YEAST AND AN EXPLANATION

[31]*Another parable he put before them, saying, "The kingdom of heaven is like a grain of mus-tard seed which a man took and sowed in his field;* [32]*it is the smallest of all seeds, but when it has grown it is the greatest of shrubs and becomes a tree, so that the birds of the air come and make nests in its branches."*

[33]*He told them another parable. "The kingdom of heaven is like leaven which a woman took and hid in three measures of flour, till it was all leavened."*

[34]*All this Jesus said to the crowds in parables; indeed he said nothing to them without a para-ble.* [35]*This was to fulfil what was spoken by the prophet:*[k]

"I will open my mouth in parables,
I will utter what has been hidden since the foundation of the world."

[36]*Then he left the crowds and went into the house. And his disciples came to him, saying, "Explain to us the parable of the weeds of the field."* [37]*He answered, "He who sows the good seed is the Son of man;* [38]*the field is the world, and the good seed means the sons of the kingdom; the weeds are the sons of the evil one,* [39]*and the enemy who sowed them is the devil; the harvest is the close of the age, and the reapers are angels.* [40]*Just as the weeds are gathered and burned with fire, so will it be at the close of the age.* [41]*The Son of man will send his angels, and they will gather out of his kingdom all causes of sin and all evildoers,* [42]*and throw them into the furnace*

of fire; there men will weep and gnash their teeth. [43] *Then the righteous will shine like the sun in the kingdom of their Father. He who has ears, let him hear."*

k Other ancient authorities read *the prophet Isaiah*

OVERVIEW: After the mustard seed is sown in the field, it grows to be larger than any herb (HILARY, CHRYSOSTOM). Believers welcome the grain of preaching and nurture the plant with the moisture of faith, causing it to sprout and shoot up in the field of the heart (JEROME). The birds of the air dwell in the branches of the tree that rises high above the ground, as the apostles have branches stretched upward by the power of Christ (HILARY).

The Lord compared himself with yeast, which is buried with the judgment of death, showing that the Law and the Prophets are dissolved in the Gospels (HILARY). The leaven, though it is buried, is not destroyed. Little by little it transmutes the whole lump into its own condition. This happens with the gospel (CHRYSOSTOM). For the three measures of flour, the Fathers offer various interpretations: the three passions of the human soul are blended into one, so that in reason we possess prudence, in anger we possess hatred toward vice and in desire the aspiration for virtue (JEROME); or the fusion of Jews, Greeks and Samaritans (THEODORE OF MOPSUESTIA). If we wish to hear Jesus and go to the house and receive something better than the multitudes did, let us become friends of Jesus, so that as his disciples come, we may also come (ORIGEN). The parables must not be explained word for word but as a whole, since many absurdities would otherwise follow (CHRYSOSTOM).

13:31 The Kingdom of Heaven Is Like a Mustard Seed

THE SEED SOWED AND BURIED. HILARY: The Lord compared his reign with a grain of mustard seed, which is very pungent and the smallest of all seeds. Its inherent potency is heightened under stress and pressure. Therefore, after this grain is sown in the field—that is, when it has been seized by someone and delivered up to death as though buried in the field by a sowing of its body—it grows up to become larger than any herb and surpasses all the glory of the prophets. ON MATTHEW 13.4.[1]

FAITH AS A GRAIN OF MUSTARD. JEROME: The man who sows in his field is interpreted by many as the Savior. He sows in the souls of believers. By others he is interpreted as one who sows in his field—that is to say, in himself and in his heart. Who is it that sows if not our mind and heart? They take up the grain of preaching and nurture the plant with the moisture of faith, making it sprout and shoot up in the field of the heart. The preaching of faith in the gospel appears to be least among all tasks. Indeed, anyone who preaches the God-man of truth, Christ who died, and the stumbling block of the cross may not think immediately of mere faith as the primary doctrine. Put this particular doctrine side by side with the teachings of the philosophers, their books, their splendid eloquence and fine discourses, and you will see just how small it is compared with the other seeds of the gospel plant. When those teachings grow, they have nothing to show that is pungent or vigorous or vital. Everything turns out weak and withering in a plant and in herbs that quickly dry up and fall to the ground. But when this tiny gospel teaching that seemed insignificant at the beginning has been planted either in the soul of the believer or throughout the world, it does not turn out to be just a plant. It grows into a tree, so that the birds of the air, which we interpret as the souls of believers or deeds dedicated to the

---

[1]SC 254:296-98.

service of God, come and dwell on its branches. COMMENTARY ON MATTHEW 2.13.31.[2]

13:32 A Small Seed Produces a Great Tree

THE LEAST, THE GREATEST. CHRYSOSTOM: Therefore he brought forward the similitude of this herb, which has a very strong resemblance to the kingdom of heaven. It indeed is "the least of all seeds, but when it is grown, it is the greatest among herbs and becomes a tree, so that the birds of the air come and lodge in the branches thereof."

Thus he meant to set forth the most decisive sign of its greatness. "Even so then shall it also be with respect to the gospel," he says. For his disciples were weakest of all and least of all. Nevertheless, because of the great power that was in them, it has grown and been unfolded in every part of the world. THE GOSPEL OF MATTHEW, HOMILY 46.2.[3]

THE GREATEST OF SHRUBS. HILARY: Now, in place of the herb, the preaching of the prophets was given to ailing Israel. But the birds of the air dwell in the branches of the tree that rises high above the ground. We see the apostles as branches stretched out by the power of Christ and overshadowing the world. The people of all nations fly there in the hope of life and, disquieted by the whirling winds—that is, by the breath and blowing force of the devil—they come to rest upon those tree branches. ON MATTHEW 13.4.[4]

THE SMALLEST OF ALL SEEDS. JEROME: I believe that the branches of the gospel tree that grew from the grain of mustard seed signify the different teachings whereon each one of the birds mentioned perches. Let us also take on the feathers of a dove so that, flying to the higher parts, we may dwell on the branches of this tree and make nests for ourselves from the different doctrines and, fleeing from earthly things, hasten to heavenly things.

Many people read that the grain of mustard seed is the smallest of all seeds. They read what the disciples say in the Gospel: "Lord, increase our faith,"[5] and the answer given to them by the Savior: "Truly, I say to you, if you have faith even like a mustard seed, you will say to this mountain, 'Move from here to there,' and it will move."[6] They wonder whether an apostle would ask for a small faith or they doubt the Lord concerning what he has to say about small faith. Yet Paul the apostle makes an even greater comparison than faith to a grain of mustard. In fact, what does he say? "If I have all faith so as to move mountains, yet do not have charity, I am nothing."[7] COMMENTARY ON MATTHEW 2.13.31.[8]

13:33 The Kingdom of Heaven Is Like Leaven

LIKE LEAVEN. HILARY: Yeast comes from flour and returns the potency it received to the batch of its own kind. The Lord compared himself with this yeast. It was taken in hand by the woman, that is, the synagogue, and buried with the judgment of death, affirming that the law and the prophets are dissolved in the gospel. This yeast, covered with three measures of flour in equal parts—that is, the law, the prophets and the gospel—makes everything one, so that what the law established and the prophets proclaimed is completed by the added ingredient of the gospel. Everything, possessing the same contents and potency, is brought about through the Spirit of God, so that there is no disunity in what is fermented in equal parts. ON MATTHEW 13.5.[9]

THE THREEFOLD MEASURE. HILARY: Many seem to believe that the three measures of flour refer not only to the sign of faith—that is, the unity of the Father and the Son and the Holy Spirit—but also to the calling of the three

---

[2]CCL 77:107-8. [3]PG 58:478; NPNF 1 10:289. [4]SC 254:298. [5]Lk 17:5. [6]Mt 17:20. [7]1 Cor 13:2. [8]CCL 77:108. [9]SC 254:298-300.

nations out of Shem, Ham and Japheth.[10] But I do not know whether reason will permit us to draw this conclusion, for, although the calling of all nations is equal, Christ is not buried in them but manifested to them, and the whole batch is not fermented in so great a multitude of unbelievers. However, in the Father and the Son and the Holy Spirit, without the need of yeast applied from without, all things are one in Christ. ON MATTHEW 13.6.[11]

HID UNTIL IT WAS ALL LEAVENED. CHRYSOSTOM: For as leaven converts the large quantity of meal into its own quality, even so shall you convert the whole world.

Note the wisdom by which Christ introduces natural things. He implies that as the leaven works, so does the flour. Do not say to me, "What shall we be able to do, twelve men, throwing ourselves upon so vast a multitude?" Rather, the most conspicuous thing about the apostles is that they were not put to flight when they mixed with the multitude. The leaven then leavens the lump when it comes close to the meal, and not simply close but so as to be actually mixed with it. He said it was not simply put in the flour but hid in it. So you also, when you come close to your enemies and are made one with them, then shall you get the better of them.

The leaven, though it is buried, is not destroyed. Little by little it transmutes the whole lump into its own condition. This happens with the gospel. Do not fear, then, that there will be many dangerous circumstances. For even then you will shine forth and be victorious. By "three measures" here he meant many, for he is prone to taking this number for a multitude. THE GOSPEL OF MATTHEW, HOMILY 46.2.[12]

THREE MEASURES OF FLOUR. JEROME: The woman who took the yeast and mixed it with three measures of flour until the whole batch of dough was fermented signifies to me either the apostolic preaching or the church, which is made up of different nations. She takes the

yeast—namely, the knowledge and understanding of the Scriptures—and mixes it with three measures of flour so that the spirit, soul and body blended into one might not differ from each other but intermingle, obtaining from the Father whatever they ask for. This point is examined also elsewhere. We read in Plato, and it is the teaching of famous philosophers, that there are three passions in the human soul: one, which we may interpret as rational; another, which we call full of anger or irascible; a third, which we call desire.[13] This great philosopher believed that our rational part resides in the brain, anger in the gall bladder and desire in the liver. Therefore, if we accept the evangelical yeast of sacred Scripture that we spoke about, the three passions of the human soul are blended into one, so that in reason we possess prudence, in anger we possess hatred toward vice, in desire the aspiration for virtue. And this all happens through the gospel teaching that holy mother, the church, offers us. COMMENTARY ON MATTHEW 2.13.33.[14]

BRINGING TOGETHER JEWS, GREEKS AND SAMARITANS. THEODORE OF MOPSUESTIA: He calls Greeks, Jews and Samaritans "three measures of meal," for when the leaven had been cast into these three it brought about one same nature and fatness in all of them. For human beings, divided from one another, were brought into the same state by my teaching, in its working. The apostle also speaks in the same way, for "in Christ Jesus" there is neither "Greek" nor "Jew" and so on.[15] FRAGMENT 74.[16]

13:34 Teaching Only in Parables

SAYING NOTHING EXCEPT IN PARABLES. CHRYSOSTOM: But Mark says, "As they were able to hear it, he spoke the word to them in para-

---

[10]Gen 9:18-19. [11]SC 254:300. [12]PG 58:478; NPNF 1 10:289. [13]Rationable, irascible, concupiscible (*logistikon, thymikon, epithymētikon*). [14]CCL 77:109. [15]Gal 3:28. [16]MKGK 121.

bles." Then pointing out that he is not making a new thing, he also brings in the prophet, proclaiming beforehand this his manner of teaching. And to teach us the purpose of Christ, how he discoursed in this way so that they might not be ignorant but that he might lead them to inquiry, Mark added, "And without a parable he told them nothing." Yet surely he did say many things without a parable, but then later nothing. And for all this no one asked him questions, whereas we know they were often questioning the prophets. They questioned Ezekiel, for instance, and many others; but of these they did no such thing. Yet surely his sayings were enough to cast them into perplexity and to stir them up to the inquiry; for indeed a very solemn punishment was threatened by those parables. Even so they were not moved. THE GOSPEL OF MATTHEW, HOMILY 47.1.[17]

13:35 Teaching What Was Hidden

I WILL OPEN MY MOUTH IN PARABLES. JEROME: As to what is said about the person of the Lord: "I will open my mouth in parables, I will utter what has been hidden since the foundation of the world,"[18] we must pay close attention to the description of the departure of the Israelites from Egypt and the narration of all the signs contained in the book of Exodus. From this we realize that all those things that were written are to be understood through parables.[19] And not only those great writings but also the signs that have been hidden will not ring clear unless we view them as parables. For the Savior promises that he will speak in parables and utter what has been hidden from the foundation of the world. COMMENTARY ON MATTHEW 2.13.35.[20]

13:36 Emboldened to Ask About the Parable of the Weeds

JESUS LEFT THE CROWDS. CHRYSOSTOM: He left the crowds and went away. Jesus "went into the house." And not one of the scribes fol-

lowed him. From this it is clear that they followed him for no other purpose than to seize him. But when they neglected to listen to his teachings, he let them be. THE GOSPEL OF MATTHEW, HOMILY 47.1.[21]

HE WENT TO THE HOUSE. ORIGEN: Now, having discoursed sufficiently to the multitudes in parables, he sends them away and goes to his own house, where his disciples come to him. His disciples did not go with those he sent away. As many as are more genuine hearers of Jesus first follow him, then having inquired about his house, are permitted to see it. Having come, they saw and stayed with him for all that day, and perhaps some of them even longer. In my opinion, such things are implied in the Gospel according to John. . . . And if then, unlike the multitudes whom he sends away, we wish to hear Jesus and go to the house and receive something better than the multitudes did, let us become friends of Jesus, so that as his disciples come, we may also come to him when he goes into the house. And having come, let us inquire about the explanation of the parable, whether of the tares of the field, or of any other. COMMENTARY ON MATTHEW 10.1-3.[22]

EXPLAIN TO US THE PARABLE. CHRYSOSTOM: When his disciples came to him "asking him concerning the parable of the tares," it seemed as though they wished to learn but were afraid to ask.[23] What was the source of their confidence to pursue the matter? They had been told, "To you it is given to know the mysteries of the kingdom of heaven."[24] So they were emboldened. They asked quietly in private, not so as to circumvent the crowd but to observe the Lord's

[17]PG 58:481; NPNF 1 10:292. [18]Ps 78:2 (77:2 LXX). [19]Psalm 78 (77 LXX), from which the Gospel citation is taken, considers the exodus of the Israelites from Egypt. Jerome links this isolated citation with the remainder of the psalm and deduces that the entire psalm is to be interpreted symbolically, as a reference to Christ and the church. [20]CCL 77:111. [21]PG 58:481; NPNF 1 10:292. [22]GCS 40:1-2; ANF 9:414. [23]Mk 9:32. [24]Mt 13:11.

wishes. For he had said "to these it is not given."

And why may it be that they let pass the parable of the leaven and of the mustard seed and inquire concerning the weeds? They let those pass because they were easier to understand, but they seemed to be attracted to the theme of the weeds. It seemed to be addressing something more that they still desired to learn. This was the second time Jesus had discussed this theme. They recognized how ominous was the danger it implied. He did not resist them but further elaborated his teaching.

And, as I am always saying, the parables must not be explained literally, since many absurdities would follow. This even he himself is teaching us here in thus interpreting this parable. THE GOSPEL OF MATTHEW, HOMILY 47.1.[25]

13:37-43 The Close of the Age

THE RIGHTEOUS WILL SHINE LIKE THE SUN. ORIGEN: But when, as we have indicated, he gathers from the whole kingdom of Christ all things that make people stumble, and the reasonings that produce lawless acts are cast into the furnace of fire, and the worse elements utterly consumed . . . then shall the righteous, having become one light of the sun, shine in the kingdom of their Father. For whom will they shine? For those below them who will enjoy their light, after the analogy of the sun which now shines for those upon the earth? Of course, they will not shine for themselves. But perhaps the saying "Let your light shine before men"[26] can be written "upon the table of the heart,"[27] according to what is said by Solomon, in a threefold way. So even now the light of the disciples of Jesus shines before the rest of humanity, and after death before the resurrection, and after the resurrection "until all shall attain to full maturity"[28] and all become one sun. Then shall they "shine as the sun in the kingdom of their Father."[29] COMMENTARY ON MATTHEW 10.3.[30]

---

[25]PG 58:481-82; NPNF 1 10:292. [26]Mt 5:16. [27]Prov 7:3. [28]Eph 4:13. [29]Mt 13:43. [30]GCS 40:3-4; ANF 9:415.

13:44-52 THE PARABLES OF THE HIDDEN TREASURE, THE PEARL AND THE NET

[44] "The kingdom of heaven is like treasure hidden in a field, which a man found and covered up; then in his joy he goes and sells all that he has and buys that field.

[45] "Again, the kingdom of heaven is like a merchant in search of fine pearls, [46]who, on finding one pearl of great value, went and sold all that he had and bought it.

[47] "Again, the kingdom of heaven is like a net which was thrown into the sea and gathered fish of every kind; [48]when it was full, men drew it ashore and sat down and sorted the good into vessels but threw away the bad. [49]So it will be at the close of the age. The angels will come out and separate the evil from the righteous, [50]and throw them into the furnace of fire; there men will weep and gnash their teeth.

[51] *"Have you understood all this?" They said to him, "Yes." [52] And he said to them, "Therefore every scribe who has been trained for the kingdom of heaven is like a householder who brings out of his treasure what is new and what is old."*

OVERVIEW: The treasure hidden in the field points toward the incarnate Lord, who is found as a free gift. The preaching of the gospel has no strings attached. The power to use and own this treasure with the field, however, comes at a price, for heavenly riches are not possessed without earthly loss (HILARY). One conquers all earthly desires by observing the heavenly discipline, no longer fearing anything that might destroy bodily life. Such is one who sells everything and buys the field (GREGORY THE GREAT). To one who has thus bought the field in faith, past possessions are no longer considered one's own (ORIGEN).

The costly pearl is the living Word, which is superior to the precious letters and thoughts in the law and the prophets (ORIGEN). The faithful seek the one pearl of everlasting life, even at the loss of all else (HILARY, PETER CHRYSOLOGUS). Many who have been entirely foreign to religion have immediately recognized, by divine grace, the greatness of Christ, in that they despise all their former things and look to this alone (THEODORE OF MOPSUESTIA). Love makes one turn away from extraneous earthly desires (GREGORY THE GREAT).

The kingdom is compared with a net that encircles every creature in the water, dragging the bottom, drawing out everything it has enclosed (HILARY). The fishing net of faith contains fish both good and bad (GREGORY THE GREAT). The variety of fish contained in the net represents Gentiles called from every nation (ORIGEN).

Those trained in Scripture are described as scribes because they understood both the new and old things—both in gospel and law (HILARY, CYRIL OF ALEXANDRIA). But one is a scribe in a deeper sense when one ascends beyond the elementary knowledge of Scripture to grasp its spiritual sense (ORIGEN). The old things are not taken away but are hidden in a storeroom. The learned scribe is now in the kingdom of God, bringing forth from the storeroom not only new and old things, but both in their relationship (AUGUSTINE, GREGORY THE GREAT).

13:44 The Treasure Hidden in a Field

ITS PLAIN SENSE AND SPIRITUAL SENSE. ORIGEN: Now a man who comes to the field, whether to the Scriptures or to the Christ who is formed both from things manifest and from things hidden, finds the hidden treasure of wisdom whether in Christ or in the Scriptures. For, going round to visit the field and searching the Scriptures and seeking to understand the Christ, he finds the treasure in it. Having found it, he hides it, thinking that it is not without danger to reveal to everybody the secret meanings of the Scriptures or the treasures of wisdom and knowledge in Christ. And, having hidden it, he goes away. Now he is focused on the heavy labor of devising how he shall buy the field, or the Scriptures, that he may make them his own possession, receiving from the people of God the oracles of God with which the Jews were first entrusted.[1] But when one taught by Christ has bought the field, the kingdom of God, according to another parable, is like a vineyard that is "taken from" the first and given to other nations bringing forth its fruits.[2] The one who bought the field in faith, as the fruit of his having sold all else that he had, no longer was keeping anything that was formerly his. For they would be a distracting source of evil to him.

And you will give the same application, if the field containing the hidden treasure is Christ.

---

[1]Rom 3:2. [2]Mt 21:43.

Those who give up all things and follow him have, as it were in another way, sold their possessions. Thus by having sold and surrendered them and having received in their place a noble resolution from God their helper, they may purchase, at great cost worthy of the field, the field containing the hidden treasure. COMMENTARY ON MATTHEW 10.6.[3]

LIKE TREASURE HIDDEN IN A FIELD. HILARY: Through the comparison of a treasure in the field of our hope, Christ points to wealth that has been covered up, for God is discovered in humanity. In compensation for it, all the resources of the world are to be sold in order that with the clothing, food and drink of the needy we may buy the eternal riches of the heavenly treasure. But we must realize that the treasure was found and hidden, for he who found it could certainly have carried it off in secret at the time he hid it; and carrying it off, there would have been no need for him to buy it. But an explanation is needed here as to both the matter concerned and what was said. Thus the treasure was hidden because it was necessary to buy the field. The treasure in the field, as we said, signifies Christ in the flesh, who was found freely. Indeed, the preaching of the Gospels has no strings attached, but the power to use and own this treasure with the field comes at a price, for heavenly riches are not possessed without a worldly loss. ON MATTHEW 13.7.[4]

SELLING EVERYTHING TO BUY THAT FIELD. GREGORY THE GREAT: See how the kingdom of heaven is compared with a treasure hidden in a field. Someone finds and hides it, and in his joy goes and sells everything he has and buys that field. We should note that the treasure, once discovered, is hidden to protect it. It is not enough to guard our pursuit of heavenly delight from wicked spirits if we do not hide it from human praise. In this present life we are, as it were, on the road by which we proceed to our homeland. Wicked spirits lie in wait along our route like

bandits. Those who carry their treasure openly on the road are asking to be robbed.

I say this, however, not because our neighbors should not see our good works, for it is written, "Let them see your good works and give glory to your Father in heaven,"[5] but that we may not seek praise from outside for what we do.

We must let our work be in the open in such a way that our intention remains secret. Then we provide an example to our neighbors from our good work, and yet by the intention by which we seek to please God alone we always choose secrecy. The treasure is heavenly delight, and the field in which the treasure is hidden is the discipline of the pursuit of heaven. One who renounces the pleasures of the body and conquers all earthly desires by observing the heavenly discipline, so that nothing his body favors is compelling any longer and his spirit no longer fears anything that might destroy his bodily life, is truly one who sells everything and buys the field. FORTY GOSPEL HOMILIES 11.1.[6]

13:45-46 One Pearl of Great Value

IN SEARCH OF FINE PEARLS. ORIGEN: Now among the words of all kinds that profess to announce truth, and among those who report them, he seeks pearls. Think of the prophets as, so to speak, the pearls that receive the dew of heaven and become pregnant with the word of truth from heaven. They are goodly pearls that, according to the phrase here set forth, the merchant seeks. And the chief of the pearls, on the finding of which the rest are found with it, is the very costly pearl, the Christ of God, the Word that is superior to the precious letters and thoughts in the law and the prophets. When one finds this pearl all the rest are easily released.

Suppose, then, that one is not a disciple of Christ. He possesses no pearls at all, much less the very costly pearl, as distinguished from

---

[3]GCS 40:6; ANF 9:416. [4]SC 254:300-302. [5]Mt 5:16. [6]PL 76:1115; CS 123:62-63 (Homily 9).

those that are cloudy or darkened. . . . The muddy words and the heresies that are bound up with works of the flesh are like the darkened pearls and those that are produced in the marshes. They are not beautiful. COMMENTARY ON MATTHEW 10.8[7]

THE PEARL ONE'S HEART WAS SET ON.
HILARY: As regards the pearl, the reasoning is the same. But this passage is of value for the merchant who has long been steeped in the law. After lengthy labors, he finds out about this pearl and abandons those things that he obtained under the yoke of the law. For he carried on business for a long time and found the pearl that his heart was set on. He must pay the price of this one pearl he desired at the expense of all his other work. ON MATTHEW 13.8.[8]

THE MERCHANT SOLD ALL THAT HE HAD.
THEODORE OF MOPSUESTIA: Many who were entirely foreign to religion immediately recognized, by divine grace, the greatness of Christ, in that they despised all their former things and looked to this thing alone, recognizing that the one who is salvation is for them. Then he adds, again, that many people, even of those who have been exceedingly zealous about religion, when they recognize the greatness of the preaching, shall turn aside from old things. Such, for instance, was Paul, who had displayed a great deal of zeal for the law, but who, when he came to see the greatness of the gospel, disdained everything having to do with the law. He himself says, "but what things were gain to me, those I counted as loss for the sake of Christ";[9] and again, "I count all things but loss, and count them as dung, that I may win Christ."[10] He seems to have said this both on account of those Greeks who were devoted to religion and, again, on account of the Jews. FRAGMENT 75.[11]

COMPARING EARTHLY PEARLS WITH HEAVENLY. GREGORY THE GREAT: Again, the kingdom of heaven is said to be like a merchant who

is seeking fine pearls. He finds one really precious pearl, and, having found it, he sells everything he has in order to buy it. In the same way, he who has a clear knowledge of the sweetness of heavenly life gladly leaves behind all the things he loved on earth. Compared with that pearl, everything else fades in value. He forsakes those things that he has and scatters those things that he has gathered. His heart yearns for heavenly things, and nothing on earth pleases him. The allure of earthly things has now dissipated, for only the brilliance of that precious pearl dazzles his mind. Solomon justly says of such love, "Love is strong as death,"[12] because just as death destroys the body, so ardent desire for eternal life cuts off the love for material things. For love makes insensitive to extraneous earthly desires the person whom it has swept off his feet. FORTY GOSPEL HOMILIES 11.2.[13]

THE KINGDOM IS LIKE A MERCHANT. PETER CHRYSOLOGUS: Let no one who hears this take offense at the name *merchant*. Here Christ is speaking of a merchant who shows mercy, not of one who is always usuriously investing his profits from capital. This merchant is the one who provides for the adornment of virtues, not the incentive of vices. He weighs the dignity of morals, not the weight of jewels. He wears necklaces of integrity, not of luxury. He flaunts not a display of sensual pleasure but the earmarks of discipline. Therefore this merchant exhibits pearls of heart and body, not in human trading but in heavenly commerce. He displays them not to trade for a present advantage but for a future one. He trades in order to gain not earthly but heavenly glory. He seeks to procure the kingdom of heaven as the reward of his virtues and to buy, at the price of innumerable other goods, the one pearl of everlasting life. SERMONS 47.2.[14]

[7]GCS 40:9-10. [8]SC 254:302. [9]Phil 3:7. [10]Phil 3:8. [11]*MKGK* 121. [12]Song 8:6. [13]PL 76:1115; CS 123:63-64 (Homily 9). [14]CCL 24:260.

13:47 A Net Thrown into the Sea

THE NET. ORIGEN: Now, these things being said, we must hold that "the kingdom of heaven is similar to a net that was cast into the sea and gathered of every kind," in order to set forth the varied character of the principles of action among people, which are as different as possible from each other. The expression "gathered from every kind" embraces both those worthy of praise and those worthy of blame in respect of their inclinations toward the forms of virtues or of vices. And the kingdom of heaven is compared with the broad and variegated texture of a net, with reference to the old and the new Scripture, which are woven together of thoughts of widely varied kinds. COMMENTARY ON MATTHEW 10.12.[15]

FISH OF EVERY KIND. ORIGEN: And this net has been cast into the waves of the sea. The waves toss about persons in every part of the world as they swim in the bitter affairs of life. Before the coming of our Savior Jesus Christ, this net was not wholly filled. The net expected by the Law and the Prophets had to be completed by him who says, "Don't think that I came to destroy the law and the prophets; I came not to destroy but to fulfill."[16] The texture of the net has been completed in the Gospels and in the words of Christ through the apostles. On this account, therefore, "the kingdom of heaven is like a net that was cast into the sea and gathered every kind of fish." In addition to what has been said, the expression "gathered from every kind" may refer to the calling of the Gentiles out of every nation. COMMENTARY ON MATTHEW 10.12.[17]

LIKE A NET. HILARY: The Lord rightly compared his preaching with a net. Coming into the world, without condemning the world he gathered those who were dwelling within it in the manner of a net. Tossed into the sea, that net is hauled up from the bottom. Encircling every

creature in that element, it draws out all those things that it has netted. It lifts us out of the world and into the light of the true sun. With the choice of righteous honor and the rejection of evil, it brings to light the scrutiny of the judgment to come. ON MATTHEW 13.9.[18]

GATHERING FISH GOOD AND BAD. GREGORY THE GREAT: Again the kingdom of heaven is said to be like a fishing net that is let down into the sea, gathering all kinds of fish. Once it is filled, the net is brought to shore. The good fish are gathered into baskets, but the bad ones are thrown away. Our holy church is compared to a net, because it has been entrusted to fishermen, and because all people are drawn up in it from the turbulent waters of the present age to the eternal kingdom, lest we drown in the depths of eternal death. This net gathers all kinds of fish because it calls to forgiveness of sins everyone, wise and foolish, free and slave, rich and poor, brave and weak. Hence, the psalmist says to God: "Unto you shall all flesh come."[19] This net will be completely filled when it enfolds the entire number of the human race at the end of time. The fishermen bring it in and sit down on the shore, because just as the sea signifies this present age, so the shore signifies its end. FORTY GOSPEL HOMILIES 11.4.[20]

13:48 Sorting the Good and Bad Fish

SORTED INTO BASKETS. GREGORY THE GREAT: At the end of this present age the good fish are to be sorted into baskets and the bad ones thrown away. Then all the elect will be received into eternal dwellings, and the condemned will be led away into external darkness, since they have lost the light of the kingdom within them. Meanwhile the fishing net of faith holds us together as intermingled fish both good and

---

[15]GCS 40:13-15; ANF 9:420. [16]Mt 5:17. [17]GCS 40:14; ANF 9:420. [18]SC 254:302. [19]Ps 65:2 (64:2 LXX). [20]PL 76:1116; CS 123:64 (Homily 9).

bad. FORTY GOSPEL HOMILIES 11.4.[21]

THE BAD FISH THROWN AWAY. GREGORY THE GREAT: Once on the shore, however, the fishing net—that is, the holy church—indicates what it has drawn in. Some fish, when they have been caught, cannot be changed. Others of us who were caught while we are wicked can become changed for the better. Let us bear this in mind as we are in the process of being caught, lest we be thrown aside on shore. FORTY GOSPEL HOMILIES 11.4.[22]

13:49 The Angels Will Separate the Evil and the Righteous

AT THE CLOSE OF THE AGE. CYRIL OF ALEXANDRIA: The calling that is through Christ is to be extended throughout the whole world. The net of gospel preaching seeks to gather together people out of every nation. People who are expert in catching fish and are mariners by trade let down their net making no discrimination, but whatever has been caught up in the meshes, wholly and entirely, is hauled by them to shore. So likewise the power of preaching and the marvelous and intricate teaching of the sacred doctrines, which the apostles, as good fishermen, wove together, draw people from every nation and gather them together for God. This net will gather all fish together until the time of consummation. Then out of all those who have been dragged out and caught, the angels appointed by God will make a separation between the wicked and the just. FRAGMENT 171.[23]

13:50 Thrown into the Furnace

THE FURNACE OF FIRE. ORIGEN: And those who attended to the net that was cast into the sea are Jesus Christ, the master of the net, and "the angels who came and ministered to him."[24] It is not until the net is filled full that they will draw it up from the sea and carry it to the shore beyond the sea—namely, to things beyond this life—but not until the "fullness of the Gentiles" has been drawn into it. But when that fullness has come, then they draw it up from things here below and carry it to what is figuratively called the shore. There it will be the work of those who have drawn it up to sit by the shore, there to settle themselves in order that they may put each of the good fish in its own proper place, into the right vessel. But they will cast outside those that are of an opposite character and are called bad. By "outside" is meant the furnace of fire, as the Savior interpreted it, saying, "So shall it be at the consummation of the age. The angels shall come forth and separate the wicked from among the righteous and shall cast them into the furnace of fire." Only it must be observed that we are already taught by the parable of the tares and the other similitudes set forth that the angels are to be entrusted with the power to distinguish and separate the evil from the righteous. For it is said above, "The Son of Man shall send his angels, and they shall gather out of his kingdom all things that cause stumbling, and those who do iniquity, and shall cast them into the furnace of fire. There shall be the weeping and gnashing of teeth."[25] But here it is said, "The angels shall come forth and sever the wicked from among the righteous and shall cast them into the furnace of fire." COMMENTARY ON MATTHEW 10.12.[26]

13:51 Have You Understood?

THEY UNDERSTOOD. HILARY: He spoke not to the crowds but to the disciples, and he gave fitting witness to those who understood the parables. He compared them with a householder, for they understood the teaching of his storeroom of things new and old. He referred to them as scribes because of their knowledge, for they understood the new and old things—that is, in

---

[21]PL 76:1116; CS 123:64-65 (Homily 9). [22]PL 76:1116; CS 123:65 (Homily 9). [23]MKGK 208-9. [24]Mt 4:11. [25]Mt 13:41-42. [26]GCS 40:14-15; ANF 9:420.

the Gospels and in the law. He brought forth both of these on behalf of the same householder and from the same storeroom. ON MATTHEW 14.1.[27]

TRAINED IN LETTER AND SPIRIT. ORIGEN: And one is a scribe "as a disciple to the kingdom of heaven" in the simpler sense, when one comes from Judaism and receives the teaching of Jesus Christ as defined by the church. But one is a scribe in a deeper sense when having received elementary knowledge through the letter of the Scriptures one ascends to things spiritual, which are called the kingdom of heaven. And as each thought is attained, grasped abstractly and proved by example and absolute demonstration, thereby one can understand the kingdom of heaven. Thus one who abounds in knowledge free from error is in the kingdom of the multitude of what are here represented as "heavens." . . . Hence, so far as Jesus Christ, "who was in the beginning with God, God the Word,"[28] has not his home in a soul, the kingdom of heaven is not in it. But when anyone comes close to admission of the Word, to that one the kingdom of heaven is near. But if the kingdom of heaven and the kingdom of God are the same thing in reality,[29] if not in idea, manifestly to those to whom it is said, "The kingdom of God is within you,"[30] to them also it might be said, "The kingdom of heaven is within you." This is most true because of the repentance from the letter to the spirit, since "when one turns to the Lord, the veil over the letter is taken away."[31] COMMENTARY ON MATTHEW 10.14.[32]

13:52 Treasures New and Old

EVERY TRAINED SCRIBE. CYRIL OF ALEXANDRIA: A scribe is one who, through continual reading of the Old and New Testaments, has laid up for himself a storehouse of knowledge. Thus Christ blesses those who have gathered in themselves the education both of the law and of the gospel, so as to "bring forth from their trea-

sure things both new and old." And Christ compares such people with a scribe, just as in another place he says, "I will send you wise men and scribes."[33] FRAGMENT 172.[34]

TREASURES IN HEAVEN. ORIGEN: One who is truly such a householder is both free and rich. He is rich because from the office of the scribe he has been made a disciple to the kingdom of heaven, in every word of the Old Testament and in all knowledge concerning the new teaching of Christ Jesus. He has these riches laid up in his own treasure house—in heaven, in which he stores his treasure as one who has been made a disciple to the kingdom of heaven. There neither moth consumes nor thieves break through and steal.[35] For the one who has such treasures laid up in heaven, not one moth of the inordinate passions can touch his spiritual and heavenly possessions. COMMENTARY ON MATTHEW 10.14.[36]

WHAT IS NEW AND WHAT IS OLD. GREGORY THE GREAT: It was the old fate of the human race to descend into the gates of hell to suffer eternal punishment for its sins. But something was changed by the coming of the Mediator. If a person really desired to live uprightly here, one could attain to the kingdom of heaven and, even though earth-born, can depart from this perishable life and be given a place in heaven. The old fate was such that by way of punishment humankind could perish in eternal punishment. The new fate was such that, having been converted, humankind could live in the kingdom.

And so we see that the Lord concluded his discourse as he began it. First he likened the treasure discovered in a field and the pearl of great value to the kingdom. Then he spoke of the punishments of the lower world and the

---

[27]SC 258:10. [28]Jn 1:1. [29]Or substance. [30]Lk 17:21. [31]2 Cor 3:16. [32]GCS 40:17-18; ANF 9:422. [33]Mt 23:34. [34]MKGK 209. [35]Mt 6:20. [36]GCS 40:18; ANF 9:422.

burning of the wicked. Then he added in conclusion: "So then, every scribe instructed in the kingdom of heaven is like a householder who brings forth from his storeroom things new and old." It was as though he had said, "That person is a learned preacher in the holy church who knows both how to bring forth new things about the delights of the kingdom and to speak old things about the terror of chastisement, so that punishments may fill with dread those not induced by rewards." FORTY GOSPEL HOMILIES 11.5.[37]

BOTH OLD AND NEW TESTAMENTS. AUGUSTINE: And now the voice of Christ speaks to the Jews through the voice of the old Scriptures. They hear the voice of those Scriptures but do not see the face of the One who speaks. Do they want the veil to be lifted? Let them come to the Lord. Thus the old things are not taken away but are hidden in a storeroom. The learned scribe is now in the kingdom of God, bringing forth from his storeroom not new things only and not old things only. For if he should bring forth new things only or old things only, he is not a learned scribe in the kingdom of God presenting from his storeroom things new and old. If he says these things and does not do them, he brings them forth from his teaching office, not from the storeroom of his heart. We then say, Those things which are brought forth from the old are enlightened through the new. We therefore come to the Lord that the veil may be removed. SERMON 74.5.[38]

---

[37]PL 76:1117; CS 123:66 (Homily 9). [38]PL 38:474; NPNF 1 6:337 (Sermon 24).

13:53-58 JESUS IS REJECTED AT NAZARETH

[53]And when Jesus had finished these parables, he went away from there, [54]and coming to his own country he taught them in their synagogue, so that they were astonished, and said, "Where did this man get this wisdom and these mighty works? [55]Is not this the carpenter's son? Is not his mother called Mary? And are not his brothers James and Joseph and Simon and Judas? [56]And are not all his sisters with us? Where then did this man get all this?" [57]And they took offense at him. But Jesus said to them, "A prophet is not without honor except in his own country and in his own house." [58]And he did not do many mighty works there, because of their unbelief.

OVERVIEW: Having come back to his own country, Jesus is no longer so intent upon miracles, so as not to inflame his detractors into more envy or condemn them more grievously. Yet he presents his teaching, which has no less of wonder than does his miracles (CHRYSOSTOM). The synagogue was astonished at his wisdom and mighty works (PETER CHRYSOLOGUS). Whether "his own country" was Nazareth, Bethlehem or Capernaum was discussed by the fathers.

If we think of Judea as Jesus' country, then we can truthfully say that all prophets have suffered dishonor in Judea (ORIGEN). The populace saw nothing in any of his relatives that would have given a clue to his remarkable accomplishments. They perceived little from his education and teaching that would lead to such wisdom and power (ORIGEN). The glory of a relative or neighbor often offends others nearby (PETER CHRYSOLOGUS, CHRYSOSTOM). He taught in their synagogue, neither separating from it nor disregarding it (ORIGEN). They did not believe that God was doing these things in a man (HILARY). Faith does not produce healing without divine power (ORIGEN).

13:53 Jesus Left His Country

COMING TO HIS OWN COUNTRY. ORIGEN: We must therefore inquire whether by the expression "his own country" is meant Nazareth or Bethlehem. It might have been Nazareth, because of the saying "he shall be called a Nazarene."[1] Or it might have been Bethlehem, since he was born there. Furthermore, I wonder whether the Evangelists could have said "coming to Bethlehem" or "coming to Nazareth." They have not done so but have named it more simply "his country." This is because of something being declared in a mystic sense in the passage about his country—namely, the whole of Judea—in which he was dishonored. This is according to the saying "A prophet is not without honor, except in his own country."[2] Jesus Christ was considered "a stumbling block to the Jews,"[3] among whom he is persecuted even until now. But he was proclaimed among the Gentiles and believed in everywhere—for his word has run over the whole world. In his own country Jesus had no honor, but among those who were "strangers from the covenants,"[4] the Gentiles, he is held in honor. But the Evangelists have not recorded what things he taught and spoke in their synagogue. All we know is that they were so great and of such a nature that all were astonished. Probably the things spoken were too elevated to be written down. Only let us note that he taught in their synagogue, not separating from it or disregarding it. COMMENTARY ON MATTHEW 10.16.[5]

IGNORED BECAUSE OF HIS PARENTAGE. CHRYSOSTOM: And what does he now call his country? As it seems to me, Nazareth. "For he did not do many mighty works there,"[6] it is said, but in Capernaum he did miracles. Thus Jesus also said, "And you, Capernaum, will you be exalted to heaven? You shall be brought down to hades. For if the mighty works done in you had been done in Sodom, it would have remained until this day."[7] THE GOSPEL OF MATTHEW, HOMILY 48.1.[8]

13:54-56 Astonished by His Teaching

HE TAUGHT THEM IN THEIR SYNAGOGUE. PETER CHRYSOLOGUS: The synagogues could not be his. A malicious and disbelieving crowd gathered there. A people full of hate rather than love came together. A group of ill-disposed and ill-mannered people assembled. "He began to teach in their synagogues, so that they were astonished." They were astonished because of indignation and not because of grace. They were amazed because of envy and not because of praise. They raged because what the proud seated on the floor were unable to discern, humility on its feet was thoroughly teaching. SERMONS 48.2.[9]

THEY WERE ASTONISHED. PETER CHRYSOLOGUS: "So that they were astonished, and said, 'Where did he get this wisdom?'" The one who speaks this way does not know God, from whom is wisdom and from whom are mighty works. Solomon points to that source of wisdom. While still young, he accepted the highest honor of the kingdom so he might rule the people entrusted to him with virtue and not with arrogance, with wisdom and not with pride, with his heart and not with his head. He wanted wisdom from God, earnestly asked for it and received it.

---

[1]Mt 2:23. [2]Mt 13:57. [3]1 Cor 1:23. [4]Eph 2:12. [5]GCS 40:20-21; ANF 9:424. [6]Mt 13:58. [7]Mt 11:23. [8]PG 58:487; NPNF 1 10:296. [9]CCL 24:265.

"Where did he get this wisdom and these mighty works?" The mighty power that gives eyesight denied by nature, that restores hearing to those drowned in silence, that unscrambles the words of those who are mute, that enables the lame to walk again and that orders souls headed for the realm of the dead to return to their bodies is from God, unless someone envious of salvation should deny it. SERMONS 48.2.[10]

IS NOT MARY HIS MOTHER? ORIGEN: And perhaps these things indicated a new doubt concerning him, that Jesus was not a man but something more divine. Yet he was thought to be the son of Joseph and Mary and the brother of four and of the others and the women as well. Yet they saw nothing in any of his relatives that would have given a clue to these gifts. They observed nothing from his education and teaching that would come to such elevated wisdom and power. For they also say elsewhere, "How does this man know letters, having never learned?"[11] which is similar to what is said here. Yet, though they say these things and are so perplexed and astonished, they did not believe but were offended by him. It is as if the eyes of their mind had been mastered by the powers that, in the time of the passion, he was about to lead in triumph on the cross. COMMENTARY ON MATTHEW 10.17.[12]

IS THIS NOT THE CARPENTER'S SON? HILARY: The Lord is dishonored by his own. Although his wisdom in teaching and his mighty works excited admiration, their faithlessness held them back from true discernment. For they did not believe that God was doing these things in a man. Moreover, they referred to his father, his mother, brothers and sisters and took offense at him.

But clearly this was the son of the carpenter who was subduing iron with fire, melting away all the might of the world with good judgment and forming the mass into every work that was humanly useful. He was molding the formless material of our bodies into members for differ-

ent ministries and for every work of eternal life. They all became irritated at these things. Among the many astonishing things he did, they were most deeply moved by his contemplativeness and his bodily self-control. The Lord said to them that a prophet is without honor in his own country,[13] because he was to be despised in Judea until the final fate of the cross. And since God's power is only with those who are faithful, he abstained from all works of divine power while he was there, because of their unbelief. ON MATTHEW 14.2.[14]

JUDGED BY PARENTAGE. CHRYSOSTOM: But having come to his own country, he is not so intent upon miracles. He does not want to inflame them into further envy or to condemn them more grievously by the aggravation of their unbelief. Yet he presents his teaching, which possesses no less wonder than his miracles. For these utterly senseless people, when they ought to have marveled and been amazed at the power of his words, instead disparaged him, because of the one thought to be his father. Yet we know they had many examples of these things in the former times, for many fathers of little note had produced illustrious children. THE GOSPEL OF MATTHEW, HOMILY 48.1.[15]

13:57 A Prophet Not Without Honor

EXCEPT IN HIS OWN COUNTRY. ORIGEN: We must inquire whether the expression has the same force when applied universally to every prophet. Does it mean that every one of the prophets was dishonored only in his own country? Or does it mean that every one who was dishonored was dishonored in his country? Or does it mean that because of the expression being singular, these things were said about only one? If these words are spoken about only one, then these things that have been said make sense in-

---

[10]CCL 24:265. [11]Jn 7:15. [12]GCS 40:22; ANF 9:424-25. [13]Mt 13:57. [14]SC 258:10-12. [15]PG 58:487; NPNF 1 10:296.

sofar as they refer to what is written about the Savior. But if the point is generalized to indicate all prophets, then it is harder to defend historically. For Elijah did not suffer dishonor in Tishbeth of Gilead, nor Elisha in Abetmeholah, nor Samuel in Ramathaim, nor Jeremiah in Anathoth. But, figuratively interpreted, this saying is absolutely true. For we must think of Judea as their country and that famous Israel as their kindred, and perhaps of the body as the house. All suffered dishonor in Judea from the Israel that is according to the flesh while they were yet in the body. As it is written in the Acts of the Apostles, "Which of the prophets did your fathers not persecute, who declared beforehand the coming of the righteous One?"[16] And Paul says similar things in the first epistle to the Thessalonians: "For you, brothers, became imitators of the churches of God in Christ Jesus which are in Judea; for you suffered the same things from your own countrymen as they did from the Jews, who killed both the Lord Jesus and the prophets, and drove us out, and displease God and oppose all people."[17] COMMENTARY ON MATTHEW 10.18.[18]

13:58 Few Works Done

BECAUSE OF THEIR UNBELIEF. ORIGEN: It seems to me that the production of miracles is similar in some ways to the case of physical things. Cultivation is not sufficient to produce a harvest of fruits unless the soil, or rather the atmosphere, cooperates to this end. And the atmosphere of itself is not sufficient to produce a harvest without cultivation. The one who providentially orders creation did not design things to spring up from the earth without cultivation. Only in the first instance did he do so when he said, "Let the earth bring forth vegetation, with the seed sowing according to its kind and according to its likeness."[19]

It is just this way in regard to the production of miracles. The complete work resulting in a healing is not displayed without those being

healed exercising faith. Faith, of whatever quality it might be, does not produce a healing without divine power. COMMENTARY ON MATTHEW 10.19.[20]

WHY JESUS HELD BACK FROM DOING MIRACLES. CHRYSOSTOM: Luke says, "And he did not do many miracles there." And yet it was to be expected he should have done them. For if the feeling of wonder toward him was growing (for indeed even there he was marveled at), why did Jesus not do them? Because he wasn't concerned with the spectacle [of miracles] but with their usefulness. Therefore when this did not succeed, he overlooked what was of concern to himself to avoid aggravating their punishment.

Why then did he still do a few miracles? That they might not say, "Physician, heal yourself."[21] Or to prevent them saying, "He is a foe and an enemy to us and overlooks his own." Or that they might not say, "If he had performed miracles, we also would have believed." Therefore he both performedd them and ceased doing so: the one, that he might fulfill his own part; the other, that he might not condemn them the more.

And consider the power of Jesus' words. Possessed as the Jews were by envy, they still admired him. And as with regard to his works, they do not find fault with what is done but invent causes that have no basis, saying, "By Beelzebub he casts out devils."[22] Even so here too they find no fault with his teaching but take refuge only in the lowly stature of his ancestors. THE GOSPEL OF MATTHEW, HOMILY 48.1.[23]

HE DID NO MIGHTY WORKS THERE. PETER CHRYSOLOGUS: Christ indeed came to his own country, because it was written, "He came among his own, and his own did not receive him."[24] In plain fact, when he says, "A prophet is not without honor except in his own country,"

---

[16]Acts 7:52. [17]1 Thess 2:14-15. [18]GCS 40:23; ANF 9:425. [19]Gen 1:11. [20]GCS 40:26. [21]Lk 4:23. [22]Mt 12:24. [23]PG 58:487; NPNF 1 10:297. [24]Jn 1:11.

he is teaching that it is a painful situation to have influence among his own. To stand out among the local denizens is similar to an inflammation. A near relation's glory burns the near relations. If neighbors have to pay homage to a neighbor, they consider it servitude. "And he did not do many mighty works there, because of their unbelief."[25] Power has no effect where unbelief does not deserve it. And while Christ does not demand a reward when he heals, he becomes indignant when injustice is shown to him instead of honor. SERMONS 48.6.[26]

---

[25]Mt 13:58. [26]CCL 24:267-68.

Early Christian Writers and the Documents Cited

The following table lists all the early Christian documents cited in this volume by author, if known, or by the title of the work. The English title used in this commentary is followed in parenthesis with the Latin designation and, where available, the Thesaurus Linguae Graecae (=TLG) digital references or Cetedoc Clavis numbers. Printed sources of original language versions may be found in the bibliography.

Apollinaris of Laodicea
Fragments on Matthew (*Fragmenta in Matthaeum*)   TLG 2074.037

Augustine of Hippo
Harmony of the Gospels (*De consensu evangelistarum libri iv*)   Cetedoc 0273
Sermon (*Sermones*)   Cetedoc 0284
Sermon on the Mount (*De sermone Domini in monte*)   Cetedoc 0274

Chromatius of Aquileia
Tractates on Matthew (*Tractatus in Matthaeum*)   Cetedoc 0218

Cyprian of Carthage
Treatises, On the Lord's Prayer (*De dominica oratione*)   Cetedoc 0043

Cyril of Alexandria
Fragments on Matthew (*Fragmenta in Matthaeum*)   TLG 4090.029

Epiphanius the Latin
Interpretation of the Gospels (*Interpretatio Evangeliorum*)

Eusebius of Emesa
Homilies (*Homiliae*)

Gregory the Great   Cetedoc 1711
Forty Gospel Homilies (*XL Homiliarum in Evangelia*)

Hilary of Poitiers
[Commentary] On Matthew (*In Matthaeum*)

Incomplete Work on Matthew (*Opus imperfectum in Matthaeum*)

Irenaeus of Lyon
Against Heresies (*Adversus haereses [liber 3]*)   TLG 1477.002

Jerome
Commentary on Matthew (*Commentariorum in Matthaeum libri iv*)   Cetedoc 0590

John Chrysostom
The Gospel of Matthew (*Homiliae in Matthaeum/Commentarius in sanctum
    Matthaeum evangelistam*)   TLG 2062.152

Maximus of Turin
Sermons (*Sermones*)   Cetedoc 0219a

Origen
Fragment (*Fragmenta*)   TLG 2042.031
[Commentary on] The Gospel of Matthew (*Commentariorum in
    Matthaeum libri 10-17*)   TLG 2042.029-030
On Prayer (*De oratione*)   TLG 2042.008

Peter Chrysologus
Sermons (*Sermones*)   Cetedoc 0227+

Severus of Antioch
Cathedral Sermons (*Homiliae cathedrales*)

Tertullian
On Idolatry (*De idololatria*)   Cetedoc 0023
On Prayer (*De oratione*)   Cetedoc 0007

Theodore of Heraclea
Fragments on Matthew (*Fragmenta in Matthaeum*)   TLG 4126.002

Theodore of Mopsuestia
Fragments on Matthew (*Fragmenta in Matthaeum*)   TLG 4135.009

BIOGRAPHICAL SKETCHES &
SHORT DESCRIPTIONS
OF SELECT ANONYMOUS WORKS

This listing is cumulative, including all the authors and works cited in this series to date.

Acacius of Caesarea (d. c. 365). Pro-Arian bishop of Caesarea in Palestine, disciple and biographer of Eusebius of Caesarea, the historian. He was a man of great learning and authored a treatise on Ecclesiastes.

Alexander of Alexandria (fl. 312-328). Bishop of Alexandria and predecessor of Athanasius, upon whom he asserted considerable theological influence during the rise of Arianism. Alexander excommunicated Arius, whom he had appointed to the parish of Baucalis, in 319. His teaching regarding the eternal generation and divine substantial union of the Son with the Father was eventually confirmed at the Council of Nicaea (325).

Ambrose of Milan (c. 333-397; fl. 374-397). Bishop of Milan and teacher of Augustine who defended the divinity of the Holy Spirit and the perpetual virginity of Mary.

Ambrosiaster (fl. c. 366-384). Name given by Erasmus to the author of a work once thought to have been composed by Ambrose.

Ammonius (c. fifth century). An Aristotelian commentator and teacher in Alexandria, where he was born and of whose school he became head. Also an exegete of Plato, he enjoyed fame among his contemporaries and successors, although modern critics accuse him of pedantry and banality.

Andreas (c. seventh century). Monk who collected commentary from earlier writers to form a catena on various biblical books.

Aphrahat (c. 270-350 fl. 337-345). "The Persian Sage" and first major Syriac writer whose work survives. He is also known by his Greek name Aphraates.

Apollinaris of Laodicea (310-c. 392). Bishop of Laodicea who was attacked by Gregory of Nazianzus, Gregory of Nyssa and Theodore for denying that Christ had a human mind.

Apostolic Constitutions (c. 381-394). Also known as *Constitutions of the Holy Apostles* and thought to be the work of the Arian bishop Julian of Neapolis. The work is divided into eight books, and is primarily a collection of and expansion on previous works such as the *Didache* (c. 140) and the *Apostolic Traditions*. Book 8 ends with eighty-five canons from various sources and is elsewhere known as the *Apostolic Canons*.

Arius (fl. c. 320). Heretic condemned at the Council of Nicaea (325) for refusing to accept that the Son was not a creature but was God by nature like the Father.

Athanasius of Alexandria (c. 295-373; fl. 325-373). Bishop of Alexandria from 328, though often in exile. He wrote his classic polemics against the Arians while most of the eastern bishops were against him.

Athenagoras (fl. 176-180). Early Christian philosopher and apologist from Athens, whose only authenticated writing, *A Plea Regarding Christians*, is addressed to the emperors Marcus Aurelius and Commodus, and defends Christians from the common accusations of atheism, incest and cannibalism.

Augustine of Hippo (354-430). Bishop of Hippo and a voluminous writer on philosophical, exegetical, theological and ecclesiological topics. He formulated the Western doctrines of predestination and original sin in his writings against the Pelagians.

Babai the Great (d. 628). Syriac monk who founded a monastery and school in his region of Beth Zabday and later served as third superior at the Great Convent of Mount Izla during a period of crisis in the Nestorian church.

Basil the Great (b. c. 330; fl. 357-379). One of the Cappadocian fathers, bishop of Caesarea and champion of the teaching on the Trinity propounded at Nicaea in 325. He was a great administrator and founded a monastic rule.

Basil of Seleucia (fl. 444-468). Bishop of Seleucia in Isauria and ecclesiastical writer. He took part in the Synod of Constantinople in 448 for the condemnation of the Eutychian errors and the deposition of their great champion, Dioscurus of Alexandria.

Basilides (fl. second century). Alexandrian heretic of the early second century who is said to have believed that souls migrate from body to body and that we do not sin if we lie to protect the body from martyrdom.

Bede the Venerable (c. 672/673-735). Born in Northumbria, at the age of seven he was put under the care of the Benedictine monks of Saints Peter and Paul at Jarrow and given a broad classical education in the monastic tradition. Considered one of the most learned men of his age, he is the author of *An Ecclesiastical History of the English People*.

Benedict of Nursia (c. 480-547). Considered the most important figure in the history of Western monasticism. Benedict founded many monasteries, the most notable found at Montecassino, but his lasting influence lay in his famous Rule. The Rule outlines the theological and inspirational foundation of the monastic ideal while also legislating the shape and organization of the coenobitic life.

Book of Steps (c. 400). Written by an anonymous Syriac author, this work consists of thirty homilies or discourses and which specifically deal with the more advanced stages of growth in the spiritual life.

Braulio of Saragossa (c. 585-651). Bishop of Saragossa 631-651 and noted writer of the Visigothic renaissance. His *Life* of St. Aemilianus is his crowning literary achievement.

Caesarius of Arles (c. 470-543). Bishop of Arles renowned for his attention to his pastoral duties. Among his surviving works the most important is a collection of some 238 sermons that display an ability to preach Christian doctrine to a variety of audiences.

Callistus of Rome (d. 222). Pope (217-222) who excommunicated Sabellius for heresy. It is very probable that he suffered martyrdom.

Cassian, John (360-432). Author of a compilation of ascetic sayings highly influential in the development of Western monasticism.

Cassiodorus (c. 485-c. 540). Founder of Western monasticism whose writings include valuable histories and less valuable commentaries.

Chromatius (fl. 400). Friend of Rufinus and Jerome and author of tracts and sermons.

Clement of Alexandria (c. 150-215). A highly educated Christian convert from paganism, head of the catechetical school in Alexandria and pioneer of Christian scholarship. His major works, *Protrepticus, Paedagogus* and the *Stromata*, bring Christian doctrine face to face with the ideas and achievements of his time.

Clement of Rome (fl. c. 92-101). Pope whose *Epistle to the Corinthians* is one of the most important documents of subapostolic times.

Commodian (c. third or fifth century). Poet of unknown origin (possibly Syrian?) whose two surviving works focus on the Apocalypse and Christian apologetics.

Constitutions of the Holy Apostles. See Apostolic Constitutions.

Cyprian of Carthage (fl. 248-258). Martyred bishop of Carthage who maintained that those baptized by schismatics and heretics had no share in the blessings of the church.

Cyril of Alexandria (375-444; fl. 412-444). Patriarch of Alexandria whose strong espousal of the unity of Christ led to the condemnation of Nestorius in 431.

Cyril of Jerusalem (c. 315-386; fl. 348). Bishop of Jerusalem after 350 and author of *Catechetical Homilies.*

Cyril of Scythopolis (b. c. 525; d. after 557). Palestinian monk and author of biographies of famous Palestinian monks. Because of him we have precise knowledge of monastic life in the fifth and sixth centuries and a description of the Origenist crisis and its suppression in the mid-sixth century.

Diadochus of Photice (c. 400-474). Antimonophysite bishop of Epirus Vetus whose work *Discourse on the Ascension of Our Lord Jesus Christ* exerted influence in both the East and West through its Chalcedonian Christology. He is also the subject of the mystical *Vision of St. Diadochus Bishop of Photice in Epirus.*

Didache (c. 140). Of unknown authorship, this text intertwines Jewish ethics with Christian liturgical practice to form a whole discourse on the "way of life." It exerted an enormous amount of influence in the patristic period and was especially used in the training of catechumen.

Didymus the Blind (c. 313-398). Alexandrian exegete who was much influenced by Origen and admired by Jerome.

Diodore of Tarsus (d. c. 394). Bishop of Tarsus and Antiochene theologian. He authored a great scope of exegetical, doctrinal and apologetic works, which come to us mostly in fragments because of his condemnation as the predecessor of Nestorianism. Diodore was a teacher of John Chrysostom and Theodore of Mopsuestia.

Dionysius of Alexandria (d. c. 264). Bishop of Alexandria and student of Origen. Dionysius actively engaged in the theological disputes of his day, opposed Sabellianism, defended himself against accusations of tritheism and wrote the earliest extant Christian refutation of Epicureanism. His writings have survived mainly in extracts preserved by other early Christian authors.

Dionysius the Areopagite. The name long given to the author of four mystical writings, probably from the late fifth century, which were the foundation of the apophatic school of mysticism in their denial that anything can be truly predicated of God.

Dorotheus of Gaza (fl. c. 525-540). Member of Abbot Seridos's monastery and later leader of a monastery where he wrote *Spiritual Instructions.* He also wrote a work on traditions of Palestinian monasticism.

Epiphanius of Salamis (c. 315-403). Bishop of Salamis in Cyprus, author of a refutation of eighty heresies (the *Panarion*) and instrumental in the condemnation of Origen.

Epiphanius the Latin. Author of the late fifth-century or early sixth century Latin text *Interpretation of the Gospels.* He was possibly a bishop of Benevento or Seville.

Ephrem the Syrian (b. c. 306; fl. 363-373). Syrian writer of commentaries and devotional hymns which are sometimes regarded as the greatest specimens of Christian poetry prior to Dante.

Eucherius of Lyons (fl. 420-449). Bishop of Lyons c. 435-449. Born into an aristocratic family, he, along with his wife and sons, joined the monastery at Lérins soon after its founding.

Eunomius (d. 393). Bishop of Cyzicyus who was attacked by Basil and Gregory of Nyssa for maintaining that the Father and the Son were of different natures, one ingenerate, one generate.

Eusebius of Caesarea (c. 260/263-340). Bishop of Caesarea, partisan of the Emperor Constantine and first historian of the Christian church. He argued that the truth of the gospel had been foreshadowed in pagan writings but had to defend his own doctrine against suspicion of Arian sympathies.

Eusebius of Emesa (c. 300-c. 359). Bishop of Emesa from c. 339. A biblical exegete and writer on doctrinal subjects, he displays some semi-Arian tendencies of his mentor Eusebius of Caesarea.

Eusebius of Vercelli (fl. c. 360). Bishop of Vercelli who supported the trinitarian teaching of Nicaea (325) when it was being undermined by compromise in the West.

Euthymius (377-473). A native of Melitene and influential monk. He was educated by Bishop Otreius of Melitene, who ordained him priest and placed him in charge of all the monasteries in his diocese. When the Council of Chalcedon (451) condemned the errors of Eutyches, it was greatly due to the authority of Euthymius that most of the Eastern recluses accepted its decrees. The empress Eudoxia returned to Chalcedonian orthodoxy through his efforts.

Evagrius of Pontus (c. 345-399). Disciple and teacher of ascetic life who astutely absorbed and creatively transmitted the spirituality of Egyptian and Palestinian monasticism of the late fourth century. Although Origenist elements of his writings were formally condemned by the Fifth Ecumenical Council (Constantinople II, A.D. 553), his literary corpus continued to influence the tradition of the church.

Fastidius (c. fourth-fifth centuries). British author of *On the Christian Life*. He is believed to have written some works attributed to Pelagius.

Faustinus (fl. 380). A priest in Rome and supporter of Lucifer and author of a treatise on the Trinity.

Filastrius (fl. 380). Bishop of Brescia and author of a compilation against all heresies.

Fulgentius of Ruspe (c. 467-532). Bishop of Ruspe and author of many orthodox sermons and tracts under the influence of Augustine.

Gaudentius of Brescia (fl. 395). Successor of Filastrius as bishop of Brescia and author of numerous tracts.

Gennadius of Constantinople (d. 471). Patriarch of Constantinople, author of numerous commentaries and an opponent of the Christology of Cyril of Alexandria.

Gnostics. Name now given generally to followers of Basilides, Marcion, Valentinus, Mani and others. The characteristic belief is that matter is a prison made for the spirit by an evil or ignorant creator, and that redemption depends on fate, not on free will.

Gregory of Elvira (fl. 359-385). Bishop of Elvira who wrote allegorical treatises in the style of Origen and defended the Nicene faith against the Arians.

Gregory of Nazianzus (b. 329/330; fl. 372-389). Bishop of Nazianzus and friend of Basil and Gregory of Nyssa. He is famous for maintaining the humanity of Christ as well as the orthodox doctrine of the Trinity.

Gregory of Nyssa (c. 335-394). Bishop of Nyssa and brother of Basil, he is famous for maintaining the equality in unity of the Father, Son and Holy Spirit.

Gregory Thaumaturgus (fl. c. 248-264). Bishop of Neocaesarea and a disciple of Origen. There are at least five legendary *Lives* that recount the events and miracles which led to his being called "the wonder worker." His most important work was the *Address of Thanks to Origen*, which is a rhetorically structured panegyric to Origen and an outline of his teaching.

Gregory the Great (c. 540-604). Pope from 590, the fourth and last of the Latin "Doctors of the Church." He was a prolific author and a powerful unifying force within the Latin Church, initiating the liturgical reform that brought about the Gregorian Sacramentary and Gregorian chant.

Hesychius of Jerusalem (fl. 412-450). Presbyter and exegete, thought to have commented on the whole of Scripture.

Hilary of Arles (c. 401-449). Archbishop of Arles and leader of the Semi-Pelagian party. Hilary incurred the wrath of Pope Leo I when he removed a bishop from his see and appointed a new bishop. Leo demoted Arles from a metropolitan see to a bishopric to assert papal power over the church in Gaul.

Hilary of Poitiers (c. 315-367). Bishop of Poitiers and called the "Athanasius of the West" because of his defense (against the Arians) of the common nature of Father and Son.

Hippolytus (fl. 222-245). Recent scholarship places Hippolytus in a Palestinian context, personally familiar with Origen. Though he is known mostly for *The Refutation of All Heresies,* he was primarily a commentator on Scripture (especially the Old Testament) and other sacred texts.

Ignatius of Antioch (c. 35-107/112). Bishop of Antioch who wrote several letters to local churches while being taken from Antioch to Rome to be martyred. In the letters, which warn against heresy, he stresses orthodox Christology, the centrality of the Eucharist and unique role of the bishop in preserving the unity of the church.

Irenaeus of Lyon (c. 135-c. 202). Bishop of Lyons who published the most famous and influential refutation of Gnostic thought.

Isaac of Nineveh (d. c. 700). Also known as Isaac the Syrian or Isaac Syrus, this monastic writer served for a short while as bishop of Nineveh before retiring to live a secluded monastic life. His writings on ascetic subjects survive in the form of numerous homilies.

Isho'dad of Merv (fl. c. 850). Nestorian commentator of the ninth century. He wrote especially on James, 1 Peter and 1 John.

Isidore of Seville (d. 636). Youngest of a family of monks and clerics, including sister Florentina and brothers Leander and Fulgentius. He was an erudite author of comprehensive scale in matters both religious and sacred, including his encyclopedic *Etymologies.*

Jacob of Nisibis (d. 338). Bishop of Nisibis. He was present at the council of Nicaea in 325 and took an active part in the opposition to Arius.

Jacob of Sarug (c. 450-c. 520). Syriac ecclesiastical writer. Jacob received his education at Edessa. At the end of his life he was ordained bishop of Sarug. His principal writing was a long series of metrical homilies, earning him the title "The Flute of the Holy Spirit." His theolog-

ical views are not certain, but it seems that he expressed a moderate monophysite position.

Jerome (c. 347-420). Gifted exegete and exponent of a classical Latin style, now best known as the translator of the Latin Vulgate. He defended the perpetual virginity of Mary, attacked Origen and Pelagius and supported extreme ascetic practices.

John Chrysostom (344/354-407; fl. 386-407). Bishop of Constantinople who was famous for his orthodoxy, his eloquence and his attacks on Christian laxity in high places.

John of Damascus (c. 650-750). Arab monastic and theologian whose writings enjoyed great influence in both the Eastern and Western Churches. His most famous writing was the *Orthodox Faith.*

John the Elder (c. eighth century) A Syriac author who belonged to monastic circles of the Church of the East and lived in the region of Mount Qardu (north Iraq). His most important writings are twenty-two homilies and a collection of fifty-one short letters in which he describes the mystical life as an anticipatory experience of the resurrection life, the fruit of the sacraments of baptism and the Eucharist.

Josephus, Flavius (c. 37-c. 101). Jewish historian from a distinguished priestly family. Acquainted with the Essenes and Sadducees, he himself became a Pharisee. He joined the great Jewish revolt that broke out in 66 and was chosen by the Sanhedrin at Jerusalem to be commander-in-chief in Galilee. Showing great shrewdness to ingratiate himself with Vespasian by foretelling his elevation and that of his son Titus to the imperial dignity, Josephus was restored his liberty after 69 when Vespasian become emperor.

Justin Martyr (c. 100/110-165; fl. c. 148-161). Palestinian philosopher who was converted to Christianity, "the only sure and worthy philosophy." He traveled to Rome where he wrote several apologies against both pagans and Jews, combining Greek philosophy and Christian theology; he was eventually martyred.

Lactantius (c. 260-c. 330). An eloquent writer known to us through Jerome. He is acknowledged more for his technical writing skills than for his theological thought.

Leander (c. 545-c. 600). Latin ecclesiastical writer, of whose works only two survive. He was instrumental is spreading Christianity among the Visigoths, gaining significant historical influence in Spain in his time.

Leo the Great (regn. 440-461). Bishop of Rome whose *Tome to Flavian* helped to strike a balance between Nestorian and Cyrilline positions at the Council of Chalcedon in 451.

Letter of Barnabas (c. 130). An allegorical and typological interpretation of the Old Testament with a decidedly anti-Jewish tone. It was included with other New Testament works as a "Catholic epistle" at least until Eusebius of Caesarea (c. 260/263-340) questioned its authenticity.

Letter to Diognetus (c. third century). A refutation of paganism and an exposition of the Christian life and faith. The author of this letter is unknown, and the exact identity of its recipient, Diognetus, continues to elude patristic scholars.

Lucifer (d. 370/371). Bishop of Cagliari and vigorous supporter of Athanasius and the Nicene Creed. He and his followers entered into schism after refusing to acknowledge less orthodox bishops appointed by the emperor Constantius.

Luculentius (fifth century). Unknown author of a group of short commentaries on the New Testament, especially Pauline passages. His exegesis is mainly literal and relies mostly on earlier authors such as Jerome and Augustine. The content of his writing may place it in the fifth century.

Macarius of Egypt (c. 300-c. 390). One of the Desert Fathers. Accused of supporting Athanasius, Macarius was exiled c. 374 to an island in the Nile by Lucius, the Arian successor of Athanasius. Macarius continued his teaching of monastic theology until his death.

Macrina the Younger (c. 327-379). The elder sister of Basil the Great and Gregory of Nyssa, she is known as "the Younger" to distinguish her from her paternal grandmother. She had a powerful influence on her younger brothers, especially on Gregory, who called her his teacher and relates her teaching in *On the Soul and the Resurrection*.

Manichaeans. A religious movement that originated circa 241 in Persia under the leadership of Mani but was apparently of complex Christian origin. It is said to have denied free will and the universal sovereignty of God, teaching that kingdoms of light and darkness are coeternal and that the redeemed are particles of a spiritual man of light held captive in the darkness of matter (*see* Gnostics).

Marcion (fl. 144). Heretic of the mid-second century who rejected the Old Testament and much of the New Testament, claiming that the Father of Jesus Christ was other than the Creator God (*see* Gnostics).

Marius Victorinus (b. c. 280/285; fl. c. 355-363). Grammarian who translated works of Platonists and, after his late conversion (c. 355), used them against the Arians.

Mark the Hermit (c. sixth century). Monk who lived near Tarsus and produced works on ascetic practices as well as christological issues.

Martin of Braga (fl. c. 568-579). Anti-Arian metropolitan of Braga on the Iberian peninsula. He was highly educated and presided over the provincial council of Braga in 572.

Maximus of Turin (d. 408/423). Bishop of Turin who died during the reigns of Honorius and Theodosius the Younger (408-423). Over one hundred of his sermons survive.

Maximus the Confessor (c. 580-662). Greek theologian and ascetic writer. Fleeing the Arab invasion of Jerusalem in 614, he took refuge in Constantinople and later Africa. He died near the Black Sea after imprisonment and severe suffering. His thought centered on the humanity of Christ.

Methodius of Olympus (d. 311). Bishop of Olympus who celebrated virginity in a *Sympo-*

sium partly modeled on Plato's dialogue of that name.

Minucius Felix of Rome (second or third century). Christian apologist who flourished between 160 and 300 (the exact dates are not known). His *Octavius* agrees at numerous points with the *Apologeticum* of Tertullian. His birthplace is believed to be in Africa.

Montanist Oracles. Montanism was an apocalyptic and strictly ascetic movement begun in the latter half of the second century by a certain Montanus in Phrygia, who, along with certain of his followers, uttered oracles they claimed were inspired by the Holy Spirit. Little of the authentic oracles remains and most of what is known of Montanism comes from the authors who wrote against the movement. Montanism was formally condemned as a heresy before by Asiatic synods.

Nemesius of Emesa (fl. late fourth century). Bishop of Emesa in Syria whose most important work, *Of the Nature of Man,* draws on several theological and philosophical sources and is the first exposition of a Christian anthropology.

Nestorius (c. 381-c. 451). Patriarch of Constantinople 428-431 and credited with the foundation of the heresy which says that the divine and human natures were associated, rather than truly united, in the incarnation of Christ.

Nicetas of Remesiana (fl. second half of fourth century). Bishop of Remesiana in Serbia, whose works affirm the consubstantiality of the Son and the deity of the Holy Spirit.

Novatian of Rome (fl. 235-258). Roman theologian, otherwise orthodox, who formed a schismatic church after failing to become pope. His treatise on the Trinity states the classic western doctrine.

Oecumenius (sixth century). Called the Rhetor or the Philosopher, Oecumenius wrote the earliest extant Greek commentary on Revelation. Scholia by Oecumenius on some of John Chrysostom's commentaries on the Pauline Epistles are still extant.

Origen of Alexandria (b. 185; fl. c. 200-254). Influential exegete and systematic theologian.

He was condemned (perhaps unfairly) for maintaining the preexistence of souls while denying the resurrection of the body, the literal truth of Scripture and the equality of the Father and the Son in the Trinity.

Pachomius (c. 292-347). Founder of cenobitic monasticism. A gifted group leader and author of a set of rules, he was defended after his death by Athanasius of Alexandria.

Pacian of Barcelona (c. fourth century). Bishop of Barcelona whose writings polemicize against popular pagan festivals as well as Novatian schismatics.

Palladius of Helenopolis (c. 363/364-c. 431). Bishop of Helenopolis (400-417) and then Aspuna in Galatia. A disciple of Evagrius of Pontus and admirer of Origen, Palladius became a zealous adherent of John Chrysostom and shared his troubles in 403. His *Dialogus de vita S. Johannis* is essentially a work of edification, stressing the spiritual value of the life of the desert, where he spent a number of years a monk.

Paschasius of Dumium (c. 515-c. 580). Translator of sentences of the Desert Fathers from Greek into Latin while a monk in Dumium.

Paterius (c. sixth-seventh century). Disciple of Gregory the Great who is primarily responsible for the transmission of Gregory's works to many later medieval authors.

Paulinus of Nola (355-431). Roman Senator and distinguished Latin poet whose frequent encounters with Ambrose of Milan (c. 333-397) led to his eventual conversion and baptism in 389. He eventually renounced his wealth and influential position and took up his pen to write poetry in service of Christ. He also wrote many letters to, among others, Augustine, Jerome and Rufinus.

Paulus Orosius (b. c. 380). An outspoken critic of Pelagius mentored by Augustine. His *Seven Books of History Against the Pagans* was perhaps the first history of Christianity.

Pelagius (c. 354-c. 420). Christian teacher whose followers were condemned in 418 and 431 for maintaining that a Christian could be perfect and that salvation depended on free will.

Peter of Alexandria (d. c. 311). Bishop of Alexandria. He marked (and very probably initiated) the reaction at Alexandria against extreme doctrines of Origen. During the persecution of Christians in Alexandria, Peter was arrested and beheaded by Roman officials. Eusebius of Caesarea described him as "a model bishop, remarkable for his virtuous life and his ardent study of the Scriptures."

Peter Chrysologus (c. 380-450). Latin archbishop of Ravenna whose teachings included arguments for the supremacy of the papacy and the relationship between grace and Christian living.

Philoxenus of Mabbug (c. 440-523). Bishop of Mabbug (Hierapolis) and a leading thinker in the early Syrian Orthodox Church. His extensive writings in Syriac include a set of thirteen *Discourses on the Christian Life*, several works on the incarnation and a number of exegetical works.

Poemen (c. fifth century) One-seventh of the sayings in the *Sayings of the Desert Fathers* are attributed to Poemen, which is Greek for shepherd. Poemen was a common title among early Egyptian desert ascetics, and it is unknown whether all of the sayings come from one person.

Polycarp of Smyrna (c. 69-155). Bishop of Smyrna who vigorously fought heretics such as the Marcionites and Valentinians. He was the leading Christian figure in Roman Asia in the middle of the second century.

Potamius of Lisbon (fl. c. 350-360). Bishop of Lisbon who joined the Arian party in 357, but later returned to the Catholic faith (c. 359?). His works from both periods are concerned with the larger Trinitarian debates of his time.

Procopius of Gaza (c. 465-c. 530). A Christian Sophist educated in Alexandria. He wrote numerous theological works and commentaries on Scripture (particularly the Hebrew Bible), the latter marked by the allegorical exegesis for which the Alexandrian school was known.

Prudentius (c. 348-c. 410). Latin poet and hymn-writer who devoted his later life to Christian writing. He wrote didactic poems on the theology of the incarnation, against the heretic Marcion and against the resurgence of paganism.

Pseudo-Dionysius the Areopagite (fl. c. 500). Author who assumed the name of Dionysius the Areopagite mentioned in Acts 17:34, and who composed the works known as the *Corpus Areopagiticym* (or *Dinysiacum*), although the author's true identity remains a mystery.

Pseudo-Macarius (fl. c. 390). An imaginative writer and ascetic from Mesopotamia to eastern Asia Minor with keen insight into human nature and clear articulation of the theology of the Trinity. His work includes some one hundred discourses and homilies.

Quodvultdeus (fl. 430). Carthaginian deacon and friend of Augustine who endeavored to show at length how the New Testament fulfilled the Old Testament.

Rufinus of Aquileia (c. 345-411). Orthodox Christian thinker and historian who nonetheless translated Origen and defended him against the strictures of Jerome and Epiphanius.

Sabellius (fl. 200). Allegedly the author of the heresy which maintains that the Father and Son are a single person. The patripassian variant of this heresy states that the Father suffered on the cross.

Sahdona (fl. 635-640). Known in Greek as Martyrius, this Syriac author was bishop of Beth Garmai for a short time. His most important work is the deeply scriptural *Book of Perfection* which ranks as one of the masterpieces of Syriac monastic literature.

Salvian the Presbyter of Marseilles (c. 400-c. 480). An important author for the history of his own time. He saw the fall of Roman civilization to the barbarians as a consequence of the reprehensible conduct of Roman Christians.

Second Letter of Clement (c. 150). The so-called *Second Letter of Clement* is the earliest surviving Christian sermon probably written by a Corinthian author, though some scholars have assigned it to a Roman or Alexandrian author.

Severian of Gabala (fl. c. 400). A contemporary

of John Chrysostom, he was a highly regarded preacher in Constantinople, particularly at the imperial court, and ultimately sided with Chrysostom's accusers. His sermons are dominated by antiheretical concerns.

Severus of Antioch (fl. 488-538). A monophysite theologian, consecrated bishop of Antioch in 522. Severus believed that Christ's human nature was an annex to his divine nature and argued that if Christ were both divine and human, he would necessarily have been two persons.

Shepherd of Hermas (second century). Divided into five *Visions*, twelve *Mandates* and ten *Similitudes*, this Christian apocalypse was written by a former slave and named for the form of the second angel said to have granted him his visions. This work was highly esteemed for its moral value and was used as a textbook for catechumens in the early church.

Sulpicius Severus (c. 360-c. 420). An ecclesiastical writer born of noble parents. Devoting himself to monastic retirement, he became a personal friend and enthusiastic disciple of St. Martin of Tours. His ordination to the priesthood is vouched for by Gennadius, but no details of his priestly activity have reached us.

Symeon the New Theologian (c. 949-1022). Compassionate spiritual leader known for his strict rule. He believed that the divine light could be perceived and received through the practice of mental prayer.

Tertullian of Carthage (c. 155/160-225/250; fl. c. 197-222). Brilliant Carthaginian apologist and polemicist who laid the foundations of Christology and trinitarian orthodoxy in the West, though he himself was estranged from the main church by its laxity.

Theodore of Heraclea (d. c. 355). An anti-Nicene bishop of Thrace. He was part of a team seeking reconciliation between Eastern and Western Christianity. In 343 he was excommunicated at the council of Sardica. His writings focus on a literal interpretation of Scripture.

Theodore of Mopsuestia (c. 350-428). Bishop of Mopsuestia, founder of the Antiochene, or literalistic, school of exegesis. A great man in his day, he was later condemned as a precursor of Nestorius.

Theodoret of Cyr (c. 393-466). Bishop of Cyr (Cyrrhus), he was an opponent of Cyril, whose doctrine of Christ's person was finally vindicated in 451 at the Council of Chalcedon.

Theophilus of Antioch (late second century). Bishop of Antioch. His only surviving work is *Ad Autholycum*, where we find the first Christian commentary on Genesis and the first use of the term *Trinity*. Theophilus's apologetic literary heritage had influence on Irenaeus and possibly Tertullian.

Theophylact of Ohrid (c. 1050-c. 1108). Byzantine archbishop of Ohrid (or Achrida) in what is now Bulgaria. Drawing on earlier works, he wrote commentaries on several Old Testament books and all of the New Testament except for Revelation.

Valentinus (fl. c. 140). Alexandrian heretic of the mid-second century who taught that the material world was created by the transgression of God's Wisdom, or Sophia (*see* Gnostics).

Valerian of Cimiez (fl. c. 422-439). Bishop of Cimiez. He participated in the councils of Riez (439) and Vaison (422) with a view to strengthening church discipline. He supported Hilary of Arles in quarrels with Pope Leo I.

Victorius of Petovium (d. c. 304). Latin biblical exegete. With multiple works attributed to him, his sole surviving work is the *Commentary on the Apocalypse* and perhaps some fragments from *Commentary on Matthew*. Victorinus expressed strong millenarianism in his writing, though his was less materialistic than the millenarianism of Papias or Irenaeus. In his allegorical approach he could be called a spiritual disciple of Origen. Victorinus died during the first year of Diocletian's persecution, probably in 304.

Vincent of Lérins (d. 435). Monk who has exerted considerable influence through his writings on orthodox dogmatic theological method, as contrasted with the theological methodologies of the heresies.

Timeline of Patristic Authors

Location / Period	British Isles	Gaul	Spain, Portugal	Italy	Africa
2nd century		Irenaeus of Lyons, c. 135-c. 202 (Greek)		Clement of Rome, fl. c. 92-101 (Greek)	
				Justin Martyr (Ephesus, Rome), c. 100/110-165 (Greek)	
				Valentinus the Gnostic, fl. c. 140, (Greek)	
				Marcion, fl. 144 (Greek)	
3rd century					Clement of Alexandria, c. 150-215 (Latin)
				Callistus of Rome, regn. 217-222 (Latin)	Tertullian of Carthage, c. 155/160-225/250 (Latin)
				Minucius Felix of Rome, fl. c. 218-235 (Latin)	Origen (Alexandria, Caesaria of Palestine), 185-254 (Greek)
				Novatian of Rome, fl. 235-258 (Latin)	Cyprian of Carthage, fl. 248-258 (Latin)
				Marius Victorinus (Rome), fl. 355-362 (Latin)	Dionysius of Alexandria, d. 264 (Latin)
4th century		Lactantius, c. 260-330 (Latin)			
					Arius (Alexandria), fl. c. 320 (Greek)
					Alexander of Alexandria, fl. 312-328 (Greek)
					Pachomius (Egypt), c. 292-347 (Coptic/Greek?)
				Eusebius of Vercelli, fl. c. 360 (Latin)	Athanasius of Alexandria, c. 295-373; fl. 325-373 (Greek)
		Hilary of Poitiers, c. 315-367 (Latin)	Potamius of Lisbon, fl. c. 350-360 (Latin)	Lucifer of Cagliari (Sardinia), fl. 370 (Latin)	Macarius of Egypt, c. 300-c. 390 (Greek)
			Gregory of Elvira, fl. 359-385 (Latin)	Faustinus (Rome), fl. 380 (Latin)	
				Filastrius of Brescia, fl. 380 (Latin)	Didymus (the Blind) of Alexandria, 313-398 (Greek)
			Prudentius, c. 348-c. 410 (Latin)	Ambrosiaster (Italy?), fl. c. 366-384 (Latin)	
				Gaudentius of Brescia, fl. 395 (Latin)	
				Ambrose of Milan, c. 333-397; fl. 374-397 (Latin)	
				Rufinus of Aquileia, c. 345-411 (Latin)	Augustine of Hippo, 354-430 (Latin)

Greece	Asia Minor	Syria	Mesopotamia, Persia	Palestine	Location Unknown
	Polycarp of Smyrna, c. 69-155 (Greek)	Ignatius of Antioch, 35- d. 107/112 (Greek)			
Athenagoras, fl. 176-180 (Greek)		Theophilus of Antioch, c. late 2nd cent. (Greek)			
				Hippolytus (Palestine?), fl. 222-245 (Greek)	
	Gregory Thaumaturgus (Neocaesarea), fl. c. 248-264 (Greek)				
	Methodius of Olympus (Lycia), d. c. 311 (Greek)		Aphrahat c. 270-350 (Syriac)	Eusebius of Caesarea (Palestine), c. 260/263-340 (Greek)	Commodian, c. 3rd or 5th cent. (Latin)
Epiphanius of Salamis (Cyprus), c. 315-403 (Greek)		Eusebius of Emesa, c. 300-c. 359 (Greek)		Acacius of Caesarea (Palestine), d. c. 366 (Greek)	
	Basil the Great, b. c. 330; fl. 357-379 (Greek)	Ephrem the Syrian, c. 306-373 (Syriac)		Cyril of Jerusalem, c. 315-386 (Greek)	
	Macrina the Younger, c. 327-379 (Greek)				
	Apollinaris of Laodicea, 310-c. 392 (Greek)				
John Chrysostom (Antioch, Constantinople), 344/354-407 (Greek)	Gregory of Nazianzus, b. 329/330; fl. 372-389 (Greek)				
	Gregory of Nyssa, c. 335-394 (Greek)				
	Evagrius of Pontus, c. 345-399 (Greek)	Nemesius of Emesa (Syria), fl. late 4th cent. (Greek)		Diodore of Tarsus, d. c. 394 (Greek)	
	Theodore of Mopsuestia, c. 350-428 (Greek)			Jerome (Rome, Antioch, Bethlehem), c. 347-420 (Latin)	

Timeline of Patristic Authors

Location / Period	British Isles	Gaul	Spain, Portugal	Italy	Africa
5th century	Fastidius, c. 4th-5th cent. (Latin)	John Cassian (Palestine, Egypt, Constantinople, Rome, Marseilles), 360-432 (Latin) Sulpicius Severus, c. 360-c. 420 (Latin) Vincent of Lérins, d. 435 (Latin) Valerian of Cimiez, fl. c. 422-439 (Latin) Eucherius of Lyons, fl. 420-449 (Latin) Hilary of Arles, c. 401-449 (Latin) Salvian the Presbyter of Marseilles, c. 400-c. 480 (Latin)		Chromatius (Aquileia), fl. 400 (Latin) Pelagius (Britain, Rome), c. 354 c. 420 (Greek) Maximus of Turin, d. 408/423 (Latin) Paulinus of Nola, 355-431 (Latin) Peter Chrysologus (Ravenna), c. 380-450 (Latin) Leo the Great (Rome), regn. 440-461 (Latin)	Cyril of Alexandria, 375-444 (Greek) Quodvultdeus (Carthage), fl. 430 (Latin) Palladius of Helenopolis, c. 363/364-c. 431 (Greek) Ammonius of Alexandria, 5th cent. (Greek)
6th century		Caesarius of Arles, c. 470-543 (Latin)	Paschasius of Dumium (Portugal), c. 515-c. 580 (Latin) Leander of Seville, c. 545-c. 600 (Latin) Isidore of Seville, c. 560-636 (Latin) Braulio of Saragossa, c. 585-651 (Latin)	Benedict of Nursia, c. 480-547 (Latin) Cassiodorus (Calabria), c. 485-c. 540 (Latin) Gregory the Great, c. 540-604 (Latin)	Fulgentius of Ruspe, c. 467-532 (Latin)
7th century					
8th century	Bede the Venerable, c. 672/673-735 (Latin)				

Greece	Asia Minor	Syria	Mesopotamia, Persia	Palestine	Location Unknown
Nestorius (Constantinople), c. 381-c. 451 (Greek)	Basil of Seleucia, fl. 444-468 (Greek)	Severian of Gabala, fl. c. 400 (Greek)		Hesychius of Jerusalem, fl. 412-450 (Greek)	
		Theodoret of Cyr, c. 393-466 (Greek)			
	Diadochus of Photice, c. 400-474 (Greek)				
Gennadius of Constantinople, d. 471 (Greek)					
		Philoxenus of Mabbug, c. 440-523 (Syriac)			
			Jacob of Sarug, c. 450-c. 520 (Syriac)		
				Procopius of Gaza (Palestine), c. 465-530 (Greek)	
		Severus of Antioch, fl. 488-538 (Greek)			
	Mark the Hermit (Tarsus), c. 6th cent. (Greek)			Dorotheus of Gaza, fl. c. 525-540 (Greek)	Pseudo-Dionysius the Areopagite, fl. c. 500 (Greek)
	Oecumenius (Isauria), 6th cent. (Greek)			Cyril of Scythopolis, c. 525-d. after 557 (Greek)	
					(Pseudo-) Constantius, before 7th cent. ? (Greek)
Maximus the Confessor (Constantinople), c. 580-662 (Greek)					Andreas, c. 7th cent. (Greek)
		Sahdona, fl. 635-640 (Syriac)			
		John of Damascus, c. 650-750 (Greek)	Isaac of Nineveh, d. c. 700 (Syriac)		
			John the Elder, 8th cent. (Syriac)		

BIBLIOGRAPHY

This bibliography refers readers to original language sources and supplies Thesaurus Linguae Graecae (=TLG) or Cetedoc Clavis (=Cl.) numbers where available.

Apollinaris of Laodicea. "Fragmenta in Matthaeum." Pages 1-54 in *Matthäus-Kommentare aus der griechischen Kirche*. Edited by Joseph Reuss. Berlin: Akademie-Verlag, 1957. TLG 2074.037.

Augustine of Hippo. "De consensu evangelistarum libri iv." Cols. 1011-1230 in *Opera omnia*. Patrologiae cursus completus, Series Latina, vol. 34. Edited by J.-P. Migne. Paris: Migne, 1861. Cl. 0273.

———. "De sermone Domini in monte." Cols. 1229-1308 in *Opera omnia*. Patrologiae cursus completus, Series Latina, vol. 34. Edited by J.-P. Migne. Paris: Migne, 1861. Cl. 0274.

———. "Sermones." In *Opera omnia*. Patrologiae cursus completus, Series Latina, vol. 38. Edited by J.-P. Migne. Paris: Migne, 1861. Cl. 0284.

———. "Sermones." In *Sermones post Maurinos reperti Studi Agostiniani*. Edited by G. Morin. Miscellanea Agostiniana, vol. 1. Rome: Tipografia poliglotta vaticana, 1930. Cl. 0284.

Chromatius of Aquileia. "Tractatus in Matthaeum." Pages 185-498 in *Chromatii Aquileiensis opera*. Edited by R. Étaix and J. Lemarié. Corpus Christianorum, Series Latina, vol. 9a. Turnhout, Belgium: Typographi Brepols Editores Pontificii, 1974. Cl. 0218.

Cyprian of Carthage. "De dominica oratione." Pages 90-113 in *Sancti Cypriani episcopi opera: pars 2*. Edited by C. Moreschini. Corpus Christianorum, Series Latina, vol. 3a. Turnhout, Belgium: Typographi Brepols Editores Pontificii, 1976. Cl. 0043.

Cyril of Alexandria. "Fragmenta in Matthaeum." Pages 153-269 in *Matthäus-Kommentare aus der griechischen Kirche*. Edited by Joseph Reuss. Berlin: Akademie-Verlag, 1957. TLG 4090.029.

Epiphanius the Latin. "Interpretatio Evangeliorum." Cols. 834-964 in Patrologiae cursus completus, Series Latina, Supplementum, vol 3. Edited by Adalberto Hamman. Paris: Édition Gernier Frères, 1963.

Eusebius of Emesa. "Homiliae." In *Eusèbe d'Émèse discours conservés en latin*, vol. 2. Edited by É. M. Buytaert. Spicilegium Sacrum Lovaniense, vol. 27. Louvain: Spicilegium Sacrum Lovaniense Adminisration, 1957.

Gregory the Great. "XL Homiliarum in Evangelia." Cols. 1075-1312 in *Opera omnia*. Patrologiae cursus completus, Series Latina, vol. 76. Edited by J.-P. Migne. Paris: Migne, 1857. Cl. 1711.

Hilary of Poitiers. "In Matthaeum." In *Sur Matthieu I*. Edited by Jean Doignon. Sources chrétiennes, vol. 254. Paris: Cerf, 1978.

———. "In Matthaeum." In *Sur Matthieu II*. Edited by Jean Doignon. Sources chrétiennes, vol. 258. Paris: Cerf, 1979.

Irenaeus of Lyon. "Adversus haereses (liber 3)." In *Irénée de Lyon. Contre les hérésies, livre 3*, vol. 2. Edited by A. Rousseau and L. Doutreleau. Sources chrétiennes, vol. 211. Paris: Cerf, 1974. TLG 1477.002.

Jerome. "Commentariorum in Matthaeum libri iv." In *Sancti Hieronymi Presbyteri Opera: Pars 1.7*. Edited by D. Hurst and M. Adriaen. Corpus Christianorum, Series Latina, vol. 77. Turnhout, Belgium: Typographi Brepols Editores Pontificii, 1969. Cl. 0590.

John Chrysostom. "Commentarius in sanctum Matthaeum evangelistam." In *Opera omnia*. Patrologiae cursus completus, Series Graeca, vol. 57. Edited by J.-P. Migne. Paris: Migne, 1862. TLG 2062.152.

———. "Homiliae in Matthaeum." In *Opera omnia*. Patrologiae cursus completus, Series Graeca, vol. 58. Edited by J.-P. Migne. Paris: Migne, 1862. TLG 2062.152.

Maximus of Turin. "Sermones." In *Maximi episcopi Taurinensis collectionum sermonum antiquam*. Edited by Almut Mutzenbecher. Corpus Christianorum, Series Latina, vol. 23. Turnhout, Belgium: Typographi Brepols Editores Pontificii, 1962. Cl. 0219a.

Opus imperfectum in Matthaeum. Cols. 611-946 in Patrologiae cursus completus, Series Graeca, vol. 56. Edited by J.-P. Migne. Paris: Migne, 1862.

Origen. "Commentariorum in Matthaeum libri 10-17." In *Origenes Werke*, vol. 10. Edited by Erich Klostermann. Die griechischen christlichen Schriftsteller der ersten drei Jahrhunderte, vol. 40. Leipzig: J. C. Hinrichs, 1935. TLG 2042.029-030.

———. "De oratione *(Peri euchēs)*." Pages 297-403 in *Origenes Werke*, vol. 2. Edited by Paul Koetschau. Die griechischen christlichen Schriftsteller der ersten drei Jahrhunderte, vol. 3. Leipzig: J. C. Hinrichs, 1899. TLG 2042.008.

———. "Fragmenta." In *Origenes Werke*, vol. 12. Edited by Erich Klostermann. Die griechischen christlichen Schriftsteller der ersten drei Jahrhunderte, vol. 41.1. Leipzig: J. C. Hinrichs, 1941. TLG 2042.031.

Peter Chrysologus. "Sermones." In *Sancti Petri Chrysologi collectio sermonum: pars 1*. Edited by Alexander Olivar. Corpus Christianorum, Series Latina, vol. 24. Turnhout, Belgium: Typographi Brepols Editores Pontificii, 1975. Cl. 0227+.

———. "Sermones." In *Sancti Petri Chrysologi collectio sermonum: pars 3*. Edited by Alexander Olivar. Corpus Christianorum, Series Latina, vol. 24b. Turnhout, Belgium: Typographi Brepols Editores Pontificii, 1982. Cl. 0227+.

Severus of Antioch. "Homiliae cathedrales." In *Les Homiliae cathedrales de Sévère d'Antioche: Homilies 91-98*. Edited and translated by Maurice Brière. Patrologia Orientalis, vol. 25. Paris: Firmin-Didot et Cie, 1943.

Tertullian. "De idololatria." Pages 1099-1124 in *Opera: pars 2*. Edited by A. Reifferscheid and G. Wissowa. Corpus Christianorum, Series Latina, vol 2. Turnhout, Belgium: Typographi Brepols Editores Pontificii, 1954. Cl. 0023.

———. "De oratione." Pages 255-74 in *Opera: pars 1*. Edited by G. F. Diercks. Corpus Christianorum Series Latina, vol. 1. Turnhout, Belgium: Typographi Brepols Editores Pontificii, 1954. Cl. 0007.

Theodore of Heraclea. "Fragmenta in Matthaeum." Pages 55-95 in *Matthäus-Kommentare aus der griechischen Kirche*. Edited by Joseph Reuss. Berlin: Akademie-Verlag, 1957. TLG 4126.002.

Theodore of Mopsuestia. "Fragmenta in Matthaeum." Pages 96-135 in *Matthäus-Kommentare aus der griechischen Kirche*. Edited by Joseph Reuss. Berlin: Akademie-Verlag, 1957. TLG 4135.009.

Subject Index

Abba, 131-32
Abraham, 3, 5, 44-45
Adam
    and Christ, 51, 56, 60-61, 174
    example of, 17-18
    and the paralytic, 174
    and sin, 175
adoption
    and baptism of Christ, 53-54
    in Christ, 13, 51, 99, 121, 132
    physical, 4
    and salvation, 134
    spirit of, 88
    and teaching, 203
    through baptism, 51, 53-54
adultery, 108-9, 112-13, 255-56
afflictions, 156-57, 208
Alexandrian School, xli, xliii, xlvi-xlviii
allegory, xxxix, xl-xli
almsgiving, 123, 125
Ambrose, xxxviii
Andrew, 70-71
angels, 63-64, 278-79, 289
anger, 44, 101-3, 109
Antiochene School, xli, xlvi-xlvii
anxiety, 144-46, 153
apostles. See disciples
Archelaus, 37
Arianism, xlv
asceticism. See piety
ask, seek, knock, 149-50
axe, 46
baptism
    and adoption, 51, 53
    and death, 185
    and family, 211

by fire, 47-48
    and forgiveness, 136
    and the Holy Spirit, 47-48, 51
    of religious leaders, 44
    of repentance, 43-49, 136
    and sanctification, 50
    sin after, 250
    and temptation, 56-57
    of water, 46-47
baptism of Christ, 49-54
baptizer, 50-51
Beatitudes, the, 79-91
beggar, 85
birds and lilies, 144
blasphemy, 249-51, 254
blessings, 83
blind men, the, 186-88
Boaz, 7-8
body
    dwelling place of, 83
    resurrection of, 278
    service of, 94
    and sin, 110
    and soul, 111, 206-7, 262
    will of the, 111
bread, 135-36, 235
bridegroom, 179-80
Cain, 102
calling, 72-73
canonization, xxxvii
Capernaum, 227
centurion, 161-63
charity, 124
children, 224-25
choice, 137, 253
Chorazin and Bethsaida, 227-28
Christ. See Jesus Christ
church
    as a body, 111
    and Christ, 8, 14, 47, 172
    and the field, 277
    as the Holy City, 93
    and Israel, 23
    as lampstand, 94
    Matthew's house as, 178
    as mother of faith, 131
    as mountain, 78
    as a net, 288-89
    peace of, 87-88
    prefigured by Rahab, 7
    as a ship, 263
    as threshing floor, 48
Clement, xli
commandments, 96-98, 109-10, 113
Commentary on Matthew

(Hilary), xliii-xliv
Commentary on Matthew (Jerome), xliv-xlv
Commentary on Matthew (Origen), xlii-xliii
compassion, 85-86
concupiscence, 71
confession, 209-10, 229-30
conscience, 105
counseling, 145
covetousness, 70, 84
creation, 87, 116
cross, 89, 212-13, 219, 256
cup of water, 214-15
Cyprian of Carthage, xxxvii
daily bread. See Lord's Prayer, daily bread
dancing and lamentation 225
darkness, 67, 94, 205
David, 3, 4, 8, 82, 235
Day of Judgment. See last judgment
"days of John," 223
death
    and baptism, 185
    and the good, 202
    the second, 206
    shadow of, 67-68
    and sleep, 184-85
    soul at, 206-7
De consensu evangelistarum (Augustine), 1
De dominica oratione (Cyprian), 1
De oratione (Tertullian), 1
De sermone Domini in monte (Augustine), 1
demoniacs, 170-72
    and faith, 188-89
    and the Gentiles, 244-45
    healing of, 188, 244-45
    identity of, 170
    and the Pharisees, 189
    speech of, 188
demons, 171-72
devil
    covenant with, 106-7
    and evil, 137
    exorcism, 246-47
    house of, 248-49
    and Jesus, 261-62
    at Jesus' birth, 32
    at Jesus' temptation, 56-58, 63-64
    kingdom of the, 246
    limitations of, 62-63
    pride of, 61
    promises of, 62

and Scripture, 61
    on seeing the, 87
    will of, 134
Didache, xxxvii
Diodorus of Tarsus, xli
disciples
    blessing of peace, 198, 200
    call of, 64-73, 191-93
    empowerment of, 191, 195-96, 201
    endurance of, 202
    as fishermen, 71
    and the gospel, 47
    healing authority of, 159
    hosts of, 197-98
    as hunters, 71
    as light, 93
    manner of calling, 70-71
    message of, 195
    mission and instruction of, 191-98, 200
    names of, 192-93
    obedience of, 195
    on the parables, 269, 283-84
    and persecution, 198-204
    provisions for, 196-97
    reception of, 198
    and sacrifices, 200
    as salt of the earth, 92
    status of, 192, 203-4
    in the storm, 169
    testimony of, 200
discipleship
    calling and response of, 72-73
    and death, 212
    and family, 166-67
    and healing, 76
    and hope, 203
    journey of, 286
    the nature of, 165-67
    and poverty, 215
    renouncing covetousness, 70
    training in, 168
disease, 75, 164, 174
divine economy, xl, 61-62
divorce, 112-13
dot (jot), 97
doves and snakes, 201
the dying girl, 181-85
"ears to hear," 224
Ecclesiastical History, xxxvii
Egypt(ians), 30-35
Elijah, 57-58, 224
Elizabeth, 17
Emmanuel, 18-19. *See also*